Tom Negrino
Popular author and Contributing Editor for Macworld magazine

With Kirk McElhearn and Kate Binder

P9-DJV-572

Microsoft Office:mac

v. X

INSIDE OUT

- **Hundreds of timesaving solutions—easy to find, easy to use!**
- **Get tips, tricks, and workarounds, plus the straight scoop**
- **Work smarter—and take your Office for Mac experience to the next level**

PUBLISHED BY
Microsoft Press
A Division of Microsoft Corporation
One Microsoft Way
Redmond, Washington 98052-6399

Library of Congress Cataloging-in-Publication Data
Negrino, Tom.
    Microsoft Office v. X for Mac Inside Out / Tom Negrino, Kirk McElhearn, and Kate Binder.
       p. cm.
    Includes index.
    ISBN 0-7356-1628-0
    1. Macintosh (Computer)--Programming.   2. Microsoft Office.   I. McElhearn, Kirk.   II. Binder, Kate.   III. Title.

  QA76.8.M3 N42   2002
  005.369--dc21   2002024400

Printed and bound in the United States of America.

1 2 3 4 5 6 7 8 9   QWT   7 6 5 4 3 2

Distributed in Canada by H.B. Fenn and Company Ltd.

A CIP catalogue record for this book is available from the British Library.

Microsoft Press books are available through booksellers and distributors worldwide. For further information about international editions, contact your local Microsoft Corporation office or contact Microsoft Press International directly at fax (425) 936-7329. Visit our Web site at www.microsoft.com/mspress. Send comments to *mspinput@microsoft.com*.

Acquisitions Editor: Kong Cheung
Project Editor: Kristen Weatherby
Technical Editor: Curtis Philips

Body Part No. X08-64094

Contents at a Glance

Table of Contents

newfeature!

Chapter 4
Office v. X: Do It Your Way 45

newfeature!

Part 2
Word 59

Chapter 5
Word Essentials 61

Chapter 6
Effective Text Editing   87

newfeature!

Chapter 7
Formatting Your Work   **123**

Chapter 10
Working with Images, Movies, Sounds, and Objects   227

Chapter 11
Using Word's Proofing Tools 263

Chapter 15
Creating Pages for the Web   363

Chapter 16
Automating Word with
Macros and AppleScripts   383

Chapter 21

Managing Your Appointments, Tasks, and Notes

507

Chapter 22

Organizing and Sharing Entourage Data

529

Chapter 23

Extending Entourage with AppleScript

545

Chapter 26
Mastering Worksheet Formatting   611

Chapter 27
Working with Functions and Formulas   637

Chapter 28
Working with Lists and Databases 659

Chapter 29
Analyzing and Presenting Data with Charts 687

Chapter 30
Adding Graphics to Worksheets 709

Chapter 31

Analyzing Data with Excel 729

Chapter 32

Collaborating with Colleagues 765

Acknowledgments

Tom Negrino

Many people contribute to a project of this size. My thanks go first to the people from my book agency, Studio B, who brought this project to me and helped shepherd it along: Neil Salkind, David Rogelberg, Stacey Barone, and Craig Wiley.

Microsoft Press has put together an amazing team who were a real pleasure to work with throughout this book. This project would not have happened without the fine work of its acquisition editors: Kong Cheung, who did the heavy lifting from its earliest beginnings and most of the way, and Alex Blanton, who carried the book through its conclusion. Kristen Weatherby, the project editor, performed almost superhuman amounts of work, did a terrific editing job, and provided just the right amount of prodding to a sometimes very weary lead author. Technical editor Curtis Philips provided a keen eye and his vast expertise along with many helpful suggestions and clarifications as he worked his way through the book. And higher praise I cannot bestow: Erin Milnes has restored my faith in copy editors.

I'd like to thank all of my co-authors for their dedication, attention to detail, and timeliness. All of you were a pleasure to work with, and I'm very happy that the fates (and in two cases, Adam Engst) brought you my way: Kirk McElhearn, who was often starting his day in France as I was winding down mine (post-midnight) in California; Kate Binder, who provided clean chapters, along with a nifty inflatable dinosaur; and unindicted co-conspirator Curt Frye, who stepped in and wrote several chapters when they were needed the most. I hope to someday actually meet you all in person!

From Microsoft's Macintosh Business Unit, big thanks to Erik Ryan, Product Manager for Office; Omar Shahine, Lead Program Manager for Entourage; and Dennis Cheung, Program Manager for Entourage. Special thanks to PR goddess Karen Sung of Waggener Edstrom.

I could not have gotten through this book without the support and love of two people. Sean Smith, the World's Best Kid™, provided lots of encouragement and put up with a drastic reduction in networked computer games with his stepdad. Finally, to my wife, best friend, and partner, Dori Smith, you amaze me every day with the depth of your wisdom and the strength of your heart.

Kirk McElhearn

I would like to thank my co-authors, Tom and Kate, for making this project an enjoyable experience. To all the unsung heroes of publishing—the editors, copy editors, proofreaders, production staff, and all the rest—thanks; I know how much work goes into making a book like this. Thanks to my agent Neil Salkind, for everything, and special thanks to Adam Engst, for all his help. Thanks also to my wife, Marie-France, and to my son, Perceval, who will think it is cool to see his name in a book.

Kate Binder

My thanks are due to lead author Tom Negrino, who invited me to join this project, and to my husband and partner, Don Fluckinger, who unlike Tom wasn't fortunate enough to be on the opposite coast while I was in the throes of writing.

We'd Like to Hear from You!

Our goal at Microsoft Press is to create books that help you find the information you need to get the most out of your software.

The INSIDE OUT series was created with you in mind. As part of an effort to ensure that we're creating the best, most useful books we can, we talked to our customers and asked them to tell us what they need from a Microsoft Press series. Help us continue to help you. Let us know what you like about this book and what we can do to make it better. When you write, please include the title and author of this book in your e-mail, as well as your name and contact information. We look forward to hearing from you.

How to Reach Us

E-mail: nsideout@microsoft.com
Mail: Inside Out Series Editor
Microsoft Press
One Microsoft Way
Redmond, WA 98052

Note: Unfortunately, we can't provide support for any software problems you might experience. Please go to http://support.microsoft.com *for help with any software issues.*

Conventions and Features Used in This Book

This book uses special text and design conventions to make it easier for you to find the information you need.

Text Conventions

Convention	Meaning
Abbreviated menu commands	For your convenience, this book uses abbreviated menu commands. For example, "Choose Tools, Track Changes, Highlight Changes" means that you should click the Tools menu, point to Track Changes, and select the Highlight Changes command.
Boldface type	**Boldface** type is used to indicate text that you enter or type.
Initial Capital Letters	The first letters of the names of menus, dialog boxes, dialog box elements, and commands are capitalized. Example: the Save As dialog box.
Italicized type	*Italicized* type is used to indicate new terms.
Plus sign (+) in text	Keyboard shortcuts are indicated by a plus sign (+) separating two key names. For example, Command+Option+F means that you press the Command, Option, and F keys at the same time.

Design Conventions

newfeature!
This text identifies a new or significantly updated feature in this version of the software.

InsideOut

These are the book's signature tips. In these tips, you'll get the straight scoop on what's going on with the software—inside information on why a feature works the way it does. You'll also find handy workarounds to different software problems.

tip   Tips provide helpful hints, timesaving tricks, or alternative procedures related to the task being discussed.

Troubleshooting

Look for these sidebars to find solutions to common problems you might encounter. Troubleshooting sidebars appear next to related information in the chapters. You can also use the Troubleshooting Topics index at the back of the book to look up problems by topic.

Cross-references point you to other locations in the book that offer additional information on the topic being discussed.

caution   Cautions identify potential problems that you should look out for when you're completing a task or problems that you must address before you can complete a task.

note   Notes offer additional information related to the task being discussed.

Sidebar

The sidebars sprinkled throughout these chapters provide ancillary information on the topic being discussed. Go to sidebars to learn more about the technology or a feature.

Part 1

Office v. X Fundamentals

Chapter 1

An Overview of Office v. X

What Is Office v. X?

Microsoft Office v. X is the first version of Office that runs on Apple's new Mac OS X operating system. A close cousin to the previous version, Office 2001, the new version has been extensively revised for peak performance in Apple's new operating system. This book covers the four main Office v. X applications:

- Microsoft Word X, the suite's word processor (Part 2)

- Microsoft Entourage X, an e-mail and personal information manager (Part 3)

- Microsoft Excel X, a spreadsheet, charting, and analysis program (Part 4)

- Microsoft PowerPoint X, for creating presentations (Part 5)

You'll also find information in this book about all of the other utility programs that come with Office v. X (or that are available on the Web) and help to support the main applications:

- Tools On The Web, a resource for updates and add-ons from Microsoft's Mac Office Web site (Chapter 3)

- Microsoft Equation Editor, which helps you create complex mathematical equations (Chapter 9)

- Microsoft Clip Gallery, an excellent repository for clip art (Chapter 10)

- Microsoft Organization Chart, for making tree-style organization charts and flowcharts (Chapter 10)

- REALBasic, a development environment for automating Office (Chapter 16)

- Office Notifications, an application that alerts you to scheduled calendar events (Chapter 21)

- Microsoft Graph, for inserting graphs into PowerPoint presentations (Chapter 36)

Finally, this book covers a bit about two Microsoft programs that are not, strictly speaking, part of the Office v. X suite, but that work closely with it:

- Microsoft Internet Explorer 5.1 (Chapter 15)

- MSN Messenger 2.1, an instant messaging program (Appendix B)

Why Office v. X?

Macintoshes have long been favorite tools of designers and graphic artists, and the myth is that these sorts of users make up the overwhelming majority of the Mac market. Not so; the vast majority of Macs are used by business and home users. Meat and potatoes applications such as word processing, e-mail, Web browsing, and spreadsheets are by far the most popular Mac programs. Like its Windows equivalent, Microsoft Office for the Mac holds the dominant position in productivity applications.

The main competition to Office v. X in the Mac market is Apple Computer's own AppleWorks 6.2. At first glance, AppleWorks seems to have a lot going for it. It's an integrated package that includes word processing, drawing, painting, spreadsheet, database, and presentation functions. It reads and writes documents in Word and Excel formats, so you're not cut off from people who use Microsoft Office. And for the budget-conscious, AppleWorks costs a fraction of the price of Office v. X.

But a closer look shows there's a lot of value in Office v. X's higher price, enough to swing the balance in Office's favor. The AppleWorks word processor is fine for short letters or reports, but it doesn't hold a candle to Word X when it comes to long or complex documents. AppleWorks lacks grammar checking as well as Word's excellent control over tables, and you have little control over the way text and graphics interact in your documents. Excel X is immensely more powerful than the AppleWorks spreadsheet module, and Excel is easier to use to boot. There's no equivalent of Entourage X's e-mail and personal information manager features in AppleWorks (though the Mail and Address Book applications included with OS X include some of the same functions). Compared to PowerPoint X, the AppleWorks presentation module is quite limited; there's very little flexibility in either creating or giving presentations. You'll also find that Office v. X performs operations quicker and lets you get your work done faster, thanks to two main factors. First, the Office applications have lots of features,

Chapter 1: An Overview of Office v. X

and they're in there for a reason—extra features save you time, because you can do your work in fewer steps. Second, the Mac Office engineers did a superb job of converting the suite to run on Mac OS X (more on that a bit later in this chapter).

AppleWorks 6.2 may be fine for younger students or for casual users. But if you need its features for serious work, you're likely to run into its limitations quickly. Office v. X is a better solution for the vast majority of people. In fact, for many business users, the availability of Office's package is a key component of the decision to upgrade to Mac OS X from Mac OS 9 or earlier.

Finding Out What's New

With every upgrade, the first question most people ask is "What's new?" For Office v. X, there are two seemingly contradictory answers: "Everything," and "Not that much." Yet both answers are correct. In order to understand why, you'll need to know a little more about Mac OS X.

In order for their software to run natively under Mac OS X, developers like Microsoft must rewrite large portions of their applications (a process called *Carbonization*), especially if they want to take full advantage of the Aqua interface. Converting just one application can take months; all the underlying code that makes the program work must be revised, and every dialog, toolbar, and window must be tweaked to look right under Aqua. And after all that effort, a developer has created a Mac OS X native application that has no new features that will entice users to upgrade except for the improved stability of OS X applications.

Office consists of the four main applications, plus several smaller ones, plus thousands of other files, and rewriting all that code required a mammoth programming effort that lasted more than a year, which meant that the Office engineers spent more time on conversion than on adding new features. Adding to the difficulty was the way that Microsoft's Macintosh Business Unit decided to go about Carbonization. They could have done a faster conversion, but to do so would not have taken full advantage of the new technologies built into Mac OS X. Instead, Microsoft's Mac developers went for the harder upgrade. The benefits of this approach are apparent as soon as you start up Office v. X. The programs launch in just a few seconds, making the Office applications some of the most responsive under OS X.

New Office v. X Features

Even though most of the effort of creating Office v. X went into converting the suite for Mac OS X, you can't say that *no* new features have been added. Entourage X leads the pack with a big facelift, and Word X has a few nice additions. In terms of brand-new features, however, Excel X and PowerPoint X have received comparatively short shrift for this revision.

A Bit About Mac OS X

Mac OS X is a huge break from the previous Mac OS, which had been developed since the Mac's debut, and culminated in Mac OS 9 (these old versions of the Mac OS are now collectively known as the Classic Mac OS). Apple needed to introduce a new operating system for a simple reason: the technology that was groundbreaking in 1984 was badly out of date in the twenty-first century. In contrast, Apple chose to build Mac OS X on the foundation of the UNIX operating system, which is more than robust enough for today's computing needs. As a result, Mac OS X is a modern operating system, with all of the features expected of such a system. Mac OS X has *protected memory,* which makes sure that applications that crash don't crash the whole machine. When something goes wrong, Mac OS X simply shuts down the offending application, letting you continue working without interruption. *Preemptive multitasking* allows OS X to allocate as much processor power as each running application needs, so the foreground application is still fully responsive while other applications crunch away in the background. For example, you can start an intensive operation like searching for a particular e-mail message in Entourage X, and then go back to Web surfing in Internet Explorer, and the search will continue in the back-ground—something that never worked well in Entourage 2001 under Mac OS 9. Sup-port for *symmetric multiprocessing* means that Mac OS X takes full advantage of dual processor Macintoshes; the operating system automatically splits up tasks between processors so that everything gets done faster. Mac OS X's modern memory manage-ment means that you no longer have to worry about how much memory an applica-tion needs; the operating system automatically allocates the right amount of memory to keep each application running smoothly.

The operating system mechanism that handles screen display is also new in Mac OS X. Called Quartz, it enables on-the-fly rendering, anti-aliasing (smoothing) of text and graphics, and PostScript-strength graphics. Quartz allows Mac OS X to use translucent controls and menus and provides excellent type handling. As an extra benefit, Quartz allows any document to be saved as a PDF (Portable Document Format) file for easy transfer to colleagues, whether or not they own Microsoft Office.

Besides its strong UNIX foundation, Mac OS X introduced a brand-new user interface—named Aqua—with a colorful, rounded 3-D look, as shown in Figure 1-1. The basic color scheme of Mac OS X is a sleek silver with blue highlights. Scroll bars look as though they're made out of bright blue glass, standing out against the windows' silver backgrounds. Not only is Aqua more colorful, it makes extensive use of large, almost-photographic icons; translucent menus that don't block your view of what's under them; and lots of rounded corners and drop shadows for windows. Icons of running applications appear in the Dock, a strip at the bottom or side of the screen that lets you switch between applications. You can even drag application icons to the Dock and launch them with a single click.

Chapter 1: An Overview of Office v. X

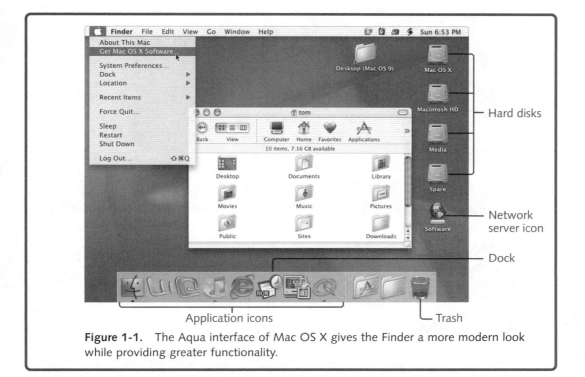

Figure 1-1. The Aqua interface of Mac OS X gives the Finder a more modern look while providing greater functionality.

Saving with Sheets

Office now uses Aqua's *sheets* for saving; sheets are special dialogs that slide down from the title bar of a document window and remain attached to the document. With sheets, you never lose track of which window a dialog applies to, as shown in Figure 1-2 on the next page.

> **note**   Incidentally, you can get a clue for how thoroughly a developer has Carbonized their application by whether or not the application uses sheets or a Save dialog.

Appending File Extensions

Another enhancement to saving is the new Append File Extension check box in the Save sheet. This helps Macintosh Office users to be compatible with their Windows-using colleagues. Although Office v. X possesses the same file format as Office XP, Office 2000, and Office 97 (as well as Office 98 and Office 2001 for Macintosh), Windows users often have problems reading documents created on the Mac, because

Part 1: Office v. X Fundamentals

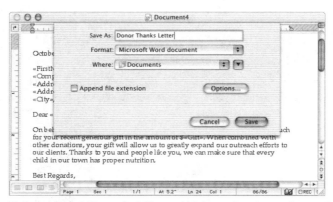

Figure 1-2. Microsoft Office v. X takes advantage of Mac OS X's new sheets when saving documents.

Mac documents have traditionally not included the three-letter file name extension that Windows uses to identify the correct application needed to open the file. Selecting the Append File Extension check box adds the extension to the files for better cross-platform compatibility.

Enhanced Project Gallery

Office 2001 introduced the Project Gallery, a handy dialog that served as a launcher for Office 2001 templates. From the Project Gallery in any Office program, you can create documents from the same program or any of the other programs. Office v. X's Project Gallery adds a Based On Recent category, which displays copies of Office documents you've created or worked on. Double-clicking a copy creates a new document that includes the text of your previous document, ready for modification, as shown in Figure 1-3.

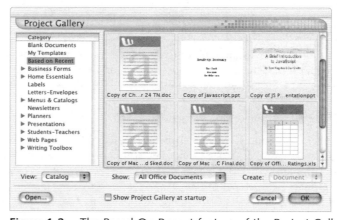

Figure 1-3. The Based On Recent feature of the Project Gallery makes it easy to create new documents from ones you've already created.

Chapter 1: An Overview of Office v. X

Tools On The Web

The new Tools On The Web feature provides all the main Office applications easy access to new services from Microsoft's Mac Office Web site. The services include downloadable new templates and clip art, reference services, and updates to any of the Office applications. Tools On The Web also includes services such as directories to help you look up people or map places.

New Word Features

Word X has just a few new features, but they're ones that have been long awaited by loyal Word users.

Noncontiguous Text Selection

The most useful new feature in Word is noncontiguous text selection, which allows you to select one or more separate blocks of text in one operation. Your next operation (such as text formatting) is applied to all of the selected text, as shown in Figure 1-4. This feature will be old hat to aficionados of Nisus Software's Nisus Writer, which has had noncontiguous selection since at least 1995, but it's a welcome addition for Word users.

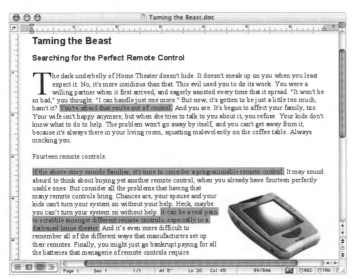

Figure 1-4. Word X's new noncontiguous text selection makes it easier to format text throughout your document.

Text Formatting Changes

Another long-overdue new feature is the ability to clear all formatting from a selection, which resets the selection to the default style for that paragraph. Winning in the category of Really Minor Change, the Highlight button has been relocated from the Standard toolbar to the Formatting Palette.

New Entourage Features

The newest of the Mac Office applications received the most attention in the change to Office v. X. A lot of the changes are under the hood, so that Entourage X would work more smoothly with other programs, but you'll be sure to notice many other changes as well.

Improved User Interface

From an interface standpoint, Entourage 2001 was not much more than Outlook Express 5 on steroids. The calendar, tasks, and notes features had clearly been shoehorned into the Outlook Express interface. No longer; Entourage X was sent to the interface doctors for an extensive facelift, as shown in Figure 1-5. Besides the Aqua look, you'll find six big buttons that switch between the five task areas (Mail, Address Book, Calendar, Notes, and Tasks). For the keyboard-oriented, each task area has a keyboard shortcut for quick switching.

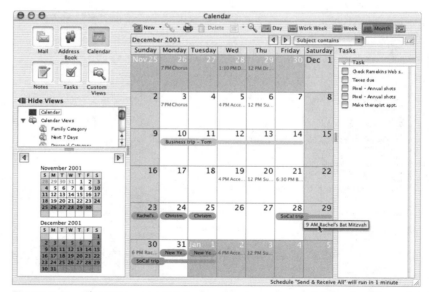

Figure 1-5. The Entourage X interface has been completely revised to match the Aqua interface, and to provide easier access to the program's main features.

Calendar Enhancements

Entourage X includes a number of nice additions and changes, especially to the calendar. Events spanning multiple days now show as banners in the calendar, rather than as a string of repeated events. Days are color coded to show workdays and weekends, and you can display a task list next to the calendar. New buttons on the toolbar switch between Month, Week, and Day views.

Custom Views

If you're using Entourage to organize your life, you need tools that help you see only the information that's most relevant to you. Each of the task areas now have dedicated Custom Views that let you show selected data, such as Mail Received Today or Events Due In The Next Week. Naturally, you can create and save your own Custom Views.

Added Mail Stability

Addressing complaints from heavy e-mail users, Entourage's mail database has been revised to improve speed and stability. This is especially good news, since rebuilding the database in Entourage 2001 was a distressingly common necessity.

Office Notifications

Because Mac OS X doesn't allow system extensions, the new Office Notifications application takes over the job of popping up and alerting users when Entourage reminders come due, as shown in Figure 1-6. Besides Entourage events, this application lets you receive notification that a buddy is available for instant messaging (if the new MSN Messenger 2.1 for Mac OS X is installed on your computer).

Figure 1-6.   Office Notifications pop up to let you know when events come due.

New Excel Features

For hardcore users, the most useful addition to Excel X is the new feature that allows you to customize keyboard shortcuts. Just as in Word, you can add, reassign, or remove shortcuts to make Excel work the way you want it to.

AutoRecover

Excel now has an AutoRecover feature that automatically saves a snapshot of your worksheets at intervals you select. If Excel crashes between your regular saves and AutoRecover data is available, all or part of your unsaved work will return when you reopen your document.

Transparent Charts and Graphics

Taking advantage of another Quartz feature, when you create charts in Excel, you can now set the transparency of bars, columns, or other chart components. This is especially useful for some chart types, such as 3-D area charts, as shown in Figure 1-7.

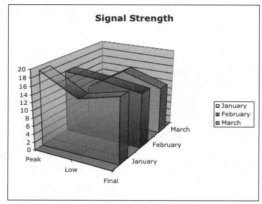

Figure 1-7. Excel X charts benefit greatly from Quartz transparency.

New PowerPoint Features

PowerPoint usually seems to be the Office program that gets the least attention lavished upon it by the Office developers, and PowerPoint X continues this dubious tradition. Its new features mainly make it easier for you to transport and export your presentations.

PowerPoint Packages

The new PowerPoint Packages feature gathers and copies your presentation file and any linked files, such as sound files or embedded QuickTime movies, into a single new folder, which can then be burned to a CD or sent via e-mail to a colleague. This feature helps you make sure that all the files you need for a presentation stay together.

Chapter 1: An Overview of Office v. X

Improved QuickTime Movie Capabilities

PowerPoint 2001 introduced the ability to turn presentations into QuickTime movies, but the movies were more limited than the original presentation, lacking interactive features such as hyperlinks and slide transitions. PowerPoint X's movies now look and act more like the presentation running inside PowerPoint. You'll also find support for the transition effects built into QuickTime, in addition to PowerPoint's slide transitions set.

Graphics Transparency

Like Excel, PowerPoint allows you to set the transparency of drawing objects or pictures. This ability is useful when you have embedded charts from Microsoft Graph on your slides, but you can also use it for regular artwork or background images.

Launching Office v. X Applications

After you install and register Office v. X, you won't have any trouble starting the programs. As you would with any other Mac application, just double-click a program's icon to launch the program.

---

tip   **Launch applications easily**

To make it easier to start any of the Office v. X applications, open the Microsoft Office X folder, which is inside your Applications folder. Then drag the icon of one or more of the Office applications to the Dock. This places a copy of the icon on the Dock. To start the program, just single-click its icon on the Dock.

Remember that once you have launched any of the Office v. X programs, you have access to all of them—and their templates—via the Project Gallery. So if you're working in Word X and you need to create a spreadsheet, open the Project Gallery (by choosing File, Project Gallery), which opens to the Blank Documents category. Then choose the kind of document you want (in this case, it's Excel Workbook), and click Open or press Return.

---

tip   **Launch Office programs automatically at startup**

It's common to want to fire up a program when you start your computer (Entourage X is an especially good candidate for launch at startup, to give you immediate access to your e-mail and calendar). To set an application to open at startup, choose Apple Menu, System Preferences, and then click the Login icon. When the Login dialog appears, click the Login Items tab. Finally, click the Add button, navigate to the Microsoft Office X folder, and select the application you want.

Let's Get Started

The combination of Microsoft Office v. X and Mac OS X is a potent one that firmly closes the door on past versions of both Office and Mac OS. If you've made the jump to Mac OS X from Mac OS 9 and earlier, you'll want the rest of your tools to be as up-to-date as the new operating system. Office v. X delivers in a big way. Read on to see how you can put Office's power to work for you.

Chapter 2

Creating and Managing Documents

The first step in working with any of the Microsoft Office v. X applications is to create documents, and as you might guess from such an important task, Office provides lots of help in making document creation easy and convenient. Besides simple blank documents, Office provides *templates*, premade documents that you can use as the basis for letterheads, brochures, fax cover letters, mailing labels, letters, spreadsheets, presentations, and dozens of other kinds of documents.

Longtime Office users who are recent upgraders to Mac OS X will find that many of the document creation and management strategies used in Office 2001 and earlier are still applicable, albeit with a Mac OS X twist.

Creating New Documents

By default, the Office v. X applications, with the exception of Microsoft Entourage X, create a new document as soon as you open the application. But the new document doesn't necessarily have to be a document of the application you have opened. Out of the box, Office v. X is set to open the Project Gallery when you launch an Office application. The Project Gallery is a dialog that allows you to create any Office document that you want, not simply a new document from the current application. The Project Gallery, which is available in all the Office v. X applications, lets you use any of the Office programs as a jumping off point to create documents in any of the other programs, without the annoyance of having to first launch the other program from the Finder or the Dock.

15

Part 1: Office v. X Fundamentals

Once you're working in any of the Office applications, you can create a new document in that application by pressing Command+N, or by choosing File, New …. The wording of the command changes depending on what application you are working in. For example, in Word, the New … command will read New Blank Document, and in Microsoft Excel X, it will read New Workbook.

Understanding the Project Gallery and Templates

When the Project Gallery opens, you are presented with a list of categories and a document area, as shown in Figure 2-1. The Project Gallery always opens to the Blank Documents category, and the main document icon for whatever program you are in is highlighted by default. For example, if the Project Gallery opens in Excel, the Excel Workbook icon will be highlighted; if you are in Word, the Word Document icon will be highlighted. Pressing Return creates a new blank document of the type selected.

If you want to create a new blank document of any other type than the default, select it in the Documents pane and press Return. Because you can choose from any of the blank document types from any of the Office applications, the Project Gallery is often the quickest way to create a new document.

---

tip   **Navigate the Project Gallery with the keyboard**

Within the Project Gallery, you can jump from the Category pane at the left to the templates in the Documents pane on the right by pressing the Tab key. The highlighting around the edge of the pane will let you know which pane is active. Once a pane is highlighted, you can navigate within the pane by pressing the Up Arrow and Down Arrow keys. In the Category pane, when you highlight a category marked by a *disclosure triangle* (as in the Finder, Microsoft Office v. X uses clickable triangles to show that more information is available in a category or dialog), press Command+Right Arrow key to expand it, or Command+Left Arrow key to collapse the category. When you've highlighted the template you want, press Return to open it.

The categories other than Blank Documents contain templates for Office documents. To see what's in each category, select it in the Category pane. The disclosure triangles next to some category names indicate that one or more subselections are available for the category. Click the disclosure triangle to see these additional choices. After you have selected a category, the templates within that category will appear in the Documents pane. Templates created by Microsoft usually, but not always, show a preview image in the Documents pane, so that you can get an idea of what the template will look like before you open it, as shown in Figure 2-2.

Chapter 2: Creating and Managing Documents

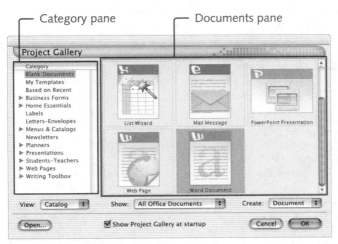

Figure 2-1.   The Project Gallery allows you to create new documents from any Office application.

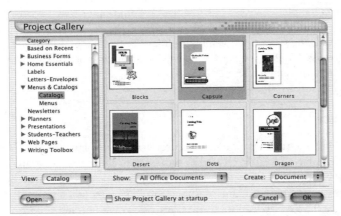

Figure 2-2.   Selecting a template allows you to preview it before use.

Once you have selected the template you want, click OK or press Return. A new document, based on that template, opens.

For more information on using, creating, and saving your own templates, see Chapter 8, "Advanced Formatting with Styles, Templates, and Themes."

> **tip**   **Do without the Project Gallery**
>
> If you clear the Show Project Gallery At Startup check box at the bottom of the Project Gallery dialog, the Office application will, instead of opening the Project Gallery, simply create a new blank document of the application's type when you launch it. If you need the Project Gallery again, you can always find it under File, Project Gallery in any of the Office programs. If you want the Project Gallery to once again always appear at startup, choose Word, Preferences, and then click the General category. Click the button next to Show Project Gallery At Startup, and then press Return to close the Preferences dialog.

In Search of Templates

You'll find the template files in a few different places on your hard disk, but all of these places are within the Microsoft Office X folder, which should be inside your Applications folder. Most of the user templates can be found within Applications/ Microsoft Office X/Templates. Inside this folder, you'll find other folders corresponding to the categories within the Project Gallery. If you want to reorganize the Project Gallery's categories, simply open the Templates folder in the Finder and have at it. The templates that are used by the Project Gallery's wizards are in Applications/Microsoft Office X/Office/Wizard Templates.

Using Based On Recent

The new Based On Recent category of the Project Gallery displays copies of Office documents that you have recently created or worked on, as shown in Figure 2-3. Double-clicking a copy creates a new document that includes the text and formatting of your previous document, ready for modification. It's really just a more convenient method of doing a Save As operation, but it does save you a few steps.

Using Wizards

Some of the templates in the Project Gallery are special templates called *wizards,* which help you create a document's content and even layout. There are Microsoft Word wizards to help you create brochures, mailing labels, business letters, menus, and newsletters. These Word wizards and the wizards for the other Office applications are listed in Table 2-1.

Chapter 2: Creating and Managing Documents

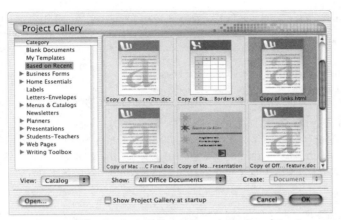

Figure 2-3. The Project Gallery's Based On Recent category automatically keeps track of documents you've recently worked on, making it easy to create similar new documents.

Table 2-1. **Office v. X Wizards**

Project Gallery Category	Wizard Name
Blank Documents	AutoContent Wizard (Microsoft PowerPoint X), List Wizard (Excel)
Business Forms/Brochures	Accessory, Bar, Blocks, Bracket, Capsule, Column, Corners, Dots, Dragon, Elegant, Forms, Marquee, Neutral, Saucer, Simple
Labels	Mailing Label Wizard
Letters-Envelopes	Envelope Wizard, Letter Wizard
Menus & Catalogs/Catalogs	Accessory, Bar, Beach, Blocks, Capsule, Corners, Desert, Dots, Dragon, Elegant, Forms, Marquee, Neutral, Phosphors, Saucer, Simple
Menus & Catalogs/Menus	Accessory, Bar, Beach, Bracket, Capsule, Column, Corners, Dots, Dragon, Elegant, Forms, Marquee, Neutral, Rocket, Saucer, Simple
Newsletters	Accessory, Bar, Beach, Blocks, Capsule, Column, Corners, Dots, Dragon, Elegant, Forms, Marquee, Neutral, Rocket, Rule, Simple

Part 1: Office v. X Fundamentals

For more information about using Excel's List Wizard, see Chapter 28, "Working with Lists and Databases." For more information about PowerPoint's AutoContent Wizard, see Chapter 34, "PowerPoint Essentials."

To create a document from a wizard, follow these steps:

1 Open the Project Gallery, select a wizard, and click OK. The wizard's window will open.

2 Enter the information that you want the wizard to place in the document it is creating, and depending on the wizard, choose things like number of pages, number of columns, and so forth, as shown in Figure 2-4.

Figure 2-4. Most wizards will ask you to enter information that the wizard will later place in the new document.

3 Press Return to exit the wizard. The wizard creates the new document to your specifications, as shown in Figure 2-5.

note Most wizards will help you create the bare bones of a document, especially documents like newsletters or brochures. The wizard will leave placeholder text such as "Lead Story Headline" that you'll need to replace with your actual text.

Chapter 2

Chapter 2: Creating and Managing Documents

Figure 2-5. You can use the Newsletter Wizard to create a newsletter like this one. After you enter the title and other information in the wizard, the text is placed automatically in the document.

Opening Existing Documents

If you want to edit an existing document and you're not already in the Office program that created the document, the fastest way to get started is to double-click the document icon. The Office program will launch and open the document.

If the Office program is already open, choose one of the following options, whichever is fastest for you at the time:

- Press Command+O.
- Choose File, Open.
- Click the Open button on the Standard toolbar.

Whichever method you choose, the standard Mac OS X Open dialog will appear, as shown in Figure 2-6 on the next page. This Open dialog looks and acts significantly different than the one used by previous versions of Office, which ran under Mac OS 9 and earlier. The Open dialog is *application modal,* that is, when it is open, you have to close it to continue using the current Office application, but you can switch to and use other applications if you want. When you return to the application, the dialog will be waiting for you to resume your work with it.

Part 1: Office v. X Fundamentals

Select the document type to list below.

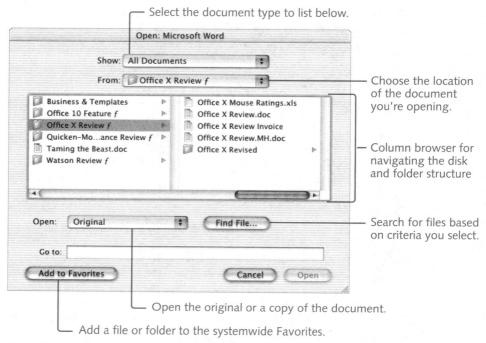

Choose the location of the document you're opening.

Column browser for navigating the disk and folder structure

Search for files based on criteria you select.

Open the original or a copy of the document.

Add a file or folder to the systemwide Favorites.

Figure 2-6. Use the Mac OS X Open dialog to find and open existing documents.

The Show pop-up menu (shown in the following graphic) allows you to choose from the types of document formats readable by Office; it is normally set to All Documents. If you choose another file type, documents not of that type will appear dimmed in the *column browser* (defined later in this section) and will not be available.

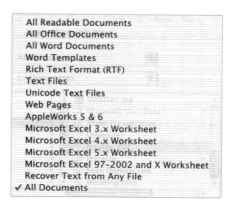

The From pop-up menu displays at the top whatever folder you are currently browsing and has three permanent entries directly below: Desktop, Home, and iDisk. Choosing one of the three entries jumps the column browser immediately to that location. Below these three locations are two areas that change depending on your work. The first, Favorite Places, is a list of all of your previously selected Favorite file locations. The second, Recent Places, changes dynamically to list the most recent folders and hard disks that you have browsed.

---

tip   **Make Favorites**

The fastest way to return to frequently used hard disks, folders, or files is to select them in the column browser, and then click the Add To Favorites button at the bottom of the Open dialog. Doing so adds the selected item to the Favorite Places section in the Open dialog's From pop-up menu. Because the Favorites list is systemwide, you'll also be able to get to the selected item from the Finder, by choosing Go, Favorites, and then choosing from the submenu.

The column browser allows you to navigate the file system; for longtime Macintosh users, the column browser is the most unfamiliar part of the Mac OS X Open and Save dialogs. Previous versions of the Mac OS Open dialog allowed you to open folders in the dialog by double-clicking them, which allowed you to descend deeper into the file hierarchy. The OS X column browser scrolls horizontally, beginning at the far left at the hard disk level. Single-clicking disks or folders scrolls the column browser to the left, revealing their contents. Selecting the target file makes the Open or Save button active.

---

tip   If you want to see more columns in the column browser, you can resize the Open dialog by moving the pointer over the bottom right corner of the dialog and dragging the corner to the size you want.

The Open pop-up menu allows you to open documents in three ways: Original allows you to open the document itself; Copy creates a copy of the document and opens it; Read-Only opens a copy of the document that can be read, but not edited.

Clicking the Find File button opens the Search dialog, which lets you search for files by their names, as shown in Figure 2-7 on the next page.

The benefit of using the Search dialog to find files, instead of Mac OS X's built-in file searching feature, Sherlock, is that you have more flexibility once you've found files that match your criteria. The results list, shown in Figure 2-8 on the next page, allows you to preview the contents of the files, and the Commands pop-up menu lets you open, print, copy, or delete a file, right from within the dialog. The Sorting command in this menu lets you specify how you want the results list sorted—by name, date, size, and so on.

Part 1: Office v. X Fundamentals

Figure 2-7. Enter the file name, choose the type of file, and select which hard disk you wish to search to find files in the Search dialog.

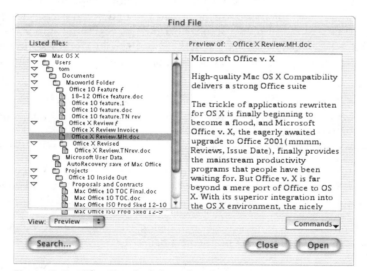

Figure 2-8. The Search dialog allows you to preview the contents of a found file.

Finally, the Open dialog's Add To Favorites button adds the selected folder or file to the systemwide Favorites list so you can find it again quickly. When you have found the file that you wish to open, select it in the column browser, and then click Open or press Return.

Chapter 2: Creating and Managing Documents

Saving Your Documents

There's nothing more annoying than working on a document for a couple of hours, having your system crash, and realizing that you had forgotten to save your work before the crash. Don't let this happen to you. Get in the habit of pressing Command+S on a regular basis.

Saving documents is so basic, that you wouldn't think that there would be anything new to say about the subject. Think again; Mac OS X has introduced a new way to save.

Using Save

The Office v. X programs use *sheets,* a new Mac OS X interface element, for saving. Sheets are special dialogs that slide down from the title bar of a document window and are connected to that document window, as can be seen in Figure 2-9. With sheets, you never lose track of which window a Save dialog applies to, and you can work on other documents from the same application even while a Save sheet is displayed. You can also switch to another application with a sheet active.

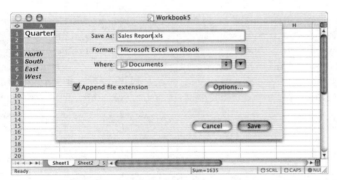

Figure 2-9. All the Office v. X programs use Mac OS X sheets to save documents.

To save a document, follow these steps:

1 Choose File, Save. The Save sheet slides down from the document's title bar.

2 Enter a name for the document.

3 If necessary, navigate in the column browser to where you want to save the document. Open the column browser by clicking the downward-pointing triangle to the right of the Where pop-up menu.

4 Click Save, or press Return.

> **tip** If you have multiple files open in Word and you want to save them all at the same time, hold down the Shift key before you choose File, Save. You'll notice that the Save command has changed to Save All. Holding down the Shift key also changes the Close command in the same menu to Close All.

InsideOut

Limit document file names to 31 characters

One of the nice new features of Mac OS X is that it lifts the Classic Mac OS's 31-character limit on the length of file names. Mac OS X supports file names up to 255 characters long. But that doesn't mean that Office does; applications need to be rewritten to handle saving long file names, and that bit of updating wasn't included in Office v. X. If you try to save new files with names longer than 31 characters, you'll get an alert that tells you that you can't, and that you should shorten the name and try again. If you've added a file name extension, such as .doc, using the Append File Extension check box, the four characters of the extension count towards the 31-character limit.

Happily, the Office programs can still open and save documents with long file names; they just can't save new documents with long file names. You can rename a file in the Finder using a long file name. Once it is renamed, Office v. X will retain the long name with future saves. It's a bit clumsy, but it works. The only drawback is that the file name in the document's window title bar has some garbage characters in it, since it won't display the whole name. But the long file name will show up correctly in the Finder.

Using AutoRecover

Those clever engineers at Microsoft suspect that you don't save your work quite as often as you need to. So they have built a feature into Word and Excel (but alas, not in Entourage and PowerPoint) called AutoRecover that automatically saves a snapshot of your documents at intervals that you select. If your system crashes between your regular saves and AutoRecover data is available, all or part of your unsaved work will return when you reopen your document.

AutoRecover is enabled by default in both Word and Excel, but you can modify the number of minutes between AutoRecover snapshots. Follow these steps to do so:

1 If you are in Word, choose Word, Preferences; in Excel it's Excel, Preferences.

2 In the Preferences dialog, select the Save category.

3 Make sure Save AutoRecover Info Every is selected, then select the number of minutes you wish to pass between each AutoRecover snapshot.

4 Click OK.

Using Save As

Save As means saving a currently open document under another name. Simply choose File, Save As, and then on the resulting Save As sheet, give the document a new name and navigate to where you want to save the document.

You'll also want to use Save As in order to save documents in a file format other than one of the native Office formats. For example, you might have to send a word processing document to a coworker who doesn't use Word, or an Excel worksheet to someone who doesn't use Excel. In Word, Excel, and PowerPoint you can save documents in non-native formats as well as older Office formats. To save a document in one of these formats, follow these steps:

1 Choose File, Save As. The Save As sheet slides down from the top of the document window.

2 Enter the name for the new copy of the document.

> **caution** If you are saving the copy in the same folder as the original, make sure to give the copy a different name so that you do not accidentally overwrite the original.

3 From the Format pop-up menu, choose the format in which you want to save the copy of the document.

4 Click Save.

> **note** The most widely read non-native format for Word documents is RTF (Rich Text Format), which can be read by virtually any word processor. The Excel equivalent is SYLK (symbolic link) format.

Saving Documents for Windows Users

Office v. X makes it easy to share documents with people using Office 97, Office 2000, or Office XP for Windows. The file formats for Word, Excel, and PowerPoint documents are identical between the Mac and Windows versions of the products, so documents can be freely exchanged between coworkers on different sides of the platform divide.

> **note** Cross-platform portability is not unique to Office v. X; the file formats for Word, Excel, and PowerPoint documents created by Office 2001 and Office 98 are also completely compatible with their Windows-based equivalents.

Yet even though the file formats are identical, Windows users often have problems reading the Office documents created on the Mac. The culprit is usually a missing or incorrect *file name extension,* that three-letter addition to the file name that Windows uses to identify the program associated with a particular document. Since 1984, Macintosh users have traditionally not needed to worry about file name extensions, because the Macintosh Finder tracked the connection between an application and its files. With the introduction of Mac OS X, with its UNIX underpinnings, Mac users have become more familiar with file name extensions. File name extensions are still not necessary to use documents under Mac OS X, but it is no longer unusual to see a file name extension appended to a document name. Table 2.2 lists common file name extensions and the kind of document with which they are associated.

Table 2-2. **Common File Name Extensions**

Type of File	Extension
Word document file	.doc
Word template file	.dot
Rich Text Format file	.rtf
Excel worksheet file	.xls
PowerPoint presentation file	.ppt
Web page file	.htm
JPEG format image file	.jpg
PNG format image file	.png
GIF format image file	.gif
TIFF format image file	.tif
QuickTime movie file	.mov
MP3 audio file	.mp3
Portable Document Format file	.pdf
Stuffit compressed archive file (Macintosh standard compression format)	.sit
Self-extracting archive file	.sea
Plain text file	.txt
Zip compressed archive file (Windows standard compression format)	.zip

Chapter 2

The Office v. X programs will add the correct Windows file name extensions to files automatically if you click the Append File Extension check box on the Save or Save As sheet.

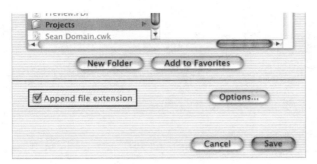

Entourage handles adding file name extensions a bit differently; for more information, see "Attaching Files and Folders to Messages," page 452.

Chapter 3

Getting Expert Help with Office v. X

Microsoft Office v. X, like many programs these days, does not come with a printed manual. But just because you won't find any dead trees in the box, it doesn't mean that you'll have any problems finding help. Office v. X provides a great deal of help resources; some available within Office, some available on the Office v. X CD-ROM, and some available from Microsoft's Web site.

If you are an experienced user of the Office applications, chances are you don't need help with the basics. Rather, you need quick help with the features that you hardly ever use. You might need to know how to do calculations in tables in Microsoft Word X, or how to animate charts in PowerPoint. Office provides several help features that will enable you to find the answers quickly.

Using the Office Assistant

The primary method for getting help while you are using one of the Office v. X programs is the Office Assistant. This animated character lives in a small window that floats above all other windows, so that help is always available. You pose questions or phrases in plain English to the Office Assistant, so there's no arcane search syntax to learn. By default, the Office Assistant is turned on and set to Max, the Office Assistant that is unique to the Macintosh version of Microsoft Office. Max, as shown in Figure 3-1, looks like an original, 1984-vintage Macintosh, with mice for feet.

Figure 3-1. Max, the default Office Assistant, is always ready to help.

Some people really like the Office Assistant, because they appreciate the way that it offers suggestions on how to accomplish tasks. Other people aren't thrilled with the Office Assistant because they feel its suggestions are more of an annoying interruption than a helping hand. Whichever description fits you, it's easy to customize the Office Assistant so that you get the kind of help you want, when you want it.

Office
Assistant

If the Office Assistant isn't visible, chances are it was turned off. You can turn it back on by clicking the Office Assistant button on the Standard toolbar, or by choosing Help, Use The Office Assistant.

If the Office Assistant is visible and you would like to get rid of it (to reduce screen clutter or just because you don't like the darn thing), click the close button in the Office Assistant window.

tip You can also get rid of the Office Assistant by Control+clicking in its window and choosing Hide Assistant from the resulting contextual menu.

InsideOut

Restore the empty Office Assistant window

Sometimes, especially when you have been switching between different open applications, the Office Assistant window is open, but there's no one home—the window is all white. This appears to be a bug caused by an interaction between Office v. X and Mac OS X. Another symptom of the bug is that when you click the close button in the Office Assistant window, nothing happens—the empty window stays stubbornly on your screen. The workaround is to close and reopen the Office Assistant window by choosing Help, Use The Office Assistant. Use this menu choice once to close the errant window, then choose it again to bring the Office Assistant back to life.

Getting Help from the Office Assistant

You can ask the Office Assistant for help with a process that you're currently working on, or with anything relating to the Office v. X application that you're in. There are four ways to ask the Office Assistant for help:

● Click in the Office Assistant window.

● Press the Help key on the keyboard.

Chapter 3

Chapter 3: Getting Expert Help with Office v. X

> **note** Not all Macintosh keyboards have the Help key. Portable Macs don't, nor do older iMac keyboards.

- Click the Office Assistant button on the Standard toolbar.

- Choose Help, Search Word Help.

No matter which method you use to invoke the Office Assistant a question dialog will appear. Type your question (remember, you can use plain English), and click Search (or press Return).

> **tip** **Use phrases rather than words**
>
> The Office Assistant understands questions that you ask it in plain English, but it does a better job of finding information if you give it a phrase or a sentence, rather than a single word. For example, you'll get better and more targeted results by entering the phrase "Calculations in a table" than by entering the single word "Calculations."

The Office Assistant responds with an answer dialog that lists help topics that match your question. If the search yields more topics than can be displayed in the answer dialog, a triangle labeled See More will appear at the bottom of the list. Click this link if none of the topics seem to be quite on target for your question.

Clicking one of the help topics brings up the Microsoft Office Help window, set to the detailed help text you requested, as shown in Figure 3-2 on the next page.

Part 1: Office v. X Fundamentals

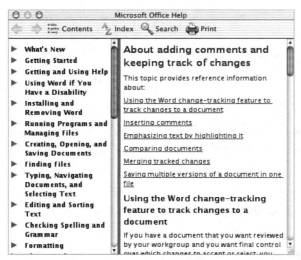

Figure 3-2. The Office Help window provides several navigation controls that let you narrow your search for help.

The Help window works a bit like a Web browser: it contains hyperlinks to further information, as well as Forward and Back buttons to let you step through Help pages. The Contents button fills the Contents pane with the names of the help sections; clicking the disclosure triangle next to a section name opens up the section for more information on that topic.

> **tip** You can get directly to the Help window, without going through the Office Assistant, by choosing Help, Word Help Contents (in Word), Excel Help Contents (in Microsoft Excel X), and so on.

The Office Assistant comes out of the box set to help you proactively, popping up tips and asking whether you need more information about certain tasks.

If the Office Assistant is set to give tips, a lightbulb will appear in the Office Assistant's window when it has a tip for you.

If you can use the help, click the lightbulb or the help button in the balloon that the Office Assistant pops up. If you're not interested in help, click the Cancel button in the balloon or simply ignore the Office Assistant.

Chapter 3

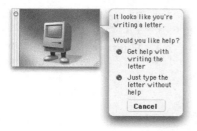

Modifying the Office Assistant

Proactive help can be good, because it can help you discover features and ways of working that you didn't know about. But for many people, the Office Assistant's eagerness to help is an annoying distraction. If you are in the Bugged by the Office Assistant camp, no problem; you can dial the Office Assistant's behavior back, or even get help without having to deal with the Office Assistant at all.

Adjusting Office Assistant Behavior

To customize the way the Office Assistant interacts with you, follow these steps:

1 If the Office Assistant isn't visible, display it by choosing Help, Use The Office Assistant.

2 Control+click in the Office Assistant window, and choose Options from the resulting contextual menu. The Office Assistant dialog appears, set to the Options tab.

3 The Assistant Capabilities section of the window controls how the Office Assistant interacts with you, as shown in Figure 3-3. The Show Tips About

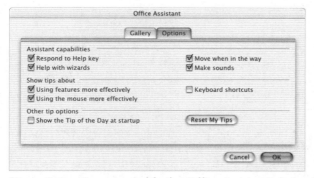

Figure 3-3. You can modify the Office Assistant's behavior with the settings on the Options tab of the Office Assistant dialog.

section controls what sort of information the Office Assistant will give you. The Other Tip Options section lets you turn the Tip Of The Day feature on or off. All the options are self-explanatory. Select the check boxes for the features that you want turned on or off, and then click OK to save your changes.

Switching Office Assistants

If you're getting tired of Max, the default Office Assistant, Office v. X comes with 12 other Office Assistants from which to choose, as shown in Figure 3-4. Each of the Office Assistants comes with its own unique animation and sound.

Max

Bosgrove   Will   Office Logo   Mother Nature

Earl   Power Pup   Rocky   Scribble

Clippit   F1   The Dot   Hoverbot

Figure 3-4. The 13 Office Assistants stand ready to make your help experience a smooth one.

> **tip** If you want to see all the animated behaviors of a particular Office Assistant, Control+ click in the Office Assistant's window. From the resulting contextual menu, choose Animate! to make the Office Assistant perform a behavior. Repeat until you are bored.

Max is the only Office Assistant that is installed with Office v. X by default. You'll need to install the rest of them yourself, and you'll find them in the Value Pack on the Office v. X CD. To install the extra Office Assistants, follow these steps:

1 Insert the Office v. X CD into your Mac.

2 Open the Value Pack folder on the CD.

Chapter 3: Getting Expert Help with Office v. X

3 Double-click the Value Pack Installer to launch it.

4 In the Value Pack Installer window, select the check box next to Office Assistants if you want to install all of the additional Office Assistants (approximately 17 MB of disk space will be required). If you don't want to install all of the Office Assistants, click the disclosure triangle next to Assistants and select the individual Office Assistants that you want from the list that appears.

5 Click Continue, wait for the Installer to finish its work, and then click Quit.

Once the extra Office Assistants are installed, you still need to switch to the Office Assistant you want. Follow these steps:

1 If it's not visible, display the Office Assistant.

2 Control+click in the Office Assistant window. From the resulting contextual menu, select Choose Assistant. The Office Assistant dialog will appear, set to the Gallery tab, as shown in Figure 3-5.

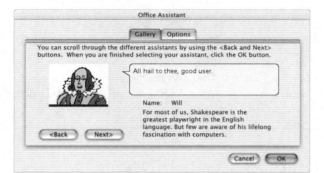

Figure 3-5. Choose a new Office Assistant in the Office Assistant dialog.

3 Scroll through the different Office Assistants by clicking the Back and Next buttons, and then click OK when you've made your choice.

note When you choose an Office Assistant for one of the Office programs, you've chosen that Office Assistant for all the programs. The Office Assistant settings are shared Office-wide, so you can't have Max in Word and Rocky in Excel.

Remembering Our Fallen Office Assistants

When software programs are upgraded, we naturally expect change. Some new features are added; other, perhaps obsolete features are deleted. So it is with Office Assistants. Office v. X says a fond farewell to two Office Assistants that previously graced our screens:

- The Genius, an Albert Einstein–like figure that appeared in Office 98 and Office 2001.

- Kairu the Dolphin, which never made it to the American desktop, but was part of the Japanese versions of Office 98 and Office 2001. Kairu was also available to our Windows Office–using friends, back in the days of Office 97.

We don't know why these fine Office Assistants were banished, while others, like the insipid Hoverbot, remain behind. The ways of Microsoft programmers are mysterious. But we certainly wish these past Office Assistants well, in whatever digital domain they now reside. I promised I wouldn't cry…

Banishing the Office Assistant

If you want to get rid of the Office Assistant altogether, clear the check mark next to Help, Use The Office Assistant. The Office Assistant will disappear until you call it back by choosing Help, Use The Office Assistant again.

Using the Help Index

The Help Index, available in the Help window, is a good way to quickly find a Help topic when you know exactly what you're looking for. It displays an alphabetical list of keywords, with help topics listed under each keyword. To use the Index, follow these steps:

1 Choose Help Contents from the Help menu. The Microsoft Office Help window appears.

Chapter 3: Getting Expert Help with Office v. X

2 Click the Index button. The Contents pane changes to an alphabetical list.

3 Click the letter corresponding to the first letter of the topic you want. The list of topics appears in the Contents pane.

4 Click the topic you want. The topic expands to show the individual Help files for that topic, as shown in Figure 3-6.

5 Click a Help file to display it in the Help Text pane.

Figure 3-6. In some cases, it's fastest to find a Help topic via the Help Index.

Printing Help Files

New to Office v. X is its ability to print Help topics. To print a Help topic, bring up the Help window using any of the techniques shown earlier in this chapter, and navigate to the specific Help topic you wish to print. Then click the Print button at the top of the Help window.

Getting Web-Based Help

Microsoft provides a vast amount of technical support information on its dedicated Mac Web site, called Mactopia. The easiest way to get to this site is by choosing Help, Visit The Mactopia Web Site from any of the Office programs. This takes you to the Mactopia home page, as shown in Figure 3-7 on the next page.

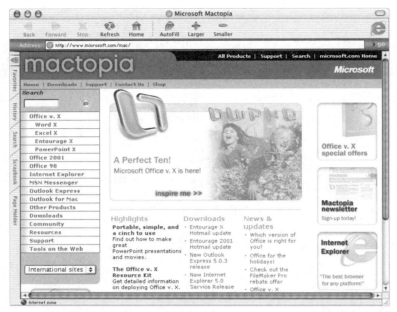

Figure 3-7. Microsoft's Mactopia Web site gives you access to downloadable updates, support information, and additional product information.

The Mactopia home page has links that will lead you to the Support area, where you can find answers to common support issues for Office v. X; the Downloads area, where you can download product updates; and links to the Community and Resources areas, which allow you to interact with other Office users.

> **tip** If all you want to do is check for product updates, there's an easier way to go directly to the Downloads page on Mactopia: choose Help, Downloads And Updates from any Office v. X program.

You'll find more links to product help by choosing Help, Additional Help Resources. Your Web browser will open and show a page (that's actually on your own machine) with links to various Microsoft Web sites, including a link to search the Microsoft Knowledge Base (Microsoft's immense repository of help articles). You'll also find links to how-to articles and, of special interest, links to special Microsoft newsgroups. You can browse these newsgroups with Microsoft Entourage X, and these newsgroups can provide invaluable interaction with other Office users.

> For more information on setting up and browsing newsgroups with Entourage, see Chapter 19, "Using Newsgroups."

newfeature!

Accessing Tools On The Web

The new Tools On The Web feature connects you to a Microsoft Web site that provides even more help resources, but also offers convenient access to a group of Internet services, such as Yellow and White pages, driving directions, the online version of the Microsoft Encarta encyclopedia, and electronic language translation. Tools On The Web is the fastest way to get to Microsoft's online Template Gallery, a library of templates for Word, Excel, and Microsoft PowerPoint X that you can download and use for your own work.

You get to this online cornucopia by choosing Tools, Tools On The Web from any of the Office v. X programs. Your Web browser will open to the Tools On The Web home page, as shown in Figure 3-8.

Figure 3-8. The new Tools On The Web feature provides a large array of up-to-date Web services.

Accessing the *Getting Started* Book on the Office v. X CD

Microsoft has provided *Getting Started with Microsoft Office X*, a manual in electronic format, on the Office v. X CD. If you are unfamiliar with using the Office applications, *Getting Started* provides a nice introduction to basic tasks.

Chapter 3

> **note** *Getting Started* is in PDF format, sometimes known as Adobe Acrobat format. PDF is one of Mac OS X's native file formats and can be read by either Apple's Preview application, or by Adobe's free Acrobat Reader; both are installed by default with Mac OS X.

The best way to use *Getting Started* is directly from the Office v. X CD. Follow these steps:

1 Insert the Microsoft Office X CD.

2 Open the Microsoft Office X folder from your Applications folder, as shown in Figure 3-9.

3 Double-click the file named *Getting Started Book.pdf*. Either Preview or Acrobat Reader will open and display the document.

Figure 3-9. You'll find the *Getting Started* quick start manual on the Office CD.

Turning on ScreenTips

By default, the Office programs show ScreenTips when you pause the mouse cursor over toolbar buttons. ScreenTips are little yellow tags that identify each button's function.

Chapter 3: Getting Expert Help with Office v. X

If you prefer, you can turn ScreenTips off, or you can keep the ScreenTips and set them to show shortcut keys as well as the button name. Here's how to do it in Word, Excel, and PowerPoint:

1 Choose Tools, Customize. The Customize dialog appears.

2 Click the Toolbars tab, as shown in Figure 3-10. Then select the check boxes for the options you want:

    ■ To turn ScreenTips off, clear the Show ScreenTips On Toolbars check box.

    ■ To add shortcut keys to the ScreenTips, select both the Show ScreenTips On Toolbars and the Show Shortcut Keys In ScreenTips check boxes.

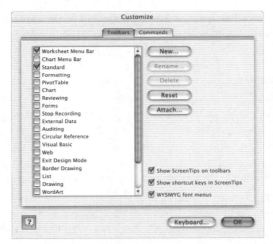

Figure 3-10. You can turn ScreenTips on in the Customize dialog.

3 Click OK. If you've turned on both options, the ScreenTips now appear when you point at a button on a toolbar, and shortcut keys will be included in the ScreenTip.

InsideOut

You can't turn ScreenTips on in Entourage's Customize dialog because, well, Entourage doesn't have a Customize dialog. Instead, choose Entourage, General Preferences, and click the General tab. Then select the Show ToolTips check box. Oddly, Entourage calls them ToolTips instead of ScreenTips, but they're the same things.

Getting the Tip of the Day

The Office programs can greet you when you start them up with a Tip of the Day, which is often surprisingly useful. You can usually discover something that you don't know that will make your work easier. There's a finite supply of tips, of course, so after a few weeks you're probably going to want to turn the Tip of the Day off. But while they're fresh, they're worth keeping around—and are occasionally even humorous, as shown in Figure 3-11.

Figure 3-11. The Tip of the Day is always good advice, but this one is better than most.

To turn the Tip of the Day on (or off), follow these steps:

1 Display the Office Assistant window.

2 Control+click in the Office Assistant window. From the resulting contextual menu, choose Options.

3 Select (or clear) the Show The Tip Of The Day At Startup check box.

Chapter 4

Office v. X: Do It Your Way

As you become more experienced with Microsoft Office v. X, you'll naturally begin looking for ways to streamline tasks and make your work easier and faster. And of course, you'll realize that some of the ways that the Office programs work aren't quite the way that you prefer to work. The good news is that, at least with Microsoft Word and Microsoft Excel, you have great control over menus, toolbars, and keyboard shortcuts, and you can make almost any modifications you want to these interface elements.

In this chapter, you'll see how to customize the Office programs so that they're more to your liking. We'll cover how to tailor toolbars, menus (including contextual menus), and keyboard shortcuts.

Wrangling Your Toolbars

Toolbars are the ubiquitous interface element in Office, and there are a great many customizations you can make to them (but there are some significant restrictions; see "Customization Limitations," on the next page). You can move toolbars where you want them; add (or delete) buttons, menus, or macros to toolbars; and even create your own toolbars.

Customization Limitations

When it comes to customizing the user interface, you've got the most latitude with Microsoft Word X and Microsoft Excel X. In these two programs, you can customize toolbars and menus, add or delete keyboard shortcuts, and record and use macros to extend the program's capabilities.

For more information about using macros in Word, see Chapter 16, "Automating Word with Macros and AppleScripts." To learn more about automating Excel, see Chapter 33, "Using Excel Macros and Add-Ins."

Microsoft PowerPoint X gives you less control; you can customize toolbars and menus, but you can't add or change keyboard shortcuts, and PowerPoint has no ability to record your own macros. You can run macros, at least theoretically, but since there's no macro recorder, you can only run macros that have been programmed from scratch. Unless you're a macro whiz, you won't be doing that, so PowerPoint's macro abilities go largely unused.

Bringing up the rear in the customization game is Microsoft Entourage. You can't customize toolbars, menus, or keyboard shortcuts, and Entourage also lacks a macro recorder. In fact, Entourage uses an entirely different automation language—AppleScript—than the other Office programs, which use a cross-platform macro language called Visual Basic for Applications. AppleScripts that you install into Entourage appear in Entourage's Script menu, and you can do surprisingly powerful things with these scripts. But you can't customize Entourage's user interface.

For more information about using AppleScripts in Entourage, see Chapter 23, "Extending Entourage with AppleScript."

There's one other customization caveat that applies to Word, Excel, and PowerPoint. Sadly, the Formatting Palette is a special type of toolbar that can't be customized. This doesn't apply to Entourage, because it doesn't have a Formatting Palette.

Displaying and Hiding Toolbars

To hide (or show) most toolbars, follow these steps:

1 Control+click one of the vertical separators, or a blank spot, on any toolbar. A pop-up menu appears, with a check mark next to active toolbars, as shown in Figure 4-1.

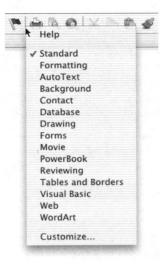

Figure 4-1. Choose from the pop-up toolbar menu to hide or show toolbars.

2 Set a check mark or clear a check mark next to a toolbar name on the pop-up menu to show or hide the corresponding toolbar.

> **tip** If the toolbar pop-up menu doesn't appear, you probably clicked a button, rather than a separator or blank part of the toolbar. Just let go of the mouse button, find a different part of the toolbar, and try again.

Alternatively, you can hide or show most toolbars by choosing View, Toolbars, and then clicking the name of the toolbar.

InsideOut

Find the hidden toolbars in Office

You look in the View menu, or Control+click on a toolbar, and you can't see the name of the toolbar you want. What gives? It turns out that the Office applications only list the "major" toolbars in the menus; "lesser" toolbars, like the 3-D Settings toolbar in Word, or the Auditing toolbar in Excel, aren't listed. The best way to view these toolbars is to choose Tools, Customize, click the Toolbars tab, and then select the check box next to the toolbar you want to display.

Chapter 4

Arranging and Docking Toolbars

At the left edge (or top edge, if the toolbar has been turned into a floating palette) of any toolbar is the move handle. Click the move handle and drag downward or to the right to turn the toolbar into a floating palette. You can also use the move handles to rearrange the toolbars; just drag the toolbars where you want them. You can get rid of toolbars or palettes by clicking the close button that's in the move handle.

> **tip** You can't overlap toolbars; if you drag one on top of another, the overlapped toolbar will slide politely out of the way. The document window will shrink to make room for toolbars, too.

Toolbars don't have to stay at the top of the screen. You can turn a toolbar into a float-ing palette and then drag the floating palette to any edge of the screen to dock it as a toolbar. The Office programs will move the document window so that docked toolbars never overlap the document you're working on. You can also change the shape and orientation of toolbars and floating palettes by using their resize handle in their lower right corner, as shown in Figure 4-2.

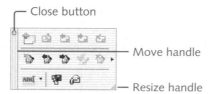

Close button

Move handle

Resize handle

Figure 4-2.   In this example, Word's Reviewing toolbar has been undocked and reshaped into a floating palette.

Adding a Button to a Toolbar

The most common way to make a toolbar work more efficiently is to add a button to it. Sometimes you'll be adding buttons that are already available on other toolbars, and sometimes you'll add buttons for commands that have no button equivalents, but should (at least, as far as you're concerned). Follow these steps to add buttons to toolbars:

1 Display the toolbar to which you want to add a button.

2 Choose Tools, Customize.

3 Click the Commands tab in the Customize dialog, as shown in Figure 4-3.

Chapter 4: Office v. X: Do It Your Way

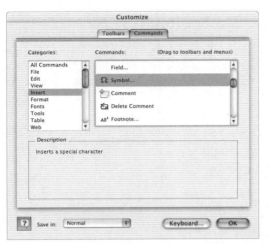

Figure 4-3. The Commands tab of the Customize dialog gives you access to all of Word's commands, so you can turn them into toolbar buttons.

4 In the Categories box, click the category for the command for which you want to create a button.

5 Scroll through the Commands box until you find the command you want, and then drag it to the toolbar you displayed in step 1. If the command has an icon associated with it (not all commands do), the icon for the command appears on the toolbar. If no icon exists, the name of the command appears as text on a new button on the toolbar.

tip If you can't seem to find a command in a particular category, select All Commands in the Categories box.

6 Click OK to close the Customize dialog.

note All of these customizations you're creating have to be saved somewhere, and that place is in the current document template. If you're not using a specialized document template, the customizations will be saved in the Normal document template. For more information about document templates, see Chapter 2, "Creating and Managing Documents."

Chapter 4

Removing a Button from a Toolbar

Sometimes you want to remove buttons from toolbars—because you never use that function, because you want to make room for your own custom buttons, or because you mistakenly placed a button. To remove a button from a toolbar, follow these steps:

1 Display the toolbar you want to modify.

2 Control+click the button you wish to remove. A pop-up menu appears, as shown in Figure 4-4.

Figure 4-4. The command modification pop-up menu lets you change toolbar buttons directly.

3 Choose Hide Command from the pop-up menu. The button disappears from the toolbar.

Moving, Copying, and Separating Toolbar Buttons

You can rearrange toolbar buttons however you want. If you want to move a button from one toolbar to another, first make sure that both toolbars are displayed, and then choose Tools, Customize to display the Customize dialog. Then, to move the button, drag the button to its new home, on the same toolbar or on a different toolbar. To copy the button, hold down the Option key while you drag the button.

If buttons seem to run together on your toolbars, you can separate them. To create a separator bar between buttons, choose Tools, Customize to display the Customize dialog, and then click a button and drag it just a little to the right or left. When you release the mouse button, the separator bar appears. To remove a separator, move the button to the right of the separator just enough to the left to touch the separator, and then release the mouse button.

> **caution** If you drag the button too far, you will end up moving the button to another toolbar or to a different place on the same toolbar. If you mistakenly move a button, just drag it back to where you started and try again.

Adding Menus to a Toolbar

If you want to get ambitious about customizing toolbars, you can add any menu to any toolbar. You're not limited to the menus that come with the Office programs; you can create your own custom menus and add them to toolbars too.

Placing a Built-in Menu on a Toolbar

You can add entire menus to toolbars, either the menus that come with the Office programs or custom menus you build yourself. Follow these steps to add one of the built-in menus to a toolbar:

1 Display the toolbar to which you want to add a menu.

2 Choose Tools, Customize.

3 Click the Commands tab in the Customize dialog.

4 In the Categories box, click Built-In Menus.

> **tip** You can add macros to toolbars, too; just choose Macros in step 4 instead.

5 Drag the menu you want to use from the Commands box to the toolbar.

6 Click OK to close the Customize dialog.

Creating a Custom Menu on a Toolbar

You can create custom menus and add them to toolbars. Just follow these steps:

1 Display the toolbar to which you want to add a menu.

2 Choose Tools, Customize. The Customize dialog appears.

3 Click the Commands tab.

4 In the Categories box, click New Menu.

5 Drag the New Menu item from the Commands box to the toolbar.

6 Double-click the New Menu item on the toolbar. The Command Properties dialog appears, as shown in Figure 4-5 on the next page.

7 In the Name box, type the new menu's title. Click OK.

8 To add commands to your new custom menu, select a category from the Categories list and then drag a command from the Commands box of the

Chapter 4

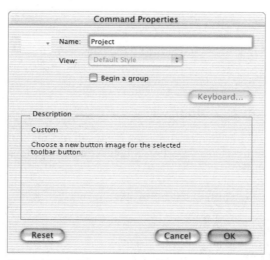

Figure 4-5. You name a custom menu on a toolbar in the Command Properties dialog.

Customize dialog to the custom menu. Wait for the menu to drop down, and then drop the command where you want it to go on the custom menu. The first time, you can only drop it in the empty box below the menu name; for subsequent commands, you can move them where you want.

> **tip** If you want a separation between two menu items, double-click the one that's lower on the menu. In the resulting Command Properties dialog, click Begin A Group.

9 Repeat step 8 until you've added all the commands you want to use on the custom menu.

10 Click OK. The new custom menu appears on the toolbar, as shown in Figure 4-6.

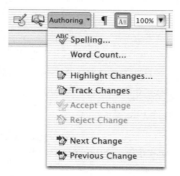

Figure 4-6. The toolbar now contains the custom Authoring menu with its set of chosen commands.

Chapter 4

> **tip** One of the great things about the Office v. X programs is that when it comes to customization, the menu bar is treated as just another toolbar. So it's easy to add your own custom menus to the menu bar, not just to toolbars.

Creating Your Own Toolbars

If customizing toolbars isn't enough for you, you can create your own. Follow these steps:

1 Choose Tools, Customize.

2 If it isn't already visible, click the Toolbars tab in the Customize dialog, shown here:

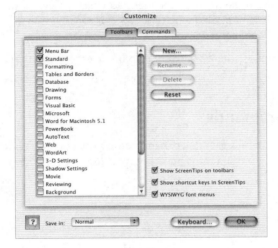

3 Click the New button.

4 Type the name of the new toolbar, and then click OK.

5 To populate the new toolbar, click the Commands tab, and then drag buttons to it, as described in "Adding a Button to a Toolbar," page 48.

Customizing Menus

Another good way to customize the Office programs is to add commands to any of the menus. For example, if your work requires a lot of scientific notation, you may want to put Word's Equation Editor on the Insert menu. To add a command to a menu, follow these steps:

1 Choose Tools, Customize.

2 Click the Toolbars tab in the Customize dialog.

Part 1: Office v. X Fundamentals

3 Select the Menu Bar check box. A customizable copy of the menu bar appears, as shown in Figure 4-7.

File ▾ Edit ▾ View ▾ Insert ▾ Format ▾ Font ▾ Tools ▾ Table ▾ Window ▾ Help ▾

Figure 4-7. A customizable copy of the menu bar allows you to make any additions or subtractions you want to Word's menus.

4 Click the Commands tab.

5 In the Categories box, select the category that contains the command you want to add to the menu. If you can't find the command in a category, select the All Commands category.

6 In the Commands box, click the command you want to add to the menu.

7 Drag the command to the name of the menu to which you want to add the command, and pause until the menu opens. A horizontal line indicates where on the menu your command will appear.

8 When the command is where you want it to be, release the mouse button.

9 Click OK.

Renaming Menu Commands

If you don't like the name of a particular menu command, you don't have to put up with it; just change the name so that it makes more sense to you. Follow these steps to rename a command:

1 Choose Tools, Customize.

2 Click the Toolbars tab in the Customize dialog.

3 Select the Menu Bar check box.

4 On the copy of the menu bar (shown earlier in Figure 4-7), double-click the command you want to change.

5 In the Name box of the Command Properties dialog, type the new name for the command.

> **note** In some menus, you may notice that ampersands (&) appear in the names of some commands. They denote *keyboard accelerators,* which are the keys that are used when you're navigating the menus entirely with the keyboard. Keyboard accelerators are not the same thing as shortcut keys. In other words, keyboard accelerators are a vestige of Office's Windows roots and are rarely (if ever) used on the Mac.

6 Press Return to close the Command Properties dialog, and then click OK to close the Customize dialog.

Creating Custom Menus for the Menu Bar

You can create your own custom menus for particular projects and add them to the menu bar. For example, suppose that you have several macros that you use frequently. You can create a custom menu that includes all of them. To create a custom menu and add it to the menu bar, follow these steps:

1. Choose Tools, Customize.

2. Click the Toolbars tab in the Customize dialog.

3. Select the Menu Bar check box to display a customizable copy of the menu bar.

4. Click the Commands tab.

5. Scroll to the bottom of the Categories box and select New Menu.

6. Drag the New Menu item from the Commands box to where you want it to appear in the copy of the menu bar.

7. To rename the new menu, double-click the New Menu item on the copy of the menu bar. The Command Properties dialog appears.

8. In the Name box of the Command Properties dialog, type the new menu's title, and then press Return.

9. Select a category from the Categories box, and then drag one of its commands from the Commands box to the new menu.

10. Repeat step 9 until you have added to the new menu all the commands you want to use. As you drag each command to the new menu, release the mouse button when the command appears in the desired position.

11. Click OK to exit the Customize dialog.

Customizing Word's Contextual Menus

Contextual menus contain commands that apply to the item the mouse pointer is resting on. You access them by holding down the Control key while clicking something on the screen. You can modify a contextual menu to contain different commands from the ones that Microsoft includes with Word X.

> **note** At press time, there was a bug that prevented you from adding new commands to contextual menus, though you could delete commands. Microsoft reported that they were working on a fix, which may be available by the time you read this. If you want to add a command to a contextual menu, make sure that you've installed the latest update to Office (by choosing Help, Downloads And Updates from any of the Office applications) and try the procedure that follows.

Chapter 4

To add a command to a contextual menu, follow these steps:

1 Choose Tools, Customize, and then click the Toolbars tab.

2 Select the Shortcut Menus check box. The Shortcut Menu toolbar appears, as shown in Figure 4-8.

Figure 4-8. The Shortcut Menu toolbar contains customizable copies of all of the shortcut menus in Word.

---

tip *Shortcut menu* is a term shared by the Windows version of Microsoft Office. In Office v. X, Microsoft has made a big effort to follow Mac terminology, but you'll still find some leftover Windows terms. Just remember that a shortcut menu is a contextual menu, and you won't be confused.

---

3 Click one of the categories (Text, Table, or Draw) on the Shortcut Menu toolbar, and then click the shortcut menu you wish to change.

4 In the Customize dialog, click the Commands tab.

5 Choose a category, and then drag a command from the Commands box to the shortcut menu.

6 Release the mouse button.

7 Click OK to accept the changes and close the Customize dialog.

To delete an item from a contextual menu, follow these steps:

1 Choose Tools, Customize, and then click the Toolbars tab.

2 Select the Shortcut Menus check box.

3 Click one of the categories (Text, Table, or Draw) on the Shortcut Menu toolbar, and then click the shortcut menu you wish to change.

4 Drag the command you no longer want off the shortcut menu.

5 Click OK to accept the changes and close the Customize window.

newfeature!
Customizing Keyboard Shortcuts in Word and Excel

Some of the shortcut keys that Microsoft thinks are logical might not make sense to you. No problem. You can change them if you don't like them. For example, if you've been using Excel for several versions, its new ability for keyboard customization will be

Chapter 4: Office v. X: Do It Your Way

especially welcome, since Office 2001 re-mapped a lot of long-standing shortcuts in an effort to make shortcuts consistent across all the Office applications. Excel's keyboard customization allows longtime users to put those familiar keyboard shortcuts, such as Command+B to blank out a cell's contents, back where they belong.

> **note** Unfortunately, shortcut key customization is only available in Word and Excel; PowerPoint and Entourage have been left out in the cold.

Follow these steps to make shortcut keys do your bidding:

1 Choose Tools, Customize.

2 Click the Keyboard button in the Customize dialog. The Customize Keyboard dialog appears, as shown in Figure 4-9.

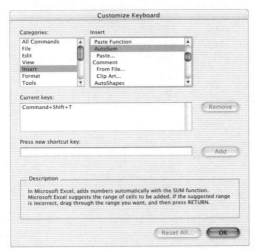

Figure 4-9.   You can change shortcut keys with the Customize Keyboard dialog (in this example, it's in Excel).

3 In the Categories box, select the category containing the command for which you want to add or change the shortcut key. If you can't find the command, select the All Commands category.

4 In the box at the right (named Commands in Word but in Excel named according to the category you selected in step 3, such as All Commands or Insert), select the command.

5 Click the Press New Shortcut Key box. If a shortcut key is already assigned for this command, it appears in the Current Keys box.

> **tip**   **Assign multiple shortcut keys**
>
> You're not limited to just one shortcut key combination per command. If you want to assign more than one key, go ahead; either key combination will then trigger the command. You might want to do this because you are used to using a particular key combination in another program and you want to reuse that knowledge in Word or Excel without replacing the Microsoft-supplied key combinations.

   6 On your keyboard, press the shortcut key combination you want to use. If the combination is already in use, a message tells you which command now has it.

   7 Click the Add button.

   8 Click the OK button to close the Customize Keyboard dialog and return to the Customize dialog, and then click OK to close the Customize dialog.

Part 2

Word

Word Essentials

Microsoft Word X is Microsoft Office v. X's word processor, and it offers an amazing array of features and capabilities that allow you to create virtually any sort of document that you can imagine. Whether you want to create simple letters and reports, Web pages and newsletters, or full-length books, Word has the tools to handle the job. Word is also a team player, effortlessly working with information from other applications to create documents that are more than the sum of their parts.

In this chapter, you'll learn how to use the different features of the Word document window, how to send Word documents via e-mail, how to use Print Preview to make sure that your documents look right before they print, and how to exercise maximum control over printing your documents.

The Word Document Window in Depth

Launching Word creates a blank document, as shown in Figure 5-1 on the next page. In addition to the menu bar and the Standard toolbar, Word provides many tools and objects in the document window itself that tell you information about the document and that allow you to manipulate the document in many different ways.

Several of the document window's elements—the menu and title bars, and the vertical and horizontal scroll bars—work in the same way as in any other Macintosh application.

> The toolbars (which you can show or hide as needed) are discussed in "Wrangling Your Toolbars," page 45. You'll find discussions of the split box and View buttons later in this chapter. The browse buttons are discussed in "Navigating with the Browse Buttons," page 114. The horizontal and vertical rulers and the Tab well are discussed in "Setting Paragraph Formatting," page 137.

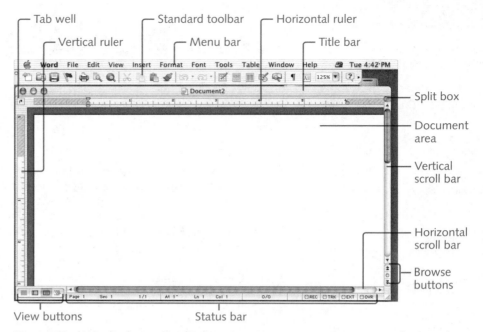

Figure 5-1. Word's document window gives you many ways to view and manipulate your document.

Word's status bar provides detailed information about the document and about what mode the program is in, as shown in Figure 5-2.

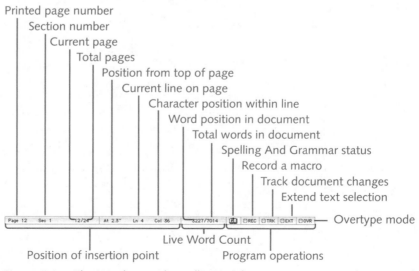

Figure 5-2. The Word status bar tells you where you are in your document, how long your document is, and what editing mode Word is in.

62

Clicking or double-clicking items on the status bar is a shortcut to quickly issue commands to Word, as detailed in Table 5-1.

Table 5-1. Command Shortcuts Available from the Status Bar

Item to Click	Action
Any of the six insertion point indicators shown in Figure 5-2 (requires double-click)	The corresponding Go To dialog opens (see "Navigating with Go To," page 115).
Live Word Count area (requires double-click)	The Word Count dialog opens (see "Getting Word Counts," page 282).
Spelling And Grammar status	Jumps to the next spelling or grammar error in your document and opens a list of suggested corrections.
REC	Begins (or stops) recording a macro (see "Recording Macros," page 387).
TRK	Turns document tracking on or off (see "Tracking Changes," page 326).
EXT	Turns Extend Selection mode on or off.
OVR	Turns Overtype mode on or off.

Getting Different Views of Your Document

Word provides lots of different ways to see what you're doing. You can see your document pages in WYSIWYG (What You See Is What You Get) mode, where there is a one-to-one correspondence between the screen and the printed page. You can look at your document in an Outline view that reveals the document's structure. And if you need a closer look at part of your document, Word can zoom in as close as you want. The key is control—you want it, and Word gives it to you.

Working with Document Views

You work with your Word documents in one of the seven *document views*. Each view provides a different way of displaying and working with the document. Page Layout view, the default view, shows you the document as it will appear when printed. You'll probably also work much of the time in the Normal view, a simplified view that concentrates on fast text entry and editing.

Table 5-2 lists the different document views, describes each briefly, and tells you how to access each view. Typically, you'll use the View menu or, for the four most commonly used views, the View buttons to the left of the horizontal scroll bar, as shown here:

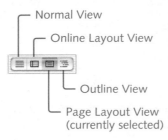

Normal View
Online Layout View
Outline View
Page Layout View
(currently selected)

Table 5-2. **Word Document Views**

View	Description	Purpose	Access
Normal	Displays pages with simple text formatting. Drawings, margins, headers and footers, and columns are not shown. Page breaks are shown as dotted lines. Also sometimes known as *galley view*.	For entering and editing text quickly. Don't use this view to check page layout or fancy formatting.	Choose View, Normal, or click the Normal View button to the left of the horizontal scroll bar.
Online Layout	Displays the page as the document would appear in a Web browser. Formatted text and graphics will appear. Text appears without page breaks and with minimal margins.	Use this view to test a page you're creating for the Web. Don't use this view as a substitute for previewing your pages in a real Web browser.	Choose View, Online Layout, or click the Online Layout View button to the left of the horizontal scroll bar.
Page Layout	Displays the document as it will appear on the printed page, with all text formatting, images, headers and footers, and other elements.	Use this view for proofing the layout and look of text and graphics before you print.	Choose View, Page Layout, or click the Page Layout View button to the left of the horizontal scroll bar.

Table 5-2. *(continued)*

View	Description	Purpose	Access
Outline	Shows the organizational structure of your document by displaying the document's headings and subheadings.	For creating and structuring the content of your document. Lets you quickly rearrange document text.	Choose View, Outline, or click the Outline View button to the left of the horizontal scroll bar.
Master Document	Displays an outline-like view of long documents made up of subdocuments.	For organizing and maintaining a long document by dividing it into several subdocuments.	Choose View, Master Document.
Document Map	Displays a document in two vertical frames. The left frame is reminiscent of Outline view, and allows you to navigate through the text in the right frame.	For moving through the document quickly.	Choose View, Document Map.
Full Screen	Displays the document window without rulers, toolbars, scroll bars, or the status bar.	Use this view to maximize your editing space. Scrolling can be accomplished using the arrow keys on the keyboard.	Choose View, Full Screen to toggle this view on and off.

tip **Improve performance in Word**

When entering text, you'll get the best performance from Word by typing in Normal view. That's because Normal view, being a simplified text view, requires less processing power from your computer than more complex views, such as Page Layout view. You'll see the performance benefit in faster scrolling through the document and in improved speed while editing text.

Zooming in on Your Document

The standard document views are useful, but sometimes you need to see your document up close and personal—or view the document from a distance. Word lets you increase or decrease the magnification of the document, which makes it easy to work with documents on your screen, regardless of the font sizes you use in the document. For example, you might want to use the 12-point Times New Roman font for your document, because it looks good when you print. But this font might not work well as a screen font because it's a little too small. Word enables you to magnify the document to make it easier on your eyes; 125% is a popular choice with many high-resolution monitors. Similarly, you can shrink the document to get an overview of the document's structure or just to fit more words on your screen. Word provides two ways to change the screen magnification: the Zoom dialog and the Zoom box on the Standard toolbar. Each method has its benefits.

To use the Zoom dialog, shown in Figure 5-3, follow these steps:

1 Choose View, Zoom.

2 Click one of the Zoom To options to set the document magnification you want; a representation will be shown in the Preview area. If none of the preset choices are what you want, you can type any number between 10 and 500 in the Percent box. Clicking Page Width is a quick way to get the document to zoom up to fit comfortably in the document window, regardless of how you have resized that window. Conversely, clicking Whole Page will zoom out so that the entire page fits within the document window. Clicking Many Pages enables a pop-up menu that allows you to drag the pointer to select how many rows and columns of pages will be sized to fit within the document window.

3 Click OK.

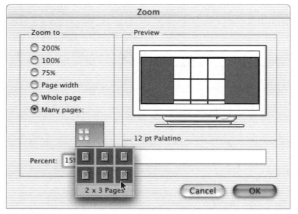

Figure 5-3. The Zoom dialog's Many Pages option allows you to fit many pages within the document window, so you can get an expansive overview of your entire document.

tip The Whole Page and Many Pages options are only available if the document is in Page Layout view.

The Zoom box on the Standard toolbar is often more convenient to use than the Zoom dialog, because it has more preset magnification choices, as shown here:

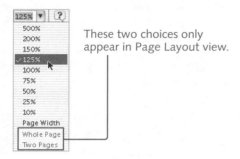

These two choices only appear in Page Layout view.

---

tip   Just as in the Zoom dialog, you can set a precise value for magnification in the Zoom box. Simply click the number in the Zoom box to select it, type a new value, and press Return.

Using the Window Menu

Word's Window menu allows you to hide or show your windows, display multiple views of the same document, split a window into two panes, or simply switch between different open documents.

Displaying Multiple Document Windows

Choosing Window, New Window creates a duplicate of your document window, which you can scroll or zoom independently. The title bar identifies the windows as "Client Letter:1," "Client Letter:2," and so on. The new windows give you a different outlook on the same document; you haven't created a new document. Because both windows are the same document, any changes that you make in one window are reflected in the other window. One especially nice aspect of this feature is that you can use different document views in each window, so that you can keep the Outline view on-screen at the same time that you are working in Normal view in the other window.

Minimizing Windows to the Mac OS X Dock

It's not unusual to have several windows open at the same time while working with Word. If you want to keep one or more documents open, but want them out of your way to reduce screen clutter, you can minimize their windows to the Mac OS X Dock.

Chapter 5

> **note** Minimizing windows to the Dock is the OS X equivalent of using the Windowshade button in the title bar of Mac OS 9 windows, which hid a window's document area, leaving only the window's title bar visible. In some ways, minimizing windows to the Dock is less convenient than windowshading them, because a windowshaded document window's title always remained visible, allowing you to select and reactivate a document with a single click. Under Mac OS X, you must slide the mouse all the way over to one edge of the screen to show the Dock, search through the Dock for the correct document, and then click the document's miniaturized icon to expand and reactivate the document.

To minimize a window to the Dock, press Command+M; choose Window, Minimize Window; or click the yellow Minimize button at the top left corner of the document window. When your pointer nears the three buttons, symbols appear within them to remind you of their function: an X in the red button, signifying close; a minus sign (–) in the yellow button, for minimize; and a plus sign (+) in the green button for maximize. You'll see the window shrink and zoom into the Dock, where it will become an icon that looks like the window.

To get the window back out of the Dock, click its iconized form in the Dock; the window will zoom out of the Dock and back to its former size.

Splitting Windows

Dragging the split box, or choosing Window, Split, divides the window into two panes, each with its own vertical scroll bar, as shown in Figure 5-4. Splitting a document in this way makes it easy to work on two widely separated parts of your document at once. You could be typing in one pane while referring to material you wrote earlier in the other pane.

> **tip** **Do quick splits**
>
> Double-clicking the split box divides the window into two evenly sized panes. To quickly return a split window to a single pane, double-click the resize bar between the two panes.

Arranging Windows

When you have several documents open at the same time, it is sometimes useful to be able to view at least part of all the documents simultaneously. Choosing Window, Arrange All tiles all the open windows so that they can be seen without overlapping, as shown in Figure 5-5.

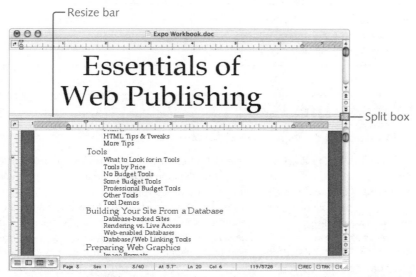

Figure 5-4. The different panes of this split document display entirely different views; the top pane appears in Normal view, at a magnification of 125%, and the bottom pane is in Page Layout view, at 100%.

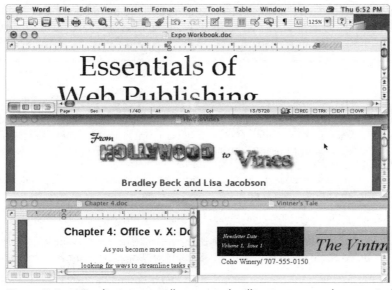

Figure 5-5. Word's Arrange All command will arrange your documents (in this case, four documents) for maximum visibility.

Chapter 5

> **tip** If you select one of the windows, making it the active window, and then choose Window, Arrange All again, the active window will be moved to the top of the screen and, if there is room, will be enlarged.

Troubleshooting

I've lost windows due to Mac OS X's window behavior.

Windows in Mac OS X act quite differently than they did in previous versions of the Mac OS, and for longtime Mac users, the adjustment to this change might be very difficult. In Mac OS 9 and earlier, clicking on any of an application's windows brought all of that application's windows to the foreground. In effect, each application and all of its windows were a single layer that acted together. Not so in Mac OS X, which treats each window as a separate layer. For example, if you are working in Entourage and you click the visible edge of a Word document that's peeking out behind the Entourage window, that Word document will become the active document, you'll see the menu bar change to Word's menu bar, and the Entourage window will become the second layer behind the Word document window. But any other Word documents that you have open will remain behind the Entourage window. If you want to get to these documents and they are completely hidden behind the Entourage window, you have to choose one of these documents from Word's Window menu to bring it to the foreground. To bring all of the Word windows in front of any other application windows you have open, choose Window, Bring All To Front.

Sending Word Documents via E-Mail

Word (and Microsoft Excel and Microsoft PowerPoint) make it easy to send documents as file attachments via Entourage or another Mac OS X e-mail program. Follow these steps:

1 With the document you want to send open, choose File, Save to make sure your latest edits are saved.

2 Choose File, Send To, Mail Recipient (As Attachment).

3 Entourage (or your default e-mail program) will open and create a new message, with the file enclosed as an attachment. Enter the address of the recipient.

4 Enter a subject for the e-mail message, and if desired, an explanatory message.

5 Click the Send button in your e-mail program.

Troubleshooting

The Mail Recipient (As Attachment) command appears dimmed.

If the Mail Recipient (As Attachment) command appears dimmed and is unavailable, there can be one of two reasons. The first is that your e-mail program isn't Mac OS X native. If you're using an older e-mail program that still runs under the Mac OS 9–based Classic Environment (such as Microsoft's Outlook Express, Bare Bones's Mailsmith, Qualcomm's Eudora, or even Entourage 2001), Office v. X can't use it to send documents as attachments. You'll need to upgrade to a Mac OS X–native e-mail program, such as (of course) Entourage X, Apple's Mail (included with Mac OS X), or Eudora for Mac OS X.

If you're already using a Mac OS X–native e-mail program, you might need to select it in the Internet panel of System Preferences. Choose Apple, System Preferences, and then click the Internet icon. Click the E-Mail tab, and on the Default E-Mail Reader pop-up menu, choose the program you want to use. If you don't see the program you want to use in the list, choose Select, and navigate to the e-mail program you want to use. Changes that you make on the E-Mail tab won't take effect until you quit and restart all of the currently running Office applications.

Flagging Documents for Follow-Up

When working on a Word document, you'll sometimes want to set the document aside and come back to work on it later. The Flag For Follow Up feature lets Word work with Entourage to create an Office Notifications reminder that appears at the scheduled time to remind you to get back to work. Office Notifications uses Entourage's events database for its scheduling.

For more information about using Entourage to work with flagged documents, see Chapter 22, "Organizing and Sharing Entourage Data."

To flag a document for follow-up, follow these steps:

1 With the document you want to flag open, choose Tools, Flag For Follow Up, or click the Flag For Follow Up button on the Standard toolbar.

2 Choose a date and time for the reminder, as shown here:

3 Click OK.

Chapter 5

Flagging a document creates a new task in Entourage. When the reminder comes due, Office Notifications will open a reminder window. You can manage the reminder in Entourage's Tasks window, or in the Office Notifications application (see the Tip that follows).

> To learn more about managing reminders with Entourage, see Chapter 21, "Managing Your Appointments, Tasks, and Notes."

tip **Manage reminders with the Office Notifications application**

You can manage your reminders using the Microsoft Office Notifications application located in the Office folder within the Microsoft Office X folder. Choose Office Notifications, Show All to display a list of reminders. You can open any item in the list, click Snooze to delay the reminder, click Dismiss to delete it, or click the file's name to reopen it.

Previewing Your Document

Print
Preview

With the exception of the simplest documents, you'll usually want to preview documents before you print them, to save time and paper. Word's Print Preview shows you how a document will look when you print it. You can check text and formatting, make sure that the document's page breaks fall where you want them, and even view multiple pages at a time. To show your document in Print Preview, choose File, Print Preview, or click the Print Preview button on the Standard toolbar.

Using the Print Preview Window

In Print Preview, the document window changes to display a full page as it will look when printed, and the Print Preview toolbar appears, as shown in Figure 5-6. The Print Preview toolbar buttons are described in Table 5-3.

Table 5-3. Print Preview Toolbar Buttons

Button	Name	Action
🖨	Print	Prints a single copy of the previewed document using the default print settings. The Print dialog does not appear.
🔍	Magnifier	Click to enlarge the document view; click again to reduce the view.
▣	One Page	Shows a single page in the document view. If the view is zoomed in, clicking this button returns the view to a full page.

Table 5-3. *(continued)*

Button	Name	Action
	Multiple Pages	Allows you to display two or more pages at once.
59% ▼	Zoom	Controls the magnification level of the displayed document. The Page Width choice enlarges the document so that it fills the Print Preview window; Whole Page reduces the document to show the entire page; Two Pages reduces the document and shows two pages side by side.
	View Ruler	Toggles the horizontal and vertical rulers on and off.
	Shrink To Fit	Avoids the problem of a small amount of text spilling onto an extra page by decreasing the font size of each font used in a document.
	Full Screen	Maximizes the viewing area by hiding the scroll bars and status bar.

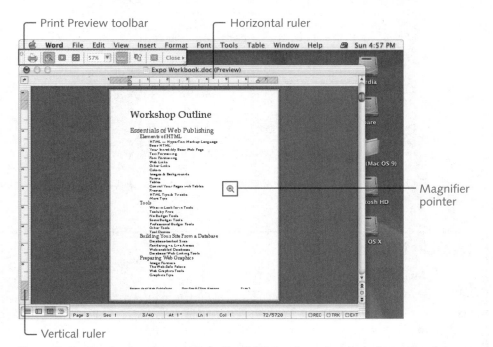

Print Preview toolbar

Horizontal ruler

Magnifier pointer

Vertical ruler

Figure 5-6. Previewing documents in the Print Preview window before you print can help you avert problems and save time.

To exit Print Preview mode, choose one of the following methods:

- Choose File, Print Preview.
- Click Close on the Print Preview toolbar.
- Press Esc.

Viewing Multiple Pages in Print Preview

Print Preview, like the Zoom command, lets you view multiple pages at once to get a bird's eye view of your document. To preview multiple pages, click the Multiple Pages button on the Print Preview toolbar, and drag to select the number of pages you wish to view. Figure 5-7 shows three rows and four columns of pages in the Print Preview window.

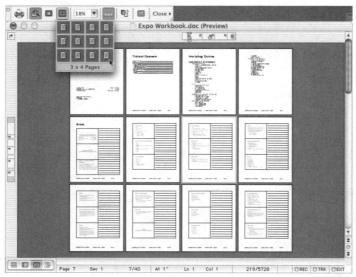

Figure 5-7. Using the Multiple Pages feature, you can get a quick overview of a large portion of your document.

InsideOut

Zoom in before making ruler changes

Note in Figure 5-7 that the rulers are only active for the page that you have selected in Multiple Pages. When there are many pages showing, the rulers are so small that they aren't as useful, so you'll probably want to zoom in on a page before you make any changes to margins or indents.

To zoom to a particular page that you're looking at in Multiple Pages view, click the page to select it, and then click the One Page button on the Print Preview toolbar.

Editing in Print Preview

You can edit text in Print Preview mode in much the same way you would edit in any of the other views. To activate the text editing mode in Print Preview, click the Magnifier button so that it is not highlighted, and then click in the document area to place the insertion point. You can now enter, delete, copy, paste, or move text or apply formatting.

> **tip** You don't have to edit in 100 percent view; you can edit in any view size. Editing in smaller sizes, especially when viewing multiple pages, makes it easy to move text or pictures from one page to another.

Adjusting Margins, Indents, and Tabs

Print Preview mode displays the rulers by default, and you can toggle them on and off by clicking the Rulers button on the Print Preview toolbar. When the rulers are displayed, you can drag the margin, indent, and tab icons on the rulers to adjust the document's margins, indenting, and tabs. You can add tabs to the document by clicking in the horizontal ruler, and remove tabs by dragging the tab's icon off the ruler.

> **tip** You can change between the five kinds of tabs (Left, Center, Right, Decimal, and Bar) by clicking the Tab well at the upper left corner of the Print Preview window, just below the window's close button.

Print Preview mode is a great place to interactively adjust the document's margins, since you can easily see how changing your margins will affect your entire document. If you want to precisely set document margins in the Print Preview window, make sure the rulers are showing, and double-click anywhere in the rulers except for in the white portion of the top ruler. The Document dialog will appear, as shown in Figure 5-8 on the next page, and you can set numeric values for the margins. If you click the white area of the top ruler, you'll accidentally insert a tab that you might not want.

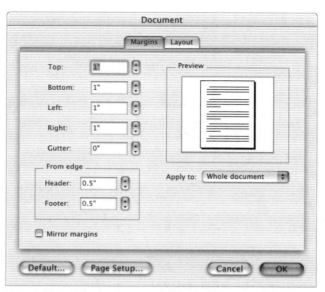

Figure 5-8. The Document dialog enables you to set precise numeric values for the document's margins.

Printing Documents

After you've reviewed and previewed your document, you're ready to print. Usually, you'll want to print the entire document. To do so, simply choose File, Print (or press Command+P) to bring up the Print dialog, shown in Figure 5-9, and then click Print. The entire document will print with Word's default settings.

InsideOut

In Mac OS 9 and earlier, you could print documents from the Finder by selecting their icons and choosing File, Print. Mac OS X doesn't have this feature, so you'll have to print documents from within their applications.

By default, Word prints one copy of the document. If you wish to print multiple copies, type a value in the box labeled Copies. For multiple copies, the Collated check box is selected by default. When collating is enabled, Word sends one copy of your print job to the printer, pauses for a moment, and then sends the next copy to the printer, and so on. This makes it easier for you, because all the pages in one copy of your document end up together in the printer's output tray. The drawback is that the entire print job takes longer to process, especially if the document contains complex formatting or graphics. If you clear the Collated check box, Word sends all copies of the first page to the printer, then all the copies of the second page, and so forth. On most laser printers,

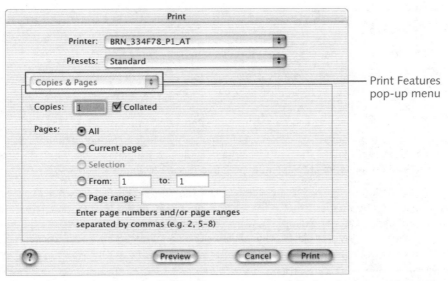

Figure 5-9. Word's Print dialog allows you a great deal of control over what you print.

the overall print job will take less time, because it is faster to print multiple copies of the same page. The drawback is that you will have to collate the copies manually.

Using the Page Setup Dialog

Word X also has a Page Setup dialog, shown in Figure 5-10. To open the dialog, choose File, Page Setup. The Page Attributes choice in the Settings pop-up menu is where you tell Word which of your printers to use to format the print job (if you have more than one printer, specify which one from the Format For pop-up menu). The most

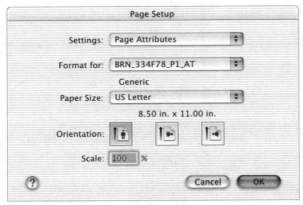

Figure 5-10. The Page Setup dialog enables you to specify paper size, orientation, and scaling.

InsideOut

Set the default paper size for your documents

Word saves the default paper size in the Normal template. If you find that your documents are being set to a different paper size than you want, open the Normal template, found in Applications/Microsoft Office X/Templates/. Choose File, Page Setup, and then choose the paper size you want from the Paper Size pop-up menu. Click OK to exit Page Setup, choose File, Save to save the changes to the Normal template, and then choose File, Close. When you create a new blank document (or open any document based on the Normal template), you'll find it is set to the new paper size.

A variation of this technique is also useful for people that regularly need to switch between two paper sizes. In that case, save a copy of the Normal template in the second paper size, for example, A4, give it a name of Normal A4, and save the template copy in the My Templates folder. The next time you need an A4-sized document, use the Project Gallery to start the document based on the Normal A4 template.

---

commonly used settings in Page Setup, however, are Paper Size and Orientation. Paper Size offers many sizes from which to choose, and when you make your choice, the size of the page is displayed below the Paper Size pop-up menu, as shown in the figure.

Orientation lets you choose between Portrait (vertical or tall page orientation) Landscape (horizontal or wide page orientation), and Rotated Landscape (horizontal page orientation, rotated 180 degrees).

You can use the Scale box to shrink or expand the printed document. Enter a value for the percentage by which you wish to scale the printed pages.

Choosing Microsoft Word from the Page Setup dialog's Settings pop-up menu allows you to set custom page sizes, as shown in Figure 5-11.

InsideOut

Print portrait and landscape pages in the same document

You can mix and match portrait and landscape pages within the same document. You might want to do this if, for example, you have a report that has most pages in portrait orientation, but a few tables that require landscape orientation. If the document is in portrait orientation, select all the text on the pages you want to print in landscape orientation. Choose File, Page Setup, and then click the landscape icon. From the Settings pop-up menu, choose Microsoft Word, and then from the Apply Page Setup Settings To pop-up menu, choose Selected Text. Click OK. Word places a section break before and after the selected text to indicate that it is a section with different formatting.

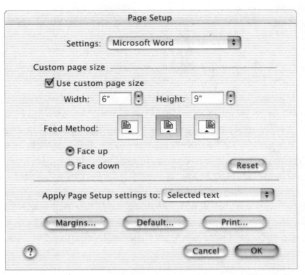

Figure 5-11. Page Setup's Microsoft Word setting allows for custom page sizes.

To specify a custom page size, select Use Custom Page Size, and then set the width and height of the paper. If necessary, choose the Feed Method (the choices are Left, Center, and Right; each can also be Face Up or Face Down). Click OK to apply your changes.

Printing Portions of Your Document

To print specific pages in sections of the document, use one of the following options in the Copies & Pages pane of the Print dialog (shown earlier in Figure 5-9, page 77):

- **All** is the default selection and prints the entire document.

- **Current Page** prints the page in which the insertion point is currently located.

- **Selection** prints the selected text only. You must first select text in your document, and then open the Print dialog, click Selection, and click Print.

- **From** has two boxes where you can enter page numbers. The numbers must be contiguous. For example, you can choose to print page 12 to page 15.

- **Page Range** prints the single pages, sections, or page ranges that you specify. You can use commas to denote noncontiguous pages to print, hyphens to denote contiguous page ranges, *s* to denote a section, and *p* to refer to pages. For example, if you enter **2-4,6,13,19-22**, Word will print pages 2 through 4, page 6, page 13, and pages 19 through 22. Entering **s2** will print all the pages in the document's second section. Entering **s4,s6** will print all pages in the fourth and sixth sections. Entering **p5s2-p2s7** will print from page 5, section 2 to page 2, section 7.

For more information about using sections, see "Working with Sections," page 151.

Simulating Duplex Printing

You can use Word's ability to print odd and even pages to print on both sides of a piece of paper. The best way to accomplish this task is with a *duplex printer,* which is a printer that can automatically print on both sides of a piece of paper. But if you don't have a duplex printer, you can use the Odd Pages and the Even Pages print options as a workaround. To accomplish this, you can print all the odd pages first, turn the printed pages over, reinsert the paper into your printer's paper tray, and then print the even pages. It's a good idea to run a test with just a few pages to make sure that you are reinserting the pages with the correct orientation.

You can also choose to print only the even or odd pages of your print selection. From the Print dialog's Print Features pop-up menu, choose Microsoft Word. Make sure the Print What pop-up menu is set to Document, and then select either Odd Pages Only or Even Pages Only, as shown here:

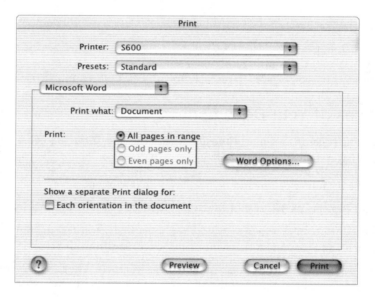

Printing Information About Your Document

Besides printing the document itself, Word can also print information about the document and about the Word environment. Follow these steps:

1 Choose File, Print.

2 From the Print Features pop-up menu, choose Microsoft Word.

3 From the Print What pop-up menu, choose one of the following:

■ Document Properties prints the document properties found under File, Properties.

■ Comments prints all the document's comments, from all reviewers.

■ Styles prints all the style names and their definitions contained within the document.

■ AutoText Entries prints all of the AutoText entries, not just the ones used in the document.

■ Key Assignments prints the customized shortcut key assignments associated with just the current document and the current document template.

4 Click Print.

Printing All Your Shortcut Keys

The Key Assignments choice in the Print dialog doesn't do the job when you want a reference list of all of the keyboard commands that are currently being used by Word. Happily, Word includes a macro that can take care of the job, and creates a new document with almost all the keyboard shortcuts, ready to be printed or saved. The exception to the printed list is that Word doesn't include shortcut keys that you assigned to macros (though it does include your other customized shortcut keys).

To print or save a list of all of the shortcut keys, follow these steps:

1 Choose Tools, Macro, Macros.

2 From the Macros In pop-up menu, choose Word Commands.

3 In the Macro Name box, scroll down and select ListCommands.

4 Click the Run button.

5 From the List Commands dialog, select Current Menu And Keyboard Settings, seen here:

6 Click OK. Word creates a new document with the list of commands and their keyboard equivalents.

7 Choose File, Save, or File, Print.

newfeature!
Printing Documents to Disk as PDF Files

One of the great new things that Macintosh applications get when they are converted to work under Mac OS X is the ability to print to PDF (Portable Document Format, also sometimes called Adobe Acrobat format). PDF files have the benefit of being able to be read and printed by other people, whether or not they have Word or any of the other Office applications. Other Mac OS X users can read PDF files with either of two programs that are included with Mac OS X: Apple's Preview application or Adobe's Acrobat Reader. Of the two, Acrobat Reader is more flexible. There are versions of the Acrobat Reader for all versions of the Mac OS, Windows, several types of UNIX, the Palm OS, and for the Pocket PC, so no matter what type of computer one of your readers is using, your Office documents will be able to be read.

To print a document to disk, follow these steps:

1 Choose File, Print.

2 In the Copies & Pages pane of the Print dialog, choose to print all or a portion of the document.

3 Click the Preview button. Word processes the document and then opens the preview in Apple's Preview application.

4 In Preview, choose File, Save As PDF.

5 In the resulting Save dialog, give the document a name, and choose where you want to save the PDF file.

6 Click Save.

7 Choose Preview, Quit Preview to return to Word.

Printing Envelopes

You can print an individual envelope with Word, and once you've got the process down, you won't want to give up that professional printed envelope look again.

> To print multiple envelopes as part of a data merge, see Chapter 14, "Automating Mailings with Data Merging."

> **tip** To see how your printer handles page orientation (so that you'll know how to feed your envelopes), print a test "envelope" with a plain sheet of paper.

To print envelopes from Word, follow these steps:

1 Choose Tools, Envelopes.

2 In the Envelope dialog, shown in Figure 5-12, fill in the Delivery Address box. Alternatively, click the Address Book button to select a name and address from Entourage's Address Book.

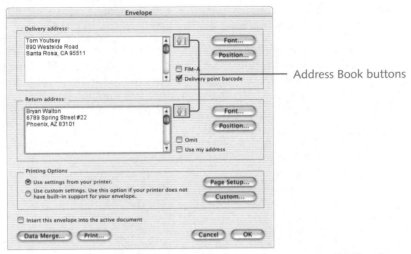

Address Book buttons

Figure 5-12. Envelope printing is a breeze, once you master the Envelope dialog.

3 By default, Word uses the name and address you entered in Word, Preferences, User Information for the return address. To use a different return address, clear the Use My Address check box and enter a new return address. If your envelopes have a preprinted return address, select the Omit check box.

4 Click the Font button next to the Delivery Address or Return Address box to set the fonts, sizes, and styles used on the envelope.

5 If you need to adjust the position of the delivery or return address, click either Position button and set the address positions, as shown here:

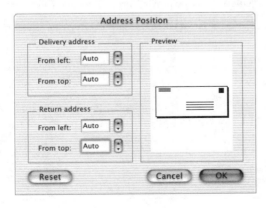

6 To set up your printer for envelopes, choose one of the following options:

▪ **Page Setup button.** If your printer driver already has support for envelope printing (most do, at least for #10 envelopes, the most common business-sized envelopes), click Page Setup, and choose the envelope size from the Paper Size pop-up menu. Try this option first.

▪ **Custom button.** If your printer doesn't have an envelope feed, or the printer driver doesn't have a provision for the size envelope you want to print, this is the choice for you. In the Custom Page Options dialog, shown next, choose the envelope size from the Envelope Size pop-up menu. Then use the Feed Method area to click the icon that matches the way that you need to feed in the envelope, and click the Face Up, Face Down, and Clockwise Rotation options as necessary. Click OK to return to the Envelope dialog.

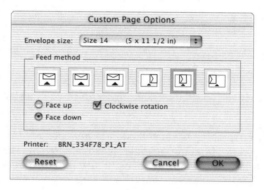

7 When you print, Word will create a new document to contain the envelope text. If you want the envelope document to be saved in the same document that you've been editing, select the Insert This Envelope Into The Active Document check box.

8 Position the blank envelope in your printer, and then click the Print button.

9 When the Print dialog appears, click Print again to print the envelope you've created.

---

tip **Speed up your mail delivery**

Selecting the Delivery Point Barcode check box next to the Delivery Address box will add a standard POSTNET barcode to the envelope, which can be read by the US Postal Service mail sorting machines. The Postal Service claims that mail with barcodes arrives sooner. If you're creating a business reply envelope, select the FIM-A check box, which adds another barcode identifying the envelope as business reply mail that also includes the POSTNET barcode.

Printing Labels

Word's Label function prints mailing labels, as expected, but it can also print other useful things. It can print business cards, file folder labels, name badges, index cards, Rolodex cards, and even labels for audio and video cassettes. Word comes with more than a thousand preset types of labels and other printed materials from many different manufacturers.

You'll often want to print mailing labels as part of a data merge, but you can also print single labels from a sheet of labels.

> To print mailing labels as part of a data merge, see Chapter 14, "Automating Mailings with Data Merging."

To print labels, follow these steps:

1 Choose Tools, Labels.

2 Type an address—or if you're printing something other than a mailing label, the information you want to print—into the Address box, as shown in Figure 5-13.

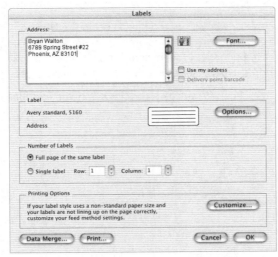

Figure 5-13. You can print one or many labels using the Labels dialog.

3 Click the Options button to select the type of label or other printed matter you're using, as shown on the next page.

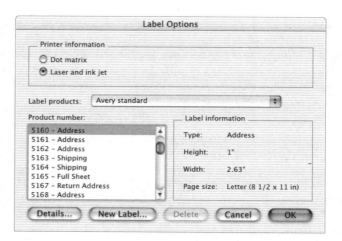

4   Select the label manufacturer from the Label Products pop-up menu, and then select the manufacturer's label code in the Product Number list. The Label Information area shows the basic dimensions of the label and its sheet size. If you want to see the complete measurements and the label layout, click the Details button. If you can't find the label in the list (possible, but not likely), click the New Label button to enter your own label measurements. Click OK.

5   If you're printing only one label, select Single Label in the Number Of Labels section, and then choose the row and column of an unused label on your label sheet. If you want to print a sheet with all of the same label (for example, for a sheet of return address labels), select Full Page Of The Same Label.

6   Make sure your label sheet is correctly placed in the printer, and then click Print.

---

tip   **Don't waste those labels**

Avoid wasting labels by printing a test page onto a plain sheet of paper, and then place the printed sheet over a label sheet and hold the two up to a light. You'll be able to see if the labels will line up. If they don't, go back into the Labels dialog, click Options, and then click Details to modify the spacing of each label.

Effective Text Editing

Microsoft Word X has hundreds of features that allow it to be used in ways far beyond the original role of a word processor. You can use Word for desktop publishing, or to make Web pages, or use it to print mailing labels. But at its heart, Word is still all about creating text documents. Word X has managed to grow in functionality without downplaying its word processing features, which are more powerful than ever.

One of the keys to using Word effectively is to enter text as quickly and efficiently as possible. Word comes with several tools you can use to enter text quickly. If many of your documents contain boilerplate text, such as introductory paragraphs or cautions that the contents of the document are privileged information, you can add that text quickly. You can also perfect the formatting of your document by using text editing tools such as Word's ability to insert copyright and other special symbols when you type simple text equivalents. Regardless of how you like to work, you can add text and formatting efficiently, reducing the number of total keystrokes and preventing most spelling and typographical errors.

Entering Text

Typing text into a document is completely straightforward, but getting to the precise location where you want to type a right-aligned date or a centered heading can be a pain. In Word X, it's much easier to enter text at a given location: as you would expect from a feature called Click and Type, you just double-click the location and start typing! Also, because the keyboard doesn't have every character you might want to include in your document, Word comes with a collection of symbols and special characters you can insert into your files.

This section of the chapter shows you how to

- Position text with Click and Type.
- Insert symbols into a document.
- Insert special characters into a document.

Using Click and Type

One of the underlying design philosophies for Word is that individuals should have as much control as possible over the contents and appearance of their documents. Most of the time, you won't need the flexibility Word offers because the program's default settings will meet your needs: the margins are set at reasonable places, the tabs are spaced appropriately, and the default font is both easy to read and familiar to most readers. Of course, when you do need to exert more influence over your document, you can. One of the ways you can control the placement of text in your document is to use Click and Type.

One of the hassles of creating a document in a word processor has always been that to add text at a given location on a page, you had to keep pressing Return until you were on the line where you wanted to add the text and then apply the paragraph formatting (usually tabs) that would position the text correctly on the page. Word X makes it much easier to create special pages, such as title pages, with its Click and Type capability. With Click and Type, all you need to do is move the pointer over the position on the page where you want to begin adding text and then double-click. Word even guesses at the proper formatting and alignment for the text. It can determine, for example, that if you double-click at the right edge of a document, you probably want right-aligned text. You can also use the familiar AutoText and AutoCorrect capabilities to add common text items, correct spelling, and speed up text entry. Even if you haven't typed another character into your document, you can double-click at the bottom right edge of the document window and begin typing text. Figure 6-1 shows what the pointer will look like when it's over the bottom right edge of a document.

> **note** Click and Type works in Page Layout and Online Layout views, but not in Normal or Outline view.

You'll see that the pointer appears as an I-beam with an additional small graphic, which in this case is the same as the Align Right toolbar button found in the AlignmentAnd Spacing section of the Formatting Palette. Depending on where

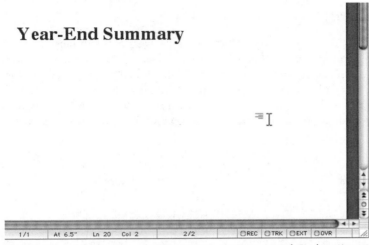

Figure 6-1. The pointer changes appearance to match its location on the page.

on the page you move it, the pointer will change to represent the formatting that will be applied to the text you enter using Click and Type, as shown here:

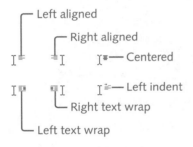

> **note** The pointer will only turn into a Click and Type I-beam if the portion of the document the pointer is hovering over is blank.

To add text to a document using Click and Type, follow these steps:

1 If necessary, choose View, Page Layout (or Online Layout).

2 Move the pointer over the portion of the document where you want to add Click and Type text.

3 When the icon matches the type of text you want to type, double-click to begin typing at that location.

Chapter 6

Inserting Symbols

The standard Macintosh keyboard lets you type every alphanumeric character, edit text, move around in a document, and insert a variety of common symbols (such as asterisks, pound signs, and percent signs). Unfortunately, many other useful symbols can't be typed with a single keystroke on a standard keyboard. You are able to add a wide range of additional symbols, which include mathematical symbols, logic symbols, and foreign language characters, using the Symbol dialog (shown in Figure 6-2).

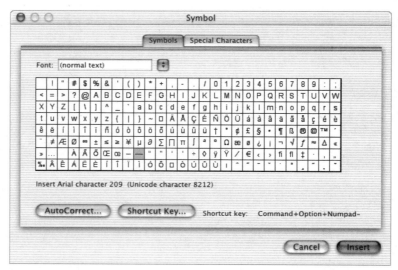

Figure 6-2. You can find many useful symbols in the Symbol dialog.

To insert symbols into your document, follow these steps:

1 Choose Insert, Symbol to display the Symbol dialog.

2 Click the Font pop-up menu to display the list of fonts from which you can choose symbols, and select a font.

3 In the symbol chart, click the symbol you want to insert into your document. When you click the symbol, Word will enlarge it so you can see it more clearly.

4 Click the Insert button to insert the symbol into your document, and close the Symbol dialog.

Inserting Special Characters into Your Document

Just as you can add mathematical and logical symbols to your document using the Symbol dialog, you can use the commands displayed on the Special Characters tab of the dialog to add other useful characters to your document. Some of the characters you can add from this tab of the Symbol dialog are the copyright symbol (©), the trademark symbol (™), and ellipses (…).

> Some of these special characters can be inserted automatically when you type keyboard abbre-
> viations; see "Applying AutoFormat Changes as You Type," page 103.

To insert special characters into your document, follow these steps:

1 Choose Insert, Symbol to display the Symbol dialog.

2 Click the Special Characters tab, shown in Figure 6-3.

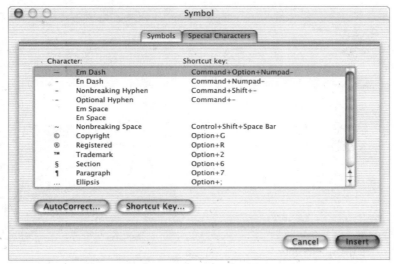

Figure 6-3. The Special Characters tab contains a list of useful characters you won't find on a standard keyboard.

3 Click the special character you want to add to your document, and then click the Insert button.

4 Close the Symbol dialog.

> For information on changing the shortcut keys associated with a special character, see
> "Customizing Keyboard Shortcuts in Word and Excel," page 56.

Copying and Pasting with the Office Clipboard

One of the strengths of Word and the other Microsoft Office programs is the ability to move text and graphics around within, or between, documents using cut and paste or copy and paste. In the past, however, the inability to put more than one item on the Clipboard at a time made it difficult to use those techniques efficiently. Although you could create a blank Word document and use it as a repository for the items you cut and copied, it was a hassle.

Office v. X removes that limitation. In Office v. X, you can use the Office Clipboard (shown in Figure 6-4) to collect and paste multiple items in any Office application. When you open the Office Clipboard, anything you cut or copy is placed on the Clipboard, up to a maximum of 60 items or 16 MB of data. If you exceed either limit, the oldest item on the Clipboard will be removed. (Office will warn you that an item will be removed from the Clipboard.) The contents of the Office Clipboard will remain available until you close every Office application.

Figure 6-4. The Office Clipboard lets you collect items from any Office application and paste them into your Word document.

To use the Office Clipboard, follow these steps:

1 Choose View, Office Clipboard to display the Office Clipboard.

2 Cut or copy the text or object you want to place on the Office Clipboard. The item you selected will appear in the top spot on the Office Clipboard, above items you had added previously. You can also drag and drop items from your document window to the Office Clipboard, and vice versa.

3 While the Office Clipboard is open, you can perform any of the following actions:

■ To paste an item from the Office Clipboard into your document, click the item you want to paste, and then click the Paste button at the bottom edge of the Office Clipboard.

■ To remove an item from the Office Clipboard, click the item you want to remove and then click the Clear button at the bottom edge of the Office Clipboard.

■ To paste every item on the Office Clipboard into your document, click and hold the Paste All & Clear All button (the small arrow button at the bottom edge of the Office Clipboard) and then select Paste All from the submenu, as shown here:

■ To remove every item from the Office Clipboard, click and hold the Paste All & Clear All button, and then select Clear All from the submenu.

caution Be careful using Clear All, because it doesn't give you any warning or ask for confirmation before it deletes everything on the Office Clipboard.

InsideOut

Reduce Office Clipboard bloat by limiting drag and drop

If you cut or copy text or graphics to the Office Clipboard, they will be stored in a much more compact form than if you drag and drop the same items to the Office Clipboard window. The reason is that Mac OS X adds extra information to dragged and dropped items that helps the system move the data between applications. The difference can be significant; for example, a short phrase from Word uses 2 KB of memory when cut or copied to the Office Clipboard window, but uses 26 KB when dragged and dropped. Similarly, a clip art image that requires a mere 16 KB when cut or copied, requires 115 KB when dragged.

Keeping a number of these bloated items on the Office Clipboard can make operations slower. The solution is simple: copy or cut items to the Office Clipboard, and avoid drag and drop.

Using the Spike to Move Many Items

The Spike is one of Word's least-known features. It's a way to move a group of text or graphics between nonadjacent locations. You can add multiple items to the Spike and then insert all of those items at once in the new location. Think of the Spike as a clipboard that you can keep adding items to, except that you always cut items to the Spike, you can't copy them.

To use the Spike, follow these steps:

1 Select a block of text or a graphic.

2 Press Command+F3. The selection disappears from the document and goes to the Spike.

3 Repeat steps 1 and 2 for each additional item you want to move to the Spike.

4 Click the insertion point where you want the Spike's contents to appear, then press Command+Shift+F3.

When the Spike's contents appear back in your document, the Spike is emptied; it doesn't retain the contents, as the Clipboard does.

> **tip** The Spike is actually a special AutoText entry; for more about AutoText, see the next section. You can insert the Spike's contents without emptying it by typing **spike** into your document, then pressing Return.

Using AutoText and AutoComplete

Creating text documents often involves significant creative effort. Of course, not every word of every document needs to be original. In fact, many documents that you create will have many elements in common with each other, such as greetings, closings, and mailing instructions. Word has two features that help you with this sort of repetitive text entry, and that help ensure that the text is consistent from one instance to the next: AutoText and AutoComplete.

The first feature, AutoText, allows you to save commonly used snippets of text or graphics as AutoText entries, which you can then insert into your documents whenever you need them. AutoText entries are stored in the current template, so they are available to all documents that use that template. Word comes with many AutoText entries that are part of the Normal template, including parts of letters, such as salutations and signature text. AutoComplete makes it even easier to insert AutoText entries; all you have to do is begin typing text until it is recognized as an AutoText entry, and then press Return to have Word insert the rest of the AutoText.

Word X has a number of predefined phrases you can add to a document using different aspects of the AutoText feature. At its simplest, you can add an AutoText entry to a document by selecting it from the submenu you open by choosing Insert, AutoText. The AutoText submenu lists several categories of AutoText; to display the entries under each category, merely point to the category of interest, as shown in Figure 6-5.

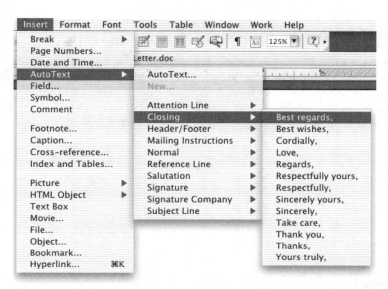

Figure 6-5. The Insert, AutoText submenus offer many AutoText entries you can add to your documents by selecting the text from the hierarchical menu.

Creating a New AutoText Entry

The default Microsoft Word AutoText entries make it easy to enter useful text for many business situations, but the entries won't necessarily meet your individual needs. For example, if you use multiline signature blocks in the memos you send out, you could create AutoText entries for each signature block. The same is true for addresses—if you want to enter an address by choosing it from the AutoText menu, just create an AutoText entry for it.

To create a new AutoText entry, follow these steps:

1 Select the text you want to define as the content of your AutoText entry.

2 Choose Insert, AutoText, New to display the Create AutoText dialog.

3 Type the name for your AutoText entry in the Please Name Your AutoText Entry box, and then click OK.

Letting AutoComplete Do the Work

In addition to using the AutoText menu to choose the AutoText term you want to add to your document, you can also begin typing a term to have Word suggest a replacement in a ScreenTip, as shown in Figure 6-6. This Word feature is called AutoComplete. It's really just an extension of AutoText; Word looks for keystrokes that match the beginning letters of an AutoText entry, then pops up a ScreenTip with the rest of the text.

> **tip**   You can turn AutoComplete on or off by choosing Insert, AutoText, AutoText, then by selecting or clearing the Show AutoComplete Tip For AutoText, Contacts, And Dates check box.

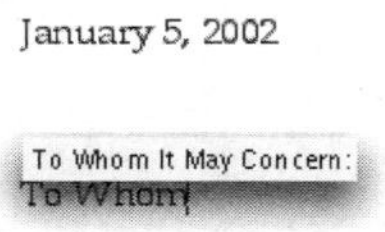

January 5, 2002

To Whom It May Concern:
To Whom

Figure 6-6.   When you begin typing a term Word recognizes as an AutoText entry, Word will display a suggested AutoComplete term as a ScreenTip. You can accept the replacement by pressing Return.

If you want to add the AutoComplete term displayed in the ScreenTip to your document, you can press Return to have Word paste the suggestion directly into the document. If you don't want to replace what you're typing with the suggested term, just keep typing.

It is possible to have a series of AutoComplete suggestions appear for a single term. For example, if you type a date beginning with a month, such as January 1, 2002, the word *January* will appear after you type **janu**, the first four characters of the month. Pressing Return will accept the suggested AutoComplete entry of January, and typing another space will cause Word to suggest the entire date in a ScreenTip. You can accept the second suggestion when it appears by pressing Return again.

> **note**   AutoComplete ScreenTips appear after you type the fourth character of an entry.

To complete data entry with AutoComplete, follow these steps:

1   Type the beginning of the term corresponding to an AutoComplete entry. When Word recognizes the term as an AutoText entry, the remainder of the replacement text will appear as a ScreenTip.

2   Press Return to accept the suggested AutoComplete phrase, or keep typing to reject the proposed change.

Adding an AutoComplete Entry

You're not limited to working with just the AutoComplete entries that come with Word. Instead, you can extend the default AutoComplete entries (which are mostly months, days, and salutations) by adding or deleting any entry you want.

To add an AutoComplete entry, follow these steps:

1 Choose Tools, AutoCorrect to display the AutoCorrect dialog, and then click the AutoText tab.

2 Type the AutoComplete entry in the Enter AutoText Entries Here box, as shown in Figure 6-7.

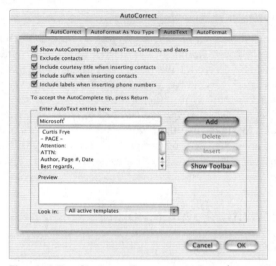

Figure 6-7. Start creating an AutoComplete entry by typing the text of the entry into the appropriate box.

3 Click the Add button to add the entry to the AutoComplete list, and then click OK.

---

tip You can insert an AutoText entry directly into your document by selecting the entry you want to add and then clicking the Insert button. A preview of the text you've selected will appear in the Preview box.

Chapter 6

Deleting an AutoComplete Entry

To delete an AutoComplete entry, follow these steps:

1 Choose Tools, AutoCorrect to display the AutoCorrect dialog, and then click the AutoText tab.

2 Select the entry you want to delete and then click the Delete button.

3 Click OK.

InsideOut

Manage AutoComplete values in multiple templates

When you save an AutoComplete value in Word X, you save the entry to the current document template, usually called Normal (it's in the Templates folder inside the Microsoft Office X folder). If you work with more than one template, you might have AutoComplete entries that are very similar, such as *confidential* in one template and *confidentially* in another template. With values that similar, the AutoComplete tip for *confidentially* would never appear and you would need to type all the way to the second *l* in *confidentially* to trigger that tip. If you want to limit the AutoCorrect entries available to you, open the Look In pop-up menu on the AutoText tab of the AutoCorrect dialog, and select the template you want to provide your AutoText values.

Inserting Text Blocks with AutoComplete

The most common use for AutoComplete is to finish entering simple terms, such as months, days, or dates, into your document. AutoComplete is actually a flexible tool you can use to insert entire blocks of text into your document. For example, let's say you work in a legal office and have a boilerplate paragraph you include in every letter indicating the information in the letter is protected by attorney-client privilege. You can select the paragraph you want to define as the replacement text for the AutoComplete entry, then define the entire paragraph as an AutoText entry. When you type the first few letters of the paragraph's text, the AutoComplete ScreenTip will pop up and allow you to insert the paragraph. To store paragraphs as AutoText so that you can use them with AutoComplete, simply select the entire paragraph, then follow the steps in "Creating a New AutoText Entry," page 95.

Fixing Common Mistakes with AutoCorrect

When you type a document, it's easy to transpose, skip, or mistype letters. Rather than make you go through your document and correct each misspelling by hand, Word's AutoCorrect feature can check your typing on the fly and correct any obvious typing or spelling mistakes it finds. As an example, if you type **spellign**, Word will detect the error and, because the most likely replacement term in its dictionary is *spelling,* will make the replacement. As with all other AutoText and AutoCorrect entries, you have the opportunity to accept or reject the change. To accept it, just keep typing; to reject it, press Command+Z or choose Edit, Undo as soon as Word makes the change.

If you often use terms (or make typos) that don't appear in the standard Word spelling dictionary, you might want to add your own AutoCorrect entries, choose which AutoCorrect rules you want Word to apply, or even turn off AutoCorrect entirely. You can use the controls on the different tabs of the AutoCorrect dialog to add or remove entries, tell Word which rules you want it to use when examining your text for potential AutoCorrect actions, and even define exceptions to some of the rules!

For information on using the spelling checker to proof your documents, see "Checking Spelling," page 263.

Creating AutoCorrect Entries

To create an AutoCorrect entry, follow these steps:

1 If you wish, select the text you want to use as the replacement text for your AutoCorrect entry. If the text should always be inserted with specific formatting, be sure the text has that formatting when you select it. Otherwise, you can type the replacement text in step 5.

2 Choose Tools, AutoCorrect to display the AutoCorrect dialog, shown in Figure 6-8.

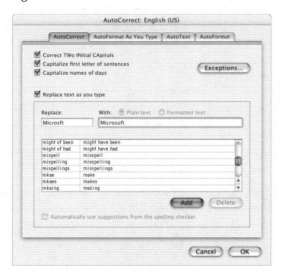

Figure 6-8. Use the AutoCorrect tab of the AutoCorrect dialog to define replacement text for common misspellings, abbreviations, or terms you type in a document.

Chapter 6

3 In the Replace box, type the misspelled or abbreviated text you want to be replaced.

4 Select Plain Text to have Word insert the AutoCorrect text as plain text, or select Formatted Text to have Word insert text with the same formatting as the text you selected before opening the AutoCorrect dialog. If you didn't select any text, Plain Text will be automatically selected.

5 If you didn't select text before opening the dialog, type the replacement text in the With box.

6 Click the Add button to create the new AutoCorrect entry. Click OK when you're done adding entries.

To delete an AutoCorrect entry, open the AutoCorrect dialog to the AutoCorrect tab, click the entry you want to remove, and then click the Delete button.

Troubleshooting

Word inserts AutoCorrect text with its original formatting.

Most times you create an AutoText entry, Word will store the entry's text without any formatting. When the text is stored without formatting, it will always take on the format of the surrounding text when you insert it. However, if you define an AutoCorrect entry with a field, symbol, paragraph mark (¶), imported graphic, or an object other than text (such as an embedded spreadsheet), Word saves the entry with its original formatting.

To force word to save an AutoCorrect entry without formatting, select Plain Text in the AutoCorrect dialog when you create the entry.

Setting AutoCorrect Options

To change your AutoCorrect options, choose Tools, AutoCorrect to open the AutoCorrect dialog, click the AutoCorrect tab, and then perform any of these steps:

- Select the Correct Two Initial Capitals check box to have Word change to lowercase the second capital letter at the beginning of a word.

- Select the Capitalize First Letter Of Sentences check box to have Word change the case of any lowercase letters beginning a sentence.

- Select the Capitalize Names Of Days check box to have Word change to uppercase the first letter of Monday, Tuesday, Wednesday, Thursday, Friday, Saturday, or Sunday.

- Select the Replace Text As You Type check box to have Word replace text using its list of AutoCorrect entries. Clear the check box to have Word ignore its list of AutoCorrect entries and wait until you run the spelling checker to attempt to correct the misspelling. Clearing the Replace Text As You Type check box makes the Automatically Use Suggestions From The Spelling Checker check box unavailable.

● Select the Automatically Use Suggestions From The Spelling Checker check box to enable automatic spelling checking and word replacement when AutoCorrect detects a misspelling. Clear the check box to have Word identify spelling errors only when you use the spelling checker. This selection will be unavailable if Check Spelling As You Type is not selected in Word's Preferences dialog.

For more information on using the spelling checker, see "Checking Spelling," page 263.

Using AutoCorrect to Save Typing

You can also use AutoCorrect to insert long boilerplate text or frequently typed phrases by typing just a few characters. For example, if you define an AutoCorrect entry to "correct" your typing of *yt* with the phrase *Yours truly,* as soon as you type **yt** and activate AutoCorrect by typing a space or punctuation character, or by pressing Tab or Return, *yt* will immediately be replaced with *Yours truly*. In this case you would type **yt,** because the comma activates the AutoCorrect entry and is also the punctuation that should follow the phrase. Of course if you don't want any punctuation to follow your AutoComplete insertion, just press the Spacebar and keep typing. Using AutoCorrect for boilerplate text or phrases is very versatile; you can use it to substitute short abbreviations for almost any sort of text:

● **Addresses** are one of the best things to make into AutoCorrect entries, because you have to type them fairly often. Simply select the address, and create the AutoCorrect entry as described previously. Be sure to give the entry an abbreviation that isn't a real word, because you don't want the address being typed accidentally. For example, on the author's Mac, the abbreviation for his address is *tnadd*.

● **Letterheads** can include graphics, as well as the text.

● **Tables** often have extensive formatting, with the table's title, header rows, and rows and columns each having specific formats. Create the table once as you want it to look, without data, save it as an AutoCorrect entry, and then you can insert perfectly formatted tables just by typing the table's abbreviation.

One of the nicest things about AutoCorrect is that it is shared by all of the Office applications, so AutoCorrect entries made in Word also work in Entourage, Excel, and PowerPoint.

Telling AutoCorrect About Exceptions

To create exceptions to AutoCorrect rules, follow these steps:

1 Choose Tools, AutoCorrect to open the AutoCorrect dialog, click the AutoCorrect tab, and then click the Exceptions button to display the AutoCorrect Exceptions dialog, shown in Figure 6-9. (The Exceptions button won't be available unless you've selected at least one of the Correct Two Initial Capitals or Capitalize First Letter Of Sentences check boxes.)

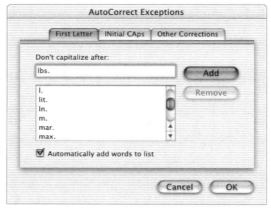

Figure 6-9. You can create exceptions to the AutoCorrect rules so you don't have to waste time undoing improper AutoCorrect changes.

2 In the AutoCorrect Exceptions dialog, perform any of these steps:

■ Click the First Letter tab, and then, in the Don't Capitalize After box, type the phrase after which you don't want Word to capitalize the first letter of the following word. This is usually used for abbreviations followed by a period, such as etc. or lbs. Click Add to add the exception.

■ Click the Initial Caps tab, and then, in the Don't Correct box, type the exact term (with appropriate capitalization) you want Word to ignore, and click Add to add the exception. This option is usually used to keep AutoCorrect's Correct Two Initial Capitals option from triggering for proper names like XPress.

■ Click the Other Corrections tab, and then type the text you don't want Word to change in the Don't Correct box, and click Add.

3 Click OK to close the AutoCorrect Exceptions dialog.

> **note** You can remove an exception from any of the AutoCorrect Exceptions tabs by selecting the term you want to remove and then clicking the Remove button.

Formatting Your Document with AutoFormat

Great content is the key to creating an effective document, but you must also pay attention to your document's formatting. Beyond using bold or italics to emphasize a phrase or indicate a book title, you can have Word make other formatting changes to ensure your document's format is consistent. For example, you can have Word format any headers in your document using the built-in heading styles, change regular quote marks to curly quotes, or change how Word presents ordinal numbers (the numerical representations of "first," "second," and so on). You can apply AutoFormat changes in one of two ways: as you type, or as part of a formatting check.

Applying AutoFormat Changes as You Type

Word can apply formatting changes immediately after you type some text. It's similar to AutoCorrect, except that what is changing is formatting, rather than text being changed or inserted. For example, if you type a URL, AutoFormat can turn it into an actual hyperlink, and clicking that link will launch your Web browser and take you to that link's Web site.

To control how Word applies AutoFormat changes as you type, follow these steps:

1 Choose Tools, AutoCorrect, and then click the AutoFormat As You Type tab, shown in Figure 6-10.

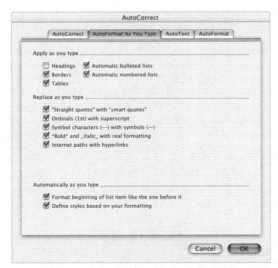

Figure 6-10. The options on the AutoFormat As You Type tab of the AutoCorrect dialog let you determine what changes Word will make to the contents of your document.

2 You can set any of these AutoFormat options to apply formatting as you type:

■ **Headings.** Word applies built-in styles Heading 1 through Heading 9 to single-line text entries you add to your document. You can identify heading levels while you work in Outline view.

For more information on working with document outlines in Microsoft Word, see "Building Documents from Outlines," page 285.

■ **Borders.** Word interprets strings of three or more hyphens, underscores, or equal signs as indications you want to apply a border to the bottom of the preceding paragraph. A sequences of hyphens or underscores is interpreted as a single-line border, whereas a string of equal signs is interpreted as a double-line border.

■ **Tables.** Word interprets strings of hyphens and plus signs as the outline of a table. For example, the string +--+--+--+, if written on a line by itself, would be interpreted as an instruction to create a table with a single row and three cells on that row (each hyphen represents a row).

■ **Automatic Bulleted Lists.** Word formats any paragraph that begins with an asterisk (*), a greater than sign (>), or a hyphen (-), as a bulleted list. Word applies the bulleted list style when you press Return at the end of the paragraph.

■ **Automatic Numbered Lists.** Word formats as a numbered list any paragraph that begins with a number or letter that is followed by a consecutive period and space.

3 Select any of these options to replace formatting that you enter with an alternate format:

■ **"Straight Quotes" With "Smart Quotes".** Word replaces straight quotation marks, which are part of the ASCII character set, with opening and closing quotes. Smart Quotes is the name of Word's feature that intelligently replaces each straight quote with either an opening or closing quote by analyzing the spacing around each straight quote to determine if it starts or ends a quoted passage.

caution Replacing straight quotation marks with opening and closing quotation marks can have unintended consequences when you cut and paste the contents of a Word document to a text-only editor, such as a third-party e-mail program. It's possible that the other program will interpret the opening and closing quotation marks as other characters.

■ **Ordinals (1st) With Superscript.** Word changes the position of the suffix of an ordinal number to superscript. For example, the ordinal number 1st would be represented as 1st.

Chapter 6

- **Symbol Characters (--) With Symbols (—).** Word replaces character representations of special characters, such as using two hyphens to represent an em dash, with the actual character. The set of replacements includes substituting a smiley face when you type **:-)**, the copyright symbol © for (c), and the superscripted trademark denotation ™ for (tm).

- ***Bold* And _Italic_ With Real Formatting.** Word replaces these plain-text representations of special formatting with the indicated format.

- **Internet Paths With Hyperlinks.** Word formats file paths and Internet addresses (such as http://www.microsoft.com/ or kristen@cohowinery.com) as hyperlinks instead of plain text.

> For more information on hyperlinks and the Web, see "Inserting and Linking Hyperlinks," page 367.

4 Select any of these options to format automatically as you type:

- **Format Beginning Of List Item Like The One Before It.** Word applies the formatting from the previous list item to the current list item. For example, if the first item in a list is italicized, then Word will italicize the next item.

- **Define Styles Based On Your Formatting.** Word creates styles based on the formatting you apply to your paragraphs.

Applying AutoFormat Changes

In the previous section, you saw how AutoFormat can react to your typing to apply formatting. AutoFormat can also operate more actively, working its way through your document and applying automatic heading styles, making bulleted and numbered lists, changing straight quotes to smart quotes, and so on. To move through your document and apply AutoFormat changes, follow these steps:

1 Choose Format, AutoFormat to display the AutoFormat dialog, shown in Figure 6-11 on the next page.

2 Click the AutoFormat And Review Each Change option to give yourself the ability to accept or reject each suggested formatting change. If you want to have Word make the AutoFormat changes without consulting you, select AutoFormat Now.

3 Open the pop-up menu in the center section of the dialog, and then select a type of document to tailor the autoformatting to your document type. You can choose from a general document, a letter, or an e-mail message.

4 Click the Options button to display the AutoFormat tab of the AutoCorrect dialog. These options are similar to those described in "Applying AutoFormat Changes as You Type," page 103.

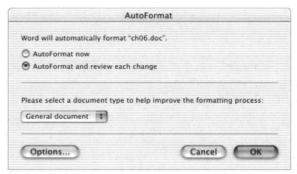

Figure 6-11. The AutoFormat dialog lets you check formatting the same way you check spelling, including the ability to accept all recommended changes or approve or reject each change individually.

5 Click the OK button to have Word make AutoFormat changes and display a second AutoFormat dialog. This dialog won't appear if you chose the AutoFormat Now option in step 2.

6 Select from these options to change your document's formatting.

■ Click the Accept All button to accept every suggested formatting change without review.

■ Click the Reject All button to decline every suggested formatting change without review.

■ Click the Style Gallery button to display the Style Gallery dialog, which allows you to copy another template's styles to your document.

■ Click the Review Changes button to look at each suggested change and choose to accept or reject it.

7 If you clicked the Review Changes button, the Review AutoFormat Changes dialog appears, as shown in Figure 6-12.

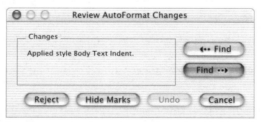

Figure 6-12. The commands in the Review AutoFormat Changes dialog let you specify which suggested formatting changes to keep and which to ignore.

8 As each formatting change is presented, select one of these commands:

- Click the Find Previous button to move back to the nearest previous suggested change.

- Click the Find Next button to find the next suggested change. This effectively means you're accepting the formatting suggestion (but you can go back to it later if you change your mind).

- Click the Reject button to decline a suggested change.

- Click the Hide Marks button to hide the formatting marks (such as paragraph marks) in the document window. When you click the Hide Marks button, Word hides the formatting marks, and the Hide Marks button becomes the Show Marks button. Clicking the Show Marks button redisplays the formatting marks.

- Click the Undo button to remove the last change you rejected and take the opportunity to review the change again and accept it.

- Click the Cancel button to close the Review AutoFormat Changes dialog.

9 The AutoFormat dialog reappears, and you should now accept the changes you allowed to stand by clicking Accept All. If you want to reject all the formatting changes, click Reject All. If you want to review the changes you've left standing one more time, click Review Changes to step through each suggested change again.

Troubleshooting

I turned off AutoFormat, but Word keeps substituting symbols for text.

Most of the time, turning off AutoFormat will prevent Word from substituting symbols such as — for text (in this case, --). However, if an AutoCorrect entry defines the same substitution, Word will make the substitution based on that rule. As always, you can reject the substitution by pressing Command+Z immediately after the substitution occurs, but you can also prevent AutoCorrect from applying the rule (and all rules) by clearing the Replace Text As You Type check box on the AutoCorrect tab of the AutoCorrect dialog.

If you don't want to turn off AutoCorrect completely, you can delete the entry by opening Tools, AutoCorrect. If the AutoCorrect dialog contains the rule replacing the selected characters, you can delete it by selecting it and clicking Delete.

newfeature!
Selecting and Editing
Text with Multi-Selection

In previous versions of Word, if you wanted to cut or copy elements from different areas of a document, you had to copy each element separately. In Word X, you can select text or objects from different parts of the document using the new Multi-selection capability. Select the first item, and then hold down the Command key and select any subsequent items. You can also use Multi-selection when finding text, checking spelling, or applying formatting.

> For more information on finding and replacing text or formatting, see "Finding and Replacing Text and Formatting," next.

To select noncontiguous blocks of text using Multi-selection, follow these steps:

1 Select the first block of text you want to copy or cut.

2 Hold down the Command key, and then select the second block of text you want to copy or cut. Repeat this step for any subsequent blocks of text you want to select.

3 When you've finished selecting, choose Copy or Cut.

4 Paste the text into your document at its new location. Even if there are multiple lines between the selections you put on the Clipboard, there will only be a single return after each block.

Finding and Replacing Text and Formatting

When your company changes the name of your main product, or when you want to change all the text in a 100 page report that's underlined into boldface, you'll be glad of Word's abilities to find and replace text and formatting.

You do need to be careful when you find and replace text, however. There can be many special cases when finding and replacing, but Word is up to the task, providing both simple and complex find and replace tools. If you don't use the additional settings on the Replace tab of the Find And Replace dialog, you won't have such options as making Word match only entire words that match the text you typed in the Find What box or only the instances of the term that are capitalized in exactly the same way as the term you typed in the Find What box.

One of the most common problems with finding and replacing text is with words that can be used as multiple parts of speech. One such word is *jack,* which can be a common noun, a proper noun (when capitalized), or a verb. If your document represents the inventory of an auto supply store owned by someone with the first name Jack, the potential for error is enormous. For example, if the owner decides he wants to use his given name, John, changing every instance of *jack* without regard to capitalization could mean you would use a "john" to raise a car to change a tire.

You can expand the Replace tab of the Find And Replace dialog to gain access to options that let you specify in greater detail the text you want to find and replace. If you want, you can also use the options in the expanded Find And Replace dialog to change the formatting of elements of your document.

Finding Text

To find text in a document, follow these steps:

1 Choose Edit, Find to display the Find And Replace dialog, as shown here.

2 Type the text you want to find in the Find What box, or open the Find What pop-up menu to display a list of terms you typed previously in the Find What box.

3 If you want, select the Highlight All Items Found In check box, and then click the button to the right of the check box to specify where Word searches for the term, such as the main document, headers and footers, or comments.

4 Click the Find Next button to highlight the first occurrence of the text in the area you decided to search. Continue clicking the Find Next button to find additional occurrences.

5 Click the Cancel button to exit the Find And Replace dialog.

Replacing Text

To replace instances of text in your document, follow these steps:

1 Choose Edit, Replace to display the Replace tab of the Find And Replace dialog.

2 Type the text you want to replace in the Find What box. You can also open the Find What pop-up menu to display a list of terms you typed previously.

3 Type the replacement text in the Replace With box. You can also open the Replace With pop-up menu to display a list of terms you typed previously.

109

4 Select any of these actions to begin replacing text:

▪ Click the Replace All button to replace every instance of the text in the Find What box with the text in the Replace With box.

▪ Click the Find Next button to find the first instance of the text in the Find What box. Click again to move to the next match.

▪ Click the Replace button to replace the highlighted instance of the text in the Find What box with the text in the Replace With box. Word will then look for the next match and highlight it. Click Replace each time you want to replace the term, or click Find Next to skip a match and look for the next match.

▪ Click the Cancel or Close button to close the Find And Replace dialog. Any replacements you accepted before closing the dialog will stay in effect.

Advanced Text Replacement

To select additional options when replacing text, follow these steps:

1 Choose Edit, Replace to display the Replace tab of the Find And Replace dialog.

2 If necessary, click the disclosure arrow to the left of the Replace All button to display additional options for finding and replacing text. The expanded Find And Replace dialog is shown in Figure 6-13.

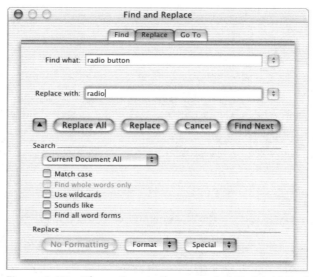

Figure 6-13. The options in the expanded Find And Replace dialog give you more control over the way Word identifies and changes text in your document.

3 Select any of these options to specify how Word should replace text in your document:

- Open the pop-up menu in the Search section to set the scope of the replace operation. Select Current Document Down to search from the insertion point to the end of the document, Current Document Up to search from the insertion point to the beginning of the document, Current Document All to search the entire document from beginning to end, or All Open Documents to search every open document from beginning to end.

- Select the Match Case check box to have Word only replace text in the document that is capitalized in exactly the same way as the text in the Find box.

- Select the Find Whole Words Only check box to have Word only replace text in the document that matches the text in the Find box and is surrounded by white space or punctuation.

- Select the Use Wildcards check box to have Word interpret wildcard characters such as *, ?, and # as wildcards and not as text. For a complete list of the available wildcard characters, see Table 6-1.

- Select the Sounds Like check box to have Word find all words that are homonyms of the word in the Find box. For example, if *there* were in the Find box, Word would identify *their* and *they're* as potential replacement candidates.

- Select the Find All Word Forms check box to have Word identify the plural form or verb forms of the word to be replaced as well as the word itself. If a word can be used as more than one part of speech (e.g., *fit* can be a verb, noun, or adjective), a list of choices will appear.

Table 6-1. Available Wildcards for Text Search and Replace

Wildcard	Description	Example
?	Any single character	**f?t** finds *fat* and *fit*.
*	Any string of characters	**f*d** finds *fad* and *fixed*.
[ ]	One of the specified characters	**f[aiu]n** finds *fan*, *fin*, and *fun*.
[-]	Any single character in this range	**[b-d]ot** finds *bot*, *cot*, and *dot*. Ranges must be in ascending order.
[!]	Any single character except the characters inside the brackets	**l[!o]st** finds *list* and *last*, but not *lost*.

(continued)

Chapter 6

Table 6-1. *(continued)*

Wildcard	Description	Example
[!x-z]	Any single character except characters in the range inside the brackets	**tr[!a-h]ck** finds *trick* and *truck,* but not *track.*
{n}	Exactly *n* occurrences of the previous character or expression	**ble{2}d** finds *bleed* but not *bled.*
{n,}	At least *n* occurrences of the previous character or expression	**ble{1,}d** finds *bleed* and *bled.*
{n,m}	From *n* to *m* occurrences of the previous character or expression	**10{1,3}** finds *10, 100,* and *1000.*
@	One or more occurrences of the previous character or expression	**ble@d** finds *bled* and *bleed.*
<	The beginning of a word	**<inter** finds *interesting* and *intercept,* but not *splintered.*
>	The end of a word	**in>** finds *margin* and *thin,* but not *intriguing.*

Replacing Formatting

To replace text formatting, follow these steps:

1 Choose Edit, Replace to display the Replace tab of the Find And Replace dialog.

2 If necessary, click the arrow to the left of the Replace All button to display further options for finding and replacing text (the dialog is shown in Figure 6-13 on page 110). Select from the following options:

■ Click the Format pop-up menu to display a list of formatting options you can use to further specify the text you want to find and replace. Select any of the items on the list, such as Font, Paragraph, or Language, to open the corresponding dialog; you can then use the settings in the dialogs to specify the exact formatting of the text you want to replace.

> **tip** If you specify only a formatting characteristic, such as italicized text, Word will find every instance of text with that format.

- Click the Special pop-up menu to add a special character, such as an en dash or nonbreaking hyphen, to the Find What or Replace With boxes. One way you can use finding and replacing special characters effectively is to locate two or more consecutive paragraph marks and replace them with a single paragraph mark, which removes extraneous blank lines.

- Click the No Formatting button to remove any formatting characteristics you defined for the Find What or Replace What boxes.

Navigating Through Your Document

Word gives you a wide variety of ways to move through your document, so you can use the methods with which you're the most comfortable. The buttons at the bottom of the vertical scroll bar, shown in Figure 6-14, let you scroll through your document, move up or down one page at a time, or move to a specific object in your document.

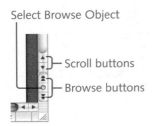

Select Browse Object

Scroll buttons

Browse buttons

Figure 6-14. The Browse buttons let you move quickly through your document in the method you select using the Select Browse Object button.

Chapter 6

You can use the following tools to navigate within your document:

● The Browse buttons, which let you move up or down a page (by default) or go to the next element (such as a heading, section, or footnote). Select an element using the Select Browse Object button.

● The Go To tab of the Find And Replace dialog, which lets you choose elements of the document to display.

● The Document Map pane (select View, Document Map), which lets you move to any heading in your document.

● Bookmarks, which you can use to establish anchor points in your document that you can quickly return to.

Navigating with the Browse Buttons

To navigate your document using the Browse buttons (shown in Figure 6-14 on the preceding page), perform any of the following steps:

● Click the Select Browse Object button, and then, from the palette that appears, shown in Figure 6-15, click the button representing the object type that you want to find the next instance of. You can move to the next table, graphic, heading, edit, page, section, comment, footnote, endnote, or field. You can also click the Find button to open the Find tab of the Find And Replace dialog or click the Go To button to open the Go To tab of the Find And Replace dialog. When you hover the pointer over a button, the name of the button appears on the face of the top button on the palette. When the pointer is not over a button, the top button is labeled Cancel; clicking the button when it reads Cancel will close the palette. When you select a browse object, the Browse buttons' names will change to reflect the object. For example, if you've selected to browse by page, the Browse buttons will be named Previous Page and Next Page. Selecting to browse by footnote will change the buttons' names to Previous Footnote and Next Footnote.

> **tip** If you hear a beep when you try to select a given type of browse object, it means that that object type does not exist in your document.

● Click the Previous button to move to the previous object selected in the Select Browse Object palette.

● Click the Next button to move to the next object selected in the Select Browse Object palette.

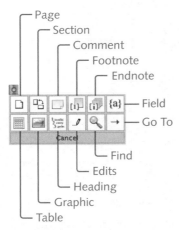

Page
Section
Comment
Footnote
Endnote
Field
Go To
Find
Edits
Heading
Graphic
Table

Figure 6-15. The Select Browse Object palette lets you choose an element of your document to view.

---

tip **Browse for comments**

The Select Browse Object palette is quite useful when you are reviewing a document with comments. Rather than take up screen space by displaying the Reviewing toolbar, you can move to the next comment by clicking the Browse By Comment button.

Navigating with Go To

As with the buttons on the Browse Objects palette, you can use the commands on the Go To tab of the Find And Replace dialog to move to specific places in your documents. The controls on the Go To tab give you a lot more control over your movements within your document than the Select Browse Objects palette, which just moves you to the next instance of the document element you select. For example, you can use the controls on the Go To tab to move to the previous instance of an element, move to the next instance of an element, or move forward or backward a number of instances that you select (e.g., "the third footnote after this one").

To navigate your document using the commands on the Go To tab, follow these steps:

1 Choose Edit, Go To to display the Go To tab of the Find And Replace dialog, shown in Figure 6-16 on the next page.

2 Click the element to which you want to move.

Chapter 6

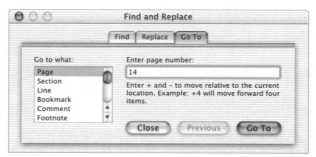

Figure 6-16. The Go To tab of the Find And Replace dialog gives you more control over your movements within a document than the Browse buttons offer.

3 Select any of these commands to go to the document element you've chosen:

■ Click the Previous button to move to the previous instance of the selected element.

■ Click the Next button to move to the next instance of the selected element.

■ Type a plus sign (+) or minus sign (–) in the Enter box and follow it with the relative number of items you want to move. For example, if you wanted to move to the fourth graphic after the current graphic, you would type **+4** in the text box and click Next. The box's label changes to reflect the item you clicked in the Go To What pane.

---

tip **Press Command+G for simpler Replace access**

If you prefer to use keyboard shortcuts in Word, you probably don't care for the Command+Shift+H sequence you have to press to display the Replace page of the Find And Replace dialog. It's much easier to press Command+G to display the Go To tab of the same dialog and then click the Replace tab.

Using the Document Map View

When you create a long document in Word, it can be difficult to remember where in the document you cover certain topics. In a yearly status report for a research project, for example, you might discuss the project's history, the results of previous years' work, and a literature review. Buried somewhere in the document is a discussion of a key point that helped you overcome an obstacle, but finding the section after you've written 70 pages can be tedious and time consuming.

Enter the Document Map (shown in Figure 6-17). The Document Map, which is a separate pane that appears at the left edge of the document window, displays all of the headings in your document. Clicking a heading moves the insertion point to the heading's location in your document. The Document Map is, in many ways, a combination of the Outline and Page Layout views. The headings let you move through the document easily while seeing the document as it will appear when printed.

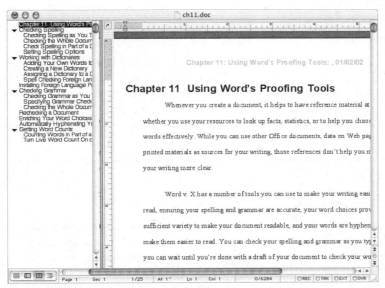

Figure 6-17. You can click a heading in the Document Map to move the insertion point to the heading's position in your document.

To navigate your document using Document Map view, follow these steps:

1 Choose View, Document Map to display the Document Map pane at the left side of your document.

2 Click any heading in the Document Map pane to display the corresponding heading in the document window.

3 Click the disclosure triangle next to a heading to display (or hide) all subheadings underneath the heading.

4 If necessary, use the Document Map scroll bar to move to parts of the Document Map that aren't visible in the pane.

Troubleshooting

Some of my headings don't appear in the Document Map pane.

Depending on how you have formatted the section and subsection headings in your document, you might find that some of the headings don't show up in the Document Map pane. For example, one publisher's style calls for third-level headings to be in italics and run on the same line as the first paragraph in the section. Those headings would not show up in the Document Map unless you had redefined one of the built-in heading styles.

Though Word does look for lines with short phrases, capitalization, and special formatting, the only way to guarantee a heading will appear in the Document Map is to either format the line with a built-in heading style or an outline level style. Word will also fail to detect any headings you have placed in the body of a table.

InsideOut

Format Document Map text

You can change the formatting of the contents of the Document Map pane by choosing Format, Style, clicking the Document Map style, and then clicking Modify. Use the controls in the Modify Style dialog to change the appearance of the text in the Document Map pane. For example, you might want to make the text in the Document Map pane smaller so more of the heading text is displayed in the pane. For more information on modifying styles, see "Defining Styles," page 165.

Using Bookmarks

Navigating your document using the Document Map makes it easy for you to jump from section to section, but it doesn't give you the pinpoint control you need to move directly to an arbitrary point in a document. Whether that point is a table in an annual report, an explanatory paragraph you want to reference from another document, or a glossary entry, you can't move there using the Document Map.

You can identify points in your document and make it possible for you and your colleagues to move to the point directly. By creating a *bookmark,* you call out a location or object of interest in your document. You can then use the Go To tab of the Find And Replace dialog or the Bookmark dialog to move to that location.

For information on creating links to bookmarked locations in your documents, see "Inserting and Linking Hyperlinks," page 367.

To manage the bookmarks in a document, follow these steps:

1 Choose Insert, Bookmark to display the Bookmark dialog, shown in Figure 6-18.

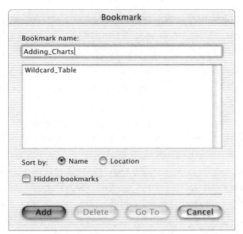

Figure 6-18. Bookmarks enable you to identify points of interest in your document. You can use the bookmarks as anchors for links from other locations in any Office document.

2 Perform any of these actions:

▨ Type the name of your bookmark in the Bookmark Name box, and then click the Add button to create a bookmark. The bookmark will be created at the location of the insertion point.

tip You can only use letters, numbers, and underscore characters in a bookmark name; you can't use spaces. If you type an unusable character in the Bookmark Name box, the Add button will be made unavailable.

▨ Select a bookmark, and then click the Delete button to delete the bookmark.

▨ Select the Name option to list the available bookmarks in alphabetical order.

▨ Select the Location option to list the available bookmarks in the order they appear in the document.

▨ Select the Hidden Bookmarks check box to list any bookmarks that Word normally hides, such as cross-references.

▨ Select a bookmark, and then click the Go To button to close the Bookmarks dialog and display the document page where the bookmark is located.

What Happens When You Cut, Copy, and Paste Bookmarks

When you manipulate text, tables, and graphics defined as bookmarks, you can sometimes get some unexpected results. The following describes the behavior of bookmarks and their constituent parts when you copy, cut, and paste bookmarked items:

- Copying all or part of an item defined as a bookmark means the bookmark will remain at its original location, and the location where the marked item is pasted will not be defined as a bookmark.

- Copying an item defined as a bookmark and pasting it into another document will cause both documents to include the item. In addition, the item will be defined as a bookmark in both locations.

- Cutting an item defined as a bookmark and then pasting it into a new location causes the bookmark to move to the new location. This change occurs regardless of whether the paste location is in the original document or a new document.

- Deleting part of the document contents defined as a bookmark won't delete the bookmark—the mark will stay with the remaining text.

- Adding text within an item defined as a bookmark will cause the new text to be included in the bookmark.

- Placing the insertion point to the right of the opening bracket of a bookmark and then typing text or adding an item will cause the addition to be included in the bookmark definition. See "Showing Bookmarks in a Document," next, to see the bookmarks in your document.

- Placing the insertion point to the right of the closing bracket of a bookmark definition and then typing text or adding an item will not cause the addition to be included in the bookmark definition.

- Adding a row to a table that is defined as a bookmark will add the row to the table definition.

If in doubt, you can always delete the bookmark that is giving you trouble and define a new one with the same name.

Showing Bookmarks in a Document

To show the bookmarks in your document, follow these steps:

1 Choose Word, Preferences to display the Preferences dialog.

2 If necessary, click the View category.

3 In the Show section of the dialog, select the Bookmarks check box, and then click OK.

Hiding Bookmark Indicators in a Printed Document

To prevent bookmark indicators from appearing when you print a document, follow these steps:

1 Choose Word, Preferences to display the Preferences dialog.

2 Click the Print category, and then, in the Include With Document section, clear the Hidden Text check box.

3 Click OK to save your change.

Formatting Your Work

Professional documents require accurate content and a professional look. Although it might be tempting to throw every formatting technique you know at a document, the hard truth is that fancy formatting tires the reader quickly. When you create a document in Microsoft Word X, you should pay particular attention to the impression the layout of your document creates. Is it professional and consistent with a little flair, or is it loud and confused? If you try a new design element in a document, be sure you get the opinion of a few of your colleagues to ensure the formatting doesn't detract from your document's content.

In this chapter, we'll look at formatting every element of your Word document—from individual characters to paragraphs to the whole document. Basic formatting, such as applying bold or italic format to a word, can be accomplished in several ways (no doubt you've found your preferred method for formatting text), but this chapter covers the whole range of techniques for formatting your document.

Browsing the Formatting Palette

Word X gives you all the tools you need to format your document exactly the way you want. And, with the Formatting Palette, Word puts all of the commonly used formatting tools in one easy-to-reach location. When you choose View, Formatting Palette (or click the Formatting Palette button on the Standard toolbar) to display the Formatting Palette for the first time, you will see the four basic categories (Font, Alignment And Spacing, Borders And Shading, and Document) into which the options are sorted.

Clicking the disclosure triangle at the left of a category heading expands the Formatting Palette to display the options available for that category; clicking again collapses the category, hiding the options. If you want, you can have all four categories open at once; the fully expanded Formatting Palette just fits at a resolution of 1024×768. However, the Formatting Palette will change to reflect the on-screen object you are editing. If you are working with an image or a list, new categories will appear with formatting tools relevant to your work.

> **tip** The Formatting Palette isn't too picky about where you click to expand and contract its sections; clicking anywhere in the category heading does the trick.

Most of the buttons and other objects on the Formatting Palette will be familiar to you, based on your previous word processing experience. If you're not sure what a particular object does (sometimes an icon's meaning isn't always clear), point at the object. After a moment, a ScreenTip will appear with the name of the object.

> For information on using the Formatting Palette to change the format of drawing objects, see "Modifying Graphics," page 251. For information on using the Formatting Palette to modify bulleted and numbered lists, see "Creating Bulleted and Numbered Lists," page 212.

Setting Font Attributes

Many times when you want to change the appearance of text, you only want to make one or two changes. Displaying text in bold or italic adds emphasis, while changing text's size can indicate a heading. You can make any of those changes using the options in the Font section of the Formatting Palette, shown in Figure 7-1.

Figure 7-1. The Formatting Palette's Font section is home to options you can use to quickly change your text's appearance.

> **tip** The Font section displays the formatting of the text you are editing or have selected, so keeping the Formatting Palette open and positioned at the edge of your document makes it easy to keep track of the current formatting.

The Font section has most of the font formatting tools you can use in Word, but not all of them. The remainder of the formatting options available to you are covered later in this chapter.

> **note** Perhaps the least-important feature change between Word 2001 and Word X appears in this section. The Highlight button has migrated from the Standard toolbar to the Formatting Palette in this revision.

Setting Alignment and Spacing

Like the Font section, the Alignment And Spacing section of the Formatting Palette, shown in Figure 7-2, gives you quick access to the most commonly used paragraph formatting commands.

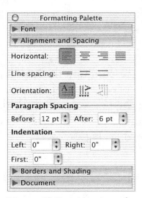

Figure 7-2. You can format your paragraphs with the options in the Alignment And Spacing section of the Formatting Palette.

> For information on choosing settings in the Alignment And Spacing section, see "Setting Paragraph Formatting," page 137.

Setting Borders and Shading

Setting apart text or paragraphs using bold or italic text, or perhaps by increasing the space between a paragraph and its neighbors, is an effective way of calling attention to the contents of the paragraph. If you want to make sure an important paragraph, perhaps one that contains instructions for filling out a form or the time of an event, catches your reader's attention, you can add a border to surround the text or color the background of the paragraph to make it stand out even more. The options you need can be found in the Borders And Shading section of the Formatting Palette, shown in Figure 7-3.

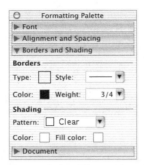

Figure 7-3. The options in the Borders And Shading section let you set important blocks of text apart from the rest of the document.

note Shading a paragraph doesn't change the color of the paragraph's text. To change the color of the text, use the Font Color setting in the Font section of the Formatting Palette.

Setting Document Properties

When you create a document, you should pay careful attention to the requirements of your audience. For example, if you are preparing a paper for publication in a conference proceedings, you should pay particular attention to the margins the printer requires to include a paper in the final collection. You can make those settings in the Document section of the Formatting Palette, shown in Figure 7-4.

Figure 7-4. Use the options in the Document section of the Formatting Palette to change your document's margins and layout.

Controlling Character Formatting

Word gives you the tools you need to format your text quickly, but the program can accommodate you regardless of your preferred method for formatting text. In addition to the settings in the Font section of the Formatting Palette, you can use the options in the Font dialog, shown in Figure 7-5, to change your text's appearance as well. Choose Format, Font to open the Font dialog.

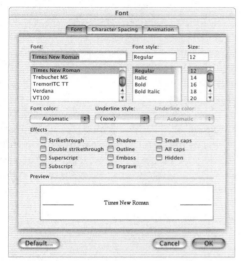

Figure 7-5. The Font dialog has a more complete collection of options you can use to format your text.

For example, many of the options in the Font dialog correspond to the options of the same name in the Font section of the Formatting Palette. In some cases the methods are different (for example, you apply a shadow using the Formatting Palette by clicking the Shadow button, whereas in the Font dialog you select the Shadow check box), but the effects are the same.

There are several considerations you should take into account when deciding whether you want to use the Formatting Palette or the Font dialog to format your text. The first consideration is whether the options you need are available on the Formatting Palette. If they are, and you already have the Formatting Palette visible on your desktop, then using the Formatting Palette will be quicker than opening the Font dialog. A parallel benefit is that, if you think of something you want to add or change in the middle of your formatting, you don't need to close a dialog; you can just move to the new location and begin editing.

Another advantage to using the Formatting Palette is that any formatting you apply to selected text in your document will be applied immediately. If you know you want to format a selection in small caps and bold, you can make those changes without delay.

The main advantage of using the Font dialog is that you can see the effect of any changes you consider before they are actually applied. The result of the current Font dialog settings appears in the Preview pane, so you don't need to select and deselect the text you want to format to see the result. Another benefit of the Font dialog is that the changes you select aren't actually applied until you click the OK button; if you click the Cancel button, the dialog disappears and you don't need to reverse your actions, as you would to remove formatting applied using the Formatting Palette. A third benefit is that you can make many formatting changes at once (for example, font, font size, and text color), and apply all the changes at once when you click OK.

Applying Basic Text Formatting Options

Whenever you want to make minor adjustments to the formatting of some text in your document, you can use the options in the Font section of the Formatting Palette (shown in Figure 7-1 on page 124) to do so. The options you select will be applied immediately to the selected text, or will be in effect for the next characters you type if you haven't selected a block of text.

To change text formatting using the options in the Font section of the Formatting Palette, follow these steps:

1 Choose View, Formatting Palette to display the Formatting Palette.

2 If necessary, click the Font category to display the options in the Font section of the Formatting Palette.

3 If you want to set attributes for text you're about to type, set the insertion point where you plan to start typing. If you want to format text you've already typed, select the text first. Then take any of these actions:

- Click the Style pop-up menu, and then choose the style you want to apply. For more information about styles, see Chapter 8, "Advanced Formatting with Styles, Templates, and Themes."

- Click the Name pop-up menu, and then choose the font in which you want the text to be displayed.

- Click the Size pop-up menu, and then choose the size, in points, in which you want the text to be displayed.

- Click the Font Color button, and then, from the palette that appears, select the color you want to apply to the text. If you want to select a color that doesn't appear in the palette, you can click the More Colors button to display the Color Picker dialog. You can use the options in the Color Picker to mix the color you want, using any one of several color systems.

For information on using the Color Picker to select Web safe colors, see "Web page background and fill colors change (or appear different) on some monitors," page 372.

- Click the Bold button to format the text in bold.

- Click the Italic button to format the text in italic.

- Click the Underline button to display the text with an underline.

- Click the Shadow button to add a drop shadow to the text.

- Click the Superscript button to display the text as a superscript.

- Click the Subscript button to display the text as a subscript.

- Click the Strikethrough button to display the text with a horizontal line through the middle of the text.

- Click the Double Strikethrough button to display the text with two horizontal lines through the middle of the text.

- Click the Small Caps button to format text as normal capitals for capital letters and small capitals for lowercase letters.

- Click the All Caps button to make text all uppercase.

- Click the Highlight button to add a highlight of a chosen color (displayed on the button's face and in the button's ScreenTip) to the selected text. The default highlight color is yellow, but you can pick a new highlight color by opening the pop-up menu and choosing the color from the palette that appears. Clicking None on that palette will remove highlighting from the selected text.

- Click the Numbering button to format text as a numbered list.

- Click the Bullets button to format text as a bulleted list.

- Click the Decrease Indent button to move an item up one level in a numbered or bulleted list, or to indent a regular paragraph one tab stop to the left.

- Click the Increase Indent button to move an item down one level in a numbered or bulleted list, or to indent a regular paragraph one tab stop to the right.

Troubleshooting

I can't underline a blank line in Word.

Word doesn't allow you to underline a blank line, so you have to resort to a variety of tricks to achieve the same result:

- **Add a border.** Use the Border feature to apply a border to the bottom of the line. You can vary the line type, style, color, and weight to produce different underlining effects. The drawback to this technique is that borders usually go across the entire width of a page, so you lack control over the length of your line.

- **Underscore.** Pressing Shift+hyphen creates underscore characters. Use as many as you need. The benefit to this technique is that you can place one or more tab stops before the underscores, so you can control both the line length and the line position. This is a quick technique for creating lines for forms, such as signature lines.

- **Nonbreaking spaces.** Pressing Control+Shift+Spacebar creates a nonbreaking space, which is a space that won't split at the end of a line. Because Word regards it as a character, these special spaces can be underlined. Create the nonbreaking spaces, and then apply underlining to them with the Formatting Palette.

Applying Advanced Character Formatting Options

If the options in the Font section of the Formatting Palette don't include the formatting options you need, use the Font dialog to make any additional changes you want. If you find it more natural to use the Font dialog to make all of your changes, you can dispense with the Formatting Palette altogether.

To set advanced character formatting options for text in your document, follow these steps:

1 Set the insertion point where you want to start typing specially formatted text, or select existing text you want to format; then choose Format, Font to display the Font dialog (shown in Figure 7-5 on page 127).

2 Follow any of these steps to modify the formatting of your text:

- Click the Underline Style pop-up menu, and then choose the underlining pattern you want to apply.

- Click the Underline Color pop-up menu, and then choose the color of the underlining you want to apply.

■ Select the Outline check box to display the selected text as an outline, rather than as solid letters.

■ Select the Emboss check box to display the text as if it were embossed onto the paper.

■ Select the Engrave check box to display the text as if it were engraved into the paper.

■ Select the Hidden check box to hide the selected text when the document is viewed or printed. You can display hidden text by selecting the Show/Hide button on the Standard toolbar; when you display hidden text, any hidden text in your document appears with a dotted underline.

■ Click the Default button to set the font properties currently displayed in the Font dialog as the default font for the active template. A confirmation dialog will appear, asking whether you are sure you want to define the current settings as the default.

caution   As much fun as it can be to add blinking words or marching ants to a document, you should strictly limit your use of the formatting options available on the Animation tab of the Font dialog. As is true when you're designing a Web page, animations most often distract the reader from the information in the document and make the files much larger than they have to be. Save the animations for your party invitations.

Adjusting Kerning and Letterspacing

With the exception of some fonts that are specially designed for large letter sizes, the majority of fonts are designed to look best in the font sizes you use in documents. Typically, that range is between 10 and 24 points. When you work with larger font sizes, the distance between letters (especially when combined with open letters such as *c* and *e*) can make the text appear uneven and harder to read. If you find your large-size text is hard to read, you can have Word adjust the spacing between the letters to improve readability. This process, known as *kerning,* takes into consideration the font, the size of the text, and the letters in a word.

note   Kerning only works for PostScript and TrueType fonts above a minimum size. The minimum size varies from font to font.

If you don't get the results you were looking for from the kerning operation, or if you want to change the appearance of text below the minimum size for a given font, you can also adjust the *letterspacing* of selected characters or words by hand.

To adjust the kerning and letterspacing in your document, follow these steps:

1 Select the text you want to format, choose Format, Font to display the Font dialog, and then click the Character Spacing tab, shown in Figure 7-6.

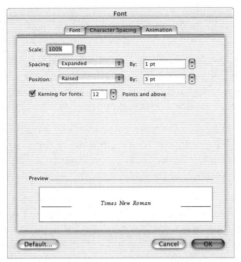

Figure 7-6. Use the options on the Character Spacing tab of the Font dialog to change the space between selected characters.

2 Follow any of these steps to change the kerning and letterspacing of the selected text:

- In the Scale box, type a percentage value representing the width of each character, as compared to the normal width of each character (equal to 100%). Changing the scale of selected text increases or decreases the width of each character, it doesn't change the space between each pair of characters.

> **note** You can also open the Scale pop-up menu to choose from a list of common values. The scale value for a font's default spacing is 100%.

- Open the Spacing pop-up menu, and then select Expanded or Condensed to either increase or decrease the amount of space between characters in the selection. (Choosing Normal removes any expansion or contraction from the selection.) After you select whether you want to expand or condense your text, use the adjacent By box to set the distance by which you want the text's spacing changed.

- Open the Position pop-up menu, and then select Raised or Lowered to either raise or lower the baseline of the selected characters. (Choosing

132

Normal returns the text to the default baseline.) After you select where you want to raise or lower your text, use the adjacent By box to set the distance by which you want to raise or lower the text.

- Select the Kerning For Fonts check box, and then type the point size at which you want to begin kerning the selected text.

note Though Word has some of the features of desktop publishing programs, it only offers automatic kerning and letterspacing. You can't kern individual pairs of letters manually, as you can with true desktop publishing programs, such as Quark XPress, or Adobe InDesign.

Specifying Superscripts and Subscripts

Whenever you work with text describing mathematical or scientific processes, you will invariably encounter exponents or ion markers (e.g., x^2 or U^{238}) that need to be written as *superscripts* (smaller text above the baseline). You might also need to display text as a *subscript* (smaller text written below the baseline), perhaps as part of the chemical equation for a compound (for example, $C_6H_{12}O_6$). You can use the options in the Font section of the Formatting Palette to format text as a superscript or subscript and then, if you want to make any additional changes to the text's appearance (such as making the subscript's font size smaller), you can do so using the other options in the Font dialog.

For more information on creating equations in Word, see "Using the Equation Editor," page 224.

Superscripts are also useful for denoting footnotes or endnotes in the body of your document, but Word has specialized tools you can use to create and edit footnotes and endnotes.

For more information on adding footnotes and endnotes to a document, see "Inserting Footnotes and Endnotes," page 310.

To format text as either superscript or subscript, follow these steps:

1 Select the text you want to format as superscript or subscript, and then choose View, Formatting Palette.

2 If necessary, click the Font category to display the Font section (shown in Figure 7-1 on page 124).

3 Either click the Superscript button or the Subscript button to format the selected text with the desired style.

For information on how to change the distance a superscript or subscript is from the text baseline, see "Adjusting Kerning and Letterspacing," page 131.

Creating Drop Caps

One typographic convention that adds to the attractiveness of the first paragraph of a chapter or section is to format the first character of that paragraph as a drop cap, as shown in Figure 7-7.

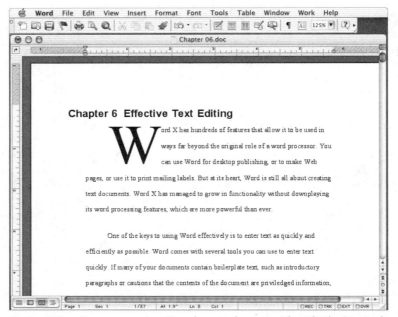

Figure 7-7. Drop caps are a time-honored way to identify the start of a chapter.

Word converts the character or characters you format as a drop cap to a larger font in a text box. After you create the drop cap, you can edit it as you would any other text.

For information on working with graphics, see "Modifying Graphics," page 251.

To add drop caps to your document, follow these steps:

1 Click to place the insertion point in the paragraph whose first character you want to display as a drop cap, and then choose Format, Drop Cap to display the Drop Cap dialog.

2 Using the options in the Drop Cap dialog, follow any of these steps:

■ Select the Dropped or In Margin button to choose the type of drop cap character you want for the paragraph.

■ Click the Font pop-up menu, and then choose the font in which you want the drop cap to be displayed.

■ Type the number of vertical lines you want the first character of the paragraph to span in the Lines To Drop box.

■ Type the distance, in fractions of an inch, you want the first character of the paragraph to be separated from the second character in the Distance From Text box.

3 Click OK to apply your changes.

tip   If you select more than one character at the start of the paragraph before you choose Format, Drop Cap, the entire selection will be turned into a drop cap. This rarely looks good, however.

Changing Text Case and Text Direction

Each language has unique rules for which words should be capitalized. The first letter of sentences and proper names are most always capitalized, but languages differ on whether common nouns, days of the week, or the names of months should begin with a capital letter or not. You can also use capitalization for effect; typing a paragraph in all capital letters, such as on a licensing agreement, indicates the text should be given close attention, whereas typing in all lowercase letters conveys a laid-back, relaxed attitude on the part of the writer.

By way of the Change Case dialog, shown in Figure 7-8, Word lets you change the case of your text according to one of several patterns. The outcome of each pattern is reflected in the way the pattern's name is written in the dialog.

Figure 7-8. The Change Case dialog lets you choose the capitalization pattern for selected text.

> **caution** When you change the case of text in your document, you are actually substituting one character for another (that is, *a* is a different character than *A*). If your text was an irregular mix of uppercase and lowercase letters and you can't reverse the change you made using the Undo button (perhaps you quit Word after you made the change), you will need to restore the capitalization by hand.

> **tip** You can cycle between lowercase, Title Case, and UPPERCASE by repeatedly pressing Shift+F3. Pressing Command+Shift+A toggles you between lowercase and UPPERCASE.

Another way to bring attention to text in your document is to change the direction in which the text is arranged. Normally, the text in your document is arranged so the top of the letters are parallel to the top of the page. You can, however, change the orientation of the text so that the top of the text is parallel to either edge of the page. Figure 7-9 shows text that has the top of the text oriented with the right edge of the page.

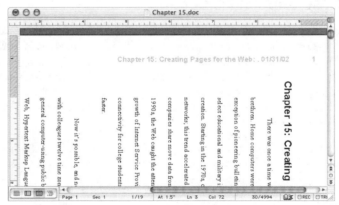

Figure 7-9. You can orient your document's text to run parallel to the right edge of the page.

> **caution** Note that changing the orientation of text in your document does not change the orientation of all elements. In Figure 7-9, for example, the header is still parallel to the top of the page. To change the orientation of the entire document, you will need to follow the instructions in "Setting Page Size and Orientation," page 148.

To change the case or direction of text in your document, select the text you want to format, and then follow either of these steps:

● Choose Format, Change Case to display the Change Case dialog. In the dialog, select the option for the case pattern you want to apply to the selected text.

● Choose Format, Text Direction to display the Text Direction dialog, shown in Figure 7-10. In the dialog, choose the direction you want to apply to the selected text. A preview of the text appears in the dialog's Preview pane.

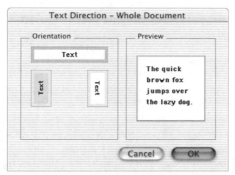

Figure 7-10. Use the buttons in the Text Direction dialog to change the orientation of your document's text.

Setting Paragraph Formatting

When you create a document, such as a business report, you can usually present most of your text in the standard, left-aligned format that reaches from margin to margin. Some organizations have more exacting standards, however, perhaps requiring you to change the line wrap for quotations, to center some text (such as chapter headings) on the page, and align page numbers with the right margin. You can do all of those things in Word, and you can do most of them with the options in the Alignment And Spacing section of the Formatting Palette (shown in Figure 7-2, page 125).

Another tool at your disposal is the horizontal ruler, shown in Figure 7-11. The horizontal ruler shows your document's margins, the left and right indents for the current paragraph, and any tab stops present in the paragraph you're editing.

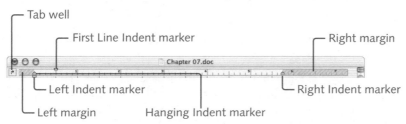

Figure 7-11. The horizontal ruler shows many of the formatting settings for the paragraph you've selected.

> **note** If you have selected more than one paragraph, the horizontal ruler will only show those settings that all selected paragraphs have in common.

InsideOut

Put the ruler under cover

Some people don't like having the ruler visible all the time, because they prefer to reserve for their document the maximum amount of space possible in the document window. That's OK; Word lets you have your cake and eat it too. If you hide the ruler by clearing the check mark next to View, Ruler, the ruler obediently disappears from your document window. But wait—if you point at the bottom of the title bar, the ruler will slide into view. Move the pointer away, and the ruler slips back to its hiding place. Point to the left edge of the document window to make the vertical ruler appear, if Vertical Ruler is selected in the Word Preferences dialog.

Using the Ruler to Set Indents

The left and right indents of a paragraph indicate where the first character of the paragraph will be placed and the point beyond which a word must be moved to the next line of the document. You can position the indents using the ruler by dragging the indent marker to the desired location—a vertical line will be drawn from the marker to the bottom of the page, showing you the location of the indent as you move it.

To use the ruler to set indents for a portion of your document, follow these steps:

1 If necessary, choose View, Ruler to display the horizontal ruler (shown in Figure 7-11 on the preceding page) at the top of your document.

2 Select the text for which you want to reset the indent, and then follow any of these steps:

- Drag the Left Indent marker to the place where you want the left edge of the paragraph to be placed.

- Drag the Right Indent marker to the location where you want to place the right edge of the paragraph. If the last character in a word would be written to the right of this boundary, the whole word will be moved to the next line.

> For information on hyphenating your document so only a portion of your word will be moved to the next line, see "Hyphenating Your Documents Automatically," page 281.

■ Drag the First Line Indent marker to the location where you want the first line of the paragraph to begin. All subsequent lines will begin at the Left Indent marker.

■ Drag the Hanging Indent marker to the right of the First Line Indent marker to create a hanging indent. (The Hanging Indent marker moves as a unit with the Left Indent marker.) When you create a hanging indent, the second and subsequent lines of the paragraph begin to the right of where the first line begins. Hanging indents are most often used in bulleted and numbered lists to place the item marker (a bullet or number) to the left of the item's text.

Using the Ruler to Set Tabs

Another way you can use the ruler to format paragraphs in your document is to set *tab stops*. A tab stop is a location you set to use as a guide to placing text in your document. For example, you can set a tab stop at the midpoint of your document to begin typing the date of a letter, or use multiple tabs to create columns of data in your document, as in a price list. You aren't limited to creating tabs that place the text you type to the right of the tab stop. Table 7-1 describes the different tab stops that are available and how they are used.

Table 7-1. Available Tab Types

Button	Tab Type	Description
	Left Tab	Text starts at the tab and continues to the right until it reaches the end of the line. Any text in the paragraph that spills over to the next line will begin at the Left Indent marker.
	Center Tab	Text is centered on the tab stop.
	Right Tab	Text begins at the tab stop and moves to the left as you type.
	Decimal Tab	Columns of numbers are aligned on the decimal point.
	Bar Tab	A vertical line (bar) is placed on every line where the tab stop is in effect. Used to draw vertical lines on a page.

To use the ruler to set tabs for a portion of your document, follow these steps:

1 If necessary, choose View, Ruler to display the horizontal ruler.

2 Select the portion of the document to which you want to assign tab stops.

3 Click the Tab well at the left edge of the horizontal ruler until the symbol representing the type of tab you want to add appears.

4 Click the horizontal ruler at the spot where you want to set the tab. If you didn't get the tab in exactly the right spot, drag it to the correct location.

> **tip**   To remove a tab, drag it from the ruler to the body of your document.

Manipulating Tab Stops

The horizontal ruler has a range of tools you can use to set and change tab stops, but it doesn't have the ability to set an absolute position for a stop or define *leader characters* that appear to the side of the tab stop (such as the periods that appear to the left of right-aligned page numbers in a table of contents). You can do all of those things, however, using the options in the Tabs dialog, which is displayed in Figure 7-12.

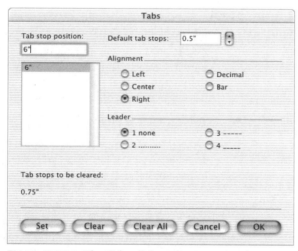

Figure 7-12.   The Tabs dialog gives you precise control over the tabs in your document.

To manipulate the tabs in your document using the Tabs dialog, follow these steps:

1 Place the insertion point in the paragraph for which you want to set or change tab stops.

2 Choose Format, Tabs, to display the Tabs dialog, and then follow any of these steps:

■ To create a new tab, type the position where you want to place the new tab stop in the Tab Stop Position box, and then click the Set button.

■ To set default tab stops at fixed intervals, type the interval (in inches) at which you want to place tab stops in the Default Tab Stops box. The default value for this box is 0.5".

■ To remove a tab, select the tab that you want to remove from the list, and click the Clear button. The tab will be added to the list in the Tab Stops To Be Cleared area, but will not actually be removed until you click the OK button.

■ To remove all tabs, click the Clear All button. The tabs will be added to the list in the Tab Stops To Be Cleared area, but will not actually be removed until you click the OK button.

■ To assign or change the alignment of a tab, select the tab you want to modify, and then, in the Alignment section of the dialog, select the desired alignment. (The tab alignments are described in Table 7-1 on page 139.)

■ To add leader characters to a tab stop, select the tab you want to modify and then, in the Leader section of the dialog, click the desired leader character.

Applying Line Spacing

Depending on the type of writing you're doing, you might want to fit as much text as you can on a single page, or you might want to leave plenty of room between lines of text so readers have room to make notes or corrections. Single-spacing is the default spacing for paragraphs in Word, but you can change line spacing to virtually whatever value you need.

To set the line spacing for one or more lines of text, follow these steps:

1 Select the text you want to format and then, if necessary, choose View, Formatting Palette to display the Formatting Palette.

2 If necessary, click the Alignment And Spacing category to expand it (shown in Figure 7-2 on page 125).

3 Select either the Single Space, 1.5 Space, or Double Space button under Line Spacing to apply the corresponding line spacing to the selected paragraphs.

> **tip** If you need finer control over line spacing, choose Format, Paragraph, then click the Indents And Spacing tab. Use the Line Spacing pop-up menu and At box to set precise line spacing values.

Adjusting Paragraph Indents, Alignment, and Spacing

The Alignment And Spacing section of the Formatting Palette holds many of the tools you need to make precise adjustments to your paragraph formatting. Although you can use the markers on the horizontal ruler to set indents, you can't specify an exact location for an indent. You can do so using the options in the Alignment And Spacing section, however.

Another useful formatting change you can make is to increase or decrease the space before and after the selected paragraphs. When you create a document from scratch, Word adds no extra space between paragraphs. In some cases, such as after a paragraph containing a graphic, you might want to add some extra space so the image stands apart from the surrounding text. If you just want to add a blank line, pressing Return is sufficient, but if you want to add more or less space, you can use the options in the Alignment And Spacing section to define the precise extra gap you want.

To adjust the indentation, alignment, and spacing of one or more paragraphs, follow these steps:

1 Select the text you want to format and then, if necessary, choose View, Formatting Palette to display the Formatting Palette.

2 If necessary, click the Alignment And Spacing category to open it (shown in Figure 7-2, page 125.)

3 To adjust the indentation, alignment, or spacing of your paragraphs, follow any of these steps:

- In the Before box, type the amount of space (in points) you want to be added above each selected paragraph.

- In the After box, type the amount of space (in points) you want to be added below each selected paragraph.

- In the Left box, type the distance that you want the left indent of the selected paragraph to be placed inside the document's left margin.

- In the Right box, type the distance that you want the right indent of the selected paragraph to be placed inside the document's right margin.

- In the First box, type the distance that you want the first line of the selected paragraphs to be offset from the left indent.

142

tip If you want a hanging indent, where the first line of a paragraph begins to the left of the left indent (where the text on subsequent lines will begin), type a negative value in the First box.

Setting Line and Page Breaks

Each time you press Return you start a new paragraph. A typical paragraph might be formatted with a first line indent or some extra spacing from the paragraph above (or both). Sometimes you want to break a line of text and start a new line without indenting or adding space; that is, without starting a new paragraph. To do this, insert a manual line break. When you insert a manual line break, the next character appears on the next line as part of the same paragraph, so it aligns with the Left Indent marker, not the First Line Indent marker. You can also have the next character appear on a new page by setting a manual page break, which also starts a new paragraph.

To set a line or page break, follow these steps:

1 Position the insertion point at the location where you want to insert the line or page break.

2 Follow either of these steps:

- Press Shift+Return to insert a manual line break.

- Press Shift+Enter or choose Insert, Break, Page Break to insert a manual page break.

note Shift+Enter only works on keyboards with separate number pads. If you're working on a portable, you might be able to use Shift+Enter if you turn on the Num Lock key; otherwise you must choose Insert, Break, Page Break.

Adding Borders to a Paragraph

When you want to set off a paragraph from the rest of your document but want the paragraph to be in the same font and not moved away from the other text, you can put a border around the paragraph. When you create the border, you can choose which edges of the selected paragraphs should have a border, how thick the lines should be, what type of line (for example, single, double, dashed, thick, thin, or combination) should be used, and what color the border should be.

To put a border around a paragraph, follow these steps:

1 Select or click in the paragraph to which you want to add a border, and then, if necessary, choose View, Formatting Palette to display the Formatting Palette.

143

2 Click the Borders And Shading category to expand it (shown in Figure 7-3 on page 126).

3 Click the Border Type button, and then select the type of border you want for the selected paragraphs.

4 Click the Style pop-up menu to choose a line style for the border. Clicking No Border, the top item on the list, will remove the border from the selected paragraph.

5 Click the Color button to display a palette of colors. You can click the More Colors button to open the Color Picker, which gives you more flexibility in choosing a border color.

6 Click the Weight pop-up menu to choose a thickness for your border. The default choice for a single border is 3/4 point.

Adding Shading Behind Text

Another technique you can use to make text stand out is to change the background color of a paragraph. In business documents you should take care to ensure the color is appropriate for your company's image and doesn't make the text too hard to read, but if you're putting together a party invitation, you should experiment with the wide range of colors at your disposal.

To add shading to a paragraph, follow these steps:

1 Select the text you want to shade, or to shade an entire paragraph click anywhere in the paragraph, and then, if necessary, choose View, Formatting Palette to display the Formatting Palette.

2 Click the Borders And Shading category to expand it (shown in Figure 7-3 on page 126).

3 Click the Pattern pop-up menu, and choose the desired saturation level for the shading.

4 To pick a different foreground color for the shading pattern (black by default), click the Color button, and then choose the desired color from the palette that appears. To choose a color that is not on the palette, click the More Colors button, and then use the options in the Color Picker to select your color.

5 To choose a different background color for the shading pattern (clear by default), click the Fill Color button, and then choose the desired color from the palette that appears. To choose a color that is not on the palette, click the More Colors button, and then use the options in the Color Picker to select your color.

6 If you want to adjust the relative mix of foreground and background colors, return to the Pattern pop-up menu, and observe that the saturation levels provide a preview of how the colors you've chosen will appear. Select the saturation level that provides the shading color you prefer.

144

> **tip** Choosing Clear from the Pattern list will shade the text with the color in the Fill Color box, whereas choosing Solid will shade the text with the color in the Color box. All other choices will result in a mix of the two colors. To remove the shading entirely, set the Fill Color box to No Fill, and then choose Clear from the Pattern box.

Formatting Using the Keyboard

If you prefer to apply formatting options using keyboard shortcuts, you can use the shortcuts listed in Table 7-2.

Table 7-2. Keyboard Shortcuts for Formatting

Shortcut	Effect
Command+B	Toggles bold formatting.
Command+I	Toggles italic formatting.
Command+U	Toggles underlining.
Command+D	Opens the Font dialog.
Shift+F3	Changes the case of selected letters. Cycles between lowercase, title case, and uppercase.
Command+Shift+A	Formats letters as all capitals. Pressing this key combination again toggles the text back to lowercase.
Command+Shift+W	Underlines all words, but does not underline spaces.
Command+Shift+D	Double-underlines text.
Control+Shift+H	Formats the selected text as hidden text.
Command+Shift+K	Formats the selected text as small capitals.
Command+equal sign (=)	Formats the selected text as subscript. (Use the equal sign in the main portion of the keyboard, not on the numeric keypad.)
Command+Shift+plus sign (+)	Formats the selected text as superscript. (Use the plus sign in the main portion of the keyboard, not on the numeric keypad.)
Control+Spacebar	Removes character formatting.

(continued)

Table 7-2. *(continued)*

Shortcut	Effect
Command+Shift+F	Activates the Font list on the Formatting Palette. Use the arrow keys to select the next or previous font in the list. Press Return when the font you want is shown, and the selected text changes to that font.
Command+Shift+>	Increases the font size to the next size in the Font Size box on the Formatting Palette.
Command+Shift+<	Decreases the font size to the next size in the Font Size box on the Formatting Palette.
Command+]	Increases the font size by one point.
Command+[	Decreases the font size by one point.

Using the Format Painter

The Formatting Palette makes it easy for you to change the appearance of your text, but it can take time to apply all of the formatting options you set on one bit of text to another selection. Fortunately, you can bypass the process and copy the format from one selection to another using the Format Painter, which you activate by clicking the Format Painter button on the Standard toolbar.

Format
Painter

To apply a format with the Format Painter, follow these steps:

1 Select the item with the formatting you want to copy, and then click the Format Painter button on the Standard toolbar. The pointer changes to an I-beam with a plus sign beside it, indicating it is carrying the format with it.

2 Select the text to which you want to apply the copied formatting.

> **tip** To apply the Format Painter to more than one selection, double-click the Format Painter button, which "locks on" the feature. Select each block of text you want to copy formatting to, and then click the Format Painter button again to release the lock.

Clearing All Formatting

When you experiment with different formatting options on text in your documents, it can be difficult, even with the Formatting Palette open, to recall exactly how you formatted your text. If you want, you can remove all of the formatting from a selected text block and start from scratch.

To clear all formatting from a selection, follow these steps:

1 Select the text from which you want to remove all formatting.

2 Choose Edit, Clear, Formats to remove the formatting from the selected item. The selected text returns to the default style (called Normal) defined in the active document template.

Revealing Formatting

Sometimes when you look at a document, you might come across a particularly attractive document element and wonder how the author managed to create the effect. Rather than sifting through the Formatting Palette or the different formatting dialogs to see every setting applied to the text you're interested in, you can have Word display the formatting for any single character or object in your document. The formatting appears in text form, with all of the details you need to recall the formatting later.

To reveal the formatting applied to text or objects in your document, follow these steps:

1 Choose View, Reveal Formatting. The pointer will change to resemble a speech balloon.

2 Click the characters or objects with the formatting you want to view. As shown in Figure 7-13, a detailed description of the formatting will appear.

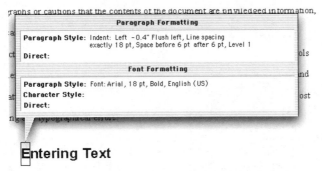

Figure 7-13. The Reveal Formatting command shows you all the gory details of how selected characters and objects are formatted.

3 Click as many areas as you want to examine, and then press Esc or choose View, Reveal Formatting again to stop viewing the formats in your document.

Formatting the Whole Document

As vital as it is to be able to change the formatting of specific elements of your document, there will be times when you want to apply a specific format to your entire document in a single go. For example, you might want to expand the margins of your document so that more text can appear on a single line, or to orient the entire document so that the long edge of the paper, not the short edge, is on top.

Setting Page Size and Orientation

Depending on the type of document you are creating and your target audience, you might need to print its contents on paper other than the standard US Letter size (8.5″ × 11″). Word X lets you choose from a variety of paper sizes, including the most common European sizes, so if you have the right paper, you can print on it accurately. You can also, if need be, switch the orientation of your document so that your text prints across the long edge of the page instead of the short edge.

To set page size and orientation for an entire document, follow these steps:

1 Choose File, Page Setup to display the Page Setup dialog, shown in Figure 7-14.

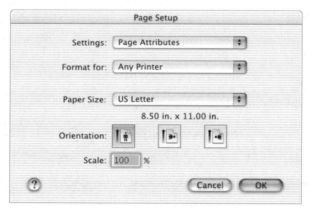

Figure 7-14. You can use the options in the Page Setup dialog to choose the size of paper you want to print on as well as how you want your document's contents oriented on the page.

2 Select any of these options to set up your document:

■ Open the Paper Size pop-up menu, and then select the paper size you want for the document. You can choose from US Letter, US Legal, A4, B5, and other sizes.

- Click the button representing the orientation you want to apply to your document.

- Type the scale, as a percentage of the normal printing size of your document, at which you want the document to be printed.

Setting Page Margins

Just as you can set indents for your text, you can set the minimum white space, called the *margins,* Word will leave at the edges of your document when you print it.

To set page margins for an entire document, follow these steps:

1 Choose Format, Document to display the Document dialog.

2 Select the Margins tab, shown in Figure 7-15.

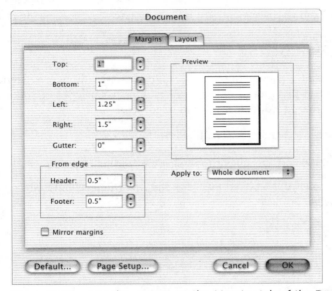

Figure 7-15. Use the options on the Margins tab of the Document dialog to set the amount of white space Word reserves at the edge of your document.

3 Use these options to set the margins in your document:

- In the Top box, enter the amount for the top margin.

- In the Bottom box, enter the amount for the bottom margin. Any additional text will appear on the next page.

- In the Left box, enter the amount for the left margin.

■ In the Right box, enter the amount for the right margin. Any additional text will appear on the next line.

■ In the Gutter box, type the additional space you want to reserve along the binding edge of your document for stapling, hole-punching, or binding. By default, this measurement is added to the left margin of each page, but you'll usually use this feature in combination with the next command, Mirror Margins.

■ Select the Mirror Margins check box if you plan to print your document on both sides of the paper and bind it book style. The Left box becomes the Inside box, and the Right box becomes the Outside box. The Gutter setting is then added to the Inside box setting so that binding or hole-punching doesn't interfere with the text.

■ Open the Apply To pop-up menu, and choose Whole Document to apply the margins to the entire document, or choose This Point Forward to change only the margins of pages beyond the insertion point.

Adding Line Numbering

When you create a document that will require precise editing or references, you might want to number the lines of your document. One instance where you might want to number the lines in a document would be for legal documents.

To number the lines in a document, follow these steps:

1 Choose Format, Document to display the Document dialog.

2 Click the Layout tab, and then click the Line Numbers button to display the Line Numbers dialog, shown in Figure 7-16.

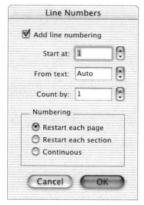

Figure 7-16. The Line Numbers dialog lets you decide how your line numbers should appear.

150

3 Select the Add Line Numbering check box to turn on line numbering.

4 In the Start At box, type the number you want to assign to the first line of your document. In most cases, the default value of 1 is appropriate.

5 In the From Text box, type the distance by which you want the line numbers to be separated from the body of the text. The default value of Auto usually provides good results, but feel free to change it if needed.

6 In the Count By box, type the increment at which you want line numbers to appear. The default value of 1 will have Word display the number of every line, but typing 5 to have Word display line numbers every fifth line reduces the visual clutter while still making it easy for readers to find the line they want.

7 Select one of these options to set the numbering pattern for your document:

- Select Restart Each Page (the default choice) to have Word begin numbering on each page from your Start At value.

- Select Restart Each Section to have Word begin numbering from your Start At value only at the beginning of a new section.

- Select Continuous to have Word number every line of the document consecutively, regardless of section breaks.

InsideOut

Download templates for legal documents from Mactopia

Unlike Word for Windows, Word X doesn't have a Pleading Wizard. So if you need to create line-numbered legal documents, also called *pleading documents,* you can download a legal pleading template from Microsoft's Mactopia site. Choose Help, Visit The Mactopia Web Site, and then type **pleading** into the Search box on the left side of the page. The site will show you where you can download the template.

Working with Sections

Except when you change the appearance of a few words or a paragraph, most of the formatting changes you make are applied to your entire document. Changes to margins, alignment, and headers and footers (discussed next) all fall into that category. Word makes it possible for you to apply those changes to a portion of your document by defining document *sections*. In a document with multiple sections, when you make a change that would normally affect the entire document, the change will affect only the selected sections.

Creating Headers and Footers

If you have text or other information you want to appear at the top or bottom of each printed page, you can add that information to the *headers* and *footers* of a section.

To add headers and footers to your document, follow these steps:

1 Choose View, Header And Footer to open the header for the current section and display the Header And Footer toolbar, shown in Figure 7-17.

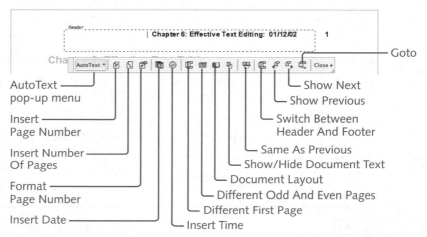

Figure 7-17. The options on the Header And Footer toolbar give you all the resources you need to format your headers and footers.

2 Type the text you want to appear in the header, and then click the Switch Between Header And Footer button on the Header And Footer toolbar to begin editing the footer for the current section.

3 Click the Close button on the Header And Footer toolbar to resume work on the main body of the document.

Adding AutoText to Headers and Footers

There are several standard types of information you can add to a header or footer, such as the file name, author, date created or printed, or page number. You can use the AutoText pop-up menu to insert this data automatically on each page. To add AutoText to a header or footer, follow these steps:

1 Choose View, Header And Footer to display the header and footer for the current section of your document, and then, if necessary, click the Switch Between Header And Footer button to move to the header or footer to which you want to add AutoText.

2 Open the AutoText pop-up menu, and then choose the AutoText you want to add from the list of available items. A list of items is displayed in Figure 7-18.

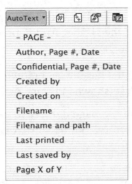

Figure 7-18. You can add commonly used information to a header or footer by selecting the item from the AutoText list.

3 Click the Close button on the Header And Footer toolbar to resume work on the main body of the document.

Positioning Headers and Footers

To change the positioning of the headers and footers in the current section, follow these steps:

1 Choose View, Header And Footer to display the headers and footers in the current section.

2 Move to the header or footer you want to position, and then follow either of these steps:

- To change the horizontal position of the current header or footer, choose View, Formatting Palette to display the Formatting Palette. Open the Alignment And Spacing category, and then click any of the paragraph alignment buttons and optionally adjust the Indentation values.

- To change the vertical spacing of the current header or footer, click the Document Layout button on the Header And Footer toolbar to display the Document dialog. Click the Margins tab, and then, in the From Edge section of the dialog, type the distance from the top of the page you want the header to begin in the Header box, and then type the distance from the bottom of the page you want the footer to display in the Footer box. Click OK to close the Document dialog.

Adding Page Numbering

You will want to add page numbers to most of your documents to enable readers to find and refer others to information easily and to help keep document pages in order. You can add page numbers using the options on the Header And Footer toolbar. To add page numbers to a document, follow these steps:

1 Choose View, Header And Footer to display the headers and footers in your document and the Header And Footer toolbar (shown in Figure 7-17, page 152).

2 Position the insertion point where you want the page number to be added and then click the Insert Page Number button to add the current page number to the header or footer.

3 If you also want to list the total pages on each page (such as *Page 3 of 35*), type the necessary text (such as *Page* and *of*), and then click the Insert Total Pages button to add the total pages to the header or footer.

Formatting Page Numbers

After you've added page numbers to your document, you can set the page formatting and numbering scheme.

To format the page numbers in your document, follow these steps:

1 Choose View, Header And Footer to display the headers and footers in your document, and then move to the header or footer with the page numbers you want to format.

2 Click the Format Page Numbers button on the Header And Footer toolbar to display the Page Number Format dialog, shown in Figure 7-19.

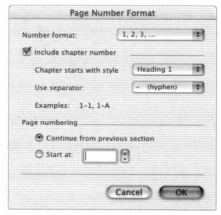

Figure 7-19. The Page Number Format dialog lets you determine how your page numbers will look when they are added to your document.

3 Use the options in the Page Number Format dialog to make any of these changes:

- Open the Number Format pop-up menu, and select the format for your page numbers. You can choose from Arabic numerals, lowercase letters, uppercase letters, lowercase Roman numerals, or uppercase Roman numerals.

- Select the Include Chapter Number check box to include the chapter number in the page number.

- Open the Chapter Starts With Style pop-up menu, and then select the heading style that marks the beginning of your chapter.

- Open the Use Separator pop-up menu, and then select the character you want to separate the chapter number and the page number. You can choose from the following characters: a hyphen (the default), a period, a colon, an em dash (—), or an en dash (–).

- Select Continue From Previous Section to have all page numbers reflect the location of the page in the overall document, not the current chapter or section.

- Select Start At to assign a starting page number for this section, and then type the starting value in the box.

---

tip **Make each chapter a separate document**

If you're preparing a longer work, such as a large report or a book, it's a good idea to make each section or chapter a separate document. Separating each chapter makes for smaller files, which are easier for your computer to keep track of when you edit them, and means that losing one file limits your losses to a chapter and not the entire book.

Troubleshooting

The style I use for my chapter headings isn't listed in the Page Number Format dialog.

If you've customized Word to reflect your work habits and requirements, you've probably created special styles to use as headings. The problem, as far as automatic page numbering goes, is that Word is only set up to recognize the nine built-in heading styles: Heading 1 through Heading 9. The best way to overcome this limitation is to redefine one of those styles, most likely Heading 1, as the style with which you begin a new chapter. If you do redefine one of the built-in heading styles, you should save the change in a new template, not in normal.dot.

Controlling the Appearance of Headers and Footers

One often-overlooked element of creating headers and footers is controlling when they appear in your document. For example, some publishers might ask you to create one header for odd-numbered pages and another for even-numbered pages. If you write a chapter for a book with multiple contributors, you might put the name of the book in the header for even-numbered pages and the chapter title and your name in the header on the odd-numbered pages.

To control when your headers and footers appear, follow these steps:

1 Choose Format, Document to display the Document dialog, and then click the Layout tab, shown in Figure 7-20.

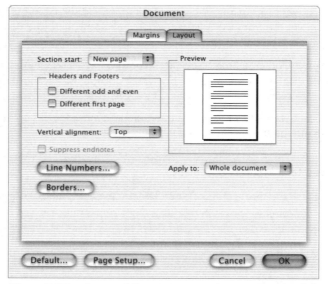

Figure 7-20. Some of the options on the Layout tab of the Document dialog let you change when your headers and footers appear.

2 Follow any of these steps to change when your headers and footers appear:

- Select the Different Odd And Even check box to have separate headers and footers for odd and even pages in the section.

- Select the Different First Page check box to define a separate header and footer for the first page in the section.

InsideOut

Hide the header and footer on a title page

Title pages can present a tricky situation when you are creating documents. You don't want a page number to appear in a header or footer on the title page, yet you want the title page to count as page 1 of the document. To create a header or footer for a section and hide the header and footer on the first page, select the Different First Page check box on the Layout tab of the Document dialog.

Inserting a Section Break

To insert a section break, position the insertion point at the desired location. Choose Insert, Break, and then, from the submenu, select the type of section break you want to create:

- Select Section Break (Next Page) to insert a section break and have the next section begin on the next page.

- Select Section Break (Continuous) to insert a section break and have the next section begin on the line after the break.

- Select Section Break (Odd Page) to insert a section break and have the next section begin on the next odd-numbered page. This break might cause you to have a blank page in your document, but it's ideal for when you want the next section to begin on a right-hand page.

- Select Section Break (Even Page) to insert a section break and have the next section begin on the next even-numbered page. This break might cause you to have a blank page in your document, but it's ideal for when you want the next section to begin on a left-hand page.

Chapter 8

Advanced Formatting with Styles, Templates, and Themes

For shorter documents, it's no problem to do all of your formatting tasks manually. All you need to do is select some text and apply the character or paragraph formatting you want. But for longer documents, it's just too laborious to apply—and reapply—formats again and again. Longer documents typically include elements that are repeated throughout the document. For example, this book has different levels of headings, figure captions, sidebars, and so forth, each of which has a very specific set of formatting characteristics. Rather than re-create these characteristics each time they needed to be used, the formatting for each element was stored as a style and applied to the text as needed. When we needed to change the look of certain elements, all we had to do was change the style for those elements, rather than manually reformat the whole document. All of the elements with the changed style automatically changed to match the new style definition.

In this chapter, you'll learn about the different kinds of styles, how to create and apply styles, and how to store them for later reuse. We'll also delve deeper into the use of templates, which work in conjunction with styles to save you even more time and effort. Finally, we'll take a look at themes, a kind of template that makes it easy to build certain specialized documents, such as Web pages.

Understanding Styles

In Microsoft Word X, *a style* is a collection of formatting commands that are grouped together and given a name and that you can apply with a single click. Word has two types of styles:

- **Paragraph styles** can be a combination of character formatting and paragraph formatting, including text alignment, indents, tab stops, line and page breaks, line spacing, borders, and shading. Paragraph formats apply to an entire paragraph at a time. They are also the most often used type of styles.

- **Character styles** can be a combination of any of the character formats that you can apply from the Font dialog. Character styles are usually applied to individual words or blocks of words within paragraphs.

You can have either or both kinds of styles in your documents, and paragraph styles can contain character styles as part of their definition.

Using the Style Area

If your document is in Normal or Outline view, you can have Word display the paragraph styles in your document in a separate *style area* at the left side of the document window. To show the style area, choose Word, Preferences, click the View category, and enter a positive number into the Style Area Width box. If the width value is 0, Word won't display the style area. The style area shows the names of the styles for each paragraph, as shown here:

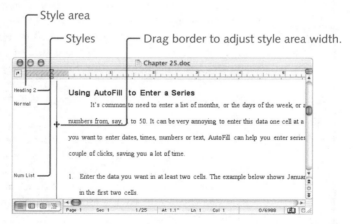

You can adjust the width of the style area by dragging the border between the style area and the document. Dragging the border all the way to the left side of the window removes the style area.

Chapter 8

Styles are stored within documents; if you create your own style (called a *user-defined style*), it is saved in your document (or in the document's template) along with Word's built-in styles. Those built-in styles, such as Normal, Heading 1 through Heading 9, and Body Text, are part of the array of styles that are provided with Word. When you create a document, it inherits all of the styles that are in the document template on which the document is based. Most of the time, you'll probably be using the Normal template, which includes more than 100 built-in styles, all of which are available for you to use in your document.

Word allows you to modify a built-in style, and the modified version is stored in the document or template where the modification was made. If a modified version of a built-in style is stored in a document, the modified version takes precedence over the unmodified version of the style that was inherited from the document's template.

The styles in your document are listed in several places; in the Font section of the Formatting Palette, in the Style dialog (accessed by choosing Format, Style), and on the Formatting toolbar. It's usually most convenient to view and apply styles from the Formatting Palette.

Applying Styles

The three ways to apply styles each have their own benefits and drawbacks:

- The Style pop-up menu on the Formatting Palette and on the Formatting toolbar is usually the easiest to use, but doesn't show you the full range of styles available to you.

- The fastest way of applying styles is to use keyboard shortcuts, but you'll have to assign the keyboard shortcuts and then remember them.

- The Style dialog shows you all available styles, displays a preview of what a style will look like when applied, and gives you a detailed description of each style. But it's the slowest method to use.

Applying Styles from the Formatting Palette

If you're just getting started using styles, it's best to use the Style pop-up menu on the Formatting Palette. Follow these steps:

1 If the Formatting Palette isn't already visible, click the Formatting Palette button on the Standard toolbar, or choose View, Formatting Palette.

2 If necessary, click the Font category on the Formatting Palette to expand the Font area.

3 To apply a paragraph style to a single paragraph, place the insertion point anywhere in that paragraph. If you want to apply the style to more than one paragraph, select part or all of each paragraph. If you are applying a character style, select the text only.

4 Click the Style pop-up menu on the Formatting Palette, and then choose the desired style, as shown in Figure 8-1. The paragraph styles show a Paragraph symbol in the upper right of each style box, and the character styles show the letter *a*. Click the style name to apply it.

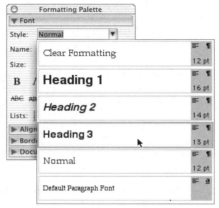

Figure 8-1. Choosing a style from the Formatting Palette's Style pop-up menu applies that style to the selected text.

As mentioned earlier, the Normal template contains more than 100 built-in styles, yet the Style menu on the Formatting Palette initially shows only six styles. That's because Word is only showing a few basic, often-used styles. You can access the entire gamut of styles by pressing Shift before you open the Style menu. Once you use a style in your document, Word always shows it on the Style pop-up menu.

---

tip If you're short on screen real estate, you can close the Formatting Palette and use the Formatting toolbar instead. The Formatting toolbar also has a Style pop-up menu, which is very similar to the one on the Formatting Palette.

Applying Styles with the Keyboard

Word allows you to apply some of the most commonly used styles in the Normal template from the keyboard, as shown in Table 8-1.

Table 8-1. Keyboard Shortcuts for Common Styles

Style Name	Keyboard Shortcut
Normal	Command+Shift+N or Option+Shift+Clear
Heading 1	Command+Option+1
Heading 2	Command+Option+2
Heading 3	Command+Option+3
List Bullet	Command+Shift+L

Eliminating WYSIWYG Styles and Fonts

You probably noticed in Figure 8-1 that styles were shown in the Style pop-up menu as they will appear in the document, a display method that Word refers to as WYSIWYG (What You See Is What You Get). Most of the time you'll want to use this WYSIWYG display, because it makes it easier to recognize and apply styles. But sometimes WYSIWYG can be a drawback, because Word has to draw the Style pop-up menu large enough to contain the biggest style element, or because some styles, such as border and shading styles, just don't look that great on the menu. You can turn off the WYSIWYG display by choosing Word, Preferences, clicking the General category, and clearing the WYSIWYG Font And Style Menus check box. Now all the style and font names listed in the Formatting Palette will display as simple text, as shown in Figure 8-2. This will also turn off the WYSIWYG display on the Font menu on the menu bar, though in order to see changes on this menu you must quit and relaunch Word.

If you have WYSIWYG display turned off for the Font menu on the Formatting Palette, you can temporarily get the WYSIWYG display back by pressing Shift before you open the menu; however, this trick no longer works for the Font menu on the menu bar.

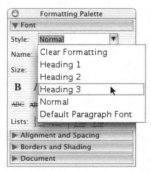

Figure 8-2. Turning off the WYSIWYG display makes the Style menu easier to read.

> **tip** You can assign keyboard shortcuts to either built-in styles or to user-defined styles;
> see "Customizing Keyboard Shortcuts in Word and Excel," page 56.

Applying Styles in the Style Dialog

The Style dialog gives you the greatest control over applying styles, but because you have to open, navigate, and close a dialog, it's the slowest way to apply a style. The Style dialog is also handy if you want to view all the settings that make up a style. To apply a style with the Style dialog, follow these steps:

1 To apply a paragraph style to a single paragraph, select the paragraph or place the insertion point anywhere in that paragraph. If you want to apply the style to more than one paragraph, select part or all of each paragraph. If you are applying a character style, select the text you want to format.

2 Choose Format, Style to open the Style dialog, shown in Figure 8-3.

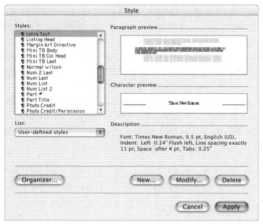

Figure 8-3. The Style dialog tells you exactly what formatting will be applied by the style you select.

3 From the List pop-up menu, choose which styles you wish to view:

- **Styles In Use** shows only styles that have been assigned in the current document.

- **All Styles** shows all user-defined and built-in styles from the current document template.

- **User-Defined Styles** shows only the custom styles in the current document and document template.

Chapter 8

4 From the Styles list, select a style that you wish to apply to your text. When you select the style, the Paragraph Preview box gives you a rough idea of what the style will look like in the context of your page when applied to your text, and the Character Preview box shows you how the text will look when the style is applied to it. The Description area gives you the details of the formatting that will be applied by the style.

5 Click Apply.

> **tip** Double-clicking a style in the Styles list will apply the style and close the Style dialog.

The list of styles shown in the Styles box in the Style dialog is dependent on any user-defined styles in the document and styles defined in the document template. Starting from a different template or document might give you a different set of styles.

Troubleshooting

The style I applied wiped out my character formatting.

If you apply a paragraph style to a paragraph whose entire text has already been manually formatted, for example, to a paragraph that was italicized, the formatting for the style will replace the manual formatting. In this example, if the style definition didn't include italic, the italicized text will be removed. The only way to fix this is to reapply the manual formatting after you have applied the style or to create an additional style that includes the base style definition plus the manual formatting. However, if you apply a paragraph format to a paragraph in which only some of the text is manually formatted or has character styles applied to it, that formatting will remain.

Defining Styles

There are two ways to create user-defined styles in Word. The first, and usually easiest, way is simply to format text or a paragraph the way that you want, and then tell Word to memorize that formatting as a style. The other method is to create and apply all the formatting in the New Style dialog.

Defining Styles by Example

Most of the time, you'll create your new user-defined styles by example. Follow these steps:

1 Place the insertion point in the paragraph that you wish to serve as the style's example. If you're creating a character style, select the text.

2 Using the Formatting Palette or Format menu, apply the formatting that you want.

For more information about formatting text, see Chapter 7, "Formatting Your Work."

3 Click in the Style box on the Formatting Palette, which will highlight the current style name. Type the new style name and press Return. The new style is added to the list of styles for the document, and to the Style pop-up menu.

Creating Styles from Scratch

The most powerful method of defining a style uses the Style dialog. With this method, you must define all the elements that make up a style manually. Follow these steps:

1 Choose Format, Style.

2 In the Style dialog, click New to open the New Style dialog, shown in Figure 8-4.

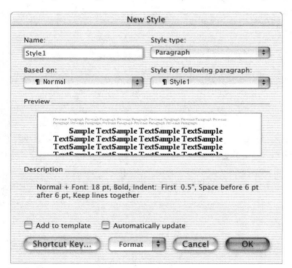

Figure 8-4. As you define the new style, the Preview area will change to show you what the style will look like.

3 Enter a name for your style.

4 From the Style Type pop-up menu, choose whether the style will be a Paragraph or Character style.

5 From the Based On pop-up menu, choose the existing style that is closest to the style that you're building. The benefit to basing your new style on an existing one is that you'll have less formatting work to do.

For more information about basing one style on another, see "Basing One Style on Another Style," on the next page.

6 On the Style For Following Paragraph pop-up menu, select the style you want to be applied to paragraphs that follow those styled with the new style. This feature can be a big timesaver, because it lets Word know whether to maintain the same style after a paragraph break or whether Word should automatically change the style for the following paragraph. For example, after a Heading style, you'll often want the following paragraph to be Normal style, for body text. By choosing Normal on the Style For Following Paragraph pop-up menu, you'll be able to type your Heading, press Return, and automatically be ready to type body text.

7 Apply the formatting for the style by clicking the Format pop-up menu and choosing each category you want to format. The seven choices on the Format pop-up menu (Font, Paragraph, Tabs, Border, Language, Frame, and Numbering) take you to the respective dialogs for that sort of formatting. (For a character style your choices are Font, Border, and Language.) For example, choosing Paragraph displays the same dialog as if you had chosen Format, Paragraph. As you apply formatting, the sample text in the Preview area of the New Style dialog changes to show you what your style will look like.

8 If you select the Add To Template check box, your new style will be saved in the template on which the document is based. Any new document that you create using this template will therefore include the new style. Otherwise, the style will be saved only in the current document.

9 The Automatically Update check box should be selected with caution. If this option is selected, any formatting changes you make to any occurrence of text formatted in the style will change the style definition, which means that *all* occurrences of text formatted in the style will change throughout your document.

10 Clicking the Shortcut Key button opens the Customize Keyboard dialog, where you can assign a keyboard shortcut to the style.

11 Click OK to save the new style. You'll return to the Style dialog, where you'll see the new style name added to the Styles list.

12 Click Apply to apply the new style to the currently selected paragraph, or click Close to close the Style dialog without applying any styles (your new style will still be saved).

Basing One Style on Another Style

As noted earlier, you can save time and effort by basing one style upon another. Here's an example. Let's say that you have a Heading 1 style that you like, defined as Helvetica 18 point, boldface, indented .5 inches. You want a similar subheading, so you define Heading 2 as based on Heading 1, but in 14 point and indented .75 inches. If you then change the font for Heading 1 from Helvetica to Lucida Grande, Heading 2 will also change to Lucida Grande. In this example, Heading 1 is the *base style* for Heading 2. But if you were to change the font size of Heading 1 from 18 points to 20 points, Heading 2 would remain at 14 points, because you explicitly set Heading 2 to 14 points. Any other formatting you haven't explicitly set for Heading 2 will change whenever you change the corresponding element in the Heading 1 style."

The Style dialog tells you whether a particular style is based on another style. Choose Format, Style, select the style you wish to examine, and look at the Description area. Figure 8-5 shows the Style dialog with the Signature style selected. The Description area shows that the Signature style is based on the Normal style, plus a 3-inch indent.

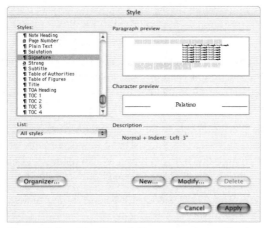

Figure 8-5. The Description area shows the base style of the selected Signature style.

You might want to reorganize some of your styles by changing the base style of one or more of your styles. For instance, you might want to base Heading 2 on Heading 1 instead of on Normal, because the two heading styles are more closely related. If you need to change the base style for a selected style, follow these steps:

1 Choose Format, Style.

2 Select the style for which you want to change the base style.

3 Click Modify.

4 In the Modify Style dialog, shown in Figure 8-6, choose the new base style from the Based On pop-up menu, and click OK.

Figure 8-6. You can change a style's base style using the Modify Style dialog.

Redefining Styles

Nothing shows off the power of styles like redefining a style and seeing the changes ripple throughout your document, especially when you are working with long documents. For example, let's say that you're working on a big report with lots of formatting: several types of headings and subheadings, figures with captions, and indented body text. You turn in the first draft of the report, and your boss tells you that the content is fine, but the formatting needs work. You need to change the size and indenting of the body text and the main headings, and italicize the figure captions. If you had manually formatted each paragraph as you wrote the report, you would be facing a huge reformatting job. But as long as you used styles, all you need to do is change the style definitions.

> **tip** You can quickly view a style's formatting settings by choosing View, Reveal Formatting and then clicking the text containing that style.

To redefine a style, follow these steps:

1 For a paragraph style, select the entire paragraph you want to redefine. For a character style, place the insertion point in the text of the character style that you want to change.

2 Using the Formatting Palette or the Format menu, make your changes.

3 In the Formatting Palette, click in the Style box, which will select the contents of the box.

4 Press Return, which brings up the Modify Style dialog, as shown here:

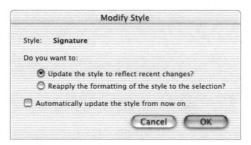

5 Leave the default option, Update The Style To Reflect Recent Changes, selected, and click OK. The other option, Reapply The Formatting Of The Style To The Selection, is useful when you have changed the formatting of the selection and you want to revert it back to the formatting found in the style's definition.

Replacing Styles

It's one thing to redefine a style, but what if you're happy with your style definitions, but you simply need to change text from one style to another style? You could go through your whole document manually, finding the text in the old style and changing it to the new style. But why bother? Word has a powerful Find And Replace feature that can find and replace styles as easily as it can find and replace text. Follow these steps:

1 Place the insertion point in the paragraph that has the style that you want to change. From the Style box of the Formatting Palette, note the style name.

2 Choose Edit, Replace.

3 In the Find And Replace dialog, click the triangle button to expand the dialog.

4 Click in the Find What box, and then from the Format pop-up menu at the bottom of the Find And Replace dialog, choose Style.

5 In the Find Style dialog, select the style you noted in step 1, and click OK.

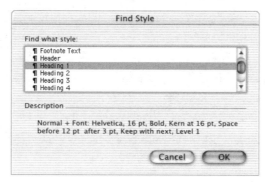

6 Click in the Replace With box, and then choose Style again from the Format pop-up menu.

7 In the Replace Style dialog, choose the target style, and then click OK. The Find And Replace dialog will now list the styles to be found and replaced, as shown here:

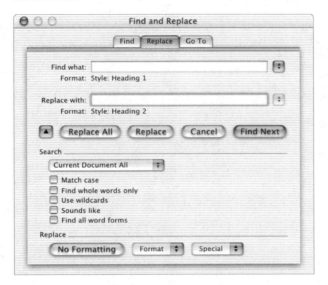

8 Click Replace or Replace All to replace instances of one style with another.

> For more information about using Find and Replace, see "Finding and Replacing Text and Formatting," page 108.

Deleting Styles

To delete a style from a document or a template, follow these steps:

1 Choose Format, Style.

2 In the Styles list, select the offending style.

3 Click Delete.

> **note** The Delete button will only be active for user-defined styles; if you select a built-in style (which you can't delete), the button will appear dimmed.

4 Click Yes in the confirmation dialog and click Apply to exit the Style dialog.

Copying Styles Between Documents and Templates

If you've created a group of styles that you like in one document, you might want to use those styles in another document, or copy the styles to a template so the styles will be included in all new documents created with that template. Word makes it easy to copy styles from one document to another, or from documents to templates. There are two ways to do the job. The first way is to use Word's Style Organizer. Follow these steps:

1 Choose Format, Style.

2 Click Organizer to open the Organizer dialog, shown in Figure 8-7.

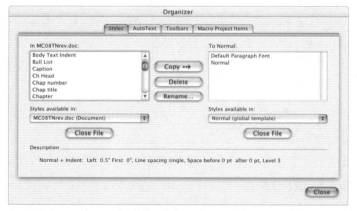

Figure 8-7. The Styles tab of the Organizer dialog allows you to copy, delete, or rename styles.

3 The styles in the current document will be shown in the box on the left, and the styles in the Normal template in the box on the right. The pop-up menus below the two boxes allow you to switch between styles in the open documents, in the templates attached to those documents, or in the Normal template. To change documents or templates, click the Close File button (which toggles to Open File) click Open File, and then choose the new document or template.

4 Select one or more styles in one box, and click the Copy button to copy them to the document or template represented by the other box. You can also use the Delete or Rename button on styles.

> **note** Word will only let you delete user-defined styles; you can't delete the built-in styles.

5 Click Close.

The Organizer is the official way to copy styles from one document to another, and it's a good way to copy styles into a template. But there's actually an easier way to get the job done between two documents. To copy a paragraph style, select an entire paragraph that is formatted with the style that you want to copy, and then paste that paragraph into the other document. Word adds the style that you pasted into the document's style list. You can then delete the text of the paragraph that you copied; the style remains. To copy a character style, select one or more characters formatted with the character style, copy them, and paste the letters into the other document. The character style is copied, and you can delete the characters without losing the style. If you want to copy several styles, select enough text from the first document to contain an example of the styles you want to copy, paste it all into the other document, and then delete the text, leaving the styles in place.

> **note** If there is an existing style in the target document with the same name as a style that you're pasting, Word will copy the text but will ignore the pasted style, giving it the formatting defined for that style in the target document.

Working with Templates

Just as styles are a collection of character and paragraph formats, a template is a special kind of document that contains a collection of styles. But that's not all a template can contain. Besides styles, templates also store your macros; AutoText entries; keyboard, menu, and toolbar customization; and many other preference settings. All Word documents are based on one or more templates; when you open up Word and it creates a new blank document, that document is based on the Normal template.

A template is the pattern for a document. Sometimes that pattern can be explicit, as when the template includes placeholder or boilerplate text. *Boilerplate* is text you tend to use over and over, such as an invoice form, a contract, or a sales pitch. Other times the pattern is implicit, as when the template provides the styles and formatting for a blank document. You can base documents on existing templates, attach templates to existing documents, and create custom templates.

Templates provide three big categories of benefits:

- **Standardization.** If all the workers in a company or organization are using the same document template, you can be assured that all of the organization's

Chapter 8

communication will have a consistent look. Depending on the degree of customization of the template, you can also create special toolbars or other customized elements tailored to your organization's needs.

- **Collaboration.** A close cousin to standardization, sharing a document template with everybody working on a particular project ensures that the documents will look and act the same for all participants. For example, for this book, Microsoft Press supplied a document template for the authors' use. This helped the writers and editors, and even benefited the book's production team, which used the styles in the Word template to match up with styles in the page layout program that produced the finished pages, ready for the printer.

- **Portability.** Templates can allow you to share your customizations with yourself. For example, if you modify the Normal template on your desktop machine, changing the default font, adding customized keyboard commands, and the like, you can copy the modified Normal template to your laptop, and bring your customized writing environment on the road with you.

Understanding the Normal Template

As mentioned before, the vast majority of documents you'll create will be based on the Normal template, which comes with Word. Regardless of what other templates you might use, the Normal template is always open and available to you. When you open Word, it looks for the Normal template in its default location, which is Applications/ Microsoft Office X/Templates/. Normally, you'll want to leave the Normal template in its default location, but if you want to, you can store it in a User Templates or Workgroup Templates folder, whose location you can specify in the File Locations category of Word's Preferences dialog. If Word can't find the Normal template in any of these locations, it automatically creates a new Normal template in the Templates folder.

The Normal template contains Word's default styles, toolbar setups, and built-in AutoText entries, which are available to you whenever you create a new blank document. When you create macros, AutoText entries, or any other customization, they are stored in the Normal template unless you specifically tell Word otherwise. The exception is user-defined styles, which are stored in the document in which they were created, unless you specifically tell Word to store the style in a particular template.

> **note** Macros, shortcut keys, or custom toolbars and menus can be stored within a document rather than within a template. Items stored in this fashion are private to that document and won't be available in other documents. AutoText entries can only be stored in a template, however.

Modifying the Normal Template

Word's default settings are fine for most documents, but what if you prefer your documents to have a different look? For example, by default, the Normal template specifies document text as Times 12 point, with 1.25-inch right and left page margins. If you prefer your documents with a different default font and smaller margins, you'll need to modify the Normal template; thereafter, all new documents based on the Normal template (which is to say, all new blank documents) will have your preferred settings. To make changes to the Normal template, follow these steps:

1 Choose File, Open.

2 Navigate to the Applications/Microsoft Office X/Templates/ folder, select the Normal template, and click Open.

3 Make the changes that you want.

4 Choose File, Save, and then close the document.

---

tip **Change the default font the easy way**

Many users want to change the default font—after all, Times 12 is hardly an inspiring typeface—and Microsoft has provided an easy way to set the default font without messing with templates. Simply choose Format, Font, set the font that you want in the Font dialog, and click the Default button. Word will present a dialog and ask you to confirm your choice, as shown here. Click Yes to change the default font stored in the Normal template.

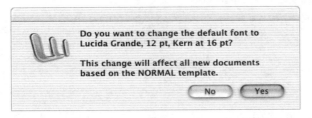

Creating Documents from an Included Template

The Project Gallery gives you access to a large quantity of built-in document templates that either came with Office v. X or that you later downloaded or copied into your Templates folder. The categories in the Project Gallery, shown in Figure 8-8 on the next page, roughly correspond to folders within the Templates folder. It's not an exact correspondence because there are two categories in the Project Gallery—Blank Documents and Based On Recent—that have no corresponding folders.

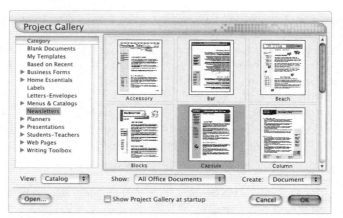

Figure 8-8. The categories in the Project Gallery provide a wide selection of templates that you can use in your documents.

To use one of the built-in document templates, choose File, Project Gallery, select the template you want, and press Return. A new document, based on that template and including all of that template's styles, formatting, and boilerplate or placeholder text opens, as shown in Figure 8-9.

Figure 8-9. This new document was based on a Book Report template downloaded from Microsoft's Mactopia Web site. Note that the template includes a table at the top of the page, extensive formatting for text, placeholder text for the body of the book report, and even includes a watermarked graphic at the bottom of the page.

For more information on using the Project Gallery, see "Understanding the Project Gallery and Templates," page 16.

Creating and Using Custom Templates

Because templates are a special kind of document, it's easy to create a new custom template. Follow these steps:

1 Create a new Word document.

2 In the new document, place the elements you wish the new template to have. You can bring virtually all of Word's tools to bear to create the template, so you can include any (or all) of the following:

- Styles
- Tabs and other ruler settings
- Margins
- Headers and footers
- Graphics
- Boilerplate or placeholder text
- Macros
- Customized menus and toolbars
- AutoText entries

3 When you're done adding the template elements, choose File, Save As.

4 From the Format pop-up menu in the Save As dialog, choose Document Template. Word will automatically change the destination of the saved template to the Applications/Microsoft Office X/Templates/My Templates folder.

5 Give the template a name, and then click Save.

To use the new template, or any of your custom templates, open the Project Gallery, select the My Templates category, select the template you want, and click OK.

Attaching Templates to Documents

If you create a document using one particular template, you're not forced to stick with that template thereafter. Word allows you to attach a new template to a document. For example, you can begin writing text for a report using the Normal template (or any template that you like) and then attach your company's specialized report template at any time. You can then use the styles and other formatting attributes of the new template to finish the report.

Chapter 8

177

To attach a new document template, follow these steps:

1 Choose Tools, Templates And Add-Ins to open the Templates And Add-Ins dialog, shown in Figure 8-10. The path to the current document template will be shown in the box in the Document Template area.

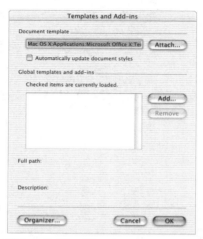

Figure 8-10. The Templates And Add-Ins dialog enables you to attach new templates to existing documents.

2 Click Attach. In the resulting Choose A File dialog, navigate to the template you want to attach and click Open.

3 Select Automatically Update Document Styles. This will make the styles in your current document change automatically to match styles with the same name in the template you just attached.

4 Click OK.

Working with Global Templates

Most of the time, you'll be working with document templates in Word. But there is another kind of template, the *global template*. These kind of templates are available to all documents, all the time. You're already familiar with one global template, the Normal template. If there are other templates that you want to be available to all your documents, you can make that template available as a global template. This means that you won't have to open the template from the Project Gallery, as you would a document template.

To load a template as a global template, follow these steps:

1 Choose Tools, Templates And Add-Ins.

2 Click Add.

3 Navigate to the template that you want to make global, select it, and then click Open. The template will appear in the Global Templates And Add-Ins list, with the check box selected to show that it is active.

4 Click OK.

---

note The preceding procedure is the same one that you would use to install *add-ins* in Word. Add-ins are programs that extend Word's feature set. For example, for Word 2001, there is an add-in that allows Word to integrate with ISI ResearchSoft's Endnote bibliographic software. The add-in inserts commands for creating and maintaining bibliographies into Word's Tools menu, enabling you to insert citations and format bibliographies right in Word.

Unfortunately, because add-ins are extra programs, they must be written for each platform, and most Word add-ins are for Windows versions only.

Keep Formatting Simple While You Write

Some templates are designed to look great when the finished document is printed, but they don't necessarily look great on your screen. Some text might be formatted at small type sizes, or as italic, or with borders and shading that make it difficult to work with on your monitor. It would be nice if you could write in a simplified format, and only apply the fancy formatting when you are ready to begin proofing the document. Because Word allows you to attach templates to documents at any time, it's fairly easy to accomplish this. Follow these steps:

1 Begin by opening the template with the fancy formatting (let's say it's called Corporate Report).

2 Immediately choose File, Save As, and save the new template with a new name, such as Simple Corporate Report. The new template will include all of the styles in Corporate Report.

3 Redefine the hard-to-read styles, reformatting them to be more screen friendly. Make sure you do not change the style names.

4 Save the changes to the new template.

5 Now add your text using the template that is easier on your eyes.

6 When you are ready to view the report in its final form, choose Tools, Templates And Add-Ins, and attach the original Corporate Report template. Remember to select the Automatically Update Document Styles check box.

Because all the styles that you used in the Simple Corporate Report template have the same names as the styles in the Corporate Report template, all the text formatted in those styles will update and reformat according to the style definitions in the Corporate Report template.

179

Using Themes

Themes are predefined collections of styles, colored backgrounds, lines, bullet styles, and so on. They can be used in any document, but they are most useful for documents that will be viewed on-screen, especially for Web pages, because each theme includes styles for hyperlinks.

> For more information about building Web pages with Word, see Chapter 15, "Creating Pages for the Web."

To add a theme to your document, follow these steps:

1 Choose Format, Theme.

2 Select one of the built-in themes in the Theme list. You'll get a preview in the large Sample Of Theme box, as shown in Figure 8-11.

Figure 8-11. Themes make it easy to format documents that will be viewed primarily on-screen.

3 If you don't like the theme's preset colors, use the Color Scheme list to change the preset colors to any of 21 other color combinations.

4 Select any of these options:

- **Vivid Colors** changes the colors used, especially for background colors, to brighter settings, providing more visual snap.

■ **Active Graphics** includes animated graphics, such as spinning or moving bullets, when the page is displayed in a Web browser. Use this feature with caution, as many viewers don't like animation on Web pages.

■ **Background Image** applies a background image or texture to the document. If you prefer to use a solid color background, clear this check box.

5 Click OK to apply the theme to the current document.

Using the Style Gallery

There are many elegant features in Word, but sadly the Style Gallery isn't one of them. The feature is poorly named, difficult to get to, and of marginal use. With a name like Style Gallery, you would think that the Style Gallery dialog would show you examples of all the styles in your current document or template. You would be wrong in thinking that, however, because that's not what the Style Gallery really does. The Style Gallery actually allows you to preview how an entire document would look if styles from another template were applied to the document. If you like the look of the preview, you can then apply the previewed template to the current document. Shouldn't it have been called the Template Gallery? And why do you get to the Style Gallery via the Theme dialog, rather than the Style dialog?

Anyway, to use the Style Gallery, follow these steps:

1 Choose Format, Theme.

2 Click Style Gallery to open the Style Gallery dialog, shown in Figure 8-12.

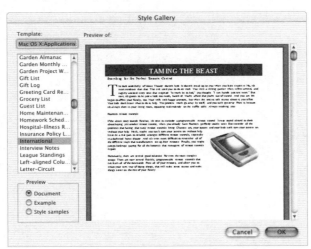

Figure 8-12. Choose a template from the list at the left to see how your current document will look with that template's styles applied.

Chapter 8

3 All of your available templates will be shown in the Template list. When you click the name of a template, a preview of your document will appear in the preview area.

4 When you find a template that you like, click OK. The template's styles will be applied to your document.

Laying Out Text

Although Microsoft Word gives you many tools to make your documents easier to read, all the formatting in the world won't help a document that is poorly organized to begin with. Word gives you several tools to help you organize and present your data, including tables, lists, columns, and text boxes, and even lets you customize these tools to fit the needs of your document. You can open a single dialog and plan out an even, orderly table from scratch, or you can draw the table freehand and make all the uneven rows and cell borders you want. Then, once you've created your table, list, or other element, you can modify its layout to best convey your message. You can change the appearance of a table using Word's table formatting tools, or by applying one of the special automatic table formats, by changing column widths or row height, or even by deleting or adding a row, column, or cell.

In this chapter, you'll learn how to create and use tables to present information efficiently, and how to format tables to present their information in the best light. You'll also see how to use Word's automatic numbered and bulleted lists. In the last section, you'll learn how to use Word's other layout features, such as text boxes and columns, to produce documents that look as though they were produced with a desktop publishing program.

Creating Tables

The secret to creating an effective table is to plan your table in advance so that when you're ready to add the table to your document, you can create the table quickly and enter your data immediately. You should pay attention to the amount of space you have available for the table, whether it should be confined to a single page or can spill over to multiple pages, whether you will need to make any calculations on the table data, and what you want the table to look like when it's completed.

183

Word provides several different ways to create a table, and you'll use different methods depending on what kind of table you need and the amount of control you need over the table's layout. The three table creation methods and their advantages are discussed in the following sections.

Creating a Simple Table

The easiest way to add a table to your document is to use the Insert Table button on the Standard toolbar. You can choose the number of rows and columns from the pop-up menu, and the table will be the width of the current column (because most documents have only one column, most of the time tables you create in this manner will span the page, from left margin to right margin). The column widths of the table will be equal. To create this type of table, follow these steps:

1 Place the insertion point where you want to create the table.

2 Click the Insert Table button on the Standard toolbar. A pop-up menu with a grid of rows and columns appears.

3 Drag the pointer down and to the right, highlighting the number of rows and columns you want to create, as shown here:

4 When you've highlighted the cells you want to create, release the mouse button. Word places the resulting table into your document, as shown in Figure 9-1.

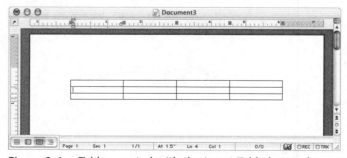

Figure 9-1. Tables created with the Insert Table button have uniform column widths, and row heights that will accommodate your default text size.

184

---

tip | **Don't worry about the number of rows**

You don't have to plan out the number of rows in your table in advance, because it's easy to add more rows to a table. All you have to do is press Tab in the last cell. Try to get the number of columns correct, though, because it is a bit harder to add columns. For more information, see "Inserting or Deleting Rows and Columns," page 190.

Drawing a Table

An alternative way to add a table to your document is to draw the table freehand, using the Draw Table button on the Tables And Borders toolbar. The buttons on the Tables And Borders toolbar are described in Table 9-1. Once you've drawn the table outline, you can add more lines to define columns and rows. If you add a line you decide you don't want, you can click the Undo button to get rid of it entirely. If you only want to get rid of part of the line, perhaps to create an uneven row or column, you can use the Eraser (also accessed through the Tables And Borders toolbar). This method provides the easiest way to create custom widths and heights for your columns and rows.

Table 9-1. The Tables And Borders Toolbar Buttons

Button	Name	Action
	Draw Table	Lets you draw a table freehand.
	Eraser	Erases unwanted column or row boundaries.
	Line Style	Sets the style for the table border lines.
1/2	Line Weight	Lets you choose the thickness of the table border lines.
	Border Color	Lets you choose the color of the border lines you draw.
	Border	Sets the border choices for selected cells of your table.
	Shading Color	Lets you set the background color for selected table cells.
	Insert Table	Displays the Insert Table dialog, which you can use to insert rows, columns, cells, or an entire table or to change column width or height.

(continued)

Table 9-1. *(continued)*

Button	Name	Action
	Merge Cells	Combines two or more cells into a single cell.
	Split Cells	Splits the chosen cell into the number of cells you specify.
	Align	Lets you change the horizontal and vertical text alignment for the contents of a table cell.
	Distribute Rows Evenly	Makes the height of all selected rows equal.
	Distribute Columns Evenly	Makes the width of all selected columns equal.
	Table AutoFormat	Displays the Table AutoFormat dialog, which you can use to change the appearance of your table by applying a preset format.
	Change Text Direction	Rotates the text in the selected cell by 90°.
	Sort Ascending	Sorts selected cells in ascending order (A–Z, 0–9, earliest to latest date).
	Sort Descending	Sorts selected cells in descending order (Z–A, 9–0, latest to earliest date).
	AutoSum	Sums the values to the left of the current cell or above the current cell and displays the total in the current cell. Values above the cell take precedence over values to the left of the cell.

To draw a table in your document, follow these steps:

1 Choose Table, Draw Table. If necessary, the document window will switch to Page Layout view, and the Tables And Borders toolbar will appear.

2 Click the Draw Table button on the Tables And Borders toolbar.

3 When the pointer changes to a pencil, drag to define the outline of your table, and then follow any of these steps to fill in the details of your table.

> **tip** To create a table in the middle of a text area and have the text wrap automatically around the table, press Option while you draw the table.

- To create a column in your table, drag down from the point on the top edge of your table outline to the corresponding point on the bottom edge.

- To create a row in your table, drag across from the point on the left edge of your table outline to the corresponding point on the right edge.

- To erase a column or row line in a table, click the Eraser button on the Tables And Borders toolbar, and then click the border you want to delete. You can also use the Eraser to erase pieces of a line that you don't want; partially erased lines allow you to create complicated tables, as shown in Figure 9-2.

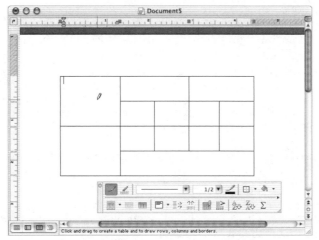

Figure 9-2. You can draw quite complex tables freehand with the Draw Table tools.

> **tip** While you're drawing a table, pressing the Shift key toggles between the pencil and eraser tools.

Inserting a Table

A straightforward way to insert a table into your document is to use the Insert Table dialog, shown in Figure 9-3 on the next page.

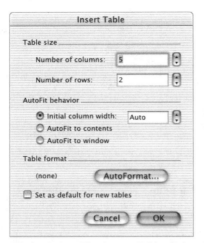

Figure 9-3. The Insert Table dialog lets you easily specify the size and format of the table and how the table's data will be formatted.

The benefit of using the Insert Table dialog is that you can create a table with the exact number of columns and rows you want, formatted the way you want, and you can even make your settings the standard settings for any table added to your document. If you're working on a report that contains many tables with exactly the same structure, defining those settings as the default will save you a lot of time.

To insert a table into your Word document, position the insertion point where you want to place the table, and then follow these steps:

1 Choose Table, Insert, Table to display the Insert Table dialog.

2 In the Number Of Columns box, type the number of columns you want in your new table.

3 In the Number Of Rows box, type the number of rows you want in your table when the table is created.

4 Follow any of these steps in the AutoFit Behavior section to set the width of the table's columns:

■ Select Initial Column Width and then, in the Initial Column Width box, type the width you want for the columns in the table.

■ Select AutoFit To Contents to have each column's width reflect the width of the cell with the widest contents.

■ Select AutoFit To Window to have the table's width adjust to the width of the document window.

5 Optionally, click the AutoFormat button to display the Table AutoFormat dialog.

For information on using the AutoFormat feature to change the appearance of your table, see "Formatting Tables," page 194.

6 If you want to define the current settings as the default settings for any new tables you create, select the Set As Default For New Tables check box. Click OK when you're finished.

---

tip **Create nested tables**

One technique you can use to gain significant control over your document's layout is to create a table within a table, which is referred to as *nesting*. For example, you could create a two-column table with a list of product categories in one column and the list of products in that category in the other. If one of the products has a number of varieties and prices, you could create another two-column table in the product's cell and list the individual varieties and prices.

Moving Around in Tables

The key to entering and editing table data effectively is to know how to move around within a table. You can always use your mouse to move to a particular spot in your table, but you can also use keyboard shortcuts to move quickly from one cell to another. When you're entering table data by hand, the one vital keyboard shortcut you need to know is that pressing Tab takes you to the next table cell and, if there is already data in the cell, selects the contents of that cell. There are other shortcuts you can use to navigate within a table, however. Table 9-2 lists those shortcuts.

Table 9-2. Keyboard Shortcuts for Navigating in a Table

Keyboard Shortcut	Action
Tab	Moves the insertion point to the next cell in the table. If the cell contains data, selects the contents of the cell. If the cell is empty, positions the insertion point in the cell. Pressing Tab in the last cell of a table creates a new row and moves the insertion point to the first cell of the new row.
Shift+Tab	Moves the insertion point to the previous cell in the table and selects the contents of the cell. If the cell is empty, positions the insertion point in the cell.
Down Arrow	Moves the insertion point to the cell directly below the current cell.
Up Arrow	Moves the insertion point to the cell directly above the current cell.

(continued)

Table 9-2. *(continued)*

Keyboard Shortcut	Action
Left Arrow	Moves the insertion point one character to the left. If the insertion point is to the left of the first character in the cell, moves to the cell to the left of the current cell or to the cell at the end of the previous table row.
Right Arrow	Moves the insertion point one character to the right. If the insertion point is to the right of the last character in the cell, moves to the cell to the right of the current cell or to the cell at the beginning of the next table row.
Control+Home	Moves the insertion point to the first cell in the current row.
Control+End	Moves the insertion point to the last cell in the current row.
Control+Page Up	Moves the insertion point to the top cell in the current column.
Control+Page Down	Moves the insertion point to the bottom cell in the current column.

Table Editing

If you've planned your table properly, hopefully you won't need to make any changes to its structure. Unfortunately, things rarely go exactly the way you plan them. You might forget you need to include a particular type of information in the table, or you might add a new column after a year of getting along with the original structure. In any event, Word makes it possible for you to change your table's structure quickly.

Inserting or Deleting Rows and Columns

If you work with Word tables often, sooner or later (probably sooner) you will need to insert or delete rows and columns. For example, if you maintain an electronic mailing list for a newsletter, you will need to create a new table row every time you add a name to your list. Similarly, you will need to add a new table column if you want to include an additional bit of information about your subscribers that you hadn't thought of earlier. You might also need to delete columns or rows that contain information you no longer need, such as subscriber birth dates or the records of individuals who have unsubscribed from the list.

To insert or delete a row or column, click in the table cell you want to use as your reference point, and then follow any of these steps:

● Choose Table, Insert, Columns To The Left to insert a column to the left of the current column.

- Choose Table, Insert, Columns To The Right to insert a column to the right of the current column.

- Choose Table, Insert, Rows Above to insert a row above the current row.

- Choose Table, Insert, Rows Below to insert a row below the current row.

- Choose Table, Delete, Columns to remove the active column.

- Choose Table, Delete, Rows to remove the active row.

---

tip **Insert multiple rows or columns**

You can add more than one row or column at a time. Simply select the same number of rows or columns as the number of new rows or columns you want to add, and then choose one of the commands presented in the preceding list to insert the rows or columns where you want.

Inserting or Deleting Table Cells

Whenever you create a table that's meant to hold a lot of data, there's a very good chance someone will forget to type in a value and throw off the alignment of the rest of the table. Although it's usually easy to tell what's gone wrong, it can take a lot of time to cut and paste the data into the correct places; not to mention the fact that moving around chunks of data introduces the possibility of even more error. One good way to fix data entry errors where the value in a cell has been skipped is to insert a new cell where the data should be. The other table cells will shift (in a manner you control) to accommodate the new cell without changing the table layout. You can also delete cells if you need to eliminate a cell where the contents were repeated in another cell.

To insert or delete table cells, click the cell you want to use as your reference point and then follow either of these steps:

- To insert a cell, choose Table, Insert, Cells to display the Insert Cells dialog, shown in Figure 9-4 on the next page. Then select one of the following options: Shift Cells Right to insert a cell and move the remaining cells in the row to the right; Shift Cells Down to insert a cell and move the remaining cells in the column down a row; Insert Entire Row to add a new row; or Insert Entire Column to add a new column.

- To delete a cell, choose Table, Delete, Cells to display the Delete Cells dialog, which is very similar to the Insert Cells dialog. Then select one of the following options: Shift Cells Left to delete the cell and move the remaining cells in the row to the left; Shift Cells Up to delete the cell and move the remaining cells up a row; Delete Entire Row to delete the row containing the selected cell; or Delete Entire Column to delete the column containing the selected cell.

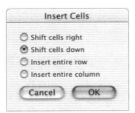

Figure 9-4. The Insert Cells dialog lets you choose how the existing table cells will shift when the new cell is added.

Selecting Table Items

Many times when you edit the contents of a table, you change the contents of one or a small number of cells. Other times, however, you need to change the contents of an entire row or column. For example, you might want to format the column headers in the first row of a table in bold to make them stand out from the rest of the table. You can drag the pointer to select entire rows or columns, but the menu system gives you an easier way to do it, especially if your table spans multiple pages.

To select a table item, click any cell in the row or column you want to select, and then follow any of these steps:

- Choose Table, Select, Table to select the entire table.
- Choose Table, Select, Column to select the column containing the active cell.
- Choose Table, Select, Row to select the row containing the active cell.
- Choose Table, Select, Cell to select the active cell.

Moving Table Rows or Columns

If you need to move an entire column or row to another part of the table, you can do so by selecting the row or column by clicking at the top edge of the column or the left edge of the row, moving the pointer over the interior of the row or column, and dragging the row or column to the desired location. As with cut and paste operations in Word X, you can use Multi-selection to move noncontiguous blocks of cells, by pressing the Command key as you select each block.

Merging and Splitting Table Cells

Tables are a great way to organize your data in a Word document, but they're also a handy tool for controlling where certain bits of text or data appear in relation to the rest of the collection. One way you can control the layout of a table is to merge two or more cells into a single cell. One circumstance when you might want to merge cells is if you have a multiple-column table and want the table's title to appear in a table cell that spans and is centered over the table as a whole, as shown in Figure 9-5. You can create that layout by merging the cells in the top row of your table and then setting a center alignment.

Figure 9-5. The title cell of this table was created by merging three cells.

You can easily merge cells by selecting the cells you want to merge and choosing Table, Merge Cells. Word also makes it easy to split cells that you've just merged or cells that have never been merged. For example, if you want to change your table's header, you can split the merged cells and add your new header and formatting as usual. To split a cell into two or more cells, follow these steps:

1 Select the cells you want to split and choose Table, Split Cells to display the Split Cells dialog, shown in Figure 9-6.

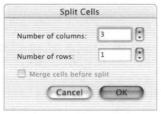

Figure 9-6. Use the Split Cells dialog to divide a cell.

2 In the Split Cells dialog, type the number of columns into which you want to split the cells in the Number Of Columns box, type the number of rows into which you want to split the cells in the Number Of Rows box.

If you've selected more than one cell to split and selected the Merge Cells Before Split check box, any data in the original cells will be arranged in the new block of cells starting in the upper left cell and extending to the cells on the right, and if necessary to the cells in the following rows.

3 Click OK when you're finished.

Splitting a Table

You might find that a table you're working on contains more data than you would like to present in a single table. For example, you might create a table listing all of your company's products by category and then decide that the information for each category should be contained in a separate table. The easiest way to create the smaller tables, one for each category, is to split your table. Splitting and merging table cells lets you control your table's layout and combine data into more or fewer cells, but neither operation lets you split a table into two or more tables. However, Word does include a command to split a table without going through the lengthy cutting and pasting that would normally be necessary.

To split a table, click anywhere in the cell you want to be the first cell in the new table, and then choose Table, Split Table. Word will insert a blank line between the old table and the new table.

Formatting Tables

After you've created your table, you might want to change its appearance to match a corporate color scheme or a team's colors, or to make the table's header row stand out from the body of the table by adding a border or background color. This section shows you how to change every aspect of your table's formatting, from the table's size to its color scheme.

Resizing an Entire Table

Whenever you're writing a report that's meant for a large print run, you'll find that the project needs to be kept within a budget. Because pages cost money, you might need to resize a table so it fits on one page instead of two. You can always change the size of your table's text, columns, and rows, but you can also change the size of the entire table at once.

> **note** When you change the size of a table by dragging the table resize handle, the table rows and columns keep their same relative widths and heights.

To resize an entire table, follow these steps:

1 If necessary, choose View, Page Layout to view the document in Page Layout view.

2 Move the pointer over the bottom right corner of the table until the table resize handle appears, shown in Figure 9-7.

Table move handle

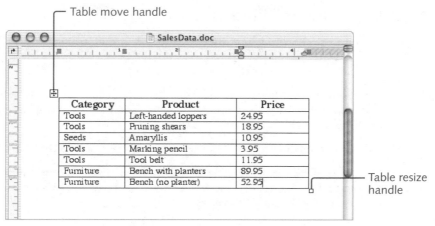

Table resize handle

Figure 9-7. Drag the table resize handle to change the size of your entire table at once.

3 Position the pointer over the table resize handle; the pointer changes to a square with arrows at the corners when it is in position.

4 Drag until the table outline reflects the desired size of your table.

Moving an Entire Table

Tables aren't required to stay where you created them; you can easily move a table to a different spot in your document. Cutting and pasting works, but you can also drag the table to any spot you want.

To move an entire table, follow these steps:

1 If necessary, choose View, Page Layout to view the document in Page Layout view.

2 Move the pointer over the top left cell of the table and pause until the table move handle appears over the top left corner of the table (shown in Figure 9-7).

3 Position the pointer over the table move handle; the pointer changes to an open hand when it is in position.

4 Drag the table until the table's outline is in the position to which you want to move the table.

Chapter 9

Adjusting Column Width and Row Height

To adjust column width and row height in a table, follow these steps:

1 Select the column or row you want to resize.

2 Position the pointer over the right border of the column or the bottom border of the row you want to resize. The pointer will change to a double-arrow bar when it is in position.

3 Drag the border until the column or row is the desired size.

tip You can also change column widths and row heights by dragging column and row markers in the horizontal and vertical rulers, as shown here:

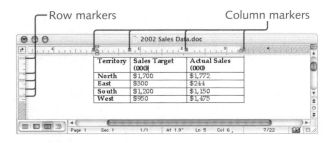

Using AutoFit

When you create a table using the Insert Table dialog, you have three choices of how you want the table to size its columns in relation to the table's contents. If you chose not to use those settings when you created the table, or if you want to change your table's AutoFit behavior, you can make one of three choices using the Table menu. The following procedure details the effects of each of those choices.

To format a table using AutoFit, follow any of these steps:

● Choose Table, AutoFit, AutoFit To Contents to adjust the table column widths to reflect the contents of the cells.

● Choose Table, AutoFit, AutoFit To Window to have the table change to reflect the width of the document window. This setting is particularly useful when you create a document that is meant to be viewed over the Web, as the table will automatically resize to match the width of the window as viewed in the Web browser.

● Choose Table, AutoFit, Fixed Column Width to make each column retain its width, regardless of the overall table width or the contents in the cells.

Adding Borders and Shading

A great way to make a table stand out from the surrounding text is to add a border and shading. Although it's easy to go overboard with the many formatting options that Word offers, such as wide, black borders and chartreuse shading, you should be able to find a mix of outer and inner borders and coloring that meets both your aesthetic and practical needs.

To add borders and shading to a table, make sure the Tables And Borders toolbar (shown in Figure 9-2, page 187) is displayed by choosing View, Toolbars, Tables And Borders. Then use any of these tools to add or modify borders and shading:

- To add a border, select one or more cells. Then click and hold the Border button. From the palette that appears, select the swatch representing the border pattern you want for the selected cells.

- To change the style of a border, open the Line Style pop-up menu. Choose the style for the selected borders from the menu items. When the pencil pointer appears, drag it over each border you want to change. Press Esc when you're finished.

- To change the weight (the line thickness) of a border, open the Line Weight pop-up menu. Choose a weight, and then drag the pointer over the borders you want to change. Press Esc when you're finished.

- To change the shading of one or more cells, select the cells. Then click and hold the Shading Color button to display the color palette. Select the color you want or click More Colors to display the Color Picker, which lets you specify any color you want from several color models.

Formatting a Table Automatically

Formatting a table can be hard work; if you're not experienced with design, or if you're starting from scratch, you can always fall back on one of the predesigned table formats that comes with Word. The available formats run the gamut of bright colors to more conservative designs meant to be viewed over the Web, but you should feel free to modify your table after applying an automatic format if you think the change will make your data easier to comprehend.

To format a table automatically, follow these steps:

1 Click anywhere in the table you want to format, and then choose Table, Table AutoFormat to display the Table AutoFormat dialog, shown in Figure 9-8 on the next page.

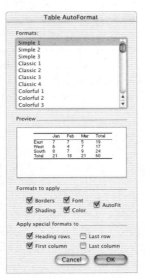

Figure 9-8. The Table AutoFormat dialog lets you choose a preset look for your table.

2 Follow any of these steps to select the AutoFormat elements to apply to your table:

■ In the Formats list, click the name of the design you want to apply to your table. A preview of the format appears in the Preview section.

■ In the Formats To Apply section of the dialog, select the check boxes representing the elements of the format you want to apply to your table. You can choose to apply or not apply the borders, shading, font, and color scheme included in the selected format. You can also select the AutoFit check box if you want the table to have AutoFit To Contents formatting.

■ In the Apply Special Formats To section, select the check boxes representing the table areas to which you want to apply special formatting. You can apply or remove special formats for headings rows, the first column, the last column, or the last row.

3 Click OK to apply the format.

> **note** Selecting a check box to apply a format to an area of a table for which the selected design has no defined formatting will have no effect.

> **tip**   **AutoFormat a new table**
>
> You can apply automatic formatting to tables as soon as you create them by first choosing Table, Insert Table (or by clicking Insert Table on the Tables And Borders toolbar). Enter the number of rows and columns you want to create in the Insert Table dialog, and then click the AutoFormat button. Select any of the styles in the Table AutoFormat dialog. When you exit both dialogs, the new table will include the format you selected.

Setting Table Properties

So far in this chapter you've seen how to change specific aspects of your table, such as its size, number of columns, or the width of those columns. You have a great deal more control than just being able to change those few items, however; in fact, you can change most any aspect of your table using the Table Properties dialog. This section discusses the options in the Table Properties dialog, plus the methods you can use to set the properties of particular columns, rows, and cells.

Defining a Table's Size, Alignment, and Text Wrapping

To set the properties for an entire table, follow these steps:

1 Click anywhere in the table for which you want to set properties, and then choose Table, Table Properties to display the Table Properties dialog.

2 Click the Table tab, shown in Figure 9-9 on the next page, and set any of these properties for the table as a whole:

- In the Size section of the dialog, select the Preferred Width check box, open the Measure In pop-up menu to define the units for the width (you can choose percent or inches), and then type the width in the Preferred Width box.

- In the Alignment section of the dialog, click the button representing the alignment you want for the table as a whole. Then, in the Indent From Left box, type the distance from the left margin you want the table to begin.

- In the Text Wrapping section of the dialog, click the button representing the way you want surrounding text to wrap around the table. To have the text stop above the table and continue below it, click the None button; to have the text flow around the table, click Around.

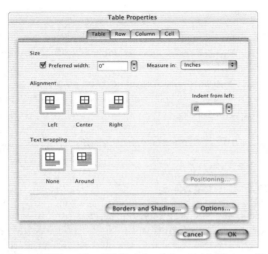

Figure 9-9. The Table tab of the Table Properties dialog gives you a great deal of control over the appearance of your table.

Controlling Table Positioning

To control the positioning of a table within a document after you have turned on text wrapping, follow these steps:

1 Click anywhere in the table you want to position, and then choose Table, Table Properties to display the Table Properties dialog.

2 On the Table tab, click the Positioning button to display the Table Positioning dialog, shown in Figure 9-10.

3 Adjust the positioning of your table in any of the following ways, and click OK when you're finished:

- In the Horizontal section of the dialog, open the Relative To pop-up menu, and then choose the document element you want to use as the reference point for positioning your table. You can choose to position the table in relation to the entire document, a margin, or a column. Then, open the Position pop-up menu, and choose how to position the table with regard to the reference you selected. You can position the table to the Left, Right, Center, Inside, or Outside of the reference.

- In the Vertical section of the dialog, open the Relative To pop-up menu, and then choose the document element you want to use as the reference point for positioning your table. Then, in the Position box, type the distance by which you want your table to be separated vertically

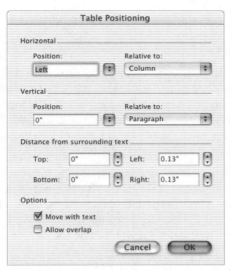

Figure 9-10. After you turn on text wrapping, use the settings in the Table Positioning dialog to control how the text wraps around the table.

from the reference you selected, or select an absolute position from the pop-up menu: Top, Bottom, Center, Inside, or Outside.

> **note** The Top and Bottom boxes are set to zero initially because the surrounding text will almost always have a small separation from the table due to normal line spacing.

- In the Distance From Surrounding Text section of the dialog, type the distance you want your table to be separated from the surrounding text in each of the four available dimensions.

- In the Options section of the dialog, select the Move With Text check box to keep the table with the surrounding text if the text is moved, and select the Allow Overlap check box if you want to be able to overlap one table on another.

> **caution** Letting one object intrude on another, such as letting surrounding text overlap a table border, makes the text hard to read and greatly de-emphasizes the table. Unless you have a specific effect in mind, you shouldn't select the Allow Overlap check box.

Setting Properties for a Table Row

To set the properties of a table row, follow these steps:

1 Click any cell in the table row for which you want to set properties, and then choose Table, Table Properties to display the Table Properties dialog.

Chapter 9

> **tip** If you select more than one row, subsequent settings will apply to the entire selection.

2 Click the Row tab, shown in Figure 9-11.

3 To set the height of the selected row, select the Specify Height check box, and then type the height in the Specify Height box. Then, click the Row Height Is pop-up menu, and select either At Least, to make the minimum row height the value in the Specify Height box, or Exactly to make the row height invariable.

4 Select the Allow Row To Break Across Pages check box if you want the selected row to be split and continued on a second page if the entire row won't fit on the first page. This option is relevant for rows with multiple lines of text. Clearing this check box will keep the row on one page, causing it to move entirely to the next page if it won't fit on the current page.

5 Select the Repeat As Header Row At The Top Of Each Page check box to have Word place the selected row at the top of every page on which the table continues. This option is usually applied when your table's first row contains column headers.

6 Click the Previous Row button to select the row above the current row, or click the Next Row button to select the row below the current row. Then make your settings for the new row you've selected.

7 Click OK to close the dialog and activate your settings.

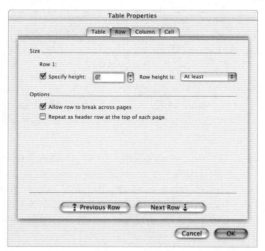

Figure 9-11. To change the properties of a table row, use the settings on the Row tab of the Table Properties dialog.

Chapter 9

Making Large Tables Easy to Read with Repeating Headers

When you create Word documents with long tables that extend for multiple pages, you can make the table data easier to read by ensuring there is plenty of white space between table values (and cell borders, if any). You can also make it much easier for your readers to understand your data by adding a header row at the top of the table and then repeating the header on every subsequent page to which the table extends. To do this, follow these steps:

1 Place the insertion point into the header row, which must be the first row in the table.

2 Choose Table, Table Properties.

3 Click the Row tab.

4 Select the Repeat As Header Row At The Top Of Each Page check box, and click OK.

With the table headers displayed on every page, your readers will only need to glance at the top of the page instead of flipping back to the start of the table to remind themselves of the values contained in your table's columns.

Setting Properties for a Table Column

To set the properties for a table column, follow these steps:

1 Click any cell in the column for which you want to set properties, and then choose Table, Table Properties to display the Table Properties dialog.

tip If you select more than one column, subsequent settings will apply to the entire selection.

2 Click the Column tab, shown in Figure 9-12 on the next page.

3 Select the Preferred Width check box to enable the settings in the dialog.

4 Open the Measure In pop-up menu, and choose Inches to have the value in the Preferred Width box represent the width of the selected column in inches, or choose Percent to have the value in the Preferred Width box represent the width of the selected column as a percentage of the total width of the table.

note Column widths in tables designed for the Web are better specified as percentages, rather than inches, to allow them to resize proportionally when the browser window is resized.

203

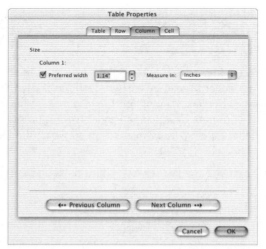

Figure 9-12. To change the properties of a table column, use the settings on the Column tab of the Table Properties dialog.

5 Type the desired width of the column in the Preferred Width box.

6 Click the Next Column button to select the column to the right of the current column, or click the Previous Column button to select the column to the left of the current column, and make your settings for that column.

7 When you're done with the columns you want to set, click OK.

Setting Properties for a Table Cell

To set the properties of a table cell, follow these steps:

1 Click anywhere in the cell you want to format, and then choose Table, Table Properties to display the Table Properties dialog.

2 Click the Cell tab, shown in Figure 9-13.

3 If you want to set the width of the selected cell, select the Preferred Width check box to enable the options in the Size section of the dialog. If you only want to set the cell's vertical alignment, skip to step 6.

4 Open the Measure In pop-up menu and choose Inches to have the value in the Preferred Width box represent the width of the selected cell in inches, or choose Percent to have the value in the Preferred Width box represent the width of the selected cell as a percentage of the total width of the table.

5 Type the desired width of the column in the Preferred Width box.

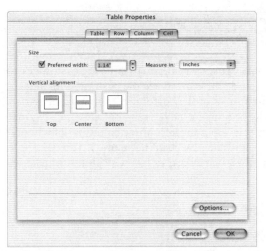

Figure 9-13. To change the properties of a table cell, use the options on the Cell tab of the Table Properties dialog.

6 If you want to set the Vertical Alignment of the selected cell, click the Top, Center, or Bottom button in the Vertical Alignment section to align the contents of the cell.

7 If you want to make further adjustments, click the Options button to display the Cell Options dialog, shown in Figure 9-14, and then use the commands in the dialog to set the cell margins. Selecting the Same As The Whole Table check box removes any changes to the margins of the current cell, whereas clearing the check box lets you type values in the Top, Bottom, Left, and Right boxes to set the inner margins of the cell (the distances between each cell border and the text inside). You can also turn on text wrapping within the cell by selecting the Wrap Text check box.

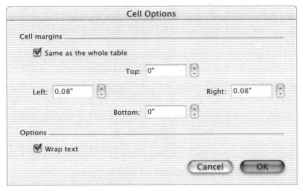

Figure 9-14. Use the settings in the Cell Options dialog to control the margins and text wrapping behavior for one or more table cells.

Chapter 9

Sorting Table Contents

Tables are a great place to store your data, but many times the table data won't be in the order you need to make sense of it. If you're entering customer contact information into a table, for example, and you want to see the customers arranged by their state, you can *sort* the table rows so all of the customers from a particular state are in sequence. You can use the options in the Sort dialog, shown in Figure 9-15, to create sorting criteria based on the values in up to three columns, which means you could sort by state, then by city, and then by customer name if you wanted. Of course, each category of information must be entered in its own column to take advantage of Word's sorting capability.

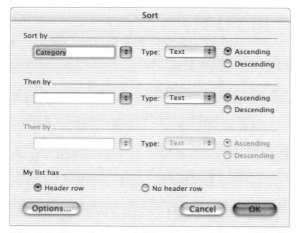

Figure 9-15. If you want to rearrange your table data on the fly, you can change the order of the rows using the settings in the Sort dialog.

To sort the contents of a table, follow these steps:

1 Click any cell in the table you want to sort, and then choose Table, Sort to display the Sort dialog.

> **tip** If you want to sort by the contents of a single column, simply select the column by which you want to sort, and then click either the Sort Ascending or Sort Descending button on the Tables And Borders toolbar.

2 Open the Sort By pop-up menu, and select the column you want to use as the primary sort criterion. Then Excel will make an educated guess about the type of data the column contains.

3 If necessary, open the Type pop-up menu, and change the data type for the column (your choices are Text, Number, or Date).

4 Select Ascending or Descending for the direction of the sort. Ascending sorts are from A to Z for text, lower to higher for numbers, and earlier to later for dates; descending sorts are the reverse.

5 If you want to sort the groups of rows that match the first criterion by a second sort criterion, open the first Then By pop-up menu, and select the column you want to use as your secondary sort criterion, and then repeat steps 3 and 4.

6 If you want to sort by a third level, open the second Then By pop-up menu, and repeat the process for selecting the third sort level.

7 In the My List Has section of the dialog, click Header Row if your table has a header row, or else select No Header Row. If you click Header Row, Word will omit the header row from the sort.

> **note** If in the Table Properties dialog you chose to repeat the header row at the top of every printed page, Word will know not to include the repetitions in the sort.

8 If you want to make advanced sort settings, click the Options button to display the Sort Options dialog, shown in Figure 9-16 on the next page, and then set any of these options:

- You can use the Sort command to sort lists that aren't in tables, and the Sort Options have two features that can help you with such lists. If you are sorting data that is character delimited text, such as names in Last Name, First Name order, in the Separate Fields At section of the dialog, select the option representing the character used to delimit your data. If the data isn't delimited by a tab or comma, you can select Other and then type the character in the Other box.

- Also for use with sorting lists that aren't in tables, select the Sort Column Only check box to change the order of the current column only, and select the Case Sensitive check box to have Word sort your data based on character order, meaning all lowercase letters will be sorted (from a to z), followed by all uppercase letters (from A to Z).

- Open the Sorting Language pop-up menu, and then select the language of your table data.

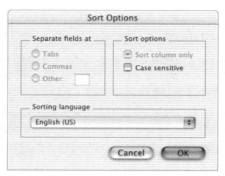

Figure 9-16.   For even more control over your sort, use the Sort Options dialog.

InsideOut

Undo a sort after you close your document

Though you can undo a sort while your document is still open, the record of the sort is lost when you close your document *and you will not be able to undo the sort when you reopen it.* This is one instance that proves the worth of having a column that contains a unique value, or *primary key,* in each table row. If you've assigned primary key field values in ascending or descending order as you went along (for instance if you reserved one column for numbering each entry sequentially or by date and time of entry), you will always be able to use a sort to put your table back in its original order.

Performing Calculations Within Tables

When you work with numeric data, such as sales totals or prices, you might want to summarize your table data by performing various calculations based on the data (perhaps to find your best sales day or the average total cost of purchases customers made in the first week of the month). You can use the Formula dialog to create those expressions, or you can use the AutoSum function to calculate simple sums of rows or columns.

Using Functions for Table Calculations

Although the mathematical heavy lifting is best done in Excel, you do have quite a few functions at your disposal in Word. Typically, you'll just want to add the contents of a row or column, but the Formula dialog gives you many other options.

To perform calculations within a table, follow these steps:

1 Click the cell in which you want to perform the calculation, and then choose Table, Formula to display the Formula dialog, shown in Figure 9-17.

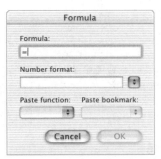

Figure 9-17. The Formula dialog makes it easy for you to summarize your table data with calculations.

2 Click the Number Format pop-up menu, and select the format you want for the value in the cell that contains the formula. A pound sign (#) represents a position that can be taken by any number, whereas dollar signs ($) and percentage symbols (%) are displayed in the cell.

3 Click the Paste Function pop-up menu, and then select the function you want to add to your formula. The function appears in the Formula box, with parentheses. Type **ABOVE** between the parentheses to apply the function to the numbers above the selected cell, such as in calculating a total.

4 Click OK to complete the formula. The result of the formula appears in the active cell of your table.

Using AutoSum

Often, you don't need to get fancy with formulas in table calculations; all you need is a quick addition of the values in a row or column. The AutoSum button on the Tables And Borders toolbar is the fastest way to get the job done. Follow these steps:

1 Click in the cell at the bottom of a column of numbers (or the rightmost cell in a row of numbers).

2 Click the AutoSum button on the Tables And Borders toolbar. Word totals the column or row and inserts the total at the insertion point.

InsideOut

Make an AutoSum current

If you change one of the values that make up the AutoSum, the total won't automatically change, as it would in Excel. To force the AutoSum to recalculate, with the AutoSum cell active, press F9. Alternatively, Control+click in the cell with the AutoSum and choose Update Field from the contextual menu.

Converting Tables

Word also has features to help you convert tables into text, or text into tables. Regardless of which direction you want to go, Word's powerful conversion features can save you considerable time in reentering and reformatting your data.

Converting Text to Tables

One of the easiest ways to transfer data from a spreadsheet to a word processing program is to convert the spreadsheet data to a series of values separated (or *delimited*) by a special character such as a comma or tab. When the data is in that form, Word can tell enough about its structure to convert the text to a table.

> For information on including an Excel worksheet in a Word document, see "Inserting Objects," page 259.

To convert text into a table, follow these steps:

1 Select the text you want to convert to a table, and then choose Table, Convert, Convert Text To Table to display the Convert Text To Table dialog, shown in Figure 9-18.

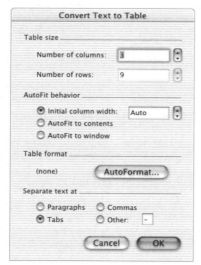

Figure 9-18. Use the Convert Text To Table dialog to transform delimited text into a new table.

2 Word will analyze the number of columns and rows in the selected text and will fill in the Number Of Columns and Number Of Rows boxes.

- If Word gets the number of columns wrong, check what character your text uses as the delimiter (comma, tab, etc.), and make sure that character is selected in the Separate Text At section. Selecting the matching character there should cause Word to correct the value in the Number Of Columns box. If necessary, select Other and type the delimiting character.

- If Word gets the number of rows wrong, make sure each row of text ends with a paragraph return.

3 In the AutoFit Behavior section of the dialog, select the option representing the AutoFit scheme you want for your table.

4 Optionally, click the AutoFormat button to display the Table AutoFormat dialog. Use the options in the dialog to choose and modify a table design.

5 Click OK to complete the text to table conversion.

InsideOut

Use Find and Replace to clean up data before converting

It's not uncommon to have data that isn't quite ready for conversion from text to table. The usual culprit is columns that are delimited with spaces, rather than with tabs. You could edit the data manually, but why bother when you can get Word to do it for you? Use Word's Find and Replace to find repeated spaces and turn them into a single tab. In most cases, it's best to use wildcards in the Replace dialog to catch repeated spaces. For more information about using wildcards and Find and Replace, see "Advanced Text Replacement," page 110.

Converting a Table to Text

Just as you can convert a block of text to a table, you can convert a table to text. To convert a table to text, follow these steps:

1 Select the table you want to convert to text by clicking any cell, and then choose Table, Convert, Convert Table To Text to display the Convert Table To Text dialog, shown in Figure 9-19 on the next page.

2 Select the character you want to use to separate each column of the table when it's converted to text. If you don't want to use a comma, tab, or paragraph mark, select Other, and then type the character in the Other box. Each table row automatically starts as a new paragraph, regardless of the character you choose to separate columns.

Figure 9-19. Use the Convert Table To Text dialog to change a table into a series of delimited text values.

3 If the table you want to convert has a table nested within it that you also want to convert to text, select the Convert Nested Tables check box.

4 Click OK to convert the table to text.

Creating Bulleted and Numbered Lists

It is quite often the case that important facts or procedures can be described in a few steps. In the case of facts, the order in which they are presented is not always important. The opposite is true of procedures, however—in most cases, as the following example illustrates, the order in which the steps are presented is quite important.

1 Ready.

2 Fire!

3 Aim.

This section shows you how to create, format, and customize bulleted and numbered lists.

Creating a List

Beginning a list is extremely straightforward. To do so, you only need to identify the current line of your document as the first item in a list.

To create a bulleted or numbered list, follow these steps:

1 Click View, Formatting Palette to display the Formatting Palette.

2 If necessary, open the Font category on the Formatting Palette.

3 Click the Numbering button to begin creating a numbered list, or click the Bullets button to begin creating a bulleted list.

Formatting Lists with the Formatting Palette

After you have created a list, you can change the appearance of any list items using the options in the Bullets And Numbering section of the Formatting Palette. You can choose from a variety of number types (uppercase Roman numerals, lowercase Roman numerals, Arabic numerals, etc.) and bullet types.

> **note** The Bullets And Numbering section of the Formatting Palette only appears when the insertion point is within a bulleted or numbered list.

To format a bulleted or numbered list, follow these steps:

1 Select the list items you want to format, and then open the Bullets And Numbering section of the Formatting Palette, shown in Figure 9-20.

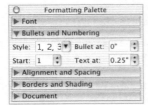

Figure 9-20. To control the appearance of your list, use the options in the Bullets And Numbering section of the Formatting Palette.

2 To change the type of numbering or the bullet character used in the list, open the Style pop-up menu and make a selection. You can even convert a bulleted list to a numbered list or vice versa by making the appropriate selection in the Style box.

3 In the Bullet At box, type the distance you want the bullet or number to be indented from the left margin.

4 In the Start box, type the number you want for the first item in the list. This box is unavailable if you've chosen a bulleted list.

5 In the Text At box, type the distance you want the list text to be indented from the left margin.

Customizing Lists Using the Bullets And Numbering Dialog

The basic lists you create in Word, which have the regular 1, 2, 3… numbering scheme or a small round bullet at the beginning of each item, are fine in many cases. But if you want to change your list's appearance, such as by choosing an image or a special character to serve as a bullet, you can do so using the options in the Bullets And Numbering dialog, shown in Figure 9-21 on the next page.

Chapter 9

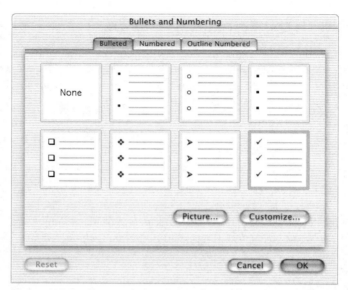

Figure 9-21. For even more control over the appearance of your bulleted list, use the settings on the Bulleted tab of the Bullets And Numbering dialog.

To use a small picture or graphic as a custom bullet character in a list, follow these steps:

1 Select the entire bulleted list.

2 Choose Format, Bullets And Numbering to display the Bullets And Numbering dialog, and click the Bulleted tab.

3 Select the button representing the bullet style you want to replace with a custom style.

4 Click the Picture button to open the Choose A Picture dialog.

5 Select the picture file you want to use as the bullet for your list. If you installed Office ClipArt on your computer, Word will display the image files available in the Bullets folder.

To choose a character from any font as your custom bullet, follow these steps:

1 Select the entire bulleted list.

2 Choose Format, Bullets And Numbering to display the Bullets And Numbering dialog, and click the Bulleted tab.

3 Click the Customize button to open the Customize Bulleted List dialog, shown next.

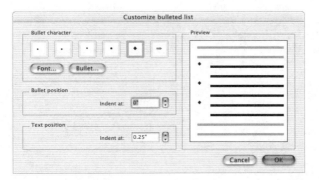

4 If you want to select a character from one of the symbol fonts, you can skip to step 5. To select a character from any other font, such as Techno or Times, first click the Font button. When the Font dialog opens, choose the font and click OK.

5 Click the Bullet button to display the characters in the font you selected in step 4. Or, if you want to use a symbol font, such as Symbol or Webdings, choose it from the Font pop-up menu.

6 When the font's characters appear, click the character you want to use as the custom bullet character, and click OK.

7 Click the Font button if you want to adjust the character's point size, weight (such as bold), or effect (such as outline or shadow), and then click OK.

8 Click OK again to close the Customize Bulleted List dialog, and the bullet character will appear in your list.

If you don't like the custom character you've chosen or grow tired of it over time, open the Bullets And Numbering dialog, click the button containing the custom bullet, and then click the Reset button to return to Word's default bullet character for that button position.

To customize a numbered list, follow these steps:

1 Select the list you want to customize, and then choose Format, Bullets And Numbering to display the Bullets And Numbering dialog.

2 Select the Numbered tab, shown in Figure 9-22 on the next page.

3 Click the button representing the numbering style you want to replace with a custom numbered list.

4 Click the Customize button to display the Customize Numbered List dialog.

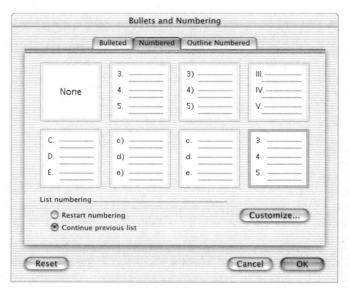

Figure 9-22. For even more control over the appearance of your numbered list, use the settings on the Numbered tab of the Bullets And Numbering dialog.

5 Use the dialog to set the font, number format, number style, starting number, number position, and number and text indents for the list.

6 Click OK, and the dialogs close, showing your new numbered list style.

Numbered lists in Word can be indented to reflect sublevels and can be numbered automatically in the form of an outline, with many possible outline formats available. To customize the outline style of a multi-level numbered list, follow these steps:

1 Click anywhere in the list you want to customize, and then choose Format, Bullets And Numbering to display the Bullets And Numbering dialog.

2 Click the Outline Numbered tab, shown in Figure 9-23.

3 Click the button representing the numbering scheme you want to assign to your numbered list, or the numbering scheme you want to replace with a custom scheme. If you're satisfied with the numbering scheme you've chosen, click OK to close the dialog. Otherwise, continue on with step 4 to customize it.

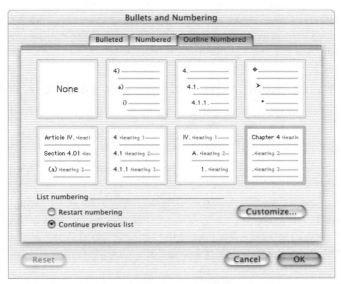

Figure 9-23. For even more control over the appearance of your outline numbered list, use the settings on the Outline Numbered tab of the Bullets And Numbering dialog.

4 To customize the numbering scheme you selected, click the Customize button to display the Customize Outline Numbered List dialog, as shown next. Use the options in this dialog to set custom properties for your outline style. Click OK to close both dialogs and see the results of your custom style.

If you customized an outline style and later decide to return to the default style, open the Bullets And Numbering dialog, click the button for the outline numbered style you customized, and click the Reset button.

Increasing or Decreasing the Indentation of List Items

To change the indent level of list items, follow these steps:

1 Click anywhere in the list item you want to move to a different level.

2 Choose View, Formatting Palette, and then click the Font category to display the Font section.

3 Click the Increase Indent button to demote the current list item to the next lower outline level, or click the Decrease Indent button to promote the item to the next higher outline level. If the list is not an outline numbered list but a simple bulleted or numbered list, only the indent level will change from one tab stop to the next.

Creating Newspaper-Style Columns

Corporate reports, memos, and academic papers are almost always single-column documents, but other document types (such as newsletters) take advantage of columns to fit the maximum amount of text onto the page as possible. Word lets you use columns in your documents as well, so you can take advantage of the layout possibilities they present.

> **tip** A good rule of thumb when creating columns is that your columns should be wide enough to allow five words per line. Any fewer words per line and the reader's eyes will move from line to line so frequently that it will disrupt their reading.

To create newspaper-style columns, follow these steps:

1 Choose Format, Columns to display the Columns dialog, shown in Figure 9-24.

2 In the Presets section of the dialog, click the column layout you want for your document.

3 If you want more than three columns, type the desired number of columns in the Number Of Columns box.

4 Select the Line Between check box to add a vertical line between each column.

5 If you don't like the equal column spacing that Word chooses by default, use the Width And Spacing section to specify the width and spacing of each column.

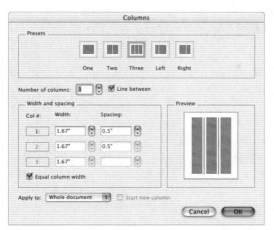

Figure 9-24. You have great control over the columns in your document; use the Columns dialog to make them look exactly right.

6 To reset each column to the same width, select the Equal Column Width check box.

7 Open the Apply To pop-up menu, and then choose Whole Document to apply the column settings to the entire document, or choose This Point Forward to leave the preceding portion of the document unchanged.

8 If you chose This Point Forward, select the Start New Column check box if you want to force the beginning of a new column.

9 Click OK to apply your column settings. The settings shown in Figure 9-24 format the text as shown here:

For information on using document sections to separate normal text from text in columns, see "Working with Sections," page 151.

Using Text Boxes

Tables and columns give you a lot of control over the placement of the text in your document, but they don't let you grab a shape containing text and put it wherever you want. You can do exactly that, however, with the aid of text boxes. A *text box* is a container you can place anywhere in your document, regardless of margins, columns, or other text.

Text boxes can also be linked to flow the contents from one box to the next box in the chain. For example, if the contents of a text box extend beyond the bottom of the box, the reader cannot see the rest of the text. If you create another text box and establish a link from the first box to the new, empty text box, the overflowing text from the first box will appear in the second box. This property of text boxes makes them very useful for creating newsletters, where you might want to start multiple stories on the front page and continue them at various points throughout the document.

You can work with text boxes using the buttons on the Text Box toolbar. The Text Box toolbar isn't listed on the View, Toolbars menu, but it appears whenever you insert or select a text box. The functions of the buttons on the Text Box toolbar are detailed in Table 9-3.

Table 9-3. **The Text Box Toolbar**

Button	Name	Action
	Create Text Box Link	Establishes a link between two text boxes.
	Break Forward Link	Removes a link between the current text box and the text box to which it is connected.
	Previous Text Box	Selects the previous text box in the document.
	Next Text Box	Selects the next text box in the document.
	Change Text Direction	Rotates the text in the text box by 90 degrees.

Creating and Deleting Text Boxes

You can add and remove text boxes easily, as follows:

- To create a text box, choose Insert, Text Box to change the pointer into crosshairs, and then drag the pointer to define the outline of the text box.

- To delete a text box, select the text box and then press Delete.

220

> **note** When you choose Insert, Text Box, the document view changes to Page Layout view and the Text Box toolbar appears.

Positioning Text Boxes

To position a text box in your document, follow these steps:

1 If necessary, choose View, Page Layout to display the document in Page Layout view.

2 Move the pointer over the edge of the text box you want to position; the pointer will change to a hand when it is in the right place.

3 Click the text box to select it, and then do either of the following to position the text box:

   ▪ Drag the text box to its new location in the document.

   ▪ Resize the text box by dragging any of the handles on the outline of the text box.

Formatting Text Inside Text Boxes

To format text inside a text box, do either of the following:

● To format all of the text inside a text box, select the text box by clicking its border; selection handles and a shaded outline appear. Use Word's formatting tools to apply the text formatting you want.

● To format some of the text in a text box, click anywhere in the interior of the box, select the text you want to format, and then format the text.

> For more information about formatting text within a text box, see Chapter 7, "Formatting Your Work."

Working with Linked Text Boxes

To manipulate linked text boxes, follow these steps:

1 To create a link between two text boxes, select the text box from which you want to create the link, click the Create Text Box Link button on the Text Box toolbar, and then click the empty text box that is the target of the link.

> **caution** The target text box (that is, the one you are linking to) must be empty so the text from the anchor text box can flow into the second box freely.

Chapter 9

2   To break a link between two text boxes, select the text box that is the anchor of the link, and then click the Break Forward Link button on the Text Box toolbar. Any text in the subsequent linked text boxes will be inserted at the bottom of the first text box.

3   To move to the next text box in a story, click the Next Text Box button on the Text Box toolbar.

4   To move to the previous text box in a story, click the Previous Text Box button on the text box toolbar.

Wrapping Text Around Text Boxes

To wrap text around a text box, follow these steps:

1   Select the text box around which you want to wrap text, choose Format, Text Box and then select the Layout tab, shown in Figure 9-25.

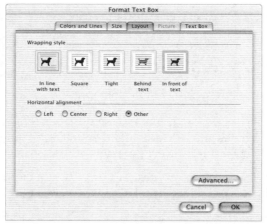

Figure 9-25.   Specify your text box's layout using the Layout tab of the Format Text Box dialog.

2   Click the button representing the text wrapping pattern you want to apply.

3   In the Horizontal Alignment section of the dialog, select the alignment you want for the text box in relation to the surrounding text.

4 If desired, click the Advanced button to display the Advanced Layout dialog, and click the Text Wrapping tab, shown in Figure 9-26. In the Wrapping Style section of the dialog, you will see two additional wrapping patterns that aren't available on the Layout tab.

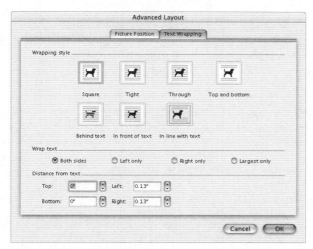

Figure 9-26. The Advanced Layout dialog gives you additional choices for wrapping text around your text box.

5 In the Wrap Text section of the Advanced Layout dialog, select which sides of the text box should be wrapped. For example, selecting Left Only would not put any document text to the right of the text box. This section is unavailable if you choose a wrapping style that doesn't put text on the left or right of the text box.

6 Use the settings in the Distance From Text section of the dialog to set the amount of white space between the edge of the text box and the surrounding document contents.

Troubleshooting

I can't see the text boxes in my document.

If you can no longer see text boxes in your document, chances are that you are in Normal or Outline view. When you choose Insert, Text Box, Word automatically switches you to Page Layout view. But if you later switch to Normal or Outline view, the text boxes will disappear.

Text boxes will also disappear if you have cleared the Drawings check box in the Show section of the View tab in Word's Preferences dialog.

Using the Equation Editor

If you are writing a report for an engineering firm, or perhaps generating a scholarly paper for a physics journal, your document might need to include equations. You can create those equations in Office using the Equation Editor, shown in Figure 9-27. The Equation Editor is a slimmed-down version of Design Science's MathType program; if you often include equations in your print and Web documents, you will find MathType has a much greater feature set. For more information about the professional version of MathType, visit the Design Science Web site at *http://www.dessci.com*.

> **note** The Equation Editor isn't part of the default installation of Office v. X. You'll need to install it using the Value Pack Installer on the Microsoft Office v. X CD.

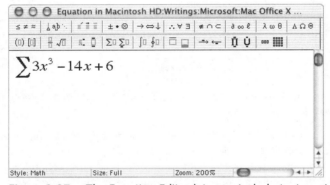

Figure 9-27. The Equation Editor lets you include text versions of advanced math functions in your documents.

> **note** Unlike the formulas you use in tables, the equations you create with the Equation Editor aren't evaluated; they are only inserted into your document as drawing objects.

To create an equation using the Equation Editor, follow these steps:

1 Choose Insert, Object.

2 Under Object Type, select Microsoft Equation and then click OK.

3 Click the button representing the template or logical character to serve as the base for your equation. Each template category has numerous frameworks you can use to create your equation.

4 Click in the text area where you want to add terms to your equation, and either type the term (such as an upper or lower bound for an integral) or use the controls to create a sub-equation that will be evaluated as part of a larger equation.

5 Choose Equation Editor, Quit Equation Editor to close the Equation Editor and make the equation you created appear in your document. The equation is inserted in your document as a graphic, so it isn't directly editable. To change the equation, double-click it in Word. The Equation Editor will reopen, enabling you to edit the equation.

tip If you don't see the specific template you need, click the buttons to display the full range of templates available in a given category.

Troubleshooting

I can't run the Equation Editor.

The Equation Editor requires a special font to run, and it will refuse to operate if that font, MT Extra, isn't installed. That font is in the Fonts folder, inside the Value Pack folder on the Office X CD. You can use the Value Pack Installer to install the font, but there's an easier way. Simply copy the MT Extra font from the Fonts folder on the CD to your hard disk in the /Library/Fonts folder.

Chapter 9

Working with Images, Movies, Sounds, and Objects

There are times when paragraph after paragraph of explanatory text can be replaced with a picture that makes everything clear. You might even be tempted to believe that people who say "a picture is worth a thousand words" are selling pictures short. In fact, they are; the original quote is "One picture is worth ten thousand words." Of course, pictures themselves rarely communicate everything you need to know. A picture of a dialog with no explanatory text doesn't let you know what you're trying to accomplish, where you are in a process, or what the result of your actions will be. It's the skillful combination of pictures and words that makes documents effective.

Just as pictures add clarity to written explanations, movies and sounds can make it much easier to understand a process. A "sound" doesn't need to be a sound effect such as crickets chirping or cats meowing; it could be a recorded explanation for a given concept, a fanfare indicating a question was answered correctly, or a response to a user action. Movies, which combine pictures, sounds, and movement into a single package, are perhaps one of the most effective teaching tools available. Seeing a process as it unfolds is a great aid to learning, if the movie demonstration of the process is well crafted, meaning it includes sufficient explanation and it is well paced. In this chapter, you'll learn how to use images, sounds, and movies to make your Microsoft Word X documents more attractive and to communicate more effectively.

Understanding Graphics in Word

Word is a powerful word processing program, but you can make your documents much more effective by adding graphics. You have a lot of flexibility in working with graphics in Word, and there are a few key concepts you should keep in mind when adding graphics and other objects to your documents. This brief introductory section describes the types of graphics available in Word and introduces *layering,* the way in which Word arranges graphics and other objects as you add them to your document.

Inline and Page Graphics

Graphics in Word fall into two general categories: *inline graphics,* which are part of the text flow and can be moved, copied, and deleted along with the surrounding text; and *page graphics,* which are anchored to a particular spot on the page and aren't connected to nearby text. There are several ways to determine whether a given graphic is an inline or a page graphic. The quickest way to tell for sure is to select a block of text starting above and ending below the graphic. If the graphic is selected in addition to the text, it is an inline graphic; if not, it is a page graphic. Another way to tell if a graphic is an inline or page graphic is to double-click the image and view the Layout tab of the Format Picture dialog.

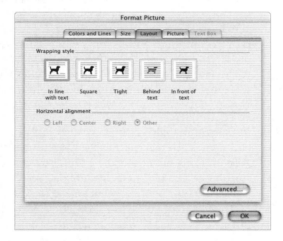

If the Behind Text or In Front of Text button is selected, then the graphic is a page graphic; if any other button is selected, the graphic is an inline graphic.

Finally, you can tell if a graphic is an inline or page graphic by displaying the document in Normal view. If the graphic appears in Normal view, it is part of the text and is an inline graphic; if the graphic doesn't appear in Normal view, but does appear in Page Layout view, it is a page graphic.

Typically, any graphic or image you insert from an external source, such as clip art from the Clip Gallery or a digital photo you downloaded to your computer, will be an inline graphic, whereas graphics you create using the drawing tools in Word (WordArt, AutoShapes, or tools on the Drawing toolbar) will come into existence as page graphics. You can change a graphic from an inline graphic to a page graphic by changing its layout properties using the Layout tab of the Format Picture dialog. To format a graphic as a page graphic, select either the Behind Text or In Front of Text layout; to format a graphic as an inline image, select any other layout.

Layering Graphics and Text

An important element of creating effective documents that include graphics is understanding how text and graphics interact. When you add an inline graphic to a document, the graphic is on the same "layer" as the text, as evidenced by your ability to cut and paste the graphic at the same time as the surrounding text. In the case of page graphics, the graphic will be on a different level than the document text. When you first add Word graphics such as WordArt or an AutoShape (more about them later in this chapter) to a document, the graphic appears in front of the text. You can move the graphic behind the text by selecting the image and then clicking Behind Text on the Layout page of the Format Picture dialog. In effect, it's as though every Word document has three layers: the graphic layer behind the text, the text layer, and the graphic layer in front of the text.

Graphics are also positioned "front to back" in relation to each other. When you add a new graphic to a document, it is placed in the graphic layer in front of the text, at the top of the stack (farthest away from the text). For example, adding a white square in front of a document with text and an existing black square would look like this:

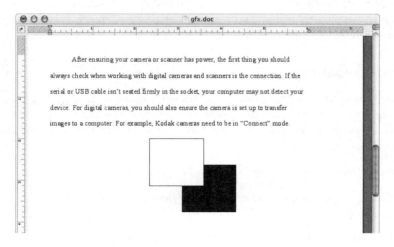

Moving the white square behind the black square would produce the following result:

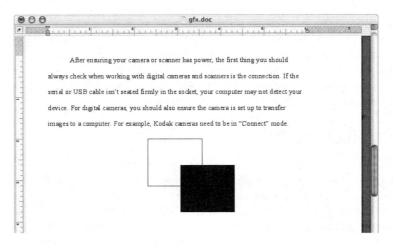

There are ways you can take advantage of this layering to produce interesting effects. For example, you can place a faint image behind your document text as a watermark (described later in this chapter), or make the image at the front of the stack partially transparent so some of the graphics and text behind it show through.

Inserting Graphics and Media Files

Whatever the type of image you want to insert into your document, you can use the tools available in Microsoft Office v. X and Mac OS X to make it happen. Office comes with a substantial collection of images you can add to your documents, but it's just as easy to bring in pictures from a digital camera or scanner. This section shows you how to import and manage all types of media files.

Using the Clip Gallery

As the name implies, the Clip Gallery is a tool you can use to display, organize, and insert clip art images. The standard installation of the Clip Gallery comes with a wide range of images in many topics. You can also store and organize movies and sounds in the Clip Gallery.

To insert an image from the Clip Gallery, follow these steps:

1 Choose Insert, Picture, Clip Art to display the Clip Gallery, as shown in Figure 10-1.

2 Click the category in which you want to look for images.

3 Select the image you want to add, and then click the Insert button to add the image to your document.

230

Figure 10-1. The Clip Gallery lets you organize and view your graphics, sound files, and movies.

---

tip You can display a full-size preview of the chosen image by selecting the Preview check box. Clearing the Preview check box will close the preview window.

Troubleshooting

I get an error message when I launch the Clip Gallery.

The Clip Gallery is one of the helper applications that is shared by Word, Microsoft Excel X, and Microsoft PowerPoint X (but not by Microsoft Entourage X). When you invoke the Clip Gallery, the application launches and comes to the foreground. When you select a clip and insert it, the Clip Gallery's job is done, and it should automatically quit. Due to an apparent bug in the Clip Gallery, you might sometimes get an error message when you attempt to launch the Clip Gallery after you have already used it once. The error dialog looks like this:

The error dialog is steering you wrong; chances are that the Clip Gallery is installed correctly and that you have enough memory to run it. In fact, given that Mac OS X

(continued)

Chapter 10

> **Troubleshooting** *(continued)* uses an advanced virtual memory system, you should never have memory limitation problems with Office v. X. What's really happening is that the bug in the Clip Gallery has prevented the Clip Gallery from quitting properly after you first inserted a graphic. The next time you attempt to insert a graphic, the error dialog appears. The solution is to look in the Dock for the Clip Gallery's icon, click the icon to bring the Clip Gallery to the foreground, and choose Clip Gallery, Quit Clip Gallery. Oh, and don't bother using the Quit command found by holding down the mouse button on the Clip Gallery's icon in the Dock; it won't solve the problem.

Viewing and Editing Image Properties

When you work with large clip art collections, its important that you be able to find the files you need. Browsing through categories can work when you have time, but you might need to make it easier to narrow your search by setting image properties such as descriptions and keywords.

To view an image's properties, follow these steps:

1 Choose Insert, Picture, Clip Art to display the Clip Gallery (shown in Figure 10-1).

2 Click the category that contains the image you want to examine.

3 Click the image you want to examine, and then click the Properties button to display the Properties dialog, shown in Figure 10-2.

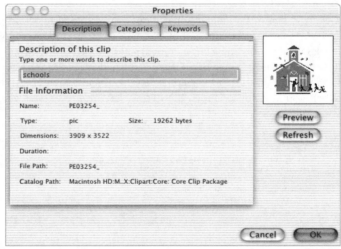

Figure 10-2. You can use the Properties dialog to view the graphic's characteristics, assign the graphic to categories, and add or delete keywords to help in searching.

232

4 Click the Description tab to display the basic facts about the image: its size, format, and description. If you want, you can type a new description in the Description Of This Clip box.

5 Click the Categories tab to display the list of categories in the Clip Gallery. The check boxes next to the categories to which the current image belongs will be selected. Select the category or categories you want.

6 Click the Keywords tab to display the keywords assigned to the current image. You can add a new keyword by clicking the New Keyword button, typing the keyword in the space provided, and then clicking OK. To remove a keyword, click the keyword, and then click the Remove Keyword button.

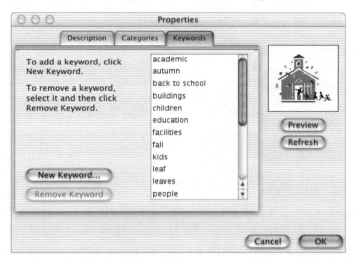

tip You can search for an image based on its keywords by displaying the main page of the Clip Gallery, typing the desired keywords in the Search box, and then clicking the Search button.

Creating a New Category

The default categories that come with Word are descriptive, but they aren't designed for every aspect of your work. For example, you might find images spread throughout the Clip Gallery that you want to use in a year-end report. Rather than memorizing where each of the clips reside, you can create a new custom category and add the images to it.

To create a new category in the Clip Gallery, follow these steps:

1 Choose Insert, Picture, Clip Art to display the Clip Gallery.

2 Click the Categories button to display the Categories dialog, shown in Figure 10-3.

Figure 10-3. Use the Categories dialog to create a new category to gather images in an order that makes sense to you, or to delete an existing category.

3 Click the New Category button to display the New Category dialog.

4 Type the name of the new category in the box, and then click the OK button to close the New Category dialog.

Adding Clips to or Removing Clips from a Category

After you've created a new category, you can add images to it by selecting the check box for that category in each image's properties. Then, when you're done working with a custom category, you can delete the category; the clips will still remain in the Clip Gallery for future use.

To add a clip to or remove a clip from a category, follow these steps:

1 Choose Insert, Picture, Clip Art to display the Clip Gallery.

2 Click the image you want to assign to a category, and then click the Properties button to display the Properties dialog.

3 Click the Categories tab and then perform either of these actions:

> ▓ Select the check box next to the name of each category to which you want to assign the image.

> ▓ Clear the check box next to the name of each category from which you want to remove the image.

---

note Unfortunately, you can't change category settings on multiple clips at once; you must change each clip separately.

Getting More Pictures Online

The clip art collection that comes with the Clip Gallery is extensive, but it's not all-encompassing. You can extend your clip art collection in several ways, but one easy way to do it is to download files from the Microsoft Design Gallery Live, available on the Web at *http://dgl.microsoft.com*. You can browse the site, view the images, and then download all or some of them at your leisure.

To get more pictures online, follow these steps:

1 Choose Insert, Picture, Clip Art to display the Clip Gallery.

2 Click the Online button to display the Design Gallery Live Web site in your default browser.

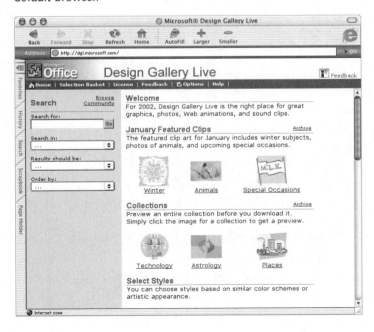

note A dialog will appear asking if it's OK to run your Web browser from Word. After seeing it a few times (or maybe even once), you will probably want to select the Don't Ask Me Again check box to eliminate this warning in the future and then click the Yes button to display the site. The first page of the site appears; you will need to read and accept the End User License Agreement to continue.

3 Click the icon representing the collection you want to download to display a list of the images in the collection. A sample collection is shown in Figure 10-4.

Figure 10-4. Click on a clip art displayed on the Design Gallery Live Web site and a preview window opens.

4 For each page of images in the collection, follow any of these steps to identify the images you want to download:

- Select the check box below an image to select it for downloading. If you want a bigger look at the image before deciding, click the image to open a Preview window

- Click the Select All hyperlink to choose all images on the page for download.

- Click the Deselect All hyperlink to clear any images on the page that you have selected for download.

5 After you have selected all of the images you want to download from all the pages, click the Download Clips hyperlink (the number of clips you've selected will be shown) at the top left of the page to display the download information page. On the new page, click the Download Now button to download the selected images. The images will download and will be placed into the Favorites category of the Clip Gallery.

6 Close the Download Manager, your browser, and the Clip Gallery.

Troubleshooting

I can't download clips from Design Gallery Live.

If your Web browser isn't configured properly for the kind of download sent by the Design Gallery Live Web site, you'll get an Unhandled File Type error dialog, as shown here in Internet Explorer:

From the wording of the dialog, not to mention its inviting Application button, you would think that all you would need to do to tell Internet Explorer how to handle Design Gallery Live files in the future would be to click the Application button, and then select the Microsoft Clip Gallery application. That's how it is supposed to work, but alas, it does not. If you click the Application button, Internet Explorer downloads the file from Design Gallery Live, and then does nothing with it. You have to configure Internet Explorer manually to get things working properly. Follow these steps:

1 If the Unhandled File Type error dialog is visible, click Cancel.

2 Choose Internet Explorer, Preferences.

3 From the category list on the left of the Preferences dialog, click the disclosure triangle next to Receiving Files to expand its list, and then click File Helpers.

4 In the File Helper Settings pane, click Add.

5 In the Description box in the Edit File Helper dialog, type **Design Gallery Live File**.

6 In the Extension box, type **.cil**.

(continued)

Troubleshooting *(continued)*

7 In the MIME Type box, type **application/vnd.ms-artgalry**. You have to type this exactly, in lowercase with no spaces.

8 In the File Type section of the dialog, click the Browse button.

9 Navigate to **Applications/Microsoft Office X/Office**, select Microsoft Clip Gallery, and then click Open.

10 In the File Type box type **CGdb**.

11 Confirm that Plain Text, Use For Incoming, and Use For Outgoing are selected.

12 The download destination should be whatever folder you usually use for downloads.

13 In the Handling section, choose Post-Process With Application from the How To Handle pop-up menu. Microsoft Clip Gallery should appear under the pop-up menu. If it does not, use the Browse button in the Handling section to select the Microsoft Clip Gallery again. The Edit File Helper dialog should now look like this:

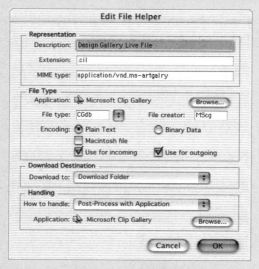

14 Click OK to exit the Edit File Helper dialog.

15 Click OK to exit Preferences.

note If you're not using Internet Explorer as your Web browser, check your browser's documentation for its MIME configuration procedure. The Extension and MIME Type information you need to enter will remain the same, no matter the browser.

Adding Images to the Clip Gallery

In addition to adding images to the Clip Gallery from the Microsoft Design Gallery Live, you can add images of other types from your computer. The Clip Gallery recognizes a wide variety of image formats, so it's very likely you can add any images you want.

To add images to the Clip Gallery, follow these steps:

1 Choose Insert, Picture, Clip Art to display the Clip Gallery.

2 Click the Import button to display the Import dialog, shown in Figure 10-5.

Figure 10-5. Browse to the graphic you want to add to the Clip Gallery with the Import dialog.

3 Navigate to the folder with the image you want to import, click the file, and then perform one of the following actions:

- Select Copy Into Clip Gallery to keep the original copy of the file and add a copy to the Clip Gallery.

- Select Move Into Clip Gallery to delete the original copy of the file and add a copy to the Clip Gallery.

- Select Add Alias To Clip Gallery to add a shortcut to the original file to the Clip Gallery.

> **tip** The Add Alias To Clip Gallery option is particularly useful when you want to add a large image to the Clip Gallery without taking up extra storage space on your computer.

4 Click the Import button to add the file to the Clip Gallery.

239

Placing Image Files

You don't need to add a picture to the Clip Gallery to place it in a Word document. If you know the location of a picture file in your computer, you can insert the file quickly using the Choose A Picture dialog. The Choose A Picture dialog displays all files of every known image type; all you need to do is identify the file.

To place an image file in a document, follow these steps:

1 Choose Insert, Picture, From File to display the Choose A Picture dialog.

2 Navigate to the folder that contains the image you want to add to your document and click the file. If you want to place a reference to the image in your document, rather than embed a copy of the image in the document, select the Link To File check box, and clear the Save With Document button. Word will still show the image in your document, but will read the image from its original location, rather than copy the image into the Word document. The benefit is that it keeps the Word document's file size smaller.

3 Click Insert.

> For information on editing images after you have added them, see "Modifying Graphics," page 251.

Working with the Drawing Tools

Adding pictures to your documents is a great way to make the documents more readable, but you probably won't be able to find a picture for everything you want to create. For example, you might want to create a banner with the name of your company's new product or service in the middle. Rather than pay a graphic artist to create a relatively simple image, you can do it yourself using the tools on the Drawing toolbar, shown in Figure 10-6.

In addition to the tools on the Drawing toolbar, these additional commands are available on the toolbar's Draw pop-up menu:

● **Format *Object*.** This command opens the formatting dialog for the selected object. The command name will change to reflect the type of object selected. If a picture is selected, the item will read Format Picture and the Format Picture dialog will open.

● **Dash Style.** Select the style of line you want to apply to a selected line or border: solid, dashed, dotted, and so forth.

● **Arrow Style.** Select the arrow style you want to apply to a selected line.

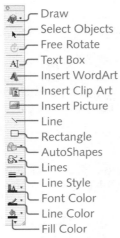
- Draw
- Select Objects
- Free Rotate
- Text Box
- Insert WordArt
- Insert Clip Art
- Insert Picture
- Line
- Rectangle
- AutoShapes
- Lines
- Line Style
- Font Color
- Line Color
- Fill Color

Figure 10-6. The tools on the Drawing toolbar enable you to create and edit a wide variety of graphics.

- **Shadow.** Select the style of shadow you want to apply to the selected object. For more control over the shadow, choose the Shadow Settings button from the submenu to display the Shadow Settings toolbar.

- **3-D.** Select the style of three-dimensional effect you want to apply to the selected object. For more control over the 3-D effect, choose the 3-D Settings button from the submenu to display the 3-D Settings toolbar.

- **Arrange.** Select how you want to change the order of one or more selected objects. Choose Bring To Front to put the object in front of (on top of) all other objects, Send To Back to put the object behind all other objects, Bring Forward to bring the object up one level at a time, Send Backward to lower the object one level at a time, In Front Of Text to put the image in front of the text it overlaps, or Behind Text to put the image behind the text it overlaps.

- **Group, Ungroup, Regroup.** These three items let you manipulate more than one object at a time. If you want to modify several objects at once, select the objects and then choose Group. To remove the grouping, select any object in the group, and then choose Ungroup; to reapply the grouping, choose Regroup.

- **Change AutoShape.** Choose a new shape for any selected AutoShapes by selecting one from the AutoShape categories listed on the submenu.

- **Edit Points.** Use this tool to change the position of points in a polygon.

- **Align Or Distribute.** Select multiple objects, and then choose their alignment or distribution. For example, choosing Align Center would align the center of each object with the center of every other selected object. In this case, the vertical positioning of the objects would not be affected. By default, the alignment options show how the objects will be positioned in relation to other objects. If you want to arrange items in relation to the page, choose Relative To Page from the Align or Distribute submenu.

- **Rotate Or Flip.** Select the amount of rotation desired, or select whether to flip the object horizontally or vertically.

- **Grid.** This command opens the Drawing Grid dialog, which you can use to modify the grid Word uses to manage object movements within a document.

> **tip** If you want to move objects with absolute freedom, click the Draw button on the Drawing toolbar, and then choose Grid to display the Drawing Grid dialog. In the Drawing Grid dialog, clear the Snap Objects To Grid check box, and then click OK.

Adding AutoShapes to a Document

Whenever you want to add a basic shape to your document, you don't need to draw it freehand. Instead, you can use one of many AutoShapes, which are ready-made graphic objects, including 3D objects. You can choose from a variety of AutoShape categories: circles, squares, stars, banners, arrows, flowchart symbols, and callouts. Each of these AutoShapes can be manipulated once you've added them to your document to modify the object's size, internal text, and coloring.

To add an AutoShape to a document, follow these steps:

1 Choose Insert, Picture, AutoShapes to display the AutoShapes toolbar. You can also use the AutoShapes button on the Drawing toolbar.

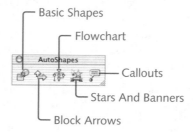

2 Click any of the buttons on the AutoShapes toolbar to display a palette containing the shapes in that category, and then click the shape you want to add.

InsideOut

Change the type of an AutoShape

When you add an AutoShape to a document, you might want to change the type of AutoShape (perhaps changing a square to an octagon so the shape will look like a stop sign). You can change the type of an AutoShape by selecting the AutoShape, clicking the Draw button on the Drawing toolbar, choosing Change AutoShape, and then choosing the AutoShape you want from the available categories.

Adding Text to an AutoShape

After you've added an AutoShape to your document, you can treat the AutoShape as a text box and add text, create links to other text boxes, and format the text inside the AutoShape.

To add text to an AutoShape, follow these steps:

1 If necessary, switch to Page Layout view, and then select the AutoShape to which you want to add text.

2 Control+click the AutoShape, and then choose Add Text from the contextual menu to begin typing in the AutoShape.

note When you add text to an AutoShape, Word treats the AutoShape as a text box; for details, see "Using Text Boxes," page 220.

Using the WordArt Gallery

When you create a document, you might find yourself wanting to add a bit more flash to the title or headings of your document. You can use the tools on the Formatting Palette to modify your text's color, positioning, size, and alignment, but you can often save time by adding WordArt that has the style you want already applied. The WordArt Gallery, like the Clip Gallery, presents the range of available effects on a page; to apply a style from the WordArt Gallery, simply click the style you want and enter the text.

To add a WordArt object to your document, follow these steps:

1 Choose Insert, Picture, WordArt to display the WordArt Gallery, shown in Figure 10-7 on the next page.

Chapter 10

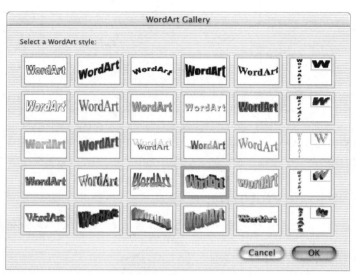

Figure 10-7. The WordArt Gallery has a wide range of styles you can use to create attractive text.

2 Click the style of WordArt you want to add to your document, and then click the OK button.

3 In the Edit WordArt Text dialog, enter your text and, optionally, change the font and point size.

4 Click OK to add the WordArt to your document, as shown in Figure 10-8.

Figure 10-8. The WordArt appears in your document as a graphic, which you can manipulate as you would any other Word graphic.

Editing WordArt Text

After you add your WordArt object to your document, you might need to edit the text in the object. You can do that by clicking the object and using one of the buttons on the WordArt toolbar, which are described in Table 10-1.

Chapter 10

Table 10-1. The WordArt Toolbar

Button	Name	Action
Edit Text...	Edit Text	Displays the Edit WordArt Text dialog.
	WordArt Gallery	Displays the WordArt Gallery.
	Format WordArt	Displays the Format WordArt dialog.
	WordArt Shape	Displays a palette of shapes for your WordArt to follow.
	Free Rotate	Lets you rotate the WordArt graphic through 360 degrees.
	Text Wrapping	Displays a submenu of patterns for wrapping the document text in relation to the WordArt.
Aa	WordArt Same Letter Heights	Toggles all letters to the same height, regardless of uppercase or lowercase. Click again to undo the effect.
Ab	WordArt Vertical Text	Toggles the alignment of your WordArt text between horizontal and vertical.
	WordArt Alignment	Displays a palette of available alignments for the text within the WordArt.
AV	WordArt Character Spacing	Displays a list of character spacing changes you can make to your WordArt text.

To edit the text of a piece of WordArt, follow these steps:

1 Select the WordArt you want to edit, which will display the WordArt toolbar.

2 On the WordArt toolbar, click the Edit Text toolbar button to display the Edit WordArt Text dialog.

3 Edit the text in the Text pane, and then click OK.

Formatting WordArt

Just as you can edit the text in your WordArt, you can change the color, size, fill pattern, and layout options of your WordArt using the tools on the WordArt toolbar. In this case, the Format WordArt button is the gateway to most of the commands you need to make your changes.

To change the appearance of WordArt, follow these steps:

1 Select the WordArt you want to format, which will display the WordArt toolbar.

2 Click the Format WordArt button on the WordArt toolbar to display the Format WordArt dialog.

3 Click the Colors And Lines tab, shown in Figure 10-9, to make any of these changes:

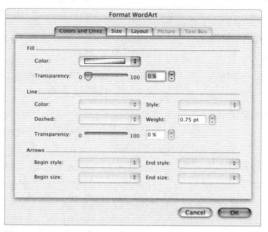

Figure 10-9. The Colors And Lines tab gives you control over the appearance of your WordArt.

■ In either the Fill or Line section, click the Color pop-up menu, and then select the color you want from the palette that appears. You can also select More Colors to display the Color Picker or select Fill Effects to display the Fill Effects dialog. The Line section settings control the outline of each text character, whereas the Fill section settings determine its inside color.

For more information on using the Fill Effects dialog, see "Adding a Background Color, Pattern, or Image to a Web Page," page 371.

■ In each Transparency box, type the percentage value representing the desired transparency for the WordArt. A value of 0 makes the WordArt totally opaque, whereas a value of 100 makes it completely transparent. If you make both the line and fill 100% transparent, your Word Art will be invisible.

4 Click the Size tab, shown in Figure 10-10, and make any of the following changes:

■ To make the WordArt a specific size, type the desired height and width for the object in the Height and Width boxes in the Size And Rotate section of the dialog.

- In the Rotation box, type the number of degrees you want the WordArt to be rotated. The WordArt will be rotated in a clockwise direction; enter a negative number to rotate the WordArt in a counterclockwise direction.

- To change the size of the WordArt by a percentage, type the percentage of the original object size you want in the Height and Width boxes in the Scale section of the dialog.

- Select the Lock Aspect Ratio check box to retain the proportions of the original object.

---

caution   Changing an object without selecting the Lock Aspect Ratio check box can cause the image to become distorted, obscuring its contents and making the image much less attractive.

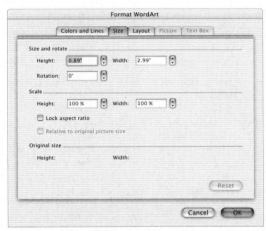

Figure 10-10.   Modify the size of your object using the Size tab of the Format WordArt dialog.

5 Click the Layout tab to change the alignment and text wrapping options for your WordArt.

---

note   The Reset button should allow you to undo any changes you make in the dialog, but due to a bug, the button never becomes active. This may be fixed in a future release of Word.

For information on using the Layout tab and the Advanced Layout dialog, which you display by clicking the Advanced button on the Layout tab, see "Wrapping Text Around Text Boxes," page 222.

Acquiring Images from a Scanner or Camera

It used to be that adding photographs or other images to a document required lots of expensive photographic and typesetting equipment. Not so in the digital world. Now you can buy an inexpensive scanner and capture digital versions of your photographs or purchase a digital camera that lets you take pictures and transfer them directly to your computer.

To acquire images from a scanner or camera, follow these steps:

1 Connect your scanner or camera to your computer, and then choose Insert, Picture, From Scanner Or Camera to display the Insert Picture From Scanner Or Camera dialog.

2 Click the Device pop-up menu, choose your digital camera from the list of devices, and then click the Acquire button to run the software that came with your camera.

3 Follow the instructions in your camera software to add the image to your document.

Troubleshooting

My computer doesn't detect my camera or scanner.

After ensuring your camera or scanner has power, the first thing you should always check when working with digital cameras and scanners is the connection. If the USB cable isn't seated firmly in the socket, your computer might not detect your device. For digital cameras, you should also ensure the camera is set up to transfer images to a computer.

Another potential problem is that your camera or scanner might not have OS X drivers available, or that it doesn't use the TWAIN image transfer protocol. If either is true, Word won't be able to connect to the device. You do have two reliable ways to bring the images into your document, however. The first way to get the image from the camera or scanner to your computer is to use the Apple Image Capture application that comes with OS X. Turn on and connect your camera, and then run Image Capture from the Applications folder. Image Capture will detect your camera and list the available images. You can save the images onto your hard disk, and then use the images in Word by choosing Insert, Picture, From File.

A second program you can use to transfer files from a camera to your Macintosh is iPhoto, which you can download from Apple's Web site (*www.apple.com/iphoto*), and comes pre-installed on newer Macintoshes. iPhoto works with most newer cameras (those made since 1999) and also lets you view and organize your images effectively. Apple's iPhoto Web page has a list of devices that are compatible with iPhoto.

Inserting QuickTime Movies

Just as you can add digital still photographs you've taken, you can add digital movies to your document. Although they do take up a lot of space on your hard disk, the information movies convey in combination with explanatory and introductory text makes them a valuable teaching tool.

To insert a QuickTime movie, follow these steps:

1 Choose Insert, Movie to display the Insert Movie dialog.

2 Select the movie you want to insert, and then click the Choose button.

---

note You can't insert a Windows Media Format movie into a Word document, because the Insert Movie command is only compatible with QuickTime. You can, however, play Windows Media movies using the Windows Media Player included on the Office v. X CD.

Troubleshooting

I can view my movie in Windows, but it doesn't play on the Macintosh.

Word can play QuickTime, MPEG, and AVI movies (AVI is a digital movie format used primarily on Windows), but you might run into trouble when you try to play AVI files that were added to a Word for Windows document you are currently viewing in Word X. When you add an AVI file to a Word document, Word translates the file to a QuickTime movie; when you add an AVI file to a Word for Windows document, it remains an AVI file, which is a format QuickTime doesn't play directly. To make the AVI file viewable in a Word document, delete the file from your document and reinsert it using the Insert Movie dialog (translating the file to a QuickTime movie in the process).

Setting Poster Frames

As the name implies, a poster frame is the frame of the movie that appears in the frame when the document is viewed in Page Layout view. If your movie has a title frame, that's a good place to start, but if you have a particularly attractive frame in the middle of the movie, you can select it and have the movie player reset to the beginning when the reader views the movie.

To set a poster frame for a QuickTime movie, follow these steps:

1 If necessary, view your document in Page Layout view, and then click the movie for which you want to set a poster frame. The Movie toolbar appears.

Chapter 10

Play

2 Click the Play button on the Movie toolbar, and then click the Play button again to pause the movie when the frame you want to display as the poster frame appears.

Set As
Poster Frame

3 Click the Set As Poster Frame button to define the displayed frame as the poster frame.

Setting Background Sounds and Music for a Web Page

As the amount of bandwidth available to the average user increases, you can add more complex design elements to your Web pages. For a humorous Web page describing the wildlife in your backyard, you might want to have a chorus of crickets chirping as visitors view the page. Remember, however, that not every user has a high-speed Internet connection and that if you slow down their Web experience, they might move elsewhere before your page finishes loading. Also remember that many people find sound on Web pages to be intensely annoying, so use this feature with discretion. Although you can add the sound in Word, you'll need to open the page in your browser to listen to it.

For more information on creating Web pages in Word, see Chapter 15, "Creating Pages for the Web."

To set a background sound or music for a Web page, follow these steps:

1 Choose Insert, HTML Object, Background Sound to display the Background Sound dialog, shown in Figure 10-11.

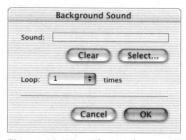

Figure 10-11. The Background Sound dialog lets you choose the file to play and how many times to play it.

2 Click the Select button to display the Choose A Sound dialog, and then navigate to the sound file you want.

3 Click Choose.

4 From the Loop pop-up menu, choose the number of times you want the background sound or music to be repeated. Choose Infinite if you want the music or sound to play continuously.

Chapter 10

5 Click OK to close the Background Sound dialog.

> **tip** To remove a background sound from a Web page, display the Background Sound dialog, and click the Clear button.

Modifying Graphics

One of the hallmarks of the Macintosh is the ease with which you can work with graphics in your documents. Word extends those capabilities by giving you a wide range of image formatting tools, grouped together in a set of handy toolbars and dialogs. In this section of the chapter, we'll look at the Format Picture dialog and the Picture toolbar.

> **note** Many of these graphic tools are also available from the Formatting Palette. The Picture category of the Formatting Palette only appears when you have selected a graphic.

Using the Format Picture Dialog

The most basic elements of an image are its size, color scheme, and interaction with the surrounding document elements. You can use the settings in the Format Picture dialog to change many of those characteristics. For example, you can change the brightness of an image to make it more or less prominent (or to correct for over- or underexposure), change the image's size without sacrificing significant image quality, and even substitute one color for another in the image.

To format a picture using the options in the Format Picture dialog, follow these steps:

1 Select the picture you want to format, and then choose Format, Picture to display the Format Picture dialog.

2 Click the Colors And Lines tab (shown in Figure 10-9), and then make any of these changes:

■ Click the Color pop-up menu in the Fill or Line area, and then select the color you want from the palette that appears. You can also select More Colors to display the Color Picker or select Fill Effects to display the Fill Effects dialog.

> For more information on using the Fill Effects dialog, see "Adding a Background Color, Pattern, or Image to a Web Page," page 371.

■ In each Transparency box, type the percentage value representing the desired transparency for the image. A value of 0 makes the image totally opaque, whereas a value of 100 makes it completely transparent.

3 Click the Size tab, shown in Figure 10-12, to make any of the following changes:

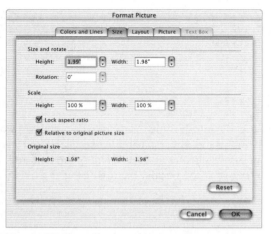

Figure 10-12.   Change the size of your object using the settings on the Size tab.

■ To make the image a specific size, type the desired height and width for the object in the Height and Width boxes in the Size And Rotate section of the dialog.

■ In the Rotation box, type the number of degrees you want the image to be rotated in a clockwise direction, or enter a negative number for counterclockwise rotation.

■ To change the size of the image by a percentage, type the percentage of the original object size you want in the Height and Width boxes in the Scale section of the dialog.

■ Select the Lock Aspect Ratio check box to retain the proportions of the original object.

---

caution   Changing an object without selecting the Lock Aspect Ratio check box can cause the image to become distorted, obscuring its contents and making the image much less attractive.

■ Click the Reset button to undo your changes without closing the Format Picture dialog.

4 Click the Layout tab to set the alignment and wrapping options for your image.

For information on using the Layout tab and the Advanced Layout dialog, which you display by clicking the Advanced button on the Layout tab, see "Wrapping Text Around Text Boxes," page 222.

---

5 Click the Picture tab, shown in Figure 10-13, and make any of these changes:

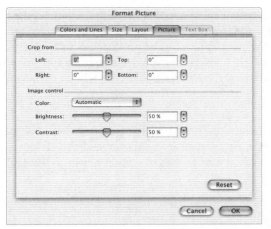

Figure 10-13. Crop or cut out pieces of your image using the settings on the Picture tab.

■ To crop the image, type the measurements for the spot from the top left corner at which you want to begin cropping in the Left and Top boxes, and then type the distance from the bottom right corner at which you want to stop cropping in the Right and Bottom boxes.

To crop images interactively, see "Cropping and Cutting Out Images," page 255.

■ To change the color scheme of the image, click the Color pop-up menu, and select Automatic, Grayscale, Black & White, or Watermark. Automatic lets Word detect the best color scheme for the image, Grayscale renders the image using 256 shades of gray, Black & White renders the image using only black and white pixels, and Watermark makes the image a background image that only appears when you print the document.

For more information on creating watermarks, see "Inserting Watermarks," page 258.

■ Drag the Brightness slider to change the brightness of your image. The change won't take effect until you close the Format Picture dialog.

■ Drag the Contrast slider to change the contrast of your image. The change won't take effect until you close the Format Picture dialog.

■ Click the Reset button to remove your changes without closing the Format Picture dialog.

6 Click the OK button to apply your changes and close the Format Picture dialog.

Chapter 10

Adding Picture Effects

Photographs or graphics often come in a distinctive style, which might not fit in with the overall design and layout of your document. Photographs are, naturally, photorealistic, whereas some graphics can be produced with a variety of illustrative techniques. Word has an extensive gallery of effects you can apply to your images to simulate many popular styles, such as watercolor, bas relief, or charcoal.

To add picture effects, follow these steps:

1 Click the image to which you want to add effects, and then click the Picture Effects button on the Picture toolbar to display the Effects Gallery. Figure 10-14 shows the Effects Gallery with a series of settings sliders on the right to adjust each effect.

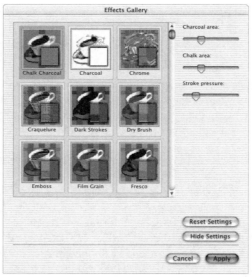

Figure 10-14. You can apply a variety of classical and modern styles to your graphics using the Effects Gallery.

2 Click the type of effect you want to apply.

3 If you don't see the sliders in the Effects Gallery dialog, click the Show Settings button. (If the settings are visible, this button becomes the Hide Settings button.)

4 Use the sliders to adjust the available settings for the effect you've chosen. The settings vary widely among effects, so you should feel free to experiment.

5 If you want to start over, click the Reset Settings button to put the sliders back to their default positions without closing the Effects Gallery.

6 When you've finished making your settings, click the Apply button to apply your changes and close the Effects Gallery. If you don't like the result, you can always undo the effect by pressing Command+Z.

Cropping and Cutting Out Images

If you don't want to change the size of an image and risk distorting it, you might want to cut away a portion of the image. You have two methods at your disposal: *cropping*, which lets you trim the edges of an image for a more pleasing composition, and *cutout*, which lets you select the portion of the image you want to keep, using the marquee selection tools. In both cases, you use the buttons on the Picture toolbar, which are described in Table 10-2.

> **note** You can use the picture tools on either the Formatting Palette or on the Picture toolbar to modify images. Because many (but not all) of the picture tools appear in both places, the Picture toolbar will only appear if the Formatting Palette is closed and when you have selected a graphic. In fact, if the Formatting Palette is open, the Picture option won't even appear when you choose View, Toolbars.

Table 10-2. The Picture Toolbar

Button	Name	Action
Format Picture...	Format Picture	Displays the Format Picture dialog.
	Free Rotate	Lets you rotate the selected picture through 360 degrees.
Picture Effects...	Picture Effects	Displays the Effects Gallery.
	Shadow	Displays a palette of shadows you can add to the selected object.
	Image Control	Lets you choose whether to format the image as an automatic color scheme, a grayscale image, a black and white image, or a watermark.
	More Contrast	Increases the contrast in the selected picture.
	Less Contrast	Decreases the contrast in the selected picture.

(continued)

Table 10-2. *(continued)*

Button	Name	Action
	More Brightness	Makes the selected image brighter.
	Less Brightness	Makes the selected image darker.
	Set Transparent Color	Renders pixels of the selected color transparent.
Color Adjustment	Color Adjustment	Displays the Color Adjustment dialog.
	Fix Red Eye	Detects and removes the "red eye" effect from flash photographs.
	Remove Scratch	Lets you smooth imperfections in the image.
	Crop	Lets you remove an edge or corner of an image by dragging a selection handle.
	Cutout	Lets you cut out an inner portion of a picture and discard the rest.
	Rectangular Marquee	Lets you select a rectangular portion of the image.
	Oval Marquee	Lets you select an oval portion of the image.
	Lasso	Lets you select a free-form portion of the image.
	Polygonal Lasso	Lets you select a polygonal portion of the image.
	Magic Lasso	Lets you select an area of similar color by clicking around the area and then cut out or edit the selected area.

To crop a portion of an image, follow these steps:

1 Select the image you want to edit, and then, on the Picture toolbar, click the Crop button.

2 The resulting Crop cursor operates on the handles of the image. Click and drag a handle to trim the image to your liking.

To cut out a portion of an image, follow these steps:

1 Select the image you want to edit.

2 Use any of the selection tools (the Rectangular Marquee, Oval Marquee, Lasso, Polygonal Lasso, or Magic Lasso) to select the portion of the image you want to keep.

3 Click the Cutout button on the Picture toolbar. Only the selected portion of the image is retained.

Adjusting the Colors of an Image

When you bring an image in from a scanner or other source, you might find that the colors of the image are slightly untrue because of the lighting used when the image was captured. Tungsten bulbs often produce a blue tint, and fluorescent bulbs often tend to green when not corrected for by your camera. If you do need to adjust the colors of your image, whether to correct for a flaw or to produce an effect, you can do so using the Color Adjustment dialog.

To adjust the colors of an image, follow these steps:

1 Select the image you want to edit, and then click the Color Adjustment button on the Picture toolbar to display the Color Adjustment dialog, shown in Figure 10-15.

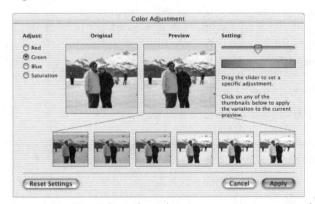

Figure 10-15. Adjust the colors in your pictures using the settings in the Color Adjustment dialog.

2 In the Adjust section of the dialog, select the option representing the aspect of the image's colors you want to change. When you select an option, the bar under the Setting slider will change to represent the range of available hues, and the previews at the bottom of the dialog will change to reflect the position of the slider. The following Adjust options are available:

- Red, which lets you change the balance between red and cyan.

- Green, which lets you change the balance between green and magenta.

- Blue, which lets you change the balance between blue and yellow.

- Saturation, which lets you change the depth or intensity of the colors in the image.

3 If the image starts looking worse than when you started, click the Reset Settings button to reset the dialog to its initial settings and start over.

4 When you've completed your adjustments, click the Apply button to apply your new settings and close the Color Adjustment dialog.

Inserting Watermarks

When you create a draft of a document, a version that's not meant to be distributed outside a certain group, it's often important that you mark the document so that everyone who handles it understands the information should not be made public. You can identify the status of the information in a document (e.g., "draft" or "proprietary") by adding a watermark to your document. A *watermark* is a light image that appears in the background of the printed page, behind the text, and imparts information without obscuring the document's contents. Oddly, you must insert a watermark into a header or footer, but the watermark isn't restricted to just the header or footer areas of your document; it can appear anywhere on the page.

To add a watermark to a document, follow these steps:

1 Choose View, Header And Footer to display the headers and footers in your document.

2 Click the Show/Hide Document Text button on the Header And Footer toolbar to hide the contents of the main document.

3 Insert the image (it can be a picture, a WordArt image, or an AutoShape) you want to use as your watermark, and then click the Close button on the Header And Footer toolbar. You can preview how your document will look when printed by viewing the document in Page Layout view or in Print Preview.

Troubleshooting

My watermark obscures the text in my document.

Adding a watermark to a document serves a variety of purposes, but none of them is to obscure the contents of the document! If you find the image you set as a watermark is too dark, you can lighten the image to fix the problem. If your watermark image contains text that is too dark, you can change the font color to a lighter shade. The same is true for the borders or internal lines of an object; if the lines are too dark, you can change the color to a lighter shade. If your watermark is an image, you can select the image (choose View, Header And Footer first), display the Picture tab of the Format Picture dialog, and lower the Brightness setting until the watermark is unobtrusive, yet still visible in your document.

Inserting Objects

Just as you can insert graphics and images into your document, you can add entire Word documents, or even files created with other programs. For example, if you were creating a project report and had some important data in an Excel spreadsheet, rather than print the spreadsheet separately and meld it with the printed report, it would be much easier to simply insert the worksheet into your Word document. With the Object dialog, you can do just that. You can also create a new, blank object and then double-click it in Word to begin editing it in its native program.

To insert a blank object into your document, follow these steps:

1 Choose Insert, Object to display the Object dialog, shown in Figure 10-16 on the next page, and then select the type of object you want to insert into your document.

2 Select the Display As Icon check box to have Word display the object as an icon reflecting the program used to create it (e.g., Microsoft Excel).

3 Click OK to insert the blank object into your file.

To insert an object based on an existing file into your document, follow these steps:

1 Choose Insert, Object to display the Object dialog, and then click the From File button to display the Insert As Object dialog.

2 Select the Display As Icon check box to display the file as an icon, or clear the check box to display the file in its own frame.

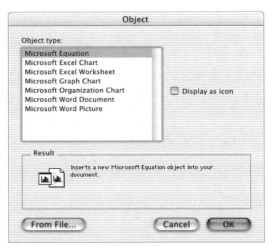

Figure 10-16. The Object dialog lets you insert files created with other programs into your document.

3 Follow either of these steps:

▨ Click the Insert button to insert a copy of the selected file into your document. Changes to this copy of the file will not be reflected in the original, and vice versa.

▨ Select the Link To File check box, and then click the Insert button to add a link to the file from within your document. Because you are creating a link to the original, all changes made to the linked file from within your document and from outside your document will be reflected.

> **tip** You can edit the contents of a linked or embedded file by viewing the document in Page Layout view and then double-clicking the file.

Using Microsoft Organization Chart

Whether you work in a large or small organization, it's important to maintain a record of the supervisory, managerial, and coworker relationships of the people in your group. Word lets you create and modify organization charts using the Microsoft Organization Chart helper application.

To add an organization chart using Microsoft Organization Chart, follow these steps:

1 Choose Insert, Object, to open the Object dialog, select Microsoft Organization Chart, and click OK to launch the Organization Chart helper application, shown in Figure 10-17.

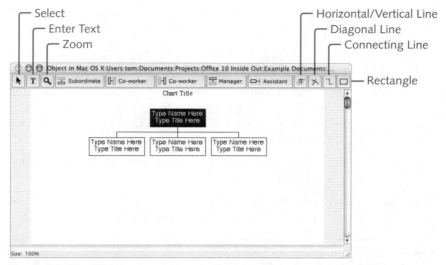

Figure 10-17. Diagram your organization or a process using the Microsoft Organization Chart helper application.

2 Follow any of these steps:

- To delete a box, select the box and then choose Edit, Clear.

- To edit the text in a box, select the box, click inside the box, and then, as desired, replace the <Name>, <Title>, <Comment 1>, and <Comment 2> markers with text. If you don't replace a marker (e.g., you don't put in any <Comment 2> text), it will be hidden when you click outside the box.

- To add a box below an existing box, select the box below which you want the new box to appear, and then click the Subordinate button. Then click the pointer in the box to add a box below it.

- To add a box to the left or right of an existing box, select the box beside where you want the new box to appear, and then click the left Co-Worker button to add a box on the left or the right Co-Worker button to add a box on the right. Then click in the box.

- To add a box above an existing box, select the box below where you want the new box to appear, and then click the Manager button. Then click in the box.

- To add a box that is attached to an existing box but does not represent a coworker, subordinate, or manager, select the box to which you want to attach the new box, and then click the Assistant button. Click the box, and a new box will be added below and to the left.

Chapter 10

▓ To draw a horizontal or vertical line on your organization chart, click the Horizontal/Vertical Line button, and then drag to define the line.

▓ To draw a diagonal line on your chart, click the Diagonal Line button, and then drag to define the line.

▓ To draw a dotted line between the edges of two boxes, click the Connecting Line button, click inside the edge of the box from which you want to draw the line, and then drag to the edge of the box to which you want to make the connection.

▓ To draw a rectangle in your chart, click the Rectangle button, and then drag to define the rectangle.

▓ To move a box, drag the box over its new manager or co-worker box. The connecting lines will be rearranged.

tip   You can use the Text, Boxes, and Lines menus to format each of those items.

3 When you are done with the organization chart, choose Organization Chart, Quit Organization Chart. If you see a dialog asking whether you want to Update the drawing, click Update. The helper application will close, and your organization chart will be placed into your Word document as a graphic. If you want to edit the chart later, double-click the graphic, and the Organization Chart program will reopen.

Chapter 11

Using Word's Proofing Tools

Whenever you create a document, it helps to have reference material at hand, whether you use your resources to look up facts or statistics, or to help you choose your words effectively. Although you can use other Microsoft Office documents, data on Web pages, or printed materials as sources for your writing, those references don't help you make your writing more clear.

Microsoft Word X includes a number of tools to help you make your writing easier to read, by ensuring your spelling and grammar are accurate, your vocabulary is sufficiently varied to make your document interesting, and your words are hyphenated correctly to make the lines flow more attractively without sacrificing intelligibility. You can check your spelling and grammar as you type, or you can wait until you're done with a draft of your document to check your work. In either case, you can choose whether to accept the suggested changes, ignore the suggestions, or make changes of your own. This chapter shows you how to use Word X's proofing and reference tools to make your documents of the highest quality.

Checking Spelling

Whenever you add text to a document in Word X, Word will identify as a spelling error any text it doesn't recognize. As shown in Figure 11-1, on the next page, Word underlines the text in question with a wavy red line. The indicator lines don't appear when you print the document; they're just there to help you correct any errors before you commit your words to paper.

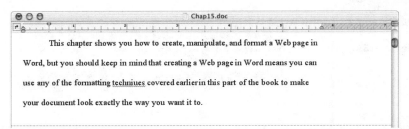

Figure 11-1. Word checks your document for spelling errors as you type. Word also marks potential grammatical errors, underlining them with wavy green lines.

> To find out how to hide the wavy lines so they don't distract you while you're typing, see "Setting Spelling Options," page 269.

Spelling And Grammar Status

When you have Word check your document for spelling and grammatical errors, the Spelling And Grammar Status icon appears on the status bar at the bottom of the Word window. The icon displays an X mark whenever there is a spelling or grammar error in your document. Even if you don't see an error on the portion of the document visible on your monitor, you should always glance at the bottom of the document window to see whether there is an error you haven't addressed.

Clicking the Spelling And Grammar Status icon highlights the first error in your document. The contextual menu that appears contains a list of suggested replacements for the highlighted word or phrase, an option to ignore the item if you want Word to bypass it, an AutoCorrect item you can select if you want to create an AutoCorrect entry for the misspelled term, and a Spelling command that opens the Spelling dialog or, for grammatical errors, a Grammar command to open the Grammar dialog.

Checking Spelling as You Type

One of the strengths of Word X is that you can set it up so you can deal with spelling errors whenever you want. If you prefer to address spelling errors when you make them, or perhaps after you finish typing a paragraph, you can have Word indicate the spelling errors as you type. Word indicates potential errors by underlining the text in question with a wavy red line; you can then edit the text manually or Control+click the underlined word to display a contextual menu with more options, as shown in Figure 11-2.

To have Word indicate spelling errors as you type, follow these steps:

1 Choose Word, Preferences to display the Preferences dialog.

2 Click the Spelling And Grammar category to display the Spelling preferences.

3 Select the Check Spelling As You Type check box to have Word underline spelling errors in your document, or clear the check box to have Word stop checking spelling as you type.

4 Click OK to close the Preferences dialog.

264

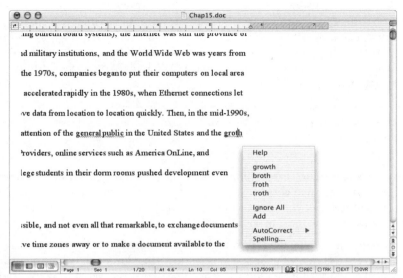

Figure 11-2. If you want to deal with spelling errors on a case-by-case basis, Control+click the word in question to display a contextual menu that provides tools to help you fix the error.

The contextual menu gives you the following options in dealing with the identified text:

● Choosing Help from the contextual menu displays the Microsoft Office Help dialog, which you can use to search for help on spelling and other topics.

> For more information on using Microsoft Office Help, see "Using the Help Index," page 38.

● Choosing one of the suggested replacement words that appears in the contextual menu will replace the misspelled word with the word you chose. This change only affects the word you clicked; if you misspell the same word later in the document, you'll need to change it separately.

> To correct the same misspelling throughout a document, see "Checking Spelling in the Whole Document," on the next page.

● Choosing Ignore All causes Word to overlook all occurrences of the indicated text in the document. Ignore All is perfect when you intentionally misspell a word or use a foreign word or unusual abbreviation. The spelling checker will ignore the word in the rest of the document without adding it to the dictionary so that you can catch the error in your next document.

> **tip**   Ignore All is also great for proper names that Word flags as misspelled but that you don't want to add to a custom dictionary.

Chapter 11

- Choosing Add instructs Word to add the term it identified to a custom dictionary. By default, Word creates a custom dictionary, snappily named Custom Dictionary, to which you can add terms. You can also create your own custom dictionaries, as discussed in "Adding Words to a Custom Dictionary," page 271.

> **note** The custom dictionary lives in the Users/*username*/Library/Preferences/Microsoft folder on your hard disk.

- Pointing to AutoCorrect on the contextual menu displays a submenu with a list of suggested corrections. Choosing a word in the submenu will create an AutoCorrect entry that will in the future cause Word to automatically replace the misspelling with the word you chose from the submenu.

- Choosing Spelling tells Word to display the Spelling dialog. You can use the controls in the Spelling dialog to perform additional actions or change your Word spelling options. The Spelling dialog is covered in more detail in the next section.

Checking Spelling in the Whole Document

Although you might prefer to deal with potential spelling errors as you type, you might instead find it more convenient to wait until you finish writing to address any spelling errors. Tackling your spelling check after you are done writing lets you keep more "in the flow" when you create your text—no distracting spelling error notifications. You can also save time by using the controls in the Spelling And Grammar dialog, shown in Figure 11-3, to identify any unrecognizable but correct words in your document so Word will bypass the terms as it moves through your document.

To check the spelling in an entire document, choose Tools, Spelling And Grammar, and then choose the appropriate option for each item presented to you:

- Click the Ignore button to have Word overlook the current misspelling but identify identical misspellings elsewhere in the document.

- Click the Ignore All button to have Word overlook every occurrence of the highlighted misspelling. Names of foreign leaders and of corporations you never expect to type again are excellent candidates for Ignore All. Plus, if you manage to misspell the word a different way later in the document, Word will alert you to your error.

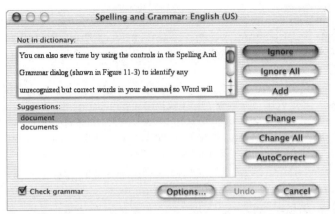

Figure 11-3. Use the controls in the Spelling And Grammar dialog to choose how to handle each item Word perceives as an error.

- Click the Add button to add the word to the current custom dictionary. Unlike Ignore and Ignore All, which only apply to the active document, adding a term to a custom dictionary means that every time you check the spelling of any document while the dictionary to which you added the term is open, Word will accept the spelling.

> **note** The custom dictionary is shared by all of the Office v. X applications, so when you've added an entry in one program, that fix will be shared by the others.

- Click the Change button to have Word replace the highlighted word in the Not In Dictionary box with the highlighted word in the Suggestions list. If the suggestion Word highlights when it encounters the misspelled text isn't the word you want to replace the error, you can identify the term you want Word to substitute for the highlighted text by clicking the term in the Suggestions list before clicking Change.

- Click the Change All button to have Word replace every instance of the highlighted text in the Not In Dictionary box with the highlighted term in the Suggestions list. As with all global operations, it's vital that you are certain you want to replace every instance of the highlighted term.

> **note** Word does protect against unintentional mass changes, as is possible with Find/ Replace, by only changing every instance of the exact term it believes is misspelled. If the text happens to be part of a longer word, Word will not change the longer word.

Chapter 11

- Click the AutoCorrect button to have Word create an AutoCorrect entry, which means that whenever you type the misspelled term in the future, AutoCorrect will automatically replace it with the selected term in the Suggestions list.

- Click the Options button to display the Spelling And Grammar pane of the Preferences dialog. The Spelling And Grammar pane, shown later in this section in Figure 11-4, lets you change how Word handles spelling and grammar checking. The controls in this pane of the Preferences dialog are detailed in "Setting Spelling Options," opposite.

- Click the Undo button to have Word reverse the last change you made and highlight the term so you can handle it differently.

- Click the Cancel button (or the Close button that replaces it once you've made your first spelling change) to close the Spelling dialog and return to the document. Note that any changes you made while the Spelling dialog was open will remain in force.

When you're done, a message box will appear indicating the spelling check is complete. Click OK to close the box.

---

tip   **Interrupt spelling check to make edits and then resume**

Sometimes inspiration will strike while you're checking the spelling of a document and you'll just have to change some text or add a few thoughts to the existing text. You have two options if you want to edit the text in your document while you are checking spelling and grammar. The spelling dialog isn't modal; therefore, you can click in the main document window and edit its contents directly. When you're ready to restart the spelling check, click the title bar of the Spelling dialog and then click the Resume button (which appears in place of the Ignore button). Alternatively, if the text you want to edit appears in the Not In Dictionary box of the Spelling dialog, click in the pane and edit the text directly. When you're done, either click the Change button to accept your change, or click the Undo Edit button (which, again, appears in place of the Ignore button) to reject your change.

Checking Spelling in Part of a Document

To check the spelling of part of a document, follow these steps:

1 Select the text you want to check and then choose Tools, Spelling And Grammar.

---

tip   Remember that if you need to select a large amount of text, it's usually easier to click at the start of the text, scroll to the end of the text you want to select, hold down the Shift key, and then click after the last word you want to select.

---

2 Use the controls in the Spelling And Grammar dialog (as displayed in Figure 11-3 and described in the previous section) to proof the selected text.

3 After you've checked the selected text, Word will display a dialog asking whether you want to continue checking the rest of the document. Clicking the No button will stop the spelling check whereas clicking the Yes button will have Word continue checking the rest of the document.

---

tip   **Skip checking a section of your document**

Just as you can have Word check the spelling of selected portions of your document, you can also have Word ignore sections of your document. To exclude a section from a spelling and grammar check, select the text to be ignored, choose Tools, Language, and then, in the Language dialog, click *(no proofing)*, the first item in the list. Click OK to finalize the operation. This technique is especially helpful when you have tables in your document with lots of text that Word would otherwise flag as errors.

Setting Spelling Options

Depending on the characteristics of the documents you produce, you might want to change how Word goes about proofing your documents. You can change the behavior of the spelling checker through the Spelling And Grammar pane of the Preferences dialog, which is shown in Figure 11-4.

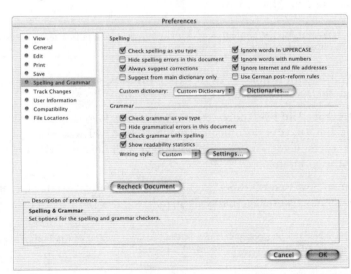

Figure 11-4. If you want to change how Word handles spelling and grammar errors in your documents, use the controls in the Spelling And Grammar pane of the Preferences dialog to specify the desired behaviors.

Chapter 11

To set the spelling options in Word X, choose Word, Preferences, and then click Spelling And Grammar in the left pane of the Preferences dialog. Then select any (or all) of these options:

- **Check Spelling As You Type.** Word underlines any spelling errors it detects in your document.

- **Hide Spelling Errors In This Document.** Word looks for spelling errors in the document but will not put wavy red lines underneath errors it detects.

- **Always Suggest Corrections.** Word lists a series of potential replacements for a misspelled word in the Suggestions list of the Spelling dialog, as shown in Figure 11-3 on page 267.

note Even if you clear the Always Suggest Corrections check box, Word will still display a list of suggested alternatives when you Control+click a word with a wavy red line underneath it.

- **Suggest From Main Dictionary Only.** Word does not consider alternative words from any custom dictionaries you have attached to the active document.

- **Ignore Words In UPPERCASE.** Word skips over any terms it finds with all capital letters. This option, which is set by default, is great if your document contains a lot of acronyms.

For information on creating a custom dictionary with acronyms you use frequently, see "Adding Words to a Custom Dictionary," opposite.

- **Ignore Words With Numbers.** Word skips any terms, such as addresses, phone numbers, or sales results, that contain numbers.

- **Ignore Internet And File Addresses.** Word skips any Web site addresses or file locations in your documents. This check box, which is selected by default, is useful if you create a Web document with links to Web sites or files on other computers.

- **Use German Post-Reform Rules.** Word follows German post-reform spelling rules for any text that contains German.

For information on using the dictionary settings in the Spelling section of the Preferences dialog, see "Assigning a Dictionary to a Document," page 273.

Working with Dictionaries

When you install Word, you install the dictionary for your local language. The spelling checker uses that dictionary when you examine a document for spelling errors. The dictionary does not contain every word in the English language, so if you work in a specialized field, such as the law or a physical science, you'll find that many terms you use won't appear in the main dictionary and will be flagged as errors. To avoid a litany of errors that aren't really errors, you can create custom dictionaries containing the specialized terms you use in your profession. You can also share these custom dictionaries with colleagues.

Adding Words to a Custom Dictionary

Besides the main dictionary, Word comes with a custom dictionary, ready for you to add your own specialized words. You'll likely add such words to the custom dictionary as proper names, technical terms, and words specific to your business.

To add a word to a custom dictionary, follow these steps:

1 Choose Word, Preferences to open the Preferences dialog, and then click the Spelling And Grammar category.

2 In the Spelling section of the Preferences dialog, click the Dictionaries button to display the Custom Dictionaries dialog, shown in Figure 11-5.

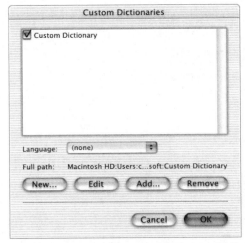

Figure 11-5. You can use the options in the Custom Dictionaries dialog to create and manipulate specialized word lists to facilitate spelling checking.

3 Select the dictionary to which you want to add a new word, and then click the Edit button to open the dictionary as a Word document. Then, with the dictionary open in its own Word document window, type each term you want to add on its own line in the dictionary.

4 When you're done adding terms to the custom dictionary, choose File, Save to save your changes. If a dialog appears notifying you that the document has some formatting that can't be saved in text format, click Save to acknowledge that you know the formatting won't be saved. After the dialog disappears, choose File, Close to close the dictionary.

5 Click the Close button twice to close the Custom Dictionaries dialog and the Preferences dialog.

Creating a New Dictionary

To create a new custom dictionary, follow these steps:

1 Choose Word, Preferences.

2 Select the Spelling And Grammar category to display the Spelling And Grammar pane of the dialog. Then, in the Spelling section of the dialog, click the Dictionaries button to display the Custom Dictionaries dialog.

3 Click the New button to open the New Dictionary dialog, which is a specialized Save dialog. Use the options in the dialog, shown in Figure 11-6, to name the new dictionary and specify the folder where it should be stored. When you're done, click the Save button.

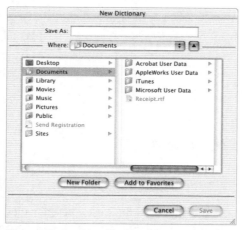

Figure 11-6. Use the New Dictionary dialog to name and assign a home to your new dictionary.

To learn how to add entries to the dictionary manually, see "Adding Words to a Custom Dictionary," page 271.

Assigning a Dictionary to a Document

You can choose which custom dictionaries to use to check a particular document. To add a dictionary to the list of dictionaries used to check spelling in a document, follow these steps:

1 Open the document to which you want to assign the dictionary, and then choose Word, Preferences to display the Preferences dialog.

2 Select the Spelling And Grammar category.

3 Click the Dictionaries button to display the Custom Dictionaries dialog.

4 Select the check box next to the name of each custom dictionary you want to use in checking the spelling of words in the active document.

InsideOut

Remove custom dictionaries without deleting them

To remove a dictionary from the list of dictionaries used to check a document's spelling, clear the check box next to the dictionary's name in the Custom Dictionaries dialog. Don't click the Remove button. If you click the Remove button, Word will delete the custom dictionary from your list of custom dictionaries (but does not delete the custom dictionary from your hard disk). If you wanted to use that dictionary again, you would have to use the Add button in the dialog to make the dictionary reappear in the dialog's list.

Checking Spelling in Foreign Languages

Unless you're a professional translator, you will probably spend most of your time working with text in your native language, or at least the language set as the default for your computer. If you do need to include some foreign language text in a document, you can identify the text's language so the spelling checker won't flag most of the words as errors.

caution Word won't actually check the spelling of foreign language text unless you've installed the dictionary for the text's language. For information on installing foreign language proofing tools, see the next section of this chapter.

Chapter 11

To identify foreign language text, follow these steps:

1 Select the text you want to identify as foreign language text.

2 Choose Tools, Language to display the Language dialog, shown in Figure 11-7.

Figure 11-7. The Language dialog contains a list of languages Word recognizes. Choosing one of the languages in the list while text is selected in the main document window marks the selected text as being in the specified language.

3 Select the language you want from the Mark Selected Text As list, and then click OK.

---

tip **Set the default language for spelling**

Clicking the Default button in the Language dialog changes the default language setting for all documents created using the active template (usually the Normal template found in the Templates folder). A confirmation dialog appears after you click the Default button, asking whether you're sure you want to change the default language for documents created with the template.

Installing Foreign Language Proofing Tools

If you work with a variety of languages in your documents, you might need to proof text in several languages. The default installation of Word X comes with a spelling dictionary, hyphenation guide, and thesaurus for your local language, but it doesn't include those proofing tools for other languages. Fortunately, the Microsoft Office X Value Pack, which comes on the Office v. X CD, does contain proofing tools for Danish, Dutch, English, French, German, Italian, Japanese, Norwegian, Spanish, and Swedish. You can install any or all of these foreign language proofing tools using the Value Pack Installer.

To install foreign language proofing tools from the Office v. X CD, follow these steps:

1 Insert the Microsoft Office v. X CD into your computer's CD-ROM drive, and then double-click the CD's icon when it appears on your desktop.

2 Double-click the Value Pack folder icon.

3 Double-click Value Pack Installer to run the installation program.

4 Select the Proofing Tools check box in the Value Pack Installer dialog. You could also click the disclosure triangle to the left of Proofing Tools to display check boxes for each available language. The expanded list is shown in Figure 11-8. The total size required for all proofing tools files is less than one-tenth of a megabyte, so you should probably go ahead and install all of the files at once.

Figure 11-8. If you don't want to install proofing files for every available language, you can select the check boxes next to the languages for the ones you want.

5 Click the Continue button to install the proofing tools. A progress box will appear with information on the installation's progress. When the installation finishes, the Value Pack Installer will display a message box asking whether you want to install any other files. Click Quit to exit the installer, or click Continue to choose other files to install.

> **note** Installing every file from the Value Pack takes up about 400 megabytes, so if you have room available on your disk, you might consider installing every extra file from the Value Pack.

Checking Grammar

Just as you can check the spelling of a Word document, you can also have Word identify and suggest corrections for common grammatical errors. You can display a list of the categories of grammatical rules Word uses to evaluate your document by displaying the Spelling And Grammar pane of the Preferences dialog, as shown in Figure 11-9. When Word locates a grammatical error in a document, it indicates the offending word or phrase by underlining it with a wavy green line.

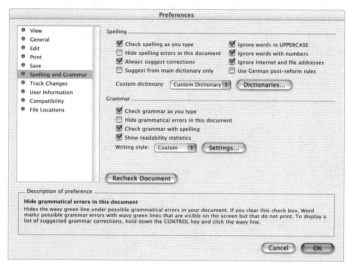

Figure 11-9.   You can use these options to specify how Word evaluates the grammar in your document.

Setting Grammar Checking Options

To set the way Word checks the grammar of your documents, follow these steps:

1 Choose Word, Preferences to display the Preferences dialog.

2 Select Spelling And Grammar in the left pane of the dialog to display the Spelling And Grammar pane, and then select any of these options:

- **Check Grammar As You Type.** Word underlines any passages that contain a grammatical error with a wavy green line as you type.

- **Hide Grammatical Errors In This Document.** Word refrains from marking any grammatical errors with a wavy green line. Word will still detect any errors, but won't mark them in the document.

- **Check Grammar With Spelling.** Word highlights grammatical errors as well as spelling errors in the Spelling And Grammar dialog.

■ **Show Readability Statistics.** Word displays measures of the document's readability after you complete your spelling and grammar check as shown here:

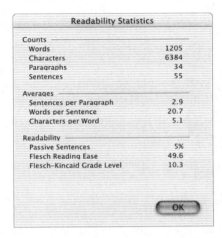

■ **Settings.** This button displays the Grammar Settings dialog. You can use this dialog to select the rules by which the grammar checker evaluates your document, as described in the next section.

Customizing Grammar Settings

To customize your desired settings for the Word grammar checker, follow these steps:

1 Choose Word, Preferences, and then select Spelling And Grammar in the left pane of the Preferences dialog.

2 Ensure the Check Grammar With Spelling check box is selected, and then click the Settings button to display the Grammar Settings dialog, shown in Figure 11-10 on the next page.

3 Open the Writing Style pop-up menu, and then choose the style you want Word to use to evaluate your document.

4 Select the check box next to each option in the Grammar And Style Options pane to have Word check for violations of that category of rules. Clear a check box to instruct Word to ignore the rules in the category.

5 In the Require section of the dialog, open the pop-up menu next to any of the listed rules and then select Always to have Word call out every instance that violates the rule.

6 Click the Reset All button to restore all grammar rules to their default settings, click the Cancel button to close the dialog without saving any settings you changed while the dialog was open, or click OK to save your new settings.

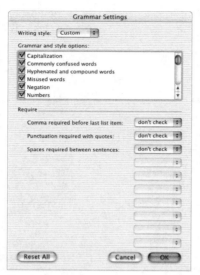

Figure 11-10. You can choose which categories of grammatical errors Word will test for when it evaluates your text.

Checking Grammar in the Whole Document

To check the grammar of your entire document in one pass, choose Tools, Spelling And Grammar, and then choose the appropriate option for each word or phrase presented to you:

- Click Ignore to have Word remove the wavy green line from underneath the marked text. When you check the document for grammatical errors in the future, Word will bypass the marked word or phrase.

- Click Ignore All to have Word ignore all instances of the error type, such as Subject-Verb Agreement, that is displayed above the upper box of the Spelling And Grammar dialog. You should note that clicking Ignore All will cause Word to ignore every instance of the displayed rule, not just the specific text displayed in the upper box.

- Click Next Sentence to skip the error displayed in the dialog without changing it.

- Click Change to replace the highlighted text with the text that appears in the Suggestions box.

- Clear the Check Grammar check box to turn off grammar checking.

- Click Options to display the Spelling And Grammar pane of the Preferences dialog.

- Click Undo to reverse the last grammatical change you made. The previous error and any suggestions appear in the dialog, and the error is marked with a wavy green underline in the document.

- Click Cancel to close the Spelling And Grammar dialog. All of the changes you made remain in effect.

Rechecking a Document

When you proof a document, you have the option of ignoring one or every instance of a spelling or grammatical error. One circumstance where you might ignore some errors is if you're creating a first draft of the document and you're not sure of the proper spelling of all terms in the file. In some cases, such as when you're writing about new products, the name of the product might not even be set until just before you create the final version of your document. In any case, you can reset your document so Word will find any potential errors you chose to ignore in previous passes through the file.

To recheck a document for spelling and grammar errors, follow these steps:

1 Choose Word, Preferences to display the Preferences dialog.

2 Select the Spelling And Grammar category.

3 Click the Recheck Document button. A message box appears, asking you to confirm that you want to recheck in the next pass through the document all grammar and spelling errors you had previously ignored.

4 Click the Yes button to close the message box, and then click OK to close the Preferences dialog.

5 Choose Tools, Spelling And Grammar to start rechecking the document.

Enriching Your Word Choices with the Thesaurus

Good spelling and grammar are vital to making a document readable, but you should also pay close attention to your word choice. If you find a word you've typed doesn't quite impart the meaning you'd like it to, you can click the term in question and then use the Thesaurus to find related words. You can search for *synonyms,* which have the same meaning (or, more precisely, almost the same meaning) as the selected word, or *antonyms,* which mean the opposite of the selected word.

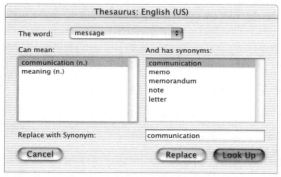

---

tip   **Use consistent terminology**

When you're preparing a technical or instructional document, it's imperative that you use consistent terminology to refer to items you're describing. Even in fiction, using too many terms to refer to the same character can be confusing, as in the following passage: *The captain walked onto the main deck of the boat, unsure of the best course to take. "Will the storm blow past us?" Steve wondered. The blond man shrugged.* Is Steve the captain? And just how many people are there in the scene?

To replace a word in your document with a synonym or antonym, follow these steps:

1   Place the insertion point anywhere in the word you want to replace.

2   Choose Tools, Thesaurus to display the Thesaurus dialog, shown in Figure 11-11.

Figure 11-11.   You can use the Thesaurus to search for the perfect word to communicate your desired meaning.

3   Click a term in the Can Mean pane of the dialog to display a list of related terms. Many words can have a variety of meanings, some of which may be different parts of speech (for example, *good* can be a noun describing a thing for sale or an adjective indicating something is of high quality), so the Thesaurus lists the range of words, including part of speech, in the Can Mean pane. If the word you selected in the document is a descriptive word, the last item in the Can Mean dialog will be *antonym*. Clicking *antonym* will list words with meanings opposite the selected word (no, the label at the top of the And Has Synonyms list doesn't change, but the Replace With Synonym box does change to Replace With Antonym).

---

tip   **Use the contextual menu to get synonyms**

You can also display a list of synonyms for a word by Control+clicking the word in your document. The contextual menu that appears will include a submenu of synonyms as well as a Thesaurus command, which you can select to open the Thesaurus dialog.

---

4 Click a word in the And Has Synonyms pane to choose it to replace the term you selected in your document. You can then click the Replace button to substitute the selected word in the And Has Synonyms pane for the selected word in the document, click the Look Up button to display synonyms for the selected word in the And Has Synonyms pane, or click the Cancel button to close the Thesaurus dialog.

---

tip   If you're not sure of the meaning of a word in your document, you can click anywhere in the word and then choose Tools, Dictionary to display the word's definition.

---

caution   When you write text in a language in which you have a limited vocabulary, it can be tempting to turn to a dictionary or thesaurus for that language and substitute words from the definition or listing. *Don't do it!* Most of the time you'll choose a word with a meaning that's sufficiently different from the original to obscure your meaning.

Hyphenating Your Documents Automatically

When you create a document in Word, you should take care to ensure the contents of the document conform to the standards of your company, institution, or organization. Some organizations require authors to use hyphens to break up words that would spill onto the next printed line. A holdover from the days of manual typewriters, hyphenation is rarely required when you create a document using a word processor program such as Word. Even so, if you do need to hyphenate a document, you can do so in Word X.

Troubleshooting

Word breaks hyphenated text where I don't want it to.

One idiosyncrasy in how Word deals with hyphenated text is that it will always break text at the hyphen if any of the characters to the right of the hyphen won't fit on the line. However, there are some pieces of information, such as phone numbers, which you should always keep on the same line, even if that means moving the entire hyphenated phrase to the next line of the document. You can type a *nonbreaking hyphen,* which Word won't use as a break point, by pressing Command+Shift+hyphen.

You can find more information on other special characters, such as nonbreaking spaces, in "Inserting Symbols," page 90.

To automatically hyphenate the contents of your document, follow these steps:

1 Choose Tools, Hyphenation to display the Hyphenation dialog, shown in Figure 11-12.

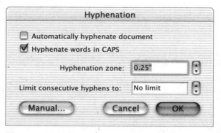

Figure 11-12. The settings in the Hyphenation dialog box control the extent of hyphenation; increased hyphenation evens the right edge of the text in non-justified text, and it evens the spaces between words in justified text.

2 Select the Automatically Hyphenate Document check box to have Word hyphenate the contents of your document.

3 Select the Hyphenate Words In CAPS check box to have Word also analyze acronyms and other words in all capital letters for potential hyphenation.

4 In the Hyphenation Zone box, type the maximum allowable space to leave between the last word on a line and the right margin. If the value in the Hyphenation Zone box is 0.25", Word will attempt to fill a space larger than 0.25" by hyphenating the word on the next line and bringing part of it to the end of the current line.

5 In the Limit Consecutive Hyphens To box, type the maximum number of consecutive lines that you want to have hyphens at the right margin. The default setting is for there to be no limit. Good practice is to limit consecutive hyphens to 2 or 3, to keep the text easy to read.

6 Click the Manual button to have Word identify each potential hyphenation. You will have the opportunity to change the position of the hyphen, to select which hyphen the word is broken after (if the word contains more than two syllables), or to bypass the instance altogether.

7 Click OK to close the Hyphenation dialog and save your new settings, or click Cancel to close the dialog without saving your changes.

Getting Word Counts

In many forms of writing, you'll be asked to write either a minimum or maximum number of words, characters, or lines. For example, you might be writing a conference paper that will be included in the conference proceedings. Because publishers of proceedings often need to keep costs in check, they will usually put an upper bound on the number of pages for each paper. You could also be writing an article for a magazine or online publication and be asked to produce a minimum number of words. Whatever the reason, you can find out how many words, characters, paragraphs, or lines of text are in a document or a portion of a document by using Word Count.

Word Count actually manifests itself in two ways—as the Live Word Count, displayed on the status bar at the bottom of the document window, and in the Word Count dialog. The Live Word Count displays two values: the position in the document of the word to the left of the insertion point, and the total number of words in the document. Word updates the counts as you type.

—Total word count of document
—Insertion point location

The Word Count dialog, shown in Figure 11-13, displays more complete information about the contents of your document.

To count the words in your document, follow these steps:

1 Choose Tools, Word Count to display the Word Count dialog.

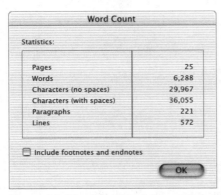

Figure 11-13. The Word Count dialog shows you statistics describing your document, which you can use to determine whether your document is of sufficient length or needs to be cut.

2 Select the Include Footnotes And Endnotes check box to have Word count the words in any references you have included in your document.

3 Click OK to close the Word Count dialog.

Counting Words in Part of a Document

To count the words in a portion of your document, follow these steps:

1 Select the text for which you want a word count.

2 Choose Tools, Word Count to display the Word Count dialog. The count reflects only the selected text.

3 Click OK to close the Word Count dialog.

Turning Live Word Count On or Off

To turn Live Word Count off or on, follow these steps:

1 Choose Word, Preferences to display the Preferences dialog.

2 Click the View category to display the View pane of the dialog, shown in Figure 11-14.

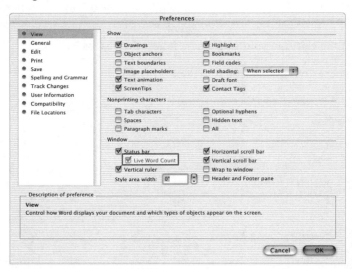

Figure 11-14. You can turn Live Word Count on and off with the controls in the View pane of the Preferences dialog.

3 Select the Live Word Count check box to turn on Live Word Count, or clear the check box to turn it off.

Mastering Large or Specialized Documents

When you begin to work on longer documents, such as books, annual reports, dissertations, and so forth, you'll discover that you need additional tools to deal with the additional complexity required of such documents. For example, a book requires a table of contents and an index, and scholarly writing usually requires elements such as footnotes. Fortunately for us, Microsoft Word X is up to the task.

In this chapter, you'll learn how to use Word's outlines to create, structure, and restructure your documents; how to use master documents to consolidate many documents into a unified whole; and how to generate indexes and tables of contents. Along the way, we'll also touch on several other tools that will help you tame long or specialized documents.

Building Documents from Outlines

Big documents need serious organization and structure. You are already familiar with one kind of structuring tool, the table of contents, as seen in virtually all books. It's easy to think of a table of contents as something that is generated after all the writing is done, and indeed you can do that with Word. But for most writers who are thinking of writing a book, creating a table of contents at the beginning of the writing process provides an indispensable roadmap for the structure of their book. Word's outlining features provide an excellent set of tools for creating tables of contents and defining the structure of your book (or any other long document).

For more information on creating tables of contents, see "Generating Tables of Contents and Indexes," page 305.

Why are outlines so great? It turns out that your high school English teacher was right all those years ago; outlines are heaven-sent for the organizationally impaired. The effort that you spend developing your thoughts in the outline will be amply repaid when it comes time to actually write your document. Word's Outline view is one of the most tragically underused of Word's features, yet paradoxically it can be of great help throughout the writing process. For example, the table of contents for this book was created in Outline view, and went through several drafts. As changes were proposed and accepted, headings and even entire chapters were added, deleted, and moved around. At least one chapter was extensively restructured after having been written, by using the Outline view to rearrange parts of the document. Outlines, in short, give you more control over creating your document, and more control over editing it, in the following ways:

- **Structural visibility** means that you see the headings in your document hierarchically arranged, with less important headings (called the *subheadings*) indented. By seeing the hierarchical structure of your document, you can easily see if you have arranged the document most effectively.

- **Detail control** allows you to show or hide headings, subheadings, and *subtext* (either subheadings or text without a heading style attached to it), which enables you to shift your focus from the overall organization of the document down to the details.

- **Editing flexibility** allows you to move entire headings around in your document, and any text or subheadings under that heading will move as well. You can promote or demote headings, according to their importance.

Applying Outline Levels to Text

When you switch to Outline view by choosing View, Outline, or by clicking the Outline View button at the bottom of the document window, the document window changes to show the document as an outline, and the Outlining toolbar appears, as shown in Figure 12-1.

The headings in Outline view correspond to Word's built-in heading styles, Heading 1 through Heading 9. The Heading 1 style is at the highest level, and is not indented. The Heading 2 style is indented slightly to the right, indicating that it is subordinate to the Heading 1 style. Each subsequent heading is further indented. Body text refers to any paragraph displayed in Outline view that has not been assigned a heading style. Word displays small icons to the left of each paragraph that tell you information about that paragraph. A plus sign indicates that it is a heading with subtext. A minus sign means the heading does not have any subtext. And a small box means that the paragraph is body text.

For more information about Word's built-in styles, see "Understanding Styles," page 160.

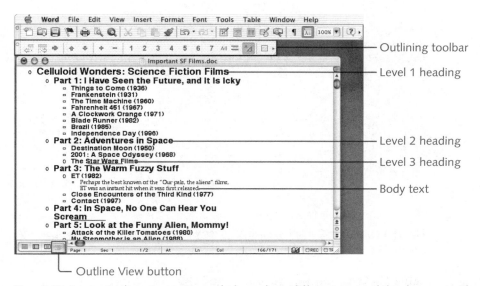

Figure 12-1. In Outline view, you can hide or show different parts of the document; the symbols before each heading indicate whether or not subheadings and subtext are hidden.

note When your document is displayed in Outline view, the content and formatting of your document doesn't actually change. Word is simply displaying the document in a different way. However, any paragraph formatting will be hidden, because the Outline view shows text in a simplified, single-spaced format.

If you're working with text that already exists in a document, and you have applied Word's built-in headings as you created the document, the document will appear with all the appropriate indents in Outline view. If you haven't already assigned headings, the easiest way to do so is to go through your document and apply heading styles by clicking in a paragraph, and then choosing the heading style you want from the Style pop-up menu in the Font section of the Formatting Palette.

When you first start typing in a blank outline, your words are formatted at the highest level in the outline, which is Heading 1. Pressing Return at the end of each heading creates a new heading. By default, Word creates the same level heading as the one you just entered, but at any time, you can *promote* a heading (thereby making it more important) or *demote* a heading (making it less important). To demote a heading, click anywhere in the heading and then press Tab; press Shift+Tab to promote a heading. You can also promote or demote a heading by pressing Shift+Tab or Tab after you press Return to create a new heading, but before you begin typing the new heading's text.

tip If you want to insert a Tab character into your outline's text, rather than use the Tab to demote a heading, press Control+Tab.

Chapter 12

2: Word

If you prefer, you can use the Outlining toolbar, as shown in Figure 12-2, to promote or demote headings, to rearrange headings in the outline, or to show particular heading levels; Table 12-1 describes the buttons on the toolbar and their keyboard equivalents.

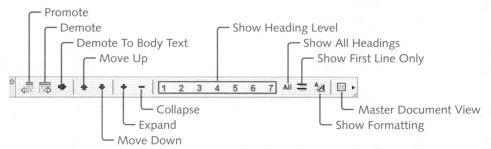

Figure 12-2.   The Outlining toolbar gives you great control over the headings in the outline.

Table 12-1. Outlining Toolbar Buttons

Button	Action	Keyboard Shortcut
Promote	Promotes a paragraph to a higher level	Control+Shift+Left Arrow
Demote	Demotes a paragraph to a lower level	Control+Shift+Right Arrow
Demote To Body Text	Demotes a heading to a lower level	None
Move Up	Moves a heading toward the top of the document	Control+Shift+Up Arrow
Move Down	Moves a heading toward the end of the document	Control+Shift+Down Arrow
Expand	Makes all text and subheadings after a heading visible	Control+Shift+equal sign
Collapse	Collapses a paragraph so that only the heading shows	Control+Shift+minus sign
Show Heading Level 1 through 7	Controls how many levels of the outline are displayed	Control+Shift+1 through Control+Shift+7
Show All Headings	Shows all the heading levels; clicking this button again after all headings are displayed toggles the display of body text	Control+Shift+A

Table 12-1. *(continued)*

Button	Action	Keyboard Shortcut
Show First Line Only	Saves space by showing only the first line of text entries	Control+Shift+L
Show Formatting	Toggles the character formatting shown in Outline view	None
Master Document View	Switches to Master Document view, and displays the Master Document toolbar	None

Expanding and Collapsing Outlines

One of the great things about outlines is that you can expand and collapse headings and subheadings so that you can view as much or as little of your outline as you desire. Word makes it easy to expand and collapse the topics in your outline:

- To expand a topic, click the heading to make sure it is selected, and then perform one of the following actions: click the Expand button on the Outlining toolbar, double-click the plus sign to the left of the heading, or press Control+Shift+equal sign.

- To collapse a topic that has already been expanded, click the heading to make sure it is selected, and then do one of the following: click the Collapse button on the Outlining toolbar, double-click the plus sign to the left of the heading, or press Control+Shift+minus sign.

InsideOut

Understand the different expand method behaviors

Double-clicking a plus sign in an outline and using the Expand and Collapse buttons work slightly differently. If you double-click a plus sign, all the levels under the current heading will be displayed (or hidden, if the subtext is already expanded). But clicking the Expand button expands the subtext one level at a time. The Collapse button also works one level at a time.

Moving Headings

Another tool for working with outlines is the ability to rearrange the headings and subheadings, which allows you to restructure your document in a flash. In fact, one of the easiest ways to make major revisions to a document is to switch to Outline view, move headings and subtext around, and then switch back to Normal or Page Layout view to do the detailed revisions.

To move headings, you can use keyboard shortcuts or the Outlining toolbar. But most of the time, you'll probably want to use the mouse to drag headings around, because it's the fastest method, allows you to promote or demote headings immediately after moving them, and gives you instant feedback.

Moving Topics Up and Down

To move part of an outline to an earlier point in your document or closer to the end of the document, you can use the Outlining toolbar's Move Up and Move Down buttons. Begin by selecting the entire part that you want to move, and then click Move Up to move the selection up one heading. If needed, continue pressing the Move Up button until the selection is where you want it. Use the same procedure to move a selection down, except, of course, use the Move Down button.

> **tip** **Move just one heading**
>
> If you want to move one heading only, and not an entire topic, click in the heading before choosing Move Up or Move Down. Word will move only the selected heading and will leave subheadings and subtext in place.

Once you get used to moving headings up and down, you might find it quicker to use keyboard shortcuts instead of the buttons on the Outlining toolbar. Refer to Table 12-1 on page 288 for the keyboard equivalents to the Move Up and Move Down buttons.

Dragging Topics to a New Location

To move headings around in an outline using the mouse, use the little icons next to each heading as handles:

● To move the heading up or down in the outline, click the icon to the left of the heading, and drag the heading where you want it in the document. As you drag, the pointer changes, showing a small box with a double-headed arrow, and a text insertion bar moves from line to line, showing you where the selection will be inserted when you release the mouse button, as shown in Figure 12-3.

● To promote or demote a heading, click the icon to the left of the heading and drag the heading to the right or to the left. As you drag, the pointer changes, showing a small box with a double-headed arrow (but this time the arrows point right and left), and a vertical text insertion bar moves from one level of heading indentation to the next.

Figure 12-3. You can move, promote, or demote headings simply by dragging them.

---

tip   **Move the parent topics; the children will follow**

Before you drag topics around, use the Show Heading Level buttons on the Outlining toolbar to show only high-level headings. You'll be able to display more of your outline on the screen and you'll have to drag what you're moving a shorter distance. Even though you're moving the high-level headings, any subheadings and subtext will move along with the heading.

InsideOut

Restart Word if you can't drag topics in Outline view

Because of what appears to be a bug in Word, sometimes while you are working on a document in Outline view the ability to drag headings up and down will stop working. You can still drag headings right and left to promote and demote them, but when you try to drag a heading up or down Word simply selects the text, rather than moving the heading.

The workaround is to save your document, quit Word, and then relaunch Word and reopen your document. This snaps Word out of its momentary confusion and allows you to begin dragging headings up and down again.

Chapter 12

Numbering Your Outline

Some outlines require numbering of topics; for example, the paragraphs in contracts are often numbered. Or you might want to add numbers in long documents while they're in their draft stages, so that people reviewing them can easily refer to specific parts of the document ("I had no idea what you were talking about in paragraph 76."). Word provides seven preset outline numbering styles; you can also create your own.

To add numbers to an outline you've already created, follow these steps:

1 If necessary, switch to Outline view.

2 Choose Format, Bullets And Numbering.

3 Click the Outline Numbered tab, as shown in Figure 12-4.

4 Choose which of the preset selections you want, and click OK.

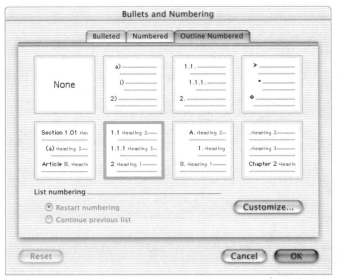

Figure 12-4. One of the seven preset outline numbering styles works for most documents.

The preset outline numbering styles include different character styles, and some of them will insert words (such as Chapter, Section, and so forth) at the start of certain levels of headings. Other styles use a mix of numbers and letters, and one style uses symbols to denote the different heading levels.

Customizing Outline Numbering

Sometimes you are required to turn in a document with a very specific format (for example, a legal document), and the preset styles don't quite match what you need. You can create your own custom outline numbering scheme. Follow these steps:

1 Choose Format, Bullets And Numbering, and then click the Outline Numbered tab.

2 Select one of the preset styles as a starting point, and then click Customize.

3 In the Customize Outline Numbered List dialog, shown in Figure 12-5, make your custom changes to each heading level. Changes are reflected as you make them in the Preview box. Click OK when you are done.

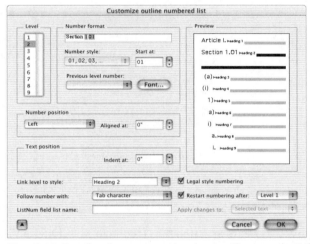

Figure 12-5. Create your own custom outline numbering styles in this dialog (expanded to show all the dialog's options).

---

tip **Use legal style numbering in your outline**

If you need to create legal documents, Word has an option that's just for you. In the Customize Outline Numbered List dialog, click the triangle button at the bottom left corner of the dialog to show the dialog's options, and then select the Legal Style Numbering check box.

Using the Document Map

Long documents are harder to navigate, so Word gives you the Document Map to make the navigation job easier. The Document Map is an interesting hybrid between Outline view and one of the other text views. When you switch to the Document Map, the document window splits vertically, showing the outline of your document in the left pane and the text of your document in the right pane, as shown in Figure 12-6.

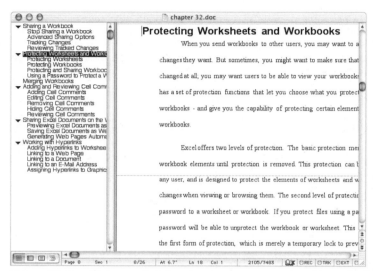

Figure 12-6. Click a section heading in the Document Map to display the section in the text pane on the right.

To navigate through a document using the Document Map, choose View, Document Map. Clicking a heading in the Document Map pane on the left jumps the text pane on the right to the corresponding spot.

> **tip** You can resize the Document Map pane by pointing at the border between the two panes. When the pointer turns into a double-headed arrow, drag the border to the right or to the left.

To use the Document Map efficiently, your document must be formatted with the built-in heading styles, just as in Outline view. These headings will appear correctly in the Document Map. If your document isn't formatted with heading styles, text will still appear in the Document Map, but it's likely to be a mass of text that won't be very useful.

Because the Document Map is in outline form, you can treat it in some of the same ways that you would if the document were in Outline view. As you can see in Figure 12-6,

Chapter 12

headings are shown with disclosure triangles next to them. To hide an open set of sub-headings, click the disclosure triangle above them. You can get even better control by using the contextual menu in the Document Map pane. Control+click in the Document Map pane to bring up a contextual menu with a familiar set of outline tools, as shown here:

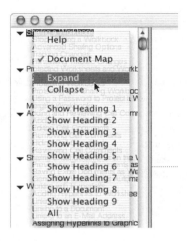

---

tip   You can also use the Document Map contextual menu to turn Document Map view off.

The text pane to the right of the Document Map can be set to Normal, Page Layout, or Outline view, but you can't display the Document Map when any additional panes are open in the document, such as the Comments or Footnotes panes. If you change the view between Normal and Page Layout, the Document Map might disappear. That's because you have to turn the Document Map on or off separately in each view.

Formatting Text in the Document Map

If the text in the Document Map is too large or otherwise difficult to work with, you can customize it to your liking. Reformatting text in the Document Map does not alter the actual heading styles in the document. To modify the Document Map text, follow these steps:

1 Choose View, Document Map to display the Document Map.

2 Choose Format, Style.

3 In the Styles box, click Document Map, and then click Modify.

4 From the Format pop-up menu, choose Font, and then make the changes you need in the resulting Font dialog.

Inserting Other Files into Your Document

Word allows you to insert the complete or partial contents of another Word or Microsoft Excel X file into your open document, as well as any other document type that Word can open. Follow these steps:

1 Place the insertion point where you want to insert the file.

2 Choose Insert, File.

3 In the resulting Insert File dialog, navigate to the file that you wish to insert, and click Insert. The Insert File dialog has two options not found in most other Open dialogs: the Link To File button and the Range/Bookmark field. Use the Link To File button to insert not the actual contents of the file but a link to the file, which takes up less room in your document. You might also choose to insert only a portion of the targeted file. If the target file is an Excel worksheet, you can type the range of cells you want from the work-sheet in the Range/Bookmark field. If the target file is another Word docu-ment, and that file contains bookmarks, you can type the bookmark name in the Range/Bookmark field.

4 If the file that you're trying to insert isn't immediately recognized by Word, the Convert File dialog will appear, asking you to select the document type, as shown here:

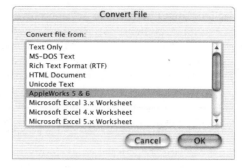

5 Select the document type, and then click OK.

Working with Master Documents

Really long documents, such as books, or documents with sections that will be contrib-uted by many different members of a team, call for a tool that can both handle the pieces and also deal with the entire project. Word's master document and subdocuments fea-tures get this big job done. With master documents, you can collect all the individual files that make up a big document (Word calls these individual files *subdocuments*), and then check spelling in, create an index for, perform search and replace in, or print all of the subdocuments that have been added to the master document. In a way, you can think of master documents in Word as roughly analogous to workbooks in Excel. Just as workbooks act as binders that contain multiple worksheets, Word's master documents contain subdocuments. Each of the subdocuments can be formatted independently and then integrated smoothly back into the overall document.

You deal with master documents using many of the same methods that you used when working with outlines; in fact, a master document is really just a specialized form of outline. Word is flexible about the way that you create master documents. You can create master documents from scratch, or you can turn existing documents into master documents.

Creating a New Master Document

To begin a new master document, follow these steps:

1 Start by creating a new document, and then choose View, Master Document. Two toolbars will appear: the Outlining toolbar and the Master Document toolbar, shown in Figure 12-7.

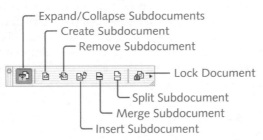

— Expand/Collapse Subdocuments
— Create Subdocument
— Remove Subdocument
— Lock Document
— Split Subdocument
— Merge Subdocument
— Insert Subdocument

Figure 12-7. The Master Document toolbar appears when you create a master document.

2 If you have a template that you want the master document and subdocuments to share, apply it now.

For more information about applying templates, see "Working with Templates," page 173.

3 Enter the headings for the document title and the subdocument titles. Word automatically creates the first heading, usually the document title, with the default style, Heading 1. It's important that each heading at which you want to start a new subdocument be the same level of heading (Heading 1, Heading 2, etc.), because Word takes the first heading in the block of text you mark for a subdocument and then creates a new subdocument each time it encounters another heading at the same level.

Chapter 12

4 If desired, create subheadings (which will become sections within each subdocument) by clicking the Demote button to assign Heading 3 to the subheading text. You can create further levels of subheadings as needed, by creating and demoting additional text.

5 Save the master document file, which should now look something like Figure 12-8.

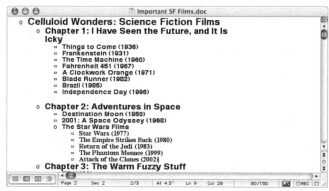

Figure 12-8.   This master document is about to be split up into subdocuments.

6 Select the block of headings and their subtext that you want converted into subdocuments. In the example shown in Figure 12-8 you would select from the Chapter 1 heading through the final chapter's text. Click Create Subdocument on the Master Document toolbar. Word will assign a new subdocument to each Heading 2 level (because that's the first heading level you selected); in this case each chapter will become a subdocument, as shown in Figure 12-9.

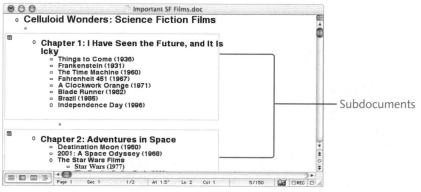
Subdocuments

Figure 12-9.   The text for each chapter has been turned into a subdocument.

7 Save the file. What isn't obvious is that Word has also created the new subdocuments, which will be saved as separate files in the same folder as the master document.

Converting Documents into Subdocuments

If you already have a document that you want to turn into a master document, begin by opening the file that you want to use, and then choose View, Master Document. The document will be shown as an outline. Organize your document's outline levels so that each level at which you want to create a subdocument starts with the same heading level. If Heading 1 is used for the title, you might want each subdocument to start with a Heading 2 subhead. Refer to the steps in the previous section to select the headings and their subtexts and create subdocuments from them.

You can also create subdocuments by importing other files into your master document. You do this by opening existing documents (which will become the subdocuments) into the master document. Follow these steps:

1 Open the master document, making sure that you are in Master Document view.

2 Place the insertion point where you want to add the subdocument. Be sure to select a blank line between subdocuments so the insert doesn't merge in with an existing subdocument.

3 On the Master Document toolbar, click the Insert Subdocument button.

4 Navigate to the file you want to import, and click Open. Word adds the subdocument to the master document at the insertion point.

5 Add additional subdocuments as necessary, and then save the master document file. Word saves both the master and the subdocuments in the same folder where the master document resides.

Navigating Master Documents

Now that you have created your master document and its subdocuments, you'll want to work with them. In the Master Document view, you can see your subdocuments, open them in separate windows, rearrange, delete, split, and combine them, and even remove them from the master document. (When working with master documents, deleting and removing subdocuments is not the same thing, as explained in "Removing and Deleting Subdocuments," page 303.)

If you open a master document, and then click the Collapse Subdocuments button on the Master Document toolbar, you see what's really going on in master documents, as shown in Figure 12-10 on the next page. Word shows you that it doesn't store everything within the single document anymore; instead the master document contains links to the subdocuments, and when you expand and work with the subdocuments within the master document, you're really working in the individual subdocument files.

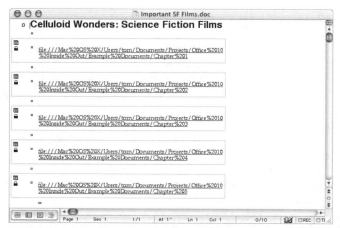

Figure 12-10. The truth behind a master document is that it contains links to the subdocuments.

When you expand subdocuments in the Master Document view, you can use all the tools on the Outlining toolbar to show, hide, or rearrange headings in the subdocuments.

> For more information about working with outlines, see "Building Documents from Outlines," page 285.

Editing and Opening Subdocuments

You can work with the subdocument directly within the master document, by clicking the Expand Subdocuments button on the Master Document toolbar, or you can work with the subdocument in its own window. To open a subdocument in its own window, simply click its link in the master document window when the master document is collapsed; when the master document is expanded, you can double-click the small icon in the upper left corner of any subdocument to open it. Then go ahead and edit it as you normally would.

InsideOut

Don't let the padlocks fool you

In Figure 12-10, you'll see little padlock icons underneath the subdocument icons. Naturally, you would guess that the padlock means that the file is locked and can't be edited. But that's not the case; you are seeing a bug in Word. If you expand the subdocument, or open it in its own window, you'll find that there's no impediment to editing it to your heart's desire.

Where Should I Make Changes?

Because you can make changes in either master documents or subdocuments, it's easy to get confused as to where you should actually make your changes. The simple rule of thumb is that you should make changes in the master document that will affect the overall document that you are creating (for example, if you're writing a book, changes that will affect the entire book), and make detailed changes in the subdocuments.

Make these sorts of changes in master documents:

- Applying heading levels
- Changing topic order
- Formatting that will affect the entire document, such as columns
- Checking spelling
- Adding headers and footers
- Setting margins and page setup for printing

Make these sorts of changes in subdocuments:

- Text editing
- Adding tables and graphics
- Adding borders and shading to paragraphs or objects

Prominent by their absence in the preceding lists are templates. That's because the subject of templates and master documents can be a bit of a can of worms. If you create your subdocuments within a master document, all of the subdocuments will have the same template as the master document. But it's possible for a subdocument that you import into the master document to have its own template, different from that of the master document. Even more confusingly, when a subdocument is expanded in Master Document view, it will share the master document's template. So for example, if you print from the Master Document view, all of the subdocuments will print using the styles from the master document's template. But when you open a subdocument in its own window, the subdocument's template will reign supreme, and the subdocument will be displayed with its own styles and other formatting.

Rearranging Subdocuments

It's easy to move subdocuments around within a master document. Follow these steps:

1 With the master document open, click the Expand Subdocuments button on the Master Document toolbar.

2 If expanding subdocuments shows too much text, show fewer headings using the Outlining toolbar.

3 Drag the subdocument icon of the item you want to move to the new location. When you release the mouse button, the subdocument will be moved to the new location.

---

tip   **Don't bury your subdocument**

When you drag the subdocument icon to move it, make sure that you drag the icon outside the other subdocuments' boundary boxes before you release the mouse button. Otherwise, Word might create a subdocument that is within another subdocument. If you accidentally do this, simply drag the subdocument icon to a new location outside any existing subdocument's boundary box.

Merging and Splitting Subdocuments

If you decide that a chapter (i.e., a subdocument) is getting too long, you can split it into two shorter documents. Follow these steps:

1 Open the master document, and choose View, Master Document.

2 Expand the subdocuments in the Master Document view. You'll see the subdocuments in outline form.

3 Click where you want to split an existing single subdocument into two subdocuments, and then click the Split Subdocument button on the Master Document toolbar.

4 Save the master document to create a new subdocument file.

Just as you can split subdocuments, you can merge two or more as well. Follow these steps:

1 Open the master document, and choose View, Master Document.

2 Expand the subdocuments in the Master Document view.

3 Move the subdocuments that you intend to merge so that they are next to each other in your outline.

4 Click the icons of the first and last soon-to-be-merged subdocuments while pressing the Shift key, and then click the Merge Subdocument button on the Master Document toolbar.

5 Save the master document, and the files will be merged into the first subdocument.

Removing and Deleting Subdocuments

In Word, removing a subdocument and deleting a subdocument are not the same thing. When you remove a subdocument, it doesn't get rid of the subdocument from your master document; instead it converts a subdocument into text within the master document. This also breaks the link between the master document and the subdocument file. To remove a subdocument, simply select the subdocument in the master document, and then click the Remove Subdocument button on the Master Document toolbar.

If you really want to delete a subdocument, which removes the subdocument from the master document file, select the subdocument's icon in the master document, and then press Delete. This only removes the subdocument from the master document; the actual subdocument file is still in the same folder where you saved it.

Creating Document Summaries with AutoSummarize

Word has the ability to automatically summarize key words in your documents, using the AutoSummarize feature. Although this feature can create a briefer version of your document, it is hardly appropriate for everything you write; it works best on highly structured documents such as reports and technical documents. AutoSummarize doesn't do an especially great job with fiction, writing meant to be read aloud, or personal correspondence.

To automatically summarize a document, follow these steps:

1 Choose Tools, AutoSummarize to open the AutoSummarize dialog, as shown in Figure 12-11.

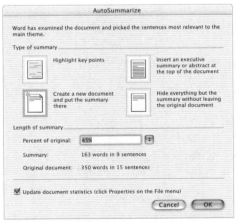

Figure 12-11. The AutoSummarize dialog provides several options for summarizing the current document.

2 Choose the type of summary you want to create. You can choose from four types of summary:

- ■ **Highlight Key Points** summarizes the current document by highlighting the summary information in yellow.

- ■ **Insert An Executive Summary Or Abstract At The Top Of The Document** inserts a summary at the beginning of the document under a new heading named Summary.

- ■ **Create A New Document And Put The Summary There** takes the summary information and puts it into a new document.

- ■ **Hide Everything But The Summary Without Leaving The Original Document** hides all of the document text except for the summary information. To show the complete text of the document again, click the Close button on the AutoSummarize toolbar.

3 In the Percent Of Original box, select the level of detail that you want to include in your summary. From the pop-up menu, you can choose 10 sentences, 20 sentences, 100 words or less, 500 words or less, 10%, 25%, 50%, or 75%. You can also type in your own custom percentage.

4 Click OK to create the summary. If you selected the Highlight Key Points option, the AutoSummarize toolbar appears, which includes a slider that enables you to adjust the percentage of the document that is highlighted. The result of a key points summary is shown in Figure 12-12.

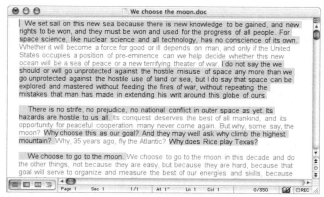

Figure 12-12. The highlighted text was chosen by AutoSummarize as the most relevant text from this portion of a speech by President Kennedy.

Generating Tables of Contents and Indexes

Tables of contents are indispensable tools for readers of long documents. The table of contents (TOC) helps readers discover what's in your document, and more importantly, tells them where to find the information they want. A TOC lists the headings in your document (and you can control the levels of headings shown in the TOC), making it perfect for finding sections of your document quickly. Tables of contents are useful not only in printed documents, but also in Web pages, because TOC headings work in Word as hyperlinks that you can click to navigate to that heading.

Indexes are another tool for readers to find information, but index entries are finergrained than TOC entries. An index is a list of important words or topics, with page numbers where those items can be found. A comprehensive index is often the best tool readers have to zero in on the information they want. Word has a wide-ranging set of features to create both tables of contents and indexes.

Creating a Table of Contents

If you have used Word's outlining feature and the built-in heading styles (Heading 1 through Heading 9) to create your document, it will be a snap to create a table of contents. If you created your document without headings, you'll have to insert them before you create the TOC. Here's a checklist that will ensure easy and effective tables of contents:

- Use Word's built-in heading styles, or create your custom styles based on them.

- Be descriptive—and short. An effective heading describes the subject clearly and is fairly short (no more than about 10 words).

Why Create Tables of Contents and Indexes in Word?

Many long documents are written in Word, but the final production takes place in a page layout program such as Quark XPress, or Adobe InDesign. If that's the case for your document, you might consider skipping the creation of a table of contents or index, because chances are good that it would be wasted effort. Most of these page layout programs cannot read the index and TOC marks that Word inserts into its documents. As a result, indexes and tables of contents are created in the page layout program.

On the other hand, if you'll be doing all of your production in Word, it makes perfect sense to create both the table of contents and the index in Word.

Follow these steps to create a table of contents from a document that contains built-in headings:

1 Place the insertion point where you want to add the table of contents. This will usually be at the start of your document.

2 Choose Insert, Index And Tables.

3 In the Index And Tables dialog, click the Table Of Contents tab, as shown in Figure 12-13.

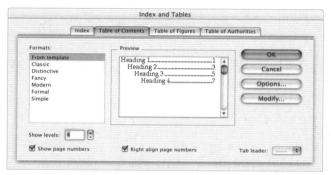

Figure 12-13. Choose the format for your table of contents in the Index And Tables dialog.

4 Choose a TOC style in the Formats box. The Preview box will change to show you the style of each choice.

5 Select the number of levels you want to show in the TOC, using the Show Levels box; this allows you to control the length of your TOC. If you want to show only the chapter names and you used Heading 1 styles for them, you would select 1 in the Show Levels box.

6 Choose whether or not to show the page numbers and whether page numbers should be right aligned. For most printed documents you want page numbers, but if you're creating a TOC that will be used on a Web page, you should turn them off.

7 Choose the style of Tab Leader you want from the pop-up menu. Tab leaders are the dotted lines that connect a heading with its page number. Your choices are periods, hyphens, underscore characters, or no leader characters.

8 Click OK to generate the table of contents, and then switch to Page Layout view to see the table of contents in all its glory, as shown in Figure 12-14.

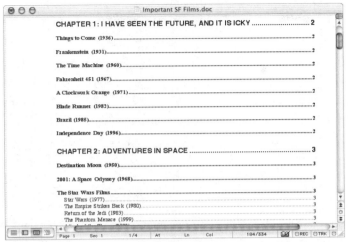

Figure 12-14. This formatted table of contents was created using the Classic TOC style.

> **note** A table of authorities is a special type of reference table that is primarily used in legal documents to track and compile legal citations. Because it is rarely used outside the legal profession, creating a table of authorities isn't covered in this book. For more information, choose Help, Search Word Help, and then type **table of authorities**.

Building an Index

There are two main steps to creating an index in Word. First, you have to mark the index entries, and then you generate the index itself, based on those entries.

Marking Index Entries

You can create an index entry in two different ways:

- To base the index entry on text that is already in the document, select the text.

- To type in your own entries, click to place the insertion point in the paragraph where you want to add the index entry.

To add index entries, follow these steps:

1 Select the text you want to use for the index entry or place the insertion point, and then press Command+Option+Shift+X. The Mark Index Entry dialog appears, as shown in Figure 12-15 on the next page.

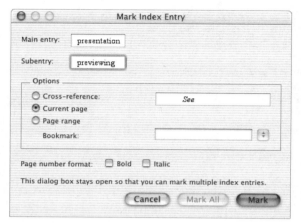

Figure 12-15. The Mark Index Entry dialog is used to enter index entries and subentries.

2 Any text that you selected before opening the Mark Index Entry dialog appears in the Main Entry box. If necessary, edit the contents of the box so that it contains the exact text that you want to appear in the index. If you placed the insertion point, type the index entry in the Main Entry box.

3 If you want to create a subentry for the main entry, type the subentry text in the Subentry box, as shown here:

Entering this example entry would create an index entry and subentry that looked like this:

Slide Sorter
using, 1

4 By default, the Current Page option is selected. This option ensures that the index entry displays the number of the page that contains the index entry.

note If you choose Cross-Reference in the Options box in the Mark Index Entry dialog, the index entry will display the cross-reference that you type into the adjoining text box, rather than a page number. For example, you could have a cross-reference that says "Shortcut menus, See Contextual menus." If you select Page Range, the index entry will show the range of pages that are marked with the bookmark selected from the Bookmark list.

5   To format the page number of the index entry, select Bold, Italic, or both.

6   Click Mark to mark the entry, or Mark All to mark all instances of the entry. Mark All is only available if you selected the index entry before opening the dialog. Because you'll usually want to continue marking index entries, the Mark Index Entry dialog stays open until you click Close.

---

note   Word marks index entries by inserting fields into the document. An index entry field contains the XE field name and is formatted as hidden text. When you mark index entries, Word ensures that you can see the hidden text by showing nonprinting characters that resemble curly brackets (this is the same as clicking the Show/Hide ¶ button on the Standard toolbar). An index entry field, with both an index entry and a subentry, looks like this:

{ XE "Slide Sorter:using" }

The colon between *Slide Sorter* and *using* indicates that the latter is a subentry. You can actually type subentries (and even multiple levels of subentries) directly into the Main Entry box in the Mark Index Entry dialog. Simply separate each level of subentry with a colon.

For more information about fields, see Chapter 14, "Understanding Fields."

Generating the Index

When you have marked all the entries that you want to include in your index, you're ready to have Word build the index. When Word compiles the index, it surveys all the entries that you have marked, paginates the document, assigns page numbers to the entries, alphabetizes the entries, and inserts the completed index into your document at the insertion point.

To generate the index, follow these steps:

1   Place the insertion point in your document where you want Word to insert the index.

2   Choose Insert, Index And Tables, and click the Index tab, as shown in Figure 12-16 on the next page.

3   Choose the type of index (Indented or Run-In) that you want, and select the index format that you want from the Formats list. As you select each index format, a preview appears in the Preview area.

4   Click OK, and Word generates the index.

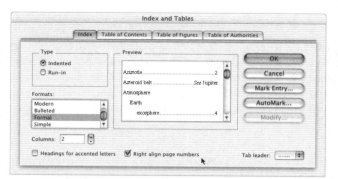

Figure 12-16. You choose the format of your index just before you generate the index.

Inserting Footnotes and Endnotes

Word enables you to create both footnotes and endnotes, annotations that provide extra explanations or citations in your document. Text for *footnotes* is placed at the end of the page that contains the reference; text for *endnotes* is placed at the end of the document.

Creating Footnotes and Endnotes

To create a footnote or endnote, you place a *reference mark* into the document. Figure 12-17 shows a footnote in Word.

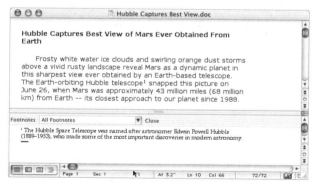

Figure 12-17. The footnote text appears in a separate pane in Word, but it prints at the bottom of the page.

> **note** Footnotes and endnotes aren't exclusive, you can combine both of them in a single document.

To insert a footnote or endnote, follow these steps:

1 Place the insertion point where you want to insert the footnote or endnote reference mark.

2 Choose Insert, Footnote to open the Footnote And Endnote dialog, shown here:

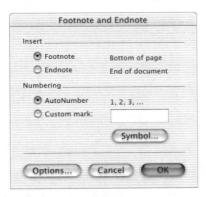

3 In the Footnote And Endnote dialog, do one of the following:

- If you want to insert a footnote, select Footnote in the Insert section.

- If you want to insert an endnote, select Endnote in the Insert section.

4 Set the numbering format; usually AutoNumber will do fine, but if you wish, you can type in a Custom Mark, or click the Symbol button, and choose a symbol from the resulting Symbol dialog.

5 If you want custom numbering, click Options. In the resulting Note Options dialog, you can choose various options for all footnotes or all endnotes. Of special note is the option on the All Footnotes tab to place footnotes beneath the text that contains the footnote reference mark, rather than at the bottom of the printed page. Click OK.

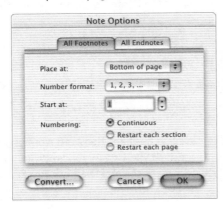

> **tip** The Convert button in the Note Options dialog enables you to convert all footnotes to endnotes, convert all endnotes to footnotes, or swap footnotes and endnotes.

6 Click OK to close the Footnote And Endnote dialog.

7 Finally, type your footnote.

> **tip** **Insert a quick reference**
>
> You can quickly insert a footnote without going through the Footnote And Endnote dialog by pressing Command+Option+F, or an endnote by pressing Command+Option+E. In either case, the reference is inserted using the default settings, or the last footnote or endnote settings you used.

Deleting Footnotes and Endnotes

To remove a footnote or an endnote, you must select the reference mark in the document and press Delete. You can't delete footnotes in the Footnote pane; if you try, Word will give you an error message. If you delete a footnote or endnote, all subsequent footnotes or endnotes will be renumbered automatically.

Customizing the Footnote Separator

Word uses a short separator line to show where the document text ends and the footnote text begins. You can change this line's color or thickness, or even add text before the line. To make any of these modifications, follow these steps:

1 Switch to Normal view, and then choose View, Footnotes to open the Footnotes pane.

2 From the pop-up menu at the top of the Footnotes pane, choose Footnote Separator, as shown here:

3 If you want to add text before the line (perhaps the word *Notes*), place the insertion point before the line, and type the text. If you want to replace the line with something a bit flashier, select the line and delete it.

4 Choose Format, Borders And Shading, and then click the Borders tab.

5 Select the line style you want, and then click OK. Usually you'll want to assign a single top line only, rather than a line around the entire footnote section.

Inserting Figure Captions

When you use graphics in your documents, you'll often want to create figure captions to identify or describe the graphics. The benefit of using Word's automatic captioning feature, instead of typing in the captions yourself, is that Word can number, remember, and even add new captions automatically. You're not limited to using captions on graphics alone, however. You can add captions to virtually any object in Word, including text boxes, tables, equations created by Microsoft Equation Editor, and organization charts created by Microsoft Organization Chart. Captions consist of two parts: the *label*, which Word generates automatically, and the *caption text*, which you enter for each caption. The label is text such as *Figure 1*; the numeral is a Word field, so it can be updated when you need to renumber your captions.

To caption an object, follow these steps:

1 Select the object you want to caption, and then choose Insert, Caption.

2 The label—in this case *Figure 1*—appears automatically in the Caption box. Type the caption text in the Caption box, as shown in Figure 12-18. If you want to change the label, choose a new label from the Label pop-up menu (your default choices are Equation, Figure, and Table; if these are not what you want, click the New Label button, and enter a new label name).

> **tip** Don't forget to type a space after the label.

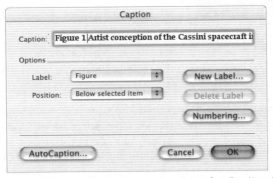

Figure 12-18. Type the caption into the Caption box, after the automatic caption label.

3 From the Position pop-up menu, choose Below Selected Item (the default) or Above Selected Item.

4 If you want to change the caption numbering scheme, click the Numbering button. The Caption Numbering dialog appears, as shown here; make your choices and click OK.

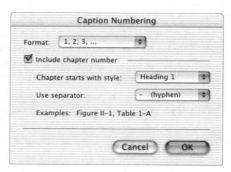

5 Click OK to insert the caption into your document, as shown in Figure 12-19.

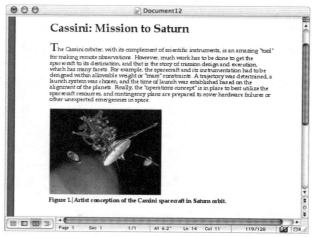

Figure 12-19. The automatically numbered caption appears in the document.

To delete a caption, you must select it, and press Delete. If you want to change all the captions throughout your document that share the same label simultaneously, that's no problem. Simply select one of the labels (for example, select *Figure 1*), and choose Insert, Caption to open the Caption dialog. Changes you make in this dialog, for example choosing a new label, will be applied to all of the captions that had the original label.

Because captions are based on fields, their numbering might need to be updated when you delete or move a caption. If you want to update a single caption, select the caption, and then press F9, the Update Field command. To update all of the captions in your document, choose Edit, Select All, and then press F9.

Word can also add captions automatically whenever you add any picture, clip art, or table to your document. Follow these steps:

1 Choose Insert, Caption, and then click AutoCaption.

2 In the AutoCaption dialog, as shown next, choose the objects for which you want Word to automatically add a caption.

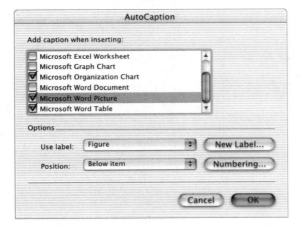

3 If necessary, choose the label and position for the AutoCaption. The New Label and Numbering buttons work the same way as in the Caption dialog. When you are finished, click OK.

> **note** Word can create a table of figures that lists all the figures in your document. Because it is rarely used, creating a table of figures isn't covered in this book. For more information, choose Help, Search Word Help, and then type **table of figures**.

Collaborating with Word

In the past, when collaborating on text documents and reports, each reviewer or colleague would pencil their comments on a printout or cross out what they didn't like and write in their changes. Incorporating all these revisions into your text was a real headache—not only understanding what each reviewer wrote, but also trying to ensure that the latest changes and comments were taken into account. Microsoft Word X has powerful tools for collaborating—tools to track changes, comments, and versions—that are modeled on the way you work by hand. Revisions are shown as text crossed out and added, and comments are shown by note marks in the text, which are linked to comments in a separate pane in the Word document window. The metaphors of making changes and revisions help you work with others on Word documents easily and naturally.

In this chapter, you will learn how to collaborate efficiently using Word's excellent functions for integrating and reviewing changes, adding and reviewing comments, comparing documents to find what changes have been made, and managing different document versions.

Working with Comments

One of the easiest ways to give and get feedback on a Word document is to use *comments*. Users can add as much text as they want to your documents, inserting comments that appear in a separate comment pane but are linked to specific points in your text. Unlike revisions added using the Track Changes feature, comments do not mark up the text with strikethrough and colored changed text. Long changes marked as revisions can make text cumbersome and difficult to read, but comments are all outside the text. Also, revisions in the text tend to

317

be changes to the actual text, whereas comments are better for saying such things as "Did you check these figures?" or "Make sure everyone is credited here." You can also choose to print comments when you print your documents, so that you can go over them away from your computer.

Adding Comments

You can insert a comment at any location in a Word document, no matter which view you are using to see your document. To insert a comment, click where you want to add the comment, and then choose Insert, Comment. Word does several things, as shown in Figure 13-1:

- Word inserts a comment mark, which is your initials in brackets followed by a number representing the number of the comment in the document. This number is sequential and depends on the location of the comment in the document, not on the chronological order in which comments were added.

- Word highlights the word before the comment mark in yellow.

- Word opens the comment pane in the bottom part of the document window.

- Word sets the insertion point in the comment pane just after the comment mark.

You can then start typing your comment in the comment pane. Enter as much text as you want. When you have finished typing, go back to your document and make any other changes you want, or insert a new comment. When you finish entering comments, click the Close button in the comment pane.

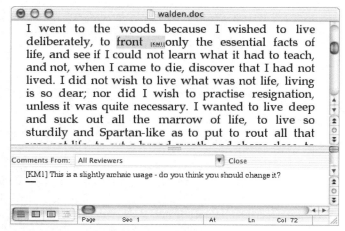

Figure 13-1. Word makes several changes when you insert a comment, both in the main text window at the top and in the bottom comment pane.

> **tip** **Add or change the name or initials for comments**
>
> Word uses your user information to enter initials and names for comments. If you want to change this information, you can do so by choosing Word, Preferences, and then clicking the User Information category. You can change the name displayed by typing a new name in the User Name field, and the initials used in the comment marks by changing the text in the Initials field.

If your comment pertains to a block of text—this can be a few words, a sentence, a paragraph, or more—select the text before inserting your comment. Word will do the same things as described earlier, but it will highlight the entire section of text you selected.

Troubleshooting

Some comments from multiple reviewers are obscured.

You can reply to comments made by others by inserting comments on their comments. The problem with this is that you cannot add a comment after an initial comment; if you click in text highlighted by comments, your new comment will appear *before* the initial comment. If you try to click after the initial comment, the following word will be highlighted, and the comment will not be attached to the same text as the initial comment. When the second comment appears before the older comment, it receives the lower number and appears to be an earlier comment rather than a follow-up comment; and, if you have ScreenTips turned on, only the ScreenTip for the second comment displays, as illustrated in Figure 13-2 on the next page. When you move the pointer over the initial comment mark, no ScreenTip displays, although the comment text is still present in the comment pane.

This means that when comments turn into conversations (which can happen often when documents are sent back and forth), they should be read in reverse order, with the last comment shown, both in the text by its comment mark, and in the comment pane, being the first one made. If you don't mind doing a little extra work, you can add the second comment, highlight the comment marker, and then drag it to the correct position. This puts the comment in the proper order and also restores a ScreenTip to both comment markers.

Another confusion occurs when you insert one comment on a long selection (a sentence, paragraph, etc.) and another comment on a word within that selection. The highlighting of the comments blends together, and It's difficult to tell the secondary comment's ScreenTip from the first comment's.

(continued)

Troubleshooting *(continued)*

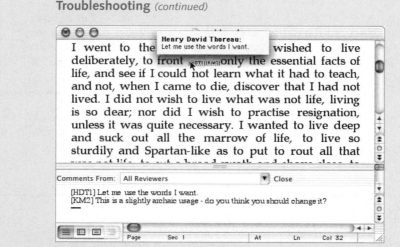

Figure 13-2. Word has trouble handling comment marks that fall directly after another comment mark. Note that the second comment is not highlighted in the document text.

Often, a better solution is to track changes (see "Tracking Changes," page 326) and add your comments after the other comments in the comment pane. Word will treat your addition to the existing comment as part of that comment, so there's no highlighting confusion, but because changes are being tracked, each person's comments will be in a different color, so there's no possibility of confusing who said what.

Reviewing Comments

Word gives you several ways to review comments added to a document. The simplest way is to view the comments by placing your pointer over a comment mark. As shown in Figure 13-2, a ScreenTip appears, showing the author and text of the comment. This ScreenTip only appears, however, if you have chosen this option in the Preferences dialog.

The problem when viewing comments as ScreenTips is that they cover part of your text. Another way to view comments is to choose View, Comments to display the comment pane below the text in your document's window. This gives you more flexibility in viewing comments, because you see each comment in its entirety and you can choose whether to view comments by all reviewers or just one person. To choose which reviewer's comments you want to view, select their name from the Comments From pop-up menu in the comment pane, as shown in Figure 13-3. You can choose All Reviewers, or the name of an individual reviewer.

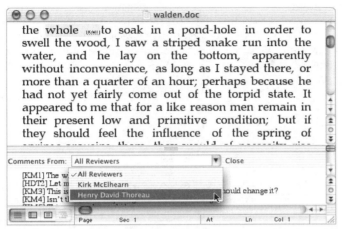

Figure 13-3. The Comments From pop-up menu lets you choose which reviewer's comments to view.

Troubleshooting

I can't see comments in my Word document.

If comments aren't displayed correctly on-screen, you need to adjust some preferences. Choose Word, Preferences, and then click View and do the following:

- To view highlighting, select Highlight in the Show section.
- To view comment marks in your text, select Hidden Text in the Nonprinting Characters section.
- To view comments in ScreenTips when moving the pointer over comment marks, select ScreenTips in the Show section. This choice affects ScreenTips in several areas of Word—ScreenTips will display for comments, but also when you move your pointer over toolbar buttons, footnotes, and endnotes.

If you still don't see comments after checking all these preferences, choose View, Comments, and choose All Reviewers in the Show pop-up menu to make sure that Word displays all comments.

When viewing comments in the comment pane, you don't need to navigate in the text section of your document. Just click anywhere in one of the comments, or press the Up Arrow or Down Arrow key, and Word scrolls to the part of the text the comment refers to. The commented text is displayed on the top line in the text pane of the window, or the first line of the commented text is moved to the top of this pane if the comment covers a long selection of text. You can edit your comment text in the comment pane—

you can delete, change, or add to this text. You can delete your own comment by select-ing the comment mark in the text pane and pressing Delete. You cannot, however, delete another's comment, although you can add strikeout or new text in another color. The way to delete another's comment is with the Reviewing toolbar, shown in Figure 13-4. To close the comment pane, click the Close button.

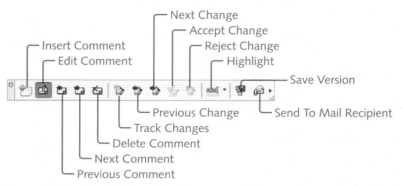

Figure 13-4. The Reviewing toolbar contains buttons for working with comments, changes, and document versions.

For more information on tracking changes, see "Tracking Changes," page 326. For more on saving versions of documents, see "Managing Document Versions," page 334.

InsideOut

Work around erratic comment behavior

Unfortunately, all is not as it should be in the land of Word comments. When review-ing comments, you might find that this feature doesn't always work as it should. First, comments sometimes display ScreenTips, but not always; sometimes you have to wave the pointer over the comment repeatedly until the ScreenTip appears, and sometimes the ScreenTip never shows up. Then, if you have two comments together (see "Some comments from multiple reviewers are obscured," page 319), Word can get stuck on one comment, such as the first of two comments at the same location, and cannot go any further. To get around this, you can click the arrow key in the direction you want to go, and then click the Next Comment or Previous Comment button to go to the next or previous comment.

The most effective way to review comments is probably to click your way through the comments in the comment pane, which will scroll the text pane to each comment. But you can't delete comments there; you must use the Reviewing toolbar or the contextual menu.

The most comprehensive tool for editing comments is the Reviewing toolbar. This toolbar contains buttons that let you add, review, and delete comments; work with changes; and save versions of your documents, as shown in Figure 13-4. The Reviewing toolbar opens automatically whenever you open a document containing comments. If you have closed it, you can also choose View, Toolbars, Reviewing.

To review comments with the Reviewing toolbar, open a document containing comments, and click the Next Comment button. Word will move ahead in the document to the nearest comment, place the insertion point at the comment, and display a ScreenTip containing the comment. If the comment pane is visible, it will move the text in this pane, as you change comments, to display the text for the comment.

Deleting Comments

To delete a comment, you must display the Reviewing toolbar. If it is not visible, choose View, Toolbars, Reviewing. Move to a comment, either by clicking the Next Comment or Previous Comment button, or by clicking in a highlighted comment in the text pane. Click the Delete Comment button on the Reviewing toolbar (see Figure 13-4), and the comment is deleted.

---

tip   **Delete comments with the contextual menu**

The main way to delete comments is to use the Delete Comment button on the Reviewing toolbar, but you can also use a contextual menu. Simply Control+click on the highlighted part of a comment in the document pane; among the choices will be Edit Comment and Delete Comment. You can also add the Delete Comment button to another toolbar, or create a keyboard shortcut for the command. If you do this, note that the command is called Delete Annotation, not Delete Comment, in the All Commands section of the Customize dialog.

For more information on adding buttons to toolbars, see "Adding a Button to a Toolbar," page 48.

Printing a Document with Comments

You can choose to print a document with its comments. When you do this, Word prints the comment marks in brackets in the text and, starting on a new page after printing the document, all of the comments. These comments are printed in the following form:

```
Page: 1
[KM1] Comment 1
[KM2] Comment 2
Page: 2
[KM3] Comment 3
etc.
```

This makes it easy for you to view comments as you read through a document on paper, because they are on separate pages and their page numbers are all clearly marked.

Comments will only print, however, if you chose this in the Preferences dialog. To do this, choose Word, Preferences, and then click Print. In the Include With Document section, select the Comments check box. This will print comments—whether or not the comment pane is visible, and whether or not highlighting is on.

Highlighting Text

Sometimes you want to draw attention to certain words or sentences. You can use bold or italic text styles, or different fonts to do this, but, just as you can use a highlighter to make text stand out on paper, you can highlight text in Word documents with one of 15 highlighting colors. Highlighting can be used to indicate specific words that you want others to notice, but you can also use it to enter annotations in the document's text, by highlighting only your annotations.

To highlight text, select any text, and click the Highlight button on the Reviewing toolbar. (It's also located on the Formatting toolbar and in the Font section of the Formatting Palette.) This highlights your text in the currently selected color. To change the highlighting color, click the arrow next to the Highlight button. The Highlight menu opens, as shown in Figure 13-5, and you can choose a color by clicking it.

Figure 13-5. You can choose from 15 colors to highlight text.

---

tip **Don't use dark highlighting colors for printed documents**

If you are highlighting text in a document to be printed in grayscale, as with most laser printers, don't use any dark colors, such as those on the second or third line of the highlighting menu. Either use one of the first three colors—yellow, bright green, or turquoise—or use 25% gray on the bottom line. If not, you will probably not be able to read your text, because any other colors will come out as dark gray.

If you want to highlight text in several locations, all in the same color, click the High-light button before selecting any text. The button will remain depressed until the next time you click it (or press Esc). The pointer changes to the Highlighting pointer, and, as you select text, it is highlighted instantly.

Removing Highlighting from Text

To remove highlighting from text, first click the arrow next to the Highlight button. Click None, and then select the highlighted text. Word will remove highlighting from your text. You can also select None, and then click the Highlight button so it stays depressed to remove highlighting from text in several locations. Click the Highlight button again (or press Esc) to turn off highlighting.

---

tip   **Remove all highlighting from a document**

If you want to remove all the highlighting in a document, first choose None in the Highlight button pop-up menu (as previously described). Then select the entire docu-ment by pressing Command+A, and click the Highlight button. Word will remove highlighting from all the text in your document, with the exception of highlighting used to show comments.

Searching for Highlighted Text

Word's Find function enables you to search your documents for highlighted text. It's very handy to be able to find text that others have highlighted without scrolling through an entire document. To find highlighted text, follow these steps:

1 Choose Edit, Find to display the Find dialog.

2 Click the triangle button in the lower left corner of the Find And Replace dialog to display additional options.

3 Click the Format pop-up menu and select Highlight.

4 Click Find Next. Word will find the next instance of highlighted text. To find more highlighted text, click Find Next again, and continue until you have found all highlighted text in your document.

For more information on finding and replacing text, see "Finding and Replacing Text and Formatting," page 108.

Tracking Changes

Word's feature for tracking changes ensures that any changes made to a document are clearly marked. The main purpose of tracking changes is to enable the original author of a document to see changes made to it and, when reviewing the document, decide whether to accept or reject them. Changes are shown in different colors, usually according to the people who made the changes; deleted text is displayed in strikethrough style, and added text is shown in a different color and underlined. In addition, vertical lines in the margin (*changed lines*), show which lines of the document contain changes.

Setting Up the Track Changes Feature

The easiest way to start tracking changes is to click the TRK button in the status bar. When you click this button, the circular *gem* to the left of TRK changes to green to show that tracking is on, as shown in Figure 13-6. Note that if you reduce the width of your window, you might not see this button—Word doesn't resize the status bar to fit the window, but merely cuts off the rightmost elements in the status bar.

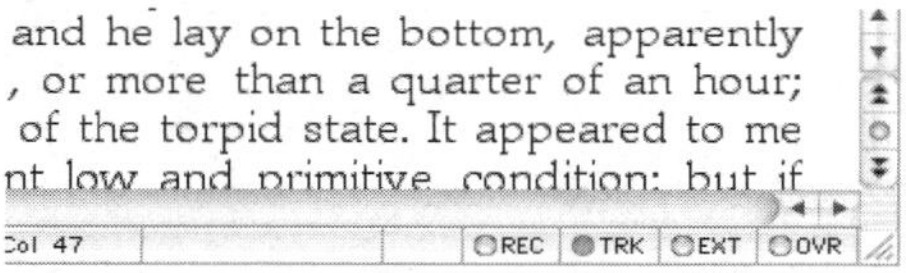

and he lay on the bottom, apparently
, or more than a quarter of an hour;
of the torpid state. It appeared to me
nt low and primitive condition: but if
Col 47
REC
TRK
EXT
OVR

Figure 13-6. The green gem in the status bar's TRK button indicates that Track Changes is active.

When you turn on tracking in the status bar, you only tell Word to record changes while editing the current document. But there are other options you can change to alter the way these changes are displayed, or whether they are displayed at all. Hold down the Control key and click the TRK button. A contextual menu appears with several options for tracking changes. If you select Highlight Changes, the Highlight Changes dialog appears, in which you can choose display options for changes, as shown in Figure 13-7.

If you select Track Changes While Editing, Word tracks the changes you make, keeping a record of all changes. If you select Highlight Changes On Screen, these changes will

Highlight Changes
Track changes while editing
Highlight changes on screen
Highlight changes in printed document
Options...
Cancel
OK

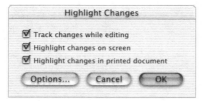

Figure 13-7. The Highlight Changes dialog lets you choose how changes are displayed or printed.

show both deleted and added text on-screen in different colors for each reviewer. Although you must select the first check box, Track Changes While Editing, in order to have changes recorded, you don't have to display them on-screen. You can have Word record these changes and choose to display them later. Selecting the third option, Highlight Changes In Printed Document, tells Word to print the change marks when you print your document.

If you click Options, Word opens the Track Changes dialog, where you can choose the type of revision marks and colors used, as shown in Figure 13-8. Each section of this dialog lets you choose what type of mark to use for that element. Each section also lets you choose a specific color or the default By Author selection, which assigns each reviewer a different color. You can choose None for any of the revision marks, which is the default that Word uses for changed formatting. (Note that you can also access the Track Changes dialog by choosing Preferences directly from the contextual menu that appears when you Control+click the TRK button.)

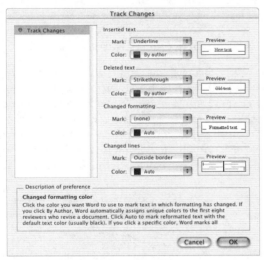

Figure 13-8. The Track Changes dialog lets you choose change marks and colors.

Reviewing Changes

When examining a document containing change marks, you will see several types of marks, as in Figure 13-9 on the next page. Changed lines in the left margin show which lines of text contain changes. Crossed out text has been deleted by reviewers, and under-lined text has been added by reviewers. The colors of the text are different for each reviewer, unless you, or a reviewer, changed the colors in the Track Changes dialog. When you move the pointer over any changes, a ScreenTip appears showing the name of the reviewer, the date and the time, in bold text, and the type of revision made.

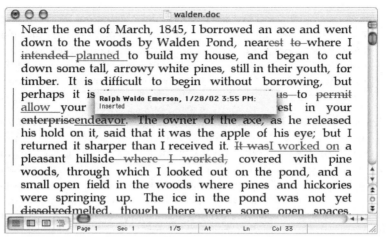

Figure 13-9. Changed lines are displayed in the left margin, and crossed-out and underlined text indicate deletions and insertions made by reviewers.

Reviewing Changes with the Accept or Reject Changes Dialog

To review changes, and choose which changes you want to keep and which to discard, choose Tools, Track Changes, Accept Or Reject Changes. The Accept Or Reject Changes dialog opens, as shown in Figure 13-10. You can use this dialog to move through changes one by one, and choose whether to accept or reject each individual change, or to accept all changes or reject all changes at once. If you wish to accept or reject all changes, click the Accept All or Reject All button. Word displays an alert asking whether you are sure you want to accept (or reject) all changes. If you are sure, click Yes.

Figure 13-10. The Accept Or Reject Changes dialog lets you review changes and decide which you want to keep.

To review changes individually, click one of the Find buttons. The top button finds from the current location toward the beginning of the document, and the bottom Find button searches toward the end. Each time Word finds a change, it stops and displays the change highlighted in the document. The Changes section of the Accept Or Reject

328

Changes dialog shows the name of the reviewer, the type of change, and the date and time of the change. To keep a change, click Accept; to discard a change, click Reject. Continue searching for changes, by clicking one of the Find buttons, until you have reviewed all changes in your document. If you want to leave a change as is, without deciding whether to accept or reject it, simply click the Find button again. The change will not be altered, and you can come back to it later.

The View section of the Accept Or Reject Changes dialog offers a useful function. It lets you choose to view your document in one of three ways:

- **Changes With Highlighting.** All changes are shown, with deleted text crossed out and added text underlined, in different colors for each reviewer.

- **Changes Without Highlighting.** The document appears as it would if you selected Accept All. All changes are integrated, but not highlighted. This makes the document easier to read if there are many changes.

- **Original.** The original document is shown with no changes. This makes the document easier to read if there are many changes, and lets you see the original as it was before any reviewers made changes.

Reviewing Changes with the Reviewing Toolbar

If you're short on screen real estate, or if you just prefer working with toolbars rather than with dialogs, you can review your changes with the Reviewing toolbar. If it isn't showing, display the Reviewing toolbar by choosing View, Toolbars, Reviewing. You can then use the Previous Change, Next Change, Accept Change, and Reject Change buttons to step through and review the document's changes (see Figure 13-4, on page 322). The Reviewing toolbar lacks many of the tools that the Accept Or Reject Changes dialog offers, so you might want to stick with the dialog for heavy reviewing sessions.

Troubleshooting

I don't see the tracked changes in my Word document.

If changes aren't displayed in a document where changes were tracked, make sure that you have selected the option to display them. Choose Tools, Track Changes, Highlight Changes. Select the Highlight Changes On Screen check box.

If changes are in hidden text or field codes, you need to make sure you have selected the option to display them. Choose Word, Preferences, and then click the View category. In the Show section, select Field Codes. In the Nonprinting Characters section, select Hidden Text.

Merging Changes from Several Reviewers

If several reviewers are editing a document, you can merge their edited documents, and view all their revisions at the same time. However, to do this, it is best to prepare the document for this purpose. Make sure everyone has a copy of the same document, not different versions. Also, it is best that all reviewers enable Track Changes before they start editing. Although you can find where a reviewer made changes by comparing documents, it is easier to merge changes when they are tracked.

For more information on comparing documents, see "Comparing Documents," opposite.

To merge changes from several reviewers, follow these steps:

1 Open the original document. This is your copy of the document, which might have your own revisions in it.

2 Choose Tools, Merge Documents.

3 In the resulting Choose A File dialog, select the file to merge, and click Open.

4 Repeat this for each copy of the document you need to merge with your copy. When you are finished, your new document will show all the changes made by all reviewers, and you can review changes.

When Word merges documents, it records all changes made by all reviewers. If multiple reviewers have made the same change, Word will display this change once for each reviewer. In Figure 13-11, you can see in the second line that two reviewers changed the word *by* to *near*; Word displays both changes, in different colors, because the reviewers were different.

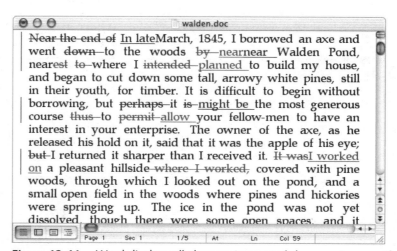

Figure 13-11. Word displays all changes in merged documents, even if different reviewers have made the same changes.

> **tip** **Track your own changes**
>
> If you want to keep track of changes you make to your own documents, turn on Track Changes and start editing. All your changes will be recorded. You can choose not to show the changes on-screen, but still record these changes, so you can go back to your original version if you want to.

> For more information on displaying changes on-screen, see "Setting Up the Track Changes Feature," page 326.

Comparing Documents

If you wish to view changes made by a reviewer, and the reviewer didn't track changes while editing, you can still display changes by comparing the edited document with your original. Comparing documents might not be quite as efficient as tracking changes, but the result is almost the same. When you compare two documents, Word examines the original and the edited document and looks for changes, and then displays these as change marks. As long as the documents are similar, this works well, but, when major formatting changes have been made, such as large changes to styles, the result is not perfect.

To compare documents, open your original document, and then choose Tools, Track Changes, Compare Documents; the Choose A File dialog appears. Select the second file to compare, and click OK. This might take a while if your document is long and complex. After Word has processed the document, it displays the original with change

Track Changes or Compare Documents?

Theoretically, the two functions should return the same results. Both display changes made to an original document and let you choose which changes you want to keep and which to discard. But, in practice, the results are slightly different. If you want to make substantial edits to a document and then return it to someone who will review your changes, you might be better off not tracking changes and having them use the compare documents function. When making changes with Track Changes turned on, it is very easy to delete spaces between words accidentally, meaning that the reviewer has to proofread the document very carefully. It can also be a bit difficult to edit a document that displays both the original text and changes, with deleted text crossed out and added text underlined. You can get around this by clearing the Highlight Changes On Screen option in the Highlight Changes dialog, but this can lead to spacing problems when dragging text from one location to another.

marks for the changes made in the second document you selected. You can then go on and review changes, choosing which ones to accept and which to reject.

For more information on reviewing changes, see "Reviewing Changes," page 327.

Protecting Documents from Changes

If you are sending a document to friends or coworkers and you want to ensure that they make no changes to the document, you can assign a password to the document that must be supplied before any changes can be made. You can also protect any document from being opened by assigning a password; if the user does not have the correct password, they won't even be able to view the document.

You can assign a password to a document when saving it. You can choose a password either the first time you save a document, or when saving a document under a new name. To add a password to a file, follow these steps:

1 Choose File, Save As (for a new document, choose File, Save).

2 Enter a new name for the document in the standard Save sheet.

3 Click Options, and the Save category of the Preferences dialog is displayed, as shown in Figure 13-12. The File Sharing Options section lets you enter a password to open the document and a different password to modify the document. (You can use the same password if you want, but that would be less secure.)

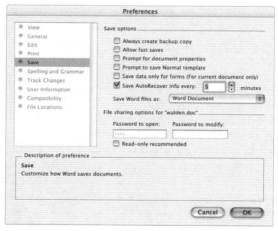

Figure 13-12. The Save category of the Preferences dialog enables you to enter passwords to protect your document.

4 Enter a password in one or both fields, and click OK. Word will display the Confirm Password dialog asking you to reenter your password. If you entered two passwords for your document, this dialog will display once for each password: first for the open password, and then for the modify password. Click OK after you enter each password.

> **note** Passwords are case sensitive and can be up to 15 characters. You can use letters, numbers, or symbols, and you can even use punctuation marks and spaces. Try to use a password that is not too difficult to remember; if you lose the Password To Open password, you won't be able to open your file.

If you select Read-Only Recommended, in the Save category of Preferences, Word displays an alert when a user opens the document, recommending that they open the file as read-only. If the user does this, they will not be able to save changes they make unless they save the document under another name. But opening the file as read-only is just a recommendation—the user can still open the document normally if they want to.

> **tip** **Assign passwords without saving**
>
> You can assign passwords without saving your document by choosing Word, Preferences and clicking Save. Enter the passwords in the File Sharing Options section.

You can change or remove the passwords assigned to a file at any time, as long as that file is open. Choose Word, Preferences, and then click the Save category. To change passwords, just enter new passwords in the open and modify password fields. Click OK, reenter your passwords to confirm, and the new passwords will be assigned. To remove passwords, simply erase the passwords in the open and modify passwords fields and click OK.

How Much Protection Do Passwords Really Give You?

The short answer: it depends. Although assigning a password to prevent a user from opening a file is relatively secure, because Word encrypts password-protected files, using a password to prevent changes is more of a bluff than real protection. Though a user without the password cannot make changes to the file, they can save the file under another name, make changes, and then change the name of that file back to the original name. If you then open this file, you won't know whether it is the original file or one with changes. So, don't count on this kind of protection.

Managing Document Versions

When editing documents, you make individual changes, but there are times when you want to freeze your documents, to send to others for review, in unique versions. You can naturally save you documents under new names, such as Report1, Report2, and so forth, or save them with dates in their names, such as Report-May-7, and so on. But Word allows you to save document versions in the file you are working on, giving you the opportunity to return to previous versions easily. It can be useful when reviewing documents to save the original version before incorporating changes, so that if you decide that you really did like that third paragraph the way you initially wrote it, you can get it back. Even after you accept or reject changes made to the file, you can still go back to a previous version, which is like a snapshot of the file at a specific time.

To save the current version of a file, follow these steps:

1 Choose File, Versions to open the Versions dialog, shown in Figure 13-13.

2 Click Save Now in the Versions dialog.

3 Word displays the Save Version dialog, where you can enter comments on the current version. It's a good idea to enter brief comments, so you know what is special about the specific version you are saving.

4 Click OK to save your version.

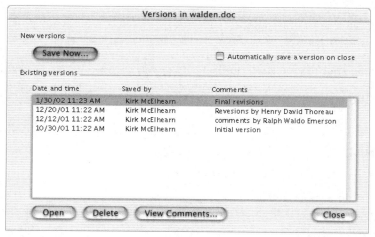

Figure 13-13. The Versions dialog lets you save the current version and lists all previous versions of your document that have been saved.

You can tell Word to automatically save a new version of your document each time the file is closed. To do this, select Automatically Save A Version On Close in the Versions dialog. This way you don't have to remember to save versions manually. However, when you save versions automatically, Word does not ask you to enter comments. It saves the version, noting the date and time, and adds the comment "Automatic Version."

To open a previously saved version, open the Versions dialog, select the version you want to open, and then click Open. When you do this, Word opens the version in a separate window, appending the date it was saved to its name, and arranges the open windows so that you can see both the original and the previous version. If you open several versions, Word will only display the original and the last version you opened, but you can choose to view the other versions by selecting their names on the Window menu. Note that you can't open another version unless you first click in the window containing the current document; if the insertion point is in the window of a version of the file, the Versions command won't be available on the File menu.

To delete a version, click it in the Versions dialog to select it, and then click Delete. You can view comments for any saved version by selecting the version and then clicking View Comments. When viewing comments in this way, you can see the full comments you entered; Word only displays the first few words of your comments in the Versions dialog. Note that once you save a version you cannot edit or delete its comments.

If you want to save a version as an individual file, open the version, and then choose File, Save As. Give the file a new name and save it. This will save only the active version in a separate file. You can compare versions, using the Compare Documents function, if you want to see what changes were made.

For more information on comparing documents, see "Comparing Documents," page 331.

tip   **Share only single-version documents**

Don't send documents with different versions to others. Not only could it be confusing, but your previous versions might contain information you don't want them to see. If you send a file containing versions, anyone can open the previous versions and see what they contain. Make sure you open and save the version you want to send under a new name, rather than just copying your original file that contains all the versions.

Automating Mailing with Data Merging

When you need to send the same letter to every member of a mailing list, you can use Microsoft Word X to create the documents quickly by performing a data merge. A *data merge* combines a list of information with a form document to produce personalized documents. In the past, data merging was one of the most confusing things you could do with Word, until Word 2001 introduced the Data Merge Manager to make the process easier. By using the Data Merge Manager tools, you can step through the process of defining your data merge. Plus, if you need to change your data source or the data you include in your merge, you won't need to create a new merge or even step back through several wizard pages—you can just make the change in the Data Merge Manager and carry on immediately.

This chapter shows you how to perform data merges to create form letters, envelopes, and mailing labels. It also goes into more detail on fields, the elements that make mail merges work. Not only can you save many hours generating letters by using data merges, you can also use fields to add automatically updatable content to any document.

Understanding Data Merges

Producing single documents takes relatively little time in Word. You can create your content, add charts, images, and graphics, and present the package in one file. However, if you need to create more than a few closely related versions of a single document, such as a thank you letter for hundreds of campaign donors, or even mailing labels for a holiday letter addressed to a dozen family members, the time required to make the changes could easily stretch into hours. You can significantly reduce the time required to create the documents by performing a data merge.

Formerly called a mail merge, because the technique is so useful for bulk mailings, a data merge lets you combine the information from a *data source,* which is a database or other collection of data, with a main document. The *main document* can be any document (but is most often a letter), labels, or envelopes, and your data source can be a table in another Word file, a Microsoft Excel X spreadsheet, or records from the Office Address Book included in Microsoft Entourage X. The connection between your data and the main document is a series of *fields,* or placeholders, in the main document that tell Word where to insert the data into your document. Combining the data source with the main document produces a series of merge documents. *Merge documents* are the individualized letters, labels, or envelopes you use as the final product of the data merge process. Figure 14-1 illustrates how the data merging process works.

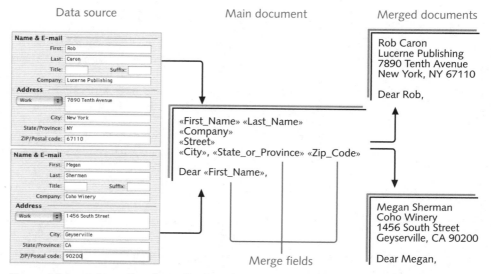

Figure 14-1. Information from the data document is combined with the main document, resulting in the merged documents.

Introducing the Data Merge Manager

Word streamlines the data merge process using the Data Merge Manager, shown in Figure 14-2. You'll use the Data Merge Manager to work with the different elements that will make up the data merge. There are several steps involved in performing a successful data merge:

1 Define a data source.

2 Create the main document, which will provide the text that will remain the same in each of the merged documents.

3 Place field codes in the main document to identify where the variable data should appear; during the merge, the fields will be replaced by the text from the data source to make each merge document unique.

4 Preview the merge and make any necessary changes.

5 Complete the data merge by sending the merge documents to the printer, saving the merge documents to a new Word document, or producing a list of addresses.

For detailed information about fields, see "Understanding Fields," page 352.

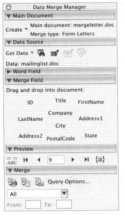

Figure 14-2. The Data Merge Manager provides a road map for the entire merge process, reading from top to bottom. If you want to change any choices you've made, you can go directly to that section and make a new selection.

Preparing Your Data Source

The first step in performing a data merge is to create the data source to provide the field structure and values for the merge. You can choose from several different types of data sources, including creating a source from scratch.

Creating a Data Source Document from Scratch

If you want to create a data source from scratch, you'll use the Create Data Source dialog. This dialog enables you to add fields from an existing list of names, or type in your own field names. Because most data merges are used to generate mailings, the list of fields includes fields for necessary items such as names, addresses, and postal codes.

To create a data source document from scratch, follow these steps:

1 Create a new document, and then choose Tools, Data Merge Manager to display the Data Merge Manager.

2 In the Main Document section of the Data Merge Manager, click the Create pop-up menu, and then select the type of merge document you want to create. You have four choices: Form Letters, Labels, Envelopes, and Catalog.

> **tip** Use the Catalog choice when you want to create a list of information from a database, such as a membership list, or a telephone directory.

3 In the Data Source section of the Data Merge Manager, open the Get Data pop-up menu, and then select New Data Source to display the Create Data Source dialog, shown in Figure 14-3.

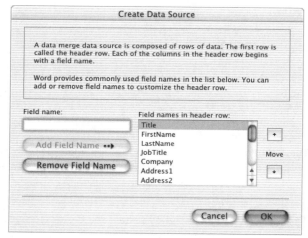

Figure 14-3. Use the Create Data Source dialog to define the structure of your new data source.

4 Word provides a list of predefined fields, which you'll probably want to edit. Define the structure of your new data source in any of these ways:

- To remove an existing field, choose the field, and then click the Remove Field Name button.

- To add a custom field, type the name of the new field in the Field Name box, and then click the Add Field Name button. Note that names cannot contain spaces, although you can link multiple words with an underscore character.

- Click the up arrow button to move a field up in the order.

- Click the down arrow button to move a field down in the order.

5 Click OK to close the Create Data Source dialog and display the Save dialog. Give the data source document a name, and then click the Save button to display the Data Form dialog, as shown here:

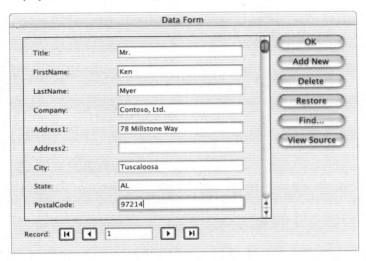

6 The Data Form dialog displays each of the fields you selected in step 4. Type the data for the first merge document in the boxes provided in the Data Form dialog. Each set of data entered into the fields of the data source document is known as a *record*. Therefore, if you're entering data to send out 20 custom letters, you will enter 20 sets of data, creating 20 records. Press Tab after filling in each field to move to the next field, and then do any of the following:

- Click OK to accept the current entry and close the Data Form dialog, when you've finished entering all your data.

- Click the Add New button to accept the current entry and create a new, blank record to fill in.

- Click the Delete button to delete the current record and display the previous record.

- Click the Restore button to undo any changes you have made to the current record.

caution If you move to another record after you make your changes, you will not be able to restore the original values.

- Click the Find button to display the Find In Field dialog. Type the value you want to find in the Find What box, select the field in which you want to find the value from the In Field pop-up menu, and then click the Find First button to display the first occurrence of the value you typed in the Find What box. After the first find, you can keep searching by clicking the Find Next button, which replaces the Find First button.

■ Click the View Source button to display your records in the Microsoft Word data source document.

caution Don't type extra spaces after the entries in the Data Form dialog. Those extra spaces, which don't show up in the data source, could throw off the structure of your merged document. For example, if you are pressed for space and need to keep every letter to a single page in length, extra white space could force a line break and push your signature block onto a second page.

tip To edit a data source you created from scratch, open the main document, and then click the Edit Data Source button in the Data Source section of the Data Merge Manager.

note When you create a data source from scratch, Word asks you to name the file where the data will be stored. The file you create is a new Word file, and the data you type into the Data Form dialog is recorded in a table. If you want, you can open that file and edit it in Word. Be careful to save your work and close the file after you're done editing; if the file is still open when you attempt your data merge, it might not work.

Using Entourage Data as the Data Source

One easy way to maintain current contact information and merge that information into a mailing is to use data from the Address Book, which is part of Entourage X.

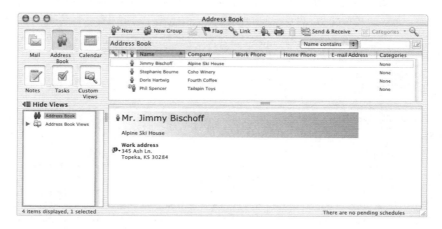

note There's a slight disagreement in terminology between Word X and Entourage X. Word's Data Merge Manager refers to the Office Address Book, but you'll only find an Address Book in Entourage. They're the same thing; the Office Address Book moniker is a leftover from the Office 98 days, when Word had a separate address book.

For more information on maintaining a list of contacts in Entourage, see Chapter 20, "Managing Your Contacts."

To use Entourage data as the data source, follow these steps:

1 Choose File, New Blank Document to create a new document, and then choose Tools, Data Merge Manager to display the Data Merge Manager.

2 In the Main Document section of the Data Merge Manager, open the Create pop-up menu, and then select the type of merge document you want to create.

3 In the Data Source section of the Data Merge Manager, open the Get Data pop-up menu, and then select Office Address Book to display the Address Book fields from Entourage in the Merge Field section of the Data Merge Manager.

Using an Excel Worksheet as the Data Source

If your data happens to be contained in an Excel worksheet, you can merge that data directly into your documents. Word will treat the columns of the worksheet as the data fields, and each row will be a data record.

To use an Excel worksheet as your data source, follow these steps:

1 Choose File, New Blank Document to create a new document, and then choose Tools, Data Merge Manager to display the Data Merge Manager.

2 In the Main Document section of the Data Merge Manager, open the Create pop-up menu, and then select the type of merge document you want to create.

3 In the Data Source section of the Data Merge Manager, open the Get Data pop-up menu, and then select Open Data Source to display the Choose A File dialog.

4 Navigate to the Excel file to use as the data source for your merge, and then click Open to display the Open Worksheet dialog, shown in Figure 14-4 on the next page.

Chapter 14

Figure 14-4. Use the Open Worksheet dialog to identify the worksheet containing the data for your merge.

5 Select the worksheet that contains the data to be used in the merge, and then click OK.

> **note** If you only want to use certain worksheet rows in the merge, type the cell references of the range containing the records in the Cell Range box.

Troubleshooting

When I try to merge data from an Excel worksheet, my field names are wrong and my first row of data is missing.

When reading merge data from an Excel worksheet, Word expects the first row of the worksheet to contain column headings (i.e., field names such as FirstName, LastName, etc.). If there isn't a row of field names above the first row of data, the values of the first data row will appear as the field names in the Merge Field section of the Data Merge Manager. To fix the problem, open the worksheet in Excel, insert a row above the first data row, and type descriptive field names for each column.

Preparing the Main Document

After you define the data source for your merge, you can go ahead and add the common text and images to your main document. When the boilerplate material, including any punctuation you want to appear after a field's value (such as a comma after a city name) is in place, you add the field codes from the Merge Field section of the Data Merge Manager to finish defining the main document's structure.

To prepare the main document for the data merge, display the document and then follow these steps:

1 Enter the text you want to appear in every printed document, and then, if necessary, click the Merge Field section title in the Data Merge Manager to expand the Merge Field section, shown in Figure 14-5.

Figure 14-5. The Merge Field section of the Data Merge Manager shows the fields available for use in your main document.

2 Drag the fields from the Merge Fields section to the body of the main document, and drop them where you want the data for the field to appear in the document. The fields appear in the main document as the field name, surrounded by double angle brackets, as shown here:

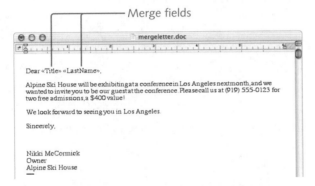

> **tip** To have the contents of a field appear in more than one place in your document, drag the field name again from the Merge Field section to each additional location in the document.

3 Type any additional punctuation or spacing around the fields as required for the field data to appear correctly in the document. For instance, you would type a space between the first and last name fields.

Limiting Records Used in a Merge

When you want to create a mass mailing, but don't want to send the letter to everyone in your data source, you can use the Query Options dialog to limit the records that appear in your merge. For example, if you wanted to send a letter to your customers in California announcing that your company would be demonstrating your newest product at a conference in Los Angeles, you could use the Query Options dialog to limit the addresses to customers in California.

To limit the records used in a merge, follow these steps:

1 Define the data source and merge fields for your merge, and then, if necessary, click the Merge section title in the Data Merge Manager to expand the Merge section.

2 Click the Query Options button to display the Query Options dialog, shown in Figure 14-6.

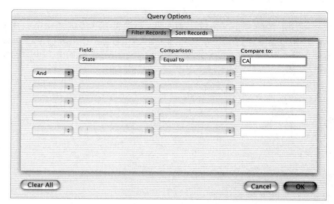

Figure 14-6. Use the Query Options dialog to determine which records will be used in your merge.

> **note** The Query Options dialog changes to match the type of data source selected. For example, if you are using Entourage's Address Book as the data source, you can only limit the data records using Entourage's Category field, or by choosing individual data records.

3 On the Filter Records tab, open the first Field pop-up menu, and then choose the first field by which you want to limit the records appearing in your merge. For instance, to limit your records to those living in California, select the State field.

4 Open the first Comparison pop-up menu, and then choose the comparison operation you want to use to compare the field value. In this example you would choose Equal To.

5 Type the comparison value for the first field in the first Compare To box. In this example you would type CA or California, depending on the format of the data in the State field.

6 You can add additional criteria by opening the first operator pop-up menu (the left-most pop-up menu on the second row of options), and choosing AND or OR. Choosing AND requires both the first statement and the new statement to be met, whereas OR requires at least one of the statements to be met.) Use the second row of Field, Comparison, and Compare To fields to complete the second criterion, and continue with additional criteria on subsequent rows of the dialog if you want.

> ## InsideOut
>
> ### Sort records in a merge data source
>
> If you want to print your records in a particular order without rearranging the data in your source file, you can do so by displaying the Data Merge Manager and clicking the Query Options button in the Merge section to display the Query Options dialog. In the dialog, click the Sort Records tab and choose up to three fields by which you want to sort and whether you want to sort each field in ascending or descending order. For example, you could sort a customer list by state, then by last name, and then by first name.

Previewing the Merged Data

After you create or define the data source and create the main document, you should preview the results of your merge to ensure all of the fields are in the right place and that no data was left out. Previewing will show the data in your main document as it will appear in the merged documents.

To preview your merged data, follow these steps:

1 Open the main document, and then, if necessary, expand the Preview section of the Data Merge Manager.

View Merged Data

2 In the Preview section of the Data Merge Manager, click the View Merged Data button to display the first record merged into the document.

3 Use these options in the Preview section of the Data Merge Manager to move through and preview the records:

- Click the First Record or Last Record button to view the first or last merged document.

- Click the Previous Record or Next Record button to step through the merged documents.

- Type the number of the merged document you want to view in the Go To Record box, and then press Return.

- Click the View Field Codes button (at the right end of the Preview section) to display the field codes in the body of the previewed document. After the codes are displayed, clicking the View Field Codes button again will hide the codes.

Printing the Data Merge

Once everything is in place, you can finish the data merge by printing the results. You can choose to print your results directly, send the results to a new Word document, or print the results on a series of envelopes or labels.

Printing Documents

To print merged documents, follow these steps:

Merge
To Printer

1 Click the Merge To Printer button in the Merge section of the Data Merge Manager to display the Print dialog.

2 Use the Print dialog to choose the settings for the print run, and then click the Print button.

> For more information on setting options in the Print dialog, see "Printing Documents," page 76.

Printing Envelopes

To print envelopes based on your merged data, follow these steps:

1 Create a blank document, and then choose Tools, Data Merge Manager to display the Data Merge Manager.

2 In the Main Document section, open the Create pop-up menu, and then choose Envelopes to display the Envelope dialog, shown in Figure 14-7.

Figure 14-7. The Envelope dialog lets you set the basic parameters for envelopes created by your data merge.

3 Verify that the address in the Return Address box is correct (edit it if it isn't), and then click OK to return to the main document. The document appears as an envelope with the return address you set and a text box in the middle of the envelope, ready to accept fields from the source file.

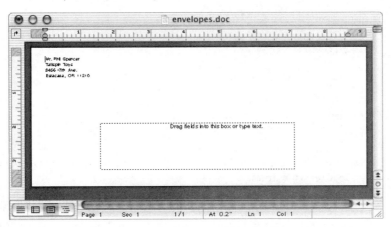

4 Use the Get Data pop-up menu in the Data Merge Manager to choose the data source for your envelopes.

5 Drag the fields from the Merge Field section onto the body of the envelope in the main document.

6 In the Merge section of the Data Merge Manager, click the Merge To Printer button to print your envelopes.

Printing Labels

To print mailing labels based on your merged data, follow these steps:

1 Create a blank document, and then choose Tools, Data Merge Manager to display the Data Merge Manager.

2 Open the Create pop-up menu in the Main Document section of the Data Merge Manager, and then choose Labels to display the Label Options dialog, shown in Figure 14-8 on the next page.

3 Select either Dot Matrix or Laser And Ink Jet to identify your type of printer in the Printer Information area.

4 Open the Label Products pop-up menu, and select the manufacturer of the labels you are using.

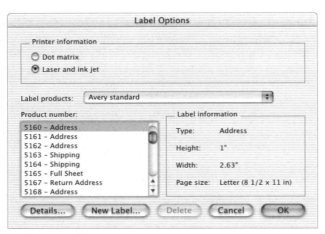

Figure 14-8. The Label Options dialog gives you complete control over how your text will appear on your labels.

5 In the Product Number pane, select the label design you are using.

6 Click OK to close the Label Options dialog and display the Edit Labels dialog, which shows a single blank label.

7 Choose fields from the Insert Merge Field pop-up menu in the Edit Labels dialog, and add any necessary punctuation or spacing.

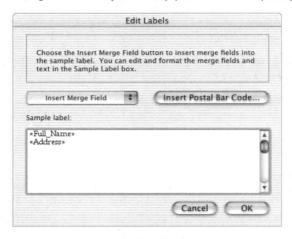

> **tip** You may be able to save yourself time (depending on your data) by using the Full Name and Address merge fields; Full Name includes the First Name and Last Name fields, and Address includes the Street, City, State, and Zip Code fields.

8 Click OK to close the Edit Labels dialog. The fields you chose will be replicated on all the labels on the sheet, and an additional field <<Next Record>>

Chapter 14

is automatically inserted on each label after the first label, so that a new record is printed on each label.

> **note** The main document will display labels with just the field codes you entered until you click the View Merged Data button in the Preview section of the Data Merge Manager.

9 In the Merge section of the Data Merge Manager, click the Merge To Printer button to display the Print dialog, from which you can print your labels.

InsideOut

Print on part of a label

If you need to limit the area of a label you print on, you can change the margins of your label by merging your labels to a document and then adjusting the layout of the document. The key to working with labels in this format is understanding that the labels are displayed in a table. You can use the techniques in Chapter 9, "Laying Out Text," to change the margins and other formatting characteristics of the table cells containing your labels.

Troubleshooting

My label doesn't appear on the list of available labels. How do I define a custom label?

If you're using a label that's of your own manufacture, or if you can't find the label in the Label Options dialog's list, you can define your own label by clicking the New Label button in the Label Options dialog. Clicking the New Label button displays the New Custom dialog. You can type a name for your new label in the Label Name box, and then define the various measurements of your labels (the graphic at the top of the dialog shows each element of the label that you can set the dimensions of). If your labels are close to another style of label, you can make that label's measurements appear in the New Custom dialog by selecting that label in the Label Options dialog; then click New Label, and modify it as needed.

Merging to a New Document

To merge your data into a new document rather than printing it directly to a printer, follow these steps:

1 Create any type of merge document using the techniques described in this chapter.

Merge
To New
Document

2 In the Merge section of the Data Merge Manager, click the Merge To New Document button. Word will write the results of your merge to a new document, which you can edit if required and save for later use. If your merge type is Form Letters, Word will merge each letter to the new file, inserting a page break after each letter.

Understanding Fields

Fields provide the power for data merges, and now that you've seen how data merges work, let's look behind the curtain and see more detail about how fields work, and how they can be used. As mentioned earlier, a *field* is a placeholder used to store information about one aspect, or *property,* of a person, place, or thing. Database tables are one example of how fields are used to describe things of interest. These tables consist of columns and rows. Each column represents a field, and each row, or *record,* contains a complete set of fields. The following graphic shows a series of records from a table named Customers.

ID	Title	FirstName	LastName	Company	Address1	Address2	City	State	PostalCode
				Customers					
0301	Mr.	Jimmy	Bischoff	Alpine Ski House	345 Ash Ln.		Topeka	KS	30284
0302	Ms.	Stephanie	Bourne	Coho Winery	12345 Valley Dr.		Dundee	OR	22841
0303	Mrs.	Doris	Hartwig	Fourth Coffee	890 Bean St.		Boston	MA	68041
0304	Mr.	Phil	Spencer	Tailspin Toys	3456 17th Ave.		Estacada	OR	11210
0305	Mr.	Bradley	Beck	Blue Yonder Airlines	67 Canyon Rd.	Ste. A4	Skokie	IL	78020
0306	Ms.	Jane	Clayton	Wingtip Toys	456 Circle Pl.		Delray Beach	FL	99302
0307	Mr.	Marc	Faeber	Alpine Ski House	345 Ash Ln.		Topeka	KS	30284
0308	Ms.	Pat	Coleman	Fourth Coffee	890 Bean St.		Boston	MA	68041
0309	Mrs.	Judy	Lew	Tailspin Toys	3456 17th Ave.		Estacada	OR	11210
0310	Ms.	Birgit	Seidl	Coho Winery	12345 Valley Dr.		Dundee	OR	22841
0311	Mr.	Paul	West	Consolidated Messenger	567 Frontage Rd.		Fort Wayne	IN	61930
0312	Ms.	Britta	Simon	Consolidated Messenger	567 Frontage Rd.		Fort Wayne	IN	61930

In this table, there are fields to represent all of the information you need to know about a customer to personalize a boilerplate letter and print an envelope with the appropriate name and address. To merge the information from the Customers table into a letter, a process described earlier in this chapter in the discussion of data merges, you could use the field names to create the main document shown here.

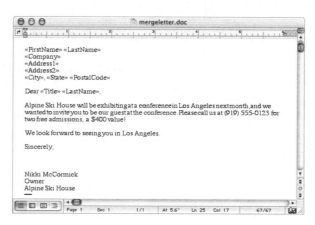

«FirstName» «LastName»
«Company»
«Address1»
«Address2»
«City», «State» «PostalCode»

Dear «Title» «LastName»,

Alpine Ski House will be exhibiting at a conference in Los Angeles next month, and we wanted to invite you to be our guest at the conference. Please call us at (919) 555-0123 for two free admissions, a $400 value!

We look forward to seeing you in Los Angeles.

Sincerely,

Nikki McCormick
Owner
Alpine Ski House

Chapter 14

The field names in this main document are created by adding field codes to your document. For example, the FirstName field in the preceding graphic is actually defined by the following field code, which contains the field name that provides the data as well as formatting information that instructs Word how to display the field's contents:

{ MERGEFIELD FirstName }

You can show the field codes if you like; press Option+F9. The result is shown here:

The remainder of this chapter discusses how to define fields to add information to your document.

> **tip**   It's important to give your fields descriptive names so that you can add the fields to your documents accurately and review the document effectively after you've been away from it for a while.

Defining Fields

In general usage, fields are containers for data about something's properties. In the context of a Word document, however, a field is a marker that identifies a location where you want to insert additional information. The actual code used to define a field is shown here:

{ TIME \@ "h:mm:ss AM/PM" * MERGEFORMAT }

The field code has four parts:

● The **field identifiers,** which are printed as curly brackets in the document. These characters are actually special characters Word creates when you insert a field using the Field dialog or by pressing Command+F9, not the regular curly brackets you type from the keyboard.

- The **field name;** in the preceding example the field name is *TIME*.

- **The field arguments,** such as the pattern in which you want the data to be displayed, or a user prompt. In the example, the string *h:mm:ss AM/PM* is the field argument, and the quotes are used so the entire string with its spaces is treated as one argument.

- **Switches** are used to control how the field's results are formatted. The switch *MERGEFORMAT*, for example, means any formatting changes you make to the contents of the field will be retained even if the field's value changes.

To define a field, follow these steps:

1 Position the insertion point where you want to add the field, and then choose Insert, Field to display the Field dialog, shown in Figure 14-9.

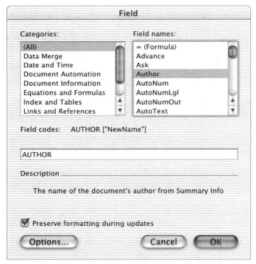

Figure 14-9. The Field dialog organizes the available fields so that you can choose the best field for the job.

2 Choose the category that contains the field you want to define, and then select the field from the list in the Field Names pane. Table 14-1 lists all fields available to you, by category.

3 Select the Preserve Formatting During Updates check box to ensure your formatting options are saved whenever field contents are refreshed.

Table 14-1. Available Fields, Listed by Category

Category	Description	Field Codes
Data Merge	Fields for use in mail merging operations.	ASK COMPARE DATABASE FILL-IN IF MERGEFIELD MERGEREC MERGESEQ NEXT NEXTIF SET SKIPIF
Date And Time	Fields in this category let you insert any combination of the current date and time into your document.	CREATEDATE DATE EDITTIME PRINTDATE SAVEDATE TIME
Document Automation	These fields enable you to move around in your document, launch macros or GoTo buttons, or print.	COMPARE DOCVARIABLE GOTOBUTTON IF MACROBUTTON PRINT
Document Information	Fields in this category let you insert information about your document, including the user who last saved it, the file's name, and the original author.	AUTHOR COMMENTS DOCPROPERTY FILENAME FILESIZE INFO KEYWORDS LASTSAVEDBY NUMCHARS NUMPAGES NUMWORDS SUBJECT TEMPLATE TITLE

(continued)

Table 14-1. *(continued)*

Category	Description	Field Codes
Equations And Formulas	These fields enable you to calculate values, insert symbols, and enter automatically incremented values.	= *(Formula)* ADVANCE EQ SYMBOL
Index And Tables	These fields let you define tables of contents, tables of authorities, and index entries. You can add these codes using the Index And Tables dialog.	INDEX RD TA TC TOA TOC XE
Links And References	These fields enable you to insert values from the AutoText list and establish links and references to external files.	AUTOTEXT AUTOTEXTLIST CONTACT HYPERLINK INCLUDEPICTURE INCLUDETEXT LINK NOTEREF PAGEREF PLACEHOLDER QUOTE REF STYLEREF
Numbering	These fields let you add autonumbered values for pages, list items, and sections. You can also add bar codes.	AUTONUM AUTONUMLGL AUTONUMOUT BARCODE LISTNUM PAGE REVNUM SECTION SECTIONPAGES SEQ
User Information	These fields display the registered user's name, address, and initials.	USERADDRESS USERINITIALS USERNAME USERPROPERTY

Fields: Not Just for Data Merging!

Using field codes in a document makes it easy for you to include information from other data sources, such as Excel worksheets, in your document. The most common use for user-inserted fields is in a mail merge, but there are many other ways you can take advantage of fields to make it easier for you to manipulate your documents.

One situation where you can use fields to your advantage is when you are generating an outline and want to move headings around without having to manually renumber the entire outline every time you make a change in structure. To do that, you use the SEQ field, which inserts a sequential value into your document. As an example, consider a list of this book's first four chapters:

Chapter 1: An Overview of Office v. X

Chapter 2: Creating and Managing Documents

Chapter 3: Getting Expert Help with Office v. X

Chapter 4: Office v. X: Do It Your Way

This list was actually created using the following combination of field codes and text:

Chapter { SEQ chapter * MERGEFORMAT }: An Overview of Office v. X

Chapter { SEQ chapter * MERGEFORMAT }: Creating and Managing Documents

Chapter { SEQ chapter * MERGEFORMAT }: Getting Expert Help with Office v. X

Chapter { SEQ chapter * MERGEFORMAT }: Office v. X: Do It Your Way

The word *chapter* is the series name argument that identifies the numbering series. Every time Word encounters a field code beginning with *SEQ chapter*, it will print an incremented value.

If you used manually entered chapter numbers and moved the fourth chapter to the second position, you would need to renumber chapters two through four. By using a SEQ field to generate the chapter numbers, however, Word will renumber the chapters for you. To trigger the automatic renumbering, however, you'll have to tell Word to update the field codes by pressing F9.

The next level of using SEQ fields to number items in your documents is to have two or more sequential numbering series going at the same time. To create a second series, you add a SEQ field code with a different series name argument. In a document where you wanted to sequentially number figures and tables, for example, you could have all figure names include the field code { SEQ figure…} and all table codes include the field code { SEQ table…}.

Using Field Switches

In addition to letting you insert fields into your documents, you can also use the Field Options dialog to set the options for the field. The options available vary for each type of field, but you can display all of the options by clicking the Options button in the Field dialog. Figure 14-10 shows the Field Options dialog for a TIME field.

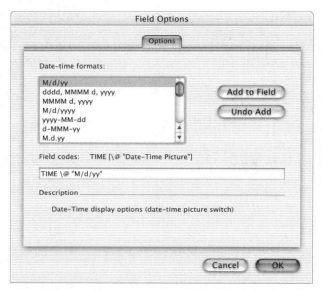

Figure 14-10. You can use the Options dialog to set the switches for a field.

To use field switches, follow these steps:

1 Choose Insert, Field to open the Field dialog, select the field you want to add, and then click the Options button to open the Field Options dialog.

> **note** Not every field has switches that can be set, so the Options button isn't enabled for every field type.

2 The Field Options dialog displays the switches you can use to format the field's contents. The specific configuration of the dialog will change depending on the field you selected in the Field dialog, but you will be able to choose from general switches and field-specific switches. Table 14-2 lists the general field code switches by category.

> **note** Clicking a switch displays a description of the switch in the Field Options dialog. Also, the same switch can have different meanings depending on the field to which it's applied.

Table 14-2. **General Field Code Switches**

Category	Switch	Description	Example
Format	*	Lets you specify the character formatting of a display field	{USERINITIALS * Upper}
Numeric Picture	\#	Lets you specify how a number will be displayed	{PAGE \# "0"}
Date-Time Picture	\@	Lets you specify how a date or time value will be displayed	{CREATEDATE \@ "MMMM d, yyyy"}
Lock Result	\!	Lets you prevent changes to BOOKMARK, INCLUDETEXT, and REF fields, even if those values have changed since the field was last updated	{INCLUDETEXT \! "mailinglist.doc"}

Viewing Field Codes

When you insert a field into a document, you will see the results of the field code and not the code itself. If you want to display one (or all) of the field codes in your document, perhaps to see the field codes used to add a specific value to the document or to refresh your memory of the argument you used for a numbering sequence, you can do so quickly.

To view field codes, follow either of these steps:

- To change the view of a single field, Control+click the field and choose Toggle Field Codes.

- To change the view of all fields in a document, press Option+F9.

---

tip **View the fields (not the field codes)**

Word can show you the fields in your documents by shading them. Choose Word, Preferences, and then select the View category. Select the Field Codes button, and then choose how you want the field codes to display from the Field Shading pop-up menu. Your choices will be Never, Always, or When Selected (which is usually the most useful choice).

Table 14-3 on the next page contains a list of the keyboard shortcuts you can use when working with fields.

Chapter 14

Table 14-3. **Shortcut Keys for Working with Fields**

Keyboard Shortcut	Action
Control+Shift+D	Inserts a DATE field into the document
Command+Option+Shift+L	Inserts a LISTNUM field into the document
Control+Shift+P	Inserts a PAGE field into the document
Control+Shift+T	Inserts a TIME field into the document
Command+F9	Inserts an empty field into the document
F9	Updates all selected fields
Command+Shift+F9	Permanently replaces field code with the current value of the code
Shift+F9	Switches between a field code and its result
Option+F9	Switches between all field codes and their results
Option+Shift+F9	Runs a GOTOBUTTON or MACROBUTTON that provides the contents for the selected field
F11	Moves you to the next field
Shift+F11	Moves you to the previous field
Command+F11	Locks a field (prevents changes)
Command+Shift+F11	Unlocks a field (allows changes)

tip To print a document including field codes (and not the field code results), choose Word, Preferences, select the Print category, and then select the Field Codes check box in the Include With Document section.

Formatting Fields

When you add a field to a document without any additional formatting information, Word will format the field's results to match the surrounding text. You can, however, add formatting instructions to the field code so that Word knows to apply that formatting to the field's results.

To format the contents of a field, follow these steps:

1 If necessary, Control+click the field, and choose Toggle Field Codes to display the field code.

2 After the last character in the field code, but before the closing curly bracket, type *** Charformat**.

3 Apply the formatting you want for the field to the first character of the field name. One example would be to type **{*TIME* \@ "h:mm AM/PM" * Charformat}**, which displays **5:36 PM**, in italic text to match the italic letter *T* in Time.

4 Control+click the field, and choose Update Field to apply your changes. If you updated more than one field, press F9 to update every field in your document.

Creating Pages for the Web

There was once a time when most computers were isolated from their brethren. Home computers were almost never connected to a network (with the exception of pioneering bulletin board systems), the Internet was still the province of select educational and military institutions, and the World Wide Web was years from creation. Starting in the 1970s, companies began to put their computers on local area networks; this trend accelerated rapidly in the 1980s, when Ethernet connections let companies move data from location to location quickly. Then, in the mid-1990s, the Web caught the attention of the general public in the United States, and the growth of Internet service providers (ISPs), online services, and connectivity for college students in their dorm rooms pushed development even faster.

Now it's possible, and not even all that remarkable, to exchange documents with colleagues 12 time zones away or to make a document available to the general computer-using public by marking up the document in the language of the Web, Hypertext Markup Language (HTML), and placing it on a Web site.

This chapter shows you how to create, manipulate, and format a Web page in Microsoft Word. You can use any of the formatting techniques covered earlier in this part of the book to make your document look exactly the way you want it to.

Building Web Pages

One of the strengths of the Microsoft Office v. X applications is that they greatly facilitate creating, manipulating, and saving documents for the Web. In fact, you can save documents as Web pages in all of the Office applications. Once you publish your files to the Web, you and your colleagues can access the documents from any Web-connected computer. Although you can create Web files in any of the Office v. X programs, you're most likely to use Word for the task. Word allows you to create Web pages that look virtually the same on the Web as they do in Word, as shown in Figure 15-1.

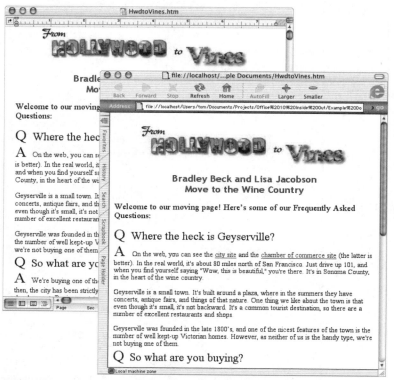

Figure 15-1. At the upper left is a Web page as created in Word, and at the lower right is the same page as it appears in Internet Explorer.

Creating Web Documents

To create a Web page in Word, follow these steps:

1 Open the document you want to convert into a Web page, and then open the Project Gallery dialog if it is not displayed already. From there you can perform any of these actions:

- To create a blank Web page, select Blank Documents in the Category pane, select Web Page in the right pane, and then click OK.

- To create a Web page based on a template from the Project Gallery, click the disclosure triangle next to Web Pages in the Category pane, select one of the subcategories of Web pages that appear, and then select the template you want to use as the base for your Web page, as shown in Figure 15-2. Choosing one of these templates creates a Web page with the layout shown in the preview pane. You can, of course, modify the Web page once you have it open in Word.

■ To open an existing Web page or Word document you want to convert to a Web page, click the Open button in the bottom left corner, and then use the controls in the Open dialog to locate and open the file you want to use as the base of your Web page.

2 Add the textual and graphic content of your Web page, editing and formatting the document using the techniques covered earlier in this part of the book.

3 Save the file as a Web page to the location where you want to access it—your local disk, a Web server, or Web hosting service.

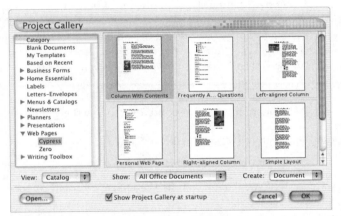

Figure 15-2. You can display the Web Pages templates available to you in the Project Gallery.

> **note** Not every element of a Word document can be transferred to HTML documents. Those elements that cannot be transferred include headers and footers, margin settings you make using the Page Setup dialog, columns, automatic hyphens, watermarks, vertical text in tables, and some character formatting and style effects such as shadow and text animations.

Opening Web Documents

Hypertext Markup Language is one of the formats built into Microsoft Word. You can take advantage of the interaction between Word and HTML by opening HTML pages in Word and editing them directly.

Hypertext Markup Language (HTML)

Hypertext Markup Language (HTML) is a method of describing how Web browsers, such as Microsoft Internet Explorer, should display the contents of a file. The display instructions are enclosed in *tags*. For example, if you wanted to instruct Web browsers to display a bit of text in boldface, you would surround the text with a pair of <bold>...</bold> tags. So, the HTML code fragment <bold>Sales for the Year</bold> would be displayed as **Sales for the Year**. You can also use HTML tags to identify structural elements of a document. An HTML document has two parts: the *head*, which includes the title of the document, and any *keywords* you want search engines such as Lycos or Google to use to index the page; and the *body*, which contains the document elements that will be displayed in the main window of a browser.

When you save a Word document as a Web page, Word analyzes your document and adds the tags required to make it look the same in a Web browser as it does in the Word document window. The translation process isn't perfect, but you can preview your document (in either Word or in a Web browser) before you commit to saving it as an HTML file and make any changes to ensure the file looks the way you want it to when it's viewed on the Web. You can also open the saved HTML file in Macromedia Dreamweaver, Adobe GoLive, or another Web page editing program.

To open an HTML document in Microsoft Word, follow these steps:

1 Choose File, Open to display the Open dialog.

2 From the Show pop-up menu, select Web Pages.

3 Navigate to the folder containing the Web page you want to open, select the file, and then click Open.

For information on searching for an existing Web page or Word document, see "Opening Existing Documents," page 21.

Adding Web Page Elements

The most important element of any Web page is the content. Many Web sites are simple lists of content on other sites or, even worse, links to pages with more lists of sites on still further sites. You can do quite a bit more with Word than put your words and images on the Web, however. In this section, you'll learn how to

- Insert hyperlinks
- Add background colors, patterns, and images
- Build Web forms

Inserting and Linking Hyperlinks

One of the strengths of the World Wide Web is the ability to reference locations else-where on the Web using *hyperlinks*. Word usually displays hyperlinks underlined and in a different color than the normal text, as shown in Figure 15-3. When a reader clicks a hyperlink, the Web browser downloads the referenced page or item. A hyperlink in a Word document has two components: the text or image that serves as the base, or *anchor,* for the hyperlink and the *URL* (Uniform Resource Locator, or address) of the target location. In Figure 15-3, the page's first hyperlink (or *link*), has the word *Sites* as its text base; the URL component isn't visible on the page, but if it were part of Microsoft's large Web site, it might be something like *www.microsoft.com/sites/ default.html*. When a reader clicks Sites, the browser retrieves the page or other item at the URL location and displays it.

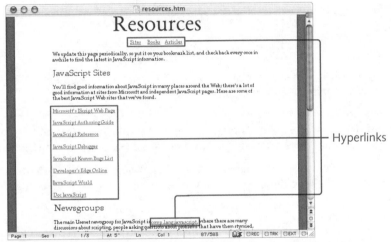

Figure 15-3. This Web page in Word includes several hyperlinks.

You can use hyperlinks to refer to a Web site, a file on another computer on your local network or your own computer, an image file, or even a different location within the current document. If you want to allow readers of your document to send you an e-mail message easily, you can also create a hyperlink with your e-mail address as the target.

To add a hyperlink to a Word document, follow these steps:

1 Select the text or image you want to use as the base for your hyperlink. If you're choosing text, it will become the underlined text that the user clicks. You can also place the insertion point at the location in the Word document where you want the hyperlink to appear and define the base text or image when you define the target of the hyperlink.

2 Open the Insert Hyperlink dialog, shown in Figure 15-4, by choosing Insert, Hyperlink or by pressing Command+K.

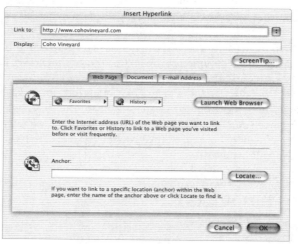

Figure 15-4. You can create many kinds of hyperlinks using the controls in the Insert Hyperlink dialog.

3 Type (or edit) the base text of the hyperlink in the Display box. You can skip this step if you are using an image as the base for the hyperlink, and if you selected text before opening the dialog, it will appear in the box automatically.

4 In the bottom section of the Insert Hyperlink dialog, select the tab that describes the type of item you want to serve as the target of your hyperlink:

■ To link to an existing Web page, click the Web Page tab.

■ To link to a document on your computer or that is reachable over a network, click the Document tab.

■ To create a link to an e-mail address, which will give the person clicking the hyperlink the opportunity to send an e-mail message to the address you define in the hyperlink, click the E-Mail Address tab.

5 If you selected Web Page in step 4, specify the target Web page using one of the following methods:

■ To specify a Web page with a URL you know, type the URL in the Link To box.

■ To select a page that is on your Internet Explorer 5.1 Favorites list, click Favorites, and then select the target Web page from the pop-up menu that appears.

■ To select a page you browsed recently, click History, and then select the target page from the pop-up menu that appears.

Chapter 15

■ To locate a page on the Web, click the Launch Web Browser button, navigate to the desired target, copy the URL from your browser's Address box, switch back to Word, and paste the address in the Link To box by pressing Command+V. You must use the shortcut key to paste the link, because the Edit menu appears dimmed while the Insert Hyperlink dialog is open.

■ To link to a specific location, or anchor, in the target Web page, click the Locate button and then use the controls in the Select Place In Document dialog to identify the anchor to which you want to link. If you don't specify an anchor, the page will be opened at its beginning, or top. If the page is long, inserting an anchor will cause the page to automatically scroll (if necessary) to the location specified when a reader clicks the link.

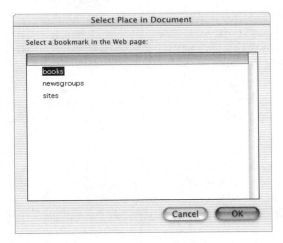

6 If you selected Document in step 4, select the target file using one of the following methods:

■ To select a file that is on your computer or is reachable over your network, click the Select button and then use the controls in the Choose A File dialog to select the file.

■ To select a file that is on your Favorites list, click the Favorites button, and then select the target file from the list that appears.

■ To link to a specific location, or anchor, in the target file, click the Locate button, and then use the controls in the Select Place In Document dialog to identify the anchor to which you want to link. Note that your document must contain one or more bookmarks (from Word, use Insert, Bookmark) for you to anchor the hyperlink to a specific location.

Chapter 15

7 If you selected E-Mail Address in step 4, select the target e-mail address using one of the following methods:

- To specify any e-mail address, type the address in the To box, such as **bob@cohovineyard.com**.

- To select an address to which you recently sent an e-mail message, click the Recent Addresses button and then select the target address from the list that appears.

> **note** The list of recent addresses comes from Entourage, the Office v. X e-mail application.

- To select an address from an e-mail application, click the Launch E-Mail Application button, and then select the address from within the application. Copy the address from the e-mail application, switch back to Word, and paste the e-mail address into the To box by pressing Command+V. You must use the shortcut key to paste the link, because the Edit menu appears dimmed while the Insert Hyperlink dialog is open.

8 To have a message appear above a hyperlink when you hover the pointer over the hyperlink, click the ScreenTip button, and then type the message in the ScreenTip Text box of the Set Hyperlink ScreenTip dialog.

9 Click OK.

You can edit an existing hyperlink by Control+clicking the text or image serving as the base of the hyperlink and choosing Hyperlink, Edit Hyperlink from the contextual menu that appears. If you want to remove the hyperlink, click the Remove Link button at the bottom left corner of the Edit Hyperlink dialog.

InsideOut

Fix an overzealous AutoFormat

When you type a URL into a Word document, the AutoFormat feature takes over and formats the text as a hyperlink. That's great if you want to make it a real hyperlink, but if not (such as when you're planning to distribute the document in print only), the change in appearance will make the hyperlink's text look different than the surrounding text. To remove the format that AutoFormat imposes, press Command+Z immediately after Word makes the change.

Adding a Background Color, Pattern, or Image to a Web Page

Clubs, companies, and organizations of all sorts usually develop a logo and color scheme for their internal documents, corporate communications, and Web site. You can use the skills covered earlier in this part of the book to add images and apply styles to the contents of your Web pages, but you can also add a background color, pattern, or image to your Web pages. For example, if you were creating a Web page with information about a new high-tech product, you could make the background of the main page advertising the product a blaring electric color, and include text in a contrasting, difficult-to-read color. Sure, this *sounds* bad, but haven't you seen color schemes just like this all over the Web? If you like this approach, or if your site will be a bit more sedate, Word can accommodate your creativity.

If you don't want the background of your page to be a solid color, you can create a background that is a pattern, a texture, or an image that repeats to fill the background. Microsoft Office v. X comes with several textures, which are used in the themes you can apply to your Office documents, or you can buy new textures from any computer graphics supply shop.

> For information on applying existing themes to your Word document or Web page, see "Using Themes," page 180.

To add a background color, pattern, texture, or image to a Web page or Word document, choose Format, Background, and then perform any of the following steps:

- To apply a standard background color to the Web page or document, click the desired color in the Background palette.

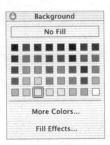

- To use the Color Picker to choose another color, or to custom-design a color, click More Colors.

- To apply a background texture, pattern, gradient, or image, click Fill Effects, and use the controls in the Fill Effects dialog to select your background. The controls on the Texture tab are shown in Figure 15-5 on the next page.

- To remove a background, click No Fill.

> **tip** You should use the standard light background and dark text on pages where the visitor will read paragraphs of information. The traditional scheme is much easier on the eyes.

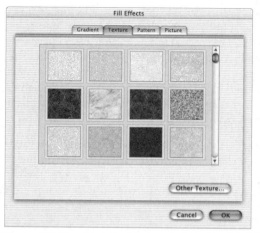

Figure 15-5. Use the Texture tab in the Fill Effects dialog to define background texture for your document, or click one of the other tabs to create a different kind of fill.

Troubleshooting

Web page background and fill colors change (or appear different) on some monitors.

The colors that appear on the standard palette in the Background palette are "Web safe" colors, meaning that most any monitor, regardless of the number of colors it is set to display (usually a minimum of 256, but often running into the millions), will display the colors accurately. Creating custom colors with the controls in the Color Picker gives you greater control over the exact color you use, but it also raises the possibility that your site visitors' monitors might not display the color accurately, rendering your carefully thought-out color scheme useless.

When you want to choose a color for use on a Web page, open the Color Picker and change to Name view. When the Color Picker is open in Name view, you can only pick colors that are "Web safe," that is, colors that will display correctly in most Web browsers. You can display the Web safe colors in a range by clicking a color close to the one you want in the multicolored vertical bar on the right side of the Color Picker dialog and then using your keyboard's Up Arrow and Down Arrow keys to move through the list one color at a time.

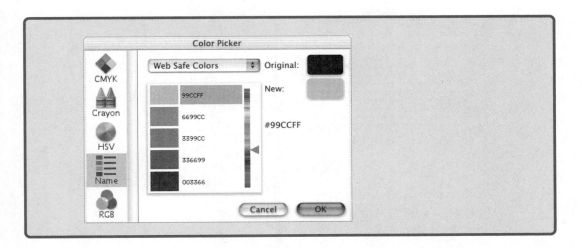

> **tip**   **Design your Web pages with smaller screens in mind**
>
> Another layout and design consideration to keep in mind is that some of your visitors might access your site using a mobile phone or personal digital assistant (PDA). If you work with more than one document at a time, do a lot of programming, or just like to have plenty of room on your desktop, you can use a 19″ or 21″ monitor at a resolution of 1024×768 or more. Remember, however, that the majority of your site's visitors will probably be viewing your work through a 15″ monitor set to 800×600, and a growing minority will be checking out your work on a screen that is smaller than the palm of your hand. Although users expect to scroll vertically to read Web pages, displaying wide tables or images on your Web pages will force some readers to constantly scroll horizontally and vertically to see all the material and might thereby drive viewers away from your site.

Building Web Forms

The original goal of HTML was to design a language to define how the elements of a Web page would be displayed in a browser. As time went by, the HTML tag set expanded to include images, tables, and forms. An HTML *form* is a special-purpose Web page that invites the viewer to interact with your Web site by filling out requests for information, ordering products, or filling out your guest book. The form can include such elements as text boxes, radio buttons, list boxes, images, and buttons. A sample form is shown in Figure 15-6 on the next page.

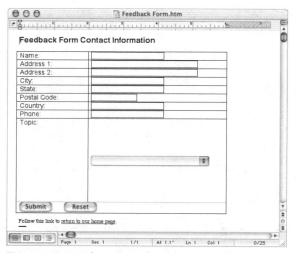

Figure 15-6. This HTML form lets site visitors type in their contact information and send feedback to the manager of the Web site.

> For information on adding movies, background sounds, images, pictures, and other elements to a Web page, see Chapter 10, "Working with Images, Objects, Movies, and Sounds."

To add a form to a Web page, follow these steps:

1 Place the insertion point at the location in the Web page where you want to place the first form element.

2 Choose Insert, HTML Object, and then select the form control you want to add to the Web page. A dialog will appear with settings you can use to set the properties of the HTML form control you just placed (for example, Figure 15-7 shows the dialog for adding a list box, which you might use to list products that a reader can click to order).

> **note** When you add the first HTML object to your form, Word inserts boundaries indicating the top of the form and the bottom of the form. Word also activates the Show/Hide Paragraph Marks button on the Standard toolbar, which displays the top and bottom of the form, paragraph marks, and other formatting information.

3 Continue adding form elements as needed.

> **note** For a complete description of the controls you can add to a form on a Web page, see the "Form Controls You Can Use on a Web Page" online help topic.

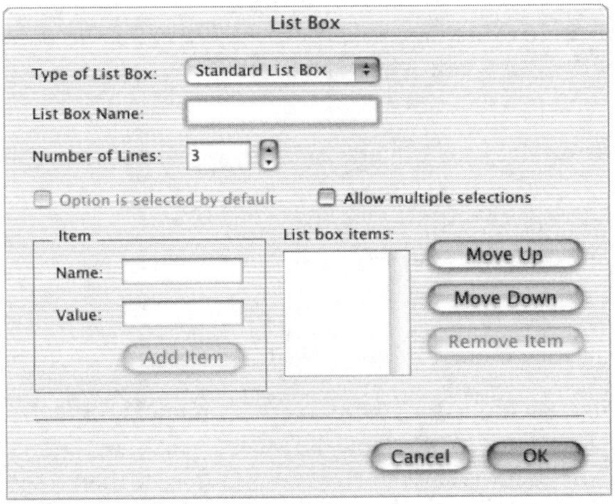

Figure 15-7. You can use the controls in this dialog to select the properties for a list box form element.

The last two HTML objects you should add to your form are a Submit button and a Reset button. Clicking the Reset button removes any of the visitor's entries and lets the visitor start over, whereas clicking the Submit button indicates that the form is complete and is ready to be processed by the server on which the form is hosted. If the Submit button isn't included, the user can't send the information to the Web site. The Submit Button dialog is shown in Figure 15-8.

When a user fills out a form on a Web page, you need a way to process the contents of the form, whether that is to send the form's contents as an e-mail message, write the user's responses to a file, or use the form's contents to generate a new page based on database data that corresponds to the visitor's responses. For example, if you want the

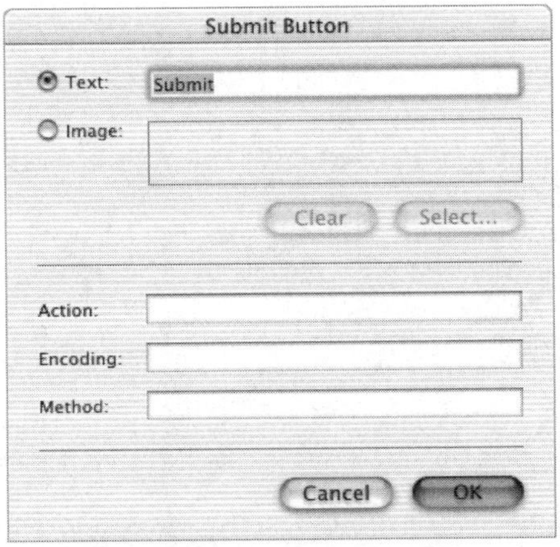

Figure 15-8. Set the properties of the Submit button using the Submit Button dialog.

form's contents sent to you as an e-mail message, you can type a *mailto* hyperlink in the Action box, such as **mailto:bob@cohovineyard.com**.

> **note** Form data can also be processed by code running on the Web server where the form is stored; you can use technologies such as CGI or Active Server Pages scripts to create dynamic content based on the form's contents.

Saving a File as an HTML File

In previous versions of Word, saving a document as a Web file was difficult. You had to save the file and then translate it to HTML. Now, however, Word includes HTML as a native format, so saving a document as a Web page is no different than saving a Word file in any other native format. And, instead of losing important document layout, graphics, and table formatting information, saving a Word document as a Web page preserves the formatting.

> For general information on saving a document in a specific format, see "Using Save As," page 27.

If you have created a new Web page or opened an existing Web page, you can save the page using the File, Save or File, Save As command. If you started with a Word document, however, you should choose File, Save As Web Page.

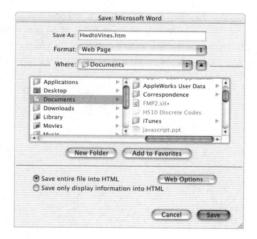

Setting Web Page Options

When you save a Web page, you can give Word specific instructions as to which elements should be saved in the file using the settings in the Web Options dialog. To display this dialog, open the Save As Web Page dialog, and click the Web Options button. You can select the settings you want by performing the following actions:

376

1 To set the title and keywords for your Web page, click the General tab, type the title for your page in the Web Page Title box, and then type the keywords for the page in the Web Page Keywords box.

---

tip   Choosing a descriptive set of keywords will help Web search engines such as Google (*www.google.com*), AlltheWeb (*www.alltheweb.com*), and AltaVista (*www.altavista.com*) index your site better, so that people searching for your site's subject matter will have a better chance of finding your site.

---

2 To change the characteristics of the Web page you're saving, click the Files tab, and then select the Update Links On Save check box to have Word refresh any links to external data. You can also have Word save only the display information that Web browsers can interpret by selecting the Save Only Display Information Into HTML check box.

---

caution   When you save only display information into the HTML file, the file loses its identity as a Word file. Opening the file in Word after saving it as an HTML-only file will not restore elements from the original document such as headers and footers that were lost when you saved the file as a Web page.

---

3 To control how Word prepares the Web page and its images for presentation over the Web, select the Pictures tab, shown in Figure 15-9 on the following page. To allow PNG images in the Web file, select the Allow PNG As An Output Format check box in the File Formats section of the dialog.

---

note   PNG (Portable Network Graphics) is a relatively new graphics format for the Web. Although virtually all current Web browsers can read and display PNG images, some older browsers cannot. If you think that your site may get many visitors using old browsers, leave this check box cleared, and Word will use GIF or JPEG formats for the images.

---

4 You can also identify the target monitor for your users (which is useful, for example, if you work for a company with an intranet and standard monitors) by opening the Screen Size pop-up menu in the Target Monitor section of the dialog and selecting the target monitor from the main list. If you want to change the resolution at which your Web page is saved, type a new value in the Pixels Per Inch box.

5 To specify the language used to display your Web page, click the Encoding tab, open the Save This Document As pop-up menu, and then select the language in which you want to save your Web page. You can define the language you chose as the default language for all of your Web pages by selecting the Always Save Web Pages In the Default Encoding check box.

Chapter 15

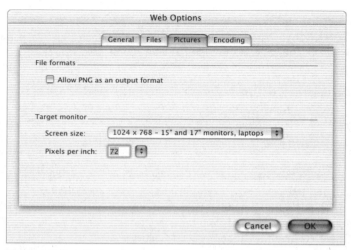

Figure 15-9. If your target audience has a well-defined, consistent hardware base, you can specify the monitor to which Word should tailor the Web pages it produces.

6 Click OK in the Web Options dialog, and then click OK in the Save dialog.

> **note** Although some newer monitors have resolutions higher than 72 dots per inch (dpi), the standard resolution of most Web pages is targeted at 72 dpi. Unless you are certain the majority of your users have monitors that display at a higher resolution than is standard, saving your Web page at more than 72 dpi increases your file size (and therefore increases the time it takes for the viewer to load your page) without any attendant benefits.

Troubleshooting

Word doesn't create backup copies of my HTML files.

When you use Microsoft Word to create HTML files, you might notice that Word doesn't create backup copies of your files, even if you selected the Always Create Backup Files check box in the Save category of the Preferences dialog. This aspect of working with HTML files in Word might trip you up if you don't create backup copies on your own. If you do want backup copies of your Web pages, be sure you save them separately, under a different file name. As with all other backup files, it's better if you can keep your archives in a separate location—perhaps on a network drive not on your computer, on a removable hard drive, or on a CD. If the file is one you simply cannot afford to lose, you should store backup copies in more than one location.

Previewing Your Web Page

Most of the time, anyone who views a Word document you save as an HTML file will view the document with a Web browser such as Microsoft Internet Explorer or Netscape Navigator. Rather than view the document in Word, you can launch your Web browser from Word and view the document directly. To view the active document as it will appear on the Web, follow either of these steps:

- Choose File, Web Page Preview to view the active document in an Internet Explorer window.

- Choose View, Online Layout in Word to view the active document as it will appear on the Web.

> For more information on using document views, see "Getting Different Views of Your Document," page 63.

Troubleshooting

My document looks great in Internet Explorer but not so great when viewed with other browsers.

The goal of the Hypertext Markup Language was to establish a standard that would let all Web browsers know exactly how to display the contents of documents on the Web. The Office applications, however, produce HTML that is tuned to look best in Microsoft Internet Explorer. Therefore, you will see differences in display between Internet Explorer, Netscape, and other browsers such as Opera and OmniWeb. In extreme cases (as with older versions of some of these non-Microsoft browsers), pages may display so poorly as to be unreadable. If you're creating a Web page that is meant to be put on the Web for public consumption, it is important that you find a document layout that looks good in all of the browsers you expect your site's visitors to use. That may require some experimentation with your Word document layout, and it's a very good idea to preview your documents in different browsers, and even in the same browser running on Macintosh and on Windows.

To a lesser extent, it is also important that you ensure your Web page is viewable in as many versions of the popular browsers as possible. You can get an idea of which browsers your site's visitors are using by examining your site's log files. Although there will always be some browsers you are not able to adjust for, you should make sure that the top 80 percent of visitors to your site will see the page as you designed it. For information on saving a file with only the information required to display it in a Web browser, see "Setting Web Page Options," page 376.

Viewing the Source Code of an HTML Page

One of the ways you can take advantage of the wide range of capabilities in Microsoft Word is to use the program as an HTML code editor. Once you have the source code for a Web page in front of you, you can change a setting in a tag so the page displays exactly the way you want it to, add or remove elements, or figure out how the author of the page pulled off a formatting trick you'd love to duplicate. Figure 15-10 shows the HTML source code used to create the form displayed earlier in this chapter.

Figure 15-10. This HTML source code was used to create the form displayed in Figure 15-6 on page 374.

To view the source code of a Web page, follow these steps:

1 Open the Web page in Word, and then choose View, HTML Source.

> **note** The HTML Source command is only available on the View menu when opening a Web page—it doesn't appear in a regular Word document.

2 Edit the HTML code for the document, if you are skilled in the HyperText Markup Language and want to fine tune the automatic HTML conversions that Word performed.

3 Choose View, Exit HTML Source to return to the Online Layout view of your file.

Publishing Your Web Pages

After you've created your Web page, you have to transfer it to a Web server to make the page available to the public. If you don't, you and anyone else on your local network (if any) who can reach the hard disk and folder where the file is stored will be able to view the document by opening it in Word or a Web browser, but no one else will be able to see it.

If you're the Web site administrator or you created your Web page on the computer that hosts the Web site, you should be able to save the file in the public directory. If not, you'll need to transfer the file to the Web server using a File Transfer Protocol (FTP) utility, by sending the Web site administrator an e-mail message (possibly with the file attached), or by using a method you and your administrator work out.

Unfortunately, there is no FTP utility in Office v. X or Mac OS X (actually, there is one built into Mac OS X, but it is only accessible from the Terminal command line, not the Aqua user interface). You can, however, download an inexpensive utility, called Fetch, from *www.fetchsoftworks.com*. From within Fetch, you can identify the server to which you want to transfer your files, connect to the server with your username and password, and put the file on the server.

caution   When you send your username and password to an FTP site, the information is not disguised in any way…it's sent "in the clear." As a result, anyone eavesdropping on your connection can read your password. Thus, you should never reuse a password for an FTP server anywhere else, and certainly not for sensitive e-mail or server accounts.

There is one good way to save HTML files you create with Word (or any Office files) onto the Web without messing with FTP programs and site administrators. Apple offers all users of Mac OS X 20 megabytes of free Web hosting space on its servers, in the form of the Sites folder on your iDisk, a virtual hard drive. Figure 15-11 shows the Sites folder in the author's iDisk. If you signed up for iTools as part of your Mac OS X setup, you already have an iDisk. For more information about your iDisk, visit *www.apple.com/itools*.

Figure 15-11.   As soon as you put HTML files in the Sites folder on your iDisk, they'll immediately become available on the Web.

Your iDisk is integrated with the Mac OS X Finder, so you can mount it on your desktop by switching to the Finder and choosing Go, iDisk. Your Mac will connect to the Internet (if you don't have a full-time connection), and your iDisk will appear on your desktop, as if it were any other hard drive. Then you can save HTML files to the Sites folder on the iDisk, just as if you were saving files to a local hard disk.

Automating Word with Macros and AppleScripts

Microsoft Word X has such a huge feature set (as detailed in previous chapters) that it's easy to think that it can do practically anything that you might need it to do. That's not far off the mark; Word might not be able to make your morning coffee, but you can wield its menus, dialogs, and other tools to meet most of your word processing, light-duty graphics, and even page layout needs. But there's no denying that the price of Word's power can be complexity. Sometimes it can take you many steps to accomplish a task. Wouldn't it be great if you could teach Word how to do a lengthy task, and then the next time you need to do that task, just have Word do the job for you? No need to wish for that ability; when it comes to saving you repetitive effort, well, Word can do that too.

The heroes of Word's automation abilities are macros and scripts. A *macro* is a series of Word commands that perform one or more actions for you as though the commands were a single command. *Scripts* can do many of the same things as macros, but in the sense that we'll be using the term in this chapter, scripts work with Word and with other applications to automate processes spanning multiple programs.

In this chapter, you'll see how you can use the power of Word's automation features to help you with repetitive tasks, discover the multiple methods of automating Word, and learn how to use scripting to get Word working with other applications (including non-Microsoft programs).

About Automating Word

Under the hood, automation is all about programming languages. Wait, don't stop reading; it doesn't mean that you have to become a programmer to use macros and scripts. Word lets you *record* your actions, and then play them back when you need them, without ever learning a bit of any programming language. Behind the scenes, Word's macro recorder writes the macro code that does the magic. If you can use menus and dialogs, you can automate Word to save you an immense amount of time and effort. Most of this chapter deals with working with recorded macros and scripts.

If you happen to be a programmer, however, the vista of things you can do with Word's automation abilities is even wider. You can create macros and scripts with their own user interface, modify recorded macros for even more power, and even create external programs that can access information in Office documents to accomplish things that you can't do within the Office programs.

Word can take advantage of three different automation methods, using three different programming languages:

- **Visual Basic for Applications** (VBA) is Word's main automation language. Word's macros are recorded or programmed in VBA. VBA is also the macro language used by Microsoft Excel X and Microsoft PowerPoint X (but not by Microsoft Entourage X). Chances are good that most of the automation you do with these three applications will be done using Word and Excel's macro recorders (PowerPoint doesn't let you record macros, so the only way to automate PowerPoint with VBA is with direct programming). All three of the VBA-capable programs allow you to create and modify macros in the Visual Basic Editor (more on that later in this chapter).

- **AppleScript** is the system-level scripting language built into Mac OS X. Word is AppleScript-aware, which means that Word is scriptable using AppleScript, but it's fair to say that Word's AppleScript support pales next to its VBA support. Fortunately, you can use AppleScript to issue individual VBA macro statements and run VBA macros. AppleScript is Entourage's only automation language.

For more information on using AppleScript with Word, see "Using AppleScript with Word," page 395. For more about using AppleScript with Entourage, see Chapter 23, "Extending Entourage with AppleScript."

- **REALbasic** is a programming language developed by Real Software that programmers can use to create applications for both Mac OS and Windows. It's a popular language for developers because it is relatively easy to program and provides many tools that ease the programmer's burden. A demo

What's the Difference Between a Macro Language and a Scripting Language?

In this chapter, we've used three different terms: *macro language, scripting language,* and *programming language*. What's the difference between all of these? Not much, actually. These different terms have come into use in association with different products, but there isn't much difference from other than a marketing standpoint. Microsoft calls programs written or recorded in VBA *macros,* but they could just as easily have called them *scripts*. AppleScripts, written in the AppleScript programming language, could be called programs, or macros. You can write programs in either VBA or AppleScript, so that makes them programming languages.

version of REALbasic comes on the Office v. X CD. Thanks to a set of plug-ins for REALbasic, you can use REALbasic applications to process data from Word, Excel, or PowerPoint, and you can use REALbasic's code editor instead of the Visual Basic Editor. To use REALbasic effectively with any of the Office applications, you must be a programmer, and it can only be used for a relatively narrow range of functions. In that sense, for most Office users, the REALbasic automation features are the least accessible.

For more information on using REALbasic with Word, see "Using REALbasic for Automation," page 399.

Using Word Macros

The most common use for macros is to record and play back tasks, so that you don't have to go through the whole process again. For example, you might be working on a project that requires you to attach a particular template to many documents. You could (every time!) perform these steps as you opened each document for editing:

1   Choose Tools, Templates And Add-Ins.

2   In the Templates And Add-Ins dialog, click Attach. In the resulting Choose A File dialog, navigate to and open the template you want to attach.

3   Select Automatically Update Document Styles.

4   Click OK.

That's not especially difficult, but if you have to do it many times, it's awfully boring. Instead, make Word record the task when you do it once, and then let Word do the repetitive work from then on.

InsideOut

Use macros to attach templates from Microsoft Windows users

Word X does a great job of transferring documents back and forth with Microsoft Word for Windows, but there's one annoyance with document templates; if you create a document in Word X, and then send it for editing to a colleague using Word for Windows, when you get it back, you'll always have to reattach the document template, even if you're both using the same template, with the same name, on both platforms. The culprit is the way that Word finds templates; it stores the document template's location with a specific path to the file. Because templates are stored in different places in Windows than they are in Microsoft Office v. X, the path is broken when you get the document back from your Windows-using colleagues. When Word can't find the correct template, it opens the document using the Normal template.

The solution is to record a macro the first time you have to reattach a document template, and then connect that macro to a toolbar button or menu item (see "Adding a Button to a Toolbar," page 48). From then on, a reattached template is just a click away.

In addition to automating repetitive processes, macros are useful in two other areas. You can use macros to make commands that Word buries in dialogs and hierarchical menus more easily accessible. For example, while writing this book, we used Word's Track Changes feature to see all the changes that each of the four or five people on the team made to each chapter. Sometimes all the revision marks made it difficult to read the current version of the document. So I recorded a macro when I opened the Highlight Changes dialog and cleared the Highlight Changes On Screen option, and then created a toolbar button for the new Tracked Changes Off macro (I also did another macro and button, Tracked Changes On). From then on, I could hide or show the revision marks with just one click.

The other good use for macros is to combine multiple commands that you might normally consider to be separate. For example, you could create a macro that would insert a table and apply an AutoFormat to it.

Macros can be saved into either documents or templates. In order to use that macro again, either that same document will need to be open or the template where the macro resides will need to be attached to the active document. If you want a macro to be available to all Word documents, save the macro in the Normal template using the Organizer. Because the Normal template, being a global template, is always open, macros in the Normal template will always be available.

For more information about the Organizer, see "Using the Macro Dialog and the Organizer," page 392. For more information about using the Normal template and global templates, see Chapter 8, "Advanced Formatting with Styles, Templates, and Themes."

Instances Where You Shouldn't Use Macros

Macros are powerful and can save you an immense amount of time, especially for repetitive tasks. But many other Word features are also designed to save you time and effort, and sometimes it's more efficient to use those other features instead of using a macro. For example, if you need to do a lot of repetitive paragraph and character formatting, don't use a macro, define a style instead. You can use a macro to insert boilerplate text or graphics, but it's better to define an AutoText entry, or even better, an AutoCorrect entry that lets you type an abbreviation that is automatically expanded to the entire boilerplate.

Recording Macros

Before you begin recording a macro, it's a good idea to take a moment to think about the process you are going to record, so that you can make sure that you'll have access to everything you'll need to get the tasks done in the easiest and most efficient fashion. Once you turn on the macro recorder, Word obediently records all of your actions—even the mistakes and any corrections that you make. Word will usually run your patched-up macro correctly, making the same mistakes and corrections you did in recording it. But why slow down your macros with a lot of extra steps? It's better to get your actions right when you record the macro. Consider taking the following actions before you start recording a macro:

● Plan the steps that you want the macro to perform.

note Word's macro recorder doesn't record mouse movements (except for clicking on buttons and making menu choices), so if your macro includes text selection or moving the insertion point, use keyboard shortcuts.

● Try to predict any alert or error dialogs that Word might display that might halt your macro when it's running. For example, in a macro that used the Find And Replace command, you would probably want to click the Expand Dialog button in the Find And Replace dialog, and then choose Current Document All in the Search pop-up menu. Otherwise, if the macro searches only up, down, or the selection in a document, the macro would stop and display an alert dialog when it reached the limit set.

● Make sure that your macro does not depend on the current document's content. If it does, your macro might not work in other documents.

● Before you record, practice the procedure.

> **tip** Macros created with Word's macro recorder are always stored in the Normal template by default.

To record a macro, follow these steps:

1 Click the REC button on the status bar, or choose Tools, Macro, Record New Macro. The Record Macro dialog appears, as shown in Figure 16-1.

Figure 16-1. The Record Macro dialog enables you to name macros and assign them to toolbars or keyboard shortcuts.

2 Enter a name for the macro. When naming macros, you must abide by the following rules:

■ The macro name must begin with a letter.

■ The macro name can contain up to 80 uppercase or lowercase letters and numbers.

■ The macro name cannot contain spaces or punctuation such as hyphens, slashes, or question marks.

> **tip** The underscore character is acceptable in macro names; use it instead of a space. For example, you could have a macro named Attach_Book_Template.

If you enter an invalid macro name, when you click OK, Word will display an error dialog that says "Invalid Procedure Name" and drop out of macro recording mode. If this happens to you, you'll have to start recording the macro again, as you did in step 1.

caution   If you give a new macro the same name as an existing macro, the new macro will replace the old macro. Word will warn you that the new macro's name duplicates an existing macro, and asks whether you want to replace the old macro with the new macro. If you're sure that you really want to eliminate the old macro, click Yes. Otherwise, click No, the default choice, and enter a different name.

3   From the Store Macro In pop-up menu, choose where you want to save the macro. You have three choices:

- **All Documents.** This is the default choice. It stores the macro in the Normal template, so that it will be available in all documents.

- **Documents based on the active template.** If you have a template loaded, you can store the macro in that template. The macro will be available only when the template is open or attached to the active document.

- **Active document.** The macro will be stored in the currently open document and will only be available in that document.

note   Macros are not stored until the document or templates where they reside are saved. If you store the macro in the Normal template, it will not be saved until you quit Word.

4   If you prefer, enter a description of the macro in the Description box. By default, Word enters the date and author of the macro in the Description box.

5   If you want to assign the macro to a toolbar button, or give it a keyboard shortcut, click the appropriate button:

- If you click the Toolbars button, the Customize dialog opens. The Commands box on the Commands tab will contain the name of your macro, with some extra text prepended to it; for example, the name in the Commands box might be Normal.NewMacros.Attach_Book_Template. Drag the macro name from the Commands box to the toolbar or menu you want (remember that in Word, the menu bar is just another toolbar). You'll probably want to rename the button at this time, so Control+click the button, and choose Properties from the contextual menu. In the Command Properties dialog, edit the button's name, and then click OK. Click OK again to exit the Customize dialog.

note   If you added the macro with the prepended text to a menu, double-click the macro name after you've placed it on the menu to bring up the Command Properties dialog and rename the menu choice.

■ If you click the Keyboard button, the Customize Keyboard dialog opens, with the macro name selected. In the Press New Shortcut Key box, enter the keyboard shortcut, click Assign, and then click OK.

> For more information about using the Customize dialog for toolbars, and the Customize Keyboard dialog for keyboard shortcuts, see Chapter 4, "Office v. X: Do It Your Way."

> **note** If you don't assign the macro to a toolbar or keyboard shortcut, the only way to run the macro will be by choosing Tools, Macro, Macros, selecting the macro name in the Macros dialog, and clicking Run.

6 Click OK to begin recording the macro. The Record Macro dialog closes, and the Stop Recording toolbar, shown in Figure 16-2, appears.

Figure 16-2. The Stop Recording toolbar has the Stop Recording button on the left and the Pause Recording button on the right.

7 Perform the actions that you want to record in the macro. If you need to you can pause the recorder while recording a macro by clicking the Pause Recording button on the Stop Recording toolbar. Click the button again to resume.

8 When you have performed all the actions that you want in the macro, click the Stop Recording button.

Running Macros

You can run a macro in any of the following ways:

● Choose Tools, Macro, Macros, select the macro name in the Macro dialog, and then click Run.

● Click a custom macro button on a toolbar (if you have assigned the macro to a toolbar button).

● Choose the macro from a menu (if you have added the macro name to a menu).

● Press a macro shortcut key (if you have assigned one).

Triggering the macro in any of these ways performs the actions that you stored in the macro.

tip   **Run a macro automatically**

You can set a macro to run automatically by giving the macro one of five special names:

- **AutoNew.** The macro runs when you create a new document based on the template containing the AutoNew macro.
- **AutoOpen.** The macro runs when you open an existing document containing the macro or a document based on a template that contains the macro.
- **AutoClose.** The macro runs when you close a document containing the macro or attached to a template containing the macro.
- **AutoExec.** The macro runs when you first start up Word if the macro is in the Normal template, or a template in the Microsoft Office X/Office/Startup/Word folder.
- **AutoExit.** The macro runs when you quit Word if the macro is in the Normal template.

You can have only one AutoExec macro, but you can have a different AutoOpen macro for each template or document. A great use for an AutoOpen macro is to activate a special toolbar that you need only in that template or document.

Avoiding Macro Viruses

One of the unfortunate consequences of a powerful programming language such as VBA is that it is possible for unscrupulous programmers to create *macro viruses*. These viruses work like other computer viruses, in that they can infect and replicate documents and templates without your knowledge or consent. Very few destructive macro viruses have surfaced for Office for Macintosh, but macro viruses have become a real problem for Windows Office users, especially those using Outlook, the e-mail program that is part of Office for Windows (Entourage, the e-mail equivalent of Outlook in Office v. X, doesn't use VBA, so it is not susceptible to macro viruses).

The bad news about macro viruses is that they can be transmitted from Windows users to Macintosh users, hitching a ride with an infected document or template. The destructive macro viruses discovered to date perform their destruction by taking advantage of specific aspects of, or vulnerabilities in, Windows, especially previous versions of Windows such as Windows 95 and Windows 98. So that's the good news: because Mac OS X doesn't have the vulnerabilities these macro viruses are looking for, macro viruses generally do nothing when opened in Office v. X.

(continued)

Chapter 16

Avoiding Macro Viruses *(continued)*   Word, Excel, and PowerPoint all have built-in macro virus early warning systems. If you open any document that contains a macro, you'll get a dialog warning you of the fact and asking how you want to continue, as shown in Figure 16-3. The default is to disable any macros contained in the document and continue to open the document. You can also choose to enable the macros in the document, or you can even choose to not open the document at all.

Figure 16-3.   The macro Warning dialog lets you know that the document you're opening contains macros.

Just because the document contains one or more macros doesn't mean that those macros are malicious. Macros are useful, so there are many legitimate reasons to attach macros to documents. What you need to do is to consider the source of the document. If the document comes from someone that you know and trust, it's probably safe to click the Enable Macros button. But if you have received the document as an e-mail attachment from someone whom you don't know, it is far better to click the Disable Macros button, or even consider not opening the file at all.

Using the Macro Dialog and the Organizer

The Macro dialog lets you run, edit, and delete macros. It also enables you to see all the macros in the active documents and templates. To run a macro, follow these steps:

1 Choose Tools, Macro, Macros. The Macros dialog appears, as shown in Figure 16-4.

2 By default, the Macros dialog always appears with All Active Templates And Documents selected in the Macros In pop-up menu, which means that all available macros show in the list box. If you want to narrow the list of macros you are viewing, make another selection from the Macros In pop-up menu, as shown here:

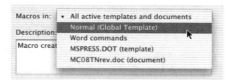

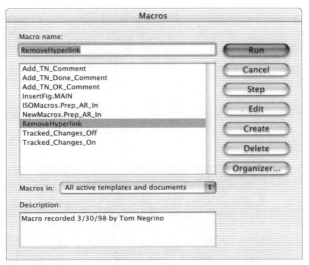

Figure 16-4. Use the Macros dialog to run, edit, or delete individual macros.

3 Select a macro in the list, and then click Run. If you want to delete the macro, click the Delete button. Word will ask you to confirm your choice.

Using the Visual Basic Editor to Edit a Macro

Word, Excel, and PowerPoint all allow you to edit recorded macros, and even create your own, in the Visual Basic Editor. If you want to see what the Visual Basic code for one of your recorded macros looks like, choose Tools, Macro, Visual Basic Editor. The Visual Basic Editor appears, as shown in Figure 16-5 on the next page.

Managing Macros with the Organizer

The Organizer dialog has a tab for managing your macros (choose Format, Styles, Organizer, and click the Macro Project Items tab). For instructions on how to use the Organizer, see "Copying Styles Between Documents and Templates," page 172. The only difference between those instructions and using the Organizer for macros is that you will of course be working on the Macro Project Items tab, and that you can't copy individual macros; you can only copy groups of macros called *macro projects*. In fact, all of the macros that you create are stored in a single macro project called NewMacros.

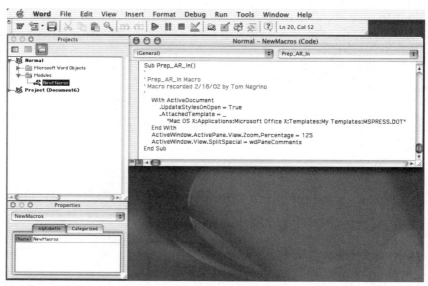

Figure 16-5. The Visual Basic Editor enables you to examine and edit macro code.

You don't have to be a programmer to make some sense of the code. The code for the macro shown in the figure is the macro that I recorded to reattach a document template when I get edited documents back from people using Windows versions of Word. Let's take a closer look at just the code from the Visual Basic Editor window:

```
Sub Prep_AR_In()
'
' Prep_AR_In Macro
' Macro recorded 2/16/02 by Tom Negrino
'
   With ActiveDocument
      .UpdateStylesOnOpen = True
      .AttachedTemplate = _
         "Mac OS X:Applications:Microsoft Office X:Templates:My Templates:MSPRESS.DOT"
   End With
   ActiveWindow.ActivePane.View.Zoom.Percentage = 125
   ActiveWindow.View.SplitSpecial = wdPaneComments
End Sub
```

This code attaches a particular template (Mspress.dot in this case), updates styles in the document to match the template, increases the screen magnification to 125%, and opens the Comments pane. If you wanted to change the magnification, you could re-record the macro, but it would actually be faster to edit the macro and change *125* to some other value.

When you are done editing your macro, choose Word, Close And Return To Microsoft Word, or press Command+Q.

For more about using the Visual Basic Editor, see "Writing Macros with Visual Basic," page 802.

Using AppleScript with Word

You can do a lot with VBA macros, but they have a significant limitation; without extra programming, they can't work across different Office applications. That's where AppleScript, Mac OS X's systemwide scripting language, comes in. AppleScript can work across applications, and Word and Excel work well with AppleScript. You can program directly in AppleScript if you like, using the Script Editor application that comes with Mac OS X, but for most people it will be easier to record an AppleScript with Script Editor.

> **note** You'll find Script Editor in the Applications/AppleScript folder.

Recording AppleScripts

You can only record AppleScripts if the applications you're using are *recordable*, which means that the application has been written to take advantage of AppleScript's recording ability. The Office applications have different degrees of recordability; Word and Excel are fully recordable, but PowerPoint is not recordable at all. Entourage appears to be recordable, but it actually records only very basic actions, such as closing, moving, and resizing windows.

> **note** Though Entourage is barely recordable, paradoxically it includes the best AppleScript support of any of the Office programs. You have to write the AppleScript by hand (or download and install scripts written by others), but there are many scripts available for Entourage that extend its abilities in various areas. For more about using AppleScript with Entourage, see Chapter 23, "Extending Entourage with AppleScript."

In the example shown next, you'll see how you can record an AppleScript that will copy a chart from an Excel worksheet and paste it into a Word document as a picture. This sort of script would come in handy if you needed to create a report every quarter based on Excel data. Naturally, your scripts will probably be different, but you can see from the example how the process would work. Follow these steps:

1 Launch Word, Excel, and Script Editor.

2 Open the Excel worksheet with the chart that you want to copy (we'll call this worksheet the *source document*).

3 Open the Word document where you will paste the copied chart (we'll call this the *target document*).

4 Make Script Editor active. You'll see an untitled script window, as shown in Figure 16-6 on the next page.

5 If you want, enter a short description of the script in the Description box.

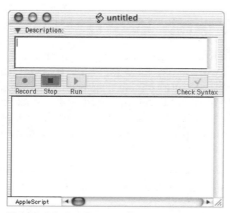

Figure 16-6. Script Editor's script window is ready to begin recording your AppleScript.

6 Click the Record button. The dot in the center of the Record button turns green to let you know recording is active.

7 Switch to Excel, select the chart by clicking on it, and choose Edit, Copy, or press Command+C.

8 Switch to Word, click where you want the chart to go, and choose Edit, Paste Special. You're choosing Paste Special here because Word's default is to paste the chart with a live link back to Excel, so that if the chart changes in the Excel worksheet, it will update in Word. You prefer a static chart in Word, because reports should not automatically change from the date they were created.

9 In the Paste Special dialog, select Picture, and then click OK. The Excel chart appears in the Word document, as shown in Figure 16-7.

10 Switch to Script Editor, and click the Stop button. The AppleScript stops recording, and the script appears in the script window, as shown in Figure 16-8.

11 Choose File, Save and give the AppleScript a name. In the Save dialog, choose Application from the Format pop-up menu, select Never Show Startup Screen (this will make it easier to run the script later), and then click Save.

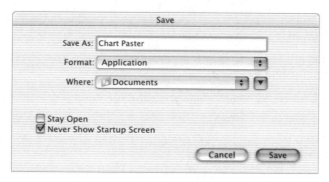

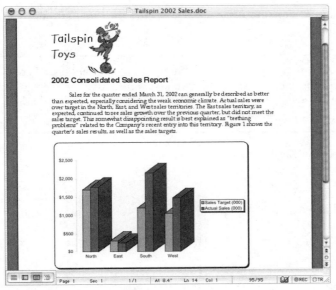

Figure 16-7. The Excel chart is copied to its new home.

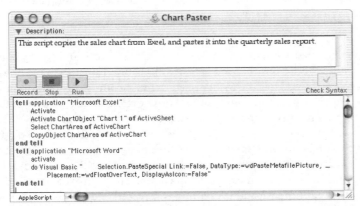

Figure 16-8. The recorded AppleScript appears in the Script Editor window.

Running the AppleScript

To run the AppleScript, you'll need to make sure that the source and target documents are open; then you can run the script in one of two ways:

- Double-click the script's icon in the Finder, as shown here.

- Launch Script Editor, open the script, and click the Run button in the script window.

> **note** You need to make sure that the source and target documents are open because you didn't specify the documents' names while you were recording the script. That's because it is better to record scripts "generically," that is, not dependent on particular documents, so that you can use the script whenever you need to.

Let's take a closer look at the text of the AppleScript:

```
tell application "Microsoft Excel"
    Activate
    Activate ChartObject "Chart 1" of ActiveSheet
    Select ChartArea of ActiveChart
    CopyObject ChartArea of ActiveChart
end tell
tell application "Microsoft Word"
    activate
    do Visual Basic " Selection.PasteSpecial Link:=False, _
        DataType:=wdPasteMetafilePicture, Placement:=wdFloatOverText, _
        DisplayAsIcon:=False
end tell
```

As you can see, the first *tell* statement gives the orders to Excel, and the second *tell* statement handles the actions in Word. The Excel portion is just a simple select and copy operation, and Excel has the ability to store those commands in the AppleScript using native AppleScript commands. In the Word portion, you see the command *do Visual Basic*, which is a key to the way that AppleScript works with Word, Excel, and VBA. The Paste Special command is specialized to Word, so there isn't a standard AppleScript command for it. AppleScript has the ability to record the VBA commands that Word or Excel uses to accomplish tasks and wrap those VBA commands inside an AppleScript. In this fashion, you can perform complex tasks in Word or Excel, and then switch to another application, and everything will record and play back properly. This ability to embed VBA inside an AppleScript is one of the most powerful aspects of using AppleScript with Office.

Troubleshooting

I get an error message when I run an AppleScript.

If an AppleScript can't run, you will get an error dialog with text that tries to indicate the nature of the problem, but is often not much help unless you're an experienced AppleScript programmer. In the previous example, you would get an error message if you had failed to open the source and target documents before you ran the script.

Troubleshooting *(continued)* You'll get different error dialogs depending on what part of the script went wrong. For example, when the source Excel worksheet isn't open when the script runs, you'll see an error dialog similar to this one:

When the target Word document isn't open, you get this error dialog:

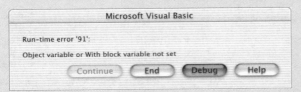

Neither of the error messages are very helpful, but the *dialog itself* tells you something. The first error dialog is from AppleScript itself, and the second error dialog is obviously a Visual Basic error. If you get the first error, you can be pretty sure that the problem is in the first part of the script, and that you should look for something wrong with the Excel portion of the task. If you get the second error, you should look for problems in Word.

newfeature!
Using REALbasic for Automation

VBA and AppleScript were available in previous versions of Office for Macintosh, and Office v. X adds a third automation choice: the ability to use REALbasic programs to work with the Office applications. REALbasic is a full-fledged programming language that creates stand-alone programs that can run on either Mac OS or Windows. Although REALbasic is considered to be a fairly easy programming language to learn and use, it still requires significant programming skills. The syntax and structure of REALbasic has many similarities to Microsoft's Visual Basic, of which VBA is a subset. Programmers like REALbasic because it has many tools that make it possible to create applications quickly, notably a visual way to create user interfaces. Even Microsoft programmers use it; the Welcome application on the Office v. X CD was written in REALbasic (though the rest of the Office programs were written in other programming languages). A demonstration version of REALbasic ships on the Office v. X CD, in the Value Pack folder.

Office v. X's REALbasic support is still something of a work in progress. Word, Excel, and PowerPoint added a new menu choice, Tools, Macro, REALbasic Editor, which launches REALbasic, if it is installed on your machine. But you can't yet use the REALbasic Editor to edit VBA macros; that will have to wait for future versions of both Office and REALbasic. Also on the horizon is the ability to write add-ins for Word and Excel with REALbasic.

At the time of this writing, you (if you're a REALbasic programmer) can create REALbasic programs that can communicate with the Office programs (except for Entourage), process data, and either display it or send the processed data back to the Office documents. For example, a REALbasic application can take data from an external database program, such as Oracle or OpenBase, analyze and digest it, and send the resulting data to an Excel worksheet for charting. Or you can do things with REALbasic applications that you can't do with the Office programs. Here's a simple example. Say that you had a Word document that you wanted to analyze on a paragraph-by-paragraph basis for word count. Word has a word count feature, of course, but it can only tell you the total numbers of words and paragraphs in your document; it can't report the statistics on each paragraph.

A REALbasic program, ParaCount, was created for this book to do the job. ParaCount reads the Word document, and then reports the number of words and characters in each paragraph, as shown in Figure 16-9.

This example is hardly earth-shaking, but it does illustrate how you can use REALbasic with Word to produce a result that you couldn't with Word alone. If teaching VBA is outside of the scope of this book, you can be certain that teaching REALbasic is *way* outside. Fortunately, there's a terrific book on REALbasic available: *REALbasic: The Definitive Guide, 2nd Edition*, by Matt Neuburg, who also created the REALbasic example shown in the figure.

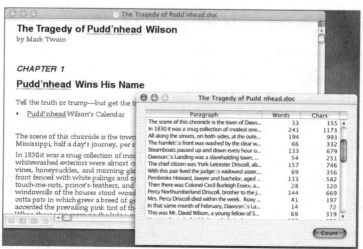

Figure 16-9. This REALbasic application analyzed the Word document in the background and reported the number of words and characters in each paragraph. Clicking a column header sorts the results by that column.

Part 3

Entourage

Chapter 17

Entourage Essentials

Microsoft Entourage X is Office's center for your e-mail and personal information. As an e-mail client, Entourage is one of the best available for Mac OS X. But Entourage can do a lot more than just get your e-mail. Entourage also has a robust set of PIM (personal information manager) features, including a contact manager, a calendar, a task manager with reminders, and an area to jot down your notes. Best of all, Entourage is well integrated with the rest of the Microsoft Office v. X suite.

In this chapter, you'll get an overview of how you can use Entourage; get an introduction to Entourage's user interface; learn how to set up Entourage to send and receive e-mail; and discover how to share one copy of Entourage between different users on the same machine.

What You Can Do with Entourage

Your life is complex, and Entourage provides a wide variety of tools to help you manage your e-mail, time, contacts, and other information.

E-Mail

Entourage X is a terrific e-mail client, one with significant improvements over the already good Entourage 2001. Entourage allows you to send and receive three types of e-mail (POP3, IMAP, and Microsoft's own Hotmail; more about these later in this chapter). Entourage can check your mail automatically, as often as you want. You can have Entourage sort and categorize your mail into mail folders to make it easier to handle, and you can set up e-mail rules so that Entourage does some of the sorting and categorizing automatically. Entourage has specialized tools to help you manage mailing lists, and a built-in junk mail filter that cuts down on the flood of unsolicited e-mail (*spam*). Because Entourage is a part of Office, it shares some of Office's text tools, such as the spelling checker and the AutoCorrect feature.

> **note** One thing that you cannot do with Entourage X is send and receive mail via an America Online account. Because AOL uses a proprietary e-mail system, Entourage can't use it.

> For more information about using Entourage for e-mail, see Chapter 18, "Mastering Your E-Mail."

Newsgroups

Before there was the Web, there was Usenet: the worldwide system of Internet message boards, called *newsgroups*. These newsgroups contain individual messages, called *news articles*. There are tens of thousands of Usenet newsgroups available, covering virtually any topic you can imagine (and probably some you never wanted to imagine). From cars to movies, wine appreciation to computer games, there's a newsgroup for it. Entourage has a flexible newsgroup reader that allows you to read news articles and post to newsgroups. You can configure Entourage to use your ISP's (Internet service provider) news server, which will typically carry a large selection of the public newsgroups, and you can also set Entourage to connect to private news servers run by companies for product support. In fact, Entourage comes already configured to use Microsoft's news server covering their Macintosh products, including newsgroups for all of the Office programs.

> For more information about using Entourage to access Usenet, see Chapter 19, "Using Newsgroups."

Contact Manager

Keeping track of your contacts is a key feature of a personal information manager, and Entourage provides you with a strong contact manager. You can track home and work addresses, as many e-mail addresses as you like, any number of telephone numbers, and a variety of personal information for each contact; you can even include a picture. If that's not enough for you, you can define up to 10 custom fields for your own needs. Contacts can be assigned to any number of categories for easy sorting and selecting. Entourage's Address Book is shared by the other Office applications (but especially by Microsoft Word X, for use in mail merges). One drawback to Entourage is that you can't share your address book with colleagues over a network, because Entourage is strictly a single-user program.

> For more information about using Entourage to keep track of your contacts, see Chapter 20, "Managing Your Contacts."

Calendar, Tasks, and Notes

Your schedule can always use extra help, and Entourage's Calendar is ready for duty. The Calendar handles single events, recurring events, and banners for events that span several days. You can view your calendar by month, week, work week, or day. Besides events, the Tasks list keeps track of your to-do's, which you can prioritize as you wish. As you complete tasks, you can check them off in the Tasks list. If you need a reminder of an event or a task, Entourage (with the help of the new Microsoft Office Notifications X application) can display a reminder dialog when you need it. Entourage also has a separate Notes list, where you can record thoughts and plans that aren't tied to a particular date or time.

As with contacts, you can't share your calendar with colleagues, because Entourage is a single-user program. There's no group scheduling; about the closest you can come is to post your calendar to a Web server.

For more information about using Entourage to handle your calendar, see Chapter 21, "Managing Your Appointments, Tasks, and Notes."

Comparing Entourage with Outlook Express

Entourage 2001 was built on the foundation of Microsoft Outlook Express 5, Microsoft's free e-mail-only application, and its heritage was readily apparent. Entourage 2001's contact and calendar portions seemed to be tacked onto the Outlook Express core, and Entourage's user interface still looked and acted almost identically to Outlook Express. Entourage X breaks with the past; its user interface was extensively reengineered when the program was updated for Mac OS X. Like the rest of the Office v. X programs, Entourage X sports a fresh Aqua interface.

The main difference between Entourage X and Outlook Express 5, however, is that Entourage X will be updated, and Outlook Express will not. Entourage X is a Mac OS X native program, and Outlook Express (like Entourage 2001) is not. Outlook Express runs (with some bugs) under Mac OS X's Classic environment, but it will not be rewritten for Mac OS X. Wisely, Microsoft has chosen not to compete with Apple Mail, the free e-mail program that ships with Mac OS X.

note Don't confuse Outlook Express with Outlook. The former is the free e-mail client for Mac OS 9 and earlier. The latter is Microsoft's client program for Microsoft Exchange Server (see the sidebar on the next page). On the Windows side, Outlook can also run independently as a PIM and e-mail program and is included with Microsoft Office for Windows. Despite the similarity of name, they are two very different programs.

Chapter 17

Entourage X Isn't an Exchange Client

Entourage X does a great job of handling Internet-based e-mail, and it is well suited to manage an individual's calendar and contacts. So it is frustrating to people in corporations with mixed Macintosh and Windows networks that Entourage doesn't work as a client program to Microsoft's Exchange e-mail/PIM server. Mac OS X users are therefore prevented from using Exchange's group scheduling and shared contact management features. In fact, at press time, Microsoft had no Mac OS X–based program that would work with Exchange Server.

There is, however, a Macintosh Exchange Server client, a different program called Outlook 2001 that can be downloaded for free from the Mactopia Web site. It works under Mac OS 8.5 or later (but not under Mac OS X). A few users have gotten Microsoft Outlook 2001 to work under Mac OS X's Classic environment, but most users report significant problems. In addition, Outlook 2001 lacks many features found in Entourage (and in the Windows version of Outlook), making Outlook 2001 an inferior solution, one best used in organizations that absolutely require the use of the Exchange Server. The obvious thing for Microsoft to do would be to add Exchange client abilities to Entourage X, and the company has stated that they're looking into that possibility for a future version of Entourage. There is also the possibility of an update to the Macintosh version of Outlook, but Microsoft has not announced any firm plans.

newfeature!
The Entourage Window in Depth

The look of Entourage X has changed dramatically from that of Entourage 2001. The program shared in the Aqua-ization of the rest of Office and looks much slicker than the past version. The most obvious difference between Entourage X and Entourage 2001 is the new navigation buttons that let you switch easily between the different Entourage features. The main Entourage window, showing the e-mail setting, is shown in Figure 17-1.

The Entourage window is divided into the following parts:

- **Navigation buttons.** These buttons switch between the five feature areas in Entourage (Mail, Address Book, Calendar, Notes, and Tasks) plus the new Custom Views area.

For more information about Custom Views, see "Using Custom Views," page 529.

- **Toolbar.** The toolbar provides buttons and other tools for common functions; what's on the toolbar changes depending on which feature you're using.

Chapter 17: Entourage Essentials

Folder list

Navigation buttons

Toolbar

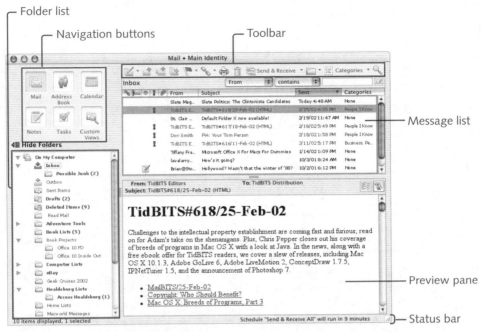

Message list

Preview pane

Status bar

Figure 17-1. The main Entourage window can be configured to display everything you need to manage your e-mail.

- **Message list/Address list.** If you are viewing e-mail, the Message list shows each message's *header* (basic information such as the sender or recipient of the message, the subject of the message, and the date sent or received). If you are viewing the Address Book, the Address list shows an abbreviated list of your contacts.

- **Preview pane.** The Preview pane shows the contents of the message selected in the Message list, or the detailed contact information for a contact selected in the Address list.

- **Status bar.** Messages in the status bar indicate when you're online or off-line, indicate when the next schedule is due to activate (if you have one or more mail schedules enabled), tell you when Entourage is sending and receiving e-mail, and alert you to any error conditions.

- **Folder list/Views list.** The Folder list is displayed when the Mail button is selected; it shows the default mail folders, your custom mail folders, your Hotmail accounts, and the Usenet news servers that you have configured, as shown in Figure 17-2 on the next page. The Views list is displayed in this location when any of the other navigation buttons are selected.

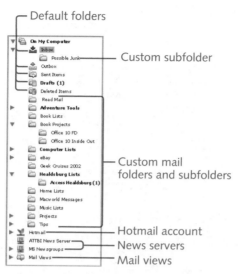

Default folders

Custom subfolder

Custom mail
folders and subfolders

Hotmail account

News servers

Mail views

Figure 17-2.   The Folder list contains Entourage's built-in mail folders, your custom mail folders, and Usenet news servers. Folders shown in bold have unread messages in them.

You'll learn more about the Folder list in "Organizing Your E-Mail," page 458.

Customizing the Entourage Window

Entourage has a pretty good interface, but you're not limited to using it only in the way that it ships. You can control which Entourage panes are visible, the width of the panes, the size of the navigation buttons, and which columns show up in list views.

To change the width of the Folder list or the height of the Preview pane, drag its border to make it larger or smaller. You can hide the Folder list by clicking the Hide Folders button at the top of the Folder list, or by choosing View, Folder List. If you prefer to work without the Preview pane, hide it in any of these ways: choose View, Preview Pane; press Command+\; or double-click the border between the Message list and the Preview pane. If you do choose to hide the Preview pane, to read messages you'll need to double-click each one in the Message list, which will open each message in a new window.

If you have a lot of mail folders, and you would like more vertical room in the Folder list, you probably would like to shrink the size of the navigation buttons. No problem; choose Entourage, General Preferences, click the General tab, and then select Display Small Navigation Buttons. The buttons shrink to small icons, but if you're not sure what they do (since they no longer have labels) point at one of the buttons until a ScreenTip (also known as a ToolTip) appears, as shown next:

Chapter 17: Entourage Essentials

You can control the width of the columns in the Message list by pointing at the border between column heads until the pointer becomes a double-headed arrow. Then simply drag the column to the desired width. You can choose which columns are visible by choosing View, Columns and then choosing the columns you want from the submenu. If you want to rearrange the columns, drag a column header horizontally. You can't change the width of the icon columns at the left of the Message list, but you can hide and rearrange them (except that the Links and Online Status columns can't be rearranged).

Entourage has a good set of keyboard shortcuts for moving around and accomplishing tasks in the application; some of these shortcut keys are listed in Table 17-1 (task-specific keyboard shortcuts are listed in their appropriate chapters). Unfortunately, Entourage doesn't offer the convenient keyboard shortcut customization that Word and Microsoft Excel X do.

Table 17-1. **Entourage Keyboard Shortcuts**

Keyboard Shortcut	Action
Command+1	Select Mail
Command+2	Select Address Book
Command+3	Select Calendar
Command+4	Select Notes
Command+5	Select Tasks
Command+6	Select Custom Views
Command+7	Open Progress window
Command+8	Open Link Maker dialog
Command+9	Open Error Log (only active when there is an error message)
Command+~ (tilde)	Cycle through Entourage windows
Command+; (semicolon)	Open General Preferences
Command+Shift+; (semicolon)	Open Mail & News Preferences

(continued)

Table 17-1. *(continued)*

Keyboard Shortcut	Action
Command+Option+Q	Switch identity
Command+, (comma)	Open Assign Categories dialog
Command+K	Send and receive all mail
Command+D	Duplicate selection
Delete or Command+Delete	Delete selection
Command+F	Open Find dialog
Command+Option+F	Open Find dialog with advanced features

Using the Entourage Setup Assistant

When you first launch Entourage (or when you create a new identity, as discussed in "Working with Multiple Users," page 418), the Entourage Setup Assistant automatically starts. It's a kind of wizard that steps you through the process of setting up your personal information and e-mail accounts, importing address book information from a previous personal information manager, and importing information from other calendar programs. Many of the screens in the Entourage Setup Assistant are self-explanatory, so we'll just skip over them lightly; other screens will get more explanation. Follow these steps as you work through the Entourage Setup Assistant:

1 In the first screen of the Entourage Setup Assistant, enter your first and last names, and then click the right arrow button to continue.

2 Enter your home address and telephone number. If you'll be using Entourage mostly from home, select This Is My Default Address.

3 Enter your work address and telephone number. If you'll be using Entourage mostly from work, select This Is My Default Address.

4 On the Welcome page, shown next, you can choose to import information from four possible sources, or choose not to import information at all.

Chapter 17: Entourage Essentials

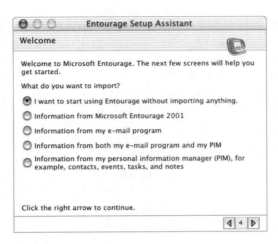

These are your choices:

- You can begin using Entourage without importing any information from other programs. Entourage assumes that you will set up your e-mail accounts manually, and steps you through setting up your initial e-mail account.

- You can import your information from Entourage 2001. Entourage will import all the information that was entered into Entourage 2001, including e-mail, address book data, calendar information, and so on.

- You can import information from another e-mail program. Entourage supports importing information from the following e-mail programs: Microsoft Outlook Express 5, Qualcomm Eudora (any version), Netscape Communicator 4 or later, or Claris Emailer 2.0v3.

- You can import information from both your e-mail program and your PIM. If you choose this option, Entourage will first step you through importing e-mail information from one program, and then through importing the contact and calendar information from another program.

- You can import information from your PIM only. Entourage supports importing information from any version of Claris Organizer, Palm Desktop, and Power On Software's Now Contact and Now Up-To-Date.

5 If you have data that you want to import from another program, skip to "Importing Data from Other Programs," page 415. If you choose to continue setting up Entourage without importing any data from another program, click the right arrow button.

6 In the Junk Mail Filter page, select Enable Junk Mail Filter. The Junk Mail Filter scans your incoming mail looking for the telltale signs of junk mail, and if it finds them, categorizes the mail as junk, which allows you to do things like automatically deleting the junk mail.

From this point, the Entourage Setup Assistant begins to step you through setting up an e-mail account, which will be covered in the next section.

Setting Up E-Mail Accounts

The Entourage Setup Assistant will step you through setting up either a POP or IMAP e-mail account. The following sidebar explains the three types of e-mail accounts Entourage can handle.

Three Kinds of Mail

There are three main types of Internet mail accounts that you might have: *POP* (Post Office Protocol), which is the most common type; *IMAP* (Internet Message Access Protocol), and *Web-based* (such as Microsoft's own Hotmail). Entourage can send and receive mail from all three kinds of accounts. You should ask your Internet service provider what kind of mail they provide; typically it will be POP or IMAP. If you have multiple accounts at one ISP, or multiple accounts at different ISPs, Entourage can handle it. You can have as many POP and IMAP accounts as you wish, in any combination.

POP Accounts

Unless your ISP specifically tells you that you have an IMAP mail account, it's a pretty safe assumption that your e-mail account uses POP. A POP server downloads your mail to your hard drive for storage and handling, and then (unless you specially set up your account for online access) deletes the e-mail from the mail server once it has successfully downloaded it to you.

IMAP Accounts

IMAP servers tend to be used more by corporations than by ISPs that cater to individuals. IMAP servers keep your e-mail on the server, so you must connect to the server to read and work with your messages. Corporations like IMAP because users can access their e-mail from anywhere, and because having all the corporate e-mail on one server makes for easy backup and archiving. The drawback to IMAP, of course, is that you can't work with your e-mail except when you're online.

Hotmail Accounts

Web-based e-mail like Microsoft Hotmail are similar to IMAP servers, because they store all of your e-mail on an Internet server. The chief benefits to Web-based e-mail accounts are that you can check your e-mail from anywhere in the world that has a Web browser and a connection to the Internet and that most Web-based e-mail accounts are free. Because Hotmail is owned by Microsoft, they've built Entourage to be able to handle sending and retrieving mail from Hotmail. In fact, you'll find that using Entourage to deal with your Hotmail account is often much faster than working with Hotmail through a Web browser. That brings up the chief drawback with Web-based e-mail accounts: they tend to be slow and clunky to use, especially in comparison to a slick e-mail program like Entourage.

SMTP Servers

Though they are not a type of Internet e-mail account, SMTP (Simple Mail Transfer Protocol) servers have a key role to play with your e-mail. SMTP servers, which can be associated with either POP or IMAP accounts (and also Web-based accounts, but these accounts hide the SMTP server from you) are the machines that take your outgoing mail and deliver it to its Internet destination. It might seem strange that one machine sends mail and another machine receives mail, but that arrangement is just one of the strange-but-true facts about the Internet.

Setting Up E-Mail Accounts with the Setup Assistant

The following instructions assume that you're continuing with the Entourage Setup Assistant from the previous section, but the information in each step is also applicable to setting up an e-mail account manually, as described in the next section. Follow these steps to set up an e-mail account:

1 Enter the name that you want to appear in the From box of your outgoing mail messages. Typically you'll want to enter your name, but that's not a requirement; an alias, such as **Slave To My Cat**, is okay too.

2 On the next page of the Setup Assistant, enter your e-mail address, or if you prefer, select the I'd Like To Sign Up For An Account From Hotmail option. If you choose the Hotmail option, the next page will include a button that you can click to open your Web browser, go to the Hotmail Web site, and sign up for an account. Then you can return to Entourage and continue entering your new Hotmail information into the Entourage Setup Assistant.

3 If you didn't go the Hotmail route, the Mail Servers page appears next, as shown on the next page. From the pop-up menu, choose POP or IMAP, depending on what kind of server your ISP uses. Then enter the address for your incoming mail server (that's the POP or IMAP server) and your outgoing mail server (that would be an SMTP server).

4 On the Setup Assistant's Account ID And Password page, enter the information that your ISP has given you. The account ID is not your e-mail address. It's usually the text in your e-mail address that comes before the at sign (@). For example, in the e-mail address *katie@tailspintoys.com*, the Account ID is *katie*. If you want Entourage to remember your password, type the password in the Password box, and select Save Password In My Mac OS Keychain.

---

tip   **Choose a good password**

Choose your password carefully, because anyone who has your password can send and receive your e-mail. Good passwords are at least six characters long, and they contain a combination of letters, numbers, and punctuation. Make sure that you don't choose easy to guess passwords such as the names of your spouse, your children, your pets, or something similar. It is also a good idea to change your password from time to time.

---

5 On the final page of the Entourage Setup Assistant, appropriately named Congratulations, enter the name of the account as you'd like it to appear in Entourage's Accounts dialog. Select the check box labeled Include This Account In My Send & Receive All Schedule, and then click Finish.

Manually Setting Up an E-Mail Account

If you need to set up additional e-mail accounts, follow these steps:

1 Choose Tools, Accounts. The Accounts dialog will appear. Make sure that the Mail tab is selected, and then click New.

2 The Account Setup Assistant, which is a subset of the Entourage Setup Assistant, starts up. Click Configure Account Manually. The New Account dialog appears, as shown next:

3 Choose the account type (POP, IMAP, or Hotmail) from the pop-up menu, and then click OK.

4 In the Edit Account dialog, shown in Figure 17-3, enter the rest of the e-mail account information, and then click OK.

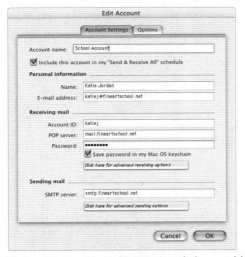

Figure 17-3. The Edit Account dialog enables you to enter all of an e-mail account's information in one place.

Importing Data from Other Programs

You can begin importing information from other programs as part of the Setup Assistant, or you can do it with the Import Assistant. The examples that follow will use the Import Assistant, but either way, the process is straightforward. Follow these steps:

1 Choose File, Import.

2 From the Begin Import page, select whether you want to import information from a program or from a text file or, if you want to import a holiday file, click the right arrow button.

Part 3: Entourage

> **note** Holiday files are text files that Microsoft makes available for download from the Mactopia Web site every year or so; they include all the holidays for a particular region (the United States, for example, or Japan), ready for importing into Entourage's calendar.

3 If you chose to import from a program, you'll be asked to choose which program your old data is in; this page, shown here, includes both e-mail programs and PIMs. Make your selection.

Depending on the program you selected, Entourage will present choices of possible data to import on the Ready To Import page, as shown here:

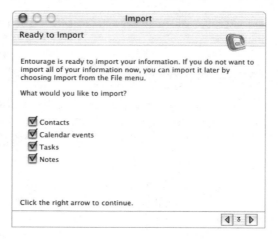

Entourage will search your hard disks for possible data files for the program you selected; if there is more than one possibility, you'll be asked to choose which data file to import from. Make the selection, and then click the right arrow button. The import will begin. When it is done, click the Finish button.

> **note** Depending on the amount of information to be imported, it could take quite a bit of time. Entourage shows a progress indicator to let you know what's going on.

4 If you chose to import from a text file in step 2, Entourage will ask whether you want to import contacts from a tab or comma delimited text file, or e-mail messages from an MBOX-format text file. Make your selection.

> **note** Entourage cannot import calendar events from a text file.

In the Import Text File dialog, navigate to the text file containing contacts, select it, and then click Import. The Import Contacts dialog will appear, as shown in Figure 17-4.

Match the fields (on the right) from the file you're importing to the corresponding Entourage fields (on the left) by dragging the field icons from the Unmapped Fields list to the correct position in the Mapped Fields list. Click Import when you're done.

5 If you chose instead to import holidays, the Import Holidays page appears with a list of holidays for various countries, regions, and religions. Select as many groups of holidays as you wish to observe or keep track of in Entourage, and then click the right arrow button. The holidays will be imported and added to the Calendar.

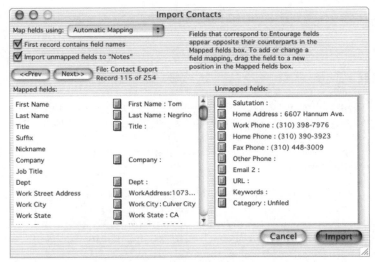

Figure 17-4. You need to show Entourage which fields in the imported file match up with Entourage's Address Book fields.

Chapter 17

Importing Mail Accounts and Messages

If your previous e-mail program was one of Entourage's supported e-mail programs, follow the importing procedure in the previous section, choosing that e-mail program in step 3. The rest of the procedure is self-explanatory.

---

tip **Import messages from Apple Mail**

Apple's Mail program, which comes with Mac OS X, isn't one of the supported mail importing programs that are built into Entourage, but that doesn't mean that you can't import e-mail messages from Apple Mail into Entourage X. Microsoft has made available an AppleScript, called Import From Mail, that will do the job. You'll find it in the Value Pack folder on the Microsoft Office v. X CD. After installing it, look in the Finder for the /Applications/Microsoft Office X/Utilities/Import From Mail folder. Open the folder, and double-click Import From Mail to run the script. The script runs automatically and places the Apple Mail e-mail in a subfolder displayed in Entourage's Folder list titled Import From Mail. You can then move the mail to any folders you prefer.

You can also import e-mail messages from programs that can export a standard kind of e-mail archive, called an MBOX file. These are specially formatted text files. Entourage can export mail folders as MBOX files, as can Eudora and many UNIX-based e-mail programs. To import messages from MBOX files, drag the MBOX file from the Finder into Entourage's Folder list. Entourage will import the file, converting it into a mail folder.

For more information about exporting e-mail from Entourage, see "Archiving Mail," page 477.

Working with Multiple Users

Entourage allows you to maintain multiple sets of user files, and to switch between them. Each set of files (which Entourage refers to as an *identity*) contains all the Entourage information for one person. For example, your Entourage identity would contain all of your e-mail, newsgroups, address book, calendar, tasks, and notes information.

If you share your computer with another person, each of you can have your own Entourage identity, with entirely different e-mail addresses, appointments, and contacts. Even if you're the only user of your computer, it's possible to have multiple identities (though there's not much need, as one identity can handle any number of e-mail addresses).

Multiple Users, Not Multi-User

Though the two terms sound similar, there's a big difference between a program that supports *multiple users* and a program that is *multi-user*. A multiple user program, such as Entourage X, allows more than one person to share use of the program (though not at the same time), with each person having their own set of files. This kind of setup makes a lot of sense with Mac OS X, because Mac OS X itself supports multiple users. Because each Mac OS X user has his or her own Documents folder (which contains the Identity folder that Entourage uses for its files), Entourage will automatically switch between different users' identities when that user logs into Mac OS X. Even within the same Mac OS X user login, you can use multiple identities within Entourage, so that different people can use Entourage without needing to log out and back in as a different user. Here's an example of how this works. When my wife and I go on the road, we both want to have access to all of our e-mail, but we don't want to bring both of our laptops. Instead, I copy my Entourage identity folder onto her PowerBook G4 (because it's the faster machine). Each of us can then have access to all of our e-mail accounts, mail rules, e-mail signatures, and other e-mail information simply by switching between our two Entourage identities.

A multi-user program, on the other hand, is one that allows many users to share and modify data at the same time. For example, Power On Software's Now Up-To-Date and Contact is a multi-user PIM that can be shared by two or more people. Changes made by one person to the calendar or address book are reflected in the copies of the data on everybody else's machines. Multi-user software typically requires a central server, which contains the data file, and client software on each machine that accesses the server.

tip **Make your identity active before running other Office applications**

The other Office applications—Word, Excel, and Microsoft PowerPoint X—are all integrated with Entourage; for example, you can use the AutoComplete feature to complete contact information or you can send Office documents via e-mail from within those applications. Word can also use your Entourage address book as a source for data merging. It's important to make sure that the correct identity is active in Entourage before you open the other Office programs. Otherwise, you might find that you have done a data merge in Word using somebody else's address book!

Creating and Switching Between Identities

It's not difficult to create a new identity for another user (or even an alternate identity for yourself). Follow these steps:

1 Choose Entourage, Switch Identity, or press Command+Option+Q.

---

caution Command+Option+Q is kind of an odd keystroke; you're more likely to press Command+Shift+Q by mistake. Since that's the systemwide command to log out of the current Mac OS X user, you don't want to do that.

---

2 If you see a dialog titled Are You Sure You Want To Switch Identities, select the Don't Show This Message Again check box, and click Switch.

---

tip **Quit other Office programs before creating or switching identities**

Because the other Office applications use the Entourage database for tasks such as calendar and contact services, you can't switch Entourage identities while Word, Excel, or PowerPoint are open. If you try, you'll get an error dialog. Simply quit the other programs and try again.

---

3 In the Entourage dialog, shown here, click New.

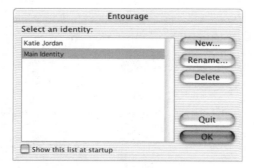

4 Enter a name for the new identity, and then click OK.

5 Entourage creates the new identity files and places them in a folder with the same name as the new identity (which by default resides in the Users/ *username*/Documents/Microsoft User Data/Office X Identities folder), where *username* is the name of the person currently logged in to Mac OS X. Then Entourage launches the Entourage Setup Assistant. Set up the new identity as described earlier, in "Using the Entourage Setup Assistant," page 410.

Once the identities are set up, to switch between different user identities, simply choose Entourage, Switch Identity, choose the identity you want to activate, and then click OK.

Moving Identity Files Between Macintoshes

One of the best things about Entourage's system of identity folders is that it allows you to easily move identities from one Macintosh to another, so it's easy to transfer your e-mail and PIM information from your desktop machine to your laptop when you hit

Chapter 17: Entourage Essentials

the road, and move the information back again when you return. There's no need to do any sort of synchronization process between machines; all you need to do is copy an identity folder from one machine to the other. You can do the job using removable media, such as a recordable CD, onto which you have burned a copy of the identity folder, but it's usually easier to make a network connection between the two machines.

---

tip　**Use your iDisk to transfer files**

If your two computers aren't connected through a network, but both computers can connect to the Internet, you might be able to use your iDisk, a file area on Apple's servers, to transfer your files. You'll need a fast Internet connection for this though, as most identity folders are dozens or even hundreds of megabytes in size. For more information about the iDisk, go to *www.apple.com/itools*.

To move an identity, follow these steps:

1 Connect both computers to an Ethernet or Airport network.

2 On either computer, mount the hard disk from the other computer as a net-worked volume.

For more information about networking two computers together, switch to the Finder, choose Help, Mac Help, type **sharing + files**, and click Ask.

---

3 Open the Users/*username*/Documents/Microsoft User Data/Office X Identities folders on both machines, and arrange the two open folders so that you can see both the source and the destination.

4 Drag the identity folder that you want to copy from the source to the desti-nation. If you have previously copied the folder, Mac OS X will ask you to confirm your copying choice. Click Replace.

---

caution　Double- or triple-check that you are dragging files in the correct direction! You don't want to accidentally overwrite the newest version of the file with the older versions.

Renaming or Deleting an Identity

To rename an identity (usually because you typed the name incorrectly when you cre-ated it, or because you want to change the default Main Identity name to your name), choose Entourage, Switch Identity, choose the identity you want to rename, and then click Rename. Enter the new name and click OK. Entourage changes the name of the identity's folder in the Office X Identities folder on your hard disk.

You can also delete identities that you no longer need. Choose Entourage, Switch Identity, choose the identity you want to delete, and then click Delete. Entourage will display a confirmation dialog. Click Delete to confirm.

> **caution**   When you delete an identity, Entourage immediately erases the folder containing the identity file from your hard disk; the folder doesn't simply get moved to the Trash. All of the e-mail, calendar, and contact information associated with that identity will be lost. Be very careful when deleting identities; there's no Undo.

Using Sound Sets

Entourage lets you know what it's doing with sounds (though you can turn them off if you want). The program has the following sounds:

- **Welcome sound** plays when Entourage is started.
- **New mail sound** plays when you receive new mail.
- **Sent mail sound** plays when you send mail.
- **Mail error sound** plays when there is a problem either sending or receiving mail.
- **No mail sound** plays when Entourage checks for mail, but sadly, there is none waiting.
- **Reminder sound** plays when an Office Notifications message comes due.

Entourage comes with a pleasant-enough sound set, but you can add your own. You can make your own if you're handy with sound-editing software, but the best place to find sound sets for Entourage is Sound Set Central (*www.soundsetcentral.com*), which has (at press time) more than 500 sound sets for a variety of applications, including Entourage and Outlook Express.

> **note**   Outlook Express sound sets work fine in Entourage, with one caveat: because Outlook Express didn't have a calendar, Outlook Express sound sets lack a Reminder sound. Sound sets created for Entourage 2001 work fine in Entourage X; if you can't find many sound sets on Sound Set Central when you search for Entourage X sets, search for Entourage sets instead.

After you've downloaded some new sound sets, install them by copying the sound set files into the Users/*username*/Documents/Microsoft User Data/Entourage Sound Sets folder.

Chapter 17: Entourage Essentials

To switch to the new sound set, follow these steps:

1 Choose Entourage, General Preferences, or press Command+; (semicolon).

2 Click the Notification tab.

3 In the Sounds section, choose the sound set you want from the Sound Set pop-up menu, as shown in Figure 17-5. You can preview the sounds by clicking on the speaker icon next to each sound type, and disable a sound by clearing the check mark next to a sound. Click OK when you're done.

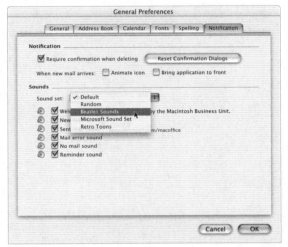

Figure 17-5. Choose your Entourage soundtrack by picking a sound set.

> **tip** New sound sets should show up in Entourage's preferences right away, but sometimes they don't. Simply quit and relaunch Entourage to get access to all of your sound sets.

Because sound sets are set via a preference, each identity can have a different sound set (though all the identities select their sound set from among the same list of sound sets, because all the identities share the Entourage Sound Sets folder, as long as those identities are owned by the same Mac OS X user).

Chapter 17

Mastering Your E-Mail

For most people, nothing in Microsoft Office v. X gets a workout more than the e-mail portion of Microsoft Entourage X. Even professional writers (like me) who use Microsoft Word X as our main tool spend as much or more time reading, writing, and replying to e-mail as we do writing in Word. Of course, the reason that we spend so much time dealing with e-mail is that we get so much of it. The volume of e-mail increases every year, with no end in sight. Organizing and winnowing this flood requires thought and care, and fortunately Entourage provides a robust set of tools to get the job done.

In this chapter, you'll learn how to create, send, and receive e-mail; how to use schedules to receive mail automatically; the best ways to organize your e-mail (and how to get Entourage to organize e-mail automatically); how to cut back on junk mail; and how to archive old e-mail that you no longer need.

Receiving and Reading Mail

In order to get and send e-mail with Entourage, you first need to configure all of the e-mail accounts that you want to work with. If you haven't already done so, see "Setting Up E-Mail Accounts," page 412.

You can receive new mail and send any mail that you've written by using Entourage's Send & Receive command. You can use three different methods to do this (of course, you need to make sure that you're in the Mail section of Entourage first):

- Choose Tools, Send & Receive All.
- Click the Send & Receive button on the toolbar.
- Press Command+K.

Entourage connects to the mail servers that you have configured, receives all mail that is waiting for you, and sends any mail that you've written that is waiting to go out. You'll know when Entourage has completed the operation because it will play a sound. Which sound it plays depends on the outcome of the mail operation; it plays one sound if it has successfully retrieved mail, another sound if there was no mail waiting, and yet a third sound if something went wrong during the mail retrieval operation.

> For more information on working with and changing Entourage's sounds, see "Using Sound Sets," page 422.

If you receive mail while Entourage is not the active application, Entourage will notify you that you've got mail by bouncing the Entourage icon, overlaid with an envelope, in the Dock, as shown here:

While mail is being sent or received, Entourage displays the Progress window, as shown in Figure 18-1. The Progress window contains disclosure triangles that you can click to see details of the operations of all of the e-mail servers with which Entourage is communicating and the progress that Entourage is making in downloading or uploading your e-mail.

Figure 18-1. The progress window lets you know what's going on in your mail operation and when the next schedule is going to trigger.

When mail is received, the names of folders in the Folder list that contain the new mail are marked in bold, with the number of unread messages listed in parentheses after the folder name. At the same time, the names of the new messages, also in bold (denoting that the messages are unread), appear in the Message list. If the message has been assigned a category (usually by one of Entourage's mail rules), the category will appear in the Message list's Categories column, and the message will also appear in the color (if any) assigned to that category.

> For more information about mail rules, see "Working with Mail Rules," page 470. For more information about categories, see "Using Priorities, Categories, and Flags," page 460.

Chapter 18: Mastering Your E-Mail

To read a mail message, select a folder in the Folder list. The folder's contents will appear in the Message list. Then, to read the contents of the message, do one of two things, depending on whether you have the Preview pane displayed—to toggle the Preview pane on and off, choose View, Preview Pane, or press Command+\ (backslash):

● If the Preview pane is active, simply select a message's name in the Message list to display the message's contents in the Preview pane, as shown in Figure 18-2. The area at the top of the Preview pane shows the e-mail addresses of the sender, the recipient, and the message's subject. Other information, such as the date sent and the message's category, are shown in the Message list.

> **tip** You can adjust the relative sizes of the Message list and Preview pane by dragging the border between them.

● If you don't like to use the Preview pane, double-click the message (or select it in the Message list and press Return) to open the message in a new window. The header area at the top of this window shows you the same information as in the top of the Preview pane. The background color of the header area is the same as the category color, and the category name also shows in the window's toolbar as the label of the Categories button; if no category has been assigned, the button is simply labeled Categories.

> **note** If you have more than one category assigned to a message, Entourage will color the message according to the color of the first category.

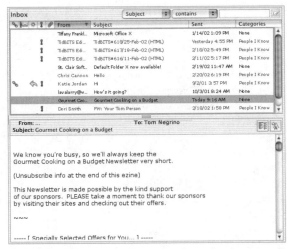

Figure 18-2. Selecting a message in the Message list displays the message's contents in the Preview pane.

Depending on whether you choose to read a message in the Preview pane or in its own window, you'll see differences in the toolbars at the top of your screen, as shown in Figure 18-3:

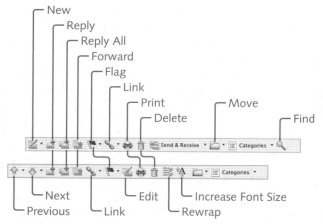

Figure 18-3. These are the toolbars as they appear when you read a message in the Preview pane (top) and in a separate window (bottom).

The different toolbars help you do much the same tasks, no matter what mode you prefer to use to read your mail. Once you have displayed a message, you can scroll through it as you read by tapping the Spacebar (press Shift+Spacebar to scroll up). When you reach the end of the message, another tap of the Spacebar changes the display to the next unread message.

InsideOut

Scroll long messages with the mouse

You can scroll down through long messages by repeatedly tapping the Spacebar, but Entourage is set to scroll rather slowly, and holding the Spacebar down, which you would think would make the message scroll continuously, perversely makes scrolling even slower. It's much faster to click and hold the down arrow in the message's scroll bar. It's even faster to click and hold *in* the scroll bar, in the blank area below the scroll bar's *thumb* (the lozenge-shaped indicator that shows your current position in the message). And if you want to get from one end of a message to the other in the fastest way, click and drag the thumb where you want it.

Chapter 18: Mastering Your E-Mail

You can also get from one message to the next by using the following keyboard shortcuts:

- If you're reading messages with the Preview pane, use the Up Arrow and Down Arrow keys to switch messages. You can also use the Home key to jump to the first message in the Message list, and the End key to jump to the last.

tip If the shortcut keys don't seem to work, it's probably because the window's focus is in the Preview pane, not the Message list (the active pane will be surrounded by a thin, colored border). Select a message in the list, and the shortcut keys should start working. You can also use Tab or Shift+Tab to move the focus.

- If you're using a separate window to read messages, use Command+[(left bracket) to go to the previous message, and Command+] (right bracket) to go to the next message. In this mode, the Home and End keys don't change messages.

note If those shortcut keys seem familiar, it's because Internet Explorer uses the same shortcut keys for the Back and Forward commands.

Entourage lets you perform many other reading operations from the keyboard; some of these keyboard shortcuts are listed in Table 18-1.

Table 18-1. **Mail Reading Shortcut Keys**

Keyboard Shortcut	Action
Return or Command+O	When the Preview pane is hidden, opens the selected message in a new window
Command+[	Displays the previous message
Command+]	Displays the next message
Control+[	Displays the previous unread message
Control+]	Displays the next unread message
Command+Option+[	Deletes the current message and displays the previous message
Command+Option+]	Deletes the current message and displays the next message

(continued)

Chapter 18

Table 18-1. *(continued)*

Keyboard Shortcut	Action
Control+Option+[	Deletes the current message and displays the previous unread message
Control+Option+]	Deletes the current message and displays the next unread message
Command+Shift+M	Opens the Move dialog to move the selected message to another folder
Spacebar	Scrolls down one screen of text, or displays the next unread message if you are at the end of the current message
Shift+Spacebar	Scrolls up one screen of text
Option+Spacebar	Scrolls down one screen of text, or deletes the current message and displays the next unread message if you are at the end of the current message
Delete or Del	Deletes the selected message in the Message list
Command+Shift+ plus sign	Increases the font size for the current message
Command+Shift+ minus sign	Decreases the font size for the current message

tip Control+clicking one or more messages in the Message list brings up a contextual menu that contains many of Entourage's commands for handling messages, and also commands from other areas of the program. Check it out!

Once you've displayed a message, the name of the message in the Message list will switch from bold to normal type. Actually, Entourage can't tell if you've really read a message simply because you've selected or displayed it, so after a respectable pause, it assumes you have. You can control this behavior in the Read tab of Mail & News Preferences. You can control this behavior by setting a preference. Follow these steps:

1 Choose Entourage, Mail & News Preferences, and click the Read tab.

2 If you want messages to switch from bold to normal type as soon as you select them, select Mark Messages As Read When Displayed In The Preview Pane.

3 If you want Entourage to wait a while before indicating you've read the message, select Mark Message As Read After Displaying For, and type a number of seconds in the box.

---

tip   **Hide the mail you've read**

You can concentrate on just the messages that you still need to read by choosing View, Unread Only, or pressing Command+Shift+O. Entourage will hide all the read messages in the Message list. Choose View, Unread Only again to display the hidden messages.

Icons in the Message list

At the left side of the Message list, you'll see five narrow columns. These columns contain icons that tell you the status of your mail messages or provide other useful information. The five columns are shown in Figure 18-4.

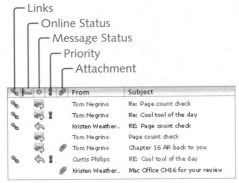

Figure 18-4. The Message list's icon columns give you valuable information about your mail.

Links

The Links column displays a chain link icon if the message has been linked to another mail message, a calendar event, task, note, or the like. See "Creating Links to Existing Items," page 535, for more information about links.

Online Status

In the Online Status column, Entourage shows you the message's status if you are working in the Online Access mode. Table 18-2 on the next page shows the different icons for Online Access mode; see "Online Access and Working Offline," page 454 for more information about what these icons signify.

Table 18-2. **Online Access Icons**

Icon	Meaning
	Message has been fully retrieved from the server.
	Message has been partially retrieved from the server.
	Message has been marked to be fully retrieved from the server at the next connection.
	Message has been marked to be deleted from the server at the next connection.

Message Status

The Message Status column is probably the most useful; it will tell you at a glance whether you have replied to, forwarded, sent, or read a message, plus much more. Table 18-3 lists all the icons that can appear in this column.

Table 18-3. **Message Status Icons**

Icon	Meaning
	The message is unread.
	You have replied to this message.
	You have forwarded this message.
	You have redirected this message.
	You have resent this message.
	The message has been sent.
	The message is in draft form and has not yet been sent.
	The message has been edited after receipt.
	The message has been flagged.

Priority

The priority of a message is generally set by the sender when the message is created, though you can set the priority automatically when you receive the message by using a mail rule. No icon in this column means the message is set to normal priority; the other five icons are shown in Table 18-4.

Table 18-4. Priority Icons

Icon	Meaning
	Message is set to highest priority.
	Message is set to high priority.
	Message is set to low priority.
	Message is set to lowest priority.
	Message is set to junk mail priority.

Attachment

The Attachment column's paper clip icon tells you whether the message includes an attached file.

Deleting Unwanted Mail

Once you've read a message (or even before you've read it if you recognize by its header that the message is junk mail), you often will want to delete it. Entourage gives you four ways to delete messages:

- Press the Delete, Del, or Command+Delete keys.
- Click the Delete button on the toolbar.
- Choose Edit, Delete Message.
- Use a mail rule to delete messages automatically.

No matter which method you use, Entourage does not actually delete the message; it merely moves it to the trash, in this case a folder called Deleted Items. Just as with the Trash in the Finder, you can open the Deleted Items folder and retrieve messages that you throw away by mistake. By default, Entourage is set to permanently delete messages in the Deleted Items folder automatically by using a schedule; the schedule deletes messages (or even folders) in the Deleted Items folder when you quit Entourage. If you want to permanently delete messages in the Deleted Items folder, perform one of these actions:

- Select a message within the Deleted Items folder, and then press the Delete, Del, or Command+Delete keys.

- Control+click the Deleted Items folder, and from the resulting contextual menu, choose Empty Deleted Items.

- Choose Tools, Run Schedule, Empty Deleted Items Folder to trigger the schedule mentioned previously.

> **tip** You can change the number of days that deleted items hang around in the Deleted Items folder before being permanently deleted. Simply change the Empty Deleted Items Folder schedule. See "Setting Up Mail Schedules," page 457, for more information.

Marking Mail

Once you have read an e-mail message, Entourage changes the message title from bold to normal text in the Message list, marking the mail as having been read. The name of the folder where the read message resides also changes from bold to normal text, assuming it does not contain any other unread messages. Entourage gives you control over this marking of messages and message folders. You can mark or unmark a single message, multiple messages, or the entire contents of a message folder. The most common reason you would want to mark a message as unread after you have read it is that you might need to put it aside temporarily and come back to it later; marking the message as unread makes the message (or the message's enclosing folder) stand out when you next scan your mail. The opposite is also true; you might want to mark one or more messages as read even if you *haven't* read them, because you never intend to read them (the most common example would be if the mail is unsolicited commercial e-mail, also known as *spam* or *junk mail*). In the Message list, select the message or messages that you want to mark, and perform one of these actions:

- To mark the selection as read, choose Message, Mark As Read, or press Command+T.

- To mark the selection as unread, choose Message, Mark As Unread, or press Command+Shift+T.

If you select a folder, you can only mark its entire contents as read. In the Folder list, select a folder, and then choose Message, Mark All As Read, or press Command+ Option+T.

---

tip **Mark the contents of a folder as unread**

If for some reason you want to mark the entire contents of a folder as unread, select the folder in the Folder list, select any message in the Message list, press Command+A to select all the messages in that folder, and then choose Message, Mark As Unread, or press Command+Shift+T.

A close relative to marking mail as unread so that you can deal with it later is flagging mail. For more information about flagging mail, see "Using Priorities, Categories, and Flags," page 460.

Replying to a Message

To reply to a message, click the Reply button on the toolbar; choose Message, Reply; or press Command+R. Entourage creates a new outgoing mail message, already addressed to the sender's return address.

If the original message was sent to you and also copied to other people, you can send your reply to the sender and all of the other people with a simple command. Instead of choosing Reply, click the Reply All button on the toolbar; choose Message, Reply To All; or press Command+Shift+R.

---

note A third option, Message, Reply To Sender, sends the reply only to the person who sent the message, so for normal mail it works in the same way as Reply. Reply To Sender is chiefly useful when you are replying to a message from a mailing list and the mailing list is set so that replies go to the entire list, rather than just to the person who posted the message. For more information about mailing lists, see "Handling Mailing Lists with the Mailing List Manager," page 468.

By default, Entourage includes the entire text of the message that you are replying to in the new message by inserting an angle bracket (>) at the beginning of each line to indicate the text is *quoted text*. Above the quoted text, Entourage adds an *attribution line,* which states the date, name, and e-mail address of the quoted text, as shown in Figure 18-5 on the next page. The quoted text and the attribution line help the recipient of your reply know what message you are replying to. Entourage also takes the message's title, prepends *Re:* to it, and inserts it as the reply's title. Finally, the insertion point is placed in the body of the message, below the quoted text.

Account pop-up menu

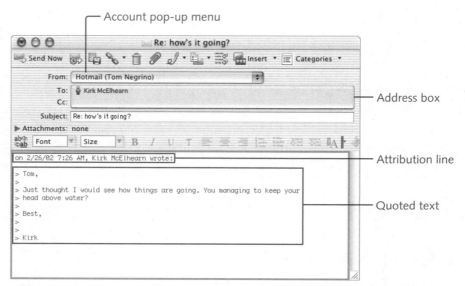

Figure 18-5. Entourage's reply window contains the text of the message to which you are replying.

You can begin typing your reply. You can also do the following:

● Choose from which of your e-mail accounts you wish to send the reply by choosing that e-mail account from the account pop-up menu. If you have only one e-mail account, the pop-up menu is unnecessary, and will not appear.

● Change the recipients of your reply by adding or deleting them in the To or Cc field in the address box.

● Edit the subject line.

● Add a file attachment.

For more about adding file attachments, see "Attaching Files and Folders to Messages," page 452.

● Edit the quoted text. It is common to do this when you want to intersperse your comments with the quoted text. This enables you to reply to the quoted text point by point, and delete quoted text that isn't relevant to your reply.

When you are done creating your reply, click the Send Now button on the toolbar (if you want Entourage to immediately connect to your mail server and send the message), or click the Send Later button if you want Entourage to send the mail at the next scheduled time (if you have mail schedules active) or the next time that you manually connect.

---

tip | **Quote less text in your replies**

Most of the time, there's no need to include the entire text of a message in your e-mail reply. In fact, according to the etiquette that has sprung up around e-mail, it is actually considered to be slightly rude to force your correspondent to wade through all the text that they had sent you in order to get to your reply. Fortunately, Entourage allows you to easily turn off quoting entire text and gives you a way to quote only the text that you select. Choose Entourage, Mail & News Preferences, select the Reply & Forward tab, and clear the Include Entire Message In Reply option. From then on, *before* you click the Reply button, select the text in the received message that you want to become quoted text in your reply. When you click the Reply button, Entourage quotes only the selected text.

Adding Correspondents to Your Address Book

When you receive e-mail, you'll often want to store the sender's e-mail address in your address book, so that it is easier for you to address future mail to that person. Follow these steps:

1 Make sure the message from the person whose address you want to add is displayed.

2 Choose Tools, Add To Address Book, or press Command+equal sign.

3 Entourage adds the e-mail address from the sender, and then opens a contact window from the Address Book, set to the contact's Summary page, as shown in Figure 18-6. If you want to add more information to the new

Figure 18-6. You can edit your new contact using the Address Book's contact window.

contact (for example, mailing addresses or other contact or personal information, you can do so by selecting the tabs in the contact window.

If there is already a contact with the *exact same name* in your address book, Entourage displays a dialog that asks whether you want to add the new e-mail address to the existing contact or create a new contact, as shown here:

4 If you added additional information to the contact, click Save on the contact window's toolbar, or press Command+S.

> For more information about working with contacts in the Address Book, see "Creating and Using Contacts," page 495.

5 Close the contact window to return to your e-mail.

InsideOut

Open most recent messages

At the bottom of the contact window, there are links that show the date that you last sent a message to that contact and the date a message from that contact was last received, as shown here. Clicking one of the links opens those most recent messages. When you add a contact's e-mail address to the Address Book, Entourage doesn't create a Last Message Received link, even though you obviously have received a message from that contact. It's not until you get the *next* message from that same contact that the link is created.

Forwarding and Redirecting E-Mail

When you want to share mail that you receive with a third party, you can *forward* it to that person. Select the message in the Message list, and then click the Forward button on the toolbar; choose Message, Forward; or press Command+J. Entourage makes a copy of the entire message, adds *FW:* before the subject line, and sets off the forwarded

Chapter 18: Mastering Your E-Mail

text of the message with "Forwarded Message" and "End of Forwarded Message" labels, as shown in Figure 18-7. You'll need to enter the e-mail address of the person to whom you want to send the forwarded mail, and add any explanation you want before the forwarded text (Entourage places the insertion point before the forwarded text). You can also edit the forwarded text however you want. Click Send Now or Send Later when you're done.

> **note** Just as with replies, if you select text before hitting Forward, only the selected text will be forwarded.

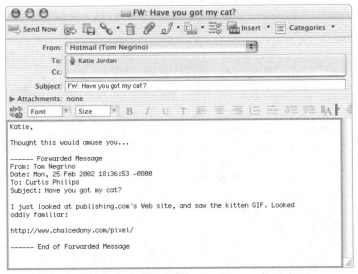

Figure 18-7. Forwarded mail includes the text of the message, preceded by your comments.

Redirecting mail is somewhat like forwarding, but with an important difference. Forwarding and redirecting mail both involve sending mail that you have received to a third person. When you forward mail, the recipient gets a copy of the message, from your e-mail address. When you redirect mail, the recipient gets a copy of the message, apparently from the *original sender's* e-mail address; your e-mail address isn't shown in the redirected message the recipient receives. This is great when you get mail by mistake, and you want to send it on to the intended recipient. With forwarded mail, if the recipient hits Reply, you will get the reply message. With redirected mail, the original sender gets the reply message. Redirecting mail is a also great way to transfer mail between two of your own e-mail accounts.

> **note** Redirected mail isn't scrubbed of all of your involvement; some mail programs (Entourage is one of them) will show a Resent header when you open the mail in a new window. Other mail programs will tell the whole tale if the recipient uses the option to view the detailed Internet headers of the mail. So don't think that you're anonymous; the recipient will know that you sent the mail on to them.

Working with File Attachments

Messages you receive can contain additional files called *attachments*. An attachment can be any type of file, and you can have more than one file attached to a message. When you receive a message with one or more attachments, you can open the attachment, save the attachment to your hard disk, or, if the attachment is a JPEG, GIF, or QuickTime movie, view the attachment in the body of the mail message.

> For information about attaching files or folders to mail you create, see "Attaching Files and Folders to Messages," page 452.

You can see at a glance that a message contains a file attachment because a paper clip icon appears in the Attachment column in the Message list. To see the attachment itself, select the message in the Message list, and click the disclosure triangle (either in the Preview pane or in the message's window). Any attachments will be visible in the Attachment pane, as shown in Figure 18-8.

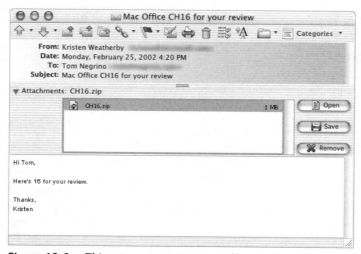

Figure 18-8. This message contains one file attachment.

Opening Attachments

To open an attachment, select the attachment in the Attachment pane, and then click Open; choose File, Open Attachment; or press Command+O. Depending on the type of file the attachment is, another program will open to display the file. For example, if the attachment is a Word file, Word will launch and open the file.

> **note** If Entourage can't find an association for a particular file type after you attempt to open it, you'll know because nothing will happen.

Saving Attachments

To save an attachment, follow these steps:

1 Open a message's Attachment pane, as described previously.

2 Select the attachments that you want to save, and then click Save.

3 In the Save Attachment dialog, navigate to where you want to save the file, and then click Save. If you selected multiple attachments in step 2, the Save Attachment dialog will return until each attachment has been saved.

> **tip** **Save all the files at once**
>
> If you know that you want to save all of the attachments in the same folder on your hard drive, select the message and choose Message, Save All Attachments. In the Choose A Folder dialog, navigate to where you want to save the files, and then click Choose.

You can also save file attachments to disk by dragging the attachments from the message's Attachment pane onto the desktop or directly into a folder in the Finder.

Removing Attachments

If you want to remove attachments from a message, perhaps because you have already saved the attachments to disk, or because some bozo has just sent you a 4-MB picture of his schnauzer, select the message in the Message list, and choose Remove All Attachments. If you want to remove just one attachment from a message that has multiple attachments, open the Attachment pane, select the offending attachment, and click Remove.

Another good reason to remove attachments is to remove attached computer viruses. A danger sign of an attached computer virus is a file with a .exe file extension from an unfamiliar correspondent, which means that the file is an executable PC program. That file is harmless on the Macintosh, but it's better to get rid of it by removing the attachment anyway so that you don't accidentally forward the message on to Windows-using colleagues, thereby infecting them with some digital nastiness. Except in some very special cases, there's no good reason for someone to send you a .exe file, these files should be considered guilty until proven innocent.

> **tip** You can create a mail rule to automatically strip attachments from messages that have file attachments that end in .exe. See "Creating Mail Rules," page 471.

Decompressing and Decoding Files

Many files you receive will be compressed or encoded. A file that has been *compressed* has been processed with a program that analyzes the file and then applies a mathematical algorithm to "squash" the file, making it smaller and quicker to send. The most common compression program on the Macintosh is called StuffIt Deluxe, made by Aladdin Systems. In fact, there's a version of StuffIt built right into Entourage. You can recognize a StuffIt attachment because it has the file name extension .sit. The most common equivalent in Windows is the ZIP format created by PKWare, Inc. These files are easily recognized by their .zip file name extension.

Files that have been *encoded* have been converted, usually by the sender's mail program, so that they can be sent over the Internet. You can recognize encoded files by their file name extensions such as .bin, .hqx, .gz, .tgz, or .uu.

Usually, all you need to do to decompress or decode one of these files is to open it in Entourage. Entourage calls upon the free StuffIt Expander program, which ships as part of Mac OS X (you'll find it in the Applications/Utilities/StuffIt Expander folder), to expand any of the file types mentioned, and many more. On occasion, opening the file from within Entourage doesn't work as well as saving the file attachment to disk and then dragging the file's icon on top of the StuffIt Expander icon.

Viewing Internet Headers

The headers that you have seen at the top of each message are generally only a fraction of the actual header information that is attached to each e-mail message. The complete header traces the message's path through the various Internet mail servers it went through between the sender and your desktop. Entourage refers to this information as *Internet headers*. Usually you won't need to view the Internet headers, but sometimes they can be helpful when you're trying to troubleshoot e-mail problems. You can view the Internet headers for a message by double-clicking it in the Message list, to open the message in a new window (you can't view Internet headers in the Preview pane), and then by choosing View, Internet Headers, or by pressing Command+Shift+H.

Working with Mail Errors

If Entourage encountered problems sending or receiving mail, processing mail, or decoding file attachments, it makes a note in its Error Log, and alerts you that there has been a problem by putting an alert icon in the corner of the status bar, as shown here:

Clicking the alert icon opens the Error Log window, which shows a list of all the currently logged error messages. As in the Message list, errors in the Error Log window appear in bold when they are unread. If you want to delete the error messages, select them, and click the Delete button in the Error Log toolbar. To read an error message, double-click it in the list. An Error Description window appears, as shown in Figure 18-9.

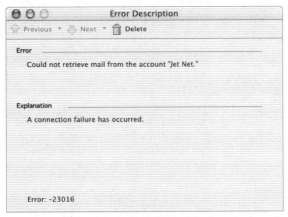

Figure 18-9. Error descriptions give you an idea of what went wrong when sending or receiving mail.

Error descriptions are well-meaning attempts to be helpful that don't always provide much real help. For example, in Figure 18-9, the explanation says that you couldn't retrieve mail from a particular account and that "A connection failure has occurred." Well, since you didn't get any mail, you already knew that (though it's helpful to know which account had problems). What can sometimes be helpful is the error number at the bottom of the Error Description window. Sometimes, but not always, you can do a search for that number in the Support section of the Mactopia Web site and find a support document that lists the error number and better explains what went wrong, so that you can fix it. Unfortunately, there doesn't seem to be a comprehensive list available of all of the possible error numbers and what they mean.

Composing, Addressing, and Sending Mail

Even if you use the Preview pane to read messages, all messages are composed in a separate message window, as shown in Figure 18-10. The message window has three sections: the message header (the To, Cc, Bcc, and subject lines), the Attachment pane, and the message body.

> **note** The To field is self-explanatory; the Cc field copies your message to others you address in this field. Both the To recipients and the Cc recipients see one another's names. Use the To field for the main recipients of your e-mail and reserve the Cc field for those whose active response is not needed, but whom you want to "keep in the loop." Just as Cc is an obsolete acronym for "carbon copy," Bcc indicates "blind carbon copy" and is used to send a copy to someone whose identity will not be visible to the To or Cc recipients (unless they examine the source code of the message).

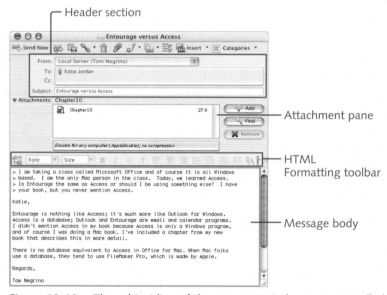

Figure 18-10. The subject line of the message window automatically becomes the window's title.

Creating a New Message

To create a new message, follow these steps:

1 Choose File, New, Mail Message. If you are already in Entourage's main mail window, you can also press Command+N or click the New button on the toolbar.

2 An untitled mail window appears, with the insertion point already placed in the To address field. Begin typing the name or e-mail address of the addressee. As you type, Entourage displays a pop-up menu showing addresses from your address book that match what you are typing. Entourage narrows your choices in the pop-up menu as you continue to type more letters. It also prioritizes addresses with which you have corresponded most recently, so for example if you have three people named Curt in your address book, Entourage will highlight the Curt with whom you corresponded last. When Entourage highlights the e-mail address that you want, press Return to move the insertion point to the Subject box.

tip Pressing the Tab key instead of Return will enable you to add another recipient in the To box. Pressing the Tab key again without entering an address moves the insertion point to the Cc box, and pressing the Tab key yet again moves the insertion point to the Bcc box.

3 Type the subject for your message, and then press Return.

4 If you want to attach a file with your message, do so now. The easiest way to do it is by dragging the file from the Finder into the message window's Attachment pane.

For more information about sending file attachments, see "Attaching Files and Folders to Messages," page 452.

5 Type the body of your message.

6 Send the message by clicking the Send Now or Send Later button on the toolbar.

Formatting HTML Mail

If you have enabled HTML mail, when you create a new message the HTML Formatting toolbar will be active in the message window, as shown next. Formatting is straightforward; you use the tools on the HTML Formatting toolbar in virtually the same way that you would in Word. All you need to do is select the text to be formatted and then click the formatting buttons on the HTML Formatting toolbar or choose the formatting commands from the Format menu.

note If the buttons on the HTML Formatting toolbar are not active, you're in plain text mode. To switch to HTML mode, click the Use HTML button at the left end of the HTML Formatting toolbar, or choose Format, HTML. You can also use these options to toggle an HTML message to plain text.

Chapter 18

Plain Text vs. HTML Mail

Entourage can display e-mail in two main ways. The first way, *plain text,* displays messages as text only, with no formatting except for underlined hyperlinks for URLs and e-mail addresses. Plain text e-mail can be read by any e-mail program, old or new. The second way, *HTML mail,* uses the HTML renderer built into Entourage to display e-mail with fancy formatting, fonts, colors, embedded pictures, hyperlinks, and more. The benefit of HTML mail is that people can send and receive messages with the sort of formatting control that they are used to with word processors such as Microsoft Word. The downside to HTML mail is that it takes a bit longer to create (because formatting a message the way you like it takes time), a bit longer to trans-mit, and depending on the complexity of the HTML, usually takes longer to appear on your screen. Another drawback is that some of your recipients, especially if they're using an older e-mail program, may not be able to read HTML e-mail.

Sending HTML mail can also be problematical for mailing lists. Many mailing list server programs cannot handle HTML mail correctly, resulting in messages being sent to the list as raw HTML code, which can be very difficult to read.

Entourage has several preferences that help you deal with HTML mail. Choose Entourage, Mail & News Preferences. On the Read tab, the two options in the HTML section enable Entourage to display complex HTML and to retrieve information (for example, download a picture) when attempting to render an HTML message. These options are enabled by default; though they will display richer messages, they will also make some HTML messages take longer to appear, sometimes as long as several sec-onds. On the Compose tab, the Mail Format pop-up menu sets the default method that Entourage will use when creating new messages, either plain text or HTML. On the Reply & Forward tab, the Reply To Messages In The Format In Which They Were Sent option overrides the default method set with the Mail Format pop-up menu.

There are three options on the HTML Formatting toolbar that are sufficiently different from their word processing equivalents to require explanation:

- The Font Size pop-up menu is limited to only five sizes, from Largest to Smallest.

- The Teletype button (the button with the letter *T* for *teletype*) turns selected text into monospaced text, which means that all of the characters take up the same width. Because HTML messages don't have true tab stops, and most fonts use variable widths for their characters, monospaced text can be useful for things like lining up columns of text or numbers.

- The Horizontal Line button draws a line across the entire message.

One other HTML formatting option is only available from the Format menu; choose Format, Headings to access a hierarchical menu with HTML heading styles, Heading 1 (largest) through Heading 6 (smallest). Choose Format, Headings, None to return to regular text.

> **note** The HTML headings produce results that use different sizes and font weights than the five HTML font sizes. You should experiment with both options to see which works best for you in a particular situation.

You can view, but can't edit, the HTML source code for incoming and outgoing messages. This capability can be useful if you are conversant with HTML and want to see the message's source code, or if you want to copy and paste the HTML source code into another application. To show the HTML source code, select a message in the Message list, and then choose View, Source. A new window opens with the source code, as shown in Figure 18-11.

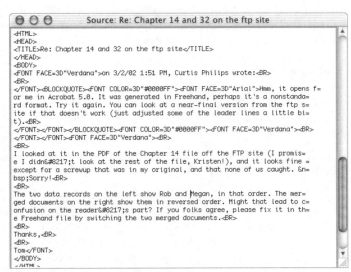

Figure 18-11. The Source window shows the HTML underlying that fancy formatting.

Checking Spelling in Messages

You have many of the same spelling checking options with Entourage as you do with Word. Entourage checks spelling as you type (this is an option that you can turn off on the Spelling tab of the General Preferences dialog) and displays misspellings in the subject line and the message body by putting a wavy red line under the misspelled word. Correct the misspelling by Control+clicking the underlined word (or by right-clicking if you have a multibutton mouse) to open a contextual menu like the one shown here:

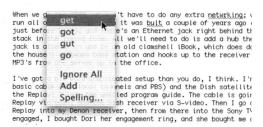

You can also check spelling throughout the message by choosing Tools, Spelling. The resulting spelling dialog is virtually identical to the one in Word. Refer to "Checking Spelling in the Whole Document," page 266, if you need more explanation.

Like the other Office v. X applications, Entourage shares all of the spelling dictionaries, including the Custom Dictionary and the AutoCorrect entries. Besides fixing common spelling mistakes, AutoCorrect is especially useful as a shortcut for typing repetitive text.

For more information about AutoCorrect, see "Using AutoCorrect to Save Typing," page 101.

If you're writing mail in HTML format, Entourage also has a subset of Word's AutoFormat commands available. To see which options are available to you, choose Tools, AutoCorrect, and then click the AutoFormat tab.

Working with Message Quoting

You've probably seen messages that have been through several recipients, each of whom quoted the message, with the levels of quoted text growing until the message becomes quite difficult to read, as shown in Figure 18-12. Each time the message changes hands another series of angle brackets is placed along the left edge to include both the formerly quoted text and the most recent text from the previous sender, which is now quoted for the first time. You can find the earliest message text by looking for the text with the most angle brackets, and trace the conversation from there by looking for successively fewer angle brackets, but it can be tedious and confusing.

When you send the message on to the next recipient, you'll be doing them a favor if you remove most of the irrelevant or outdated quoted text, keeping just enough to make the meaning clear. Follow these steps:

1 In the outgoing message, select the text, and then choose Edit, Auto Text Cleanup, Remove Quoting. All of the quote marks will be stripped from the selection.

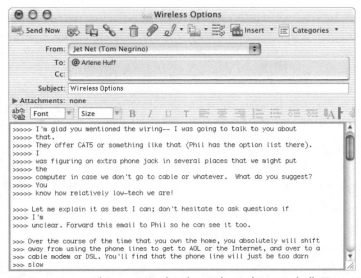

Figure 18-12. This message has been through quote hell. Time to cut those quotes down to size.

2 You will want some quoting (just not so much as to make things unreadable), and different paragraphs will need different amounts of quoting, so select the text that needs the most quoting, and choose Edit, Auto Text Cleanup, Increase Quoting.

3 One level of quoting will be applied to the selection. Repeat on this paragraph until you have all the quoting you need to get the idea across, and then select the next paragraph and repeat the process.

4 To make the text look good, you should rewrap the text lines so that the text breaks pleasingly. Select all of the text, and then choose Edit, Auto Text Cleanup, Rewrap Paragraphs. The cleaned and rewrapped text will look something like this:

```
>> I'm glad you mentioned the wiring-- I was going to talk to you about that.
>> They offer CAT5 or something like that (Phil has the option list there).  I
>> was figuring on extra phone jack in several places that we might put the
>> computer in case we don't go to cable or whatever.  What do you suggest?  You
>> know how relatively low-tech we are!
>>
> Let me explain it as best I can; don't hesitate to ask questions if I'm
> unclear. Forward this email to Phil so he can see it too.
```

tip **Clean up your quoted messages faster**

Instead of using the menu commands to clean and rewrap text, you can Control+click the selected text and use the Auto Text Cleanup command on the contextual menu. You can also use the Rewrap Text button found on the message's toolbar, or the Rewrap Paragraphs button in the Preview pane's header.

You can also copy plain text from one message and paste it as quoted text in another message—very useful when you are replying to a long message and you don't want to quote the entire text of the original back to the sender (that's another bit of e-mail etiquette). Copy the text, switch to the new message, and then choose Edit, Paste Special, Paste As Quotation, or press Command+Shift+V.

Other reformatting commands, also found on the Edit menu's Auto Text Cleanup submenu, include the following:

- **Straighten Quotation Marks** changes curly or smart quotes to straight quotes, which can be better read by some older e-mail programs.
- **To UPPERCASE** changes the selected text to be all uppercase.
- **To lowercase** changes the selected text to be all lowercase.

Saving Message Drafts

If you want to save the message that you are working on for more work later, you can save it as a message *draft,* which puts it automatically into the Drafts folder. Messages in the Drafts folder will not be sent until you open them and click the Send Now or Send Later button. To save a message draft, perform any of these actions while composing a message:

- Press Command+S.
- Choose File, Save.
- Click Save As Draft on the message window's toolbar.

The first two actions keep the message window open for further writing; use these to periodically save your work on a long letter. The Save As Draft command saves and then closes the message.

> **note** If Entourage crashes while you are writing a message, when you relaunch the program, it usually (but not always) will reopen a recovered copy of the message draft, even if you hadn't specifically saved the draft. It's reminiscent of Word's AutoRecover feature.

Using Signatures

Signatures are text that you can append to the end of your e-mail messages such as your name and address, your company's name and contact information, a legal disclaimer, or a favorite quote. To create a signature, follow these steps:

1 Choose Tools, Signatures to open the Signatures dialog.

2 Click the New button.

3 In the Name box, enter a name for the signature to help you identify it in the future.

4 Type the text of your signature in the large box.

---

note Like any other message, a signature can be formatted using HTML or can be left as plain text. You can only add an HTML signature to an HTML message, but you can add a plain text signature to either an HTML message or a plain text message. You can also switch the format of a message by toggling its Use HTML button and then choose a matching signature.

---

5 If you want to use the signature randomly, select the Include In Random List option.

When you sign a message, you choose the name of the signature from the Signature pop-up menu on the message's toolbar. Signatures can be staid or fun; if you lean toward the fun, you might also want to take advantage of Entourage's ability to choose a signature at random. If you choose the Include In Random List option, you can later choose Random from the Signature pop-up menu on a message's toolbar to have Entourage insert one of your random bon mots.

6 Close the window to save the new signature.

---

tip **Use a signature for boilerplate messages**

You can use signatures to quickly insert a block of text, as long as that block of text will be at the end of a message (but that text can also be the *entire text* of a message). Simply create a new signature, enter its text (or drag in the text from Word or another program), and then give it a name and save the signature. When you need to create a fast boilerplate message, create a new message, choose the signature from the toolbar, and hit Send Now. This method is even faster than using AutoCorrect to enter boilerplate text.

You can attach a default signature to each of your e-mail accounts. For example, e-mail you send from a work account can be created with your work signature already attached and messages sent from your home account can have a less formal home signature attached. Follow these steps to establish a default signature for an e-mail account:

1 Choose Tools, Accounts.

2 Double-click an account to edit it.

3 In the Edit Account window, select the Options tab.

4 Make a selection from the Default Signature pop-up menu, and then click OK.

Attaching Files and Folders to Messages

You can also send files and folders (including all of that folder's contents, including files and subfolders) as attachments to your e-mail. Follow these steps:

1 Create a new mail message.

2 If necessary, click the Attachments disclosure triangle to open the Attachment pane.

3 Do one of the following:

   ■ Drag a file or folder into the Attachment pane from the Finder.

   ■ Click the Add button, navigate to the file or folder you want to attach, and then click Choose.

You can repeat the process to attach as many files or folders as you wish.

Compressing and Encoding Files and Folders

Files can be sent as is, but folders cannot. They must be compressed to be sent. When you add a folder as an attachment, Entourage displays this dialog to make sure that you meant to send an entire folder:

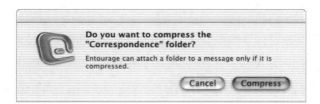

Click Compress to add the folder as an attachment. Attachments are compressed using the Stuffit format. If you want to compress the attached files as well as the folders, click the wide button at the bottom of the Attachment pane to open the encoding and compression dialog shown in Figure 18-13. Click the Macintosh (StuffIt) button in the Compression section of the dialog, and then click the dialog's close box.

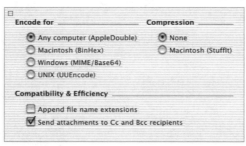

Figure 18-13. The encoding and compression dialog lets you set file attachment options.

You can also use the encoding and compression dialog to encode attachments. *Encoding* is the process of converting the files into another format, which makes them easier to send over the Internet. Entourage supports four encoding schemes:

- **Any computer (AppleDouble)** should be your first choice. This encoding format is designed to work with all computers and is a good choice for sending files to most other Macintosh or Windows users.

- **Macintosh (BinHex)** is a Macintosh-only encoding format. You might need to use this format if your correspondent uses an older Macintosh with an old e-mail program.

- **Windows (MIME/Base64)** format is used by Windows e-mail programs. You should try to use AppleDouble first, but if the file doesn't go through correctly, try sending the file again in this format.

- **UNIX (UUEncode)** is rarely used, because it cannot properly send many Macintosh files, but it is sometimes appropriate for sending e-mail to UNIX computers.

Solving Windows Users' Compatibility Problems

It might have happened to you. You send a file to a coworker who uses a Windows machine. They can't open the file, and tell you so. While trying to figure out the problem, your colleague makes a snide comment about how it must be the Macintosh's fault, and "if you used a real computer...." The next thing you know, you're dueling at 10 paces. This will never do; eliminating colleagues is at best bound to get you talked about, and at worst, could become a sticky legal issue. As Macintosh users, we're in the minority, so it's incumbent on us to make life easier for our Windows-using brethren and sistren.

There are two things we can do to help ensure good e-mail file compatibility between platforms. The first is to use the correct file encoding options, as discussed in this section. The other is to make sure that your Windows friends can decompress Stuffit archives, so that you can send them compressed files and folders. Fortunately, there's a great, free tool for Windows users, called StuffIt Expander for Windows (it is compatible with all versions of Windows since Windows 98). It also comes in versions for Macintosh (Mac OS 8.1 and later, and Mac OS X), Linux, and Solaris. Tell your Windows-using friends to download StuffIt Expander for Windows from *www.stuffit.com* and solve their compression and encoding problems forevermore. As a bonus, the program can decompress or decode virtually any type of file formats (including Windows ZIP files, UNIX Gzip files, and of course Macintosh Stuffit archives), so it's a great replacement for less-capable file utilities your friends might have been using previously.

In the Compatibility & Efficiency section of the dialog, the first option, Append File Name Extensions, makes it easier for Windows users to use Macintosh files. Because Windows depends on file name extensions, such as .doc to denote a Word file, selecting this option tells Entourage to append the proper file name extensions so that files will open in the proper program when they arrive on Windows machines. Clear the other option, Send Attachments To Cc And Bcc Recipients, if you only want attachments to go to your primary addressees.

Sending Your Messages

After doing all that work to create a message, sending it is simplicity itself. Click the Send Now or Send Later button to speed the message on its way. If you click Send Now, Entourage will immediately connect to your Internet service provider, connect to your ISP's outgoing (SMTP) mail server and send the message. If you click Send Later, Entourage will wait until the next time that you connect to the Internet by choosing Send & Receive All or until your next mail schedule triggers.

When you send mail and the e-mail doesn't go through, perhaps because of a temporary mail server failure on the recipient's end, you might want to send the message again. You can *resend* the message, as long as you are the original author, the message was sent successfully by your ISP's SMTP server, and the message was sent from a POP account. When you resend a mail message, you can send it to the original recipient, or you can readdress it to a new recipient.

> **note** You will most often want to resend a message when you have received a *bounce message* from the recipient's mail server. These automated messages tell you that the server couldn't deliver the mail, for various reasons. For example, one good reason would be that the recipient's mailbox is full.

To resend a sent message, highlight it in the Message list, and choose Message, Resend. The message opens in its own window, enabling you to change the recipients and even edit the text, if needed. Click the Send Now or Send Later button to resend the message.

Online Access and Working Offline

As you recall, the difference between a POP and IMAP account is that the POP account downloads all of its messages to your hard disk, and IMAP accounts let you work with e-mail that is kept on the server. But you can also set up a POP account so that it works somewhat like an IMAP account; this is called *online access* mode. Online access enables you to retrieve messages without removing them from the POP server. Better yet, Entourage can download only the message headers, which enables you to check the subject lines and select which messages you want to download in their entirety. This

Chapter 18: Mastering Your E-Mail

feature is an amazing timesaver when you're on the road and forced to use a slow dial-up connection. Not only are you freed from the necessity of downloading unimportant mail and attachments, but because the mail stays on the server, you can download it again when you get back home to your fast connection.

For more information about the differences between POP and IMAP accounts, see "Setting Up E-Mail Accounts," page 412.

To set up a POP account for online access, follow these steps:

1 Choose Tools, Accounts.

2 In the Accounts window, double-click the name of the account you wish to change.

3 In the Edit Account window, select the Options tab.

4 Select the Allow Online Access option, and then click OK.

Entourage puts a new icon in the Folder list, with the name of the account you just changed. This is the online access icon for that account. To have Entourage check for new messages in this account, click this icon in the Folder list. Entourage connects to the Internet and downloads the message headers—but not the contents—of any waiting e-mail, putting the names of the messages in the Message list. If you see a message that looks interesting, select it in the Message list. Entourage then downloads the entire message and displays it in the Preview pane.

To delete e-mail from an online account, select one or more messages in the Message list, and then press the Delete key. An icon will appear next to the deleted messages showing that they are marked for deletion the next time that you connect to the server.

For a list of the message icons associated with online access, see Table 18-3, page 432.

Most of the time you will be working with e-mail interactively, that is to say, you'll be reading and replying to e-mail messages while you are connected to the Internet. But sometimes you want to work with Entourage when you don't have an Internet connection. It's no problem to read and reply to previously downloaded messages, but Entourage, trying to be helpful, will try to connect to the Internet however often you've told it to with its Schedules feature. Because you can't connect, you'll get an error message, and that will happen whenever your schedule triggers. To avoid this, you can switch Entourage to *offline* mode by choosing Entourage, Work Offline. When you're working offline, schedules are disabled, and any mail or replies that you write are stored in your Outbox, to be sent the next time you go online. To switch back to online mode, choose Entourage, Work Offline again, to clear the check mark next to the menu item.

Printing Mail Messages

Even in the age of electronic mail, sometimes you need a paper copy of one or more of your messages. Select one or more messages in the Message list, and then choose File, Print, or press Command+P. The Print dialog appears, with a preview of how your page will look when printed, as shown in Figure 18-14.

> **note** If you choose more than one message to print, only a preview of the first message will be shown in the Print dialog.

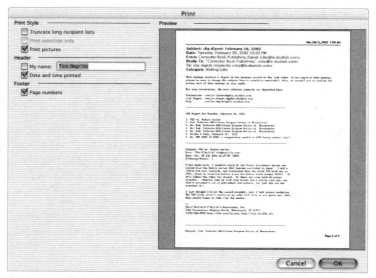

Figure 18-14. Preview your print job in the Print dialog.

InsideOut

Avoid this buggy print option

In the Print dialog, there is an option titled Truncate Long Recipient Lists. This option shortens the list of addressees when printed in order to allow more space on the page for the message body. This option works fine when the list includes only a few addressees, but invoking it when the list is long can cause Entourage to freeze up. It's best not to select this option until Entourage is updated to fix this bug.

Setting Up Mail Schedules

Entourage can perform a variety of tasks automatically, at times that you specify. These schedules can retrieve and send mail without your intervention, permanently empty the Deleted Items folder, and much more.

To create a schedule, follow these steps:

1 Choose Tools, Schedules.

2 Click New.

3 In the Edit Schedule dialog, shown in Figure 18-15, enter a name for the schedule.

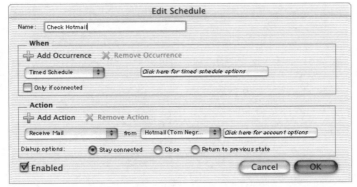

Figure 18-15. This schedule will be set to check for e-mail from the author's Hotmail account.

4 In the When section, specify when the schedule will run, from the following choices:

- **Manually.** You will trigger the schedule yourself by choosing it from the Tools, Run Schedule hierarchical menu.

- **At Startup.** The schedule will run when Entourage launches.

- **On Quit.** The schedule will run when you quit Entourage.

- **Timed Schedule.** The schedule will run on days that you specify at specific times, as shown on the next page.

Part 3: Entourage

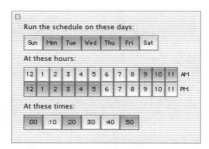

■ **Repeating Schedule.** The schedule will run at the specified time interval, as shown here:

■ **Recurring.** Use this option if you have complex scheduling requirements or if you need a schedule to run only for a specific number of times, as shown here:

5 You can specify additional times for the schedule to run by clicking Add Occurrence.

6 In the Action section, specify the events that will occur when the schedule runs, choose which account will be used for the action, and then click OK.

Organizing Your E-Mail

The key to organizing your e-mail with Entourage is to create a good set of folders and subfolders so that you can organize mail the way that you want and that makes the most sense to you. Proper filing of your messages according to a scheme makes it much easier to find messages again when you need them.

Entourage starts you off with five default folders: Inbox, Outbox, Deleted Items, Sent Items, and Drafts. To these, you can add as many folders and subfolders as you like.

Using Folders

To create a folder, choose File, New Folder, or press Command+Shift+N. The new folder appears in the Folder list with the name Untitled Folder, which is selected and ready to be typed over. Rename the folder the way you want, and then press Return.

To create a subfolder, select the folder in the Folder list that will be the containing folder, and then choose File, New, Subfolder. The new subfolder will appear in the Folder list, indented immediately below the containing folder, and titled Untitled Folder. Again, type over the name to give the folder the name that you want.

Moving Messages

To file your messages in folders or subfolders, select the messages in the Message list and drag them to the target folder. If you hold down the Option key while dragging a message, you'll make a copy, which will appear in the target folder while the original message stays in the original folder.

Alternatively, after selecting the messages, you can choose Message, Move To, and then choose the folder name from the hierarchical menu. This menu only lists the most recently used folders, so if the folder that you want isn't listed, choose Message, Move To, Move To Folder, or press Command+Shift+M. The Move To Folder dialog appears, as shown in Figure 18-16.

Figure 18-16. The Move To Folder dialog enables you to access all your folders, so that you can move messages to older, less frequently used folders.

Chapter 18

> **tip** One of the most useful things that you can do with mail rules is to move messages to folders automatically; for more information about mail rules, see "Working with Mail Rules," page 470.

Moving and Deleting Folders

To move a folder within the Folder list, simply drag it up or down in the list as needed. You can drag a folder on top of other folders to make the first folder a subfolder of the second folder.

> **tip** In order to take a subfolder out of a containing folder and make the subfolder a regular folder, you must drag the subfolder all the way up the Folder list and drop it on the On My Computer icon at the top of the Folder list.

The easiest way to delete a folder is to Control+click it, and then choose Delete Folder from the contextual menu. Like deleted messages, the folder is not immediately deleted from your hard drive, but rather is moved to the Deleted Items folder, where you can retrieve it if you decide that you made a mistake.

Using Priorities, Categories, and Flags

Priorities, categories, and flags are all ways for you to mark messages so that you can filter, sort, organize, and search those messages later.

Priorities

You can set one of five priority levels for messages that you have received. These levels are Highest, High, Normal, Low, and Lowest. Once a priority has been assigned to a message (oftentimes with a mail rule) you can sort messages by priority in the Message list by clicking the Priority column. You can set a message's priority manually by selecting it in the Message list and then choosing from the Message, Priority menu.

Categories

Categories help organize all of the items in Entourage, not only e-mail messages. Contacts, calendar events, notes, and tasks can all share the same category with an e-mail message. You can sort and search for items by category. Each category has its own color, which tells you at a glance what category an item belongs to, whether it is in an e-mail Message list, in the Tasks list, or in the Calendar. You can assign multiple categories to a single item (though the item will only take on the color of the first category). Entourage comes with nine categories by default, but you can add as many more as you need.

To assign a category to an item, follow these steps:

1 Select the item.

2 Assign the category by performing any of the following actions:

- Click in the Categories column for an item, and then choose one or more categories from the list.

- Click the Categories button on the toolbar, and then select categories from the Assign Categories dialog.

- Choose a category from the Edit, Categories menu.

- Control+click the item, point to Categories on the contextual menu, and then select a category from the submenu.

To create a new category, follow these steps:

1 Choose Edit, Categories, Edit Categories.

2 In the Categories dialog, shown in Figure 18-17, click New.

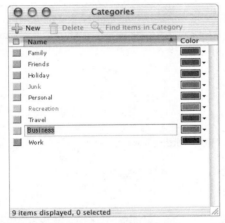

Figure 18-17. You can add as many categories as you like in the Categories list.

3 Enter a name for the category, and press Return.

4 Choose a color for the category from the pop-up menu in the Color column, and then close the Categories dialog.

Flags

There are two types of flagged messages in Entourage, both of which help you keep track of messages (or other items) that you want to mark for later action. When you flag a message, a little red flag appears in the Message Status column in the Message list, and also next to the folder that contains it in the Folder list. To flag a message, select it in the Message list, and choose Message, Flag, or press Command+' (apostrophe).

Flag For Follow-Up attaches a reminder to the e-mail message using the new Office Notifications application to pop up a notification dialog at a later date that you specify. To flag a message for follow-up, select the message in the Message list, and then choose Message, Flag For Follow-Up, or press Command+Shift+' (apostrophe). A follow-up window appears, in which you can set the due date and reminder for the follow-up, as shown in Figure 18-18.

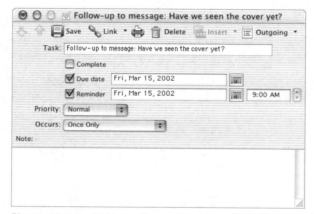

Figure 18-18. You create an Office Notifications reminder in the Follow-up To Message dialog.

Flagging E-Mail for Follow-Up

As with documents in the other Office v. X programs, you can flag e-mail messages for follow-up later. When you set a Flag For Follow-Up, Entourage creates an Office Notifications reminder that appears at the scheduled time to remind you to get back to work.

To flag Entourage messages for follow-up, follow these steps:

1 Select the message that you want to flag, and then choose Message, Flag For Follow-Up, or press Command+Shift+" (quote).

2 Choose a date and time for the reminder, as shown here, and then click OK.

Chapter 18: Mastering Your E-Mail

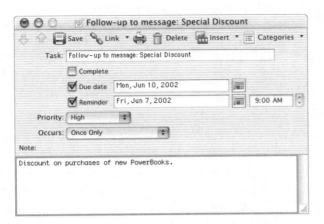

Sorting and Filtering the Message List

You can sort messages in the Message list by clicking the column header you want to sort by. Click the same column header again to reverse the sort order. For example, if you click the column header for the Sent column in the Inbox and you see a down arrow, you're viewing the newest mail at the top of the Message list. If you click again the arrow points up and the oldest mail is displayed at the top of the list—the order reverses each time you click. You can sort using any of the column headers except for the Links and Online Status columns.

---

tip   **Clear your attachments**

Sorting with the Attachment column is especially useful when you want to get rid of a bunch of file attachments. Clicking the column groups all the messages with file attachments together. Then you can select them in the Message list and choose Message, Remove All Attachments.

You can filter messages in the Message list using the two pop-up menus and the text box located directly above the Message list's column headers. This filter enables you to quickly find a message or group of messages, as long as you know what folder the message you are looking for is in. To filter the Message list, follow these steps:

1 In the Folder list, select the folder that you want to filter.

2 From the first pop-up menu at the top of the Message list, select the part of the message with which you want to filter. Your choices are Subject, From, To, or Category Is. In the example shown on the next page, *From* was chosen.

Part 3: Entourage

3 From the second pop-up menu, choose either Starts With or Contains (unless you chose Category Is in step 2, in which case you should pick the category name from the pop-up menu). In the example *contains* was chosen.

4 In the text box, type the text with which you wish to filter. Entourage will filter the list appropriately. In the example, only messages containing the string *kristen* are shown.

Troubleshooting

I can't see some e-mail messages in the Entourage Message list.

When you can't see some messages that you know are in the Message list for a particular folder, chances are that you have applied a filter to that particular list. Messages that don't pass through the filter won't be shown. If the words *Filter Applied* appear at the top of the Message list, then the list is under the influence of a custom filter. Click the Clear button next to the text box in the filter area to remove the filter.

If the problem isn't a custom filter, you might have run afoul of one of the built-in filters from the View menu. Those filters allow you to view Unread Only or Flagged Only messages. If a check mark appears next to either of these two items on the View menu, select them to toggle them off.

Searching Your E-Mail

When you can't find messages by simply filtering the Message list, you'll need to search through the messages themselves. That's when you'll need Entourage's Find capabilities. You have both a basic and an advanced find from which to choose. Thanks to Mac OS X's multitasking nature, you can start a search in Entourage, switch to another application, and the search continues at nearly full speed in the background, a feat that Entourage 2001 couldn't match.

To do a basic search in Entourage, follow these steps:

1 Choose Edit, Find, or press Command+F.

2 In the Find dialog, type your search string into the Find box, as shown in Figure 18-19. To find the search string in the currently selected message, select Current Item. To search in a particular area of Entourage (such as Messages,

Chapter 18: Mastering Your E-Mail

Contacts, Calendar Events, Tasks, or Notes) choose it from the pop-up menu. You can also choose All Items, but be aware that this type of search will take some time. To speed up the search, select the Search Subjects, Titles, And Names Only check box. The Find dialog also has an option to search in only the currently selected folder.

3 Press Return or click Find to start the find operation. The results will appear in a Search Results window.

Figure 18-19. The basic Find dialog provides a surprising amount of searching power.

Sometimes the basic Find feature doesn't give you enough power; you need to search for several very specific criteria at once. For example, you might want to find all the messages that come from a particular domain, that have an attached file, and that contain the phrase "propeller beanie." That kind of search is beyond the capabilities of Find, so you'll need to turn to Entourage's Advanced Find.

To do an advanced search in Entourage, follow these steps:

1 Choose Edit, Advanced Find, or press Command+Option+F.

> **tip** You can also get to the Advanced Find dialog by clicking the More Options button in the basic Find dialog.

2 In the Item Types section of the Advanced Find dialog, select the areas of Entourage where you would like to search, or click All Items to select all the areas in one step.

3 In the Location section, choose This Folder, and then choose which folder to search from the second pop-up menu, or choose All Folders. This option is only available if you've selected only the Messages item type; otherwise all locations within each item type will be searched. If you've chosen a specific folder, you can also choose whether to include its subfolders in the search.

4 In the Criteria section, use the first pop-up menu to select the area you'll be searching. In the second pop-up menu choose the way you'll be searching for the text you enter in the text box to the right; for example, you might want to search for messages that contain, or perhaps do *not* contain, the text you enter in the text box.

5 If you want to search by more than one criterion, click Add Criterion, and repeat the process in step 4. Repeat as necessary until you are done adding criteria.

6 If you've used more than one criterion, the Match pop-up menu can be used to control how Entourage weighs the criteria; for example, you could find only information that matches all the criteria, or information that matches any of the criteria. Figure 18-20 shows an advanced Find dialog that will show messages that match any of three criteria.

7 Click Find. The results will appear in a Search Results window.

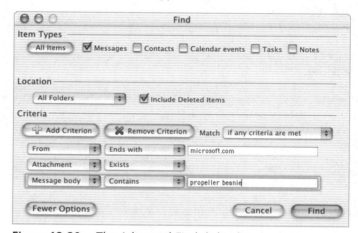

Figure 18-20. The Advanced Find dialog lets you narrow your search as much as you want.

For more information about searching for Entourage information, see "Creating a Custom View," page 531.

Using the Junk Mail Filter

The Junk Mail Filter is deceptively simple, yet it has a powerful effect; it uses a variety of rules and algorithms to identify junk mail and flag it for you (you can't access or change these rules directly). You can perform a variety of actions using mail rules on messages that have been classified as junk mail. For example, you can create mail rules that automatically move junk mail into the Deleted Items folder, so that you never see the junk mail at all. The Junk Mail Filter is enabled by default in Entourage. To view it, choose Tools, Junk Mail Filter. The Junk Mail Filter dialog appears, as shown in Figure 18-21.

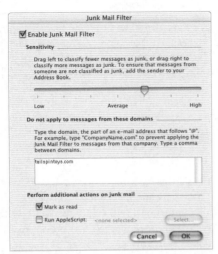

Figure 18-21. The Junk Mail Filter is your first line of defense against spam.

> **tip** **Make small changes to the Junk Mail Filter's sensitivity**
>
> Begin using the Junk Mail Filter at its default setting, which is right in the middle. After a few days, if it isn't screening as much junk as you would like, bump it up a notch. See how things go over the next several days, then modify the setting again, if needed. The reason you want to make gradual changes is that the nature of junk mail is variable; some days you'll get lots of the kind of mail that gets caught by the Junk Mail Filter, other days you won't. By waiting a few days between setting changes, you get a larger sample of junk mail.

Drag the Sensitivity slider to the left to make the Junk Mail Filter less vigilant for junk mail and to the right to increase its paranoia. In the box below the Sensitivity slider, you can enter domains (the part of an e-mail address after the @ symbol) to exclude all mail from those domains from the Junk Mail Filter. For example, you can put your company's domain in this box, so that messages from colleagues are never classified as junk mail. Finally, you can select either of the options at the bottom of the dialog, to mark all junk mail as read, or to run an AppleScript automatically when Entourage thinks a message is junk mail. Click OK when you are done. If you changed any settings, Entourage will ask whether you want to apply the new settings to the messages currently in your Inbox.

The Junk Mail Filter works fairly well, especially at its higher settings. It will probably not screen out all of the junk mail that you get, but it is a good start in the battle against spam.

> **note** One of the criteria that the Junk Mail Filter looks for is whether the e-mail address for the sender of a message is in your address book. If it is, then the message will never be classified as junk. You can use mail rules to further process those messages.

Handling Mailing Lists with the Mailing List Manager

If you subscribe to any Internet mailing lists, Entourage has a tool that makes dealing with them a treat. An Internet *mailing list* is a discussion group you and others subscribe to by signing up with the list manager. These lists enable the list members to discuss a topic of common interest via e-mail. Unlike an e-mail reply that goes only to the original sender, e-mail replies to a mailing list e-mail message are sent to everyone on the list, so that members can carry on a group discussion. You might think of a mailing list as an e-mail version of a Usenet newsgroup, with a list manager that controls the list's membership; the manager can also exercise some control over the list's content. Entourage's Mailing List Manager enables you to specify the handling instructions for messages that you get from mailing lists and has tools to handle mailing lists' special needs. You need to set up a separate mailing list rule in the Mailing List Manager for each mailing list.

You can use the fact that an e-mail message is from a mailing list as the criterion for invoking a mail rule (see the next section). For example, you can create a mail rule that recognizes all messages from a particular mailing list and performs such actions as automatically setting the priority for the mailing list messages to low, setting the messages so that they won't be classified as junk mail, and automatically stripping off any file attachments.

To create a mailing list rule, follow these steps:

1 In the Message list, select a message from the mailing list.

2 Control+click the message, and then choose Create Mailing List Rule from the resulting contextual menu.

3 In the Edit Mailing List Rule dialog, shown in Figure 18-22, enter the name of the list. Some of the information in this dialog will already be filled in for you, such as the List Address.

4 If you want to move messages from the list to a folder (a good idea to collect all the list's messages in one place), select the Move Messages To Folder option, and then select or create a folder from the pop-up menu.

5 If you want to pick a category for the mailing list's messages, set those options in the Set Category pop-up menu.

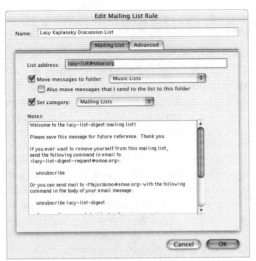

Figure 18-22. Adding a mailing list rule will make it much easier for you to manage your mailing lists.

6 If you have any notes about the mailing list, enter them in the Notes box, and then click OK.

---

tip   **Use the Notes box to your advantage**

The Notes box is a terrific place for you to copy and paste the subscription instructions that almost all mailing lists send to you automatically when you subscribe. These instructions tell you such things as how to reply to list messages, how to change options for the list, and how to unsubscribe if you no longer want to participate.

There are a number of options on the Advanced tab of the Edit Mailing List Rule dialog, most of which are self-explanatory. One that needs explaining is the Burst Digests Into Individual Messages option. Mailing lists can send out messages in one of two ways. One way is to send out each message individually. The other is to group several messages into a *digest,* which is then sent out to the members of the mailing list. Most mailing lists offer both individual and digest versions. A mailing list server will typically generate a digest either at a specified time period (for example, once a day) or when enough messages have accumulated to make the digest a particular size. Many people prefer to subscribe to the digest version of a list, especially if the list gets a lot of messages. The Burst Digests Into Individual Messages option breaks apart, or *bursts,* mailing list digests into individual messages, which makes it easier to reply to a particular message.

To change the settings for a mailing list rule, choose Tools, Mailing List Manager. Double-click the list name to edit the list's rule.

Working with Mail Rules

Mail *rules* (also referred to as *filters*) are one of the best things about Entourage. They allow you immense flexibility in handling and organizing your e-mail. A good set of mail rules can save you a tremendous amount of time and effort by filtering, filing, and categorizing your e-mail—all automatically. For example, you can create a rule that moves all of the mail that you receive from a client to a project folder, or another that scans a message to see if it meets multiple criteria, and if it does, forwards the mail to another correspondent.

Mail rules begin in the Rules window, shown in Figure 18-23. You can create as many rules as you want, and rules can handle both incoming and outgoing messages. Rules for POP, IMAP, and Hotmail accounts are separate and must be created separately on the different tabs of the Rules window. You can't copy or paste rules from tab to tab.

Figure 18-23. The Rules window looks like a simple list, but under the surface it provides a tremendous amount of power for handling your e-mail.

> You can also use the Rules window to create rules to work with messages from Usenet newsgroups. See "Using Newsgroup Rules," page 492.

Mail rules have two parts: the If section applies some sort of test to the message. Depending on the result of the test (usually if the result of the test is true), the second section, the Then section, is activated and performs one or more actions on the message. Here's an example: you can set up a rule that checks to see if a message comes from someone on a specific list of people. If the message is not from anyone on that list, the test fails, and the rule stops working; the message is then passed on to the next rule in the Rules list. If the message comes from someone on your list, the actions in the Then section of the rule are applied to the message, such as setting the message to a high priority, filing the message in a specified mail folder, or assigning a category.

For information about the priority of mail rules, see "Prioritizing Rules," page 473.

Creating Mail Rules

To begin creating a mail rule, follow these steps:

1 Choose Tools, Rules to open the Rules window.

2 In the Rules window, select the tab for the kind of rule that you wish to create: POP, IMAP, or Hotmail. (Outgoing rules will be described in "Using Outgoing Mail Rules," page 476, and News rules are described in "Using Newsgroup Rules," page 492).

3 Click the New button on the Rules window's toolbar.

> **tip** You can also choose to create a POP, IMAP, or Hotmail rule directly from the pop-up menu next to the New button.

4 The Edit Rule dialog appears. Enter a name for the rule in the Rule Name box.

5 In the If section, set the selection criteria for the rule. There is a very wide range of selection criteria available to you. Depending on your choice in the pop-up menu displaying All Messages by default, one or more other pop-up menus or entry fields might appear to the right for the selection criteria that you're building. For example, if you want to select all the messages from people at a particular domain (the part of an e-mail address after the @ symbol), you could choose From in the first pop-up menu, Ends With in the second pop-up menu, and then enter, for example, *tailspintoys.com* in the entry field.

> **tip** If you select a message in the Message list before you begin creating a rule, information from the selected message that matches the selection criteria you choose will be automatically placed in the entry field.

6 If you want to add another selection criterion, click Add Criterion.

7 Repeat steps 5 and 6 until you've created all your selection criteria.

8 If you created more than one selection criterion, make a choice from the Execute pop-up menu to indicate whether or not the message rule should apply if (or unless) *any* of the criteria are true, or if (or unless) *all* of the criteria are true.

9 In the Then section, you'll enter the actions that will be performed on the message if it matches the criteria in the If section. By default, two actions are created for you; Change Status To Not Junk Mail and Set Category To None. Feel free to change these to actions that you want, delete them by selecting the action and clicking Remove Action, or add new actions with the Add Action button. Figure 18-24 shows a completed dialog for a new rule.

10 Make sure that the Enabled check box is selected, and then click OK.

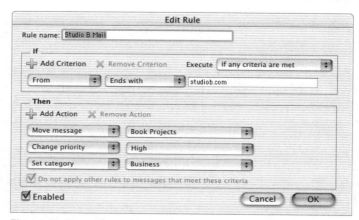

Figure 18-24. This completed mail rule moves, prioritizes, and categorizes any mail from my agent.

Filtering Out Spam

You can use mail rules to cut way down on the annoying flood of junk mail that you get. The Junk Mail Filter does a decent job of identifying junk mail, and can even mark that mail as having already been read, but you need a mail rule to get rid of the junk mail by moving it into the Deleted Items folder. Follow these steps:

1 Create a mail rule as described in the previous section.

2 In the If section, select the criterion Is Junk Mail.

3 In the Then section, set three actions: Move Message To Deleted Items, Change Status To Read, and Do Not Notify.

When the message rule executes, any mail caught by the Junk Mail Filter will be deleted, marked as read, and Entourage won't even let you know that the mail arrived. This would seem to be a satisfying way to get rid of spam, except that the Junk Mail Filter isn't perfect; sometimes it categorizes mail that you want as junk, especially things like the first message from a mailing list to which you just subscribed. A good solution is to make a folder called Possible Junk, and move messages classified as junk to that folder. Then you can browse that folder from time to time to see if there is any

Chapter 18: Mastering Your E-Mail

mail you want to keep. You can extend the automation further by making another rule that automatically sends messages that have been in the Possible Junk folder longer than, say, 10 days (plenty of time for you to check the mail for items you might want to rescue from purgatory) to the Deleted Items folder.

My favorite rule to get rid of spam is a rule that takes advantage of the way that spam works. The majority of spam that is sent to you will have your e-mail address in the Bcc (blind carbon copy) line, so that you can't see the other recipients of the message. To attack spam in this way, follow these steps:

1. Create a rule with these two criteria in the If section:

    ■ Select Any To Recipient, Does Not Contain, and type your e-mail address in the text box.

    ■ Select Any Cc Recipient, Does Not Contain, and type your e-mail address in the second text box.

2. If you use more than one e-mail address, repeat these two criteria for each of your e-mail addresses.

3. Make sure you set the Execute pop-up menu to require that all criteria are met.

4. You can choose your own actions, but you should probably choose these two actions: Set Category, Junk; and Move Message, Possible Junk (or Deleted Items).

If your e-mail address doesn't appear in a message's To or Cc lines, it must appear in its Bcc line, which makes it a prime spam suspect.

Prioritizing Rules

When Entourage retrieves your mail, mail rules are applied only after two related Entourage features filter your mail: the Mailing List Manager and the Junk Mail Filter. So every message passes through three levels of checks before ending up in one of your mail folders:

1. The Mailing List Manager checks to see if an incoming message is from a mailing list, and if that mailing list is one for which a mailing list rule has been created. If so, the Mailing List Manager applies the actions specified in the mailing list rule. Note that by default, once the Mailing List Manager deals with a message, that's the end of the message's journey; it won't be affected by the Junk Mail Filter or your mail rules. If you want mailing list messages to be operated upon by your mail rules, in the Mailing List Manager, clear the Do Not Apply Rules To List Messages option on the Advanced tab of the Edit Mailing List Rule dialog.

2 If the message wasn't from a mailing list, the message next passes through the Junk Mail Filter, which can mark it as read, but can't move the message to someplace like the Deleted Items folder. You'll let that happen in the next step.

3 Final disposition for the message is left up to the Rules feature.

Mail rules are executed from top to bottom in the Rules list. It's important to understand that rules toward the bottom of the list might not execute as you expect if messages are caught by rules higher up in the list. It helps to think of each mail rule as a filter, and the Rules list as the container for the filters. Messages enter the Rules list at the top, and pass through each mail rule in turn. Each rule performs a test on the message, and if the result of the test is false, the message passes down to the next rule. If the result of the test is true, the message gets "caught" in the filter, and only that rule's actions are applied to the message. Mail that gets through the gauntlet of your mail rules drops into your Inbox.

> **note** The preceding analysis assumes that mail rules have the Do Not Apply Other Rules To Messages That Meet These Criteria option enabled. If this option is not enabled, actions can be applied to messages by more than one rule. Though this can be quite useful, it also makes your mail rule prioritization task more difficult, because it makes it harder to know which rules were applied to a message when you are trying to troubleshoot mail actions.

You can rearrange the priority of a mail rule by moving it up or down in the Rules window. The easiest way to do that is to select the rule you want to move and drag it up or down; the outline of the rule and a line across the Rules window indicate where the rule will end up, as shown in Figure 18-25. You can also move rules by selecting them and using the Move Up or Move Down button on the toolbar of the Rules window.

Figure 18-25. The rule being moved up in the Rules list will end up above the Amazon Reports rule.

Applying Rules Manually

Normally, mail rules are run automatically on incoming mail messages. But there are cases in which you might want to run a mail rule (or run all mail rules) on a message that you have already received. The usual reason for wanting to run mail rules manually is that you have modified one of your rules and you would like to test the modification by running just that one rule on one or more messages in a mail folder. Another good reason is to be able to run a mail rule that is not enabled in the Rules list. A disabled rule doesn't run automatically when you receive mail, but it can be run manually.

To manually apply a mail rule, follow these steps:

1 Select one or more messages in the Message list.

2 Choose Message, Apply Rule, and then choose the name of the rule that you wish to apply from the hierarchical menu.

> **tip** You can also Control+click the selected messages and choose Apply Rule from the resulting contextual menu.

3 Alternatively, if you want to run all the mail rules on the selected messages, choose Message, Apply Rule, All Rules.

> **tip** **Use All Rules to simulate receiving mail**
>
> When you modify a mail rule and then choose Message, Apply Rule, All Rules, all of the mail rules are applied, as you would expect, but the message is also sent through the Mailing List Manager and Junk Mail Filter. It's a perfect way to test what would have happened to that message if you had received it after you had made the rule changes. This also enables you to test changes you make to the Mailing List Manager or Junk Mail Filter.

Disabling, Duplicating, and Deleting Rules

You can turn a mail rule off when you don't need it anymore, or when you need to suspend it for a while. For example, you might have a recurring project with a particular person. When the project is active, you want the project mail rule to file all the mail from that person in a particular folder. But when the project is done, that person's mail can start landing in your Inbox again. You could delete the rule and re-create it again the next time the project occurs, but why bother? Just turn it off until you need it again. To disable a mail rule, open the Rules window and clear the check box next to the mail rule you want to turn off.

> **tip** Pressing the Spacebar, Right Arrow, or Left Arrow key while a rule is selected toggles the rule's check box.

You can duplicate rules, so that you don't have to re-create complex rules from scratch when you want to reuse a rule with a slightly different set of criteria or actions. To duplicate a rule, select the rule in the Rules list, and from the menu bar choose Edit, Duplicate Rule, or press Command+D. The new rule will appear in the list, with the same name as the old rule, plus the word "copy" appended. Double-click the duplicate rule to edit it.

To delete a rule, select the rule in the Rules list, and click the Delete button on the Rules window toolbar, or press Delete. Entourage asks you to confirm the deletion; click the Delete button.

Using Outgoing Mail Rules

Rules for outgoing mail work much the same as incoming mail rules, except that there are fewer options, as you would expect. You can create mail rules that do the following:

- Move, copy, print, or delete messages.
- Set the message's category.
- Forward or redirect the message.
- Save or remove attachments.
- Notify the user by playing a sound, animating the program icon, or displaying a text dialog.
- Run an AppleScript.

Outgoing mail rules are especially useful to make sure that mail that you send is moved automatically to a particular folder, assigned a category, or both. For example, when I'm doing a book project, I want all of the mail for that project to go to the project's mail folder. I define two rules: one for all the incoming mail from the project's team members, which moves their mail into the project folder. The second is the outgoing mail rule, which moves all mail that I send to the project's team members to the project folder, and also assigns a category (and therefore a color) to my mail. I can tell at a glance which mail was sent to me, and which was sent from me.

To create an outgoing mail rule, follow these steps:

1 Choose Tools, Rules.

2 In the Rules window, select the Outgoing tab.

3 Click New, or press Command+N.

4 In the Edit Rule dialog, give the new rule a name.

5 In the If section, choose the first criterion, and choose the execution conditions. If you want to add more If criteria, click Add Criterion and repeat this step.

6 In the Then section, choose the actions you want the rule to take if the If criteria are satisfied. If you want to add more Then actions, click Add Action and repeat this step.

7 Select the Enabled option.

8 Click OK, and then close the Rules window.

Archiving Mail

Archiving mail is the act of saving one or more messages (or more commonly an entire folder) outside of Entourage. The reasons you might want to do it are many:

● You want to transfer mail messages to someone else, so that they can import them into their mail program.

● You want to make a copy of the mail folder from a completed project, so that you can delete the project folder from within Entourage.

● You want to make additional backups of especially important mail folders.

● You want to convert a folder of mail messages into one Word file for quick text searching.

Entourage makes it easy to archive mail folders in the industry-standard MBOX format. All you need to do is select a mail folder in the Folder list, and drag it to the desktop. Then move the file to where you want it.

---

tip   You can import MBOX folders into Entourage just as easily; simply drag the MBOX file into Entourage's Folder list.

If you want to export Entourage messages to a Word file, you'll need to work a little harder. In order to accomplish the task, you'll need to download and install a free AppleScript from *www.applescriptcentral.com*. Go to the site, and search for a script called Entourage Many to Word. Download the script, and install it into the Users/ *username*/Documents/Microsoft User Data/Entourage Script Menu Items folder.

For more information about using AppleScript with Entourage, see "Finding and Installing Cool Scripts," page 547.

To use the script, select the messages that you want to archive (one limitation of the script is that you must select messages, not message folders), and then from the Scripts menu (shown next), choose Entourage Many To Word. Word will open, and the selected messages will be transferred and concatenated into a single Word document. You can then save the Word document wherever you like.

 —— Scripts menu

Rebuilding the Entourage Database

There are two reasons why you might want to rebuild Entourage's database. The first reason is to reclaim disk space after you have deleted e-mail messages or file attachments from Entourage. This isn't exactly a compelling reason, as the following sidebar describes. Entourage stores all of its message information (including file attachments) in a single database file, which helps the program's performance. The drawback to this scheme is that the database file doesn't automatically shrink when you delete items. In order to shrink the database and reclaim disk space, you have to rebuild the database file.

> **note** Each Entourage Identity has its own, separate database file.

The other reason for rebuilding Entourage's database file is that on occasion the file can become corrupted and Entourage will refuse to open. This doesn't happen often, but when it does it can be a scary experience. Rebuilding the database generally cures the corruption and restores Entourage to working order.

Rebuild Only When Necessary

Rebuilding the database file should be a rare occurrence. It isn't very often that you will delete enough messages to make much of a difference in the database file's size. For example, while writing this book I sent or received approximately 1,300 e-mail messages, about 300 of which had compressed file attachments. At the end of the project I archived the project folder, deleted it from Entourage, and rebuilt Entourage's database. The database, containing approximately 20,000 messages, began at 225 MB, and after the rebuild had lost only about 25 MB. Compared to the total capacity of the 80-GB hard drive that's in my Power Macintosh G4, 25 MB is practically a rounding error. And considering that the rebuild took approximately 20 minutes, it wasn't worth the effort. I recommend that you only rebuild the Entourage database if you suspect file corruption or Entourage refuses to open.

Chapter 18: Mastering Your E-Mail

To rebuild Entourage's database, follow these steps:

1 If Entourage is open, choose Entourage, Quit Entourage, or press Command+Q.

2 Open the Microsoft Office v. X folder, inside your Applications folder.

3 Hold down the Option key, and double-click Entourage's icon.

4 The dialog shown next appears. In the vast majority of cases, a Typical Rebuild, which is the default selection, is all that will be required. If this is the first time that you're attempting a rebuild, select Typical Rebuild and click Rebuild.

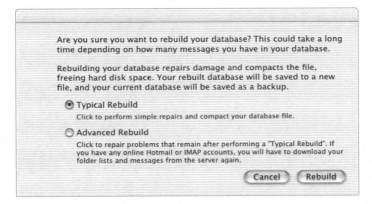

5 Entourage will rebuild the database, showing you a progress dialog as it goes. When the rebuild is complete, a dialog will appear, explaining that the rebuild is done and that the old database files have been renamed and can now be thrown away.

6 In rare cases, the Typical Rebuild won't be enough, and you'll have to perform an Advanced Rebuild. In this event, follow steps 1 through 4, but this time select Advanced Rebuild.

7 After either rebuild is complete, switch to the Finder and open the Users/*username*/Documents/Microsoft User Data/Office X Identities folder. This is the location of the database files for the Entourage Identity that was just rebuilt. The old files are renamed Old Database and Old Database Cache and can be moved to the Trash.

Chapter 19

Using Newsgroups

If you ask the average person on the street what the Internet is, chances are they will tell you about the Web. If you probe a little more, you'll hear about e-mail. But long before the Web existed (since 1981, in fact), there was *Usenet*. You can think of Usenet as being a worldwide bulletin board system, where people from everywhere compose messages and join discussions about subjects of common interest. Each topic area within Usenet is organized into one or more *newsgroups,* and individual messages in a newsgroup are called *news articles*. The machines that host newsgroups are called *news servers*.

In this chapter, you'll learn about using Microsoft Entourage X as a *newsreader,* which is a program that can read and post to newsgroups.

About Usenet

Usenet is big. Really big. How big is it? Nobody really knows, because Usenet doesn't hold still long enough to be meaningfully counted. I know there are at least 34,209 newsgroups, because that's how many my ISP carries. And that's what really matters; how many newsgroups you can read with Entourage. But unless you have the same ISP that I do, you'll almost certainly have a different number of newsgroups available to you. Given the number of newsgroups, and the incredible variety of subjects that they cover (and I do mean incredible; there is a newsgroup devoted to *ketchup,* for pity's sake), you are certain to find some that have interesting discussions.

> **note** Actually, you're not limited to just the newsgroups that you can read with Entourage;
> Google, the Web search engine, provides a Web interface to Usenet, called Google
> Groups, that covers every newsgroup it can find. If you're interested in a newsgroup
> that your ISP doesn't carry on its news server, you might be able to find it by going to
> *http://groups.google.com* with your Web browser. Google also maintains a searchable
> archive of more than 700 million Usenet messages, going back to 1981. News servers
> run by ISPs or Usenet-only providers retain only recent messages dating back a few
> days to a few months, depending on the popularity of each newsgroup and the stor-
> age capacity of the providers' news servers.

To find a newsgroup that interests you, you have to know a little about the structure
of newsgroup names. Usenet has a hierarchy of names, and Table 19-1 shows the most
common top-level newsgroup names.

Table 19-1. Common Top-Level Newsgroup Names

Name	Discussion Subjects
alt	Subjects that don't fit into any of the other, official categories; contains the most newsgroups, but many are poorly conceived and not actively visited; lots of bizarre stuff, some of genuine interest and some in poor taste
biz	Business products and services
comp	Computer hardware and software
humanities	Fine art, literature, music, philosophy, and more
misc	Miscellaneous subjects, including job listings and classified ads
news	News about Usenet
rec	Recreational hobbies, games, and arts
sci	Scientific discussions
soc	Social issues and culture
talk	Debates about current issues

The top-level names above are the ones agreed upon by the loose affiliation of volun-
tary groups that administer Usenet (as much as any group can be said to administer it).
Though there are exceptions, you'll find most newsgroups in one of these categories.

Chapter 19: Using Newsgroups

The most common exceptions to the official newsgroup hierarchy are private newsgroups run by companies, colleges and universities, and even some private citizens. All of these organizations have realized how useful Usenet discussion groups can be, and they have created their own newsgroups outside the official hierarchy. Some of these newsgroups are private, existing behind corporate firewalls. Others are public and available for anyone to use, as long as their ISP's news server carries the newsgroup. Microsoft, for example, has a set of public newsgroups to support its products. Entourage comes preset to use the Microsoft News Server, where you'll find more than 1,800 newsgroups devoted to virtually every Microsoft product, including its Mac products. Some ISPs also carry popular private newsgroups such as Microsoft's in whole or part in addition to carrying the public Usenet newsgroups.

Individual newsgroups are named by tacking onto the right of the top-level name several qualifying names that narrow down the subject in a hierarchical manner, with each name separated by a period. Table 19-2 shows a few examples of specific newsgroups and their general topic of interest.

Table 19-2. Sample Newsgroup Names

Newsgroup Name	Subject
alt.fan.pooh	Fans of Winnie the Pooh
comp.lang.javascript	The JavaScript computer language
comp.sys.mac.apps	Macintosh applications
humanities.lit.authors.shakespeare	Discussions about Shakespeare and his works
rec.arts.sf.movies	Science fiction movies
sci.nanotech	Nanotechnology

News articles, or messages posted to newsgroups, are usually text messages. Each newsgroup usually posts periodically a long message detailing its rules or *bylaws* for content and behavior in what's called a *FAQ,* which stands for Frequently Asked Questions. Usenet etiquette suggests that you should read and follow each group's standards before you post your own messages to it; one of the worst offenses (for which you'll be reprimanded in a very public fashion) is to post graphics or other attachments in groups that are designed for text-only discussions. You will, however, find many newsgroups that welcome attachments, often with the word *binary* or *pictures* in their names, containing files of computer programs, images, photographs, or drawings.

Although the Usenet used to be text-based because of a lack of bandwidth, these new groups will accept pictures of your recent vacation, your pet, or the priceless antique you found at a recent garage sale; but be forewarned that some of these graphics groups are of a decidedly adult nature. When you post an article with an attachment, Entourage automatically encodes it properly before sending it to the news server.

Newsgroup articles are grouped in *threads,* which are a series of messages in response to a beginning post. For example, if I were to post an article named "Hubble telescope repair" to the sci.space.policy newsgroup, any responses from other people with the title "Re: Hubble telescope repair" would be part of the message thread. You can set Entourage's Message list to view articles in newsgroups as threads (which will show responses indented from the original post), or simply in the order that the articles were posted to the newsgroup.

Setting Up a News Account

Setting up a news account tells Entourage how to use the news server and which of your e-mail accounts will be associated with the news account. The process is much like setting up a new e-mail account.

To set up a news account, follow these steps:

1 Choose Tools, Accounts.

2 Select the News tab in the Accounts dialog, and then click New.

3 The Account Setup Assistant starts up. Click Configure Account Manually. The Edit Account dialog appears, as shown in Figure 19-1.

4 Enter the Account Name. It's common to use the name of your ISP, followed by News Server, for example, Comcast News Server.

5 Choose the e-mail account that you want to be associated with the news account. The e-mail address for this e-mail account will be included in posts that you make to newsgroups.

> **caution** There are good reasons why you do not want to use your primary e-mail account for news posts. See "Using a Separate E-Mail Account for News," page 486.

Chapter 19: Using Newsgroups

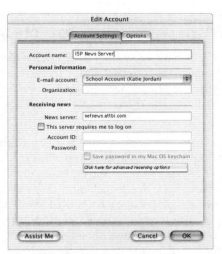

Figure 19-1.   Setting up a News account is similar to creating an e-mail account.

6 The Organization field is optional. It is usually used to state your company or school affiliation and will be included in posts that you make to newsgroups.

7 In the Receiving News section of the dialog, enter the name of the news server, as given to you by your ISP or your systems administrator. This sometimes takes the form of news.*ispname*.com or news.*ispname*.net, where *ispname* is an ISP name, such as earthlink, but check with your ISP to be sure of the format it uses.

8 If your news server requires you to log on (most don't), select the This Server Requires Me To Log On option, and then fill in your account ID and password (you will have gotten them from your ISP or your systems administrator if you needed them). Click OK. Entourage will place an icon of the news server in the Folder list, as shown here:

Using a Separate E-Mail Account for News

One of the problems with Usenet is that it is constantly being scanned by automated robot programs (or *bots*) used by spammers to collect e-mail addresses. If you use your real e-mail address when posting to Usenet newsgroups, you virtually guarantee that you will soon be deluged with junk mail. There are three good ways to get around the problem:

- **Use a fake e-mail address.** Create a completely phony e-mail account in Entourage, one that has a bogus e-mail address such as *nobody@nowhere.goaway*. Then choose that account in the Edit Account dialog. The drawback to this approach is that nobody will be able to contact you directly (although they will still be able to reply to your posts in the newsgroup). There are times when it makes sense to receive a direct e-mail reply, such as when the sender wants to share something confidential or when the topic is wandering away from the group's topic area and wouldn't be of interest to the rest of the group. Entourage enables you to do either, as described in "Composing and Replying to Messages," page 490.

- **Use a disposable e-mail account.** Sign up for a free, Web-based e-mail account, such as a Hotmail or Yahoo! Mail account, and live with the fact that it will be a spam magnet. On the rare occasions when you might expect a personal reply to a newsgroup post, you can check the disposable account (and if the account is a Hotmail account, you can even check it from within Entourage), but otherwise you can ignore the account and spare yourself the spam.

- **Garble your e-mail address.** If you need to be able to have people contact you, you can use your real e-mail account, but insert the word NOSPAM or SPAMFREE or the like somewhere in your e-mail address, and then give instructions in your signature for what people should do to get your real e-mail address. This takes advantage of the fact that spam robots aren't nearly as smart as real people.

Downloading the Newsgroup List

The first time that you click a new news server icon, Entourage asks whether you want to download the list of newsgroups from that server. Click Receive. Entourage connects to your news server and downloads the entire list of newsgroups. If you're on a dial-up connection, this can take quite a while, as there can easily be tens of thousands of newsgroups in the list. Downloading the newsgroup list generally only needs to be done once, though you can update the list at any time by choosing View, Get New Newsgroups or by clicking the Update List button on the toolbar.

> **tip** If you need to download the entire list again, you can do so by choosing View, Receive Complete Newsgroup List, or by pressing Command+L.

Chapter 19: Using Newsgroups

When the newsgroup list finishes downloading, the newsgroups appear in the newsgroup list on the right side of the Entourage window, as shown in Figure 19-2.

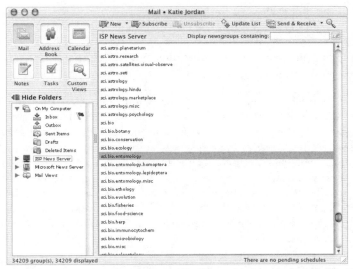

Figure 19-2. When the newsgroup list is displayed, the total number of groups appears in the status bar.

Selecting and Subscribing to Newsgroups

It's certainly possible to scroll and browse through the list of newsgroups until you find what you want, but it's better to use Entourage's ability to filter the list. At the top of the list, start typing a topic into the box labeled Display Newsgroups Containing. As you type, Entourage filters the list to show only newsgroups whose names contain what you typed. For example, if you are interested in astronomy, you could type **astro** in the filter box. That would show the newsgroups about astronomy, but also newsgroups about astrology and about the Houston Astros baseball team. Typing **astro** narrows the list down to about 80 newsgroups, which is easy for you to browse. You could type the entire word **astronomy**, but it turns out that if you do, you would be casting your net too narrowly; you would miss potentially interesting newsgroups such as sci.astro.amateur.

When you have browsed or filtered the list and found newsgroups that look interesting, you'll want to *subscribe* to them, which means that Entourage will keep a list of the newsgroups that you want to follow.

> **note** The term *subscribe* is a bit misleading; the newsgroup isn't informed that you're following it, and there are no subscription fees involved.

To subscribe to a newsgroup, select it in the newsgroup list, and then do any of these actions:

- Choose Edit, Subscribe.

- Click the Subscribe button on the toolbar.

- Control+click the name of the newsgroup, and choose Subscribe from the contextual menu.

When you subscribe to a newsgroup, two things will happen. First, the name of the newsgroup in the newsgroup list will be displayed in bold. Second, a disclosure triangle will appear next to the name of the news server in the Folder list. Clicking the disclosure triangle shows the names of the newsgroups on that news server to which you have subscribed. If you click (a single click is all that is required) one of the newsgroup names, Entourage will download the headers of the newsgroup articles and show you how many unread articles are in the group, in much the same way that it shows you how many unread e-mail messages are in an e-mail folder. Because newsgroup names can be long, placing the pointer over a newsgroup name pops up a ToolTip with the entire newsgroup name, as shown here:

Reading News Messages

Just as with e-mail, with newsgroups you can use the Preview pane or read all the articles in a separate window. If you're using the Preview pane, select the article in the list that you want to read, and Entourage connects to the news server, downloads the article, and displays it in the Preview pane, as shown in Figure 19-3.

If you want to read the news article in a separate window, toggle off the Preview pane (by choosing View, Preview Pane, or pressing Command+\), and then double-click the news article in the Message list.

> **note** Because Entourage only downloads and stores the headers of the messages in newsgroups, you must be online and connected to your ISP to read the message contents. Each message's contents are retrieved when you click the message in the Message list, which accounts for the slight delay before each message appears.

Chapter 19: Using Newsgroups

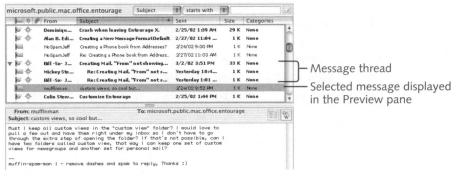

— Message thread

— Selected message displayed
in the Preview pane

Figure 19-3. Directly above the selected article in the Message list, you can see a message thread, with an initial post and two replies.

To save time and limit the amount of bandwidth that Entourage uses, it only downloads a subset of the total article headers available. For example, a newsgroup that is new to you might contain thousands of articles. Entourage will only download headers for the most recent 300 articles. You can tell Entourage to retrieve another 300 headers from the newsgroup by choosing View, Get More News Messages. If you want to change the number of headers retrieved each time, double-click the news account in the Folder list, and select the Options tab when the Edit Account dialog opens. Set the number in the Server Options section to the number of headers you want to download at one time.

Article Selection Strategies

There are several techniques that you can use to browse and read newsgroup articles more efficiently:

- Don't use the Up Arrow and Down Arrow keys to scroll through the article list. If you do, Entourage will download each article as it is highlighted. Instead, scroll the list and select articles with the mouse.

- You don't have to read every message; you can often tell by the subject alone that a message or group of messages won't interest you. You should mark these messages as having been read so that Entourage doesn't show them to you the next time that you read the newsgroup. Select the unwanted messages in the Message list, and press Command+T. Then choose View, Unread Only; or press Command+Shift+O. Only messages that interest you and that you haven't read will then be shown in the Message list.

- Turn on threaded view, so that you can see which messages are replies to others, by choosing View, Threaded. When you turn on threaded view, the Message list is sorted by Subject, and disclosure triangles appear next to

(continued)

> **Article Selection Strategies** *(continued)*
>
> articles that have replies. You can click individual disclosure triangles to view the replies for that one topic, or you can choose View, Expand All, which has the same effect as clicking all the disclosure triangles.
>
> ● You can sort the Message list by any column by clicking the column header, but threaded view is turned off if you sort by any column other than Subject. If you sort by another column and then click Subject, you won't return to a threaded view; select View, Threaded instead. Clicking the column header more than once toggles it between an ascending and descending sort.
>
> ● You can highlight articles according to criteria that you select by applying newsgroup rules to them. For example, you can apply a category to articles authored by a particular person (thereby changing the color of the articles' headers and making them easy to spot). For more about newsgroup rules, see "Using Newsgroup Rules," page 492.

Composing and Replying to Messages

Writing articles to be posted to newsgroups is much like writing e-mail. As you do with e-mail, you open a new message window, address and write your article, and then send it off. Follow these steps:

1 In the Folder list, select the newsgroup to which you want to post an article.

2 Choose File, New, News Message, or press Command+N.

3 In the window for the new message, which is already addressed to the newsgroup, enter the Subject line. This text is what people will see in the headers they download, so make it as descriptive as you can in a few words.

4 If you want to add an attachment to the article, drag the file from the Finder into the attachment area.

> **note** It's possible to attach Stuffit-compressed folders to newsgroup messages, but few people will be able to read such an attachment. Avoid annoying other readers of the newsgroup in this fashion.

5 Type your message in the message body. Your message might look something like Figure 19-4.

6 If you want to add a signature to the message, choose it from the Signature pop-up menu on the toolbar. You should generally stick to plain text for both your messages and your signatures; many newsgroups and newsreaders can't handle HTML-formatted messages.

Chapter 19: Using Newsgroups

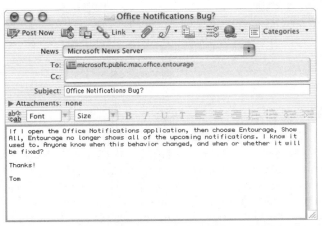

Figure 19-4.   This message is ready to be posted to a newsgroup.

7   Click the Post Now button on the toolbar, or choose Message, Post Message Now; or press Command+Return.

---

tip   Newsgroup articles aren't posted to news servers as quickly as e-mail arrives when you send it. Your messages might take minutes, hours, or even days to be seen by some readers. Don't make the mistake of sending your message repeatedly because it hasn't appeared on the news server. Send it once, and have faith.

To post a reply to a newsgroup article, follow these steps:

1   In the Message list, click the article to which you want to reply. It's considered polite to quote a portion of the message to which you are replying so that other readers know the context of your message. On the other hand, it's rude to quote an entire message if it's long, so quote just the relevant portions by selecting only the text that you need before the next step.

2   Click the Reply To Newsgroup toolbar button; choose Message, Reply; or press Command+R.

3   Just about everything's completed for you except your reply. Type that in the message box.

---

tip   Don't change the Subject line. If you do, newsreader programs won't know that your reply is part of a thread; they'll think that it is the first post in a new thread, and other people won't be able to follow the conversation.

---

4   Click the Post Now button on the toolbar.

> **tip** If you want to reply to the article's author directly via e-mail, choose Message, Reply To Sender in step 2. If you want to send the reply both to the newsgroup and to the author via e-mail, choose Message, Reply To All.

Using Newsgroup Rules

You can create newsgroup rules that help you include or exclude articles. Rules that exclude articles are especially useful because many Usenet newsgroups contain spam, and worse yet, contain people who are regular posters and who are annoying beyond belief. Imagine a person who loves to argue about picayune things. Then imagine that they have a mean streak, and enjoy goading reasonable people. Finally, imagine that this person gets to hide behind the relative anonymity of a made-up name, or *handle*. Such a person is a perfect candidate for a newsgroup rule that blocks all their messages. Newsgroup rules that do this are colloquially known as *bozo filters*.

To create a newsgroup rule, follow these steps:

1 Choose Tools, Rules.

2 In the Rules window, select the News tab.

3 Click the New button on the Rules window's toolbar.

4 In the Edit Rule dialog, enter a name for the rule in the Rule Name box.

5 From the Newsgroup pop-up menu, select the newsgroups for which you want the rule to apply. If you choose anything other than All Newsgroups, you'll need to enter a criteria string. For example, if you want the rule to apply only to Microsoft newsgroups, you could choose Starts With from the pop-up menu, and then you would enter **microsoft** in the text box that appears to the right of the pop-up menu.

6 In the If section, set the selection criteria for the rule. Your choices are All Messages, From, Subject, Size, Date Sent, or Category.

> **tip** If you select an article in the Message list before you begin creating a rule, and you choose From, Subject, or Date Sent, the corresponding information from the selected message will be automatically placed in the text entry field that appears to the right of the pop-up menu.

7 If you want to add another selection criterion, click Add Criterion.

8 Repeat steps 6 and 7 until you've created all your selection criteria.

9 If you created more than one selection criterion, make a choice from the Execute pop-up menu to indicate whether or not the message rule should apply if (or unless) *any* of the criteria are true, or if (or unless) *all* of the criteria are true.

10 In the Then section, you'll specify the actions that will be performed on the message if it matches the criteria in the If section. By default, two actions are created for you: Change Status To Not Junk Mail and Set Category To None. Feel free to change these to actions that you want, delete them by selecting the action and clicking Remove Action, or add new actions with the Add Action button. Figure 19-5 shows a bozo filter ready to be put into action.

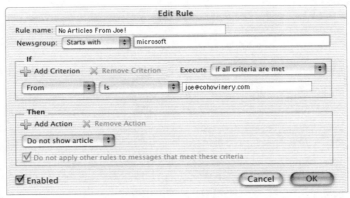

Figure 19-5. This completed newsgroup rule screens out any articles posted from a particular e-mail address.

11 Make sure that the Enabled check box is selected, and then click OK.

Chapter 20

Managing Your Contacts

The personal information manager (PIM) capabilities of Microsoft Entourage X begin with its Address Book. This feature began (in Entourage's former incarnation as Outlook Express) as merely a place to store your e-mail addresses, but with the transformation of Outlook Express into Entourage 2001, the Address Book was expanded to store names, mailing addresses, phone numbers, e-mail and Web addresses, and many other bits of personal information for your contacts.

In this chapter, you'll discover how to add contacts to the Address Book, use Entourage X to manage your personal contacts, how to import and export contacts from Entourage, and how to print contacts.

Creating and Using Contacts

You can access Entourage's Address Book by clicking the Address Book navigation button, or by pressing Command+2. Entourage switches to its Address Book view, as shown in Figure 20-1 on the next page.

The figure shows the Preview pane turned on, so that you can see the detailed information of the contact selected in the Address Book list, but you can toggle the Preview pane off by pressing Command+\ (backward slash), which will show your contacts in one big list. Double-click on a contact to open it in a new window, as shown in Figure 20-2 on the next page.

Part 3: Entourage

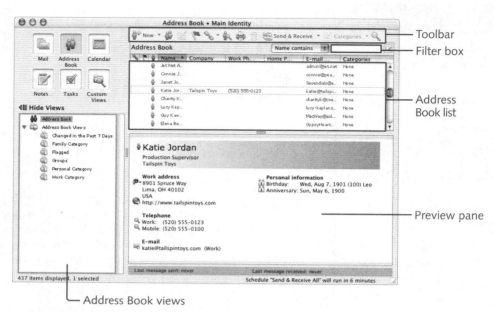

Toolbar

Filter box

Address
Book list

Preview pane

Address Book views

Figure 20-1. Like Entourage's Mail feature, Address Book enables you to view information in both list and detailed formats.

---

tip Drag the border between the Address Book list and the Preview pane to change their relative sizes.

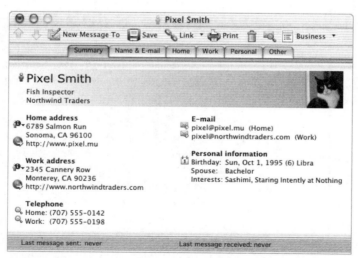

Figure 20-2. You can enter or edit information in a separate contact window by selecting the appropriate tabs.

Chapter 20: Managing Your Contacts

> **note** You can't customize Entourage's toolbars or menu commands, as you can with the other Microsoft Office v. X applications, but you can make some changes to the window. For information about hiding or showing columns in the Address Book list, or resizing columns, see "Customizing the Entourage window," page 408. As with the other Entourage list views, you can sort by any column (except the Links column) by clicking its header. Clicking the column header again reverses the sort direction.

Typically, when you first begin working with Entourage, you will import contact records from whatever PIM you were previously using. Of course, you can create new contacts in Entourage as well.

> **For more information about importing contacts into Entourage, see "Importing and Exporting Contacts," page 504.**

To create a new contact, follow these steps:

1 Choose File, New, Contact; click the New button on the toolbar; or press Command+N.

2 In the short form of the Create Contact dialog, enter the contact's name and e-mail address, phone numbers, and mailing addresses, as shown here. You can enter additional information for this contact by clicking the More button, which changes the Create Contact dialog into a long form with multiple tabs, as shown in Figure 20-2.

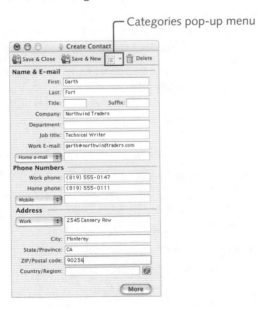

Categories pop-up menu

> **note**   If you click the More button, there's no way to return to the short form of the Create Contact dialog.

3   You can assign a category to the contact by choosing it from the Categories pop-up menu in the toolbar.

4   If you're done entering information for this contact, click the Save & Close button. If you want to create additional contact records, click Save & New.

To edit the contact record, double-click it in the Address Book list. The contact will open in a separate window. Click the tab that contains the information you want to change, enter the information, and then click the Save button on the toolbar.

> **tip**   **Start with an existing contact**
>
> Many of the new contacts you create will have some of the same information as an existing contact (for example, a person that works for the same company as another contact). Rather than enter the common information again, select the existing contact in the Address Book list, and then choose Edit, Duplicate Contact, or press Command+D. Then edit the duplicate contact, changing only the different information.

Setting Defaults

Contacts can have multiple mailing addresses and e-mail addresses. You can choose which ones you want to use as the defaults; that is, the ones that Entourage always uses first when using the contact record.

You can use either a person's home or work address as their default mailing address. To set either address as the default address, open the record, select either the Home or Work tab, and then select the Default Address option, as shown here:

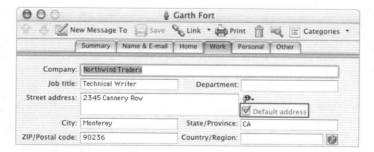

The first e-mail address that you enter for a contact will be the default e-mail address. When you enter an e-mail address for an outgoing message, the default address is always listed first in the pop-up address list in the To, Cc, or Bcc fields of the e-mail composition window. To make a different e-mail address the default, switch to the contact's Name & E-Mail tab, select the e-mail address, and click Make Default.

Working with the Personal Tab and Custom Fields

You can use the Personal tab to enter your contact's birthday and anniversary, as well as the name of their spouse, their children, and a little about their personal interests. If you enter a birthday, such as 10/5/57, Entourage automatically changes it to Sat, Oct 5, 1957, and calculates and enters the Age and Astrology Sign fields for you. Clicking the little calendar icon to the right of the Birthday and Anniversary fields opens a pop-up menu that presents a small calendar for easier date selection (choose Insert Date), allows you to insert today's date (choose Insert Today's Date), or lets you add the birthday or anniversary to Entourage's Calendar so that you don't forget the event (choose Add To Calendar).

InsideOut

Use four-digit years for post-2000 dates

The Birthday and Anniversary fields on the Personal tab of a contact window don't handle years past 2000 well. If you enter **5/6/01** into either of these fields, when you tab out of them Entourage changes the date to show Wed, Aug 7, 1901. Adding insult to injury, if you enter that post-2000 date into the Birthday field, Entourage calculates the Age field as 100. The workaround is to enter four-digit years for any date later than January 1, 2000, for example, **5/5/2001**.

The square field to the right of the other fields is for a picture; you can drag a picture in any format that QuickTime understands (typically you use a JPEG format, however) from the Finder into the picture field. The picture will then show up on the Summary tab of the contact window, in the Preview pane, and when you print your address book.

Entourage includes eight custom text fields and two custom date fields that you can rename and use however you like. For example, if you're managing subscriptions, you can use one of the date fields for the subscription's expiration date. To rename any of these fields, open a contact record and click the underlying title of one of the fields, such as Custom Date 1 on the Other tab. In the Edit Custom Label dialog, enter a new name, and then click OK. The new name will appear in all the contact records.

There are also four custom labels for phone labels, which enable you to add labels such as Toll-Free, or Customer Support. Open a contact record to either the Home or Work tab, click in the Label column, and choose Edit Custom Labels from the pop-up menu that appears. Enter the custom phone labels in the Edit Custom Phone Labels dialog. The new labels will be available when you add phone numbers for any of your contacts.

Defining Address Groups

An address *group* is created in the Address Book, but is actually used for e-mail. A group is two or more contacts that are grouped together so that you can contact all of them by selecting a single Address Book contact. Rather than individually adding the names of each contact to an outgoing message as message recipients, you can simply enter the group name. Entourage will send the message to each of the contacts in the group.

To create an address group, follow these steps:

1 In the Address Book list, select the contacts that you want to add to the group. You can select noncontiguous contacts by pressing Command and clicking each contact.

2 Choose File, New, Group, or click the New Group button on the toolbar.

3 In the untitled group window, enter the name for the new group.

4 The contacts that you selected in step 1 will already be entered in the group window, as shown here:

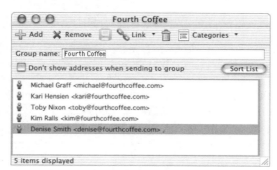

5 If you need to add additional contacts, click the Add button, and begin typing the contact information. Entourage will display a list of all matches as you type; press Return to select a contact and add it to the group.

> **note** Keep the following in mind when you're working with groups: an e-mail address doesn't have to be in your address book for you to add it to a group; a contact can belong to as many groups as you wish; and you can include a group as a member of another group.

6 If you don't want message recipients to see the addresses of the other group members, select the Don't Show Addresses When Sending To Group option.

7 If you add a contact by mistake and want to remove it, select it in the group window, and then click Remove. Removing a name from a group does not remove it from your address book. Click the Save button when you're done.

To use the group, create a new mail message, and then enter the group name in any of the To, Cc, or Bcc address fields of the message form.

InsideOut

Use a better group sort

The Sort List button in a group window sorts the list of people in the group, but it sorts the people by first name, and even then it displays some quirks that defy all sorting logic. If you want a more useful way to sort Entourage groups, you'll need to turn to an AppleScript. Freely downloadable from AppleScript Central (*www.applescriptcentral.com*), the Group Sort X script will sort the group members of one, many, or all of your groups in one pass. Download the compressed script, install it into your Users/*username*/Documents/Microsoft User Data/Entourage Script Menu Items folder, and then invoke the script from Entourage's Scripts menu. The script will sort e-mail-only addresses from left to right and will sort contacts by their last name. If you need more information about using AppleScripts in Entourage, see "Finding and Installing Cool Scripts," page 547.

For more information about addressing e-mail, see "Creating a New Message," page 444.

Searching for Contacts

Most of the time when you want to find a contact you'll remember the contact's name or company name, and the fastest way to find contacts using this information is to enter the search text into the filter box at the top of the Address Book list. Follow these steps:

1 From the pop-up menu next to the filter box, pick one of the three choices (Name Contains, Company Contains, Category Is).

2 If you chose Category Is, choose the category from the pop-up menu that appeared. Otherwise, in the filter box, type the search text. As you type each letter, Entourage narrows the choices shown in the Address Book list. At the same time, the label (Filter Applied) will appear at the top of the Address Book list to let you know that you're not viewing your entire set of contacts, as shown in Figure 20-3:

Figure 20-3. Filtering the list for *coffee* shows both addresses and a group matching the criteria.

> **note** Choosing Name Contains searches in either the contact's name or in any of the e-mail addresses.

3 When the Address Book list is narrowed enough so that you see the contact that you want, select the contact to view its detailed information in the Preview pane, or (if you don't have the Preview pane turned on) double-click the contact to open the contact window.

4 When you are done viewing the contact's information, click the Clear button next to the filter box to return the Address Book list to showing all contacts.

When a simple filtering isn't enough, for example, when you need to search for information in a contact's notes, or find all the contacts with e-mail addresses from a particular domain, you'll need to use Entourage's Find or Advanced Find feature. These features have already been covered earlier in this book, in "Searching Your E-Mail," page 464. Refer to that section for step-by-step instructions. Note that in the Find dialog (see Figure 18-21, on page 467), you'll need to choose Contacts from the pop-up menu to tell Entourage to search through the Address Book, and in the Advanced Find dialog (see Figure 18-22, on page 469), you'll need to make sure that Contacts is selected in the Item Types section.

Using Contact Actions

You might have noticed that on the Summary tab of the contact window (the same information shows up in the Preview pane) there are small icons next to several of the data fields. These five kinds of icons, shown here, are *contact actions*, and they enable you to work with your contact data in a variety of interesting ways.

● Next to each street address you'll see an information icon. Clicking this icon opens a pop-up menu with four choices: Show On Map, Driving Directions From Home, Driving Directions From Work, Copy Name And Address To Clipboard. The first three options open Microsoft's Expedia Web site (*www.expedia.com*) in your Web browser and display, respectively, the contact's address on a map, a map and written instructions of how to get from your home address to the contact's address, or how to get from your work address to the contact's address.

● Next to each URL is an icon that looks like a globe with an arrow on top of it; clicking this icon launches your Web browser and brings you to the associated Web page.

● Next to each e-mail address is an e-mail icon; clicking this icon creates a new e-mail message addressed to the selected e-mail address.

● Next to each phone number is a magnifying glass icon; clicking this icon opens a new window with a magnified version of the phone number, so that you can read it easily while dialing your phone.

● Next to each date is a calendar icon that indicates that a recurring event and reminder have been placed in the Entourage Calendar.

For more information about repeating events, see "Working with Recurring Events," page 519.

Working with vCards

A *vCard*, which stands for virtual business card, is a cross-platform, industry-standard file that includes contact information and can be sent via e-mail. You can send your own information, or that of any of your contacts, to someone else as an attachment to an e-mail message, and if the recipient has a vCard-compatible contact manager, they will be able to open the vCard and add the contact to their contact manager. It saves a lot of typing. A vCard file has the file extension .vcf.

note You can learn more about the vCard format at the Internet Mail Consortium's Web site, *http://www.imc.org/pdi*.

A vCard includes most, but not all, of the contact information that Entourage stores. It does not include the following:

● Personal: age, astrology sign, anniversary, spouse, interests, children

● Custom fields

Interestingly, a vCard *can* include the contents of the Picture field, which it converts to the JPEG format and encodes within the vCard. This means that vCards with embedded pictures can potentially be quite large, though most vCards are only 1 KB or so.

Obviously, Entourage is compatible with vCards, both for sending and receiving. So are Outlook and Outlook Express for Windows, so it's fairly easy to transfer contact information back and forth between these programs.

To send a contact as a vCard, select the contact in the Address Book list, and then choose Contact, Forward As vCard. Entourage creates a new e-mail message, with the .vcf file already created and set as a file attachment. Address and send the message as you normally do.

> **tip** To send multiple vCards in one message, select all of the contacts you want to send before you choose Contact, Forward As vCard.

You can also save vCard files to your hard disk by dragging the record from the Address Book list onto the desktop or into a folder on your hard disk.

To import into the Address Book a vCard that you receive with an e-mail message, follow these steps:

1 Double-click the message in the Message list to open it in its own window.

2 Click the disclosure triangle to open the attachment area.

3 Click the Address Book navigation button, or press Command+2.

4 Drag the .vcf file from the attachment area of the message to the Address Book list.

> **tip** When you import a vCard, Entourage just creates a new record, and does not check to see if it is a duplicate of an existing contact record. You'll have to check for that manually, by sorting the Address Book and looking for duplicates. Then delete the duplicate.

Importing and Exporting Contacts

Importing data into the Address Book from other contact managers and from tab or comma delimited text files, is covered in "Importing Data from Other Programs," page 415. Refer there for more information.

Entourage can export contacts as a tab delimited text file, which can be read by virtually any other contact manager (as well as by any word processor). You have very little control over this process; unlike some other contact managers, you can't modify or limit the amount of information that Entourage exports for each contact, nor can you export a subset of your records. All you can do is export your entire contact list. All the information in your contact file will be exported, with the exception of the picture information and any children's names that you might have entered.

> **note** At the end of the list of fields that are exported are several fields, including Bloodtype and fields labeled "furigana;" these are used in Japanese installations of the program and will normally be empty of data in English contacts lists.

To export your contact information, choose File, Export Contacts. In the Save dialog, give the export file a name, or accept the default name of Contacts Export. Click Save.

Printing Contacts

You can print the Address Book in a variety of formats to match popular paper organizer books, in either address book or phonebook style. You can choose to print all contacts, or only a subset, and you have some control over what information is printed.

To print your contacts, follow these steps:

1 If you want to print only one record or a selected number of records, select the records in the Address Book list. You do not need to make a selection if you want to print all records.

2 Choose File, Print.

3 The Print dialog, shown in Figure 20-4 on the next page, has a large Preview area that changes as you select different options in the Print Style area of the dialog. Choose one or more of these options:

   - From the Print pop-up menu, choose Selected Contacts, All Contacts, or Flagged Contacts.

   - From the Style pop-up menu, choose Address Book or Phone List.

   - From the Form pop-up menu, choose the style of organizer for which you'll be printing: Day Runner Classic (5.5 x 8.5), Day Runner Entrepreneur (8.5 x 11), Day Timer Junior Desk (5.5 x 8.5), Day Timer Senior Desk (5.5 x 11), Default (8.5 x 11), Franklin Classic (5.5 x 8.5), or Franklin Monarch (8.5 x 11).

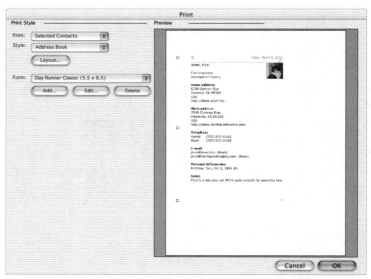

Figure 20-4.   You can work with the interactive preview in the Print dialog to format your address book the way you want before you commit it to paper.

■ To specify which fields of information you want to print and other information about the print job, click the Layout button. The Print Layout dialog will appear, as shown here. The options in this dialog are self-explanatory. Make your choices, and then click OK.

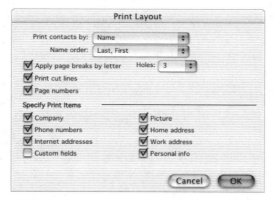

4 Click OK in Entourage's Print dialog. The Mac OS X Print dialog will appear. Make your selections from this dialog, and then click Print.

Chapter 21

Managing Your Appointments, Tasks, and Notes

A personal information manager (PIM) needs to be able to store and work with the information concerning the people that you deal with, and with the things that you do. In Chapter 20, you saw how Microsoft Entourage X works with your contacts, and in this chapter you'll see how Entourage enables you to manage your appointments (which Entourage calls *events*) and to-do's (which are called *tasks*). Entourage handles appointments in its Calendar section, your things-to-do in its Tasks area, and for good measure allows you to jot down notes in the Notes section. Notes are just that—text snippets that are not connected to any particular time.

In this chapter, you'll learn how to create calendar events, tasks, and notes; how to use Entourage's different calendar views to get different perspectives on your schedule; how to set reminders; and how to import events and holidays into Entourage.

Working with Calendar Views

To switch to Entourage's Calendar, click the Calendar navigation button, or press Command+3. (If you want to open the Calendar in a new window, so that you can simultaneously see your e-mail (or address book), press Command+Option+3.) The Calendar, shown in Figure 21-1 on the next page, has a large calendar pane where you can view and edit your events. At the upper left of the window, the Views list includes custom views that deal specifically with calendar events (for more

Part 3: Entourage

about custom views, see "Using Custom Views," page 529). Below the custom views, you'll see the mini-calendar pane, which can show one or more months to let you look quickly to a past or future month. Like all Entourage windows, you also have the navigation buttons and the toolbar at the top of the window.

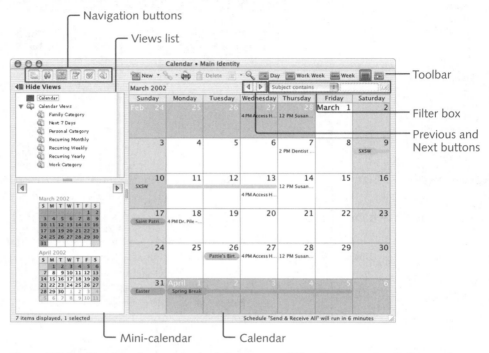

Figure 21-1. You can view your schedule in many different ways using Entourage's calendar.

> **note** Figure 21-1 (and some other figures in this chapter) shows small versions of Entourage's navigation buttons in order to show more calendar details. You can control the size of the navigation buttons by choosing Entourage, General Preferences, and selecting or clearing the Display Small Navigation Buttons option on the General tab.

You can view the calendar area in any of five views:

●   **Month** shows an entire month at a time. Working days are shown with a white background; non-work days (usually weekends, unless you've changed the working days on the Calendar tab of General Preferences) display in a light purple color; and days outside of the month being displayed have a gray background. Today is shown with a salmon-colored background.

Chapter 21

Chapter 21: Managing Your Appointments, Tasks, and Notes

- **Week** shows the seven days in a week as columns, with events displayed as bars in the columns, as shown here:

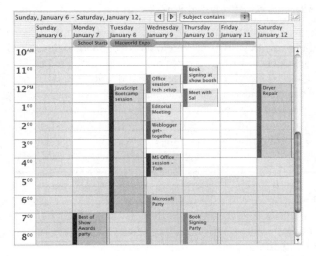

- **Work week** zooms in on just the days in the work week for a single week.

- **Day** shows all of the events in a single day, with bars showing how appointments span the hours of a day.

- **List** view shows your events in a long scrolling list.

You can switch between the different views by clicking a view's button on the toolbar; pressing Command+3 repeatedly to cycle through the (in order) month, day, week, and work week views; or choosing the view you want from the Calendar menu. The last method is the only way to display the List view.

To get from one time period to the next (from month to month, or day to day), click the Previous and Next buttons (see Figure 21-1), or press Command+[(left bracket) or Command+] (right bracket), respectively. As you move through the time periods, the mini-calendar in the lower left pane will change as needed to keep up. The mini-calendar isn't just for show, either; you can use it to quickly show a particular date in the main Calendar by clicking that date in the mini-calendar. Clicking a weekday in the mini-calendar scrolls that week to the top of the Month view, enabling you to scroll through the calendar week by week. Clicking a month name in the mini-calendar switches the Calendar to Month view and displays that month. And if you select an arbitrary range of days in the mini-calendar, Entourage will display only those days in its calendar area, which is great for zooming in on just a couple of weeks (actually, you can select up to six weeks), or even three or four days.

Chapter 21

InsideOut

Print mini-calendars to get previous and next months

The unfortunate thing about the mini-calendar is that it doesn't work like a mini-calendar in a traditional paper day planner, and therefore isn't quite as useful as it could be. You can adjust the mini-calendar to show one or more months, but you can't view the previous month and the next month without the current month (you don't need the current month shown in the mini-calendar, because you already have it in front of you in the Calendar pane). It would also be helpful if the mini-calendar displayed days with events differently from those without, perhaps by showing those days in bold type. Interestingly, when you print a monthly calendar, Entourage does show the previous and next months in the mini-calendar on the printed page along with the current month.

You can also choose to view or hide the Tasks pane, shown in Figure 21-2, which shows you the upcoming tasks that you've set. Although Tasks has its own navigation button in Entourage, it often makes sense to view the Tasks pane in conjunction with the Calendar to help in scheduling your activities. To toggle the Tasks pane, choose Calendar, Tasks Pane. Your future tasks appear in the Tasks pane; select the check box next to a task to mark it as completed. You can mark multiple tasks as completed by selecting them in the Tasks List, and then Control+clicking them. Select Mark As Complete in the resulting contextual menu.

Like the panes for the Views list and the mini-calendar, you can resize the Tasks pane by dragging the gray border between it and the calendar. Or you can Control+click the

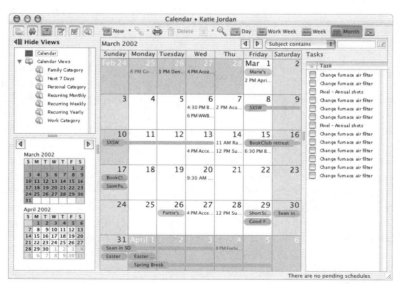

Figure 21-2. The Tasks pane shows you upcoming tasks; you can check them off as you complete them.

border to select it and then click anywhere to the left or right to resize the Tasks pane to that width.

The interaction between the different Calendar views and the Tasks pane can be a bit confusing until you figure out the pattern. Displaying or hiding the Tasks pane in the Month view affects its display only in the Month view; the List view works the same. However if you display or hide the Tasks pane in any of the Day, Work Week, or Week views, all three of those views will share the same Tasks pane setting. Entourage remembers the status of the Tasks pane for these three viewing groups (Month, List, and Day/Week views) so that when you return to a view the Tasks pane will appear as you last set it.

You can jump quickly to any date in the past or future by choosing Calendar, View Date, or by clicking the View Date button on the toolbar. In the resulting View Date

Making Room for the Calendar

If you don't have an especially large screen, the Calendar window can get pretty crowded—especially when you show the Tasks pane, the Views list, and the mini-calendar. You can expand the area for your calendar by clicking the Hide Views button, or by choosing Calendar, Folder List (if you really want a stripped-down window, you can even get rid of the toolbars by clearing the Show Toolbars option on the General tab of General Preferences). The Views list and the mini-calendar are hidden, and the navigation buttons are arranged vertically, allowing you to see more of your calendar, as shown here. To display the Views list and the mini-calendar again, click the Show Views button at the bottom of the column of navigation buttons, or choose Calendar, Folder List.

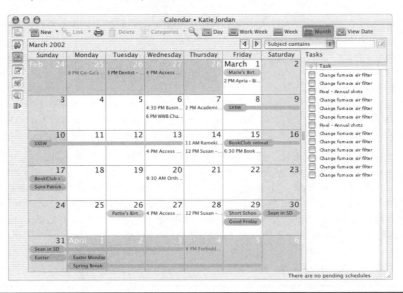

Chapter 21

dialog, enter the date that you want to go to, and press Return. The View Date dialog shows dates in the form Wed, May 29, 2002, but you can enter 5/29/02 with no problems. Finally, in any of the views, you can press Command+T, or choose Calendar, Go To Today to jump immediately back to today's date.

Importing Calendar Information

By far the best way to enter existing calendar data from another calendar program is to import it into Entourage. Otherwise, you must enter your calendar information manually. Entourage supports importing calendar data from the following programs:

- Entourage 2001
- Power On Software's Now Up-To-Date
- Palm Desktop
- Claris Organizer

Unfortunately, there's no way to import calendar data into Entourage by reading it from a tab or comma delimited text file. To import data into the Calendar from one of the programs listed, and to import lists of holidays into the Calendar, see "Importing Data from Other Programs," page 415.

see "Importing Data from Other Programs," page 415.

Troubleshooting

Entourage imported too much data into my Calendar.

Entourage's feature for importing data from other calendar programs isn't especially flexible; there's no way to control or limit the data that you bring in from the other programs. For example, there's no way to import only events and tasks from the last year. So if you have been using one of the other programs for several years, Entourage will grab and import *all* of its data, including tasks and events that you've long since forgotten. Worse, when importing data from Now Up-To-Date, Entourage imports reminders incorrectly, flagging all of them as undone and in most cases overdue, triggering new Office Notifications for each reminder.

The solution is to do some data pruning in the other program *before* you attempt to import into Entourage. See if the other program allows you to easily delete large amounts of data. If it does, make a backup copy of the data from that program. Then open the copy, not the original file, and delete all of the data that you don't want. Then you'll be ready to import that data file into Entourage. If the other program doesn't allow you to delete chunks of data from within the program, consider exporting the data as a text file, editing the text file in Microsoft Word X, re-importing it into the original program as a new file, and then importing it into Entourage.

Entourage does not always import information from other programs correctly, which might require you to do some calendar editing after you've imported the data so that events or tasks are listed correctly. For example, when importing data from Now Up-To-Date, Entourage doesn't understand that events spanning more than one day should be treated as banners. The only way to deal with this incorrect import is to edit the first day's event to become the correct length (which makes it a banner) and then delete the leftover events, as shown in Figure 21-3.

Figure 21-3. Entourage imported an event spanning several days as discrete events (top). After editing, the event becomes a proper banner (bottom).

> For more about banner events and other recurring events, see "Working with Recurring Events," page 519.

Recurring tasks from other programs might also not be imported correctly. In Figure 21-2 on page 510, two tasks ("Change furnace air filter" and "Pixel – Annual shots") are repeated several times because they weren't properly recognized as the same recurring task when they were imported to Entourage from Now Up-To-Date. As with banner events, you'll need to turn the first task in the series into a recurring task, and then delete the rest of the tasks from the Tasks pane.

Importing Holidays

When you install Microsoft Office v. X, the Entourage installation includes a file that contains holidays for 36 countries or regions, as well as Christian, Islamic, and Jewish religious holidays. The holiday file lists holidays from the year 2001 through 2005 (presumably, Microsoft thinks that you will have upgraded to a future version of Entourage by then!). By default, none of these holidays show up in the Calendar; you must import the ones that you want. To import holidays, follow these steps:

1 Switch to the Calendar by clicking the Calendar navigation button, or by pressing Command+3.

2 Choose File, Import.

3 In the Import dialog, select Import Holidays, and then click the right arrow button.

4 If you're asked to find the Holidays file you want to import, navigate to it in the Choose A File dialog. You'll find it in the Applications/Microsoft Office X/Office folder; the file is named Holidays. Click Choose.

5 The Import Holidays dialog appears, as shown in Figure 21-4. Select the check boxes next to the regional or religious holidays that you want to import, and then click the right arrow button.

Figure 21-4. Select the regional or religious holidays you wish to import into the Calendar.

6 Entourage imports the holidays and informs you that it has completed the task with a dialog. Click OK, and then click Finish to close the Import dialog.

The holidays appear in your calendar, already assigned to two categories—the generic Holiday category and a new category called Holiday-[*region* or *religion*]. For example, if you imported Canadian holidays, they are categorized as Holiday and Holiday-Canada.

Creating and Editing Calendar Events

You can create entries in Entourage's Calendar for any kind of event—a meeting, an interview, an appointment, your birthday, whatever. Entourage can remind you before the event, so that you don't forget it; can make it easy to schedule recurring events; and can even send e-mail to invite other people to meetings.

> **note** To Entourage, a calendar event and a task are similar, but not the same. Both are things that happen at a time that you specify. The difference is that a calendar event has a duration, and a task might or might not have a date and time when it is due.

Chapter 21: Managing Your Appointments, Tasks, and Notes

To create a calendar event, follow these steps:

1 With the Calendar showing (if it isn't, press Command+3), click the New button on the toolbar, or press Command+N.

> **tip** If you select a date in one of Entourage's calendar displays before creating a new event, Entourage will use that date as the starting date for the event and will assume it's an all-day event rather than a shorter appointment; if you don't select another date, today's date will be entered. If you select a range of dates (for a multi-day event like a conference, for example), Entourage will fill in both the beginning and end dates.

2 In the new event window, enter the Subject of the event. As you type the subject, it becomes the title of the window.

3 In the Location field, enter where the event will take place.

4 If you selected a date in the calendar before you created the event, Entourage has already filled in the Start date. If you didn't select a date first, enter the date. Use the format **5/6/02** to enter dates; because of an apparent bug, other day formats can result in odd dates. If you leave off the year, for example, enter **7/22**, Entourage assumes that you want the current year. You can also click the small calendar icon next to the date field, which pops up a small calendar. Clicking a date on the calendar will insert the date into the Start field and close the calendar.

> **tip** If you want to change the date in the Start and End fields by only a few days forward or backward, you can do it by pressing your keyboard's plus or minus key, respectively.

5 If the event is not an all-day event, such as a meeting or other shorter appointment, clear the All-Day Event check box and enter the Start time.

6 Enter the End date and time as necessary. An easy way to avoid figuring out the End time is to use the Duration field and pop-up menu to specify how long the event will last in minutes, hours, or days.

7 If you want Entourage to display a reminder before the event, select the Reminder check box, and specify how many minutes, hours, or days before the event you want to be reminded. By default, Entourage is set to deliver reminders 15 minutes before the event. If you want to turn off these default reminders or change their timing, you can do it on the Calendar tab of the General Preferences dialog.

8 If you want to allow travel time for the appointment, select the Travel Time check box and enter the travel time, specifying whether the travel time is both before and after, only before, or only after the event. If you specify

Part 3: Entourage

travel time before an event, Entourage will include the travel time when it calculates when to display the reminder; for example, if travel time is 30 minutes and the reminder is set to 15 minutes, you'll be notified 45 minutes before the event is to start. The travel time feature, new in Entourage X, shows the travel time as pale yellow bars around the event in the Date, Work Week, or Week views, as shown here:

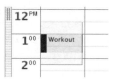

9 If this will be a recurring event, choose the frequency of the recurrence from the Occurs pop-up menu, as shown here:

If one of the standard intervals doesn't meet your needs, choose Custom from the Occurs pop-up menu. The Recurring Event dialog appears, as shown in Figure 21-5.

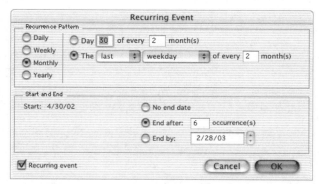

Figure 21-5. The Recurring Event dialog gives you a great deal of flexibility in scheduling your repeating events.

The options in the Recurrence Pattern section of the dialog change depending on whether you select Daily, Weekly, Monthly, or Yearly. The Start And End section of the dialog lets you indicate how long the event will keep repeating; these options are self-explanatory. Click OK to close the Recurring Event dialog.

10 In the Notes box at the bottom of the event window, enter any text that you want associated with this event.

11 From the event's toolbar, select the category to which you wish to assign this event.

12 Optionally, if you want to send somebody an e-mail message about this event, click the Invite button on the toolbar. Enter the names or e-mail addresses of the people you want to invite in the To box and press Return. Two items will be added at the top of the event window, both familiar from Entourage's e-mail window:

■ The From pop-up menu allows you to choose from which of your e-mail accounts you want to send the message.

■ The Invite field is the same as the To field in an e-mail message. Click the field to add or edit the list of invitees.

> **note** When you invite someone by sending them an e-mail message, you also have the opportunity to attach a file to the message. For more information about file attachments, see "Attaching Files and Folders to Messages," page 452.

13 Click Save (or press Command+S), and then close the event window. The result should look something like Figure 21-6.

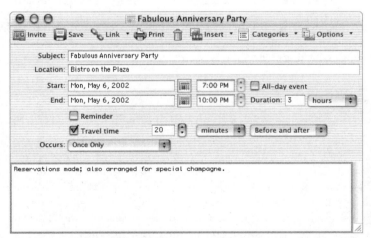

Figure 21-6. The completed event has all the information you'll need.

> **tip** You can create an event from a birthday, an anniversary, or a custom date field in a person's contact record. See "Using Contact Actions," page 502, for more information.

Editing and Deleting Calendar Events

To edit an event, all you need to do is double-click it in any of the Calendar views. The event window opens. Make your changes, click Save, and then close the window. You can move an event in the Calendar by dragging it to where you want it to go.

> **tip**   **Save and close at the same time**
>
> It's kind of annoying to always have to first save, and then close the event window. The first time you forget and try to close the window without saving first, Entourage will pop up an alert dialog asking whether you want to save your changes. Click the Always Save Changes Without Asking check box to save yourself an extra step in the future.

Unfortunately, there's no way to directly duplicate calendar events; unlike virtually all other Macintosh PIMs, you can't even Option-drag an event to duplicate it. Once again, there's an AppleScript ready to come to the rescue. Freely downloadable from AppleScript Central (*www.applescriptcentral.com*), the Duplicate Calendar Events X script will do the job. Download the script, install it into your Users/*username*/Documents/Microsoft User Data/Entourage Script Menu Items folder, and then invoke the script from Entourage's Scripts menu.

> If you need more information about using AppleScripts in Entourage, see "Finding and Installing Cool Scripts," page 547.

To delete an event, select it in any of the Calendar views, and then press Delete. Entourage will pop up an alert dialog asking whether you are sure. Click Delete. Pressing the D key is the same as clicking Delete in this dialog.

InsideOut

Select and change multiple events

One of the big annoyances about Entourage is that you can't select multiple items in any of the Calendar views. That means that there isn't a good way in the Calendar to change the category of many items at once (you can change the category of an individual event in the Calendar by Control+clicking it and then choosing the category from the resulting contextual menu), or to delete several items that you no longer need (perhaps because Entourage imported them incorrectly).

There is a good workaround, however; you can use the Advanced Find feature to search for and display all the items that you want to change. Then you can select multiple items in the Search Results list and apply the changes you want. For more information about using Advanced Find, see "Searching Your E-Mail," page 464.

Working with Recurring Events

You set up an event's recurrence while creating the event. But when you go to edit or delete an event, recurring events act a bit differently than single events. Editing or deleting the recurring event brings up an alert dialog that asks you to make a decision about the event chain, as shown here:

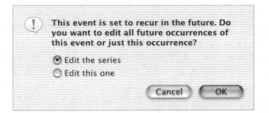

If you choose Edit The Series (the choice will be Delete All if you are deleting the item), your changes will affect all the future occurrences of the event. Choosing Edit This One (or Delete This One) affects only the event you are working with.

newfeature!
Working with Office Notifications

When reminders come due, the Office Notifications dialog appears, as shown in Figure 21-7. This dialog is generated by a new program, Microsoft Office Notifications, that works with another program that is always running in the background and that launches automatically when you start your Macintosh.

> **note** You can see the name of the program that launches at startup (though you can't see it in the Dock or switch to it, because it has no user interface) by choosing Apple, System Preferences; choosing Login; and then clicking the Login Items tab. The application called Microsoft Database Daemon is the program that runs automatically at startup, and that triggers Microsoft Office Notifications to do its work. If for some reason you didn't want Microsoft Database Daemon to run at startup, you would select it and click Remove on the Login Items tab.

Figure 21-7. The Office Notifications dialog appears no matter what application you're using, and floats over all other applications until you click Snooze or Dismiss.

In the Office Notifications dialog, you can choose to open the item, click and hold the Snooze button to display a pop-up menu with options to delay the reminder (the default delay is five minutes, which is what happens if you just click the button), or click the Dismiss button to acknowledge and delete the reminder. If there is more than one reminder due, you can also click and hold the Dismiss button to open a pop-up menu and choose the Dismiss All option.

Sending Invitations and Getting RSVPs

When you send invitations to people when you are creating an event, Entourage sends an e-mail message that includes a special *vCalendar* attachment. The vCalendar, which includes all the information about your event, is similar to the vCard, in that both are cross-platform, industry-standard files that include PIM information and can be sent via e-mail.

> For more information about vCards, see "Working with vCards," page 503.

Entourage is compatible with vCalendar attachments, both for sending and receiving. So are Microsoft Outlook and Microsoft Outlook Express for Windows, so it's fairly easy to transfer events back and forth between these programs.

> **note**   If you send an invitation to someone who is using an e-mail program that doesn't understand vCalendar attachments, he or she will receive a message with the event title in the subject line and the start time, end time, and notes in the message body.

When you get an e-mail message with a vCalendar attachment, Entourage shows the message with a Calendar icon in the Message Status column, as shown here:

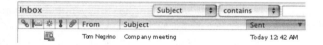

Opening the message (you have to double-click it to open it in its own window; you can't work with the invitation in the Preview pane), you'll see a link at the top of the message form called Show Calendar Event. If you click the link, you'll see that the event has inserted itself into your calendar.

On the toolbar of the message, you'll see three new buttons:

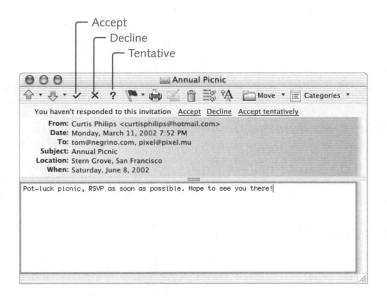

These buttons, Accept, Decline, and Tentative, generate a reply e-mail message to the person who sent you the invitation. You'll also see a line with a pale yellow background that includes three links, Accept, Decline, and Accept Tentatively, which you can click instead of the toolbar buttons. If the invitee accepts or tentatively accepts the invitation, the message shown next appears. Accepting an invitation isn't of much use if you don't tell the sender about it, so you should click OK. If you decline the invitation, a dialog appears that allows you to send your regrets (or not, as you choose).

When the person who sent the invitation receives your reply, they will be able to open the calendar event, which will now have a link called Show Attendee Status. Clicking that link opens a window with all the attendees listed, as shown here:

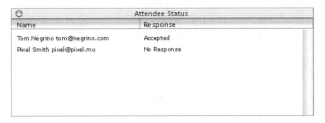

521

Clicking on the response next to an attendee's name (in the Response column) makes a pop-up menu appear; opening the pop-up menu reveals four possible responses: No Response, Accepted, Tentative, Declined. If an invitee has replied with an e-mail program that isn't vCalendar savvy, you can update their status manually using this pop-up menu. If the person is using a vCalendar-enabled program, the status will be updated automatically.

If your event is cancelled, Entourage can handle that, too. Simply open the event in the Calendar, and click the Cancel Invitations button on the toolbar. Entourage will ask whether you want to send cancellation messages to the people you've invited. Of course you must inform invitees that you've cancelled the event, so click OK unless you're planning to contact them in another way, such as by phone.

Printing Your Calendar

You can print the Calendar in a variety of formats to match popular paper organizer books. You can choose to print the following, each with starting and ending dates:

- **Daily Calendar** prints individual days; it's the most detailed view.

- **Weekly Calendar** prints one week per page. It includes a mini-calendar for the current month.

- **Monthly Calendar** prints the entire selected month. It also prints small calendars for the previous and next months.

- **Calendar Event List** prints the events in list form.

To print your calendar, follow these steps:

1 Choose File, Print.

2 The Print dialog, shown in Figure 21-8, has a large Preview area that changes as you select different options in the Print Style area of the dialog.

3 From the Print pop-up menu, choose Daily Calendar, Weekly Calendar, Monthly Calendar, or Calendar Event List.

4 Choose the appropriate Start and End dates.

5 From the Form pop-up menu, choose the style of organizer for which you'll be printing: Day Runner Classic (5.5 x 8.5), Day Runner Entrepreneur (8.5 x 11), Day Timer Junior (5.5 x 8.5), Day Timer Senior (5.5 x 11), Default (8.5 x 11), Franklin Classic (5.5 x 8.5), or Franklin Monarch (8.5 x 11).

Chapter 21: Managing Your Appointments, Tasks, and Notes

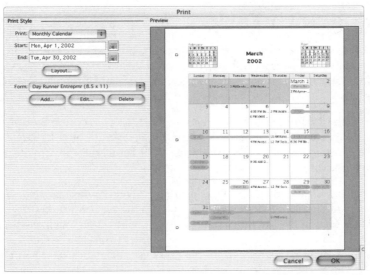

Figure 21-8. You can work with the interactive preview in the Print dialog to format your calendar the way you want before you commit it to paper.

6 To specify which items will print and other information about the print job, click the Layout button. The Print Layout dialog will appear, as shown here:

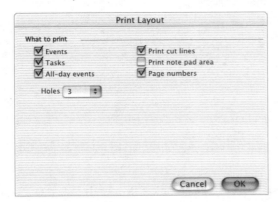

7 Select the calendar elements you want to print, whether you want the pages marked for hole-punching, and then click OK.

8 Click OK to close Entourage's Print dialog. The Mac OS X Print dialog will appear. Make any selections for your printer from this dialog, and then click Print.

Working with Tasks

Tasks are things that you want to accomplish, and that might or might not have a due date, but do not have a duration. You can track your tasks in Entourage, see which tasks have yet to be done, and mark tasks as completed. You can attach notifications to tasks, have a task be recurring, and you can assign one of five priority levels to a task.

To switch to Entourage's Tasks area, click the Tasks navigation button, or press Command+5. Figure 21-9 shows Tasks views in the left pane and the Tasks list in the right pane. Completed tasks are shown in the Tasks list with a check mark and strikethrough text.

Tasks work differently in the Tasks list than they do in the Tasks pane in the Calendar. When you select a check box next to a task in the Tasks list to mark it as completed, the task stays in the list, but is struck through with a line. When you mark a task as completed in the Tasks pane, the task disappears from the screen. Because the task will still show (with strikethrough) in the Tasks list, the inconsistent handling of the same action can be a bit unsettling at first.

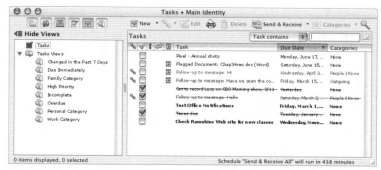

Figure 21-9. You can view tasks yet to do as well as completed tasks in the Tasks list.

The five narrow columns at the left edge of the Tasks list show you different attributes of each task:

- The **Links** column displays a chain link if the task is linked to any other Entourage items.

- The **Status** column contains check boxes that you can mark to indicate that a task is completed.

- The **Priority** column uses the same priority icons as e-mail. See Table 18-4, on page 433, for details.

- The **Recurring** column displays an icon if the task is set to repeat.

- The **Reminder** column displays an alarm clock icon for each task that has a reminder associated with it.

Creating Tasks

You can create tasks manually, but you will also often create tasks through follow-ups from the other Office programs. If you see tasks in the list that you didn't create in Entourage, it's probably because you chose Flag For Follow Up while working with a document in Word, Excel, or PowerPoint. The names of these tasks will always begin with "Follow-up to," which makes them easy to spot.

To create a task, follow these steps:

1 Choose File, New, Task. If Tasks is selected in Entourage, you can also click the New button or press Command+N.

2 In the untitled window that appears, enter a title for the task. As you type, your entry becomes the title of the window.

3 If the task has a due date, select the Due Date check box, and set the date.

4 If you want to set a reminder for the task, select the Reminder check box, and set the date and time for the reminder.

5 Set the task's priority level.

6 If the task will recur, choose the recurrence interval from the Occurs pop-up menu. If none of the preset intervals is what you want, click Custom on the Occurs pop-up menu, and create your own recurrence schedule.

7 You can set the category for the task with the Categories button on the toolbar. The task should now look something like Figure 21-10.

8 Click Save, and then close the window.

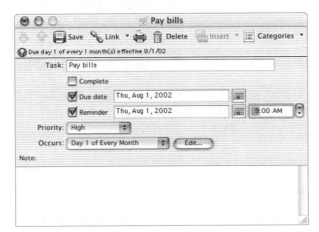

Figure 21-10. Creating a new task is very similar to creating an event in the Calendar.

Printing Tasks

Printing tasks is very much like printing Calendar events, with minor changes in the Print dialog that are specific to the job of printing tasks. To print tasks, make sure that you are displaying the Tasks list, and then choose File, Print. For detailed instructions about the resulting Print dialog, see "Printing Your Calendar," page 522.

Working with Notes

Notes are completely free-form text notes that you can create in Entourage. They're like sticky notes that you might have stuck to your monitor, but they offer the benefit of being able to be searched by Entourage's Find tools.

Like practically everything else in Entourage, notes can be assigned to one or more categories and linked to any other item. You can insert pictures, sounds, movies, or hyperlinks into notes, and they are written with the same rich text tools as Entourage uses for HTML e-mail.

To display your notes in Entourage, click the Notes navigation button, or press Command+4. Figure 21-11 shows the different Notes views in the left pane and the Notes list in the right pane. You can sort the Notes list by title, date created, or category by clicking the appropriate column header.

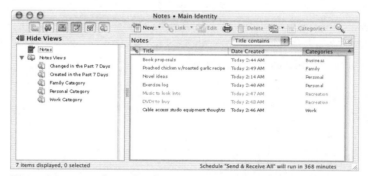

Figure 21-11. Like tasks, notes are displayed by Entourage in the right pane, and the left pane displays views for filtering your notes.

Creating Notes

To create a note, follow these steps:

1 Choose File, New, Note. If the Notes list is displayed in Entourage, you can also click the New toolbar button or press Command+N.

2 In the untitled window that appears, enter the title for the note. As you type, your entry becomes the title of the window.

3 Enter the text of the note. You can format the text of the note using the Format menu or the Formatting toolbar shown in Figure 21-12, and you can use the Insert pop-up menu on the toolbar to insert graphics, media files, or hyperlinks from Internet Explorer into the body of the note.

4 Click Save when you're done, and then close the note window.

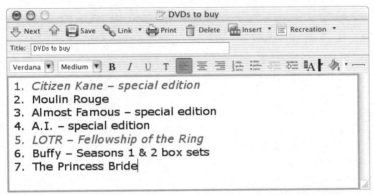

Figure 21-12. You can format the text in your notes; the auto-numbering feature is especially handy for lists.

Printing Notes

Printing notes is like printing Calendar events or tasks, with minor changes in the Print dialog that are specific to the job. To print notes, make sure that you are displaying the Notes list, and then choose File, Print. For detailed instructions about the resulting Print dialog, see "Printing Your Calendar," page 522.

Chapter 22

Organizing and Sharing Entourage Data

After you've used Microsoft Entourage X for a while, you will have amassed a large amount of information, considering all of your e-mail, contacts, calendar events, tasks, and notes. Entourage offers many tools to help you organize this data, such as folders, mail rules, and categories, and previous chapters have shown how to use these tools. In this chapter, you'll learn about one more feature, Custom Views, which enable you to leverage all the other tools to view or access data efficiently.

Entourage is only one of the tools that you use daily, and you can use Entourage as a hub to help you manage your projects. You can also share Entourage data with the other Office programs and post your calendar on a Web site.

In this chapter, you'll learn how to create custom views so that you can find information quickly; how to create links to your Entourage data to help you manage all the pieces of a project; how to use your Entourage contacts in Microsoft Word X documents; and how to share your Entourage calendar with colleagues over the Web.

newfeature! Using Custom Views

Custom Views is probably the most unknown of Entourage's major features—at least as unknown as a feature can be, given that it has a navigation button devoted to it. Custom views themselves are not new to Entourage X, as they existed in Entourage 2001. What is new is the feature's new prominence in the Entourage X user interface.

529

Part 3: Entourage

A *custom view* is a search, run from the Find or Advanced Find dialog, that you have saved. What you have saved is not the *results* of the search; rather, the *search criteria* so that the search can be easily run again. Saving these criteria can be beneficial in many ways. For example, say that you want to regularly review all the correspondence that you get from the people at a particular company, or from all members of your family. In the former case, you could do a search for all messages from, say, microsoft.com, and then save the search as a custom view. In the latter case, you could do a search for all messages that were assigned the Family category. Even though members of your family might have different last names, the search will find everybody.

Of course, because Entourage has a single database for all of its information, you're not limited to simply searching e-mail messages. You can create custom views that include any of the information that Entourage stores, in any combination. So, for example, you could construct a custom view that shows you Calendar events or tasks, but not e-mail messages, that occurred or were created in the last seven days.

Entourage comes with many useful custom views already created for you, which you can access by clicking the Custom Views navigation button, or by pressing Command+6, as shown in Figure 22-1.

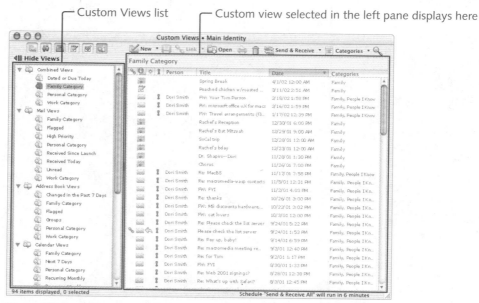

Custom Views list   Custom view selected in the left pane displays here

Figure 22-1. The name of the custom view appears at the top of the right pane.

The Custom Views list in the left pane shows Combined Views at the top, which returns search results from more than one of the Entourage task areas. In addition to the Combined Views group, you'll find Mail Views, Address Book Views, Calendar Views, Notes Views, and Tasks Views. Each of these view types also appears in it's respective task areas. But combined views can only be accessed from the Custom Views list.

Chapter 22: Organizing and Sharing Entourage Data

Creating a Custom View

In order to create a custom view, you'll need to do a search first. You can search using either a simple Find or an Advanced Find, but in this example, we'll use an Advanced Find.

> For more details about finding information in Entourage, see "Searching Your E-Mail," page 464.

Follow these steps to perform a search, and save it as a custom view:

1 Choose Edit, Advanced Find, or press Command+Option+F.

> **tip** You can also get to the Advanced Find dialog by clicking the More Options button in the basic Find dialog.

2 In the Item Types section of the Advanced Find dialog, select the areas of Entourage where you would like to search, or click All Items to select all the areas in one step. If you select more than one area, you will create a combined view.

3 In the Location section, choose This Folder, and then choose which folder to search from the second pop-up menu, or choose All Folders. The Location section will only be available if you've selected only the Messages item type. If you've chosen a specific folder, you can also choose whether to include its subfolders in the search.

4 In the Criteria section, use the first pop-up menu to select the first type of information that you're searching for, such as the sender of an e-mail or the last name of a contact. Depending on your selection in the first pop-up menu, another pop-up menu, and perhaps a text box might appear. In the second pop-up menu, choose the way you'll be searching for the text you enter in the text box to the right; for example, you might want to search for items that start with, or perhaps end with, the text that you enter in the text box.

> **note** If you had selected more than one area in step 2, the only criteria available from the first pop-up menu will be the ones that are common to all of the areas, namely Title, Date, Category, Person, and Body (which means the message body for e-mail, or the notes section in calendar events, tasks, or notes).

5 If you want to search by more than one criterion, click Add Criterion and repeat the process in step 4. Repeat as necessary until you have finished adding criteria.

6 If you've used more than one criterion, the Match pop-up menu can be used to control how Entourage combines the criteria; for example you could find only information that matches *all* the criteria, or information that matches *any* of the criteria.

7 Click Find. The results will appear in a Search Results window, as shown in Figure 22-2.

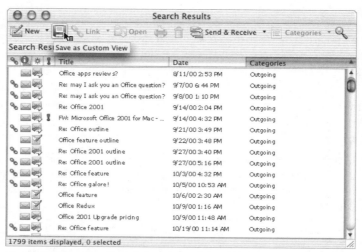

Figure 22-2. The Search Results window enables you to save the search criteria as a custom view.

8 Choose File, Save As Custom View.

9 In the resulting Edit Custom View dialog, shown in Figure 22-3, enter the name of the custom view in the Name box, and then click OK.

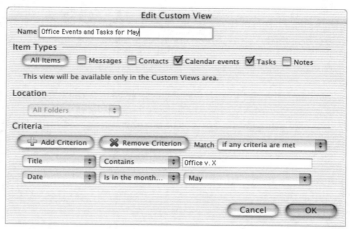

Figure 22-3. Save the custom view in the inappropriately named Edit Custom View dialog.

To use the custom view you just created, click the Custom Views navigation button, or press Command+6, and then select the custom view in the list. The results of the search will appear in the Search Results list. If you created a custom view that only uses one of Entourage's areas, the custom view will also appear in the left pane of that area.

Search Tips, Tricks, and Oddities

Here is a potpourri of Entourage search tips that will help you construct custom view searches:

- In order to stop a search in progress without losing the search results already found, press Command+period.

- You can customize any custom view by sorting, changing, and rearranging columns, just as you can with any other Entourage list. Entourage saves any changes you make when you exit the view.

- If you want to use a date as one of your criteria, you can only specify a particular date by entering a number of days since the event; you can't enter a date such as 1/1/02 to find items dated this year. The exception to this is that you can specify Today, Yesterday, Tomorrow, or Is In The Month Of, which then provides a pop-up menu with the 12 months.

- When searching for messages, you can use the Any Header criterion to select messages based on the IP addresses of the mail servers the messages passed through on their way to you. You can even select messages based on part of the IP address; for example, the 211.x.x.x set of addresses are assigned to China and are notorious as being a major source of spam. In this case, you would choose the Any Header criterion, then Contains from the middle pop-up menu, then enter **211.** in the text box.

- If you search Messages and select All Folders under Location, Entourage will also return the names of Usenet newsgroup messages that you have retrieved from the news server. There doesn't seem to be a way to exclude newsgroup messages from such a search.

- When searching Contacts, don't overlook the Full Name criterion. It searches the First Name and Last Name fields simultaneously.

- If you want to find all of the messages that have either been sent to or received from one of the people in your address book in one step, select the person's name in your address book and choose Edit, Find Related Items. The results appear in a standard Search Results window. If you like, you can then save the results as a custom view.

Editing or Deleting a Custom View

Changing or deleting custom views works just as you would expect. To edit a custom view, follow these steps:

1 In the Custom Views area or the individual task areas, find the custom view you want to change.

2 Control+click the icon next to the custom view, and then choose Edit Custom View from the contextual menu.

> **tip** If you click the name of a custom view, pause briefly, and then click it a second time, you can edit the name.

3 Make the changes you want in the Edit Custom View dialog, and then click OK.

To delete a custom view, select the custom view, and then choose Edit, Delete Custom View, or press Delete.

Linking Information

One of the benefits of Entourage, which includes an e-mail program and a PIM, is that you can link items together so that you can view and work with the related information. In Entourage, every item can be linked to any other item, or to multiple other items. For example, you can link a calendar event to one or more e-mail messages you sent and received while you were arranging the event. Or you can link a task with the people in your address book that will be working on the task with you. You can also link any Entourage item with external files, such as a Microsoft Excel or Adobe Photoshop file, so that you can see all the supporting documents that you'll need for an important meeting. Links in Entourage are two-way connections; for example, if you link a contact to a calendar event, you can view the links associated with the contact and see the event, or open the event's links and see the contact information.

When you link an Entourage item, a little chain link icon appears in the Links column next to the item, as shown here:

Once you've set up a link, you can use it to quickly open the linked items. For example, if you link an event with all of the e-mail messages sent in support of that event, you can open any of the messages in one step, rather than having to do a search for the messages.

Creating Links to Existing Items

To create a link to one or more existing items, follow these steps:

1 Select the item for which you want to create a link.

2 Choose Tools, Link To Existing, and then from the submenu choose Message, Calendar Event, Task, Note, Contact, Group, or File.

3 The Link Maker window appears, with the name of the item that you have selected displayed in the Link From area. Find the item (or items) that you want to link to (if necessary, you can switch to another Entourage area, such as the Address Book, or the Calendar), and drag its name into the Link To area of the Link Maker window, as shown in Figure 22-4.

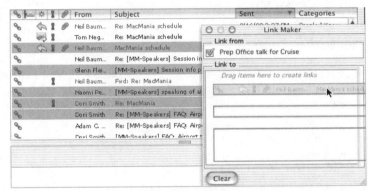

Figure 22-4. Drag items to the Link Maker window to create links to an existing item.

> **tip** You can drag one or more files from your desktop into the Link Maker window, instead of choosing the File choice from the Link To Existing submenu.

4 After a moment, the words "Link Created" will appear in the Link To area. If you want to create more links to the item in the Link From area, continue to drag additional items to the Link To area. Then close the Link Maker window.

> **tip** In any Entourage list, if you click in the Links column next to an item, a menu will open that contains both the Link To Existing and Link To New choices.

Creating Links to New Items

You can also create new items that are automatically linked to a currently selected item. Follow these steps:

1 Select an item for which you want to create a link.

2 Choose Tools, Link To New, and then from the submenu choose Mail Message, News Message, Calendar Event, Task, Note, Contact, or Group.

3 The new item window for whatever sort of item you selected will appear. Fill it out as usual, and then save and close the window.

If you prefer using the toolbar, you can use the Link button on the toolbar to create links to either existing or new items. Click the arrow next to the Link button, point to either Link To Existing or Link To New, and choose from the submenu.

Showing an Item's Links

Once you've created links to an item, you want to be able to access them easily. You have these ways of working with an item's links:

- To open a specific link in one step, click the chain link icon that appears in the Links column for that item, and then choose the linked item you want from the hierarchical menu, as shown here:

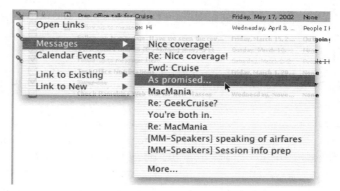

- To view a list of all an item's links and then choose from the list, select the item and choose Tools, Open Links, or click the icon next to the item and choose Open Links.

The Open Links command opens the Links To window, as shown in Figure 22-5. This window groups and totals the selected item's links according to their type. Click the disclosure triangle next to a group to expand or collapse the linked items. Select any linked item to open it, remove its link, or link it to other existing or new items.

Chapter 22: Organizing and Sharing Entourage Data

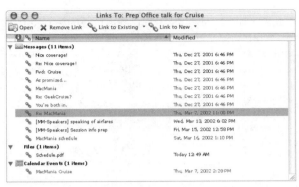

Figure 22-5. The Links To window enables you to examine, open, modify, or add links to the selected item.

Using Entourage
Contacts in Word Documents

Because Entourage's Address Book is shared by Microsoft Word, you can draw on the Address Book to fill in names and addresses while writing letters in Word. Follow these steps to insert a name in your Word document:

1 In Word, choose View, Toolbars, Contact.

2 Create a new document, or place the insertion point in the place in the document where you want to insert information from Entourage.

3 On the Contact toolbar, click where it says Type Contact Name, and then type the first few letters of the name of the contact whom you want to insert. As you type, a menu appears below the text box that narrows in scope as you type more letters, as shown here:

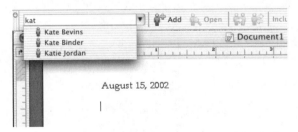

4 Choose from the list, either with the mouse or by pressing the Down Arrow key, and then pressing Return. The name is inserted into your document.

5 If you want to add any or all of the addresses, phone numbers, or e-mail addresses of the contact to the Word document, click the corresponding buttons on the Contact toolbar. If there are multiple addresses or phone numbers from which to choose, the buttons will become pop-up menus listing the information. Choose which you want, and Word inserts it into the document, as shown in Figure 22-6.

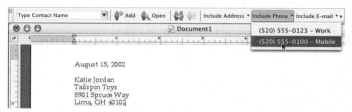

Figure 22-6. The Contact toolbar draws from Entourage's Address Book to save you typing.

> **note** The information inserted in the Word document is inserted as one or more fields and can't be edited in Word. If you want to change some of the information, change and save the contact record in Entourage, and then return to Word, Control+click on the inserted data, and choose Update Field from the contextual menu.

> For more information about using fields in Word, see "Understanding Fields," page 352.

Publishing Your Calendar on the Web

You can share your Entourage calendar with others by saving it as a Web page and placing it on a Web server. The calendar includes hyperlinks for events, which you can click to view the event's details in the list displayed on the right side of the Web page.

> **note** You can't publish your tasks along with your calendar.

To publish your calendar as a Web page, follow these steps:

1 Click the Calendar navigation button, or press Command+3.

2 Choose File, Save As Web Page.

3 In the Duration section of the Save As Web Page dialog, shown next, set the Start Date and End Date for the Web calendar. You can either type the dates in the format 7/22/02 or use the small calendar icons next to each date to open a pop-up calendar from which you can select dates.

Chapter 22: Organizing and Sharing Entourage Data

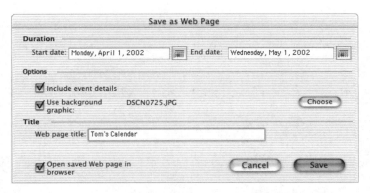

4 In the Options section, optionally select one or both of these check boxes:

■ **Include Event Details** includes the information in the notes field of your calendar events (not to be confused with the notes that you make in the Notes area of Entourage) on the Web page. Initially, these are collapsed on the Web page, but can be displayed by clicking the disclosure triangle for the event in the Appointment And Event Details pane.

■ **Use Background Graphic** puts a background image on the Web page. If you select this option, you must click the Choose button and find a graphic for the background of the calendar. Background graphics must be in JPEG, GIF, or PNG format, and if the graphic isn't big enough to fill the space required by the calendar, the graphic will be *tiled,* or repeated as many times as is needed to fill the space.

5 In the Web Page Title field, enter the title that will appear at the top of the calendar.

6 Make sure the Open Saved Web Page In Browser option is selected. This ensures that when the calendar is saved as a Web page, your browser will open so that you get a preview of what the calendar will look like on the Web.

7 Click Save. In the Save dialog, give the calendar file a name. You must follow the usual rules for naming a Web page: just one word, and you must not include spaces or slashes in the name. After naming the file, click Save. Your browser will show the result of your handiwork, as shown in Figure 22-7 on the next page.

---

note   Even though there is no option to append a file name extension in the Save dialog, Entourage automatically appends the .htm extension to the calendar page you save. Entourage also creates a folder, with the same name as the page, that contains additional HTML and graphics files that are needed to display the calendar as a Web page.

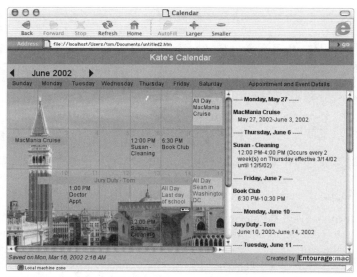

Figure 22-7. You can dress up your Web calendar with any background image, as long as it is in JPEG, GIF, or PNG format.

Once you've saved your Web page and its associated folder, you'll need to upload it to your Web server. This usually requires the use of an FTP (File Transfer Protocol) program, such as Fetch (available from *www.fetchsoftworks.com*). From within Fetch or another FTP program, you can log onto the server to which you want to transfer your files and put the files on the server.

If you don't want to fiddle with an FTP program or pay for a Web site, Apple offers all users of Mac OS X, as part of its iTools service, 20 MB of free Web hosting space on its servers on a virtual hard drive called your iDisk. You can mount the iDisk on your Mac OS X desktop by switching to the Finder and choosing Go, iDisk. You can then save the calendar files in the Sites folder on your iDisk, just as though the iDisk were a regular hard drive attached to your Macintosh. If you signed up for iTools as part of your Mac OS X setup, you already have an iDisk. For more information about your iDisk, visit *www.apple.com/itools*.

Synchronizing Entourage to Your Palm Device

The popularity of handheld computers based on the Palm OS, such as the units from Palm Computing, Handspring, Sony, and others, provides a unique opportunity for Entourage users. Your PIM data can break free of its desktop shackles and slip into your pocket, purse, or briefcase so that it is always with you. And this data isn't taking

Chapter 22

a one-way trip, either; changes that you make to your schedule, tasks, or contacts on the handheld while you are on the road can be synchronized with your desktop machine when you get back to your home or office.

Entourage 2001 synchronizes Calendar events, Address Book information, the Tasks list, and Notes to and from your Palm handheld, and Microsoft has said that Entourage X will do the same. Unfortunately, this book was finished before Palm Computing released its updated software, called *conduits,* which Entourage needs to transfer information from the desktop back and forth to the Palm handheld. As with Office itself, the Palm conduits needed to be rewritten for Mac OS X, and at press time the new conduits had not been completed. As a result, Microsoft had not yet released an update to Entourage enabling Palm support. Microsoft has confirmed that they do indeed intend to support Palm synchronization in Entourage X, with a free upgrade that will be downloadable from the Mactopia Web site (*www.mactopia.com*). You can check to see if the update is available from within Entourage by choosing Help, Downloads And Updates.

When the update is available, I will write instructions for synchronizing Entourage to your Palm handheld and you will be able to find those instructions on my Web site (*www.negrino.com*). Look for the Books link, and then find this book in the list. There will be a link to the synchronization information.

> **note** Entourage does not synchronize with devices that use Microsoft's Pocket PC platform, and Microsoft has not announced any plans to support Pocket PC handhelds with Entourage X. As this book goes to press, the only solution is a product from Information Appliance Associates (*www.pocketmac.net*), called PocketMac Pro, which is in beta testing and will offer Pocket PC support for Entourage.

Using Entourage Contacts with Your iPod

The Apple iPod is primarily a stylish portable music player with a large capacity; as of press time, there were two different models of iPod that had 5-GB or 10-GB internal hard disks, so you can carry 1,000 or 2,000 MP3 songs in your pocket. In March 2002 Apple made the iPod more useful when it announced a firmware update for the unit that allows the iPod to accept and display contact files in vCard format. This enables you to bring your contacts along with your music, which is surprisingly handy, as you don't need to lug around multiple portable units for music and contacts. Apple also released an application that will extract contacts from Entourage and write them out to the iPod's internal hard disk as vCards. Unlike Entourage's forthcoming Palm synchronization feature, data from Entourage that goes into your iPod has taken a one-way trip; there's no way to make changes on the iPod and synchronize them back to Entourage.

Before you can transfer Entourage contacts to your iPod, you'll need to do some preparation. First, you'll need to update the firmware in your iPod to version 1.1 or later, and you'll also need to update your copy of iTunes 2, Apple's music player that imports music CDs to MP3 files, creates playlists, burns music CDs, and synchronizes music with the iPod. Download the latest iPod firmware update from *www.apple.com/ipod* and install it, according to its included instructions, to your iPod. Then, from Apple's iTunes 2 site, *www.apple.com/itunes,* download the latest version and install it, too.

> **note** It is not strictly necessary to get the latest version of iTunes 2, but because it is used to control how the iPod appears on the Mac OS X desktop, it's a good idea to make sure that you're up-to-date with all pieces of the process.

From the iPod site, you must also download the Entourage To iPod application, which will do the work of extracting contacts from Entourage and copying them to your iPod's hard disk. This application uses AppleScript to do its work, so if you have problems finding the Entourage To iPod application, look for a link that refers to AppleScripts that make Entourage work with the iPod.

> **tip** The Entourage To iPod application is written using the free AppleScript Studio, which makes it possible for you to modify the program and change the information it takes from Entourage and sends to the iPod. For more information about AppleScript Studio, see "Where to Learn More," page 556.

Once you're sure that you're running the latest versions of iTunes 2 and the iPod firmware, follow these steps to transfer your contacts:

1 Launch iTunes 2, and then connect your iPod to your Macintosh with the FireWire cable. As usual, iTunes will automatically synchronize your music with the iPod. If necessary, wait until this process is complete; you'll know because iTunes 2 will report iPod Update Is Complete at the top of its window.

2 In the Playlists column of iTunes 2, select your iPod, and then, in the lower right corner of the iTunes 2 window, click the iPod button, as shown here:

└ iPod Preferences

3 In the resulting iPod Preferences dialog, select Enable FireWire Disk Use. You'll get an alert dialog informing you that FireWire disk mode will require you to manually unmount the iPod from your desktop after each use; click

Chapter 22: Organizing and Sharing Entourage Data

OK, and then OK again to exit the iPod Preferences dialog. Your iPod will appear on the desktop as if it were a hard disk (as indeed it is).

4   If it isn't already open, launch Entourage. If you have multiple Entourage identities, switch to the identity that contains the contacts that you wish to import.

5   Switch to the Finder, and launch the Entourage To iPod application that you previously downloaded. As you can see in Figure 22-8, it's a simple program, with only two options.

This application will import contact information from Microsoft Entourage into your iPod.

Quit   Import

Figure 22-8.   Your only choices with the Entourage To iPod application are to import or not.

> **note**   When you launch the Entourage To iPod application, it automatically hides all of the other visible applications, including Finder windows.

6   Click Import. A sheet appears asking you to select the iPod that you wish to update with contacts. This is because it is theoretically possible to have more than one iPod connected to your computer at once. In this unlikely event, choose the iPod you want; otherwise the only one connected will be already selected.

7   Click Select. If this is the first time that you have copied contacts to your iPod, skip to step 8. If you have previously sent contacts to the iPod, a sheet will appear letting you know that, and when the contacts file was created, as shown here:

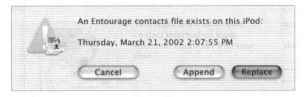

An Entourage contacts file exists on this iPod:

Thursday, March 21, 2002 2:07:55 PM

Cancel   Append   Replace

Choose Append to add the contacts in your Entourage file to the existing file or Replace to erase the old contact information from the iPod and replace it with a new file.

Chapter 22

Part 3: Entourage

You can use Append to add the contacts from more than one Entourage identity to your iPod.

8 Choose how you want your contacts to be listed, as shown here, and then click Select:

9 A progress sheet will appear. When the process is done, the progress sheet will be replaced by another sheet informing you that the contacts file has been updated. Click Done, which will close the Entourage To iPod application.

10 In the Finder, select the iPod's icon, then choose File, Eject, which unmounts the iPod from your desktop. Disconnect the FireWire cable from your iPod. When the iPod restarts, choose Contacts from the iPod's main menu to view and browse your contacts.

note Entourage supports pictures as part of its vCards; these pictures will *not* be transferred to your iPod.

Chapter 23

Extending Entourage with AppleScript

Microsoft Entourage X is an exceptionally capable e-mail and PIM program, but even the best program doesn't always do everything that you want it to. Fortunately, there is a way to *make* Entourage do practically anything that you want it to, by using AppleScript, the systemwide scripting language built in to Mac OS X.

In this chapter, you'll learn about Entourage's support for AppleScript; see how to use AppleScript to extend Entourage's abilities; learn how to find, install, and use AppleScripts in Entourage; and find out where to learn how to create your own AppleScripts.

About Entourage's AppleScript Support

Of all the Microsoft Office v. X programs, Entourage has by far the most extensive support for AppleScript. But paradoxically, it also has the worst support for AppleScript. How can this be? It's because of the difference between a scriptable application and a recordable application. A *scriptable* application is one that exposes most or all of its inner workings to the AppleScript language, so that AppleScript programmers can use AppleScript to tell the application to do a wide variety of things. A *recordable* application allows the user to turn on AppleScript recording (via the Script Editor application that comes with Mac OS X), perform a series of actions, and then save those actions as an AppleScript that can later be played back. If you have used the macro recorder in Microsoft Word X or Microsoft Excel X, you've already seen an example of recordability. (However, the macro recorder uses Visual Basic for Applications, the *other* scripting language that Word, Excel, and Microsoft PowerPoint X support but that Entourage does not.)

> For more information about automating Word, see Chapter 16, "Automating Word with Macros and AppleScripts." For information about automating Excel, see Chapter 33, "Customizing and Automating Excel."

Entourage is an exceptionally *scriptable* application; it has an extensive AppleScript *dictionary,* which defines the AppleScript commands that the application will understand. Dictionaries also define all the *objects* that programmers can manipulate with AppleScript commands. Objects can be all sorts of things within Entourage, such as windows, contact records, individual fields, e-mail account setups, calendar events, and so on. Because Entourage is so scriptable, programmers can write scripts to extend Entourage's capabilities in many ways, enabling the program to perform actions that it otherwise could not. For example, there's no way within Entourage to duplicate a calendar event. But you can easily download and install a script that will do just that.

Entourage, however, is not especially *recordable*. Its support for recording AppleScripts is limited to fairly simple things like resizing and closing windows. That can be useful in some special cases—for example, I recorded an AppleScript for Entourage to automatically resize windows so that they were uniform when I captured the screen shots for this book—but for the most part AppleScript recording in Entourage isn't terribly useful. It's a bit frustrating that Entourage has all this AppleScript power available to it, but that power is locked away from the average user who isn't a programmer.

> **note** Scripts that were originally written for Entourage 2001 often, but not always, will work in Entourage X. The best way to tell if a given script will work is to try it. When these older scripts don't work, it's usually because the scripts rely on a scripting addition that hasn't been updated for Mac OS X. A *scripting addition* is a special file that has its own dictionary of commands, which are added to AppleScript's built-in set of commands. Like many other programs, scripting additions need to be rewritten to work with Mac OS X.

Teaching AppleScript is beyond the scope of this book, so unfortunately the rest of this chapter won't show you how to write your own AppleScripts. But you will see how you can use the power of AppleScript within Entourage, even if you're not a programmer, by using scripts written by people who *are* programmers.

Finding and Installing Cool Scripts

You can download AppleScripts from many places on the Web, but there are a few sites that stand out.

- AppleScript Central (*www.applescriptcentral.com*) has a large collection of AppleScripts for both Entourage X and Entourage 2001 and many other programs. Updated frequently, this site should be your first stop when looking for useful AppleScripts for Entourage.

- Allen Watson's AppleScripts (*http://homepage.mac.com/allenwatson*) is maintained by Allen Watson, a major contributor to AppleScript Central, and he has written many of the Entourage scripts featured on that site. You can download more than 200 scripts that he's written for Entourage X and Entourage 2001.

- Mactopia (*www.mactopia.com*) is Microsoft's own Web site for all things Macintosh. Some AppleScripts are available on the Downloads page of the site. Choose Help, Downloads And Updates to open the Mactopia Downloads page in your Web browser, and then look for AppleScripts. Remember that scripts listed as working in Entourage 2001 will probably work fine in Entourage X.

Follow the links on any of these sites to download scripts to your hard disk that look useful to you, and then follow these steps to install them:

1 In the Finder, open the folder to which you downloaded the script.

2 Often (but not always) scripts that you download will be enclosed in a folder that includes both the script file and a short text file that explains more about the script, as shown in Figure 23-1. Open this folder.

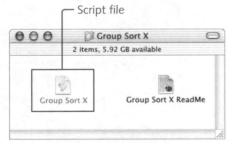

Figure 23-1. The script file is the only file that you need to copy into Entourage's Script Menu Items folder.

Part 3: Entourage

3 Drag the script file to the Users/*username*/Documents/Microsoft User Data/Entourage Script Menu Items folder.

> **tip** If you want to copy the script file into the Entourage Script Menu Items folder, rather than moving it, hold down the Option key as you drag.

4 Switch back to Entourage and make sure that the script appears in Entourage's Scripts menu.

Scripts menu

Entourage's Scripts menu is the menu furthest to the right on Entourage's menu bar. Instead of a name, it shows up on the menu bar as an icon that looks like a scroll.

If you have used Entourage 2001, you might notice that one difference between that program and Entourage X is that scripts appear immediately in Entourage X's Scripts menu; with Entourage 2001, you have to quit and relaunch the program to get new scripts to appear.

Troubleshooting

A script doesn't show up in Entourage's Scripts menu.

If a script doesn't appear in the Scripts menu, there are two possible reasons. First, the file might not be an AppleScript at all. You can tell by looking at its icon; if it doesn't look like one of the icons shown in Figure 23-2, it wasn't created by Script Editor, and Mac OS X will not recognize it as an AppleScript.

Secondly, the file must have been saved as a *compiled script*. Script Editor can save files in any of three ways:

● Application makes the script a double-clickable application icon that you can run from the Finder.

● Compiled Script saves the file in a form that AppleScript can run without further processing.

● Text saves the file as a standard text file, which can be opened by any program that can read text files (such as Microsoft Word or Text Edit).

My Script   My Script   My Script.txt

Figure 23-2. Script Editor creates three types of AppleScript files. From left to right, they are applications, compiled scripts, and text files.

Entourage will only recognize compiled scripts in the Entourage Script Menu Items folder. AppleScripts in the form of applications or text files will not show up in the Scripts menu.

Using the Scripts Menu

Not only does Entourage's Scripts menu appear as an icon rather than text, it is also the only menu in Entourage that can be customized. Unlike the other Office v. X applications, Entourage does not allow you to customize toolbars, shortcut keys, or menus, with the sole exception of the Scripts menu. You can add or remove scripts from the Scripts menu, and you can also assign shortcut keys to those scripts.

InsideOut

Organize your AppleScripts

If you add many AppleScripts to Entourage, the Scripts menu can easily grow to an unmanageable length. You can organize scripts within the Scripts menu by adding folders inside the Entourage Script Menu Items folder and then moving scripts into those folders. For example, if you have many scripts that affect messages, you could create a folder inside the Entourage Script Menu Items folder called Message Scripts, and move the messaging scripts into that folder. On Entourage's Scripts menu, you'll see a hierarchical menu named Message Scripts, as shown here:

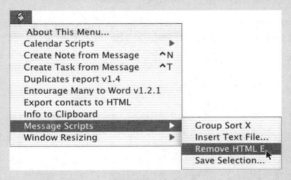

All the scripts that you run within Entourage will appear in the Scripts menu, and you run those scripts by choosing them from that menu. Typically, you'll need to select something in Entourage before you can run a script; for example, if you wanted to run a script that would export selected e-mail messages to a Word file, you would need to select those messages first. Similarly, to run a script that duplicates a calendar event, you would need to select the event first.

When an AppleScript can't run, you'll see an error dialog. In many cases the dialogs are technical and only list the line of code where the AppleScript failed. If you run an AppleScript in Entourage and receive this kind of error message, about all you can do is click the dialog's OK button, scratch your head, and try running the script again. Better-written AppleScripts will give you a more intelligible error message when you do something wrong. For example, if a script needs you to select a message before you run the script, and you forget to do so, a well-written script will pop up a dialog that will tell you to do the right thing, and then run the script again.

> For more information about interpreting AppleScript error dialogs, see "I get an error message when I run an AppleScript," page 398.

You can add a shortcut key to any of the scripts that you add to the Scripts menu. You do so in a very unusual fashion: by modifying the name of the script in the Finder. Follow these steps to add a shortcut key:

1 Open the Entourage Script Menu Items folder, and find the script to which you want to assign a shortcut key.

2 Select the script's icon, press Return, and then press the Right Arrow key to place the insertion point at the end of the script's name.

3 Type a backslash, followed by the keyboard modifier that you want to use, followed by the shortcut key, and then press Return. The modifiers are as follows:

- m or no modifier for Command
- s for Shift
- c for Control
- o for Option

For example, if you wanted to assign Command+Shift+D to a script, you would append \msD to the script's name. To assign Control+E, you would append \cE to the script's name. Strictly speaking, you don't have to capitalize the shortcut key, but it makes it easier to recognize and modify at a later time, if needed.

> **caution** Entourage does not check if you've chosen one of its built-in shortcut keys for a script shortcut key, nor does it check against other scripts' shortcut keys. If you accidentally duplicate a shortcut key combination, you might get unpredictable results.

Anatomy of a Script

The power of using AppleScript in Entourage is that it can add abilities to Entourage that it doesn't otherwise have. In this section, we'll break down a script line by line to show you how Entourage can be extended to do something new and useful with the help of a relatively short AppleScript. In this case, it's a script that automatically stores your replies to messages in the same folder as the originals. For example, if you've created a mail folder for a particular project, you've probably also made a rule that automatically routes incoming messages from people in the project to that folder. The trouble is that Entourage puts your replies to messages into the Sent Mail folder, not the project folder. It would be better if all of the correspondence for a project were in the same folder. Using the Mailing List Manager, Entourage can automatically file replies to mailing list messages in the original folder, but otherwise there's no way to do the job with Entourage's rules. AppleScript to the rescue! The script, File Reply in Original's Folder, uses Entourage's Links feature to identify replies, and is run by an outgoing rule. This script will work only with POP account messages, which are filed in local folders. It will not work with IMAP account messages, which are stored on the server.

> For more information about links, see "Linking Information," page 534. For more information about rules, see "Using Outgoing Mail Rules," page 476.

Figure 23-3 shows the entire script in the Script Editor window. If you want to create the script on your machine, you can type all of the text in the numbered steps on the next page into Script Editor, which you'll find in the Applications/AppleScript folder.

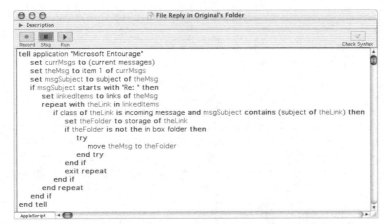

Figure 23-3. For this picture, the text in Script Editor has been made larger, so that it is easier to read on this printed page.

> **note** This script was written by, and provided courtesy of, Paul Berkowitz, one of the leading experts on AppleScript and Entourage. This and many other of Mr. Berkowitz's scripts can be downloaded from AppleScript Central (*www.applescriptcentral.com*), where he is a frequent and valued contributor.

To create and use this script, follow these steps:

1 Launch Script Editor from the Applications/AppleScript folder.

2 In the untitled Script Editor window, type the first line of the script:

```
tell application "Microsoft Entourage"
```

> **note** The lines of code shown here highlight key words of the AppleScript language in bold text to make the code easier to read. Type the lines without any bold or special formatting.

You need to let AppleScript know where to send the script's commands. This *tell* command points AppleScript to Entourage.

> **note** Your code won't automatically take on the formatting (which includes color coding) shown in Figure 23-3 on the preceding page until you check its syntax after entering all the code. If you try to check before completing the code entry, you'll receive syntax error messages, due to the lack of balanced *end tell*, *end if*, and *end repeat* statements for the *tell*, *if*, and *repeat with* statements.

3 Type these two lines:

```
set currMsgs to (current messages)
set theMsg to item 1 of currMsgs
```

In these two lines you are setting two variables. *Variables* are objects within a program that contain values. For example, you could have a variable called *myName* that has the value *Tom*. You can use variables in AppleScript to store values that will be updated or manipulated by other commands in the script. The two variables being set here are *currMsgs* and *theMsg*.

In these lines, *(current messages)* is the way to refer either to messages selected in a folder, or the message or messages being filtered by a rule. It's always a list, so the message being filtered by a rule is always *item 1* of that list. You first need to set the *currMsgs* variable to *(current messages)* to be able to evaluate it, and then you set the *theMsg* variable to *item 1* so that you can refer to the message again.

Chapter 23: Extending Entourage with AppleScript

4 Type this line:

```
set msgSubject to subject of theMsg
```

This line extracts the subject line of the message, and then puts that value into another variable, *msgSubject*.

5 Type this line:

```
if msgSubject starts with "Re: " then
```

The *if* command (it's one of a group of commands known as *conditionals*) runs a test to see if a condition is true. If the condition is met, then the script continues with the actions within the conditional; if not, the script skips to the next part of the script (following the next-to-last line, *end if*). The subject of a reply (*msgSubject*) will always start with *Re:* , and will contain the original message's subject. If the subject of this message doesn't begin with *Re:*
it's not a reply, so the test fails and the script ends without doing anything.

6 Type this line:

```
set linkedItems to links of theMsg
```

This first command within the conditional sets another variable, *linkedItems*, to include the links of the message that the script is working on.

7 Type this line:

```
repeat with theLink in linkedItems
```

The *repeat* command starts a *loop*, which lets you repeat an action a specified number of times, or until a particular condition is met. Links to the original message are automatically created by Entourage. But there may be other links—to the sender if it's a contact, or added manually by you. So you need a *repeat* loop to find links that are received messages, and to check the subject, both of which happens in the next line.

8 Type this long line as one long line; in this book we have to break it onto two lines, but you shouldn't:

```
if class of theLink is incoming message and msgSubject
        contains (subject of theLink) then
```

This line checks to make sure that *theLink* is an incoming message and that the variable *msgSubject* actually contains the subject of the linked message. If all's well, the loop continues with the following lines; if not, the code skips to the corresponding *end if* and executes the code from that point on.

9 Type this line:

```
set theFolder to storage of theLink
```

This line gets the folder location of the original message and puts that information into the variable *theFolder*. In this line, *storage* is a *property*; that is, information that Entourage knows about the message, and is the name of the folder the message is in.

10 Type this block of code, in multiple lines as shown:

```
if theFolder is not the in box folder then
try
move theMsg to theFolder
end try
end if
```

We don't want to store replies in the main Inbox, so these lines do another conditional test, which begins with the *if* statement, and ends with the *end if* statement. The conditional starts by posing the test "If the original message's folder is *not* the Inbox, then do the next statement." Within the conditional, the *try* command attempts to move the current message. This is actually a trick to make sure that the message isn't either an IMAP message or a Hotmail message; if it is, the *try* will fail, and the script will end.

11 Type these lines:

```
exit repeat
end if
end repeat
end if
end tell
```

These lines exit the *repeat with* loop, end the *if* conditional that was begun in step 5, and, with the *end tell* command, end the script.

12 Click the Check Syntax button in Script Editor. This will add the formatting to the script, including coloring different parts of the text and adding the indentations to make it easier to see how the conditionals and loops work. If you've made any typing errors, you might see incorrect coloring or receive syntax error messages. Correct your code, using Figure 23-3 on page 551 as a guide.

13 Choose File, Save. In the Save dialog, choose Compiled Script from the Format pop-up menu, and give the script the name **File Reply in Original's Folder**. Save the script in the Entourage Script Menu Items folder in the Users/*username*/Documents/Microsoft User Data folder.

14 Switch to Entourage, and choose Tools, Rules. In the Rules window, click the Outgoing tab, and then click New.

15 In the Edit Rule dialog, name the new rule **File Replies** or something similar.

Chapter 23: Extending Entourage with AppleScript

16 In the If section, you can leave the criterion set to the default, which is All Messages.

> **note** If you have other outgoing rules that might need to run on messages that meet certain criteria, you'll need to add a more specific criterion here, for example selecting *Subject* and *Starts with* in the pop-up menus, and typing **Re:** (include a space after *Re:*) in the text box. That way, non-replies could still be handled by other outgoing rules.

17 In the Then section, set the first pop-up menu to Run AppleScript. Click the Script button, and navigate to your File Reply in Original's Folder script in the Entourage Script Menu Items folder. Click Select. The Edit Rule dialog should look like the one shown in Figure 23-4.

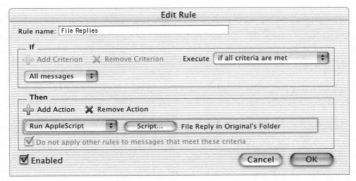

Figure 23-4. This outgoing rule triggers the File Reply in Original's Folder AppleScript.

18 Make sure the Enabled check box is selected, and then click OK.

19 In the Outgoing Rules window, drag the new rule above any other rules that move messages or run scripts, but lower than any rules that do other things like set categories. (Those types of rules allow other rules to run after them, and rules run in the order of top to bottom.)

> **caution** Rules that run AppleScripts do not allow other rules to run on messages that meet their criteria, so if you leave it as All Messages, it's the only outgoing rule that will run, even on non-replies. That's why you need to move rules that set categories higher than the rule you've created, so that the set category rules have a chance to run first.

Now you're all set up, and everything will take care of itself. Simply send out your replies and watch your sent messages immediately appear in the folders where the original messages are, except for replies to messages in your main Inbox, which will still appear in Sent Items.

Where to Learn More

If this chapter has whetted your appetite for more AppleScript information, it's not difficult to find more about scripting Entourage specifically, scripting other applications, or even scripting Mac OS X itself.

There are many Web sites devoted to AppleScript. Here are some of the best:

- Apple's main AppleScript page (*www.apple.com/applescript*) is the mothership of AppleScript information. You'll find links to tutorials, AppleScript mailing lists, AppleScript language reference guides, and of course, links to lots of scripts, including scripts for Apple's iPhoto and iTunes.

- AppleScript Studio (*www.apple.com/applescript/macosx/ascript_studio*) is one of the most recent, and exciting, additions to the AppleScript universe. It's a development tool that enables you to write full-fledged, double-clickable Mac OS X applications with AppleScript that sport all of the Aqua user interface elements.

- MacScripter.net (*www.macscripter.net*) is updated nearly every day with the latest news, information, links, and discussions about AppleScript.

- Mac.scripting.com (*http://mac.scripting.com*) is another news site that covers not only AppleScript news, but also news about other scripting languages and products for the Macintosh, such as Perl, Userland Frontier, JavaScript, REALbasic, PHP, and more.

- The AppleScript Sourcebook (*www.applescriptsourcebook.com*) isn't being updated, but still contains much valuable information about AppleScript.

The range of books explaining AppleScript is not as robust as with other programming languages, unfortunately. The following books are all valuable resources, but you might be able to glean much of their information from online sources.

- *AppleScript for Applications: Visual QuickStart Guide*, by Ethan Wilde
- *AppleScript in a Nutshell: A Desktop Quick Reference*, by Bruce W. Perry
- *AppleScript for the Internet: Visual QuickStart Guide*, by Ethan Wilde

Part 4

Excel

Excel Essentials

Microsoft Excel X is an electronic spreadsheet application, perfect for calculating, organizing, and analyzing your data. When you open Excel, the empty worksheet you see is like an artist's blank canvas, opening worlds of possibilities. Behind the cells in the workbook, you'll find hidden power and complexity. Though it is relatively easy to do simple things with Excel—keep records, make simple calculations, do sums and averages—what is most interesting is the power lurking under the hood. You can do complex financial and scientific calculations, create striking charts, and prepare reports with complex formatting to best highlight your data and figures.

Excel is full of features that help you enter data quickly, move around efficiently, and format your results effectively. Some of these features have been around for years, but Excel X adds some essential new features to your toolbox, such as customizable keyboard shortcuts, so you can do common tasks more efficiently, and AutoRecover, to save your changes and protect your work. Whatever your analysis needs, from a simple expense report to a complex financial statement, Excel can do it all.

> For more information on customizing keyboard shortcuts in Excel X, see Chapter 33, "Customizing and Automating Excel." For more details on AutoRecover, see "Using AutoRecover," page 568.

Introducing Excel's Workspace

When you open a new Excel document, you see the default *workbook* displayed with the Sheet1 worksheet visible. A new workbook contains three *worksheets,* each of which can contain up to 256 columns and 65,536 rows. A worksheet is easily recognizable by its column and row headers and its grid lines. The grid lines represent the physical boundaries of the *cells,*

559

which contain numbers and formulas. Each cell is referenced by its *cell name*: these names are made up of a combination of the cell's column reference and its row reference. You can also assign your own names to cells. In Figure 24-1, cell A1 is selected—this is the cell found at the intersection of column A and row 1. The Name box at the left edge of the Formula Bar shows the reference of the selected cell, chart item, or drawing object or the name you have given to a cell or *range* of cells.

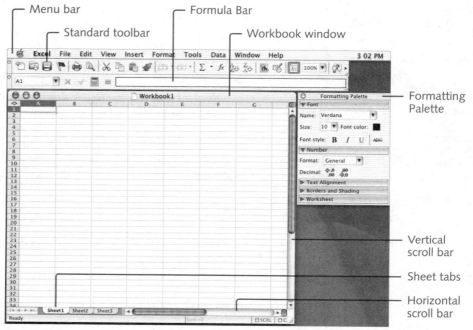

Figure 24-1. The standard blank Excel workbook includes a variety of tools to help you create your spreadsheet.

> **tip** You can also set up your own templates to use preformatted workbooks when you open new Excel files. For information about using templates, see Chapter 26, "Mastering Worksheet Formatting."

The standard Excel interface, as seen in Figure 24-1, contains several elements:

- **Menu bar.** This bar contains all of Excel's menus and their commands.

- **Standard toolbar.** This toolbar is one of many available in Excel. It contains buttons and menus that give you quick access to some of the most commonly used commands. Other toolbars can be displayed by choosing View, Toolbars and selecting the toolbar you want to show.

> **tip** **Show off your toolbars**
>
> You can quickly show or hide other toolbars by Control+clicking on a blank portion of any toolbar (if you have a mouse with more than one button, using the right mouse button is the same as Control+clicking in all the Office v. X applications). A pop-up menu will appear listing all of the toolbars available. The visible toolbars are marked with checks next to their names. Simply choose a toolbar to make it appear or disappear. If, when you Control+click, you instead get the Command Customization pop-up menu (recognize this menu by its Run Command menu choice), you've accidentally clicked on a button instead of the toolbar. Just try again; the easiest place to click is on one of the vertical separator bars that separate groups of buttons.

- **Formula Bar.** This is a special toolbar that you use to enter and edit formulas, data, and text in cells or charts. The Name box, at the left, shows the reference of the selected cell, or the first cell in a multiple selection, or the name of the selected chart or drawing object. This toolbar also contains the Calculator button; the calculator helps you create formulas easily.

> For more information on the Formula Bar and the calculator, see Chapter 27, "Working with Functions and Formulas."

- **Workbook window.** This window contains the active workbook. It has scroll bars at the right and bottom to navigate within the active worksheet and tabs at the bottom with the names of the worksheets it contains. You switch between the worksheets by clicking the tabs.

- **Formatting Palette.** This palette gives you quick access to most of the formatting functions in Excel. You can change font formatting (font name, size, style, color), number formatting for cells, text alignment (as well as orientation and text wrapping), borders and shading, and print margins and other print settings. If the Formatting Palette is not visible, choose View, Formatting Palette to display it, or click the Formatting Palette button on the Standard toolbar. To hide the Formatting Palette, click its close button. When the Formatting Palette is visible, it floats over your open workbook windows and is always available.

> **note** The Formatting Palette in Excel X (and also the ones in Word and PowerPoint—Entourage doesn't have a Formatting Palette) is just a specialized toolbar. Like all toolbars, it automatically becomes invisible if you switch to another application, to reduce screen clutter.

Working with Worksheets

The worksheet is where you do the vast majority of your work in Excel, so you'll need to know how to add and delete worksheets, and how to move smoothly around the entire Excel workspace. If you've used Excel at all, you probably know many of these techniques, but we'll try to show you some new ways of working with workbooks.

Adding and Deleting Worksheets

Although the default workbook contains three worksheets, you can add many more, each of which can be formatted differently and can contain different data, calculations, or charts. The tabs at the bottom of the window allow you to see how many worksheets are in your workbook, and their names; to move to a different worksheet, simply click one of these tabs.

You can insert a new worksheet into your workbook at any time by choosing Insert, Worksheet. New worksheets are added before the currently active worksheet in your workbook and are numbered sequentially. If, for example, you have three worksheets in your workbook and Sheet1 is the active worksheet when you insert a new worksheet, Excel will add a new worksheet, called Sheet4, before Sheet1. However, if you have already added and deleted worksheets in your workbook, the name of the new sheet will take this into account. So, if you have added two worksheets, and then deleted them, the next new worksheet you insert will be called Sheet6, rather than Sheet4.

> You can change the name of this new worksheet, and any other worksheet; see "Naming and Renaming Worksheets," page 569.

---

tip　**Use Control+click to add a new worksheet**

Another way to add a new worksheet is to hold down the Control key on your keyboard and click one of the worksheet tabs. This will display a contextual menu, which allows you to insert a new worksheet and offers other functions. Contextual menus of this type are available in many areas of Excel and provide you quick access to some of the most common functions.

You can delete any of the worksheets in your workbook. Select the sheet you want to delete by clicking its name tab, and then choose Edit, Delete Sheet. You can also delete a worksheet by holding down the Control key and clicking the sheet tab. Select Delete from the resulting contextual menu to delete the worksheet.

---

caution　When you delete a worksheet, it is permanently removed from your workbook. You cannot undo this operation, so make sure you really want to delete it before doing so.

Navigating Worksheets and Workbooks

You already know how to get around Excel's workspace by scrolling and by using the arrow keys, as well as Page Up and Page Down. In the following sections we describe some other ways to get around.

Moving Around in a Workbook

If you have a lot of worksheets in your workbook, or if your workbook window is small, not all the sheet tabs for the different worksheets will be visible. Excel provides several ways for you to adjust the tab area at the bottom of the window.

The first way is to move the *tab split bar*. When you pass your pointer over the tab split bar, it changes to the double-arrowed split pointer, as shown in Figure 24-2. Drag the split bar to the right and the tab sheet display will become wider. You can then select a worksheet from one of the tabs.

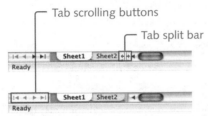

Figure 24-2. Here are some of Excel's workbook navigation tools—at the top, the tab split bar and, at the bottom, the tab scrolling buttons.

> **tip** To move quickly among worksheets in a workbook, use the keyboard shortcuts, such as Control+Page Up and Control+Page Down, which take you to the previous and next worksheets, respectively. For a full list of keyboard shortcuts for navigating worksheets and workbooks, see Table 24-1 on page 565.

If you have a large number of worksheets, the easiest way to display hidden tabs is by clicking the tab scrolling buttons to the left of the sheet tabs. You can use these to scroll through the sheet tab display. Click one of the single arrows, and the tab display will move one tab in that direction. Click one of the end scroll buttons, and the display will move to the first or last sheet. Scrolling through the tabs doesn't activate a different worksheet, though; to do this, you need to click a sheet tab.

> **tip** You can also easily select an active worksheet by holding down the Control key and clicking in the tab scroll button area. A contextual menu will appear with the names of all the worksheets in your workbook. Select a worksheet, and it will become active.

563

Moving Around the Worksheet

No matter how large or small your worksheet is, you will need to be able to move around it to enter data, edit formulas, and change formatting. Although you can simply scroll vertically or horizontally to find the cells you want to work on, Excel has many shortcuts to get you where you need to go as quickly as possible. In some worksheets you might have hundreds of columns and thousands of rows of data; moving to the right place quickly will save you a lot of time.

To activate a cell, you must *select* it, or click it. An *active cell* is the one where you can enter data or formulas in the Formula Bar. You can always tell which cell is active (or which cells, if several are selected) by looking in the Name box. In Figure 24-3 the active cell is C4, which means it is the cell at the intersection of column C and row 4.

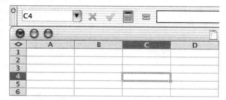

Figure 24-3.   The active cell is shown by its reference in the Name box and by the high-lighting around the cell.

To move to a new adjacent cell, press one of the arrow keys on the keyboard. For example, if you press the Left Arrow key in the worksheet shown in Figure 24-3, the active cell will become B4; if you press the Up Arrow key, the active cell will become C3.

There are two easy ways to go quickly to the active cell in your spreadsheet, depending on your working style. If you're keyboard-oriented, simply press Control+Delete on your keyboard. If you prefer using the mouse, click in the Name box, and then press Return on your keyboard. In both cases, your worksheet will move instantly to the active cell. In addition, Excel provides a full range of keyboard shortcuts for moving around in worksheets and workbooks, as Table 24-1 shows.

Depending on your keyboard, some shortcut keys might not be available. The Apple USB keyboard included with some Macintoshes is a streamlined keyboard that does not have all of the keys listed in the table. On PowerBook and iBook keyboards, you will need to press the Fn key to access such keys as Home, End, Page Up, and Page Down.

Table 24-1. Keyboard Shortcuts for Navigating Worksheets and Workbooks

Keyboard Shortcut	Action
Arrow keys	Moves one cell up, down, left, or right
Control+arrow keys	Moves to the edge of the current data region or to the beginning or end of a row or column if there is no data
Return	Moves down one cell
Shift+Return	Moves up one cell
Home	Moves to the beginning of a row
Control+Home	Moves to the beginning of the worksheet, cell A1
Control+End	Moves to the last cell in the data region of the worksheet (the cell at the intersection of the rightmost column containing data and the bottom-most row containing data)
Page Down	Moves down one screen
Page Up	Moves up one screen
Option+Page Down	Moves one screen to the right
Option+Page Up	Moves one screen to the left
Control+Page Down	Moves to the next sheet in the workbook
Control+Page Up	Moves to the previous sheet in the workbook
Control+Tab	Moves to the next workbook or window
Control+Shift+Tab	Moves to the previous workbook or window
F6	Moves to the next pane in a worksheet that has been split
Shift+F6	Moves to the previous pane in a worksheet that has been split
Control+Delete	Moves to the active cell
Control+G	Displays the Go To dialog
Command+F	Displays the Find dialog

InsideOut

Save your worksheet to find its final data cell

When using the Control+End keyboard shortcut, you will go to the last cell in the data region of your worksheet. In most cases, this is the bottom right cell of your data region. But Excel has a small problem with this if you have entered and then deleted data in cells. Say you have data in cells A1 to C12, but had entered data in cell E15, which you later deleted. Pressing Control+End will take you not to C12, the bottom right corner of your data region, but to E15. Because this cell once had data in it, Excel considers it part of the worksheet's data region. There is a simple workaround for this: save your workbook. You don't even need to close it. Excel will update its internal map of the data region. When you press Control+End, you will go to the real end of your data region.

Moving Worksheets

If you don't want a worksheet to stay in its location, you can click its tab and drag it to a new position in the workbook. Click the sheet tab, and start dragging it along the row of tabs to the new location. The pointer will change into a document icon, showing that you are moving an object. A triangle above the tab row will show you where the sheet is, and when you release the mouse button, the sheet will be placed in the new location.

You can easily move several worksheets simultaneously, as shown in the following procedure:

1 Click the tab for the first worksheet you wish to move.

2 Hold down the Shift key, and then click the tab for the last worksheet. The two worksheets, and any worksheets between them, will be selected, and the window's title bar will show that there are grouped worksheets.

3 Drag the worksheets to the new location. The pointer will change to show that you are moving multiple objects.

4 Release the mouse, and the worksheets will now be in their new locations. Figure 24-4 illustrates the process.

> **tip** You can also select two or more nonadjacent worksheets and move them. To do this, click the tab for the first sheet, hold down the Command key, and then click the other sheets you want to select. They will be grouped as in the earlier example. You can then move them wherever you want in your workbook.

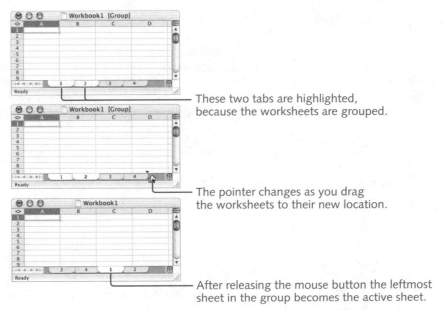

These two tabs are highlighted, because the worksheets are grouped.

The pointer changes as you drag the worksheets to their new location.

After releasing the mouse button the leftmost sheet in the group becomes the active sheet.

Figure 24-4. You can move adjacent worksheets in a workbook as a group.

There is another way to move worksheets that can be very useful if your workbook has many sheets in it. First select a worksheet by clicking its tab. Choose Edit, Move Or Copy Sheet to bring up the Move Or Copy dialog, as shown in Figure 24-5. Click on the sheet before which you want to move your worksheet, or click Move To End if you want to move it to the end of your workbook, and then click OK. As you can see in Figure 24-5, you can also create a copy of a worksheet or move it to another workbook. For information on creating a copy of a worksheet, see the next section.

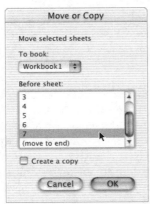

Figure 24-5. Use the Move Or Copy dialog to move worksheets within your workbook.

Copying Worksheets

You might want to copy a worksheet within your workbook so you can have the same formatting or data in a new sheet. To do this, select the worksheet by clicking its tab. Hold down the Option key, and drag the tab to the new location. The pointer will change to show you are moving an object, and a small plus sign will show that you are making a copy. When you release the mouse button, the worksheet you have moved is in the new location, and its name is followed by *(2)* showing that it is a copy, as shown in Figure 24-6.

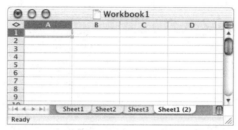

Figure 24-6.   You can copy a worksheet by Option+dragging its tab.

As you probably surmised from its name, you can also use the Move Or Copy dialog to copy a worksheet. Choose Edit, Move Or Copy Sheet to open the dialog, shown earlier in Figure 24-5. Select the sheet you want to copy and the location where you want to place the copy. Select the Create A Copy check box, and then click OK. The worksheet will be copied to the selected location.

> **caution**   Don't try to use the Copy command, or its keyboard shortcut Command+C, to copy a worksheet. Even though you select a worksheet by clicking its tab, there is always at least one cell selected within the worksheet. If you use the Copy command, the selected cell, not the selected sheet, will be copied.

newfeature!
Using AutoRecover

One of the most useful new features in Excel X is the AutoRecover feature, which has existed in Word for some time. It saves your work in the background, in invisible work files, so you can recover your work in the event of a crash or power failure. Although you should still save your work regularly, AutoRecover helps you by saving these work files automatically at the interval you select. If you have a crash or power failure, the next time you restart your Mac and open Excel it will open any unsaved files you might have been working on, with their changes, up until the last AutoRecover save.

To turn on AutoRecover, or to adjust the amount of time between saves, choose Excel, Preferences. Click the Save category, and then make sure the Save AutoRecover Info check box is selected. You can set the amount of time between saves by entering a number in the time box or by clicking one of the arrows to increase or decrease the amount of time between saves.

Getting the Most Out of Workbooks

Excel's use of workbooks to collate and organize worksheets allows you to have a wide variety of data—figures, text, charts, and so forth—in one file. Each new workbook contains three worksheets by default, but you can add and delete these worksheets as well as copy sheets from other workbooks. With Excel, you can put as many as 255 worksheets in a single workbook, though you will rarely need more than a dozen or so. This allows you not only to easily store related data in files, but also to link data from one worksheet to another within your workbook. You can have sales figures in one worksheet, averages in another, charts in a third, and projections in a fourth worksheet.

> **tip** It's a common—and useful—practice in workbooks that include multiple active worksheets to have the first worksheet serve as a summary sheet. The summary sheet contains data linked from the subsequent sheets.

Another advantage to multiple worksheets is the number of print layouts you can set up in a workbook. You can copy worksheets and create special printing layouts, retaining the data in standard row and column form on the original.

> **For more information on printing with Excel, see "Printing Worksheets," page 576.**

To set the number of sheets in a new workbook, select Excel, Preferences, click the General category, and then enter a number in the Sheets In New Workbook field. If you always use only one worksheet in your workbooks, set this value to one, but if you regularly find yourself adding sheets to your workbooks, you should set it to a higher number.

Naming and Renaming Worksheets

If you are the only person using your workbooks, you will know what each worksheet contains and how many sheets are in the workbook. But Excel files are often sent to other users. When setting up workbooks that you will be distributing, you should keep these users in mind and design worksheets so they can be easily understood. Here are some tips for creating worksheets that are easy to follow:

● Make sure your worksheet names are clear at a glance. Don't use cryptic names, like B02Q1 for First Quarter 2002 Budget, unless you are sure other users will understand them.

● Keep your names short. Excel allows you to use up to 31 characters to name your worksheets, but, if their names are this long, their tabs will take up most of the space in the sheet tab section at the bottom of the worksheet. Instead of a long name, like First Quarter 2002 Budget, use something like 1st Q 2002 Budget.

● Don't use too many worksheets if you can avoid it. It is easier for other users to find the information they need if it is presented on only a few worksheets; if they have to constantly scroll back and forth among the different worksheets they might get lost.

● If you have a lot of data to present, consider using multiple workbooks. This technique is especially useful if you have one workbook with data that changes, such as sales figures, and another that does not change, such as a price list. But remember that if you are distributing your workbooks to other users, you need to make sure they have all the workbooks with linked data, or they will not be able to effectively use your files.

As mentioned, you can use up to 31 characters to name your worksheets. By default, each worksheet in a new workbook, and each additional worksheet you add is named Sheet*N*, where *N* is a number. You can rename any worksheet by double-clicking a worksheet tab. The tab will be highlighted, and you can type a new name and press Return.

InsideOut

Watch how Excel names your worksheets

There are some quirks to the way Excel names new worksheets. If you open a new, default workbook, you will have three sheets: Sheet1, Sheet2, and Sheet3. Delete Sheet2, and, if you insert a new worksheet, it will be called Sheet4. But, if you delete Sheet2, save the file, close it, and reopen it, when you insert a new worksheet it will be called Sheet2.

Using Multiple Workbooks at Once

Though you can use one workbook with several worksheets, you can also use several workbooks at once. You might have workbooks with price lists, others with invoices, and still others with sales data. Or you might have some with certain financial formulas or simulations that you use occasionally. Whatever your uses, you can open many workbooks at once the same way you open files normally, either by double-clicking their icons or by choosing File, Open and selecting the workbooks to open.

When you have several files open in Excel, one of them will be in the front. You can choose other open workbooks by selecting in the Window menu, as shown in Figure 24-7. The bottom of this menu shows the files that are open—the checked file is the one at the front.

Figure 24-7. This Window menu shows two files open; the check mark before the file name Sales 2000.xls means that workbook is in the front.

You can view two or more files at the same time by choosing Window, Arrange. The dialog that appears offers several display options. If you choose Vertical, your windows will be displayed side by side. If you choose Horizontal, your windows will be displayed one above the other, as shown in Figure 24-8 on the next page. The choice between these two displays depends on the type of data and layout in your workbooks.

You can also choose to have your windows tiled—if you have more than two workbooks open, each workbook will be sized as equally as possible to fill your screen space as tiles would. If you choose Cascade, your windows will be overlapped so you can see the title bar of each window. This display style is useful if you need to switch between windows a lot.

You can hide the window of any open workbook by choosing Window, Hide. The window will no longer be displayed, and its name will be removed from the list at the bottom of the Window menu. To show the window again, choose Window, Unhide, and then select the workbook to unhide; it will then be displayed again.

No matter how your workbooks are displayed, there are some easy ways to move from one to the other. You can cycle forward through the open windows (those which are not hidden) by pressing Control+Tab, and you can cycle backward through the open windows by pressing Control+Shift+Tab.

For a complete table of keyboard shortcuts, see Table 24-1, "Keyboard Shortcuts for Navigating Worksheets and Workbooks," page 565.

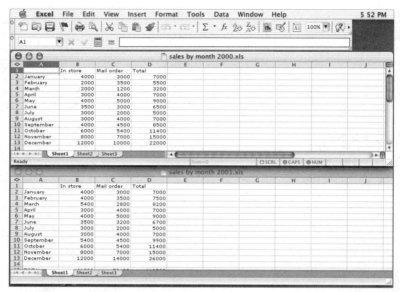

Figure 24-8. It's easier to compare two worksheets when you arrange their windows horizontally.

Getting Different Views

Excel allows you to view your worksheets in many ways. You can view one worksheet at a time, the basic view; you can view several worksheets in different windows; or you can split a worksheet into two panes, horizontally or vertically, so you can simultaneously see data in different areas of a worksheet.

Changing Window Views

To view several worksheets in different windows, choose Window, New Window. A new window will be displayed, initially the same as the current active window, and its title bar will have a *:2* at the end of the file's name. You can view a different worksheet in this window, or scroll to a different location, while keeping the original window open behind it.

To split a window into two panes, move your pointer over the split bar. The split bars are located above the vertical scroll bar and to the right of the horizontal scroll bar. The pointer will change, showing you that you can move this bar. Drag it to the location you want; you can then scroll either pane to view any section of the worksheet.

> **tip** To restore a split window to a single pane, you don't need to drag the split bar back to the edge of the window. Simply double-click anywhere on the split bar that separates the panes. It will return to the single view.

You can split a window into four panes by dragging the vertical split bar to one location and the horizontal split bar to another. However, when you do this, you will not be able to see four different sections on your worksheet. Although you can scroll each pane horizontally to different areas on your worksheet, you cannot scroll vertically in the same way. When scrolling horizontally, you can move each section of your window separately, but the side-by-side sections will always show the same rows on both sides of the vertical split.

If you split your window into four panes, you can move the two split bars around together. Simply move the pointer over the intersection between the split bars. It will change to a four-way arrow, as shown in Figure 24-9, and you can drag the split bar intersection wherever you want. If you want to restore a four-pane window to a single pane, double-click the intersection between the two split bars.

Figure 24-9. The four-way arrow cursor lets you change the panes in a four-pane window.

> **tip** You can easily switch among the different panes in your worksheet by pressing F6, to go to the next pane, or Shift+F6, to go to the previous pane.

Freezing Panes

When you have worksheets with many rows and columns, and your top row and leftmost column contain headers, it can become frustrating to scroll around and not be able to see the labels for your data. If you freeze the panes in your window, you will be able to move around in your data while retaining labels or headers. You can freeze panes horizontally, vertically, or both. If you want to freeze the top row of your worksheet, click in cell A2, and then choose Window, Freeze Panes. Row 1 will be frozen, and you will be able to vertically scroll the rest of your worksheet while still seeing the headers in the first row. If you want to freeze column A, click in cell B1, and then choose Window, Freeze Panes. Column A will be frozen, and you will be able to scroll through the rest of your data. You can also freeze rows and columns at the same time, if you want to keep a certain part of your worksheet visible. Click in the cell below and to the right of the row and column you want frozen, and then choose Window, Freeze Panes. Remember that you can only freeze a pane on the top or left or top left part of your worksheet. To unfreeze the panes, choose Window, Unfreeze Panes.

Using Custom Views

If you find yourself resizing panes often and switching between different views of your windows, you should save custom views of the windows you use most. Custom views save the attributes for your workbook: column widths, display options, window size, splits, and panes, as well as any hidden rows and columns or print settings you might have recorded. Custom views cover an entire workbook—not just one worksheet. So, if you have hidden any worksheets, the custom view will take this into account as well.

1 To save a new custom view, choose View, Custom Views. In the resulting Custom Views dialog, click the Add button.

2 Enter a name for your view, and decide whether you want to select the Print Settings and Hidden Rows, Columns And Filter Settings options.

3 Click OK, and your view will be saved. Now, whenever you want to select that view, choose View, Custom Views, and select your view from the list.

InsideOut

Record a macro to change views easily

Unfortunately, the only way to change views is to choose View, Custom Views, select a view, and click OK. This is three steps. If you find you change views often, it would certainly be more practical to be able to do this easily. There is a simple way to automate this procedure, though: record a macro that performs the three steps to change views, and apply a keyboard shortcut to it. With the press of a few keys you can switch views instantly. See Chapter 33, "Customizing and Automating Excel," for an example of a macro that will do this.

Sending Excel Documents via E-Mail

It is easy to send documents as attachments by e-mail to colleagues or friends with an e-mail program. Excel lets you save a few steps and do it with only a few clicks. With the document you want to send open, choose File, Send To, and then select Mail Recipient (As Attachment). Excel will tell Entourage X (or another e-mail client, if you have chosen a different program as your default mail program) to create a new e-mail message with the Excel file as an attachment. Simply enter the recipient's e-mail address, and you can send your file.

> **note** You can only send documents as attachments if your e-mail program is a native Mac OS X application, such as Entourage X. If you're still using an e-mail program that runs in the Classic environment, such as Microsoft Outlook Express 5, Eudora, or even Entourage 2001, you will have to save the Excel document, and then send it by switching to the e-mail program, creating a new message, and then attaching the file.

newfeature!
Flagging Workbooks for Follow-Up

Excel works hand in hand with Entourage X to help you manage your work. You can tell Excel to flag a workbook for follow-up, and Entourage will display a reminder at the date and time of your choice. This is a good way to make sure you update your workbooks or enter new data when needed. To do this, with the workbook for which you wish to be reminded open, click the Flag For Follow-Up button on the Standard toolbar. Set the date and time you want to be reminded in the dialog, and then click OK.

Flag For
Follow Up

When the time comes for your reminder, the new Office Notifications window will appear, showing you the flagged document's name, as shown in Figure 24-10. You can click Open Item, to open the document; Snooze, to choose an amount of time for the reminder to delay before reappearing; or Dismiss, to dismiss the reminder. You can also click the link containing the document's name to open it.

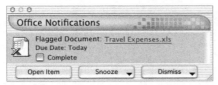

Figure 24-10.   This Office Notifications window reminds you to check a flagged Excel workbook.

> **tip**   **Make sure Office Notifications is active**
>
> Make sure you haven't turned off Office Notifications; if you have, you won't get a reminder. You can turn notifications on and off in Entourage X, on the Entourage menu. If you see a menu item called Turn On Office Notifications, this means they have been turned off. Select that menu item to turn them back on.

Printing Worksheets

Excel's vast range of functions for calculating and presenting data and information are nearly equaled by the wide variety of printing options available. You can choose from a number of formats, you can decide how much of a worksheet or workbook you want to print, the orientation of pages, the size of your margins, whether to use headers or footers, and much more. Excel's printing options let you create printed reports exactly the way you want to best present your data.

Setting Up Worksheets for Printing

Excel's Page Setup dialog lets you customize many formatting options for your workbook. Choose File, Page Setup to open this dialog, shown in Figure 24-11. The options in this dialog are discussed in the following sections.

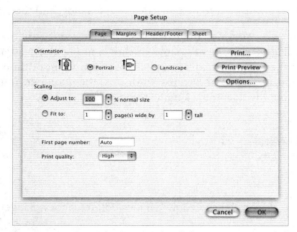

Figure 24-11. The Page tab of the Page Setup dialog includes orientation and scaling options.

Page Orientation and Scaling

Orientation tells the printer which way to print your page on the paper. You can choose to have your pages printed either in Portrait mode (vertically oriented), for data that covers a small number of columns and many rows, or in Landscape mode (horizontally oriented), for data that covers only a few rows but many columns. For complex worksheets, you might want to try both and see which presents your data best. You can check to see how your data is laid out in either orientation, before printing, by clicking the Print Preview button on the Standard toolbar.

> **tip** Each worksheet in a workbook can have its own printing orientation; you're not limited to having all worksheets set as portrait or all as landscape.

576

Scaling allows you to adjust the printing size in two ways. The first is by choosing a percentage from the Adjust To box. In most cases, you will use this to fit a worksheet onto one or several pages. The best way to use scaling is with the Print Preview button. Try a percentage, and then look at the preview. If your data will not fit on the number of pages you want to use, try another percentage, and check the preview again. An easier way to do this, however, is to use the Fit To box to select the number of pages you want to print. Enter a number of pages wide and pages tall, and your worksheet will be printed accordingly.

---

tip   **To make text more legible, use Adjust To**

The Fit To option won't make your data and text print any larger. If you only have a small amount of data, and tell Excel to print 2 pages wide by 2 pages tall, it will still only print one page. If your data is set in a small type size, and you want to make it more readable, use the Adjust To box, and increase the size to print your text larger.

You can set page numbering from this tab as well. By default, page numbering is set to Auto, but if you enter a number in the First Page Number box, numbering will begin at the number you choose. This is useful if you are printing several workbooks as part of a report, and you want to number the pages sequentially throughout the entire report.

Setting Margins

The Margins tab of the Page Setup dialog, shown in Figure 24-12, lets you choose the size of your page margins. Enter numbers, in inches, in the boxes for the different margins. The page shown in the middle of the margin boxes gives you a thumbnail preview of your data—shown as empty cells—with the margins you've set. This preview will change as you change the margins, giving you an idea how the page will look when printed.

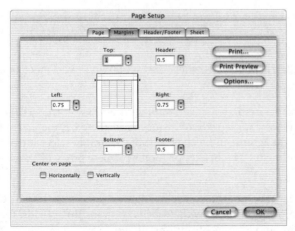

Figure 24-12.   The Margins tab of the Page Setup dialog allows you to set the blank space around the edge of the worksheet on the printed page.

Dealing with Headers and Footers

Excel lets you add headers and footers to any of your documents for printing. Unlike Word, however, Excel does not enable you to insert headers and footers and see them on-screen as you work. Headers and footers only show up when printing. Excel gives you many choices for the type of information you can use in headers and footers. In addition to text that you type yourself—your company name, the name of a report, and so forth—you can use variables, such as page numbers, dates, times, and worksheet names. There are two ways to access the Header/Footer tab shown in Figure 24-13: you can either choose this tab in the Page Setup dialog, or you can select View, Header And Footer.

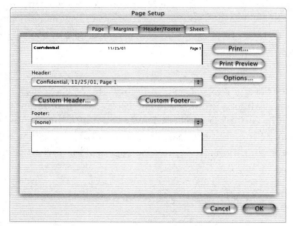

Figure 24-13. The Header/Footer tab is where you set up your worksheet's header and footer information.

Excel gives you a choice of more than a dozen built-in headers and footers. These use variables such as the name of your workbook, your name, the date, the page number, and so on. To use one of these built-in headers or footers, simply select it from the Header or Footer pop-up menu. The header or footer preview box will show you how they will appear.

You can make custom headers and footers by clicking the Custom Header or Custom Footer button. The customization window that opens contains three fields, for the Left, Center, and Right sections, and a series of buttons, as shown in Figure 24-14. These buttons insert field codes, which correspond to variables, in the selected header or footer sections. Each of the buttons is described in the following list:

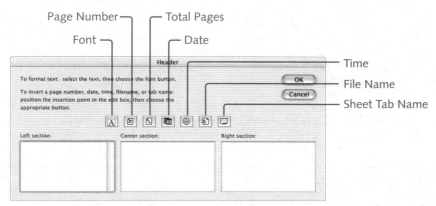

Figure 24-14.   The Header dialog lets you set headers and adjust text styles (the Footer dialog is similar).

- **Font.** If you select text in any of the header or footer sections, and then click this button, the Font dialog opens. Choose the font, style, and size from this dialog.

- **Page Number.** If you click this button, an &[Page] field code will be entered in the active header or footer section. This dynamic field code will print the page number of the current document. You can add arguments to this field code to start numbering at a page other than page 1; by using a plus (+) or minus (−) sign, plus additional numbers, you change the first number in the sequence. For example, to start numbering the first page as page 3, type **&[Page]+2**; to make page 4 print with the number 3, type **&[Page]−1**.

- **Total Pages.** Clicking this button inserts a field that displays the total number of pages being printed. Use this button if you want to have your header or footer read Page *x* of *xx*.

- **Date.** Clicking this button adds the current date to the header or footer.

- **Time.** Clicking this button adds the current time to the header or footer.

- **File Name.** Clicking this button adds the name of the file, that is, the name of the workbook you are printing. If you are printing several files sequentially, this information helps you identify each printout easily.

- **Sheet Tab Name.** Clicking this button adds the name of the worksheet being printed. This information is usually only useful when you are printing the name of the file as well; it can help you identify sections of long printouts.

---

tip   **Use ampersands carefully**

You probably noticed that each of the field codes used for headers and footers contains an ampersand (&). If you want to use the ampersand character in your header or footer—say for a company name, such as "Smith & Sons"—you must enter two ampersands; for example, you must type **Smith && Sons** for Excel to understand that the ampersand is not a field code mark but an ampersand character.

After you have created your custom header or footer, you can preview it by clicking the Print Preview button, or you can go ahead and print your document by clicking the Print button.

InsideOut

Save custom headers and footers in a template

Unfortunately, you cannot save custom headers and footers in the Header or Footer pop-up menus. When you create a custom header or footer, it is saved in your file, but if you choose one of the built-in headers or footers, your custom header or footer will be erased. Also, when you create a custom header, it will not appear in the custom footer list, and vice versa. The best way around this, if you make complex headers or footers and want to reuse them, is to save your document as a template. For more information on templates, see Chapter 26, "Mastering Worksheet Formatting." There is a workaround for saving your customizations to headers and footers: simply copy the text from each of the text boxes in the custom header or footer dialog (refer to Figure 24-14 on the preceding page), with all the field codes, and paste it into cells in your workbook or into another file, such as a Word document. You can then copy and reuse your headers and footers in any other Excel workbook.

Adjusting Page Breaks

Before printing your worksheets, you might want to adjust the page breaks to make sure that data is not split at inappropriate locations—it is impractical to have a totals row printed on the page following a list of data. When your worksheet contains more cells than can be printed on a single page, Excel adds page breaks automatically, sending the following data onto the next page. These page breaks are added both vertically and horizontally as needed.

You should first check where the page breaks fall. Choose View, Page Break Preview to switch the display of your workbook. You will see a reduced preview of your workbook, with dashed lines indicating the page breaks and with the names of the pages (Page 1, Page 2, etc.) shown over each page, as Figure 24-15 shows. To go back to normal display, choose View, Normal; you will notice that your page breaks are now shown by dashed lines.

Figure 24-15. This page break preview shows a worksheet that will be printed on three pages.

The easiest way to manipulate page breaks is to drag the dashed blue lines in the preview. Move the pointer over one of the lines, and it will change to a double arrow. Drag the page break to a new location. Note that page breaks can only occur on the borders of cells—you cannot place a page break in the middle of a row or column. Note that when you move a page break, other page breaks might also move with it. You should check the page break preview after moving page breaks to make sure that breaks later in your document are in the right places.

---

tip   **Edit in Page Break Preview mode**

When you are in Page Break Preview mode you can edit your data and layout just as you can in Normal view—the only difference is the reduced size of the display and the page break lines. If you need to change the sizes of some columns or rows to make them fit pages, you can do so in this mode. You can also move, cut, copy, and paste cells. You can even edit data in cells; the worksheet display is small, but when you click a cell its content is displayed in the Formula Bar as it is in Normal view.

When editing your data and laying out your worksheets, you can add page breaks manually at any location. Click in the cell below and to the right of the row and column where you want to start a new page. Choose Insert, Page Break. A page break will be inserted above and to the left of the active cell. The position of the pages will be shown by black dashed lines.

---

tip   **Restore default page breaks**

If you are in Page Break Preview mode and have changed some of the page breaks from the default page breaks, you can easily reset them all to their automatic locations. Press the Control key and click in any cell. In the contextual menu that is displayed, select Reset All Page Breaks, and all your page breaks will be removed and replaced with automatic page breaks.

Chapter 24

Specifying the Print Area

One of the most powerful printing features in Excel is the ability to precisely choose which area or areas you want to print. Though you can easily print an entire worksheet, with all of your data, information, and charts, you can also choose to print only those areas that you want to print. This feature is extremely flexible; you can choose to print large areas of your worksheet, individual rows or columns, or even just a few cells.

There are three ways to specify the print area. Each method has advantages and weaknesses, but which one you use depends on the complexity of the print area you wish to choose.

- The first way is to select the range of cells you want to print by clicking and dragging your pointer across the worksheet from the top left cell in the area you want to print to the bottom right. You can select multiple, nonadjacent areas on the same worksheet by selecting a first range of cells, and then holding down the Command key as you select the additional ranges. However, this method is best if you need to select only one cell range. After you have selected the cells you want to print, choose File, Print Area, Set Print Area. The area you have selected will become the print area. You can check this by choosing File, Print Preview.

For more information on the Print Preview function, see "Previewing the Print Job," page 584.

- The second way is to choose File, Page Setup, and then click the Sheet tab. Click the small button to the right of the Print Area box; the window will roll up, and you will see this box and your worksheet only. Click and drag in the worksheet to select a range of cells, and then click the button next to the Print Area box again. The window will roll down, and your print area will be selected. You can select multiple, nonadjacent areas on the same worksheet by selecting a first range of cells, and then selecting additional ranges while holding down the Command key.

> **tip** **Clear the print area selection**
>
> You can clear the print area at any time by choosing File, Print Area and then selecting Clear Print Area from the submenu. This erases all of your print area selections. If you are in Page Break Preview mode, you can Control+click anywhere in the worksheet and select Reset Print Area from the contextual menu to erase your selection. Clear Print Area and Reset Print Area do exactly the same thing.

- The third way to select a print area is to choose View, Page Break Preview and then select the area you want to include. Press the Control key and click in the selected cell range, and then choose Set Print Area from the contextual menu that is displayed. If you want to select multiple cell ranges with this method, before you bring up the contextual menu, press the Command key and select another cell range (or ranges). Then Control+click inside one of the areas and select Add To Print Area.

---

tip **View the print area**

No matter how complex the print area is in your worksheet, there is an easy way to view it with just one click. When you set a print area, it is named. (For more information on naming, see "Using Named Cell Ranges in Formulas," page 656.) Like any named cell range, the print area is quickly accessible by selecting its name from the Name box in the Formula Bar. Click the Name box pop-up menu, and select Print_Area. You will immediately move to the selected print area. If your print area contains nonadjacent cell ranges, they will all be selected and the last one (the one closest to the bottom right of your worksheet) will be displayed.

Exploring Other Printing Options

The Sheet tab of the Page Setup dialog gives you some other important options for printing your worksheets. Use these options to decide whether certain elements are printed, such as gridlines or headings, to choose the printing quality, and more. Table 24-2 describes the print options that aren't obvious.

Table 24-2. **Worksheet Printing Options**

Option	Action
Print Section	*(Note: by default, all of these Print options are turned off.)*
Black And White	Selecting this option prints your worksheet in black and white, even on a color printer.
Comments	Select an option from the pop-up menu: None will print no comments. At End Of Sheet will print comments at the end of your worksheet. As Displayed On Sheet will print comments at the location where they are inserted on your worksheet.
Page Order Section	
Down, Then Over	As shown in the graphic to the right after selecting this check box, the pages of your worksheet will be printed down starting at the top left, then down again from the next page section, and so on. This is the default page order.
Over, Then Down	As shown in the graphic to the right after selecting this check box, the pages of your worksheet will be printed across starting at the top left, then across again from the next page section, and so on.

Previewing the Print Job

After you have set the print area and laid out your worksheet for printing, you can preview your print job before printing it. This is a good idea for any long print job—Excel's print options are complex, and, if you do not preview your print job you might find yourself printing dozens of pages of a report before you discover that you needed to make one tiny formatting change.

To preview the print job, choose File, Print Preview. The Print Preview window will open, as shown in Figure 24-16. This window shows exactly how your worksheet will be printed. If you are printing more than one page, the first page will be displayed, and the arrows in the Print Preview toolbar will be activated to move from one page to another.

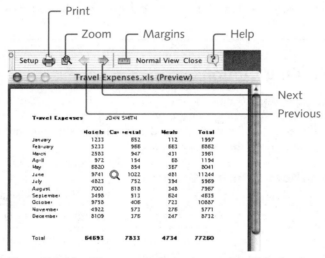

Figure 24-16. You can see how your page will look when printed, and make any necessary changes, with the Print Preview window and its toolbar.

When in the Print Preview window, the pointer changes to a magnifying glass, as you can see in Figure 24-16. Click anywhere in your preview, and the display will zoom in so you can get a closer look. You can then scroll around the window to check how your document will look when printed. Click again to zoom out. You can also zoom in and out by clicking the Zoom button on the Print Preview toolbar.

You can view your document's margins by clicking the Margins button on the Print Preview toolbar; this displays the margins in your document as dotted lines. You can adjust the margins by clicking one of the margin handles, on the edge of the document, and dragging it where you want. If you need to make any other changes to your print setup, click the Setup button on the Print Preview toolbar. This opens the Page Setup dialog, where you can make many changes to the setup and layout of your page.

> For more information on the Page Setup dialog, see "Setting Up Worksheets for Printing," page 576.

If you are satisfied with your print preview and want to print your document, click the Print button on the Print Preview toolbar. If not, you can click the Close button to close the Print Preview window and return to the previous view. If you were in Normal view before selecting File, Print Preview, the toolbar will contain a button labeled Page Break Preview—clicking this button takes you into Page Break Preview mode.

> For more information on Page Break Preview mode, see "Adjusting Page Breaks," page 580.

If you were in Page Break Preview mode before going into Print Preview mode, this button will be labeled Normal View. Clicking this button will return you to a normal worksheet view.

> **note** If your document contains charts or text in color, the print preview will only display these in color if a color printer has been selected. If your printer is black and white, you will only see black and white data and charts in the print preview. The preview shows you exactly how your document will print.

Printing the Worksheet

The first way to print your active worksheet quickly is to click the Print button on the Standard toolbar. Unlike many other Macintosh programs, Excel X does not use a Print dialog or screen that gives you a choice of various options for your printer. It merely prints all the data on the active worksheet, or, if you have selected part of the worksheet, the selected data. This method is good for quickly printing all or part of a worksheet to check data, but it offers you no control over any of the print options.

To have more control over your printing options, choose File, Print, or, if in Print Preview mode, click the Print button on the Print Preview toolbar. Make sure you have selected the appropriate printer from the Printer pop-up menu, if more than one printer is available.

The bottom part of the Print dialog consists of several sections, which are accessed through the Print Features pop-up menu that is initially labeled Copies & Pages. The sections that will be available to you on the pop-up menu depend on the printer driver associated with the printer you've chosen from the Printer pop-up menu. For example, if you are printing to a directly connected color inkjet printer, you may have sections labeled Color Options, Quality & Media, and so forth. If you have a PostScript printer, you'll have a section labeled Output Options. The description that follows is typical for a PostScript laser printer.

The Copies & Pages pane of the Print dialog is displayed first. Here you can choose the number of copies to print and indicate exactly what you want to print: a selection, active sheets, or the entire workbook. You can also choose to print only certain pages. If you select the Collated check box and print several copies of a multiple-page document, your printout will be collated. This means that each copy will be printed in order—that is, page 1, 2, 3, …—rather than printing all copies of page 1, then all copies of page 2, and so on.

If you select Layout from the Print Features pop-up menu, you can choose several layout options for your print job. You can choose the number of pages per sheet from another pop-up menu, and also choose a border to print around each page, if you wish.

If you select Output Options from the Print Features pop-up menu, you can choose to save your print job as a file. You have two choices: a PDF file, which can be opened with Adobe Acrobat, or a PostScript file, which can be opened by any program that can read this file format. PDF is a good format for files you will be sending to people who do not have Excel or for files with complex formatting that you will be sending to people to whom you do not want to send your original workbooks.

tip Because PDF is a native file format in Mac OS X, anyone running this operating system will be able to read PDF files using the Mac OS X Preview application, included with the OS.

Editing a Worksheet

Building a Microsoft Excel X worksheet requires entering, selecting, and editing data. You begin with empty cells and gradually create complex documents by entering figures, text, formulas, and functions. Excel has many powerful ways to do these common tasks, such as ways to quickly enter data into a group of cells, and features that complete series of data for you. In this chapter, you'll learn Excel's essential techniques for editing worksheets, and how to use Excel's many tools to make entering and formatting data easier.

Selecting Information

The basic way to select information in your worksheet's cells is to click a cell. This makes the cell *active*; when a cell is active, you can manipulate the cell and the information it contains in many ways. You can change the text or data, you can change the formatting, or you can copy or move the cell's data, formulas, or formatting.

There are four ways you can see that a cell is active; all four are shown in Figure 25-1 on the next page.

- The color border around the active cell or cells is the most obvious indicator that the cell or cells are selected. For the border's color, Excel uses the Highlight Color setting in System Preferences under General.

- The active cell is at the intersection of a row and a column; their headers are highlighted when any cells are selected. In Figure 25-1, row 4 and column B are highlighted.

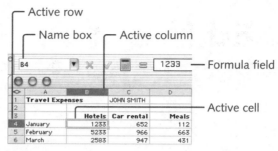

Figure 25-1. An active cell is indicated in four ways.

● The cell reference appears in the Name box; in the figure, it's B4.

● The cell's formula is shown in the Formula field. In this case, because the cell contains only a number, the "formula" is understood as =1233, or just 1233; but if the cell contained a formula involving calculation, the formula would appear in the Formula field, whereas the cell would show the value calculated by the formula.

Selecting a range of cells is just as easy as selecting a single cell. Click the first cell of the range you want to select and drag your pointer to the last cell. When you release your mouse button, the cell range will be selected and the first cell in the range will be the active cell. In range selections, the only indication of the selection is the highlighting of the cells and the row and column headers—the Name box shows the cell reference of the top left cell, and the Formula field shows the formula in that cell.

---

note When you select only one cell, it always becomes the active cell, but when you select several cells they do not all become active. Although you can select many cells at a time—you can even select an entire worksheet—only one cell can be active at one time.

---

tip **Select a specific cell**

If you need to select a specific cell, and you know its reference, you can just type this reference into the Name box and press Return. The cell will be selected, and the part of the worksheet visible in the window will immediately be shifted to display that cell.

If you have named a cell or a range of cells, you can easily activate it by selecting its name from the Name box pop-up menu. This menu shows all named cells and cell ranges, and also shows the print area, if you have set one, as Print_Area.

For more information on naming cells and cell ranges, see "Naming Cell Ranges," page 602. For more information on setting the print area, see "Specifying the Print Area," page 582.

You can select an entire row or column by clicking the row or column header. The header and the entire row or column is highlighted. Click a row or column header and drag the pointer to select multiple rows or columns. Table 25-1 shows how to select text, cells, and groups of cells.

Table 25-1. Selecting Text, Cells, Ranges, Rows, and Columns

Item	Selection Method
Text in a cell	Double-click the cell, and then select the text in the cell. You can edit the text directly in the cell or in the Formula Bar.
A single cell	Click the cell, or press the arrow keys to move to the cell.
A range of cells	Click the pointer in one corner of the range you want to select, and then drag across the cells.
All cells on a worksheet	Press Command+A; choose Edit, Select All; or click the diamond where the row and column headers meet.
Nonadjacent cells or cell ranges	Select the first cell or range of cells, and then press the Command key and select the other cells or ranges.
A large range of cells	Click the first cell in the range, press the Shift key, and click the last cell in the range. You can scroll to make the last cell visible.
An entire row	Click the row header.
An entire column	Click the column header.
Adjacent rows or columns	Click and drag across the row or column headers. Or select the first row or column, and then press the Shift key and select the last row or column.
Nonadjacent rows or columns	Select the first row or column, and then press the Command key and select the other rows or columns.
More or fewer cells than the active selection	Hold down Shift and click the last cell you want to include in the new selection. The rectangular range between the active cell and the cell you click becomes the new selection.

Selecting Cells That Contain Particular Contents

Although you can select cells manually in your worksheets, you can also use a different technique to select cells that contain particular contents: formulas, comments, constants, and so forth. Begin by selecting the part of your worksheet that contains the area in which you want to select special cells, as shown in Figure 25-2 on the next page.

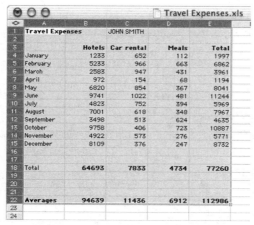

	Hotels	Car rental	Meals	Total
Travel Expenses	JOHN SMITH			
January	1233	652	112	1997
February	5233	966	663	6862
March	2583	947	431	3961
April	972	154	68	1194
May	6820	854	367	8041
June	9741	1022	481	11244
July	4823	752	394	5969
August	7001	618	348	7967
September	3498	513	624	4635
October	9758	406	723	10887
November	4922	573	276	5771
December	8109	376	247	8732
Total	64693	7833	4734	77260
Averages	94639	11436	6912	112986

Figure 25-2. The highlighted area shows the part of the worksheet that is selected.

Say you want to then select, from within this selection, all of the cells containing formulas to apply specific formatting to them. Choose Edit, Go To, and then click the Special button in the Go To dialog. The Go To Special dialog will appear, as shown here.

If you select Formulas, and then click OK, only the cells containing formulas will be selected, as shown in Figure 25-3. You can then apply formatting to those cells only. This is also a good way to look for cells with formulas in a worksheet you have not designed, or to look for many other special types of cells; study the available options in the Go To Special dialog.

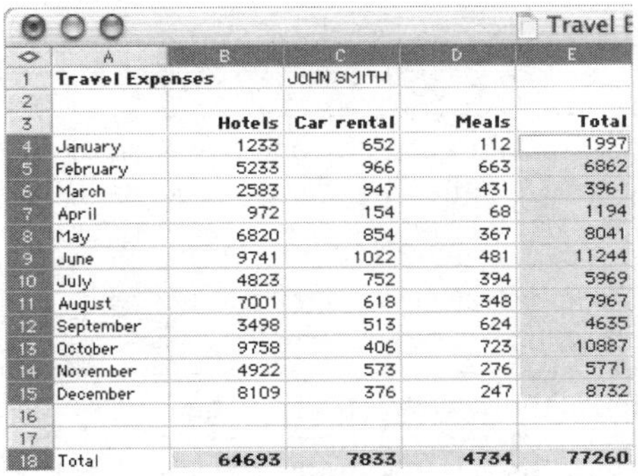

Figure 25-3. After making a selection in the Go To Special dialog, only the cells containing formulas are selected.

InsideOut

Select only visible cells

If you have hidden some of the cells in your worksheet, you can use the Go To Special dialog to select only the visible cells. This is useful when you want to copy data from your worksheet and paste it into another document, but don't want your hidden cells to be included. Just make your selection, then choose Edit, Go To, and click Special, and select Visible Cells. Excel will select only the visible cells in your selection—you won't notice the difference, because the unselected cells will remain hidden, but if you then copy these cells and paste them into another document you will see that the hidden cells were left behind. This tip only works when you're selecting cells; if you select columns or rows, the hidden areas will be copied anyway.

Using the Keyboard to Select Cells

You don't need to use your pointer to select cells—you can make many of your selections right from the keyboard, as explained in Table 25-2 on the next page. Using the keyboard can be much faster than using the mouse, especially when you want to extend a selection to an entire row or column.

note Depending on your keyboard, some of the shortcut keys listed in Table 25-2 might not be available. The Apple USB keyboard included with some Macintoshes does not have all of these keys, notably the Home, End, Page Up, and Page Down keys. On PowerBook and iBook keyboards, which share some key functions to save space, you will need to press the *fn* key to access Home, End, Page Up, and Page Down.

Table 25-2. Keyboard Shortcuts for Selecting Cells

Keyboard Shortcut	Action
Shift+arrow key	Extends the selection by one cell. (Use the Up Arrow key to extend up, the Down Arrow key to extend down, and so forth.)
Control+Shift+arrow key	Extends the selection to the last nonblank cell in the same column or row as the active cell.
Shift+Home	Extends the selection to the beginning of the row.
Control+Shift+Home	Extends the selection to the beginning of the worksheet.
Control+Shift+End	Extends the selection to the last cell used on the worksheet (lower right corner).
Control+Spacebar	Selects the entire column.
Shift+Spacebar	Selects the entire row.
Command+A	Selects the entire worksheet.
Shift+Delete	Selects only the active cell when multiple cells are selected.
Shift+Page Down	Extends the selection down one screen.
Shift+Page Up	Extends the selection up one screen.
Shift+F8	Adds another range of cells to the current selection. After selecting the first range, click Shift+F8 (*ADD* will appear in the status bar), and then select another range by dragging with the mouse. Instead of dragging with the mouse, you can use the arrow keys to move to the start of the new range you want to add, press F8 (*EXT* will appear in the status bar), and then use the arrow keys to highlight the next range.

Entering Information in Cells

Excel lets you enter data into cells in two ways—either by directly typing into the cells, or by selecting a cell and entering information into the Formula Bar. The first method is best when you are entering text or numbers only; the second is better when you have formulas, because you can more easily see the whole formula, especially if it is long one.

But Excel also gives you an easy way to enter data into ranges of cells. Say you have a worksheet with a list of months, from January to December, and want to enter data for each of these months in the following two columns, B and C. Select the cell range, as shown in Figure 25-4. You can see that the active cell is B1; this is where the first data you enter will be placed. Enter the data you want in this cell, and then press Tab. The active cell will move to the next cell in the range, C1. Enter data in this cell, and then press Tab again. Now, the active cell is B2—Excel moves the active cell through the cell range from left to right, and then down to the next row.

Figure 25-4. Select a cell range to enter data quickly by restricting the data to the highlighted cells.

---

tip **Change Excel's default cell moving behavior**

In the example of filling a cell range in Figure 25-4, you saw that the Tab key moves you across to the next column. To instead move down to the next cell in the same column, press Return instead of Tab. When Excel reaches the end of the cell range, it moves up to the first cell in the next column.

You can also change the direction the active cell moves after pressing Return. By default, the next cell down is set to become the active cell. But you can set it to be the next cell up, right, or left if you prefer. Choose Excel, Preferences, and select the Edit category. Choose the direction the selection will move after pressing Return by selecting the Move Selection After Return check box and then selecting the direction from the Direction pop-up menu. You can also turn this function off by clearing the check box—if you do, when you press Return the active cell will remain selected.

Keyboard Shortcuts for Entering Data

There are many keyboard shortcuts that can help you enter data more quickly and efficiently. Table 25-3 on the next page lists handy keyboard shortcuts for entering data.

Table 25-3. **Keyboard Shortcuts for Selecting and Editing Cells**

Keyboard Shortcut	Action
Return	Completes a cell entry and moves one cell down.
Control+Option+Return	Starts a new line in the same cell. The cell expands vertically to accommodate the additional text.
Shift+Return	Completes a cell entry and moves one cell up.
Tab	Completes a cell entry and moves one cell right.
Shift+Tab	Completes a cell entry and moves one cell left.
Esc	Cancels a cell entry.
Delete	Deletes cell contents.
Arrow keys	Moves one cell up, down, left, or right. When editing a cell's contents, the Right or Left Arrow key moves the insertion point one character or digit at a time.
Home	Moves to the beginning of the current row.
Control+D	Fills the active cell with the contents of the cell above it.
Control+R	Fills the active cell with the contents of the cell on the left.
Control+F3	Defines a name.
Control+Shift+F3	Creates names from row and column labels.
Command+Y	Repeats the last action.

Using AutoFill to Enter a Series

It's common to need to enter a list of months, or the days of the week, or a series of numbers from, say, 1 to 50. It can be very annoying to enter this data one cell at a time. Whether you want to enter dates, times, numbers, or text, AutoFill can help you enter series with just a couple of clicks, saving you a lot of time.

1 Enter the data you want in at least two neighboring cells. The example here shows January and February in the first two cells:

2 Select these two cells, and move the pointer to the handle at the bottom right corner of the selection, called the *fill handle*. The pointer changes to show you can drag the handle.

3 Click and drag the fill handle. As you do this, the series will be extended, and a ScreenTip will display the last entry in the series.

4 When the ScreenTip indicates the final value of the series that you want to enter, release the button, and the values will appear.

You can use AutoFill to enter all kinds of series, from dates to days of the week, from numbers to years. Table 25-4 on the next page shows the type of data you can enter using AutoFill.

Table 25-4. **AutoFill Extended Series**

Initial Selection (data separated by commas is in separate cells)	Extended Series (partial series examples shown)
Dates and Times	
9:00	10:00, 11:00, 12:00
Mon	Tue, Wed, Thu
Monday	Tuesday, Wednesday, Thursday
Jan	Feb, Mar, Apr
Jan, Apr	Jul, Oct, Jan
Jan-96, Apr-96	Jul-96, Oct-96, Jan-97
15-Jan, 15-Apr	15-Jul, 15-Oct, 15-Jan
1994, 1995	1996, 1997, 1998
Numbers and Variables	
text1, textA	text2, textA, text3, textA,…
1st Period	2nd Period, 3rd Period,…
Product 1	Product 2, Product 3,…
1, 2	3, 4, 5, 6,…
1, 3	5, 7, 9,…
100, 95	90, 85, 80,…

Advanced Series

AutoFill can extend many of the series you need based on pre-established lists. But there are ways to go even further with this function: if you use any kind of series often—data, text, dates, times, and so forth—you can create custom lists and save lots of time entering your data. You can see Excel's built-in series by choosing Excel, Preferences, and then selecting Custom Lists. You will then see four lists: two with days of the week, and two with months of the year.

You can add custom lists by following these steps:

1 Click the Add button, and then enter your list data.

2 Type each entry on one line, and then press Return to go to the next line.

3 After you have completed your list, click the Add button again, and the list will be shown in the Custom Lists box, as shown in Figure 25-5. Note that you cannot name your lists; the Custom Lists box shows the first few entries. You can click one of these lists to display all of its entries in the List Entries box.

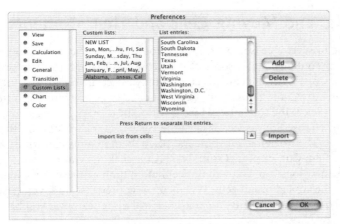

Figure 25-5. Use the Preferences dialog to add a custom AutoFill list.

If you already have your list in a worksheet, you can import it rather than retype it. Just click the Collapse Dialog button (the upward-pointing triangle) next to the Import List From Cells box. The Preferences dialog will roll up, giving you access to your worksheet. Select the cells containing your list, and then click the Expand Dialog button (the downward-pointing triangle) to restore the dialog. The selected cell range will appear in the Import List From Cells box. Click Import to create the new Custom List.

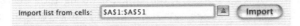

InsideOut

Create custom lists that contain only numbers in text format

Custom lists can contain either text or text and numbers, such as Part 1, Part 2, and so forth. If you want to create a custom list that contains only numbers, do the following: Select enough empty cells in your worksheet to hold the list. Choose Format, Cells and click the Number tab. In the Category box, click Text and click OK. Type your list of numbers in the formatted cells, and then create your list as shown in the preceding discussion.

Editing Cell Contents

Most people don't think about the layout of their worksheets when they start creating them. You might put a few numbers here, some labels there, and some totals down below. After a while, though, you will want to organize your information in a more coherent manner. Excel lets you copy, paste, cut, and move your cells and their content in many ways, from using menus to clicking and dragging with the mouse to using keyboard shortcuts.

Copying, Pasting, and Moving Cells and Their Contents

If you select one or several cells in a worksheet, you can copy, paste, or move either the cells and their contents or just some of their contents (data, formulas, formatting, comments, etc.). Copying and pasting is easy: simply select the cells you want to copy and press Command+C; or choose Edit, Copy; or click the Copy button on the Standard toolbar. Select the top left cell where you want to start pasting and press Command+V; or choose Edit, Paste; or click the Paste button. To cut cells, that is, to remove them from their original location and place them in a new location, select the cells and choose Edit, Cut; or press Command+X; or click the Cut button. Then paste the cells into the new location. You will notice that, in both of these cases, a marquee is active around the copied or cut cells. When copying, press Esc after you paste to remove this marquee; when cutting, the marquee will disappear after you have pasted the cells into a new location.

> **note** When you copy or cut data in this way, Excel copies all the cell's contents, including any formulas, formats, comments, or values. If the selected area contains hidden cells, these cells are also copied. For more information on hidden cells, see "Hiding and Unhiding Rows and Columns," page 606.

You can easily move cells to a new location by selecting the cells and dragging them to a different spot on your worksheet. Doing so is the same as cutting and pasting, but moving is more practical when you can see both the original location and the new location. Select the cells you want to move, and place the pointer on one of the borders of your selection. The pointer will change to a hand, as shown in Figure 25-6. Click and drag the selection wherever you want—as you drag it, the hand pointer will close into a fist, a gray border will appear around the new location as you move it, and a ScreenTip will show the new cell range. Release the mouse button, and the cells will be placed in the new location.

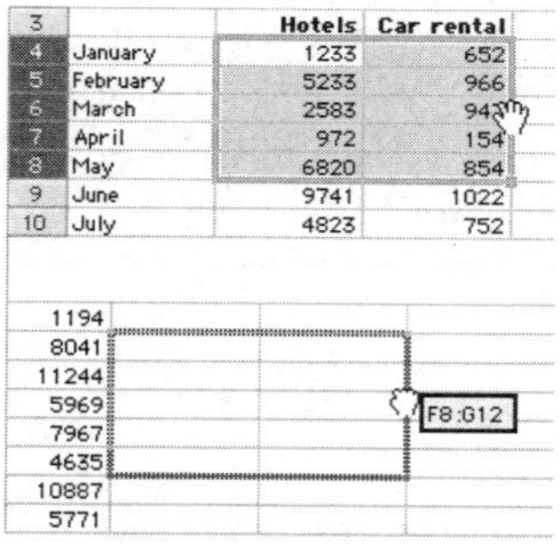

Figure 25-6. You can quickly move a block of cells by dragging them.

---

tip   **Use keyboard shortcuts while dragging cells**

If you drag cells to move them, you can use a few keyboard shortcuts to perform additional tasks. If you hold down the Option key while dragging cells, they will be copied to the new location, not moved. The original cells will remain unchanged. If you hold down the Shift key when dragging cells, you can insert them between existing cells. If you hold down the Shift and Option keys while dragging, you can copy the originals and insert them between existing cells. Finally, if you want to drag your cells to another worksheet, hold down the Command key, and drag your selection to a sheet tab. This displays the worksheet for this tab, and you can then drag your cells wherever you want on this sheet.

When you copy cells, everything they contain is copied: their text or data and their formulas, formatting, comments, and values. You can choose instead to paste some of these contents into a new location. This is useful if you want to copy a formula or formatting, for example, from one cell and paste it into another.

---

tip   **Decide when to move and when to cut**

Moving cells does the same thing as cutting and pasting them. So why should you use one rather than the other? Cutting and pasting is best when you are transferring data over long distances—from the beginning to the end of a worksheet, for example, or from one sheet to another. Moving is more practical when you are moving cells only a few rows or columns away, when you can see both the original location and the new location.

To paste only specific types of cell content, follow these steps:

1   Copy the cell or range of cells you want to paste.

2   Instead of pasting, press the Control key and click the top left cell where you want to begin pasting.

3   Select Paste Special from the contextual menu, and the Paste Special dialog will be displayed. This dialog, shown in Figure 25-7 on the next page, enables you to choose which of your cells' contents you paste.

4   Select one of the options in the Paste section, and then click OK to paste.

Table 25-5 on the next page lists the types of contents you can paste and describes the additional options available in the Paste Special dialog.

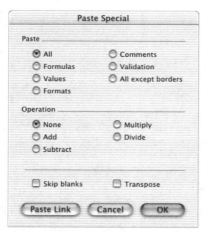

Figure 25-7.   You can choose to paste only specific cell contents with the Paste Special dialog.

Table 25-5. Paste Special Dialog Options

Option	Action
All	All the contents of the cells you have copied are pasted.
Formulas	Only the formulas from the cells you have copied are pasted. Note that when Excel pastes formulas, it changes the cell references they contain to relative values. If you copy the formula A1+A2 from cell A3, and then paste it into cell B3, the pasted formula will be B1+B2.
Values	Only the values displayed in the cells are pasted. If the cells contain a formula, the result of the formula is pasted. This is useful when you want to copy results and remove formulas at the same time.
Formats	Only the formats of the cells are pasted. Formats include the number formats; any text formatting such as font, style, and size; and any border, pattern, and color formatting.
Comments	Only the comments attached to the cells are pasted.
Validation	Only the validation rules that you have applied using the List Manager are pasted. For more on validation, see Chapter 28, "Working with Lists and Databases."
All Except Borders	All the contents of the cells are pasted, with the exception of any cell borders you have applied to the original cells.

Table 25-5. *(continued)*

Option	Action
Operation section	You can choose to add, subtract, multiply, or divide the contents of cells by the contents of other cells. If you copy a cell containing the value 2, Control+click a destination cell containing the value 4, select Paste Special, and then select Divide, the cell you paste in will contain the value 2 (4 divided by 2).
Skip Blanks	If you select Skip Blanks and some of the cells you copied were blank, the cells in the location you are pasting to that would normally be replaced with blank cells will keep their former values. Only the nonblank cell values will be pasted to the corresponding cells in the new location.
Transpose	If you select a vertical cell range, select Paste Special, and then click Transpose, your cells will be pasted horizontally. This is a useful feature if you need to change columns to rows and vice versa.
Paste Link	This button is only available if you have not chosen any of the preceding options. It will paste a link into the new location, that is, cell references for the cells you have copied. These cells will be updated if any of the data in your original cells changes.

InsideOut

Copy and paste data to several worksheets at once

You can copy data from one worksheet and paste it into several worksheets in your workbook at the same time. Open the worksheet, and select the data you want to copy and paste. To paste to a neighboring sequence of worksheets, press Shift and click the last worksheet in the range. To paste to one or more noncontiguous worksheets, press the Command key, and click each worksheet's sheet tab. This will *group* the selected worksheets, and their sheet tabs will be highlighted. Choose Edit, Fill, Across Worksheets. The Fill Across Worksheets dialog will enable you to choose whether to copy the contents, formats, or all. Click OK, and your data will be pasted into all the worksheets you have grouped, in the same cell ranges as the original data.

Deleting Cells and Clearing Cell Data

In Microsoft Word terminology, you *delete* data to remove it from a table cell. The equivalent Excel function is *clearing* a cell—the cell remains, but its contents are erased. The menu command to perform this action is Edit, Clear, Contents. Excel's menu choice of delete (Edit, Delete) is quite different. When you *delete* cells, the cells (and their contents and formatting) are removed from the worksheet. To remove the data only and not the cell itself, you must clear cells. Most of the time people want to clear cells and not delete cells, so Excel is set up to interpret pressing the Delete key as invoking the Edit, Clear, Contents command

If you select one or more cells, and then press Delete, Excel clears the contents of the cell, but leaves the formatting and comments. If you then put new data into the cell, it will be formatted according to the choices you made for the old data. If you want to control how much you clear from a cell, choose Edit, Clear, and then select All, Formats, Contents, or Comments. If you want to clear only the contents from your selection, it's usually quicker to skip the menu and press the Delete key. This will remove the cell data only.

In contrast, when you delete cells, they are removed from your worksheet. Choose Edit, Delete, and select one of the options in the Delete dialog. Because a worksheet can't have a "hole" where a cell used to be, you must choose to shift the remaining cells on the right to the left, to shift the remaining cells below upward, to delete the entire row, or to delete the entire column. When you shift cells, Excel moves all the cells to the right of or below your selection to replace the deleted cells. When you delete an entire row or column, Excel deletes the row(s) or column(s) corresponding to your selection, even if you have only selected one cell.

Naming Cell Ranges

Naming cells and cell ranges is a shortcut that enables you to both go to specific cells and cell ranges quickly and use simple names to refer to your cells in formulas. You can name any cell or cell range. Simply select the cell or cell range you want to name, type a name in the Name box on the Formula Bar, and press Return. Figure 25-8 shows a selected cell range and its corresponding name.

For more information on using names in formulas, see "Using Named Cell Ranges in Formulas," page 656. For more information on selecting named cell ranges, see "Selecting Information," page 587.

There are some limitations to naming cells and cell ranges:

● The first character of a name must be a letter or an underscore character (_). You can use any letters or numbers for the remainder of the name, as well as periods and underscores.

● You cannot name a cell range in the manner of a cell reference—you cannot use B4, or C3E9, for example.

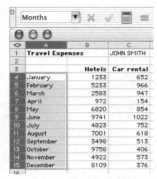

Figure 25-8. The range of cells containing January through December has been named Months in the Name box.

- You can use more than one word, but you cannot use spaces. So, if you want to name a range Year End Profits you should use underscores between the words: Year_End_Profits.

- Your name can contain up to 255 characters; but names this long will be unwieldy, especially if you are planning to use them later in formulas. If your name contains more than 253 characters, you will not be able to select it from the Name box.

- Names are not case sensitive. If you name one range Average and another AVERAGE, the more recent one will replace the former.

Naming Cell Ranges Automatically

If your worksheet has headers identifying your data, you can name cell ranges easily according to these headers. Select a cell range and its header, as shown in Figure 25-9. Choose Insert, Name, and select Create. A dialog will let you choose where the name will get its text from: the top row, left column, bottom row, or right column. In this example, you would click Top Row, and then OK. Excel will name your cell range according to this

	A	B	C
1	Travel Expenses		JOHN SMITH
2			
3		Hotels	Car rental
4	January	1233	652
5	February	5233	966
6	March	2583	947
7	April	972	154
8	May	6820	854
9	June	9741	1022
10	July	4823	752
11	August	7001	618
12	September	3498	513
13	October	9758	406
14	November	4922	573
15	December	8109	376

Figure 25-9. The highlighted cell range has been named Car_rental using its header as the name.

text; in this case, because the name has a space, it will be called Car_rental. If you select the name from the Name box, only the data will be selected—Excel applies the name to the entire range minus the top row, which you chose as the name.

Changing Name References

If you have named cell ranges, and deleted or inserted cells, rows, or columns, Excel automatically updates the references in your named ranges. But, if you want to include additional data in a named range, you need to do this manually. To add cells to a named range, follow these steps:

1 Choose Insert, Name, Define. The Define Name dialog displayed in Figure 25-10 shows a list of all named cell ranges and allows you to define your named ranges.

2 Select one of the names in the list. The Refers To box will show the current cell references for this name.

3 To change these references, click the Collapse Dialog button, and the dialog will roll up to let you access the worksheet.

4 Select the new cell range on your worksheet, and then click the triangle button again (or press Return). Click OK.

The name will now apply to the new cell range.

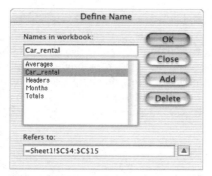

Figure 25-10. You can change references to a named cell range using the Define Name dialog.

Working with Rows and Columns

The basic building blocks of Excel worksheets are rows and columns—cells are only intersections between them. Rows and columns can be inserted, deleted, copied, pasted, and moved. You will probably do these operations often, because part of making efficient worksheets is arranging their data logically and coherently.

Inserting Rows and Columns

To insert a row in your spreadsheet, click on a cell or row below where you want the inserted row to be placed. Rows are always added above your selection. Choose Insert, Rows, and a new row will be inserted. If you want to insert several rows, select more than one cell or row. Excel inserts as many new rows as you have selected.

The same goes for columns, except that these are inserted to the left of your selection. To insert one column, click on a cell or column, and then choose Insert, Columns. To insert several columns, select more than one cell or column.

You can also insert rows and columns by holding down the Control key and clicking the header for a column or row. Select Insert from the contextual menu, shown in Figure 25-11, and a row will be inserted if you clicked on a row header, and a column will be inserted if you clicked on a column header. You can insert multiple rows or columns by selecting several rows or columns before Control+clicking.

Figure 25-11.   Choose Insert from this contextual menu to insert rows or columns.

Deleting Rows and Columns

To delete rows or columns, select the row or column you want to delete, and then choose Edit, Delete. You can also hold down the Control key and click on a row or column header, and select Delete from the contextual menu.

Copying, Pasting, and Moving Rows and Columns

When you copy and paste a row or column, you are only copying and pasting its contents into an existing row or column—you are not copying a row or column of cells and inserting the cells when pasting. Simply select the row or column by clicking its header. Copy the data, by pressing Command+C or choosing Edit, Copy, and then paste the data wherever you want. You can move rows and columns by cutting their data, and then pasting it elsewhere. However, this will leave a blank row or column in

Changing Rows to Columns, or Columns to Rows

There is an easy way to change the orientation of all or part of your worksheet. In Figure 25-12, in the table labeled *Before*, the row headers contain numbers and the column headers contain letters. To change the orientation of the table, while keeping all the data, formulas, and formatting in the same relative cells, follow these steps:

1. Select the cells you want to change, and choose Edit, Copy.
2. Click the cell where you want to start pasting (the top left cell of the new range).
3. Choose Edit, Paste Special, select the Transpose check box on the dialog, and click OK.

As Figure 25-12 shows, the cells still correspond to their headers, the table has just been rearranged.

	A	B	C	D	E	F	G	H	I	J	K	L	M
1	**Before**							**After pasting with Transpose**					
2		A	B	C	D	E			1	2	3	4	5
3	1	A1	B1	C1	D1	E1		A	A1	A2	A3	A4	A5
4	2	A2	B2	C2	D2	E2		B	B1	B2	B3	B4	B5
5	3	A3	B3	C3	D3	E3		C	C1	C2	C3	C4	C5
6	4	A4	B4	C4	D4	E4		D	D1	D2	D3	D4	D5
7	5	A5	B5	C5	D5	E5		E	E1	E2	E3	E4	E5

Figure 25-12. The Transpose command can quickly switch rows and columns and place the data in the correct cells.

the original location. If you want to remove the blank row or column, you need to delete it. See the previous section, "Deleting Rows and Columns," for details.

Sometimes you will want to cut or copy a column or row and insert it between another column or row (without overwriting the data that's already there). Cut or copy as usual, but instead of pasting, click where you want to insert the row or column, and select Insert, Cut Cells (or Copied Cells) from the menu. The selected column will move to the right to make room for the new column, or the selected row will move down to make room for the new row.

Hiding and Unhiding Rows and Columns

You might find that you have too much data on your worksheet to see clearly, or that you don't want other users to see certain rows or columns either on-screen or when printing. You can hide any of your rows and columns by selecting a row or column, and then choosing Format, Row, Hide (to hide a row) or Format, Column, Hide (to hide a column). You can determine whether a column or row is hidden by looking at the headers—if you hide column C, you will see column B and then column D. There is no other indication of hidden rows or columns. To display a hidden row or column, you select cells on both sides of it—in the preceding example, you would select cells in columns B and D. You don't need to select the entire columns; one cell on each side will do. Choose Format, Column, Unhide. The hidden column will be visible again.

> **tip**   **Unhide all hidden rows and columns**
>
> If you have hidden many rows and columns and want to display them all, you don't need to do so one row and one column at a time. Simply select your entire worksheet by pressing Command+A; choose Format, Row; and then select Unhide to display all your rows. Choose Format, Column, and then Unhide to display all your columns.

Finding and Replacing Information

Just as in Word, you can find and replace information in Excel. You can look through your worksheets and workbooks for specific data, formulas, or comments, and replace data. The Find dialog, shown in Figure 25-13 on the next page, is opened by pressing Command+F, or by choosing Edit, Find. Enter the data you are looking for, and then click Find Next. If you want to refine your search, you can choose several options in this dialog, as described in Table 25-6.

Table 25-6. Options for Finding Information

Option	Action
Search By Columns	Excel searches down the first column, then down the second column, and so on, through the worksheet.
Search By Rows	Excel searches across the first row, then the second row, and so on, through the worksheet.
Look In Formulas	Excel searches only in formulas.
Look In Values	Excel searches only in values, that is, data you have entered, or the results of formulas.
Look In Comments	Excel searches only in comments.
Match Case	Excel finds only data in the same case. For example, if you search for *Hotel*, the word *hotel* will not be found.
Find Entire Cells Only	Excel looks for the complete search string in one cell, with no other data. For example, if you look for *Hotel*, and select this option, the cell containing *Heartbreak Hotel* will not be found.

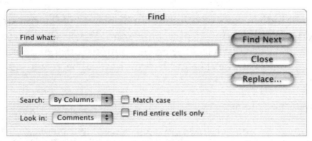

Figure 25-13. The Find dialog contains several options for finding the exact data you are looking for.

To replace information, click the Replace button in the Find dialog. The display changes to contain a Find What field and a Replace With field. There are fewer options when replacing data; the Look In pop-up menu is not available. You can also click Replace All, which replaces all instances of your search string with the replace string.

Checking Spelling

Excel provides you with a spelling checker, so you can easily correct any spelling errors you might have made when entering information. Excel's spelling checker works in the same way as the spelling checker in Word. Choose Tools, Spelling, and the Spelling dialog will open. Any words not in the spelling checker's dictionary will be flagged and presented to you in the Spelling dialog. You can respond to each item in the following ways:

- Click Ignore to skip the item once
- Click Ignore All to skip the item throughout the worksheet.
- Click Change to change the item to the word displayed in the Change To box.

> **note** The Change To field initially contains the first word in the Suggestions list. If that's not correct you can click another word in the Suggestions list, or simply type your correction directly in the Change To box.

- Click Change All to change all occurrences of the misspelled word to the word displayed in the Change To field.
- Click Add to add the flagged word to your custom dictionary.
- Click AutoCorrect to let Excel choose the word it thinks is best from those available in the Suggestions list.

The two options at the bottom of the Spelling dialog are Always Suggest, which ensures that Excel suggests words whenever possible, and Ignore UPPERCASE, which will cause Excel to ignore any words that are all in uppercase letters.

tip **Check spelling on all your worksheets at once**

When you check spelling with Excel, it only checks the active worksheet. You can easily check all of your worksheets together. Press the Control key, and click one of your sheet tabs. Choose Select All Sheets from the contextual menu; the worksheets will be *grouped*. Then, when you check spelling, Excel will check all of your worksheets, one after another. Make sure you ungroup your worksheets when you have finished—if you don't, you could inadvertently make changes to one sheet that are repeated through-out your entire workbook. To ungroup your worksheets, press the Control key, and click one of the sheet tabs. Select Ungroup Sheets, and only one worksheet will be active.

InsideOut

Use Word to modify your Excel custom dictionary

Although you can add words individually to your custom dictionary as you check spelling, Excel offers no way for you to edit this dictionary. You can, however, edit the custom dictionary using Word. Find the dictionary—its file path is shown in the Spelling dialog—and open it with Word. You can add as many words as you want, by typing them and pressing Return after each word. Save this dictionary, and you will now have more custom words that will not be flagged by the Excel spelling checker.

Mastering Worksheet Formatting

No matter what you use your worksheets for—whether you create complex financial reports, personal budgets, catalogs, or inventories—the information and data they contain is only part of the picture. Using worksheets efficiently calls for effective formatting, so you can find what you need at a glance, and so your data stands out and is easy to read when you print your worksheets. Though some of the formatting you apply to an Microsoft Excel worksheet affects the way it calculates data, other formatting only changes the way your data and information are displayed. In this chapter, you'll learn Excel's techniques for formatting worksheets, and how to make your data stand out both on-screen and on paper.

Formatting Cells

Excel allows you to format your cells, and the data and information they contain, at two levels. On the surface, you format the way the data looks—the fonts, styles, and sizes of the text and figures in the cells, as well as the alignment and orientation of information. But on another, deeper level, you can format cells to tell Excel what kind of information they contain: this can be text, numbers, currency values, percentages, dates, times, and more. This formatting is essential for Excel to calculate your data correctly, and, as in most of Excel's functions, you have a wide variety of choices.

Using the Format Painter

Format
Painter

Excel's Format Painter is a powerful tool that lets you copy formatting from cells and paste it into other cells. The Format Painter copies all of the formatting contained in a cell or range—and only formatting—it does not copy any data or information. To use the Format Painter, select the cell or range containing the formatting you want to copy. Click the Format Painter button on the Standard toolbar and select the cell or range to which you want to paste the formatting. All of the formatting is immediately applied to the target cell or range. If you change your mind and decide not to paste the formatting to other cells, press the Esc key to turn off the Format Painter.

---

tip   **Apply the Format Painter to multiple selections**

When you use the Format Painter to copy formatting, it turns off once you have copied the formatting to the target cell or range. This makes it a bit complicated to paste the formatting to other cells. To copy formatting to several cells or ranges, simply double-click the Format Painter button on the Standard toolbar, and then select the cell or range from which you are copying formatting. The Format Painter will stay on after you paste the formatting to the first cell or range, and you can paste it to other locations as many times as you like. To turn off the Format Painter, just click its button again, or press the Esc key.

Specifying Number Formats

Excel lets you specify number formats for any combination of cells or ranges. There are many number formats to choose from; your choices affect the way data is displayed and calculated. For simple worksheets, you might not need to change any number formatting. If you are using only basic numbers without special requirements, such as a precise number of decimal places, percentages, or currency symbols, you can probably use the default number format. But once you start creating more advanced worksheets, you will need to use number formats to ensure both correct calculations and display.

To apply a number format to a cell or range, select the cell or range, and then choose Format, Cells. The Format Cells dialog is displayed, as shown in Figure 26-1. If the Number tab is not active, click this tab. You can then choose from a dozen number formats. Many of these formats include options for you to choose from, such as the number of decimal places, the currency symbol, and more. Table 26-1 gives you an overview of what these formats do.

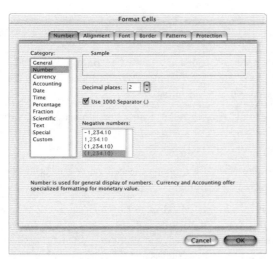

Figure 26-1. The Format Cells dialog allows you to format worksheet cells in an almost infinite variety of ways.

Table 26-1. **Excel's Number Formats**

Format	Result
General	The General format is the default number format for all new worksheets. Text is roman, and numbers are right-aligned.
Number	The Number format is used to display numbers. You can choose from several options to modify the way numbers are shown: you can set the number of decimal places, choose whether a comma is used to separate thousands, and choose how negative numbers are displayed.
Currency	The Currency format lets you choose the number of decimal places and how negative numbers are displayed, as in the Number format, but it also lets you choose a currency symbol or code for your figures. You can select None from the pop-up menu, if you don't want to specify a currency, or you can select one of dozens of currency symbols, from dollars to pounds, from yen to euros. If you scroll down the pop-up menu, you will find several dozen standard international currency codes.
Accounting	The Accounting format is similar to the Currency format—you choose a number of decimal places and select a currency symbol. But it also lines up your numbers by their decimal points and currency symbols. This is especially useful for worksheets that you will be printing.

(continued)

Table 26-1. *(continued)*

Format	Result
Date	The Date format lets you select one of 15 date formats, such as March 14, 2002, or 3/14/02, with many additional choices. Some Date formats also include times.
Time	The Time format lets you select from eight time formats, from 12-hour or 24-hour formats to hour:minute:second formats and more. Some Time formats also include dates.
Percentage	The Percentage format multiplies the cell value by 100 and displays the result with a % symbol.
Fraction	The Fraction format lets you display numbers as fractions and lets you select the denominator that will be used. With this format you can enter numbers in two ways: if you enter a fraction (such as 7/22), Excel converts this fraction to a decimal number for calculations. If you enter a decimal number, Excel converts it to a fraction for display. In both cases, the decimal number is retained for calculations. For example, if you enter a decimal number, such as .6648, and choose to round it to one digit by selecting Up To One Digit in the Number Format dialog, it will display in the cell as 2/3. But Excel remembers that this is .6648 for all of its calculations. Your number is only rounded off for display purposes.
Scientific	The Scientific format uses scientific notation for very large numbers. You select how many decimal places are used.
Text	The Text format treats numbers and formulas as text; the display shows exactly what is entered in the cell.
Special	The Special format lets you select one of four ZIP code, phone number, or Social Security number formats, for tracking list and database values.
Custom	The Custom format lets you make your own formats using Format Codes. For more information on Custom Formats, see "Creating Custom Number Formats," page 616.

The Formatting Palette gives you the quickest access to many cell formatting functions. You can use the pop-up menu in its Number section to choose between the 12 types of number formats. The Formatting Palette also has buttons for increasing or decreasing the number of decimal places displayed. The Formatting toolbar, preferred by some users because it takes up less screen space, offers a bit more flexibility and the most-used number formatting buttons, as shown in Figure 26-2.

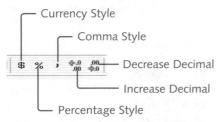

Currency Style
Comma Style
Decrease Decimal
Increase Decimal
Percentage Style

Figure 26-2. If you prefer the Euro Style over the Percentage Style, open the Preferences dialog and select Show Euro Tool from the Edit category.

Setting the Currency Symbol Excel Uses

If you want to change the currency symbol used in Excel (and in other Mac OS X programs), there's a systemwide setting you can use. Follow these steps:

1 From System Preferences on the Apple menu, click the icon for the International panel.

2 Click the Numbers tab.

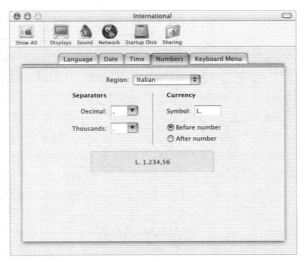

3 From the Region pop-up menu, choose a country or region.

4 Make a selection from the two pop-up menus in the Separators section.

5 If one is not already listed, enter a currency symbol.

If you're using a U.S. keyboard layout, and you wish to enter the Euro symbol, you'll find it by pressing Shift+Option+2.

6 You'll need to quit and restart Excel for the changes to take effect. But when you do, you'll see that applying the Currency number format to cells uses the currency you just set.

InsideOut

Pick the most efficient formatting method

As do all of the Microsoft Office v. X applications, Excel X gives you multiple ways to do things, in this case format one or more cells. Which method is the best? As usual, it depends on what you want to accomplish. The Formatting Palette is quickest for choosing a basic number format and increasing or decreasing decimal places, but it has little flexibility if you need to fine-tune your number formatting. For example, Excel includes many different options for date formatting and can display them all. But from the Formatting Palette, you can select only the default choice for each type of number format. The Formatting toolbar is little better. For the most control, you must use the Format Cells dialog, because it's your only means to the full range of Excel's formatting power. So if you want a quick format, use the Formatting Palette, or if you like it better, the Formatting toolbar. When you need the most control over your formatting, however, turn to the Format Cells dialog.

Creating Custom Number Formats

In addition to the 11 basic number formats you can choose, Excel lets you create your own custom number formats using Excel's special formatting codes. The best way to begin building a custom number format is to use an existing number format as a launching pad for your own format. To create a custom number format, follow these steps:

1 Select a cell or range, and then choose Format, Cells.

2 Click Custom at the bottom of the Category list. You will see a list of custom number formats, and, above this list, a sample of what the first cell in your selection will look like according to the number format selected in the Type box, as shown in Figure 26-3.

3 Type a number, and format it using the built-in format (from the Number tab of the Format Cells dialog) that is closest to the custom format you want to create.

4 Click the Custom category. The format you selected is highlighted in the Type list, which represents the code equivalent of the format that you want to modify.

5 Start typing in the Type box; don't worry about typing over what is there—it won't be deleted. Table 26-2 explains what codes are available and how to use them. The Sample box above the Type box will change as you add number format codes; you can see exactly what your codes do to the selected number.

6 When you have finished creating your custom number format, click OK and it will be saved at the bottom of the list of custom number formats.

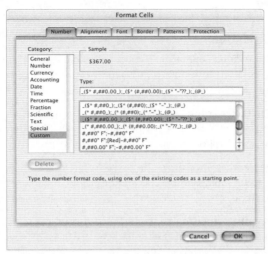

Figure 26-3. You choose custom number formats in the Format Cells dialog.

Table 26-2. **Custom Number Format Codes**

Format Code	Description
#	**Digit placeholder.** It does not display insignificant zeros, that is, zeros at the end of the decimal portion of a number. If a number has more digits to the right of the decimal point than there are number signs in the format, the number in the cell will be rounded. Example: if you enter **###.###**, the number 367 will be displayed as *367*, and the number 367.123456 will be displayed as *367.123*.
0	**Significant digit placeholder.** If a value lacks a digit in its place, this code will fill that place with a zero. This code is used to align numbers and to fit a specific number of decimal places. You can also use this to indicate leading zeros on numbers. Example: if you enter the code **00000**, the number 367 will be displayed as *00367*.
?	**Digit placeholder.** This code adds spaces for insignificant zeros on either side of the decimal point so that decimal points align. Example: if you enter **?????.00**, the number 367 will be displayed as __*367.00* (these two underscore characters represent the two blank spaces that are actually displayed in the cell).
.	**Decimal point.** This symbol determines how many digits (0 or #) appear to the right and left of the decimal point.

(continued)

Table 26-2. *(continued)*

Format Code	Description
Comma (,)	**Thousands separator.** The comma indicates that commas are to be used to separate thousands. Example: you would enter **###,###** to display 367000 as *367,000*.
"Text"	**Character string.** Any text you enter, in quotes, will be displayed exactly as entered. Example: if you enter **### "units"**, the number 367 will be displayed as *367 units*.
%	**Percentage indicator.** The percent sign indicates that the number is to be multiplied by 100 and displayed in percentage format. Example: if you enter **###%**, 367 will be displayed as *36700%*.
E- E+ e- e+	**Scientific notation characters.** If a format contains one 0 or # to the right of any of these characters, Excels displays the number in scientific notation and inserts E or e in the displayed value. The number of 0s or #s to the right of the E or e determines the number of digits in the exponent (if additional digits are necessary to express the number the format will be overridden). Use E- or e- to place a minus sign by negative exponents; use E+ or e+ to place a minus sign by negative exponents and a plus sign by positive exponents.
$ + - / ( ) *space*	**Formatting characters.** These symbols type these characters directly into the formatted result.
m, d, y, h, s	**Date and time placeholders.** These letters indicate, respectively, month, day, year, hour, second. These codes are used in date and time formats. Doubling, tripling, or even quadrupling the placeholders results in longer formats of the respective value. Example: entering **m/d/yy** would display a date such as *6/2/02*, but specifying **mmmm dd, yyyy** would display *June 02, 2002*.
[Black] [Blue] [Cyan] [Green] [Red] [Magenta] [Yellow] [White]	**Color indicator.** These eight colors within square brackets set the color for a section of the number format. Separate sections of a number format using a semicolon. The color code must be the first item in the section. Color coding is especially useful to highlight numbers if they meet certain conditions. For example, if you want a number to be shown in black if it is positive, and red if it is negative, you could use **$#,##0;[Red]$#,##0**.

Manage unfriendly custom number formatting

There is something unsettling—and un-Maclike—about Excel's procedure for creating a custom number format. The only way to create a new custom number format is to edit an existing one. There is no New button, and no Save button. So, when you edit a custom number format, you might worry about losing the built-in formats. Never fear, they cannot be deleted. Even if you click Delete, the built-in formats remain.

But there's another hurdle: understanding and correctly using the cryptic symbols needed to create custom number formats. Unfortunately, there is no easy way to do this—it certainly would be easier to select codes from a pop-up menu than type these confusing characters. So, if you need to create your own, the best way is to start with the existing custom number format that is closest to what you want and make changes to it.

Applying Borders and Shading

Borders and shading are excellent ways to highlight certain cells, rows, and columns on your worksheets. They allow you to make key cells and ranges stand out, and help users better understand the purpose of complex worksheets and forms. You can put borders around cells and ranges, and choose from a variety of different line styles. And you can add patterns and colors to cells to make them stand out even more.

tip **Check out the example templates**

To get a better idea of the way you can use borders and shading, check out some of the templates that Excel installs by default. To do this, choose File, Project Gallery, and select Excel Documents from the Show pop-up menu. If you click on the different categories to the left of the Project Gallery, you will see some of these templates. Only a few of these categories contain Excel workbooks; try clicking Business Forms, and then Fundraising. The Budget Worksheet is a good example of how you can use borders and shading to highlight different sections of a worksheet. Use this as inspiration.

Applying Borders

You can apply borders to a single cell or a range of cells. To do this, select the cell or cells, choose Format, Cells, and then click the Border tab, as shown in Figure 26-4 on the next page. This dialog has three sections: Presets, Line, and Border. The Presets section gives you three basic border options: None, which removes any borders you have applied, Outline, which applies borders to the outside edges of the selection, and Inside, which applies borders only to the gridlines between the selected cells. If you click both Outside and Inside, borders will be applied to all the gridlines around and between the selected cells. To clear the borders at any time, click None.

Chapter 26

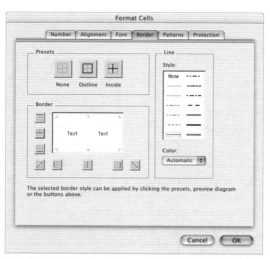

Figure 26-4. The Border tab of the Format Cells dialog lets you add borders to one or more cells.

The Border section gives you more power in applying borders; you can choose exactly which gridlines get borders. You can choose only the tops or bottoms, any or all of the cell's sides, or inner gridlines only; you can even choose diagonal borders that run through the selected cells. Click any combination of the border buttons (or click on borders directly in the preview box), and then view the preview box to see what your cells will look like. To clear the borders at any time, click None in the Presets section above. To remove a single border, click the corresponding border or border button a second time.

The Line section lets you choose what kind of lines your borders will use. There are 13 choices, plus None. After you have selected your borders from the Presets or Border sections, click a line style in the Style box, and, if you want a color other than black, choose a color from the Color pop-up menu. Then apply the new color and line type by selecting each border you want to change in the Border section.

To remove any borders from your cells, select the cells, choose Format, Cells, and then click the Border tab. Click the None button in the Presets section, and the borders will be erased.

Using the Border Drawing Toolbar

Although you can apply borders to your cells using the Format Cells dialog, there is a quicker way to do the same thing. Choose View, Toolbars and select Border Drawing. This toolbar, shown in Figure 26-5, floats over your worksheet, and you can use it to quickly apply borders without having to open the Format Cells dialog. With the toolbar visible, click the Draw Border button, and select the type of lines and color, if any, from the Line Style and Line Color pop-up menus. Drag the pencil icon over the cells you want to apply borders to, and the borders appear around your cells. If you want to have borders between the selected cells, toggle the Draw Border button to the Draw

Chapter 26

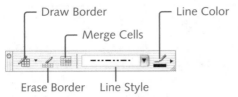

Figure 26-5. The Border Drawing toolbar makes it easy to apply borders to selected cells.

Border Grid button by clicking the Draw Border button and selecting the Draw Border Grid button from the submenu that appears. You can also click on individual borders to apply the selected border style to that segment only. To erase the borders from your cells, click the Erase Border button, and drag the eraser icon over the cells with borders.

Applying Shading

You can apply shading to a single cell or a range of cells. To do this, select the cell or cells, choose Format, Cells, and then click the Patterns tab. You can choose a color and a pattern for your cell shading. Click on the color you want to use in the color palette, and select a pattern and color from the Pattern pop-up menu. The Color selection sets the color for the cell background, and the Pattern color is the color of the pattern lines and dots. You can see how this looks in the Sample box on the right, as shown in Figure 26-6.

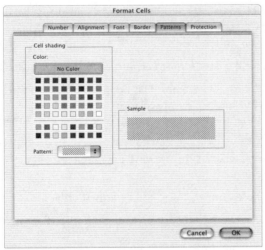

Figure 26-6. This setting of the Patterns dialog will apply a cross-hatch pattern.

> **note** Remember that if you choose color shading and patterns for your worksheets, and then print on a black and white printer, the result might not be what you expect. You should always print a test sheet in such cases to make sure your worksheet data and information remain readable.

A Nice Angled Border Trick

When you're doing tables of information, there's often an empty cell up at the table's upper left corner. Why not put that cell to work with a couple of labels, as in the example below?

◇	A	B	C	D	E	
1	Yearly Sales by Region (in thousands of dollars)					
2						
3	Year 1998 1999 2000 2001 Sales Region					
4	North	100	110	105	115	
5	South	60	75	70	80	
6	East	95	105	105	100	
7	West	125	115	135	140	
8						
9						
10						

There's a bit of a trick to it, but it isn't difficult. Here's how to do it:

1 Click in the cell that you want to format, and then increase the cell height by dragging the bottom edge of the row header down. (The row header is the numbered cell at the left edge of the worksheet.)

2 Type about a dozen space characters into the cell. You'll need to adjust the number of spaces later (to control the horizontal alignment of the first text label), but this will get you started.

3 Type the text you want for the label for the columns across the top of the table.

4 Press Control+Option+Return a few times. This adds line breaks to the cell, but doesn't kick you out of the cell, as a regular Return would. Again, you'll probably want to adjust the number of line breaks later (to control the vertical alignment of the second text label).

5 Type the second text label, which is for the rows down the left edge of the table, and then press Return.

6 Select the cell again, choose Format, Cells, and click the Border tab.

7 Select the line style you want, and then click the upper left to lower right angled border button.

8 Click the Alignment tab, click the Wrap Text button, and then click OK.

You can get the two labels to go exactly where you want by adjusting the column width and row height, as well as by adding or subtracting spaces before the first text label and line breaks before the second label.

Changing Alignment, Text Orientation, and Text Wrapping

Although you can't control text with Excel the same way you can with Word, you can do some interesting things with Excel. In addition to giving you text alignment and wrapping options, Excel lets you orient text almost any way you want. This helps you make your worksheets more readable, by allowing you to set text in almost any direction.

Excel's text alignment, orientation, and wrapping functions are all available from the Format Cells dialog, shown in Figure 26-7. By default, Excel aligns text to the left in cells, and aligns numbers to the right. You can change alignment for any cell or range by selecting the cell or range, choosing Format, Cells, and then clicking the Alignment tab. This tab contains three sections: Text Alignment, Text Control, and Orientation.

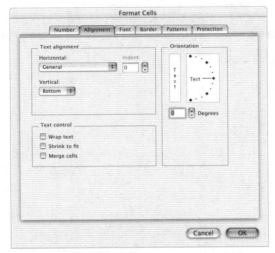

Figure 26-7. The Alignment tab of the Format Cells dialog controls how text will be displayed within cells.

To change text alignment, select one of the options from the Horizontal pop-up menu. Figure 26-8 on the next page shows an example of each of these alignment options, and Table 26-3 explains how each of them works.

Table 26-3. Excel's Text Alignment Options

Option	Text Display
General	The General format is left aligned, and, if the text is longer than the cell containing it, the portion spilling into the next cell is covered if that cell contains any data. If the next cell is empty, the text will extend into that cell and beyond, if necessary.
Left (Indent)	The Left (Indent) format is left aligned, and, if text wrap is selected, each line is flush left in the cell.

(continued)

Table 26-3. *(continued)*

Option	Text Display
Center	The Center format centers text within a cell and, if text wrap is selected, centers each line in the cell.
Right	The Right format aligns text to the right of the cell. If text wrap is selected, each line is flush right in the cell.
Fill	The Fill format is similar to the General format: the text is left aligned, but it will not run over into adjacent cells, even if they are empty.
Justify	The Justify format aligns text to the left and right, filling the cell.
Center Across Selection	The Center Across Selection format centers the text in the cell containing it and runs the text over on both sides of the cell if these adjacent cells are empty.

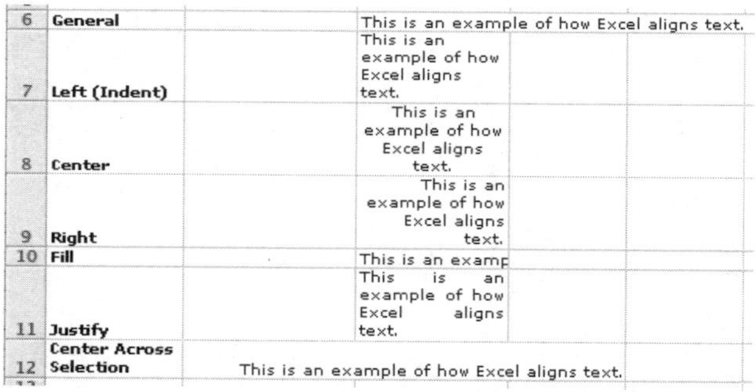

Figure 26-8. Here are several examples of text alignment options within Excel. To better show how text would behave, Text Wrap was turned on for the Left, Center, and Right options.

> **tip** Many of the text alignment options—but not all—are available in the Text Alignment section of the Formatting Palette, which is often quicker to use.

You can also align text within cells so it is displayed at the top, center, or bottom of the cell, or so that it is vertically justified. Select the alignment option you want to use from the Vertical pop-up menu. Figure 26-9 shows the results of these four options.

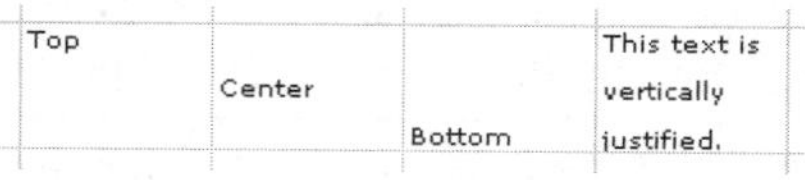

Figure 26-9. The vertical text alignment options allow you to position text precisely, no matter the height of the row.

To wrap text, that is, to ensure that the text will cover as many lines as necessary in the cell, expanding the height of the row where it is located, select the Wrap Text check box in the Text Control section of the Alignment tab. Figure 26-8 shows how text wraps according to different horizontal alignment options.

---

tip   **Break lines where you want**

When you tell Excel to wrap text in a cell, it starts new lines as needed to fit the text to the width of the cell. But sometimes you might want new lines to begin after specific words. Instead of changing the cell width to make it wrap correctly, do the following: click in the cell at the point where you want the text to move to a new line. Press Control+Option+Return, and a line break will be added at that location. You can now control the text wrap so that your lines break exactly where you want.

You can shrink text to fit cells by selecting the Shrink To Fit check box in the Text Control section of the Alignment tab. This changes the size of the text to fit in your cell. But use this feature sparingly—if you have a lot of text and choose this option, the text will be very small and difficult to read.

Excel lets you orient the text in your cells in almost any direction, as shown in Figure 26-10. Select the cell or cells containing your text, choose Format, Cells, and then click the Alignment tab. Click a degree point in the compass display or drag the text orientation indicator to the position you want. The preview shows you the precise angle of display. You can also enter a number of degrees in the Degrees box. To display the text vertically in a single column of letters, click the vertical Text box to the left of the compass display. To reset the orientation to the normal, horizontal position, click the diamond degree point at the "East" position on the compass display, or enter 0 in the Degrees box.

Figure 26-10.   These examples of text orientation are but a few of the options available.

Troubleshooting

I can't rotate text in Excel.

If you find that the text rotation options under Orientation are not available, it is likely that your cells are formatted as Center Across Selection or Fill. If you select a range that contains cells formatted in either of these manners, text rotation will be available, but it will not affect the cells formatted as Center Across Selection or Fill; only the other cells will be changed.

625

Chapter 26

> **tip** **Go further with text orientation**
>
> If you combine text orientation with horizontal and vertical alignment options, you can put your text just about anywhere in your cells, at any angle. Try some of these different options to see how flexible this formatting is.

Merging Cells

When you open a new workbook, each of the worksheets contains cells at the intersections of each row and column. But you can merge cells at any location on your worksheet, combining several cells into one, as shown in Figure 26-11. This ability is useful for formatting worksheets: when you merge cells you can fit a large block of text all in one cell. To merge cells, select the cells you want to merge. Open the Text Alignment section of the Formatting Palette, and then click the Merge Cells button. Excel merges these cells into one, using the top left cell reference for the new, larger cell. If these cells contain any data or information, Excel will display an alert telling you that it will only keep the data in the upper leftmost cell after merging. If you click OK, all the data in the other cells will be deleted. You can also un-merge any merged cells by clearing the Merge Cells check box.

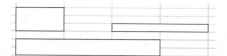

Figure 26-11. Borders have been added to better show these merged cells.

Formatting Rows and Columns

When you open a new workbook, Excel creates worksheets with set row heights and column widths. But these default sizes will not be right for all of your data. So, as you can do with everything else in your Excel worksheets, you can change the sizes of both rows and columns, both manually and automatically.

Adjusting Row Heights

To adjust the height of one or several rows, select the row or rows you want to change by clicking on their headers. The row headers are the numbers that run down the left column of the worksheet, and the column headers are the letters that run across the top of the worksheet. Choose Format, Row and then select Height. The Row Height dialog lets you enter the new height, in points, for the selected rows. Click OK, and the rows will change to the height you have chosen.

The preceding method is fine if you know the exact height, in points, that you want to apply. If not, the easiest way to change a row height is to move the pointer along the headers to the bottom boundary of a row. The pointer changes to a double-headed arrow, showing that you can adjust this boundary, as shown in Figure 26-12. Click your mouse and drag in either direction; if you drag up, your row height will decrease, if you drag down your row height will increase. As you drag the row header, a ScreenTip shows the height of the row.

Figure 26-12.   Drag the double-headed arrow to adjust row height interactively.

If you want to interactively change the height of several rows at the same time, select the rows you want to adjust by clicking your pointer on one row header and dragging in either direction. You can select nonadjacent rows by holding down the Command key and clicking on several rows. Move the pointer to the bottom boundary of any of the selected rows and drag it up to decrease the height of the rows or down to increase their height. As you drag the row header, a ScreenTip shows the height of the rows.

Adjusting Column Widths

To adjust the width of one or several columns, select the column or columns you want to change by clicking on their headers. Choose Format, Column and then select Width. In the Column Width dialog, enter the new width, in the average number of digits 0–9 that fit in the cell, for the selected column. Click OK, and the columns will change to the width you have chosen.

The above method is fine if you know the exact width that you want to apply. If not, the easiest way to change column widths is to move the pointer along the column headers to the right boundary of any column. The pointer changes to a double-headed arrow, showing that you can adjust this line. Click your mouse and drag in either direction; if you drag left, your column will become narrower, if you drag right your column will become wider. As you drag the column header, a ScreenTip shows the width of the column, as shown in Figure 26-13.

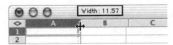

Figure 26-13.   Drag the double-headed arrow to adjust column width interactively.

---

tip   **Fit a row or column to its contents**

To make a row's height or column's width fit its contents, simply double-click on the boundary below the row or to the right of the column you want to adjust.

If you want to interactively change the width of several columns at the same time, select the columns you want to adjust by clicking your pointer on one column header and dragging in either direction. You can select nonadjacent columns by holding down the Command key and clicking on several columns. Move the pointer to the right boundary of any selected column, and drag it left to decrease the width of the columns or right to increase their width. As you drag the column header, a ScreenTip shows the width of the columns.

---

tip   **Adjust all the rows or columns in a worksheet**

To quickly change all the row height or column widths in a worksheet, select the entire worksheet by pressing Command+A, and then drag any row or column boundary to the size you want for all of them.

Using AutoFit

Although you can carefully adjust the column widths and row heights to ensure that your worksheet presents your data as concisely as possible, AutoFit can save you a lot of time by making all the adjustments with a couple of clicks. AutoFit sets the row heights or the column widths to the size of your data. If you have a column with several rows, one of which is much longer than the rest, AutoFit will set the column width for the all columns to accommodate this row. All the rows and columns will be set so that all your data is visible.

To use AutoFit, select all or part of your worksheet. You can apply AutoFit to rows or columns. Choose Format, then either Rows or Columns, and then select AutoFit. Your rows or columns will be adjusted to fit the widest or tallest data.

Using the Formatting Palette

Excel's Formatting Palette is a special toolbar that gives you one-click access to many (but not all) formatting options. It allows you to format fonts, numbers, text alignment, borders and shading, and worksheets. When the Formatting Palette is visible, it floats over your worksheet windows, giving you access to its functions at all times. You can expand it and reduce it, section by section, and hide it completely when you don't need it.

---

note   Even though the Formatting Palette is a kind of toolbar, you can't customize it as you can all of Excel's other toolbars.

If the Formatting Palette is not visible, choose View, Formatting Palette to display it. Figure 26-14 shows three views of the Formatting Palette: the first shows all tabs closed, and the second and third show the functions available under different tabs. Table 26-4 lists the functions you can perform from the Formatting Palette.

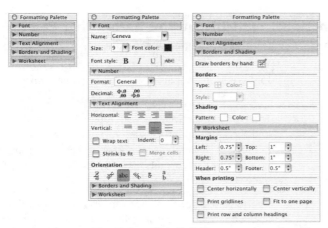

Figure 26-14. The Formatting Palette expands and contracts as needed to display just the formatting options you want.

InsideOut

Open the Formatting Palette in sections to fit your screen resolution

Depending on your screen resolution, you might not be able to display the Formatting Palette with all its tabs open—unfortunately, it was not designed to be used on any screen size. If your screen is set to less than 1024×768 pixels, the Formatting Palette will be too tall to fit entirely on your screen. You will have to open and close its tabs as needed.

Advantages and Disadvantages to the Formatting Palette

Excel's Formatting Palette is another of several ways to apply formatting to your worksheets. All of the functions available on the Formatting Palette can also be accessed elsewhere—by choosing menu commands, by using keyboard shortcuts, from toolbars, or by adjusting settings in dialogs. The Formatting Palette is not meant to replace any of these methods, but it gives you quick access to some of the most widely used formatting functions. Since you can't do all your formatting with the Formatting Palette, it won't replace these other methods entirely. But, because it floats over your workbook windows, you will find it saves you a lot of time when applying simple formatting, such as fonts and styles, number formats, and borders.

Table 26-4. Functions Available on the Formatting Palette

Palette Section	Formatting Functions Available
Font	The Font section lets you select the font, type size, and font color and apply bold, italic, underline, and strike-through styles.
Number	The Number section lets you apply number formats to cells, and the Decimal buttons let you decrease and increase the number of decimal places shown in cells. For more information on number formats, see "Specifying Number Formats," page 612.
Text Alignment	The Text Alignment section lets you set horizontal and vertical alignment of text in cells, wrap text, indent text, shrink text to fit, and merge cells. The Orientation area lets you choose from six text orientation settings. For more information on text alignment, see "Changing Alignment, Text Orientation, and Text Wrapping," page 623.
Borders And Shading	The Borders And Shading section lets you set borders for your cells either by drawing them or by selecting them and then clicking the Type button to choose the type of border you want. You can choose border colors from the Color button, and you can set shading patterns and colors in the Shading subsection. For more information on borders and shading, see "Applying Borders and Shading," page 619.
Worksheet	The Worksheet section lets you set print margins and lets you choose from several print options, such as centering your worksheet, printing gridlines, and more. For more information on print options, see "Printing Worksheets," page 576.

Letting AutoFormat Do It

Okay, so you have a worksheet full of data—you've just finished your report, but you have no time to make it look good before you print it. Or, maybe, you can't think of a good way to present your data. Excel's AutoFormat function saves you time and gives you modern, effective formatting in just a few clicks. Your documents will look professional, and all you need to do is choose one of the many formats available.

To use AutoFormat on your worksheet, you must first select the range you want to format. Then choose Format, AutoFormat. A dialog opens showing a list of table formats to the left and a sample of how these table formats look in the center, as shown in Figure 26-15. Click the different table formats to see how they look. If you like one of these formats, click OK, and your data will be formatted automatically.

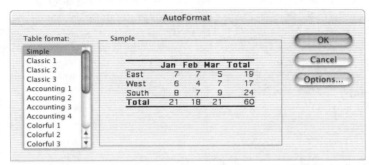

Figure 26-15. The AutoFormat dialog lets you add complex formatting to a selection with just a few clicks.

> **tip** If you don't like the result of the AutoFormat, choose Edit, Undo to return the selection to its previous state.

When you choose a table format under AutoFormat, you don't have to use all the formatting it includes. Click Options, and an additional section will be displayed at the bottom of the dialog. This box, called Formats To Apply, lets you choose which of the six formatting elements you want to use. Clear any of the check boxes to not use one of these elements. Say you want to use the fonts you have already applied to your data. Clear the Font check box, and your fonts will be used, instead of those specified for the table format you choose.

> **note** AutoFormat offers many color formats. If you don't have a color printer, these will probably not look good when printed in black and white. Even in color, some of them might not look very good, so think of printing a test page before you print any long documents.

---

tip **Touch up AutoFormats**

The table formats available in the AutoFormat dialog apply six different formatting elements to your selected data at the same time. But AutoFormat is merely a shortcut for applying this formatting. Not only can you choose to not apply certain elements, such as the font, borders, patterns, and so forth, but you can also change the formatting afterward. Say you like the formatting of one of the color tables but don't like the colors used. You can select only the color cells and change their color. You can change any or all of the formatting elements after AutoFormat applies them—they are not locked together, but are all individual.

Using Styles in Excel

You can spend a lot of time formatting your worksheets. Changing fonts, number formats, borders, colors, each of these can keep you busy. Creating and saving your own styles can save you time and enable you to apply several formatting elements to cells in a jiffy. Excel lets you create custom styles that include most of the formatting elements you need.

Creating Custom Styles

The easiest way to create a custom style is to apply all the formatting you want to a cell or range of cells, and then select it. Choose Format, Style, and the Style dialog opens, as shown in Figure 26-16. If you have not applied any custom styles, the Normal style will be chosen. To create a new style, simply type a new name in the Style Name box. The formatting elements for this style appear in the Style Includes section. When you enter a new name, the formatting elements will change to reflect those applied to the selected cell or range. To save this style, click OK.

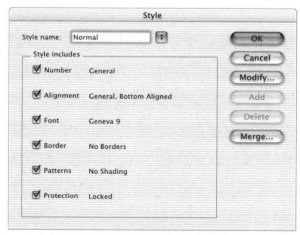

Figure 26-16. You can create custom styles, and modify existing styles, in the Style dialog.

You can choose which formatting elements are used in your custom style. When you display your style in the Style dialog, the Style Includes section shows six formatting elements. By default, all of these are selected. If you clear any of the check boxes, those elements will not be added to your custom style.

You can modify any of your styles, as well as any of the default styles. Choose Format, Style, and select the style you want to modify from the Style Name pop-up menu. Click Modify, and the Format Cells dialog will open. All the formatting choices you make now will be added to your custom style. Click each of the tabs for the formatting you want to change, and modify the current choices. When you click OK, these changes will be shown in the Style Includes section of the Style dialog. Click OK in this dialog to save your changes.

Applying Styles

When you have created your own custom styles, you will certainly want to reuse them. To apply a style, first select a cell or range, and then choose Format, Style. The Style dialog appears. Select the style you want from the Style Name pop-up menu, and then click OK.

InsideOut

Apply styles with just one click

Though Excel uses styles similarly to Word, the basic way of applying them—choosing Format, Style, selecting the style from a pop-up menu, and clicking OK—is a bit tedious. Unlike Word, Excel does not have a Style button on any of its toolbars. If you find yourself using styles a lot, you should probably add a Style Name pop-up menu to one of the toolbars you use regularly. For more information on how to customize toolbars, see "Customizing Excel Toolbars," page 789.

Merging Styles

When you create custom styles, they remain in the workbook where you created them. But if you want to use these styles in another workbook, you don't need to go through the entire process to re-create them in the other file. You can merge styles from one workbook to another and reuse your custom styles easily.

To do this, you must first have two workbooks open—the one containing the style and the one to which you want to copy the style. The latter workbook must be the front window. Choose Format, Style and then click Merge. The Merge Styles dialog opens, as shown in Figure 26-17 on the next page. Click the name of the workbook containing the styles you want to copy, and then click OK. All styles you have created in this workbook will be copied into the front workbook.

Figure 26-17. Use the Merge Styles dialog to transfer styles from one workbook to another.

---

tip　**Keep your custom styles in a safe place**

If you create many custom styles, it is a good idea to keep them all together in one workbook—that way it will be easier to copy them into other workbooks when you need them. You can assemble your custom styles by creating a new, blank workbook and copying the styles from other workbooks into it. Call this workbook something like Style Vault, and your custom styles will always be on hand.

There is another way to keep styles together and have them available—you can put them all into a template. For more information on templates, see "Using Templates," on the following page.

Using Conditional Formatting

Sometimes you might want certain data to stand out on your worksheets if it meets specific conditions—if it is negative, if it is greater than a certain value, or if it is equal to a certain cell. Conditional formatting is how Excel indicates negative numbers. When you choose number formats, you choose whether you want negatives to be displayed in parentheses, in red, or with a minus sign before them.

Conditional formatting lets you apply any kind of formatting to cells that meet certain conditions. Say you want to have cells containing more than a specific value show up in red, but you can't just format the cells as red because their results are dynamic and depend on other data. Select the cell you want to apply conditional formatting to. Choose Format, Conditional Formatting. The Conditional Formatting dialog will appear. Select how you want the first condition to work. In Figure 26-18, the condition is that the cell value is greater than 50000. To decide how to format cells meeting this condition, click Format. The Format Cells dialog will open, and you can choose any kind of formatting for fonts, borders, and patterns. Click OK after you have made your formatting choices, and then click OK to close the Conditional Formatting dialog.

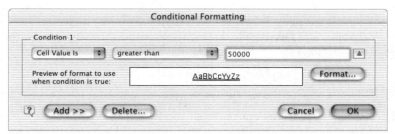

Figure 26-18. The Conditional Formatting dialog applies formatting based on up to three criteria.

You can use more than one condition when applying conditional formatting. Simply click Add, and a new section will appear. You can set this second condition, and the conditional formatting whose conditions are met will be applied. Excel lets you use up to three conditions.

---

tip   **Copy conditional formatting to other cells**

Like any kind of formatting, conditional formatting can be copied to other cells. The easiest way to do this is to use the Format Painter. For more information on the Format Painter, see "Using the Format Painter," page 612.

Using Templates

Some people create totally new files every time they need a new workbook, because they use these files for different things every time. But you might need to use the same workbooks over and over for different data. If you have invested a lot of time formatting and laying out these workbooks, it is logical to want to reuse them. Also, if you have created many custom styles and have merged them into one workbook to keep them all handy, it makes sense to use this workbook as often as possible.

Excel lets you save workbooks as reusable files called *templates*. When you open the file, only a copy of it is opened; the original remains unchanged. The advantage of using templates in Excel is that you can apply complex formatting to a file, create styles, and even add macros and be able to quickly and easily use that file as the basis for new files. Ideally, you want your templates to be devoid of any data—you want to retain formatting, formulas and functions, layout, styles, and macros. Then, when you open the template, you simply enter your data, and the workbook does the rest.

You can save any Excel workbook as a template. With the file you want to save open, choose File, Save As. The Format pop-up menu provides a number of formats in which you can save your workbook. Select Template, and the Where pop-up menu will change to My Templates—this is your personal template folder inside the Templates folder of the Microsoft Office X folder. Click Save, and your workbook will be saved as a template.

When you open a template, Excel merely opens a copy of the original file. So, when you make any changes, and save the file, a standard Save sheet will appear. You can then save your new version of the file under any name.

tip **Display templates in the Project Gallery**

If you have the Project Gallery appear when you start up Microsoft Office v. X, it's better to have previews of your Excel templates show up there, rather than just have them appear in the My Templates section with a generic Excel workbook icon. To do this, when saving your template, choose File, Properties, click the Summary tab, and select the Save Preview Picture check box.

Chapter 27

Working with Functions and Formulas

Functions and formulas are the primary elements used to make calculations in your worksheets. You enter raw data, and then tell Excel what to do with it, how to crunch the numbers. From functions as simple as SUM, which adds a series of numbers and displays the result, to more complex mathematical, statistical, and financial functions, Microsoft Excel X provides you with a library of more than 200 predefined functions that will meet most of your calculation needs. This chapter will tell you how to use Excel's built-in functions and how to make your own formulas when these functions don't fit your needs. You'll also find out how to streamline formulas so that they are easier to write and simpler to understand.

Understanding Functions and Formulas

Functions and formulas do the same things; the difference is that functions are built-in to Excel and provide simpler ways to do complex calculations. You write your own formulas, but you can use Excel's functions in your formulas or on their own. The simplest function in Excel is SUM. This function adds all the numbers in a range of cells and displays the total. A formula using SUM can be written as follows: =SUM(A1:A3). This tells Excel to apply the SUM function to the cell range in parentheses.

You could also write the same formula as follows: =A1+A2+A3. The result would be the same, but the difference is that, in the first case, you call up Excel's SUM function, and, in the second case, you are merely adding numbers. The difference is minimal for such a simple calculation, but the more complex your needs, the more time and power you gain by using functions. When you use functions, you don't need to know what formulas are behind them. You don't need to know statistics, or compound interest, or trigonometry. Functions encapsulate complex math in easy-to-use packages, giving you Excel's full calculation power with just a few keystrokes.

Using Functions

Excel's *functions* are predefined formulas that return calculations based on data in cells or ranges. They use specific values, called *arguments,* in a specific order or *syntax.* Arguments can be numbers, text, logical values such as TRUE or FALSE, arrays, error values such as #N/A, or references to individual cells or ranges. These references can be to cells on the worksheet using the function, to other worksheets in the same workbook, or even to data in other workbooks. You can use functions in formulas, and you can even *nest* functions, that is, include functions as arguments for other functions.

Functions must be part of formulas, and every function must be entered using specific syntax. The following is an example of SUM function syntax:

=SUM(A1,B4,C7:C15)

The equal sign indicates that the worksheet cell contains a formula, as opposed to simply text entered in a cell. Then comes the function name, SUM. This function adds all the values in the arguments contained within the parentheses and returns this sum, which is then displayed in the cell containing this formula. Parentheses are used to enclose arguments, and commas separate each argument. The colon is used to indicate a range of cells, in this case, from cell C7 through cell C15. In this example, Excel totals the values in cells A1, B4, and cell range C7 to C15. The result of this calculation is then displayed in the cell, and this result can be used elsewhere, in other formulas.

Employing the AutoSum Function

AutoSum

One of the most commonly used Excel functions is the AutoSum function. This feature is so popular that Microsoft gave it its own button on the Excel Standard toolbar. This button actually gives you quick access to several other functions, in addition to calculating sums. You can click the AutoSum button to access its pop-up menu with four other common functions, AVERAGE, COUNT, MAX, and MIN, or you can select More Functions, which opens the Paste Function dialog.

InsideOut

Use the button that is also a menu

The AutoSum button, like several other buttons on Office toolbars, is actually an odd hybrid of a button and a pop-up menu (indicated by the small triangle to the right of the button icon). Clicking and holding down the mouse button pops up a menu that contains additional functions. Working with this tool can be a bit disconcerting because its two parts (the button and the triangle) act differently. A single quick click on the button part triggers the AutoSum function. Clicking and holding down the mouse button on the button pops up the menu with more functions, after a short delay. But if you click and hold the mouse button on the triangle, the menu pops up immediately. Oddly, this behavior for the AutoSum control is different from the behavior of similar controls in Excel, Microsoft Word, and Microsoft PowerPoint, namely, the Undo and Redo toolbar buttons. On these controls, clicking and holding the mouse button on the button part doesn't activate the pop-up menu at all; when you release the mouse button, the result is the same as if you had quickly clicked the button. The only way to activate the pop-up menus with these controls is to click and hold their triangles. Buttons with pop-up menus on Entourage's toolbar act like Excel's AutoSum button. So the best way for you to figure out how one of these controls will act in one of the Office applications is to try it, since the behaviors aren't consistent.

To insert the AutoSum function into a cell, do the following:

1 Click the cell where you want to place your AutoSum.

2 Click the AutoSum button. If you just want a sum, clicking this button will enter the SUM function in the Formula Bar. If you want an AVERAGE, COUNT, MAX, or MIN, select one of these functions from the pop-up menu next to the AutoSum button.

3 Excel will examine your worksheet and try to determine which cells should be used for your AutoSum. If you have selected a cell at the bottom or to the right of a range of numbers, Excel will automatically assume that this range is what you want to use in the SUM function, as shown in Figure 27-1 on the next page. If Excel's selection is not exactly what you want to use, select a range of cells with your pointer, and then press Return. If you decide you want to cancel the AutoSum function, press Esc.

Chapter 27

639

4: Excel

Figure 27-1. When you choose the AutoSum function in cell B17, Excel automatically suggests the cell range surrounded by the marquee.

> **tip** You can select nonadjacent cells for the AutoSum function by holding down the Command key and selecting any cell or cell range.

Instant Totals (and More) on the Status Bar

Whenever you have two or more cells with numeric values selected, Excel displays the sum of the selection in the AutoCalculate area of the status bar at the bottom of the worksheet's window, as shown here.

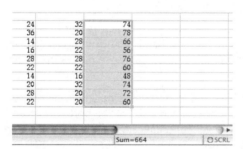

The AutoCalculate area usually shows the sum of the selected values, but clicking the area opens a menu with other choices. You can choose to display the average of the selected cells, count the number of selected cells (but not empty cells), count only the selected cells with numeric values, find the maximum value, or find the minimum value.

Inserting Built-in Functions

Excel has more than 200 functions to make just about every type of calculation imaginable. In most cases, you will find that Excel's functions meet your calculation needs. If not, you can write your own formulas. (For more information on writing your own formulas, see "Building Formulas," page 644.) Excel's functions are organized in nine categories, as shown in Table 27-1.

Table 27-1. Excel's Built-in Functions

Category	Calculation
Financial	Carry out financial calculations, such as calculating interest and depreciation for loans.
Date & Time	Work with dates and times, calculating things such as the number of days between two dates, or the number of minutes between two times.
Math & Trigonometry	Return and calculate a wide variety of mathematical values, such as sines and cosines, and can round numbers, return logarithms, and raise numbers to powers.
Statistical	Provide calculations for averages, medians, distributions, and trends.
Lookup & Reference	Identify data in tables and move cells around.
Database	Give you powerful ways to work with cell ranges within Excel that you define as databases.
Text	Carry out many kinds of operations on text data, such as concatenation, substitution, and finding and replacing.
Logical	Return true and false values, let you create IF tests, and more.
Information	Test cells to see what kind of information they contain.

Each function has a specific syntax, that is, specific rules, and requires arguments to make calculations: these arguments can be numbers, text, cell references, cell ranges, or nested functions. Each function uses different types of arguments—you cannot use text arguments in an AVERAGE function, nor can you use Boolean arguments (TRUE, FALSE, etc.) in numeric functions. In addition, each function has a limit to the number of arguments it can handle. The AVERAGE function can use up to 30 arguments, whereas the SIN function, which returns the sine of an angle, uses only one argument.

The syntax of some functions, such as the AVERAGE function, is relatively simple:

AVERAGE(**number1**,number2,...)

where *number1, number2*, and so on represents 1 to 30 numeric values. This is a simple function, but other functions are much more complex. The YIELD function, which returns the yield on securities that pay periodic interest, has the following syntax:

YIELD(**settlement,maturity,rate,pr,redemption,frequency**,basis)

The arguments in bold type are required for the function; the others are optional. The security's settlement date is represented by *settlement; maturity* is the security's maturity date; *rate* is the security's annual coupon rate; *pr* is the security's price per $100 face value; *redemption* is the security's redemption value per $100 face value; *frequency* is the number of coupon payments per year (for annual payments, *frequency* = 1; for semiannual, *frequency* = 2; for quarterly, *frequency* = 4); and *basis* is the type of day count basis to use.

> **note** YIELD is part of the Analysis ToolPak, which is an optional installation. To install the Analysis ToolPak, use the Value Pack Installer on the Microsoft Office v. X CD.

As you can see from this function, you need to know a lot of information in advance, not all of which will necessarily be in your worksheet. You can enter some of these arguments manually, and others can be entered as cell references. The Formula Palette helps you enter these arguments by giving you information about each argument and showing which are required (bold type) and which are optional.

To insert a function into a cell, follow these steps:

1 Select a cell and choose Insert, Function.

2 The Function Category list shows the different categories of functions. Click a category, and then select a function from the Function Name list. Click OK, and the Formula Palette appears.

3 The Formula Palette is a kind of assistant that helps you enter the correct arguments into your function. In Figure 27-2, the Formula Palette is displayed for the MAX function. The Formula Palette explains what the function does and indicates which arguments are needed. The Formula Result section at the bottom of the Formula Palette gives you the result of your function as your compose it.

4 Click OK to insert the function into your worksheet.

To enter arguments into a function, you can either enter data manually or select cells and use the data they contain. If you enter data manually, just type it into one of the Number fields. To add cell references, click the triangle button next to a number field, and the Formula Palette rolls up showing your active worksheet. Select the cell or range

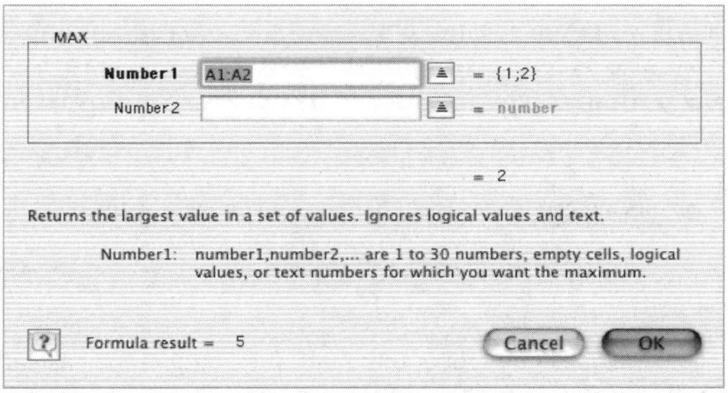

Figure 27-2. The Formula Palette enables you to enter arguments into functions easily.

you want to use for this argument in your function, and then press Return or click the triangle button again to return to the Formula Palette. Figure 27-3 shows the SUM function with three arguments.

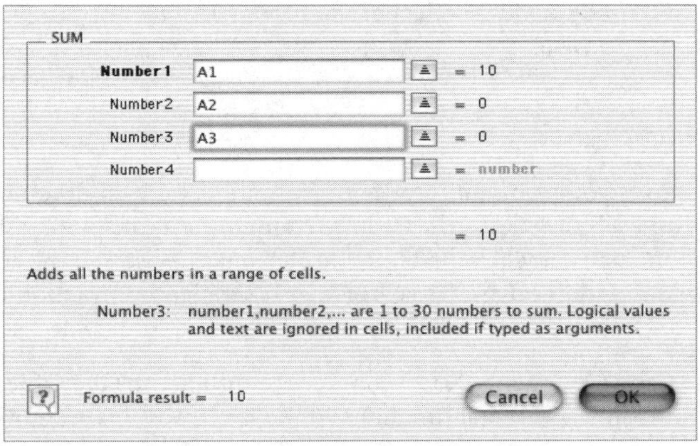

Figure 27-3. Excel populates the Formula Palette with as many arguments as needed to make the formula or function work. Here, the SUM function shows three arguments.

Troubleshooting

Where's the Formula Palette?

Some users might find the Formula Palette only sticks out a bit beneath the menu bar at the top of the screen. It seems that Excel X was optimized for a 1024x768 screen resolution. If you are using an 800x600 resolution, you might see only the bottom of the Formula Palette. This is annoying, but you can still use the Formula Palette. Just click anywhere on the palette and drag it into view. You can then use it as explained. You can avoid this difficulty by shifting your screen resolution to 1024x768, but not all Macs let you do this. Clamshell iBooks, for example, will only display at 800x600.

If you know which cells you want to enter into your function, you can simply type their references into the fields in the Formula Palette. You can also enter names of cell ranges into these fields. Just type a name, and its value will be displayed to the right of the field.

For more information on naming cell ranges, see "Naming Cell Ranges," page 602.

tip   **Insert functions manually**

You can insert functions manually by typing them into the Formula Bar, instead of selecting them from the function list. This method is much faster if you are familiar with functions and the arguments and syntax they call for. When inserting a function manually, make sure you include an equal sign at the beginning of your formula. When you type a function name, Excel will automatically display it in uppercase letters, even if you type it in lowercase letters. In fact, this is a good way to check that your functions are spelled correctly—if they are, Excel will recognize them as functions and change their case. If not, and the letters of the name remain lowercase, you will know that you made a mistake.

Going Further with Functions

Excel's online help gives you plenty of information about its built-in functions, much more information on each function than we have room to fit in this book. Choose Help, Excel Help Contents, and click the Function Reference section in the contents pane. Each of Excel's function categories is listed, with detailed information on each function: how it works, its arguments, its syntax, and examples of how to use it.

In addition, your Microsoft Office v. X CD contains an installer for the Office Value Pack, which contains some additional functions in the Excel Add-ins section, including the YIELD function discussed earlier. Run the Value Pack Installer to find out what these additional functions are.

Building Formulas

Although Excel's more than 200 built-in functions will certainly be sufficient for many of your calculations, you can't do everything with them. They can calculate logarithms, interest, and various statistical functions, but they can't do $A + B - C \times D$. Formulas let you calculate just about anything, using dynamic data from your cells and ranges, or data you enter in your formulas. Excel formulas can be very simple, such as $x + y$, or very complex, containing functions within formulas, calling on several cells from different worksheets, and even different workbooks.

Using the Formula Bar

Though you can type formulas directly into cells, it is much easier to use the Formula Bar, shown in Figure 27-4. Click the cell where you want to enter a formula, and start typing in the Formula Bar. (If the Formula Bar is not visible, choose View, Formula Bar to display it.) To start composing a formula, the first thing you need to do is enter an equal sign (=). This tells Excel that the text you are entering is a formula; if you omit this sign, everything you enter will be treated as data (if it is numbers) or text. When you click in the Formula field and enter the equal sign, you will see several changes on your worksheet. The equal sign is entered in the active cell, a shadow highlights the active cell, and a ScreenTip appears showing the reference of this cell.

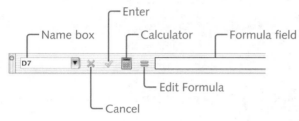

Figure 27-4. Use the Formula Bar to enter formulas in cells.

In addition to the equal sign, formulas can contain as little as a cell reference, or any combination of values, operators, cell references, functions, and names (of cells or ranges). Formulas can refer to cells on the same worksheet, or to cells on other worksheets in the same workbook, and even to cells in other workbooks. (For more on referring to cells in other worksheets and workbooks, see, "Linking Data Between Worksheets and Workbooks," page 656.)

Figure 27-5 shows the different elements that can make up a formula:

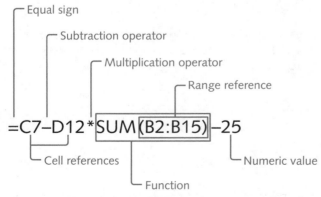

Figure 27-5. Excel formulas can be as simple or as complex as you need them to be.

To build a formula, you enter the necessary elements in the Formula Bar in the appropriate order. This order follows basic algebraic logic, but it must also take into account Excel's order of evaluation of mathematical operators.

For more information on the order of evaluation of operators, see "Understanding Operators and Their Order," opposite.

The following is an example of how to build a simple formula. Cells A1 and A3 in the following graphic will be added, the range B1 to B3 will be subtracted from this amount, and then the result will be divided by cell A2.

1 Select the cell where you want to place the formula, and enter an equal sign in the Formula Bar.

2 Click the cell you want to use first in the formula; in this example it is A1. To add cells and ranges together in a formula, you don't need to enter a plus sign—simply click the cell you want to add and it is entered automatically. In this example, you would click cell A3.

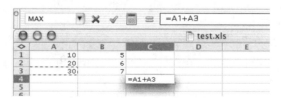

3 Enter a minus sign (–). Type **SUM**, type an open parenthesis, select the cell range B1 to B3, and then type a closing parenthesis. This enters the SUM function, which adds the values in the range in parentheses.

4 Enter a division sign: a slash (/). Select the cell that will be the divisor. In this example, it's A2.

5 Because you want all of the addition and subtraction to be carried out before the division, you must put parentheses around this first part of the formula. Click in the Formula Bar and enter parentheses around A1+A2.

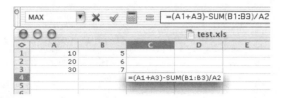

6 Because you want the result of the first two operations to be divided by cell A2, you must put these operations in parentheses. Type an open parenthesis before A1, and a closing parenthesis after the closing parenthesis of the SUM function.

7 Press Return. The result (1.1) will display in the cell containing the formula.

Though the preceding example presents only a simple formula, you can compose complex formulas that use many functions, cells, and values and that even get some of their data from cells in other worksheets and workbooks.

---

tip **Streamline formulas by using named ranges**

Every Excel worksheet you use contains data, some of it in individual cells, some of it in ranges. You might have columns or tables that are inseparable—say you have a record of sales by month for different departments in a store. Rather than select the cells of this range each time you want to enter them in a formula, give the range a name. Not only will it be quicker to compose your formulas, but they will be easier to understand and edit. For more on naming cells and ranges, see "Naming Cell Ranges," page 602.

For more information on using data in other worksheets and workbooks, see "Linking Data Between Worksheets and Workbooks," page 656.

Understanding Operators and Their Order

Excel formulas use standard mathematical operators to carry out basic calculations in standard algebraic order, as shown in Table 27-2 on the next page. If two operators with the same precedence—the same priority in the order of evaluation—appear in a formula, Excel performs these operations from left to right.

Table 27-2. **Order of Evaluation of Arithmetic Operators**

Order of Evaluation	Operator	Description
First	–	Negation (as in –2)
	%	Percent
	^	Exponentiation
	* and /	Multiplication and division
Last	+ and –	Addition and subtraction

> **tip** **Use parentheses to enter negative numbers in formulas**
>
> Though you can enter negative numbers by typing a minus sign before them, it can be easier to surround them with parentheses. Excel will understand the following formula:
>
> =7+–2
>
> as being 7 plus –2, and return 5. But if you enter this formula as
>
> =7+(–2)
>
> it will be easier for you, and others, to understand when editing the formula, especially if you use many negative numbers.

For example, if you enter this in a formula:

2*2+8/4+5^2

Excel will calculate the result in the order shown next. Italics represent the operation to be performed, and bold indicates the result:

2*2+8/4+5^2
*2*2+8/4+**10**
4+*8/4*+10
4+*2*+10
6+10
16

Using Parentheses

You can use parentheses to force Excel to first calculate the contents of the parentheses before following the standard order of evaluation. If, in the previous example, you want to add 2 plus 8 and 4 plus 5 before multiplying and dividing, you would need to type your formula as follows:

2*(2+8)/(4+5)^2

Excel will calculate the operations in parentheses first. The result will be

2*(2+8)/(4+5)^2
2*10/9^2
2*10/81
20/81
.2469135

As you can see, this answer is very different from that of the formula without parentheses.

If you're in doubt as to the order in which Excel will process a sequence of operators, use parentheses, even if they aren't strictly necessary. As an added benefit, using parentheses makes it easier for you to read a formula, which will make it easier to change the formula later, if necessary.

note Parentheses must always be entered in pairs—for every opening parenthesis there must be a closing parenthesis. In many cases, Excel's Formula AutoCorrect function will be able to detect unbalanced parentheses and will display an error message offering to correct your formula if any are missing.

Troubleshooting

I receive error messages when I create Excel formulas.

Many common errors can occur when working with Excel formulas. Some of them might be the result of mistakes in entering formulas, but others might be caused by the way you display your worksheet or by missing cell references. Excel uses eight error codes to indicate the type of error encountered, as shown in the table below.

Error Code	Meaning	How to Correct the Error
#####	• A number, date, or time is wider than the cell.	• Increase the cell width by dragging the right boundary of the column header.
	• A cell contains a date and/or time formula that produces a negative result.	• Check your date or time formula and values.

(continued)

Troubleshooting *(continued)*

Error Code	Meaning	How to Correct the Error
#VALUE!	The wrong type of argument or operand is used, or the Formula AutoCorrect feature cannot correct the formula.	Make sure you are using the correct arguments or operands for your formula. Some formulas require single cells and will return this error when a range is used as an argument. This error can also appear when you need to use a numeric value but your cell reference contains text.
#DIV/0!	A formula divides by zero.	Check your cell references. If a cell is empty, Excel considers its value to be zero.
#NAME?	Excel doesn't recognize text in a formula.	This error appears when you type the wrong range name; check the spelling of your range name. This error also appears when you fail to enclose text used in a formula in quotes. In this case, Excel interprets this text as a range name.
#N/A	This error occurs when a value is not available to a function or a formula.	If any cells on your worksheet will contain data at a later time, but you still want to include them in a formula, enter #N/A in those cells. Formulas referring to those cells will return #N/A instead of attempting to calculate a value.
#REF!	A cell reference is not valid.	Check your cell references. This error occurs when you delete cells that are referred to in a formula, or when you paste or move cells to a cell reference in a formula. If this appears immediately after deleting, pasting, or moving cells, choose Edit, Undo to return the cells to their original location, and then check your formula.
#NUM!	There is a problem with a number in a formula or function.	This error usually occurs when you have entered an incorrect argument in a function that requires a numeric argument. Check the syntax of the function.
#NULL!	The intersection of two areas specified in a reference do not intersect.	This error occurs when you incorrectly enter multiple range references. These must be separated by commas when more than one range appears in a function.

650

Putting the Calculator to Work

Excel has a useful tool called the calculator, shown in Figure 27-6. You can access it by clicking the Calculator button on the Formula Bar. The calculator, which looks like a standard handheld calculator, lets you build formulas in a familiar interface. You can click number and operator keys (the plus, minus, division, and multiplication signs) and click in your worksheet to select cells and ranges for your formula. The calculator's formula box (the large window at the top of the calculator) contains an equal sign to start you with your formula, and the Place In Cell box shows the active cell or range. In addition, the calculator gives you a real-time result in the Answer box as you compose your formula.

> **note** The calculator doesn't enable you to do anything more than you can when you enter formulas in the Formula Bar. It's just a nice interface trick for people who aren't very experienced with Excel.

Figure 27-6. The calculator makes entering formulas easy.

To use the calculator, follow these steps:

1 Click the cell, or select the range where you want to enter your formula.

2 Click the Calculator button on the Formula Bar to display the calculator.

3 Compose your formula in the same way as you would using the Formula Bar—click cells and ranges to enter them in the formula, and click the number and operator keys on the calculator to enter them. You can check your formula as you go by looking at the Answer box.

Chapter 27

4 The calculator lets you enter conditions and functions in your formula.

■ To enter a condition, click the If button. The calculator will widen to display the If section. Enter the condition you want to test, and then click Insert.

■ To enter a sum, click the Sum button. The calculator will widen to display the Sum section. Select the cells you want to add, and then click Insert.

■ To enter any other function, click the More button. The Paste Function dialog will appear. Select your function, and then click OK. The Formula Palette will be displayed. (For details, see "Inserting Built-in Functions," page 641). When you have finished inserting your function, the calculator appears again with the function in the Formula box.

5 When you have completed your formula, click OK, and it is entered in the cell or range you selected.

---

tip **Edit formulas with the Formula Calculator**

Though you can edit formulas in the cells that contain them, or in the Formula Bar, you can also use the calculator for this. Simply click a cell or select a range containing a formula, and click the Calculator button on the Formula Bar. The calculator opens and displays the formula from the selected cell or range, ready for editing.

Troubleshooting

The calculator prevents me from seeing my worksheet!

The calculator is a very useful tool, but, unfortunately, it is very large—it is as wide as four columns of a default Excel spreadsheet. If you use an 800x600 screen resolution, it covers more than one-third of the screen width and almost covers your entire worksheet height if you have two toolbars visible. In addition, when you click the If or Sum button, it widens to cover almost eight columns. This makes it very difficult to use. Because you must have access to your worksheets to click and select cells and ranges, you will find yourself moving the calculator out of the way and scrolling to select cells. Unfortunately, the only workaround to this is to use a higher screen resolution, if possible, such as 1024x768. But even at this resolution, the calculator still takes up too much room in its wide form, for conditions and sums. Try it out, and see what works for you. The best balance is probably not to use the calculator all the time; it will be most effective when you are composing formulas using cells that are relatively close to each other.

Understanding Cell References

Excel uses several types of cell references to know where to look for data in worksheets and workbooks. Excel uses the A1 reference style by default. This style refers to cells by the intersections between rows and columns. These might be simple references, such as A1, which refers to the cell at the intersection of column A and row 1. Cell ranges are represented by a pair of cell references separated by colons, with the first part of the reference the top left cell, and the second part the bottom right cell. For example, the reference B3:M25 refers to a cell range beginning at B3 at the top left and extending to M25 at the bottom right. Table 27-3 shows the different ways you can refer to cells and ranges.

Table 27-3. References to Cells and Ranges

To Refer to	Use
The cell in column A and row 4	A4
The range of cells in column A and rows 4 through 10	A4:A10
The range of cells in row 10 and columns B through E	B10:E10
All cells in row 2	2:2
All cells in rows 2 through 4	2:4
All cells in column D	D:D
All cells in columns D through H	D:H
The range of cells intersected by columns A through C and rows 4 through 10	A4:C10

Excel lets you also name cell ranges. You can choose any name you want for a range, and you can even name individual cells and use these names in formulas and functions.

For more information on naming cells and ranges, see "Naming Cell Ranges," page 602.

Working with External and Remote References

Excel lets you use references to cells in other worksheets, other workbooks, and even other programs. References to data in different workbooks are called *external references,* and references to data in other programs are called *remote references*. This ability gives you a great deal of flexibility in how you organize your data. You can have workbooks that contain data, such as catalogs, that are fed into other workbooks making calculations. This is one way to use Excel to make invoices—your product information and prices can be in an external workbook, and, whenever you change prices, the current prices are automatically reflected in your new invoices.

For more information on using external references, see "Linking Data Between Worksheets and Workbooks," page 656.

Chapter 27

The R1C1 Reference Style

Excel has another cell reference style you can use called R1C1. R and C stand for row and column. In this system, you specify cells by the letter R, followed by the row number, and then the letter C, followed by the column number. For example, cell B5 in the A1 system would become R5C2 in the R1C1 system. To use the R1C1 cell reference style, choose Excel, Preferences, and select General. In the Settings section, select the R1C1 Reference Style check box.

The R1C1 cell reference style is efficient for computing row and column positions in macros, but it is a bit confusing for regular use. This is because Excel creates a special kind of relative reference when this style is used. Excel makes references in the R1C1 style relative to the cell where your formula is entered. These references are in the form R[x]C[y], where x is the number of rows above or below the current cell, and y is the number of columns before or after the current cell. For example, if you enter a formula in cell E5 and want to include cell C11 in this formula, Excel shows this cell as R[6]C[−2]. This is because it is in row [5 + 6] and column [5 − 2]. These references do not change if you move that cell, or copy that formula; they are relative to the cell to which they are copied.

Working with Relative and Absolute References

Excel can use both *relative* and *absolute* cell references when you create formulas. By default, relative references are used. When you create a formula, such as in the following example, where cell A3 contains the sum of cells A1 and A2, Excel notes that the two cells in the formula are located at certain positions relative to the cell containing the formula. (Excel does this in the background; you never see it, but it keeps track of these references in relation to the cells where they are found, similar to the R1C1 reference style.)

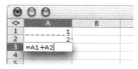

If you copy that formula to another cell, Excel translates the relative cell references and converts them to correspond to the new position. This formula, when pasted into cell B3, changes to be relative to the same cells in column B. Instead of reading =A1+A2, it now reads =B1+B2.

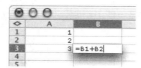

Sometimes, however, you don't want Excel to change your references when you copy formulas to other cells. In this case, you need to use absolute references. An absolute reference is one that tells Excel the exact cell or cells you are referring to. In the preceding example, if you want to keep the A1 and A2 references absolute, you need to write them as follows: =$A$1+$A$2. If you then copy this formula and paste it in another cell, the references will not change.

You can easily change relative references to absolute references. To do this, click a cell containing a formula, and select a cell reference in the Formula Bar or in the cell. Press Command+T; this command cycles from relative to absolute references. If you keep pressing Command+T, you will loop through the various combinations available: absolute column and absolute row ($A$1); relative column and absolute row (A$1); absolute column and relative row ($A1); and back to relative column and relative row (A1).

Chapter 27

---

tip   **Not sure which reference to use?**

Relative references work well with many calculations that you'll need to perform in a worksheet: sums, averages, percentages, and so on. If you only use your formula in one location in your worksheet, you don't need to worry about relative and absolute references. But if you are planning to copy a formula to a different location, you'll need to make the right choice. Relative references are best when you have tables, with similar data in several rows or columns, and you want to calculate totals for each of these rows or columns. If, however, some of your references refer to data that is found in only one cell or range, you must use absolute references. If not, your calculations will be wrong, because Excel will be using data from different, relative cells instead of the precise cells you require.

Copying and Pasting Formulas

When you move or copy a formula, the way the formula is pasted depends on whether you used relative or absolute cell references. If you used absolute references, these references will not change. If you used relative references, however, they will change to correspond to their new location.

For more on relative and absolute references, see "Working with Relative and Absolute References," opposite. For more on copying, pasting, and moving, see "Copying, Pasting, and Moving Cells and Their Contents," page 598.

Using Named Cell Ranges in Formulas

If you want to use specific cells in formulas, and copy them to different locations in your worksheet, the best way is to use named cells or ranges. When Excel pastes a formula into a new cell, it uses relative references (unless you have entered absolute references, as described in "Working with Relative and Absolute References," page 654). But if you use named cells or ranges in your formula, Excel does not change them. They are treated as absolute references. Using named cells and ranges also makes them easier to remember, and can speed up writing formulas—it is much easier to enter DATA_2001 than remember that this name refers to the range G17:V84.

For more on naming cells and cell ranges, see "Naming Cell Ranges," page 602.

Troubleshooting

Excel returns errors when I enter names in formulas.

If you use the Formula Palette to enter arguments in your functions, and enter the names of cell ranges manually, you might sometimes get a #NAME? error. This error means that you have used a name that is not defined in your workbook. Sometimes, the cause of this error is simply a spelling mistake—check the spelling of your name and make sure the correct spelling is used in the function. Other times this error can arise when you have deleted named ranges. You can click the triangle on the Name box to make sure that your names are still in the list. For more information on Excel error codes, see "I receive error messages when I create Excel formulas," page 649.

Linking Data Between Worksheets and Workbooks

Excel lets you use data from any location in your worksheet in a formula. You can also use cells from other worksheets, and even other workbooks. Consider an example in which two different workbooks are open: Sales 2000.xls and Sales 2001.xls. Suppose that each of these workbooks contains a worksheet with similar data, and you want to calculate an average for the yearly totals in these workbooks and place the result in a cell in Sales 2001.xls. You would do the following:

1 Click the cell of Sales 2001.xls where you want to place the result of your calculation.

2 Enter =, and then click the first cell of your calculation (in this example, cell B15 in Sales 2001.xls).

3 Now, enter **+**, since you want to add this cell to another cell.

4 Click once on the other workbook to activate it, and then click the cell with the data you want to use in your calculation (suppose that here, as in the first workbook, this is cell B15).

Excel automatically creates an *external reference* to the cell in the other workbook, Sales 2000.xls, in the form shown here:

'[Sales_2000.xls]Sheet1'!$B$15

The first part of this reference, *[Sales_2000.xls]*, is the name of the workbook being referenced, surrounded by square brackets. Following this is the name of the worksheet in that workbook, *Sheet1*, and this external reference is followed by an exclamation point. Then comes the cell reference, *$B$15*, with dollar signs, which indicate that it is an absolute cell reference. All of this information tells Excel which workbook, worksheet, and cell to look for. You can easily link data and information between workbooks, either by entering this type of reference manually or by simply clicking the cell or range in the external workbook.

caution   External references contain information about the exact location of the external workbook. If you move any of the files used in such references, Excel will no longer be able to make the calculations in your formula. If you open a file containing formulas using external references, and Excel cannot find the external workbook, it will display a dialog asking whether you want to update your linked information. If you click Yes in this dialog, you will be prompted to find the external file. It is much easier, though, to try to make sure that you keep all the necessary files in the same folder. If you use external references often, you might even want to set up one folder containing all of these files, to keep from losing them.

Chapter 28

Working with Lists and Databases

You might work with large amounts of related information in your business: parts lists, contact information, prices, or inventories. Or you might have a collection of objects such as stamps, coins, or records. In both of these cases, you can use Microsoft Excel X to store this information, track it, and manipulate it in many ways. Excel provides extensive tools for managing *lists,* sets of information organized in worksheets. Excel uses two kinds of lists: The first, which is the one you would use to maintain inventories and stamp collection records, is a *database*; Excel uses the term *list* for this. The second type of list in Excel is one created by the List Wizard and maintained by the List Manager. This type of list is used to maintain data integrity and use Excel's powerful, easy-to-use sorting and filtering functions.

This chapter will show you how to create lists, how to use the List Manager, how to sort data according to specific fields, how to select and filter data, and how to organize your lists for maximum efficiency. You will also learn how to use external data in Excel—how to import data from other database programs as text files, from the Web, and from Apple's FileMaker Pro, and how to use Excel as a Word data merge source. You will see how Excel does more than simply calculate data; it can organize any kind of data and function as a powerful database tool.

Building Lists with the List Manager

An Excel list is a simple database made up of rows and columns, like all information stored in worksheets and workbooks. Each row is a record in the list, and each column is a field. The intersection of a row and a column is the field of a

A Little Database Terminology

Databases have their own terminology, which you'll need to know. But there are only three basic things to worry about: fields, records, and databases. You're already familiar with all three in a real-world application that you've used at one time or another: your address book. The entire address book, with all its information, is the *database*. Inside the database, each individual's set of name, address, and phone numbers makes up that person's *record*. And within that record, the individual bits of information—the first name, the last name, the street address, the city, the state, and so on—are the *fields*. So a bunch of fields make up a record, and a bunch of records make up the database.

specific record in the list. The Excel List Manager lets you easily create lists, maintain their data, sort them, filter them, and find data within them.

When you create a list in the List Manager, it is surrounded by a *list frame,* a special border that looks like a window border, which displays when the list is active. When it is not active, this border becomes blue, to indicate that it is a list. Figure 28-1 shows two lists in an Excel worksheet—the list to the left is active, the list to the right is not. Lists created with the List Manager can also be used to create PivotTable Reports.

Tips for Efficient List Layout

Keep these guidelines in mind as you go about creating your lists:

- **One worksheet = one list.** It is best to have only one list per worksheet, unless you use the List Manager. Some list management functions, such as filtering, only work on one list at a time.

- **Think ahead.** Design your list so all rows have the same information in the same column. Remember, a list is a database; each column is a field, and each row is a record.

- **Separate your lists from other data.** Separate your list from other worksheet data by at least one blank column and one blank row. Excel can more easily detect and select the list when you sort, filter, or insert automatic subtotals.

- **No blank rows or columns.** Make sure your lists contain no blank rows or columns (individual blank cells are fine, if a given field is empty). This helps Excel select the list more easily.

- **Put headers and labels above or below the list.** Avoid placing critical data, such as headers and labels, to the left or right of your lists. This data might be hidden when filtering the list.

- **Show rows and columns.** Make sure all your hidden rows and columns are displayed before making changes to the list. It's easy to inadvertently delete hidden rows and columns.

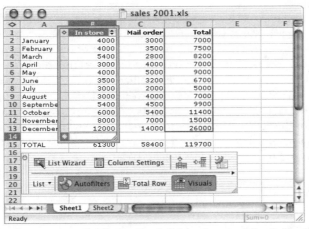

Figure 28-1. The list to the left is active, and the list to the right is not. The List toolbar is also displayed.

For more information on PivotTables, see "Creating PivotTables," page 729.

Creating a List

To create a list, follow these steps:

1 Select the data you want to include in your list. This can be one or several columns of data.

2 Choose Insert, List. This graphic shows a list being created for the Mail Order column shown in Figure 28-1.

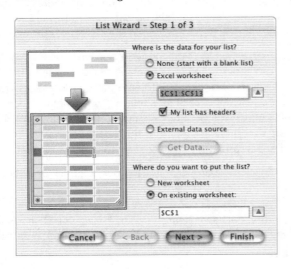

The first page of the List Wizard appears, with the selected cells chosen as the source for the list. You have several options in this window. If your list has headers directly above the selected data, or as part of the selected data, select the My List Has Headers check box. This tells Excel that the headers are not part of the list data. Then choose whether you want your list to be placed in a new worksheet or in the existing worksheet. If you choose the latter option, you can either leave the list in its existing location or select a new location for the list by clicking the triangle button next to the bottom text box and selecting the location for the list from the Formula Palette that appears. When you have made your choices, click Next.

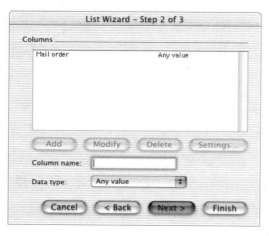

3 The Columns page lets you add, modify, and delete columns in your list, as well as change settings for them. To add a column, enter a name in the Column Name box, select the type of data the column will contain in the Data Type pop-up menu, and then click Add. To change settings for any column, select the column and click Settings to open the Column Settings dialog.

The Column Settings dialog lets you choose many types of settings for your list column. You can choose the type of data it contains in the Data Type box. The choices range from text to different number formats, as well as dates, times, and calculations. Each selection has other options, such as formatting, default values, whether unique values only are allowed, and so on. These options are accessible according to the data type chosen. You can also apply conditional formatting or validation to your list column.

When you have finished making changes to your columns, or settings, click Next.

For more information on using conditional formatting, see "Using Conditional Formatting," page 634. For more information on data validation, see "Using Data Validation," page 665.

```
              List Wizard – Step 3 of 3

  List Options
     List name                    Mail Order List

       Autoformat list after editing    AutoFormat...

       Repeat column headers on each printed page
       Show totals row

     Show list visuals            Auto

     Cancel      < Back      Next >      Finish
```

4   The third page of the List Wizard lets you choose a name for the list, its for-
    matting, and whether totals and visuals are displayed. List visuals are the
    special borders around lists. It is useful to display these borders, because they
    also contain special menus at the tops of your lists that you can use to sort
    and filter the list's data. When you have made these choices, click Finish, and
    your list will be created and displayed in the location you chose.

The final page of the List Wizard lets you choose AutoFormatting for your list. For more information on AutoFormatting, see "Letting AutoFormat Do It," page 630.

InsideOut

You can't use external data sources yet

External data comes to Excel X from a data source that, not surprisingly, resides somewhere outside Excel. Examples include data from other database programs, such as SQL
Server, Oracle, Access, or Informix. Typically, you would run a *query* in Excel, which is an
information request that asks the external database to provide the data that Excel wants.
Excel can retrieve information from any database program for which it has an Open
Database Connectivity (ODBC) software driver. The nice thing about ODBC queries is
that every time you run the query, Excel reaches out to the external database and grabs
the latest data, and then incorporates the updated information into your worksheet.
Queries can also make sure the grabbed data is formatted correctly for use by Excel.

Here's the bad news: as of press time, external data queries using ODBC can't be done
with Excel X. You should be able to select the External Data Source option, on the first
page of the List Wizard, and then click Get Data to create a query to import external
data. The problem is that the ODBC software drivers needed to interface with external
databases are not yet available; they need to be rewritten for Mac OS X. So, in the
meantime, the only solution is to either format your Web data so that you can paste it
into a worksheet first, or use the Get External Data command, discussed in "Importing
Text Files," page 677. If you're importing data from Apple's FileMaker Pro, you can use
Excel's Import From FileMaker Pro command, as discussed in "Importing Data from
FileMaker Pro," page 680.

When your list is created, Excel surrounds it with special borders and displays menus at the top of its columns (if you have selected Show List Visuals). It also displays the List toolbar. This toolbar, shown in Figure 28-2, which gives you quick access to some list functions, displays automatically whenever you click a cell in the list and hides when you click outside the list. Table 28-1 describes the tools on the List toolbar.

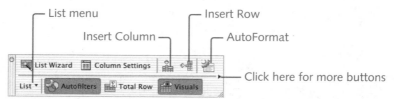

Figure 28-2. The List toolbar, which appears automatically when you click in a list, gives access to many list features.

Table 28-1. Actions Available from the List Toolbar

Button	Action
List Wizard	Click this button to open the List Wizard and make changes to your list.
Column Settings	Click any cell, and then click this button to select the entire column and change its settings.
Insert Column Insert Row	These buttons let you insert columns or rows into your list.
AutoFormat	Click this button to open the AutoFormat dialog and apply AutoFormatting to your list.
List menu	This menu gives access to many list functions, as well as other functions commonly used with lists, such as Chart, PivotTable, and so forth.
AutoFilters	If you click this button, pop-up menus appear at the top of the list columns. These menus let you filter your data quickly and easily.
Total Row	If you click this button, Excel displays a total row at the bottom of each column of numerical data.
Visuals	Clicking this button causes Excel to display special list borders and menus; otherwise a thin blue border surrounds the list.

tip **Get to your list in a jiffy**

If you name your list, you can easily get to it by selecting its name from the Name box in the Formula Bar. Even if you are on a different worksheet in your workbook, you will go to it immediately. For more on naming cell ranges (after all, a list is simply a cell range with delusions of grandeur), see "Naming Cell Ranges," page 602.

Using Data Validation

When you create a list, you can choose to use *data validation* for your different cells. This enables you to specify *restrictions* that must be met when data is entered in a list. You can restrict data to such things as an amount below a certain ceiling, a date before a certain limit, a text limited to a certain length, and more. You can specify very detailed restrictions for validating data, and, if the data entered does not meet these restrictions, it will not be accepted. You can also show input messages when cells are selected and create your own personal error messages to alert users to incorrect data. Data validation is an excellent way to protect your worksheets from erroneous data entry.

To use data validation in a list, follow these steps:

1 Start creating a list as described in "Creating a List," page 661. When you reach the second page of the List Wizard, select the column you want to apply validation to and click the Settings button.

2 In the Column Settings dialog, which is displayed next, click Validation.

The Data Validation dialog appears, with three tabs.

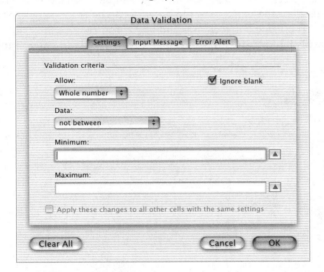

- The first tab, Settings, lets you choose the validation criteria for your data. The Allow pop-up menu lets you choose such data types as whole numbers, decimals, date, and so forth. The Data pop-up menu lets you select the type of condition: between, equal to, above, below, and more. Depending on the restriction you select, one or two fields will be displayed below this menu. They will be labeled Minimum, Maximum, or Value; you enter the values you want to use here.

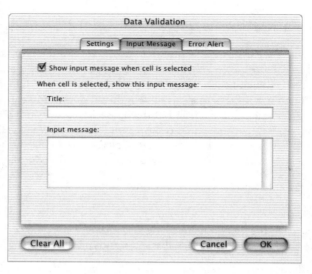

- The Input Message tab lets you choose to have a message displayed when a cell is selected. This message can be as simple as the name of the cell or the type of data to enter or can be more complex, such as "Enter a value between 100 and 500." You can use this tab to provide detailed information to users on the type of data to enter in the cell.

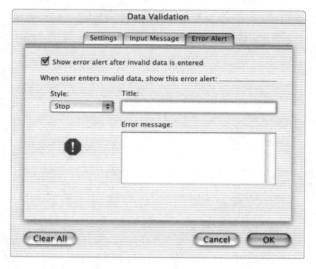

- The Error Alert tab lets you display error messages when incorrect data is entered. These can be Stop, Warning, or Information messages, and you can compose your own text in the Error Message field. Choosing a stop alert from the Style pop-up menu prevents the user from entering data that does not meet conditions. The warning alert displays the

warning message you choose, but allows data entry. The information
alert displays information to the user, but allows data entry.

3 When you have finished entering this information, click OK to return to the
Column Settings dialog, and then click OK to return to the List Wizard.

Troubleshooting

Excel doesn't validate copied data.

Even if you have set up strict validation rules, it is still possible for users to enter data
that doesn't meet the criteria you have set. If a user copies data and pastes it into a cell
with validation rules, or drags cells to a location where validation rules were applied,
Excel simply accepts the new data *and* deletes the validation rules in place. Make sure
you tell users to enter data with the keyboard and not copy and paste data from other
cells to prevent this.

Sorting Columns and Rows

You can see the real power of the List Manager when using it to sort columns and rows.
Though Excel's sort functions are available from the Data menu by choosing the Sort
menu command, the List Manager lets you sort data in lists with just a click of the mouse.
The advantage of using the List Manager is that it groups your data together as a database
and adds special menus to your lists, allowing you to perform database tasks easily.

Figure 28-3 shows a simple list: Sales and Returns data is shown for each of the months
in a year. At the top of each column, a pop-up menu lets you select from a number of
sort possibilities. Clicking one of the pop-up menus lets you choose from many sort
and display options.

Month	Sales	Returns
January	5000	820
February	7500	450
March	4000	280
April	3600	200
May	6000	300
June	5800	250
July	4700	420
August	3800	360
September	6200	420
October	7000	540
November	8200	480
December	9400	640

Figure 28-3. This simple list has pop-up menus at the top of each column to sort data.

If you choose Sort Ascending or Sort Descending from one of the pop-up menus,
as shown in Figure 28-4 on the next page, Excel sorts the records in your list in either
ascending or descending order. When you sort the data in a list in this manner, Excel

Chapter 28

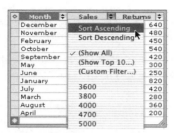

Figure 28-4.   The list pop-up menus make it easy to sort data.

rearranges the entire list: the values that are part of the same record in the list before the sort remain in the same rows after the sort. All of your records are sorted together, not only the column where you select the menu. This means that when sorting the Sales column, the entire list will be rearranged according to the values in this column.

---

tip   **Remove duplicates from a list**

If you have a list that contains duplicate records, there is an easy way to remove all these doppelgangers so that you have only one copy of each record in your list. This tip doesn't work for lists that use the List Manager; you must use it on plain lists. Select the entire list, choose Data, Filter, and then select Advanced Filter. Make sure the Copy To Another Location option is selected. Select another location (only on the active worksheet; you cannot copy to another worksheet), select the Unique Records Only check box, and then click OK. Excel filters your list and copies it to the new location, retaining only unique records, that is, one of each record.

Note that if you don't copy your list to a new location, Excel merely hides the rows containing the duplicates, and does not remove them from the list.

Troubleshooting

Excel sorts days and months in a list incorrectly.

When a list contains a column with either days or months, the sort options available from the list pop-up menu, ascending and descending sorts, will sort the days or months in *alphabetical* order, not in *chronological* order. This behavior means you cannot go back to your original display easily if you want to view your data in chronological order once more. To re-sort your data in this way, follow these steps:

1   Choose Data, Sort.

2   In the first sort section of the Sort dialog, select the name of the column containing the days or months. In the other columns, select None from the pop-up menus.

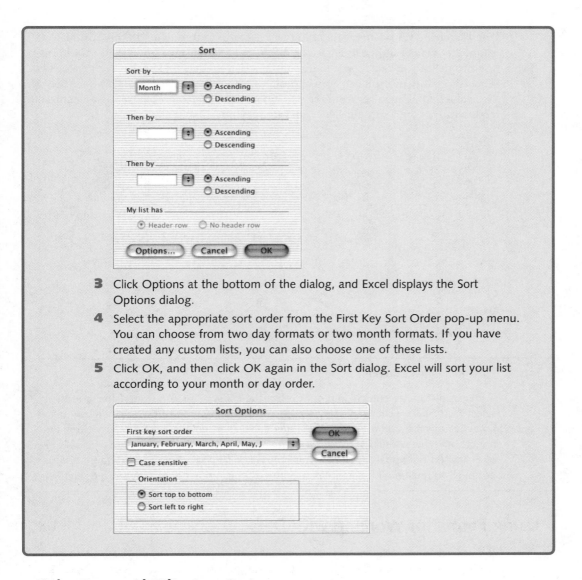

3 Click Options at the bottom of the dialog, and Excel displays the Sort Options dialog.

4 Select the appropriate sort order from the First Key Sort Order pop-up menu. You can choose from two day formats or two month formats. If you have created any custom lists, you can also choose one of these lists.

5 Click OK, and then click OK again in the Sort dialog. Excel will sort your list according to your month or day order.

Selecting and Filtering Data

The List Manager's pop-up menus give you several ways to select and filter data. You can choose Show Top 10, which displays only the records with the 10 highest values. You can select one of the values from the lower section of the list, to display only those records containing the selected value in the column you are sorting. If you have done this, you can then select Show All to display all records again.

You can create your own custom filter by selecting Custom Filter. In the Custom AutoFilter dialog, shown in Figure 28-5, you can select from a number of conditions in the two fields: you can choose to display data that is equal to, less than, or greater than a specific value, and you can even choose two conditions to display data that is between two values. Other choices from the pop-up menus let you choose data that begins with, ends with, contains specific values, and more.

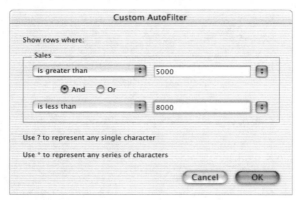

Figure 28-5. Use this dialog to create a custom filter to sort data in a list.

---

tip **Filter individual columns**

If you want to filter one column only, select the column, choose Data, Filter, and then select AutoFilter. Excel will display a pop-up menu at the top of the selected column, and you can sort data in the same manner as you sort data in a list. However, this sort affects only the selected column—since the data is not a List Manager list, the cells in each row do not remain together. This method of sorting lets you sort data that does not need to remain with neighboring cells, but does not work for any list-type data.

Using Forms for Working with Data

If you have long, complex lists, Excel has a function that lets you find, add, change, and delete records: Excel calls this Data Forms, or just Forms. Although this term is a bit ambiguous, the function is powerful and lets you easily access data in lists and work with it. When you choose Data, Form, Excel displays a special dialog, the Form dialog, shown in Figure 28-6, which gives you quick access to the data in your lists.

You can scroll through the records in your list by clicking the arrow buttons on the vertical scroll bar, or by clicking in the scroll bar to move 10 records at a time. If you want to delete a record, click the Delete button when the record is displayed. If you want to create a new record and add it to your list, click the New button, and then enter the

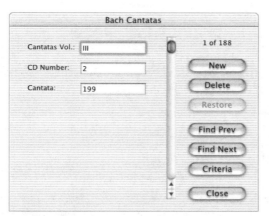

Figure 28-6. The Form dialog is displayed with the name of the active worksheet in its title bar.

data in the record fields. Excel adds new records at the bottom of the list. Though you can add new records simply by typing into your list, using Forms can be more practical in many cases—if you have a large number of fields in your records that extend beyond your window, you don't need to scroll around the worksheet.

You can find data in your list by clicking Criteria. Doing so enables you to create a simple filter to look for specific data in your list. In the blank record that displays, enter criteria in any of the fields, and then click Find Next. The Form dialog displays the first record that matches these criteria. You can move through the rest of the records found by clicking Find Prev or Find Next. You can use operators such as < and > in any of the criteria fields containing data values, and you can use wildcards in fields with text strings. The ? wildcard can be used to match any character, and the * wildcard to match any string. So, if you want to find any city whose name begins with "New," enter **New***. If you want to find any part number whose name contains "XDM," where part numbers are listed in the form 12XDM345, enter ***XDM***.

---

tip   **Remove List Manager formatting**

If you have created a list with the List Manager, you can always remove its formatting and return to a standard worksheet view. Select your list, and then, on the List toolbar, select Remove List Manager from the List pop-up menu. Excel will display a warning, telling you that you will lose column settings defined by the List Manager. Click OK. Your data will now be in standard worksheet form. However, if the List Manager has added any names to the columns, it won't remove these names. You will have to delete the row or cells that contain the name to get back to exactly where you were before you created the list.

Chapter 28

Using DFunctions to Extract List Data

Excel has a set of functions that analyze data in lists and databases. Collectively, these 12 functions are called DFunctions, or database functions. Each of these functions acts on data in a range that meets specific criteria specified in the function's arguments.

The syntax for all of these functions is the following:

Dfunction(database,field,criteria)

All of the arguments in parentheses are required.

- *Database* is the range of cells containing the list or database.
- *Field* is the column used in the function. Because these functions work only on lists and databases, each column is a field. There must be a header in the first row of the field.
- *Criteria* is the range of cells that specify the conditions of the function. The function returns data that matches the conditions in this range. This can either be a cell range, such as A1:B8, or a name, if you have named a cell range. You can use a variety of conditions, from a series of text values, each in its own cell in the range, to numerical values, either unique or in series, and you can also use numerical operators with values, such as >100, or <55. You can even use a formula in a cell as a criterion.

For more information on using DFunctions, see the online help topic "Database Functions."

Subtotaling Data

Excel's Subtotal function lets you analyze and summarize data by inserting intermediate totals, averages, maximums, and minimums into lists of data. This function can also add grand totals at the end of your data and can group and outline your list to make it easier to view and analyze. This function does not work with lists created with the List Manager, however. To use Subtotals, you need to work with raw data on your worksheet.

To add subtotals to a list on a worksheet, follow these steps:

1 Sort your data to group similar records—you might want to sort by month, by sector, by region, or by salesperson. Do this by selecting Data, Sort and choosing the sort keys for the column you want to sort by.

2 Select the data you want to add subtotals to. In Figure 28-7, quarterly sales data for four years is sorted by salesperson and selected.

672

		northwest sales.xls			
	A	B	C	D	E	F

	A	B	C	D	E	F
1	Northwest Region Sales		1998	1999	2000	2001
2	John	Q1	27,317.56	26,949.98	16,479.18	28,856.22
3	John	Q2	22,405.31	29,787.60	28,854.78	32,115.68
4	John	Q3	36,611.23	20,070.10	45,782.66	63,190.68
5	John	Q4	11,157.50	21,717.28	30,056.96	26,390.38
6	Mary	Q1	17,498.50	24,546.10	20,463.45	19,366.60
7	Mary	Q2	17,280.55	15,430.35	36,703.73	56,355.26
8	Mary	Q3	23,662.83	21,981.44	23,956.15	52,637.22
9	Mary	Q4	49,924.20	51,134.33	24,283.80	21,313.54
10	Steve	Q1	20,895.87	25,532.39	28,138.38	28,753.04
11	Steve	Q2	25,195.72	22,513.07	32,586.57	44,433.56
12	Steve	Q3	44,288.22	66,920.98	32,792.46	31,695.19
13	Steve	Q4	35,877.06	28,932.96	32,931.71	44,710.78
14						

Figure 28-7. This worksheet contains data sorted by salesperson.

3 Choose Data, Subtotals to open the Subtotal dialog, shown in Figure 28-8. In this dialog you can choose which columns will be used for subtotals and which function is used. Several options allow you to select whether current subtotals are updated, whether page breaks are added, and whether summaries will be added below data. Select the columns you want to add subtotals to and choose the function. The functions are described in Table 28-2 on the next page.

Figure 28-8. In this example, Excel will display subtotals for each of the four columns selected.

4 Click OK. Excel calculates subtotals and enters them below each section. In the following example, subtotals are added after each salesperson, and a grand total is added at the end.

Chapter 28

	A	B	C	D	E	F
1	Northwest Region Sales		1998	1999	2000	2001
2	John	Q1	27,317.56	26,949.98	16,479.18	28,856.22
3	John	Q2	22,405.31	29,787.60	28,854.78	32,115.68
4	John	Q3	36,611.23	20,070.10	45,782.66	63,190.68
5	John	Q4	11,157.50	21,717.28	30,056.96	26,390.38
6	**John Total**		97,491.60	98,524.96	121,173.58	150,552.96
7	Mary	Q1	17,498.50	24,546.10	20,463.45	19,366.60
8	Mary	Q2	17,280.55	15,430.35	36,703.73	56,355.26
9	Mary	Q3	23,662.83	21,981.44	23,956.15	52,637.22
10	Mary	Q4	49,924.20	51,134.33	24,283.80	21,313.54
11	**Mary Total**		108,366.08	113,092.22	105,407.13	149,672.62
12	Steve	Q1	20,895.87	25,532.39	28,138.38	28,753.04
13	Steve	Q2	25,195.72	22,513.07	32,586.57	44,433.56
14	Steve	Q3	44,288.22	66,920.98	32,792.46	31,695.19
15	Steve	Q4	35,877.06	28,932.96	32,931.71	44,710.78
16	**Steve Total**		126,256.87	143,899.40	126,449.12	149,592.57
17	**Grand Total**		332,114.55	355,516.58	353,029.83	449,818.15

> **note** Once you have added subtotals, you can make changes to your data, if you want to make projections or extrapolations. If you click any of the subtotal cells, you will see that they contain formulas. Your data, its subtotals, and grand totals are fully dynamic.

Table 28-2. **Subtotal Functions**

Function	Description
Sum	Generates a total for each group.
Count	Counts the number of items in each group.
Average	Averages the values of each group.
Max	Displays the largest value in each group.
Min	Displays the smallest value in each group
Product	Multiplies all the values in each group.
Count Nums	Displays the number of records in the group that contain numeric data.
StdDev	Estimates the standard deviation of a population, where the list is the sample.
StdDevp	Calculates the standard deviation of a population, where the list is the entire population.
Var	Estimates the variance of a population, where the list is the sample.
Varp	Calculates the variance of a population, where the list is the entire population.

Grouping and Outlining Data

When worksheets contain a lot of data, with subtotals and totals, you don't necessarily need to see all the data. Often the totals are sufficient. But you cannot erase the raw data, since it is used to calculate totals. You can use the Group and Outline functions in Excel to better organize your data on complex worksheets, and, with a simple click of the mouse, you can hide and show large sections of data. If you Outline a worksheet, you can use a full range of different hierarchical views to examine your data.

Figure 28-9 shows a worksheet with sales information by salesperson and by quarter, over four years, with totals in various locations on the worksheet. If you want to group all of the data in the columns so you can easily hide everything but the totals in column G, select columns A to F, and then choose Data, Group And Outline, Group. Click Columns in the Group dialog and click OK. The selected columns are grouped, and the worksheet now has level bars above it.

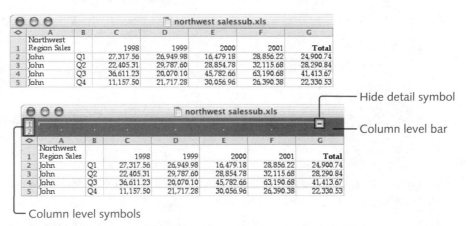

Figure 28-9. Two views of the same worksheet. At the bottom, the worksheet's columns have been grouped.

If you click the hide detail symbol above the worksheet, the grouped columns—in this example, columns A to F—will be hidden, and only the Total column will be displayed. If you do this, the hide detail symbol changes from a minus to a plus sign; click this symbol, and the hidden columns will be displayed again. If you click the column level symbols, you can easily toggle between different views. In this example there are only two views, but, if you have several levels, each column level symbol changes the display to show more or fewer levels. See Figure 28-10 on the next page for another example of an outlined worksheet.

To ungroup rows or columns, simply select the rows or columns you want to ungroup, and choose Data, Group And Outline, Ungroup. In the Group dialog, choose whether you want to ungroup rows or columns. Click OK, and your data will be ungrouped.

Chapter 28

Automatic Outlining

Though you can easily group rows and columns to create a personalized outline, Excel can also do it for you automatically with just a few clicks. Either select the range you want to outline, or click anywhere in your worksheet if you want the entire worksheet to be outlined. Choose Data, Group And Outline, Auto Outline. Excel examines your worksheet and creates an outline based on the subtotals and totals it contains. Figure 28-10 shows how Excel automatically outlines the worksheet shown in Figure 28-9 on the preceding page. You can see that it has created two levels for the columns—one showing all the columns, another showing the first two columns and the Total. For the rows, it has created three levels: one with the Grand Total, another showing all the rows, and one in between that shows the subtotals.

		A	B	C	D	E	F	G
	1	Northwest Region Sales		1998	1999	2000	2001	Total
	2	John	Q1	27,317.56	26,949.98	16,479.18	28,856.22	24,900.74
	3	John	Q2	22,405.31	29,787.60	28,854.78	32,115.68	28,290.84
	4	John	Q3	36,611.23	20,070.10	45,782.66	63,190.68	41,413.67
	5	John	Q4	11,157.50	21,717.28	30,056.96	26,390.38	22,330.53
	6	John Total		97,491.60	98,524.96	121,173.58	150,552.96	116,935.78
	7	Mary	Q1	17,498.50	24,546.10	20,463.45	19,366.60	20,468.66
	8	Mary	Q2	17,280.55	15,430.35	36,703.73	56,355.26	31,442.47
	9	Mary	Q3	23,662.83	21,981.44	23,956.15	52,637.22	30,559.41
	10	Mary	Q4	49,924.20	51,134.33	24,283.80	21,313.54	36,663.97
	11	Mary Total		108,366.08	113,092.22	105,407.13	149,672.62	119,134.51
	12	Steve	Q1	20,895.87	25,532.39	28,138.38	28,753.04	25,829.92
	13	Steve	Q2	25,195.72	22,513.07	32,586.57	44,433.56	31,182.23
	14	Steve	Q3	44,288.22	66,920.98	32,792.46	31,695.19	43,924.21
	15	Steve	Q4	35,877.06	28,932.96	32,931.71	44,710.78	35,613.13
	16	Steve Total		126,256.87	143,899.40	126,449.12	149,592.57	136,549.49
	17	Grand Total		332,114.55	355,516.58	353,029.83	449,818.15	372,619.78
	18							

Figure 28-10. Excel's Auto Outline function creates an outline for this worksheet according to its totals and subtotals.

Now that your worksheet is outlined, you can easily toggle among various views to display only subtotal or total rows and columns or all of the data used in these calculations. Simply click the hide detail and show detail symbols to hide or display your data, or click the row level or column level symbols to collapse or expand the outline. For example, you can reduce the worksheet shown in Figure 28-10 to that shown next by hiding one level of data horizontally and one level vertically. Your data remains in the worksheet, but you don't see it.

		A	B	G
	1	Northwest Region Sales		Total
	6	John Total		116,935.78
	11	Mary Total		119,134.51
	16	Steve Total		136,549.49
	17	Grand Total		372,619.78
	18			

676

Using External Data

Excel is a powerful tool for formatting, calculating, and analyzing data, but if your data is somewhere else, you need to get it into a worksheet to use all of these functions. Excel has tools to import text files, data from FileMaker Pro databases, and data from the Web.

Importing Text Files

Because Excel can import text files, you can take data from almost any program and use it in your worksheets—most programs that handle text or data let you save it in text format. Depending on the way this data is saved, you might be able to use it right away, or you might have to move it around to make it accessible. For example, if the original data was saved from a database program and contained a lot of blank fields, you might have many empty rows or columns.

---

tip   **Import data from Word tables into Excel**

If you have data in a Word table, it is a breeze to import this data into Excel. Simply select all the data in the table, switch to Excel, and paste it onto your worksheet. For more on using tables in Word, see Chapter 9, "Laying Out Text."

To import a text file, follow these steps:

1 Choose Data, Get External Data, Import Text File. Select the text file you want to import in the Choose A File dialog, and click Get Data to open the Text Import Wizard.

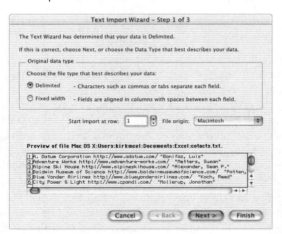

This wizard examines your file and determines, if possible, what type of data it contains. The Original Data Type section shows the type of file you are importing. If the Text Import Wizard thinks it is a tab- or comma-delimited file, it chooses Delimited. If the wizard thinks it is a fixed width file, with fields aligned in columns and spaces between each field, it chooses Fixed Width. If you do not agree with this choice, select the option that corresponds to the file format.

2 Use the pop-up menu to specify whether the file was created on a Macintosh, Windows, or DOS or OS/2 computer. This choice helps Excel know how to handle special characters such as returns and line breaks. You can also choose at which row the import will begin. If the text file has headers, you might not want to include the first row. At the bottom of the Text Import Wizard page is a preview window, which shows what the data is in the file. When you have finished making your choices on this page of the wizard, click Next to go to the second page of the wizard.

3 This page of the Text Import Wizard is where you can see the real power of this wizard. Excel lets you choose among several types of delimiters to separate your data into cells. Though the symbol used as a delimiter is often a tab or comma, it can also be a semicolon, a space, or any other character. You can even choose several delimiters—if the original data uses both tabs and spaces to separate fields, select both check boxes. You might need to import data containing several tabs—for example, multiple tabs that were entered between certain fields to align data. With the Treat Consecutive Delimiters As One option, you can clean up even these messy files. Select this check box, and any time multiple delimiters are found they will be reduced to a single delimiter. As you make your selections on this wizard page, the Data Preview section will show you what your data will look like when imported.

When you have completed these selections, click Next to open the third page of the Text Import Wizard.

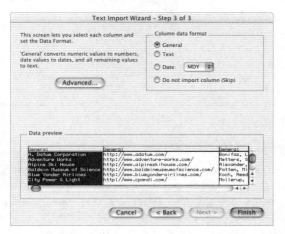

4   The final page of the wizard gives you some additional options for the way Excel handles and formats the data being imported. Click the Advanced button if you want to choose the characters that are to be used to recognize decimal and thousands separators in the imported data. The Data Preview section shows the different columns that will be used when your data is imported. The first column is selected initially. Set the data format for each column by selecting a column in the Data Preview section and then selecting one of these options in the Column Data Format section:

- Choose General to convert numeric values to numbers, date values to dates, and leave all other values as text. This is the default data format, and is best for most data.

- Choose Text to treat all data as text. Numbers and dates are imported in text format as well.

- Choose Date to convert date values to dates, in the order you choose from the pop-up menu.

- Choose Do Not Import Column to skip the selected column. You can easily leave out any of the columns of your data by selecting this option.

5   Click Finish. The Import Data dialog appears as shown on the next page, letting you choose whether you want to import the data into the current worksheet or a new worksheet. If you click Properties, you can set several query, refresh, and layout properties for the data. When you click OK in the Import Data dialog, Excel imports your data and displays the External Data toolbar.

Troubleshooting

The zeros disappeared in my imported data.

If you want to import any data containing leading zeros (such as part numbers that begin with zeros, ZIP codes, or some international phone numbers), and you merely choose the default import settings, Excel will treat the cells containing these numbers as numerical values, and drop the leading zeros. If this data needs to remain as is, with the leading zeros, on the third page of the Text Import Wizard, select Text format for the column with the numeric data, and Excel will retain the zeros.

Importing Data from FileMaker Pro

FileMaker Pro is the most popular database program for Macintosh, and quite popular on Windows. If you work with this program, you can integrate it with Excel by importing your data directly from FileMaker Pro database files into Excel. With other databases you must save files in a format that Excel can import—text, SYLK, DIF, and so forth—but Excel can read native FileMaker Pro files. After importing, you can refresh data in your Excel worksheet to reflect changes in the FileMaker Pro database.

To work with FileMaker Pro files, you must have a version of FileMaker Pro installed on your computer. When importing data, Excel opens FileMaker Pro, and then imports the data. It doesn't matter whether you have a Mac OS X version of FileMaker Pro; if you have a Mac OS 9 version, it will open in the Classic Mac OS environment and you can import the file as though you have the Mac OS X version.

To import a FileMaker Pro database into Excel, follow these steps:

1 First create a new workbook.

2 Choose Data, Get External Data, and then select Import From FileMaker Pro. Select your FileMaker Pro file from the dialog, and then click Choose. The FileMaker Import Wizard opens, as shown in Figure 28-11. This wizard shows all the fields in the FileMaker Pro database for each of the layouts in the database file.

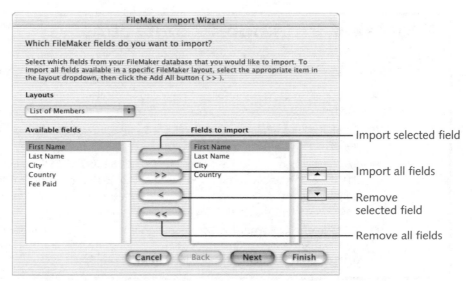

Figure 28-11. The FileMaker Import Wizard lets you choose which fields to import into your Excel Worksheet.

3 Choose a FileMaker Pro layout from the Layouts pop-up menu. The list of available fields shows which fields are used in this layout, and you can choose which of these fields you import.

4 To import a field, click the field in the Available Fields list, and then click the single arrow button to move the field name to the Fields To Import list. To import all the fields, click the double arrow button. After you choose the fields to import, click Next.

5 The second page of the FileMaker Import Wizard lets you filter the records you import from your database. You can choose up to three criteria; each criterion is applied to a field, and you can choose from a number of mathematical operators, or the contents of a field. After you have applied any filter criterion, click Finish.

6 Excel asks where you want to insert the imported data. You can choose from a location on the active worksheet or a new worksheet in the same workbook. Click OK, and Excel inserts the data into your worksheet.

Importing Web Data

You can use Excel to import data directly from the Web using special Web query files. These files retrieve data from the World Wide Web or from a local intranet. You can refresh this data regularly, or automatically—because it is external data, it might be updated often at its source. Several Web query files are installed when you install Office X. You can find them in the Applications/Microsoft Office X/Office/Queries folder.

FileMaker Pro Import Limitations

When you import FileMaker Pro data into Excel, you should be aware of the following limitations:

- Excel only imports the results of FileMaker Pro calculations, not the formulas used in the calculations.
- Excel does not retain the FileMaker Pro sorting order. You will have to re-sort your data after importing it into Excel.
- Excel worksheets can be a maximum of 65,536 rows by 256 columns. If your FileMaker Pro database contains more than 65,535 records or 256 fields, only the first 65,535 records and 256 fields from FileMaker will be imported. The first row on the worksheet is reserved for field names.
- A cell in an Excel worksheet can contain up to 32,767 characters. FileMaker Pro text fields that contain more than 32,767 characters are truncated, and only the first 32,767 characters are imported into Excel.

To see how Web queries work, you can open one of them in a blank worksheet. To do this, create a new workbook. Choose Data, Get External Data, and then select Run Saved Query. The Choose A Query dialog will open with the Queries folder selected. Select the query called MSN MoneyCentral Major Indices. A dialog appears asking where you want to put the data. You can either put it in the active worksheet, or choose to create a new worksheet. Click OK, and Excel will connect to the Web to retrieve that data for the query. In a few seconds (depending on your Internet connection), the query data will appear in your worksheet, as shown in Figure 28-12.

You can copy the data at any time and use it in another worksheet, create a chart, or paste it in any kind of document, such as a Word file or an e-mail message. You can format the data in any way you want, changing the size of columns and rows, changing fonts, or hiding cells, or make any other changes you wish.

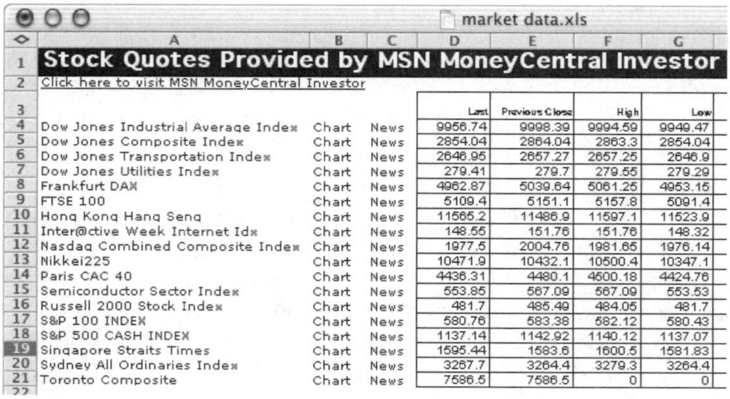
market data.xls

Stock Quotes Provided by MSN MoneyCentral Investor

Click here to visit MSN MoneyCentral Investor

			Last	Previous Close	High	Low
Dow Jones Industrial Average Index	Chart	News	9956.74	9998.39	9994.59	9949.47
Dow Jones Composite Index	Chart	News	2854.04	2864.04	2863.3	2854.04
Dow Jones Transportation Index	Chart	News	2646.95	2657.27	2657.25	2646.9
Dow Jones Utilities Index	Chart	News	279.41	279.7	279.55	279.29
Frankfurt DAX	Chart	News	4962.87	5039.64	5061.25	4953.15
FTSE 100	Chart	News	5109.4	5151.1	5157.8	5091.4
Hong Kong Hang Seng	Chart	News	11565.2	11486.9	11597.1	11523.9
Inter@ctive Week Internet Idx	Chart	News	148.55	151.76	151.76	148.32
Nasdaq Combined Composite Index	Chart	News	1977.5	2004.76	1981.65	1976.14
Nikkei225	Chart	News	10471.9	10432.1	10500.4	10347.1
Paris CAC 40	Chart	News	4436.31	4480.1	4500.18	4424.76
Semiconductor Sector Index	Chart	News	553.85	567.09	567.09	553.53
Russell 2000 Stock Index	Chart	News	481.7	485.49	484.05	481.7
S&P 100 INDEX	Chart	News	580.76	583.38	582.12	580.43
S&P 500 CASH INDEX	Chart	News	1137.14	1142.92	1140.12	1137.07
Singapore Straits Times	Chart	News	1595.44	1583.6	1600.5	1581.83
Sydney All Ordinaries Index	Chart	News	3267.7	3264.4	3279.3	3264.4
Toronto Composite	Chart	News	7586.5	7586.5	0	0

Figure 28-12. This Web query retrieves indices for leading world stock markets.

You can also save the Excel workbook containing this query. If you do so, and want the file to refresh automatically when you open it, choose Data, Get External Data, and then select Data Range Properties. Select the Refresh Data On File Open check box, and the data will be refreshed automatically when you open the file.

---

tip   **Create your own Web queries**

Web queries are made from forms in Hypertext Markup Language (HTML). If you know how to make these forms, you can easily make your own Web queries to retrieve external data. You can use the sample Web queries in the Office/Queries folder as a guide. Modify these files with any text editor by changing the HTML code to make your own queries.

Because external data from the Web or a FileMaker Pro database is dynamic and might be updated regularly at its source, you can choose to refresh the data by choosing Data, Refresh Data. Each time you refresh the data, Excel will connect to the Web, or reread the FileMaker Pro database, to retrieve the latest data. Excel will not, however, indicate that there are changes in any of the data—it will simply refresh its display if necessary.

Using Excel Data as a Word Data Merge Source

Microsoft Word allows you to import data from files and merge it with your letters, envelopes, mailing labels, and other documents. You can use Excel to create files to use as a data merge source for Word documents and ensure that the formatting and layout is perfect, whether it be for just a few contacts or for large documents with hundreds of records.

What is most important in this task is that you structure your Excel worksheet so Word's Data Merge Manager can import the data smoothly. To do this, ensure that your data meets the following conditions:

- In most cases, you will want to use only one data source. Though you can use several data sources, it is simpler to have all your data in one file.

- The first row of your worksheet should contain column headers. These should be clear, so you know exactly what data they contain. Use headers such as Title, First Name, Middle Name, Last Name, Address 1, Address 2, ZIP Code, and so forth.

- Each field name should be unique. Don't have two fields called Address; name them Address 1 and Address 2. Don't have a field with full names if you need to handle the first and last names separately. Also, if you have separate first and last name fields, you can use the last name in the address; in an Attention: field in the address; and in a salutation, such as Dear Mr. Smith.

● Each bit of information you use should be in its own field. Don't put an entire address in one field; split it by lines, and call them Address 1, Address 2, and so on. Think of adding a third address field if your addresses might contain more than two lines.

● Don't leave any blank rows in your worksheet.

> For more information on merging data into Word documents, see "Introducing the Data Merge Manager," page 338.

Exporting Data from Excel

Though you can easily import data from files created by other programs, you can also save Excel worksheets in other formats for use in different programs. When exporting data, Excel saves only the active worksheet, and, in most cases, removes all formatting except for number formatting.

To export data from an Excel worksheet, choose File, Save As. A standard Save dialog appears. You can choose a different name for your worksheet by entering a name in the Save As field, and you can select a location by choosing a folder from the Where pop-up menu or by navigating through the column browser. You can choose among a wide variety of formats in the Format pop-up menu. Table 28-3 presents these formats and discusses features not saved when exporting data.

Table 28-3. Excel Export Formats

Format	Export Information
Previous Excel version formats	You can save your worksheet in a variety of Excel formats. These files files can be opened with previous versions of Excel, but not all information and data on your worksheet will be retained. For more information on saving files in older Excel formats, see the online help topic "Formatting and Features not Transferred in File Conversions."
Text	Excel can save files in several text formats: Formatted Text (Space Delimited), Text (Tab Delimited), Text (Windows), and Text (OS/2 Or MS-DOS). If you save a worksheet in one of these text formats, Excel only saves the text and values as they are displayed in the worksheet. Formulas are not saved, nor are any formatting, graphics, charts, or other objects. If you save as Tab Delimited, Excel separates cells with tab characters, and rows with return characters. Tab delimited format is the most commonly used of the text-only export formats; it can be read by many other programs, on many different computing platforms. If you choose Space Delimited, Excel inserts spaces to align the contents of the cells. The Windows and OS/2 Or MS-DOS text formats convert Macintosh character sets into the appropriate character sets.

Table 28-3. *(continued)*

Format	Export Information
CSV	If you save a worksheet in Comma Separated Values (CSV) format, Excel only saves the text and values as they are displayed on the worksheet. Formulas are not saved, nor are any formatting, graphics, charts, or other objects. Excel separates cells with commas, and rows with return characters.
DBF	DBF formats are used to save Excel worksheets so that they can be opened by different versions of the dBase database program. Excel saves only the text and values as they are displayed on the worksheet. Formulas are not saved, nor are any formatting, graphics, charts, or other objects. There are three DBF formats: DBF 2, 3, and 4. All rows are saved, but the number of columns saved depends on the format chosen: ● DBF 2 (dBASE II): 32 columns ● DBF 3 (dBASE III): 128 columns ● DBF 4 (dBASE IV): 256 columns
DIF	The DIF (Data Interchange Format) format saves only the text, values, and formulas as they are displayed on the worksheet. If worksheet options are set to display formula results in the cells, only the formula results are saved in the converted file. To save formulas, display the formulas on the worksheet before saving the file by choosing Excel, Preferences, and then select the Formulas check box in the View section.
SYLK	The SYLK (Symbolic Link) format saves only the text, values, and formulas as they are displayed on the worksheet, and some cell formatting. All rows are saved; up to 255 characters are saved per cell. If an Excel function is not supported in SYLK format, Excel calculates the function before saving the file and replaces the formula with the resulting value.
Web Page	You can save your worksheet as an HTML file that can be viewed on the Internet or an intranet by any Web browser. Several additional options are available when saving worksheets as Web pages. Click the Web Options button in the Save As dialog to set these options. For more on saving Excel workbooks as Web pages, see the online help topic "Save Microsoft Excel Data on a Web Page."

Chapter 28

Analyzing and Presenting Data with Charts

If a picture is worth a thousand words, a chart is certainly worth a hundred cells. Rows and columns of data can be confusing, but a well-designed chart can make data understandable in one glance. The powerful and flexible chart functions in Microsoft Excel X let you create many different types of charts, both to analyze and present your data graphically. You can enhance your charts with legends and gridlines and print them in black and white or in color. In this chapter, you will learn how to create all kinds of charts, including the basic techniques for designing effective charts, how to format charts, and how to print them, so that your data can speak for itself.

Understanding Chart Types

Excel lets you choose from more than a dozen different types of charts, and a number of variations of these basic charts, some of them in two dimensions and others in three dimensions. Each type of chart is designed to present a specific type of data and to highlight certain relationships between the values displayed in the chart. Some charts, such as column charts, are ideal for displaying data by period, while others, such as pie charts, show data as part of a whole. You will want to choose the type of chart that best fits your data, but until you've gained some experience with charts, you might find it useful to try different chart types to see which one works best for you. Table 29-1 on the next page shows the different standard chart types and describes the kind of data they present best.

Table 29-1. **Excel Chart Types and Their Uses**

Icon	Chart Type	Description and Use
	Bar Chart	Bar charts show unique values. They are very useful when comparing values, such as sales, over different periods and for different items. Stacked bar charts, like area charts, display both individual values and the sum of several values for a given item. There is a 2-D and a 3-D version of this chart.
	Column Chart	Column charts, like bar charts, show individual items and their relationship. They are very useful for showing variations over time. There is a 2-D and a 3-D version of this chart.
	Pie Chart	Pie charts show proportional relationships between several values and a whole, often as percentages. There is a 2-D and a 3-D version of this chart.
	Line Chart	Line charts show data trends over time or other intervals. They are good for showing variations in values, such as stock prices. There is a 2-D and a 3-D version of this chart.
	Area Chart	Area charts show the magnitude of change over time, displaying both individual values and the sum of all values in the chart. This type of chart is good for showing both unique and cumulative values together. There is a 2-D and a 3-D version of this chart.
	3-D Surface Chart	Surface charts are useful when you want to find optimal combinations of two sets of data. This type of chart is especially practical when you want to examine how two axes of data interact to give a third result.
	Stock Chart	Stock charts are akin to column charts, but show the high, low, and average values over a given time period.
	Radar Chart	Radar charts show the relationships of several values to a central point. They show data for several criteria for each of a number of items.
	(XY) Scatter Chart	Scatter charts show the relationships among several data series plotted as x-y coordinates. They are most often used for scientific and statistical data.

Table 29-1. *(continued)*

Icon	Chart Type	Description and Use
	Bubble Chart	Bubble charts are a kind of scatter chart. Data markers are plotted on two axes, and the size of the data marker indicates a third value.
	Doughnut Chart	Doughnut charts are like pie charts, but their concentric circles allow them to display several data series, often with each ring being a time period or other category of data.
	3-D Cylinder Chart	Cylinder charts are a three-dimensional version of column and bar charts, and and are useful when you want to present your data more dramatically.
	3-D Cone Chart	Cone charts are a three-dimensional version of column and bar charts.
	3-D Pyramid Chart	Pyramid charts are a three-dimensional version of column and bar charts.

Chart Design Tips

Choosing the right kind of chart is not always simple. Although your choices might be limited for some kinds of data, for others, many possibilities might fit your data and how you want to present it. Here are some tips to help you make the right choices:

● Think of what kind of data you are presenting, and what aspect of this data you want to highlight. If you are presenting data where totals are more important than the individual values that make them up, area charts and stacked bar charts are best. If you are showing percentages, only pie charts really fit the bill.

● If you have many data series to present, keep in mind that your chart might be hard to read if you use a 3-D chart. Each bar or column takes up more space because of the 3-D effects.

● If you plan to print your chart, rather than simply insert it into a Microsoft Word document that will be viewed on-screen or in a Microsoft PowerPoint presentation, you should think about the colors you use and how good they will look on paper. Make a few test prints of your chart and adjust your colors if necessary. If you have to print in black and white, you are better off using patterns than colors.

For more information on printing charts, see "Printing Charts," page 708.

(continued)

Chart Design Tips *(continued)*

- Use colors that contrast well. Don't use, say, red, orange, and yellow for a chart with three data series; use red, blue, and green. The more contrast, the easier the data is to read.

- Make sure your charts are big enough to be easily read. Consider pasting them into their own chart sheets, rather than leaving them on the worksheets that contain their source data, so that you can enlarge them as much as possible.

- Think about the culture of the people who will be seeing your charts. In Western countries, we are accustomed to interpreting column charts, which show data over time, by reading them from left to right. But in Asian and Middle Eastern countries, people generally read from right to left, and might not perceive the changes shown in your charts in the same way.

- Make sure you have the right perspective when using 3-D pie charts. When you create a chart like this, the segment closest to the front of the chart is exaggerated, and might even look bigger than an equivalent-sized segment at the back of the chart. Of course, you might want to take advantage of this effect if you want your data to look better.

- Perspective counts with 3-D bar and column charts too. If you have a lot of data series, viewers can be confused, because each bar or column has two lines along the axis showing its value—one is the real value, the other is the line used for the 3-D effect.

Creating Charts

The quickest way to create a chart with Excel is to select the data you want to display and press F11. When you use this shortcut, Excel will create an express chart using the default chart settings and paste it into a new chart sheet (called Chart1, or Chart*n*, if you already have other chart sheets in your workbook). This shortcut is very useful for a quick view of your data, and is also good if the default chart settings fit your needs. You can always create your chart in this manner, and then change its settings. For more on tweaking charts, see "Chart Formatting," page 695.

InsideOut

Choose and customize the default chart settings

If you often need to make charts, and always use the same type of data and want the same type of chart, the quick chart method described above can be a timesaver. By changing the default chart settings, you can make sure that you get the chart that you want.

To modify the default settings, click in a chart to make the Chart item appear on the Excel menu, and then click Chart, Chart Type. Select a chart type from the Chart Type list, and then click the Set As Default Chart button. Excel will display a dialog asking you to confirm this change. Click OK if you are sure that you want to make the change. From this point on, every time you make a chart by pressing F11, it will be the type you have selected as the default type.

Using the Chart Wizard

Excel's Chart Wizard walks you through the steps to create a chart. If you want more flexibility than you get by pressing F11 and making a default chart, the Chart Wizard gives you access to many more choices to create and format your charts. To create a chart with the Chart Wizard, follow these steps:

1 In the worksheet, select the data that you want to display in your chart. Make sure that you only select raw data, not totals or subtotals. If you select these amounts, Excel will make a chart with the totals and the data used to make them, which usually results in a chart that doesn't accurately represent the data. If your worksheet has header rows or columns, select them as well—Excel will use these as labels for the chart.

	A	B	C
1		In store	Mail order
2	January	4000	3000
3	February	2000	3500
4	March	2000	1200
5	April	3000	4000
6	May	4000	5000
7	June	3500	3000
8	July	3000	2000
9	August	3000	4000
10	September	4000	4500
11	October	6000	5400
12	November	8000	7000
13	December	12000	10000

Chart
Wizard

2 Click the Chart Wizard button on the Standard toolbar, or choose Insert, Chart. The first page of the Chart Wizard appears, as shown in Figure 29-1 on the next page.

3 Select a chart type either from the Standard Types tab or the Custom Types tab. Each chart type also has several sub-types; in many cases there are 3-D versions of basic charts, as well as other variants. If you select a standard type, click the Press And Hold To View Sample button to get a preview of what your chart will look like. If you don't like it, choose another chart type. When you have chosen your chart type, click Next.

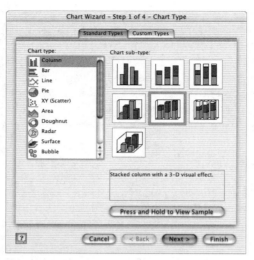

Figure 29-1. Get started creating a chart by selecting a chart type from the first page of the Chart Wizard.

4 On the second page of the Chart Wizard, shown in Figure 29-2, Excel examines your data to determine whether the data series are in rows or columns, indicates its decision by selecting either the Rows or Columns Series In button, and displays a preview of your chart based on the data range you selected. If Excel's choice is wrong, select the other Series In option.

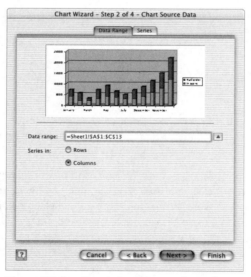

Figure 29-2. Excel shows a preview of your chart based on the selected data range.

5 Click the Series tab, and you can see Excel's choices for the names of your data series and their values. If these choices are not correct, click the appropriate triangle button to select different cells on your worksheet. When finished with this page, click Next.

6 The third page of the Chart Wizard enables you to define many options for your chart:

■ On the Titles tab, choose a name for the chart, if you want one to be displayed, and names for the different axes. These titles are text box objects that you can move around on your chart.

■ The Axes tab lets you choose which axes are displayed. This does not affect all types of charts. Change the settings to see the result in the preview box.

■ The Gridlines tab enables you to choose from several options that affect the display of gridlines. Change the settings to see the result in the preview box.

■ The Legend tab enables you to choose whether to display a legend, and where you want it displayed.

■ The Data Labels tab enables you to choose whether to display data labels. Data labels are useful if you absolutely need to display your values in labels, but, if you have many values, they might clutter up the chart and be hard to read.

■ The Data Table tab enables you to choose whether you want a data table displayed beneath your chart, containing the values shown in the chart. Such a table is easier to read than data labels.

When you have finished setting the options on this page, click Next.

7 The final page of the Chart Wizard enables you to choose where to place the chart. You can either put it on a new sheet (and choose the name for this sheet), or have it inserted as an object on any sheet of your workbook. You cannot, however, have it placed in a new workbook. Click Finish, and Excel creates your chart.

A *chart sheet* is a special sheet in a workbook that contains only a chart. When you create a chart and place it on a chart sheet, the chart displays alone, with no cells around it or behind it. However, this chart is linked to the data you selected when creating it, and whenever that data changes the chart changes as well. Depending on the size of the chart, you might or might not see all of the labels. In Figure 29-3 on the next page, for example, not all of the months are displayed because there is not enough room. If you enlarge the view, by using the Zoom pop-up menu on the Standard toolbar, you will be able to view all the labels.

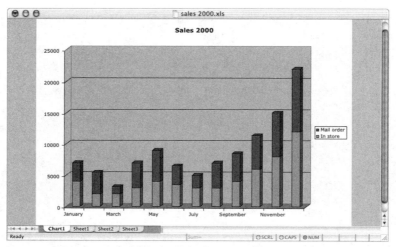

Figure 29-3. Because of the width allotted in the chart sheet to this stacked bar chart, only every other month is labeled.

---

note When you create a chart sheet, it shows up as Chart*n* in the sheet tab area at the bottom of the workbook window. You can switch to the chart at any time by clicking its tab, and you can also rename or rearrange chart sheet tabs in your workbook as you would any other sheet tab. For more information, see "Getting the Most Out of Workbooks," page 569.

InsideOut

Display the Chart toolbar

If you are used to Excel 2001, you might have noticed that in Excel X, when you create a new chart, the Chart toolbar is not displayed automatically. This is because most of the commands on the Chart toolbar are now found on the Formatting Palette, so if the Formatting Palette is open, the Chart toolbar doesn't automatically appear. You can still open the Chart toolbar, though, by choosing View, Toolbars and selecting Chart.

Creating Embedded Charts

If you choose to create your chart on a worksheet, it is called an embedded chart. An *embedded chart* is an object, similar to any graphic you add to your worksheets. Like a chart placed on its own chart sheet, embedded charts are updated automatically when worksheet data used to define them changes. The main difference between a chart on a chart sheet and an embedded chart is that you can move the embedded chart around and change its size more easily. You can increase or decrease its size by clicking its border and dragging one of the handles. To move the embedded chart, select it by clicking on its border. When the selection handles appear, click the chart on its border (but not directly on one of the selection handles), and drag it to a new location.

Another advantage to using embedded charts can be seen in Figure 29-4. When you select the plot area of an embedded chart, a blue border appears around the data used to define the chart. You can click one of the handles on this border and drag it to dynamically change the data included in your chart, and see the changes immediately without having to switch to a chart sheet.

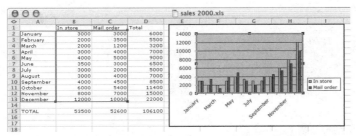

Figure 29-4. When the plot area of an embedded chart is selected, a border appears around the cells used in the chart.

Chart Formatting

When you create a chart with the Chart Wizard, you can choose many formatting options. But most of the advanced formatting options can only be accessed after the chart has been created. You can change the chart's colors, fonts, and gridlines; adjust its legend; change its titles; and add text. You can also make certain charts transparent to give them a contemporary, professional appearance and improve their readability.

Working with the Chart Menu and Chart Toolbar

Whenever you create a chart, and the chart is selected, the Chart menu replaces the Data menu on the Excel menu bar. This menu gives you access to many chart options and enables you to change such things as the chart type and the source data and gives you access to chart formatting options.

Accessing Your Chart Options Quickly

There are two quick ways to access chart formatting options: the Chart toolbar and the Formatting Palette. Both of these toolbars include buttons that give you easy access to formatting options and other chart functions. The Chart toolbar is more compact, but the Formatting Palette provides more functions, such as letting you choose legend placement and gridlines. Figure 29-5 shows both the Chart toolbar and the Formatting Palette next to a chart.

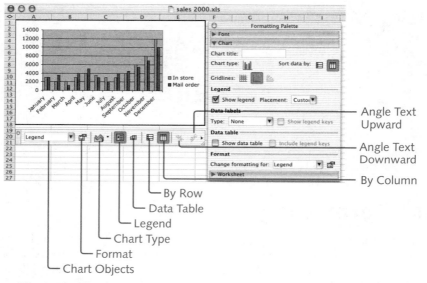

Figure 29-5. The Chart toolbar is shown beneath the chart, and the Formatting Palette is to the right.

---

tip   If the Chart menu goes away, and the Data menu replaces it, it means the chart is not selected (even though it might look selected). Click somewhere else, and then click back in your chart. The Chart menu should return.

Changing Chart Formatting

To change the formatting of any part of a chart, select the object you wish to change, and then click the Format button on the Formatting Palette, shown in Figure 29-6. (Examples in this section will use the Formatting Palette, but most of the same functions are available on the Chart toolbar.) You can either select the object by clicking it or by selecting it from the Chart Objects pop-up menu. The pop-up menu is easier to use, because it shows all the chart objects that you can format. Click the Format button next to that menu to access the formatting options available for the object you've chosen.

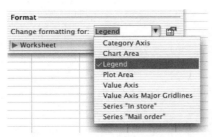

Figure 29-6. Select a chart object from the Chart Objects pop-up menu on the Formatting Palette.

Changing Chart Types

You can change chart types easily by selecting your chart and then clicking the Chart Type button on the Formatting Palette. When you click this button, a new menu opens, showing icons for the basic Excel chart types. If you want to try out several different chart types, click the handle on this menu (as shown next). The menu turns into a floating palette. You can position it where you like, and you can more easily click the different Chart Type buttons to try out different charts.

The Formatting Palette (and the Chart toolbar) only give you access to Excel's basic chart types. If you want to access all of the available chart types, and their sub-types, select the chart and then choose Chart, Chart Types. The Chart Type dialog appears, as shown in Figure 29-7 on the next page, where you can choose among 14 standard chart types and 20 custom types, with dozens of sub-types. Choose a chart type from the list at left, and then select a chart sub-type from those displayed at right. Click OK, and your chart will be configured according to your new selections.

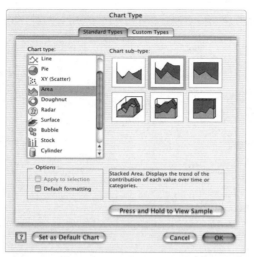

Figure 29-7. The complete set of chart types is only accessible from the Chart menu.

Changing the Perspective of 3-D Charts

When you create a 3-D chart, Excel uses a default perspective to display the chart and its data. The angle at which it is displayed is good for most charts, but you might want to change it to suit your data. To do this, click in the chart to select it, and then choose Chart, 3-D View. The 3-D View dialog opens, as shown in Figure 29-8. You can click the arrow buttons in this dialog to change the elevation, perspective, and rotation, and set the height of the chart to a percentage of the default value. The preview section of this dialog shows you the angle of your chart as you make changes, but the way it looks is not always very clear from this preview. If you want to see your chart as you make your changes, move the 3-D View dialog as far to one side of your screen as possible so you can see all or part of your chart behind it. As you make changes, click Apply, rather than OK. When you click OK, the dialog closes and the changes are applied, but when you click Apply, the dialog remains open, and you can see your chart and make further changes if necessary.

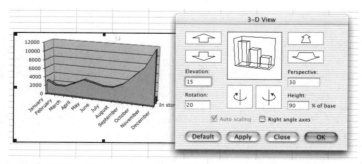

Figure 29-8. If your chart is small enough, you can see it along with the 3-D View dialog as you apply changes.

Chapter 29

Changing Titles and Other Text

If you did not give your chart a title when you created it with the Chart Wizard, or if you created it quickly using the F11 shortcut, you can give it a title now. If you give the chart a title, this text will be displayed above the chart by default. The Formatting Palette has a text field marked Chart Title where you can enter a title easily. Type your title in this field, and press Return.

The title is initially displayed in large, bold type. To change this, select the title either by clicking it or by selecting Chart Title in the Chart Objects pop-up menu on the Formatting Palette. Click the Format button. The Format Chart Title dialog opens. This dialog contains three tabs: Patterns, Font, and Alignment. These tabs are available when formatting any text on your chart.

- **Patterns.** The Patterns tab enables you to choose a border to place around the text. Title and Legend text objects on charts are in text boxes. You can choose a line style, color, and weight and you can make this box display with a drop-shadow behind it by selecting the Shadow check box. A preview of your text box display is shown in the Sample section. The Area section lets you choose a color for the text box. If you click Fill Effects, you can choose from a number of advanced shading styles, color blends, and transparency. Other tabs in the Fill Effects dialog let you choose textures, patterns, and even pictures to place behind your text.

For more on using transparency with charts, see "Setting Chart Transparency," page 702.

- **Font.** The Font tab is a standard font dialog. You can choose a font, style, size, and color, and you can select from a number of underlines and other effects, such as outline and shadow. The Sample box shows how your text will look as you make your changes.

- **Alignment.** The Alignment tab lets you choose a precise orientation for your text, as well as its alignment.

Depending on the text object you format, the tabs might be different. When formatting a legend, the Alignment tab is replaced by the Placement tab, which lets you choose where on the chart your legend is displayed. If you are formatting an x- or a y-axis, the Scale and Number tabs appear in the dialog.

Adding Legends to Your Chart

A chart *legend* explains the significance of the colors or patterns you've used in your chart, which makes it much easier to understand the data you're presenting. Legends contain *legend keys,* small squares containing patterns or colors that match the data series they refer to. If you didn't choose to have a legend displayed when creating your chart with the Chart Wizard, you can still choose to display a legend at any time.

Using Angled Text to Show More Category Labels

In the chart shown earlier, in Figure 29-3, not all of the labels of the category axis are visible because the names of the months are too long to fit horizontally in the available space. If you angle the text, you can display them all, making your chart easier to read. To set these labels at an angle, click the text to select the category axis, and then click the Angle Text Upward button on the Chart toolbar (this function is not available on the Formatting Palette). The text will be displayed at a 45° angle, and all the names of the months will be visible.

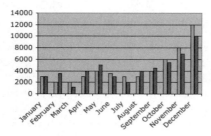

In some cases, if your chart is very small, you will still not be able to see all the labels. To enlarge the chart, click near one of the chart area borders, and drag one of the handles to expand the chart. To adjust the text angle even more precisely, select the category axis, as in the preceding process, and then click the Format button on the Chart toolbar or the Formatting Palette. Click the Alignment tab in this dialog to adjust the alignment precisely.

Simply select the Show Legend check box on the Formatting Palette. The legend will be displayed by default at the right of your chart. To change its location, click the Placement pop-up menu on the Formatting Palette, and choose a new location, or simply drag it to the exact place you want it.

If your data has text headers above its columns, and you select these headers with the data when creating your chart, Excel automatically interprets these headers as the text to use for legends. If, however, you either don't have headers or didn't select them, the legend displayed will be Series1, Series2, and so forth. You can still change this legend by renaming the data series. Just follow these steps:

1 Click in your chart to activate it, and then choose Chart, Source Data.

2 Click the Series tab, shown in Figure 29-9, and select one of the data series.

3 Enter a name for the series, or click the triangle button and select a header or other text on your worksheet.

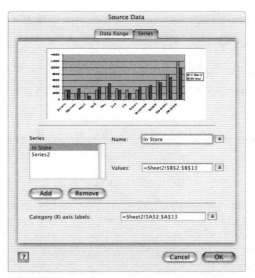

Figure 29-9. You can name data series in the Source Data dialog.

4 Click the next series and name it, and continue until you have named all your data series.

5 Click OK, and these names will appear in your legend.

---

tip **Change legend names**

Even if you have selected headers on your worksheet to use in your chart's legend, you can still change the names. You can leave the headers on your worksheet and have different labels displayed on the chart. To do this, select the chart by clicking anywhere in it, and choose Chart, Source Data. The Series tab will show cell references as the names for the data series. Type over the cell references in the Name field with the names you want to display for each series in your chart and click OK. These new names will display in the legend, and the headers on your worksheet will remain unchanged.

Adding Gridlines

Most of Excel's charts display gridlines by default. Two-dimensional charts use gridlines for the category axis and value axis, and three-dimensional charts add gridlines on the series axis. You can easily hide and display gridlines from the Formatting Palette by clicking one of the Gridlines buttons, shown in Figure 29-10 on the next page. When one of these buttons is depressed (darker in appearance), those gridlines are active and displayed.

Figure 29-10. Gridlines buttons on the Formatting Palette enable you to quickly change which gridlines appear in your chart.

InsideOut

Use gridlines with caution in three-dimensional charts

When Excel creates three-dimensional charts, it uses effects of perspective to give an impression of depth. When you use value axis gridlines on a three-dimensional column chart, you will notice that these lines do not correspond exactly to the values shown by the columns. The effect of perspective skews the positioning of these lines a bit. If it is important that people seeing the chart make the connection between the columns and the precise values shown in the value axis gridlines, think of using data labels on your columns. Data labels will display exact values above the columns. To display data labels, select Value from the Data Labels Type pop-up menu on the Formatting Palette. You might need to enlarge your chart to display these labels correctly; if the values are long, they will overlap.

You can change the type of gridlines used for any of your chart's axes. In the Format section of the Formatting Palette (or the Chart toolbar), select Value Axis Major Gridlines, if you want to change the gridlines for the value axis; select Series Axis Major Gridlines, to change the gridlines for the series axis; or select Category Axis Major Gridlines, to change the gridlines for the category axis. (You can only change the formatting of these gridlines if they are displayed. If not, they will not appear on the Chart Objects pop-up menu.) Click the Format button, and you can adjust the style, color, and weight of the gridlines on the Patterns tab. If you click the Scale tab, you can adjust the gridline scale, or the separations and values used for each gridline.

new feature!
Setting Chart Transparency

One of the most striking new features in Excel X is the possibility of using transparency in charts. (Actually, this feature makes chart data series translucent, not transparent.) This feature takes advantage of Mac OS X's advanced Quartz 2-D drawing technology. It's a cool feature, but it isn't the easiest one to implement in your charts. The benefits are often worth it, however, especially if you are displaying your charts on-screen, rather than printing them. The following steps explain how to make a data series in your chart transparent:

1 Select the data series you want to make transparent on the Chart Objects pop-up menu of the Formatting Palette, and then click the Format button.

2 The Format Data Series dialog appears. If the Patterns tab is not selected, click it. If you want to change the data series' current color, click one of the colors in the Area section. Click the Fill Effects button to display the Gradient tab of the Fill Effects dialog:

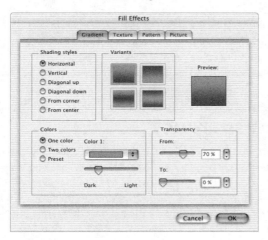

3 Choose one of these methods to add transparency to the data series:

■ If you want to use a single transparent color, select One Color in the Colors section. Choose your color from the Color 1 pop-up menu, and move the slider to select how dark or light you want it to be.

■ If you want to use a two-color gradient fill, select Two Colors in the Colors section. Choose your colors from the Color 1 and Color 2 pop-up menus.

■ If you want to use a preset color gradient fill, select Preset. Choose one of the preset gradients from the Preset Colors pop-up menu.

4 Select a direction for the gradient from the Shading Styles section, and then click the orientation of the gradient in the Variants section. The Preview box shows you what your color will look like.

5 Set the transparency range by adjusting the From and To sliders. This sets the transparency for the one or two colors (or the preset) chosen in the Colors section. Click OK.

6 This brings you back to the Format Data Series dialog. Click OK to see the transparency effect.

InsideOut

Make a data series transparent with one color and no gradient

When you create a transparent data series, Excel considers that it is best to use a gradient. When you choose just one fill color, the only choices possible include gradients. To use a single color with no gradients, choose Two Colors in the Colors section of the Fill Effects dialog, but select the same color for both. The preview will now show a single color, and, when you apply your change, your data series will be filled with one color only. Make sure you set the same level of transparency for both colors, or your data series will have a line through it separating the two sections with different transparencies.

When to Use Transparency

Transparency looks great, but it is not ideal for all charts. It probably works best with 3-D area charts, because this type of chart shows data series as solid objects across the category axis. If your data is higher in the front of the chart than in the back, the transparency will let you partially see through it and better spot the differences between given data series. However, if most of the data is higher in the front of the chart, you would be better off using a different type of chart, or reversing the stacking order when feasible. Even though the transparency helps you "see through" data series, it does not necessarily make it easy to appreciate specific values.

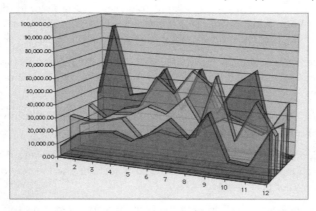

Chapter 29

You should also use care in choosing colors. Ideally, you want each data series to be a different color from the next, otherwise, even with transparency, you will not make them out clearly. If you only have a few data series, use contrasting colors, such as red and blue, or green and orange. If you have many data series, try the Roy G. Biv approach—set the colors as red, orange, yellow, green, blue, indigo, and violet (Roy G. Biv is a mnemonic that helps you remember the order of the colors). This approach not only makes a good contrast between data series, but the familiar progression of colors helps the viewer appreciate changes over time when each data series represents a month, year, or other time period.

Troubleshooting

I changed a data series color and my chart's transparency disappeared.

After you have gone through the long process to make a transparent data series, you might decide you want to change its color, after you see the result in front of or behind another color. If you change its color on the Patterns tab of the Format Data Series dialog only, your transparency will be removed, and the series will be displayed as a solid color. Any time you want to change a color and maintain transparency you need to make the change in the Fill Effects dialog and reset the transparency. The easiest way around this is to go straight to the Fill Effects dialog (click Fill Effects on the Patterns tab of the Format Data Series dialog), and change the color on the Color pop-up menu. Doing so will retain your level of transparency, although you will probably need to adjust it if the color is very different.

Transparent chart elements will look good when viewed in Excel X on Mac OS X, but won't look as good in Excel 2001 in Mac OS 9, or in Excel in any version of Windows. These operating systems can't handle the extra information that allows for transparency. As a result, transparent chart elements will appear as dithered or as gradient patterns in Excel for these other platforms, as shown in Figure 29-11 on the next page.

Chapter 29

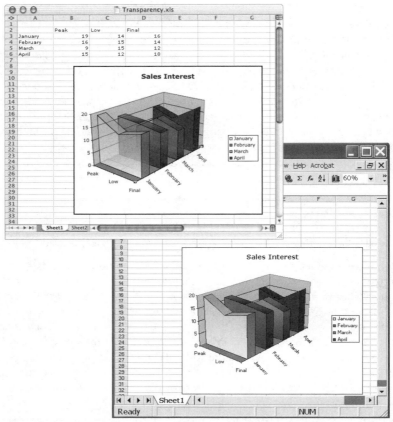

Figure 29-11. Transparent chart elements look good in Excel X (top), but show as dithered or solid gradient patterns on other platforms (as in Excel 2000 in Windows XP, bottom).

Creating Combination Charts

Combination charts are charts where one data series is presented in one chart type, and another chart type is used for a different data series. You can combine several chart types, one per data series, but if you use too many different chart types your chart will be confusing. To create a combination chart, you must first create a chart using one of the chart types you want in the combination chart. Select one of the data series, and choose a different chart type from the Formatting Palette.

Figure 29-12 shows a chart using a column chart for one data series and a line chart for another. This gives a good contrast between the two data series. This kind of chart is best when data is not directly related, such as sales per store and number of sales. It is not very logical when comparing, for example, sales from one year to the next, because the use of two different chart types makes the viewer assume that the type of data is different.

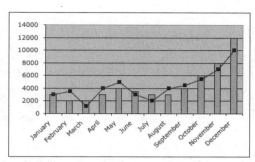

Figure 29-12. This combination chart uses a line chart and column chart.

> **note** You cannot combine 2-D and 3-D chart types. If you have used a 3-D chart type in your chart and try to change a data series to a 2-D chart type, Excel displays a message asking whether you want to change the entire chart to 2-D.

Another type of combination chart is one using a *secondary axis*. This type of chart plots data on two y-axes across the same x-axis, as shown in Figure 29-13. The column chart shows sales data in dollars using the left axis, and the line chart shows the number of sales made in units on the right axis. If both sets of data were plotted on the same axis, the line chart values would all be at the bottom of the chart, because the values are much smaller than the dollar values on the left axis. By using a secondary axis, you can keep the relationship of the two data series in better perspective. If you use a secondary axis, you'll want to add labels to each of the axes, so that the reader knows what each axis represents. In the example, the left axis label would be "Sales (in dollars)" and the right axis label would be "Sales (in units)."

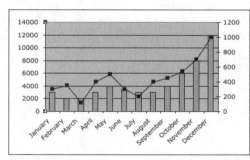

Figure 29-13. This combination chart adds a secondary axis to the previous chart.

Chapter 29

Printing Charts

Excel gives you several ways to print your charts. You can either print charts alone or as part of a worksheet, if your charts are embedded in worksheets. If you want to print a chart alone, whether from a chart sheet or an embedded chart, display the sheet containing the chart. If it is an embedded chart, click in it once to select it, and then choose File, Print; only the chart will print. If your chart is on a chart sheet, simply choose File, Print.

If you want to print an embedded chart and the surrounding data on a worksheet, click anywhere in the worksheet to make sure that the chart isn't selected, and then choose File, Print. Excel will print your worksheet and the chart, as it is displayed.

When you print a chart alone, Excel prints it to fill the page by default. To change this, click in the chart to select it, and then choose File, Page Setup. Click the Chart tab. Click Custom, in the Printed Chart Size section, and then click OK. Excel will print the chart at its actual size, and not enlarge it.

For more on printing worksheets, see "Printing Worksheets," page 576.

Tips for Chart Readability When Printing

Although almost any chart looks good on-screen, printed charts are a different story. With color printers, the colors might not be exactly what you see on-screen. With black and white printers, you are limited in the way you can format your charts for optimum readability. Whereas a color chart enables you to differentiate data series easily, using a different color for each data series, the same chart in black and white presents a variety of grays, most of which look the same. The best way to print charts in black and white is to use patterns rather than colors for your data series.

To use patterns, double-click a data series to bring up the Format Data Series dialog, click the Fill Effects button, then click the Patterns tab in the Fill Effects dialog. You will find almost 50 different patterns to choose from. By selecting different types of patterns for your data series—say, one made up of lines, another of dots, another with check marks—you can easily differentiate the data on your chart.

Another way to make charts easier to read on paper is to change the color of the plot area. By default, Excel sets this to a dark gray. To change this color, select Plot Area from the Formatting Palette's Chart Objects pop-up menu, and click the Format button. The Format Plot Area dialog appears. Select a color from the Area section. If printing in color, choose a lighter gray than the default color. If printing in black and white, you will have the best results with a white background—that way, all your data series will stand out clearly, whether they are displayed with bars, lines, or points.

Adding Graphics to Worksheets

Although charts can help highlight your data, and make it stand out in striking ways, graphics can spruce up both charts and worksheets, and give your information additional visual power and focus. You can add elements such as boxes and lines to emphasize and draw attention to different areas of worksheets. You can add text boxes to charts, to present additional information about the data they display, and use eye-catching text effects to go even further. You can also add all kinds of pictures either within your worksheets and charts or as backgrounds and even use movies to give animated examples of your data and information. Microsoft Excel X gives you a wealth of possibilities to use graphics in your documents, including text boxes, AutoShapes, and WordArt, so you can use stylized text in your worksheets and charts as well. In this chapter, you will learn how to use all of these to make your documents stand out, either on-screen or on paper.

Managing Images

Excel comes with a set of tools that helps you manage, organize, and insert images into your worksheets. The images can be the clip art graphics that Microsoft Office v. X installs on your computer, images that you import from other files, graphics that you scan, or pictures you take with a digital camera.

Adding Pictures and Clip Art

Worksheets and charts give you many ways to present data and information, either for on-screen use, presentations, or in printed reports. Although your data might be clear using just basic layout and charts, sometimes you might want to add pictures or clip art to illustrate it and make it even easier to understand. Excel lets you add graphics to worksheets or charts to highlight your data or information, or simply to make it look better.

---

tip　**Use graphics to add, not to distract**

If your data is complex, graphics might not help make it any easier to understand. Graphics are fine for simple data, but complex data requires that viewers pay attention and think about how it is related. Pictures and clip art can detract from this, especially in presentations, when viewers don't have a lot of time to look closely at your slides. Use graphics sparingly, and they will help make your documents better; overuse them, and they will only end up confusing viewers.

To insert clip art into a worksheet, follow these steps:

1 Choose Insert, Picture, and then select Clip Art. (Make sure your worksheet is active. If a chart is selected, you will not be able to access the Clip Art function.) After a brief wait, the Clip Gallery appears.

---

note　The Microsoft Clip Gallery is a separate helper application that is shared by Microsoft Excel X, Microsoft Word X, and Microsoft PowerPoint X.

Chapter 30

2 The Clip Gallery contains all of the clip art installed by the Microsoft Office Installer, organized by category. You can click the different categories in the Category section at left, and the thumbnails of the clip art graphics in each category display at right. Click one of the graphics to select it. If you select the Preview check box, the graphic opens in a separate window at full size so that you can see what it looks like. To hide the preview window, clear the Preview check box.

3 If you can't find the graphic you want by browsing through the categories, enter one or several words in the Search field. All the clip art in the Clip Gallery is marked with keywords to help you search for graphics. When you enter one or several words, and then press Return, the Search Results category displays thumbnails of the graphics that correspond to your keyword(s) in the section at right.

4 When you find the graphic you want to use, select it by clicking it in the section at right in the Clip Gallery, and then click Insert. The graphic appears on your worksheet, at full size, and, when you click it to select it, the Picture toolbar appears. (If the Formatting Palette is visible, the Picture toolbar will not appear; the Picture section of the Formatting Palette will appear instead.)

Troubleshooting

There's no clip art in the Clip Gallery.

If you try to import clip art into a worksheet, Excel opens the Clip Gallery, which organizes your clip art. But if the Clip Gallery is empty when it opens, don't fret. This just means that when you installed Office v. X, you didn't install the clip art package. Run the installer again, and choose a custom installation. Select the Clip Art check box, and then click Install, and several sets of graphics will install. If you want more, you can run the Value Pack Installer in the Value Pack folder on the Office X CD. The Value Pack includes more than 7,000 clip art graphics.

Inserting Other Types of Graphics in Worksheets

You can insert all kinds of graphics in your worksheets by choosing Insert, Picture, and then selecting From File. Navigate until you find the file, and then click Insert. Excel supports the following graphics formats:

- Joint Photographic Experts Group (JPEG)
- Graphics Interchange Format (GIF)
- Portable Network Graphics (PNG)
- Tagged Image File Format (TIFF)
- Macintosh Picture (PICT)
- Macintosh Paint (PNTG)
- Windows Bitmap (BMP)
- Device Independent Bitmap (DIB)
- Encapsulated PostScript File (EPSF)
- Windows Metafile (WMF)
- Enhanced Windows Metafile (EMF)
- Photoshop Document (PSD)
- Silicon Graphics Incorporated (SGI)
- QuickTime Image Format (QTIF)
- Targa (TGA)
- FlashPix (FPX)

Besides these image formats, Office uses Apple's QuickTime media architecture, so whenever Apple updates QuickTime to understand a new type of image or media file, the Office applications can also use the new format.

Adjusting Graphic Position and Size

If you need to move a graphic after you insert it (you usually will), simply click and drag it to the desired location. When you move the pointer over the image, the pointer will turn into a grabber hand.

When you import clip art through the Clip Gallery, it is displayed at its full size. In most cases, this will be too large for your needs. If you import other graphics, such as images from a file, a scanner, or digital camera, you might also need to adjust the size of the image. To do this, click the graphic to select it. Resizing handles will appear around the image. Click one of the handles, and drag it to change the image size. The pointer will change when you move it over the handles to show you which way the image size will change, as shown in Figure 30-1.

Figure 30-1. The pointer shows which way the image size will change when you click and drag a handle.

If you click and drag one of the corner handles, the image will change in size proportionally, that is, its height and width will change together so the image is not distorted. But if you click and drag one of the side handles, the image will change size only in the direction you drag it—if you drag a side handle, only the width of the image will change; if you drag a top handle, only the height of the image will change.

If you want to change the size of a graphic more precisely, click the image to select it, and then click the Format Picture button on the Picture toolbar (or the Formatting Palette). In the Format Picture dialog, click the Size tab to access size and scale functions.

You can change the size of the graphic by entering a precise height or width in the Height and Width fields of the Size And Rotate section of this dialog, or you can scale it to a specific percentage by entering a percentage in the Height and Width fields of the Scale section. If you select Lock Aspect Ratio, you only need to adjust either the height or width—the two are locked, and when one changes, the other changes proportionally. Click OK to apply your changes.

Chapter 30

InsideOut

Insert clip art into charts by copying from a worksheet

You might notice that if you select a chart, the Clip Art menu item is not available from the Insert, Picture menu; this means that you cannot insert clip art directly into a chart. But, there is a simple workaround for this. Insert your clip art into your worksheet, click it to select it, and then copy it. Click the chart in which you want to place this graphic, and then paste the graphic. You can now move the image wherever you want in the chart, resize it, and apply any effects you want to it. In the chart shown here, the store and mail images are clip art that was pasted into the chart.

Adding Picture Effects

After you have inserted graphics into your worksheet or chart, you can apply a variety of picture effects to personalize them and give them a totally different look. Click a picture, and then click the Picture Effects button on the Picture toolbar (or the Formatting Palette). The Effects Gallery dialog appears, as shown in Figure 30-2.

The Effects Gallery contains 48 effects, which apply filters to your image to change its relief, its texture, make it look like charcoal or stained glass, and more. These effects are similar to those found in high-end graphics programs. Although you don't have a lot of

InsideOut

Reserve the Picture Effects tool for casual use

Although Excel's Picture Effects are many and powerful, you cannot see what your image will look like before applying the effect. You also cannot see how the different parameter adjustments change the image until you apply them. This is a big drawback with this feature, and limits its usefulness to casual, occasional use. If you need to apply this kind of effect often to your graphics, you will be better off using a professional graphics program, and then importing the result of your image editing to Excel.

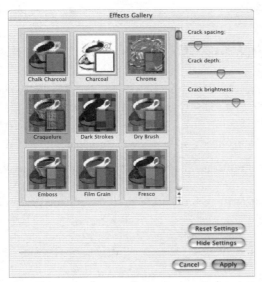

Figure 30-2. The Effects Gallery includes dozens of effects that equal those found in high-end graphics programs.

control over them, each effect does let you adjust one or several parameters. In Figure 30-2, the Craquelure effect is selected. You can adjust three parameters for this effect using these sliders: Crack Spacing, Crack Depth, and Crack Brightness. Other effects let you adjust different parameters. After you have selected an effect and adjusted its parameters, click Apply to see the effect.

Adding Drop Shadows to Graphics

You can add drop shadows to any graphics you insert into a worksheet to add dimension and give them a more professional look. To add a shadow, click on a graphic to select it, and then click the Shadow button on the Picture toolbar (or the Formatting Palette).

Shadow

The Shadow palette appears. Select one of the shadow options, and a shadow is added to your graphic immediately. If you click the Shadow Settings button on the Shadow palette, the Shadow Settings toolbar appears. This toolbar lets you turn shadows on or off, nudge shadows in different directions so they look better, and choose shadow colors and transparency. Figure 30-3 shows two examples of drop shadows. Bear in mind, when

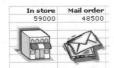

Figure 30-3. These two examples of shadows behind graphics show how the color and direction of the shadow can be adjusted.

Chapter 30

Importing Your Own Graphics into the Clip Gallery

If you have graphics or clip art you use often, and want to have easy access to them, you can import these graphics into the Clip Gallery. Open the Clip Gallery by choosing Insert, Picture, Clip Art. Click the Import button in the Clip Gallery dialog, and choose your graphic file from the Import dialog.

You have three choices in the Import dialog as to how your graphic is imported:

- Copy Into Clip Gallery copies the image into the Clip Gallery and leaves the original in its location.
- Move Into Clip Gallery copies the image into the Clip Gallery and deletes the original from its location.
- Add Alias To Clip Gallery makes an alias of the original image and places it in the Clip Gallery. (Note: if you move or delete the original, the Clip Gallery will no longer be able to find it.)

After you choose how you want to import the image, click Import. A properties dialog will open for this image. You can enter a description on the Description tab, assign your art to one or more categories on the Categories tab (or create a new category by clicking the New Category button), and assign keywords to your image on the Keywords tab. These keywords will help you find the image if you enter one of the keywords in the Search field of the Clip Gallery. Click OK to import your image.

applying shadows to graphics, that they look best if all the graphics on a worksheet have shadows of the same color going in the same direction.

Inserting Scanned Images

You can insert images directly from a scanner or digital camera by choosing Insert, Picture, and then selecting From Scanner Or Camera. Excel will call up the driver for your scanner or camera and open its dialog or software. This method only works if the correct driver for your scanner or camera is installed on your computer.

note Scanner and camera drivers must be rewritten (usually by the device's manufacturer) in order to work in Mac OS X. Generally speaking, if your device will work in other OS X applications (for example if your digital camera is recognized by Apple's Image Capture or iPhoto application), it will work fine in Office. If the device doesn't work, check the manufacturer's Web site for updated drivers.

You can also insert pictures from a digital camera directly into Excel. If your camera lets you mount it like a hard disk, do this, choose Insert, Picture, and then select From File. Navigate to the mounted disk for your camera, and choose a picture. You can then insert it into your worksheet and apply effects or resize the image as you would any other graphic. If your camera's images have been imported by Apple's Image Capture program, you'll have to find the photos in whichever folder Image Capture is set to store images in (usually it's the Users/*username*/Pictures folder).

> For more information on applying effects and changing image sizes, see "Adding Picture Effects," page 714, and "Adjusting Graphic Position and Size," page 712.

Adding Movie Files

You can add movie files to any of your worksheets, just as you can add pictures and other graphics. You can use these to give animated visual information that complements your data. But beware—movie files can be very large. If you add large movies to your workbooks they can take much longer to save or to send by e-mail or over a network.

To add a movie file, choose Insert, Movie. Find the movie file you want to insert in the Insert Movie dialog, and then click Choose. The movie file is added in the same way as a graphic; a small movie icon in the lower left corner indicates that it is a movie and not a graphic, as shown in Figure 30-4. You can reposition this movie and change its size as well, the same way you can with other graphics.

> For more information on moving and resizing graphics, see "Adjusting Graphic Position and Size," page 712.

Figure 30-4. Movie files are displayed with a small movie icon to show that they are not graphics. The Movie toolbar appears when you click the movie object.

To play a movie, click the Play button on the Movie toolbar, shown in Figure 30-5 on the next page. To stop playing, simply click the Play button again. For more control when playing, and to set the sound volume, click the Show Controller button on the Movie toolbar to show the QuickTime controller. You can format the movie's display by clicking the Format Picture button.

Chapter 30

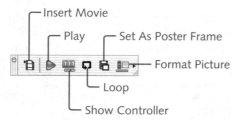

Insert Movie
Play — Set As Poster Frame
Format Picture
Loop
Show Controller

Figure 30-5. The Movie toolbar appears when a movie is selected, enabling you to control the movie's playback.

Setting Background Images

You can add your own background images to your Excel worksheets. These can be photos, clip art, or simple patterns. Bear in mind, however, that backgrounds must be used with caution—background images can make your data difficult to read. Background images do not interfere with embedded charts, however, because these charts are graphic objects that are displayed on top of your worksheets. If you use a simple pattern, you must make sure that it does not conflict with your data, especially if you are planning to print the worksheet. If you use a picture or clip art as background, make sure that your data is displayed in an area that is not too busy.

To insert a background image, choose Format, Sheet, Background. Navigate to the image you want to use, and then click Insert. Your image will appear in the background of your worksheet. Excel inserts the image in the top left corner of your worksheet and then repeats the image throughout the worksheet. If your image is not big enough to cover the part of the worksheet you want to display or print, Excel will tile the image to fill the space, as shown in Figure 30-6.

Types of Movie Files You Can Insert

You can use the following types of movie files in Excel worksheets:

- QuickTime movies
- QuickTime VR movies
- MPEG movies
- Windows AVI files

When inserting AVI files, Excel converts them to QuickTime format and saves a copy in your workbook, leaving the original file unchanged. However, when you open a file with AVI files that was saved in Excel for Windows, Excel X will not be able to play the files and will only display a poster frame. If you want to see the movie, you need to reinsert it in Excel X.

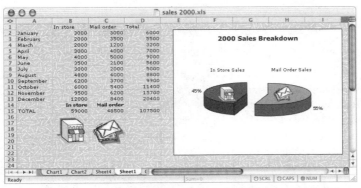

Figure 30-6. The background pattern behind this worksheet does not interfere too much with viewing the data.

Troubleshooting

Scrolling in files with graphics is very slow.

Excel can sometimes be lethargic when scrolling through files that contain graphics and charts. If you must have graphics in your files, it is probably best to add them when you have already entered and formatted all your data. But, if you need to edit your data later, after you have added graphics, there is a way to speed things up a bit. Choose Excel, Preferences, and click the View category. Select Show Placeholders in the Objects section, and click OK. Now, instead of displaying charts, Excel displays only gray rectangles. However, graphics are still displayed—this doesn't make sense, but that's what happens. The only way to keep graphics from being displayed is to select Hide All in the Objects section of the View window. All graphics and charts will be hidden. The drawback to this view is that you don't know where the graphics are; with placeholders you can at least see the graphics' positions.

You can set graphics to be displayed again after you have finished editing your data. Also, make sure that graphics are visible before you print your worksheet; Excel only prints what is visible.

Note that Excel has a strange way of applying this change to graphic display: due to an apparent bug, when you change the view of graphics it sometimes only applies to the active worksheet. If you want to hide graphics on other worksheets you must reselect this option with each worksheet active. Other times, it seems to work as it should; hopefully this will be fixed in a future update.

Tips for Working with Background Images

Using background images can be tricky. Here are some tips for handling them:

- Background images are tiled to fill your worksheet, so, if you have a large worksheet with lots of data, your image will be repeated, unless it is as big as the worksheet. The solution is to scale the background image in proportion to how big the worksheet will be displayed (for example, if the worksheet will be printed, you'll want to scale the background image to the paper size; if the worksheet will be mainly used on screen, scale the image to a bit bigger than the screen size).

- When using background images, you might want to turn off gridlines. To turn them off, choose Excel, Preferences, and then, on the View tab, clear the Gridlines check box in the Window Options section.

- When you insert a background image in a worksheet, you have no control over the image. If it is too small, too large, too dark, or too light, you cannot change it as you can change other graphics in Excel. The best way to work with background images is to edit them in a graphics program first, to make sure they are in the form you want to be displayed, and then insert them in your worksheet. And, as always, remember that if you are printing color images to a black and white printer, your printed results might not look like what you see on-screen.

Using the Drawing Tools

Excel includes a suite of drawing tools that provides a full range of functions from simple tools to draw lines and shapes to more advanced functions found in dedicated illustration software. Though workbooks and worksheets do not usually call for a lot of drawing and graphic functions, Excel provides the tools you need to create shapes and graphic objects to highlight and enhance your data and information. These tools enable you to make simple shapes and lines, smooth curves, three-dimensional boxes, and all kinds of arrows and give you a great deal of control over these objects and how they are aligned, rotated, presented, and viewed.

The Drawing toolbar is the nerve center of all these tools. To display it, choose View, Toolbars, and then choose Drawing. This toolbar gives you quick access to all the basic drawing tools. In addition, many of its buttons can be *torn off* to create their own floating palettes to give you easy access to their functions without having to go back to the Drawing toolbar and reopen them.

Drawing objects with Excel is a snap and works the same way it does in any drawing program. Simply click one of the buttons on the Drawing toolbar to select a tool, and then click and drag your pointer on your worksheet to use the tool. This technique works for basic lines, rectangles, and ovals, as it does for drawing AutoShapes. If you want to draw the same type of object several times, double-click its button. It will remain active as long as you want; To deactivate it, click it again or press Esc.

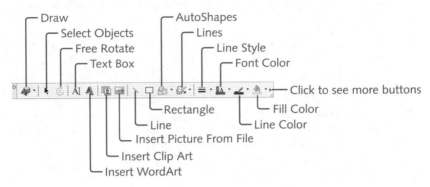

InsideOut

Distinguish between the Line and Lines tools

Some things in Excel are needlessly confusing. The Drawing toolbar contains two buttons that let you draw lines: One is called Line, and, if you click this button, you can draw a straight line. The second is called Lines; if you click this button, a pop-up menu appears with six choices of line types, including the same Line button that is found nearby on the Drawing toolbar. So what's the deal? Well, there's no difference between the two straight-line Line functions—they both draw straight lines. Perhaps the idea is to have a simple line button for quicker access, or it might be a relic from an earlier version of Excel before AutoShapes were introduced. If all you need is a simple straight line, click either Line or Lines, but if you want more power and flexibility in choosing your line type, open the Lines pop-up menu, and select one of the other five line types. You can even tear off this menu to make a separate palette if you have lots of lines to draw.

The Rectangle tool is similar—with it you can only draw simple rectangles or squares, which you can also draw by selecting Rectangle from the AutoShapes pop-up menu's Basic Shapes category. In this case, the Rectangle tool provides much less flexibility than its AutoShapes counterpart.

If you hold down the Shift key when drawing objects (see Figure 30-7 on the next page), their dimensions are constrained in different ways, as follows:

- **Lines and Arrows.** You can draw lines that are either perfectly horizontal or vertical, or diagonal lines that are constrained to 15-degree intervals. If you have already drawn a line or arrow, and resize it while holding down the Shift key, the line will remain at the exact angle it was before you started resizing it. You can no longer constrain it to specific intervals.

● **Rectangles.** You can draw perfect squares. If you have already drawn a rectangle or square, and resize it from a corner while holding down the Shift key, it will resize proportionally, that is, the height and width will change in the same ratio as you resize it.

● **Ovals.** You can draw perfect circles. If you have already drawn an oval or circle, and resize it from a corner while holding down the Shift key, it will resize proportionally, that is, the height and width will change in the same ratio as you resize it.

● **AutoShapes.** You can constrain AutoShapes to remain symmetrical in the same manner as squares and circles. Some AutoShapes might act differently, though, because of the many types of shapes available. In most cases, if you hold down the Shift key while resizing AutoShapes, the AutoShapes change size in the same way as lines, rectangles, and ovals.

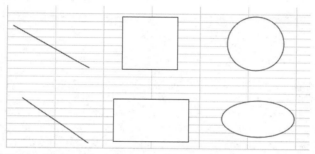

Figure 30-7. The objects on the top were drawn while pressing the Shift key, while those on the bottom were drawn without pressing the Shift key.

If you hold down the Shift key when moving objects, their movement is constrained to the same horizontal or vertical position as before you move them. Also, if you hold down the Shift key you can select multiple objects by clicking on them.

If you hold down the Command key when drawing objects (See Figure 30-8), their dimensions are constrained in different ways, as follows:

● **Lines and Arrows.** You can draw lines that extend from the corner of one cell to the corner of another cell. Click the Line button, click in the starting cell, and drag to an end cell. The line will fit perfectly between the cell corners.

● **Rectangles.** You can draw rectangles and squares that fit perfectly on cell borders.

● **Ovals.** You can draw circles and ovals that fit perfectly within cell borders.

● **AutoShapes.** You can draw AutoShapes that either fit between cell corners, if they are lines, or fit within cell borders for geometric objects. Some AutoShapes might act differently, though, because of the many types of shapes available.

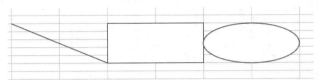

Figure 30-8. These objects were drawn while pressing the Command key.

InsideOut

Don't worry about the contextual menu that appears when you draw while pressing the Command key

Yep, that's what happens. Is it a bug or a feature? I don't know. As soon as you release the mouse button, after drawing while holding down the Command key, the same contextual menu appears as when you hold down the Control key (the usual way of getting a contextual menu) and click an object. This result isn't new; the same thing happens in Excel 2001. There doesn't seem to be anything to do other than just grin and bear this interface oddity (and then press Esc to close it).

Adding AutoShapes

AutoShapes are a set of dozens of built-in graphic objects that you can add to your worksheets. They include basic figures, such as squares, rectangles, and circles; all kinds of lines and arrows; connectors; flowchart symbols; callout boxes; and stars and banner shapes. You can use some AutoShapes as text boxes and others as graphic objects. To use AutoShapes, follow these steps:

1 Click the AutoShape button on the Drawing toolbar to open the pop-up menu.

2 Point to a category from the submenu to open its palette, and then select one of the shapes.

3 If you plan to use many different AutoShapes, you can tear off the AutoShapes menu into its own toolbar. To do this, click the AutoShapes button once; when the menu appears, move the pointer over the handle, and click and drag it where you want. When you release the mouse button, the AutoShapes toolbar appears, as shown in Figure 30-9 on the next page.

If you are going to use one of these AutoShape categories frequently, you can in turn tear off its pop-up menu from the AutoShapes toolbar. In the figure, the Flowchart palette is about to be detached from the AutoShapes toolbar.

Chapter 30

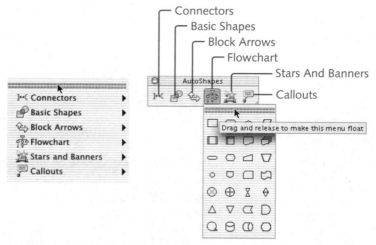

Figure 30-9. Displayed on the left is the AutoShapes pop-up menu before being detached from the Drawing toolbar. On the right, the AutoShapes toolbar has been detached, and the Flowchart palette is about to be detached from the toolbar.

There are six AutoShape categories:

- **Connectors** are lines, some with arrows, that link shapes used in flowcharts. Connectors link to specific *connection points* on the shapes. The nice thing about connectors is that they are "sticky," that is, the ends of the lines stay connected to their connection points when you move the shapes with the connection points. The connector will automatically grow or shrink, bend, or do whatever else it has to do to stay connected.

- **Basic Shapes** include squares and rectangles, circles and ovals, triangles, parallelograms, brackets, and some 3-D shapes such as cylinders and cubes.

- **Block Arrows** are outline-style (hollow) arrows in different proportions and combinations. These arrows can be made any size, and you can add text to them easily.

- **Flowchart** includes a full range of standard flowchart symbols.

- **Stars And Banners** can be used to highlight sections of your worksheets. You can add text to these shapes easily.

- **Callouts** are special text boxes attached to connector lines that you can use to point to other objects. You can enter text in the callouts to label data or information—you can even use special callouts designed to portray cartoon speech or thought bubbles.

Many AutoShapes include one or several yellow diamonds called *adjustment handles* that appear when you select the object. These diamonds are different from the usual handles that appear around graphic objects, and their function depends on the AutoShape. They generally enable you to change the shape of the object, and, in many cases, let you alter objects along several axes. Some AutoShapes, such as the more complex block arrows, have up to three adjustment handles, allowing you to change different parts of the object.

You can apply most of the other drawing tools to an AutoShape; for example, you can control the line width, line color, or fill color; rotate or flip the AutoShape; or group AutoShapes together.

Adding Text to AutoShapes

You can add text easily to most AutoShapes. Although they are similar to text boxes, AutoShapes can be many different types of graphic forms, whereas text boxes can only be squares or rectangles. Text boxes are discussed next. To add text to an AutoShape, click the Text Box button on the Drawing toolbar, click in an AutoShape, and then start typing your text. (When you create callouts, you can start typing right away—Excel immediately places the insertion point in the callout.) You can add text to all the AutoShapes that are hollow objects. Some examples are shown in Figure 30-10. You can also add text boxes next to connectors and brackets, but the text is not included in those objects.

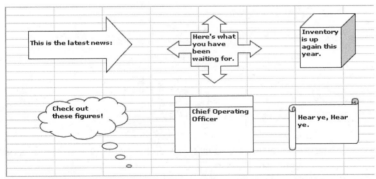

Figure 30-10. These are just a few examples of the many types of AutoShapes that can contain text.

Using Text Graphics

In addition to the many graphic functions available in Excel, the program enables you to use text graphics, that is, text that functions as a graphic or sits in a movable frame like a graphic. Of course, you can format text in worksheet cells and display it in the font, size, and color you want, but you can also place text outside of the cells (in essence, *superimposed* over an area of the worksheet). In addition to using AutoShapes, which are graphic objects that can contain text, you can also add simple text boxes or insert WordArt, with which you can create stunning, dynamic text effects.

For more information on formatting text in cells, see "Formatting Cells," page 611.

Adding Text Boxes

Text boxes enable you to insert text free of the constraints of particular cells to explain or highlight the data and information in your worksheets and charts. These boxes are independent of the data in your cells, yet they are anchored in the location where you place them. To add a text box, click the Text Box button on the Drawing toolbar. Click in your worksheet or chart at the location where you want to add the text box, and then drag the pointer until the box is the desired size. Start typing in the box. Your text will wrap automatically, but the box will not change in size if you enter more text than it can hold. To view text that doesn't fit, you must change the size of the text box by dragging one of its handles.

You can format the text in text boxes in many ways. You can change the font, color, style, and alignment, and you can even change the orientation. You can make all of these formatting changes from the Formatting Palette. Figure 30-11 shows some examples of text boxes and different kinds of formatting.

> **For more information on using the Formatting Palette, see "Using the Formatting Palette," page 628.**

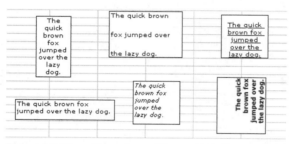

Figure 30-11. Many formatting options are available for text in text boxes, including styles, alignment, and even orientation.

Inserting WordArt

You can use WordArt to add special text objects to your worksheets and charts. WordArt is text that is inserted as a graphic object. You can choose from dozens of bright and playful styles to add eye-catching text to your worksheets and charts. To insert WordArt on a worksheet, follow these steps:

1 click the WordArt button on the Drawing toolbar.

2 Choose a style from the WordArt Gallery, and then click OK.

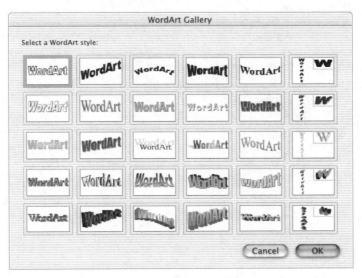

3 Enter your text in the Edit WordArt Text dialog, and choose a font and size. You can also choose to display the text in bold or italic style. Click OK.

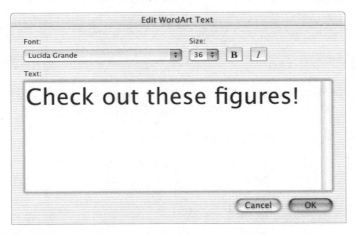

4 The WordArt text is displayed over your worksheet as a graphic object. When you select this text, the WordArt toolbar appears. Use the tools on the WordArt toolbar to edit the text, change the shape and style of the text, rotate the text, and much more.

2000	2001	2002	
45	78	45	
34	89	65	
67	99	23	
23	102	12	
169	368	145	

For more information about WordArt text styles, see "Using the WordArt Gallery," page 243.

Analyzing Data with Excel

Although Microsoft Excel X is first and foremost a tool for organizing and calculating data and information, and displaying it in worksheets and charts, it also contains powerful functions for analyzing data. No matter how complex your data, Excel can help you get a clearer view of it to better understand trends that might not be apparent at first glance. Excel's PivotTable Reports are powerful tools for analyzing data, and What-If analysis lets you examine scenarios, find the data needed to meet specific goals, and solve complex calculations to reach the results you want. In this chapter you will learn how to use these tools to get the most out of your data and find the answers you need.

Creating PivotTables

PivotTables are interactive tables that provide summaries of large amounts of even the most complex data. When you *pivot* a PivotTable, you rotate its row and column headers to show data in different ways, changing the presentation of your data without having to move cells and ranges around on your worksheet, giving you different insights into the relationships underlying your data. By rotating these tables' rows and columns, you can examine different summaries of the data. You can also filter the data by displaying different pages and display the data in many ways to highlight specific categories or elements, and of course, you can perform calculations on the data in the PivotTable. PivotTables let you change your perspective on data by altering its *hierarchy,* the way different fields are presented in relation to others.

By moving the fields of your PivotTable, you can see how different trends result from looking at the data from new angles. Say you have some raw data about a basketball team and which players score at different times in the game. You can look at each player and see how many points they score; you can look at each period and see which players score more points early in the game and later; you can look at free throws and see who scores more; you can look at three-point shots and see whether they are scored more often in the first period or the fourth period. Each time you pivot the table, you look at its data from a different angle.

Preparing Data to Make a PivotTable

When making a PivotTable, the first thing to consider is the type of data you want to present and analyze and whether it is arranged well for use by a PivotTable. The table in Figure 31-1 is a simple presentation of sales data by store in 10 stores, over 4 categories with totals by store and by category. This data is clear and easy to understand in this simple table form, yet, if you try to create a PivotTable from this worksheet, you will not end up with anything useful.

	Store	Books	CDs	DVDs	Misc	Total
1	Store	Books	CDs	DVDs	Misc	Total
2	1	2700	4800	2900	1000	11400
3	2	3500	5600	4600	1200	14900
4	3	4600	3700	4800	900	14000
5	4	1800	5200	1800	2300	11100
6	5	2900	4100	5600	1400	14000
7	6	3200	3800	5700	1200	13900
8	7	4100	4200	3900	1100	13300
9	8	2000	3900	4500	1300	11700
10	9	1800	5100	6400	1800	15100
11	10	2300	5400	3900	1200	12800
12		28900	45800	44100	13400	

Figure 31-1. This simple table presents data clearly, but is not ideal for creating a PivotTable.

Data for PivotTables must, oddly, be in a much more raw form than that shown in Figure 31-1. The data in Figure 31-2 is much better for a PivotTable—in this format, the data is repetitive, with subcategories as entries in a single column category. Here, the Department column includes the Books, CDs, DVDs, and Misc categories, and the Month column includes each of three different months repeated for each store. Excel creates PivotTable fields from the various columns and looks for repetitions in the data in order to create *items*, which are subcategories of these fields. You can't lay this type of data out in a normal two-dimensional chart; if you put Stores in the rows and Months in the columns, you still couldn't handle the Departments without a third dimension. You could create a series of two-dimensional charts that looked at various permutations of two groups at a time, but that isn't as flexible (or useful) as a PivotTable. Because PivotTables require a different layout of your data than you would use for a normal table on a worksheet, you need to rethink exactly what you want to examine and how to best prepare your data to make effective PivotTables. As you will see, this raw data gives you much more power to examine your information with a PivotTable than a simple worksheet or chart.

	A	B	C	D
1	**Store**	**Month**	**Department**	**Total**
2	1	October	Books	5400
3	1	October	CDs	9600
4	1	October	DVDs	5800
5	1	October	Misc	2000
6	1	November	Books	5400
7	1	November	CDs	9600
8	1	November	DVDs	5800
9	1	November	Misc	2000
10	1	December	Books	5400
11	1	December	CDs	9600
12	1	December	DVDs	5800
13	1	December	Misc	2000
14	2	October	Books	7000
15	2	October	CDs	11200
16	2	October	DVDs	9200
17	2	October	Misc	2400
18	2	November	Books	1680
19	2	November	CDs	1920
20	2	November	DVDs	2400
21	2	November	Misc	600
22	2	December	Books	1800
23	2	December	CDs	4800
24	2	December	DVDs	2520
25	2	December	Misc	2280

Figure 31-2. This raw, repetitive data is more suited for PivotTables.

Using the PivotTable Wizard

To create a PivotTable report, you use the PivotTable Wizard. Follow these steps to create a PivotTable:

1 When you have prepared your data for use in a PivotTable report, select your data and its headers, and choose Data, PivotTable Report.

2 Page one of the PivotTable Wizard appears. You can choose where to get the data for your PivotTable report. You have four choices:

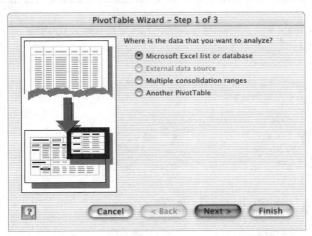

- **Microsoft Excel List Or Database.** This is data contained in your worksheet or in another worksheet or workbook.

> For more information on using lists and databases, see Chapter 28, "Working with Lists and Databases."

■ **External Data Source.** This can be an external data source such as a database, a text file, or another source, including sources on the Internet.

■ **Multiple Consolidation Ranges.** This is data from several tables, lists, or worksheets that you consolidate into a single PivotTable.

■ **Another PivotTable.** You can use one PivotTable as a source for another PivotTable, which allows you to create several tables with the same data presented in different ways. This is useful if you need to print your PivotTable in several iterations showing different data relationships.

InsideOut

Update Excel before using external data sources to create a PivotTable

As of press time, the external data source function is not available. On the first page of the PivotTable Wizard, the External Data Source option appears dimmed. You should be able to select this option and import external data to create a PivotTable, and then choose its location from the next page. This data can come from an external data source such as an Oracle or FileMaker Pro database, a text file, or another source, including sources on the Internet. The ODBC middleware, which is the intermediate software needed to interface with external databases, is not yet available. When it is, Microsoft will create an upgrade and make it available for downloading from the Mactopia Web site.

Because you selected a range of cells in step 1, select Microsoft Excel List Or Database and click Next.

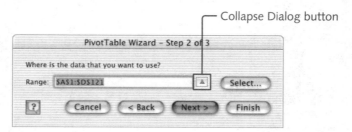

3 The second page of the PivotTable Wizard appears. If you selected your data in step 1, you will not need to do anything here. But if you want to change your data range, or select data in a different workbook, click Select, navigate to the workbook you want to use, and then click Next. If you want to select data on your current worksheet, click the Collapse Dialog button (the button with the upward-pointing triangle next to the Range box); the dialog is rolled up so that you have more room to select data. Select the data, and then click the Expand

Dialog button (this triangle points downward) to expand the dialog. Your selected cell range will be displayed in the Range box. Then click Next.

4   Page three of the PivotTable Wizard enables you to choose where to put the PivotTable and gives you access to several options concerning its layout and functions. Select New Worksheet or Existing Worksheet for the location of the PivotTable. It is more practical to put PivotTables on separate worksheets; it makes them easier to work with and does not interfere with your data. Though you can click the Layout button to lay out your PivotTable at this point, it is easier to adjust the layout after the table has been created. Click Finish.

> For more information on laying out your PivotTable, see the next section, "Laying Out the PivotTable." For more information on PivotTable options, see "Formatting PivotTables," page 743. These options can be chosen after creating the table.

Your PivotTable is created in the location you chose in step 4. A new blank PivotTable, as shown in Figure 31-3, is displayed, and the PivotTable toolbar also appears. The sections of the table include instructions that indicate what items to drag to each table section.

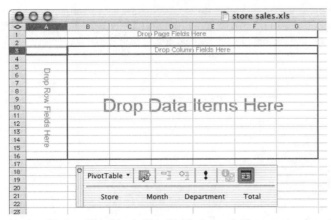

Figure 31-3. This blank PivotTable is ready for you to drag fields and items to it. The PivotTable toolbar shows the available fields.

Laying Out the PivotTable

The blank PivotTable is like a template waiting for you to add items to it. All of the available fields are shown on the PivotTable toolbar, which also gives you access to many PivotTable functions and options, as shown in Figure 31-4.

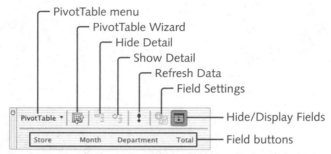

Figure 31-4. The PivotTable toolbar provides tools to change the PivotTable and contains the field names to be dragged to the table.

To lay out your PivotTable you must first decide what the main focus of your table will be. In Figure 31-3 on the preceding page, the table is being built from four fields: Store, Month, Department, and Total. The primary interest here is the total, not the store (which is just an identifier) or the month (which is just a time period), or the department (which gives you information about how the totals are broken down). What you want to examine are the totals that arise from different combinations of these fields; therefore, you want to change their relationship to see different totals. To do this, you must place the totals in the data area. The easiest way to do this is to drag the Total field to the section marked Drop Data Items Here last, after dragging the row and column fields. Follow these steps:

1 Start by dragging the Store button to the Drop Row Fields Here section. The pointer changes as you do this to show that you are moving a field, and the different sections on the PivotTable are highlighted as you move the pointer over them.

2 Now drag the Month button to the Drop Page Fields Here section and the Department button to the Drop Column Fields Here section. You will notice that the table resizes slightly to accommodate the fields that you add.

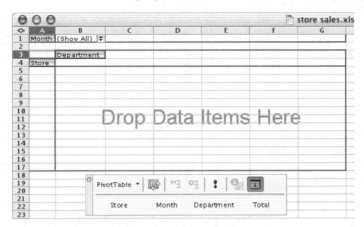

3 To examine different totals and how they change when these fields are combined in various ways, drag the Totals button to the Drop Data Items Here section. The PivotTable will now be displayed according to the way you have laid out the different fields.

Troubleshooting

The field buttons on the PivotTable toolbar disappeared.

Figure 31-4 shows the PivotTable toolbar as it should normally appear (except, of course, your field buttons will have different names unless you're following this example). But sometimes the field buttons disappear. These buttons only appear when the Display Fields button is selected, but, in some cases, you can click this button and the field buttons still don't appear on the toolbar. If this occurs, click outside the PivotTable, anywhere on the worksheet, and then click inside the table again. The field buttons should now be displayed correctly.

Understanding the Elements of PivotTable Reports

To understand how to use PivotTables, it is important to know what each element is and what purpose it serves. These elements are shown in Figure 31-5 on the next page.

Row field
Data field
Page field

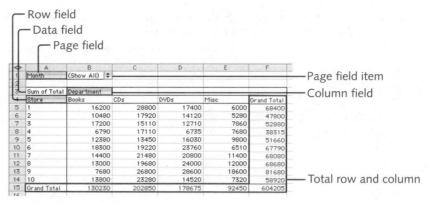

Page field item
Column field
Total row and column

Figure 31-5. Several elements make up a simple PivotTable.

The main elements of a PivotTable are the following:

- **Row fields.** These fields come from the source data and are assigned row orientation in a PivotTable report. In the example used earlier, the Store column is assigned to the row field. This means that data is sorted according to Store first, and then according to the column fields. If there is more than one row field, as in the example that follows, these are called outer and inner row fields. The outer field is the Store field, and the inner field is the Month field. The inner field is repeated for each outer field, so, for each store, you can see the three months included in the source data.

	A	B	C	D	E	F	G
1			Drop Page Fields Here				
2							
3	Sum of Total		Department				
4	Store	Month	Books	CDs	DVDs	Misc	Grand Total
5	1	October	5400	9600	5800	2000	22800
6		November	5400	9600	5800	2000	22800
7		December	5400	9600	5800	2000	22800
8	1 Total		16200	28800	17400	6000	68400
9	2	October	7000	11200	9200	2400	29800
10		November	1680	1920	2400	600	6600
11		December	1800	4800	2520	2280	11400
12	2 Total		10480	17920	14120	5280	47800
13	3	October	9200	7400	9600	1800	28000
14		November	3600	5400	1020	2760	12780
15		December	4400	2310	2090	3300	12100
16	3 Total		17200	15110	12710	7860	52880

- **Column fields.** These fields come from the source data and are assigned column orientation in a PivotTable report. In the example just described, the Department column is assigned to the column field, and the Department field shows beneath it several items that the PivotTable picked up from the source data. A PivotTable can have multiple column fields as it can have multiple row fields.

- **Item.** An item is a subcategory or member of a PivotTable field. In the example, Books, CDs, DVDs, and Misc are items belonging to the Department field. Items appear as menu items on the pop-up menus that appear next to page fields.

- **Page Fields.** These are fields assigned to a page orientation. When you assign a field to be a page, it acts as a filter; you can choose to display any one of its items individually, and the PivotTable shows only the data related to that item. In the example, the Month field is assigned to the page field. You can choose to display each month separately.

- **Page Field Items.** These items are the various members of the page field. You can choose one of these items from the Page Field pop-up menu to display only the data related to a particular item.

For more information on using page fields, see "Using Page Fields," page 742.

- **Data Field.** The data field is the column of the source data that is being summarized. In the example, the Total field is the data field, and this is indicated by the label Sum Of Total. By default, Excel PivotTables summarize numeric data using the SUM function and summarize text data using the COUNT SUMMARY function. You can change the function used by changing the field settings for this field.

For more information on changing field settings, see "Changing PivotTable Field Settings," page 744.

Refreshing PivotTable Data

PivotTables are based on source data found in a worksheet, a workbook, or an external data source. Unlike charts, they do not refresh automatically. If the source data changes, you need to refresh your PivotTable manually. To do this, select any cell in the table, and click the Refresh Data button on the PivotTable toolbar shown in Figure 31-6.

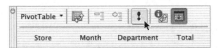

Figure 31-6. Clicking the Refresh Data button on the PivotTable toolbar updates the table based on changes made to the source data.

---

tip **Be careful with Excel Help**

For some reason, Excel's online help contains some strange things. If you look at the help topic "Elements of a PivotTable Report," you will see a screen shot that does not exist in Excel X. In fact, it looks strangely like a Windows screen shot, because PivotTables in the Windows version of Excel have pop-up menus next to the row and column field headers, but the Mac version does not. Be careful when using Excel Help. Most of it—probably about 99% of it—is exact, but there are occasional bits and pieces that aren't quite right.

Rearranging PivotTable Data

PivotTables are most useful for quickly and easily rearranging their fields, giving you different perspectives on the data they contain. If they were simply two-dimensional tables containing row and column data, they would be little different from a standard worksheet layout. But the power of PivotTables comes from the way they can display data in different levels and in different relationships and show subtotals and grand totals automatically.

Moving Fields Around

The way to change the orientation of a PivotTable is to move its fields around. To move row fields to columns and vice versa, simply drag a field from one section to another. You can also change the order of row and column fields to change their hierarchy by dragging a field to a different position in its current section.

> **tip** **Move fields using the contextual menu**
>
> In some cases, you might find it difficult to insert a field in the precise location you want, especially if you have several fields together. If you click a field header while holding down the Control key, and choose Order, you can change the hierarchy from the menu that opens.

Analyzing Data with PivotTables: Four Examples

The beauty of using PivotTables is the way you can change the analysis of complex data by just dragging a field from one location to another. You can examine different relationships among your data and discover unexpected trends and results. Here are four ways of looking at the same data. As you can see, each one gives a different outlook on the same data. These examples use the data that was shown previously in this chapter—sales data for 10 stores over 3 months in 4 departments.

In the first example, shown next, the data is arranged by store and then by month, and the column field shows the departments. As you can see, data is displayed first for each store, and then for each of the three months of the source data within each store. Looking across the table you can see the exact sales figures for each department, for each month and store. This develops a hierarchy that goes from store to month to department. Subtotals are automatically created after each store, and grand totals at the end of each row correspond to monthly totals.

Sum of Total		Department				
Store	Month	Books	CDs	DVDs	Misc	Grand Total
1	October	5400	9600	5800	2000	22800
	November	5400	9600	5800	2000	22800
	December	5400	9600	5800	2000	22800
1 Total		16200	28800	17400	6000	68400
2	October	7000	11200	9200	2400	29800
	November	1680	1920	2400	600	6600
	December	1800	4800	2520	2280	11400
2 Total		10480	17920	14120	5280	47800
3	October	9200	7400	9600	1800	28000
	November	3600	5400	1020	2760	12780
	December	4400	2310	2090	3300	12100
3 Total		17200	15110	12710	7860	52880

If you switch the Month and Department fields, the table changes, as shown here:

Sum of Total		Month			
Store	Department	October	November	December	Grand Total
1	Books	5400	5400	5100	15900
	CDs	9600	9600	9600	28800
	DVDs	4800	4200	5800	14800
	Misc	3000	3600	2000	8600
1 Total		22800	22800	22500	68100
2	Books	7000	1680	1800	10480
	CDs	11200	1920	4800	17920
	DVDs	9200	2400	2520	14120
	Misc	2400	600	2280	5280
2 Total		29800	6600	11400	47800
3	Books	9200	3600	4400	17200
	CDs	7400	5400	2310	15110
	DVDs	9600	1020	2090	12710
	Misc	1800	2760	3300	7860
3 Total		28000	12780	12100	52880

The PivotTable now displays a hierarchy from store to department to month. You can examine sales data for each department by store and for each month, and the totals at the end of each row correspond to sales in each department over the three-month period.

Change the table again by switching the Store and Month fields, and the following table is displayed:

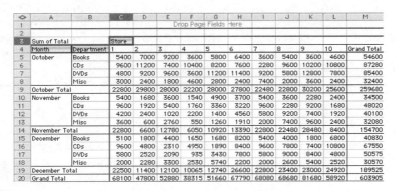

Sum of Total		Store										
Month	Department	1	2	3	4	5	6	7	8	9	10	Grand Total
October	Books	5400	7000	9200	3600	5800	6400	3600	5400	3600	4600	54600
	CDs	9600	11200	7400	10400	8200	7600	2280	9600	10200	10800	87280
	DVDs	4800	9200	9600	3600	11200	11400	9200	5800	12800	7800	85400
	Misc	3000	2400	1800	4600	2800	2400	7400	2000	3600	2400	32400
October Total		22800	29800	28000	22200	28000	27800	22480	22800	30200	25600	259680
November	Books	5400	1680	3600	1540	4900	3700	5400	3600	2280	2400	34500
	CDs	9600	1920	5400	1760	3360	3220	9600	2280	9200	1680	48020
	DVDs	4200	2400	1020	2200	1400	4560	5800	9200	7400	1920	40100
	Misc	3600	600	2760	550	1260	1910	2000	7400	9600	3600	32080
November Total		22800	6600	12780	6050	10920	13390	22800	22480	28480	8400	154700
December	Books	5100	1800	4400	1650	1680	8200	5400	4000	1800	6800	40830
	CDs	9600	4800	2310	4950	1890	8400	9600	7800	7400	10800	67550
	DVDs	5800	2520	2090	935	3430	7800	5800	9000	8400	4800	50575
	Misc	2000	2280	3300	2530	5740	2200	2000	2600	5400	2520	30570
December Total		22500	11400	12100	10065	12740	26600	22800	23400	23000	24920	189525
Grand Total		68100	47800	52880	38315	51660	67790	68080	68680	81680	58920	603905

This time, the focus is on sales by month, and then by department for each store. The totals at the end of each row are global totals for each department over all stores, and the totals at the bottom of each column show totals for each store for the three-month period. Subtotals present total sales per month for each store.

In the final, simplest example, only the Store field is in the row section, and the Month and Department fields are in the column section.

	A	B	C	D	E	F	G	H	I	J
1									Drop Page Fields Here	
2										
3	Sum of Total	Month	Department							
4		October				October Total	November			
5	Store	Books	CDs	DVDs	Misc		Books	CDs	DVDs	Misc
6	1	5400	9600	4800	3000	22800	5400	9600	4200	3600
7	2	7000	11200	9200	2400	29800	1680	1920	2400	600
8	3	9200	7400	9600	1800	28000	3600	5400	1020	2760
9	4	3600	10400	3600	4600	22200	1540	1760	2200	550
10	5	5800	8200	11200	2800	28000	4900	3360	1400	1260
11	6	6400	7600	11400	2400	27800	3700	3220	4560	1910
12	7	3600	2280	9200	7400	22480	5400	9600	5800	2000
13	8	5400	9600	5800	2000	22800	3600	2280	9200	7400
14	9	3600	10200	12800	3600	30200	2280	9200	7400	9600
15	10	4600	10800	7800	2400	25600	2400	1680	1920	2400
16	Grand Total	54600	87280	85400	32400	259680	34500	48020	40100	32080

This gives a more "standard" view of the data. Data for each store by month and then department is displayed, with subtotals by month in columns. This type of display is a bit less practical, though, because the table stretches across the worksheet and requires scrolling to view the entire table. It is therefore more practical to use multiple row fields rather than multiple column fields, because they are easier to view on-screen.

Troubleshooting

Excel takes a long time to update my changes when I move fields.

Because you can make PivotTables from very large amounts of data, Excel might need to take a long time—several seconds, or more—to update changes to your PivotTable when you move fields around. One workaround for this is to do your layout in the PivotTable Wizard. Select any cell in your PivotTable, and then click the PivotTable Wizard button on the PivotTable toolbar. Click the Layout button on the wizard page. You can move your fields around on this screen, and Excel will only update them after you click OK, and then Finish, rather than dynamically after each change.

Displaying Data Field Details

Although you will most often want to see the global view of your data that PivotTables provide, at times you might need to look back at individual data entries from your source data. You can easily see the original data by double-clicking on a data item. A new worksheet will open showing the data used to make up that item, as shown in Figure 31-7. Excel calls this *drilling down* to the details behind data items.

Worksheets, Worksheets Everywhere!

Although Excel's drilldown function is very useful, enabling you to examine specific data items in your source data, it can also be annoying. Each time you use this function, Excel creates a new worksheet with the source data rather than simply going to the original data and highlighting it. The feature was probably designed this way because Excel cannot show the actual source data if your data source is external, so copying it to a new worksheet ensures that it can be viewed. The problem with this design is that if you drill down many times, you will have dozens of worksheets in your workbook. The only thing you can do is delete them afterward, because they won't go away on their own. However, you can turn this function off by choosing the PivotTable menu on the PivotTable toolbar, selecting Table Options, and clearing the Enable Drilldown check box.

	A	B	C	D	E
1				Drop Page Fields Here	
2					
3	Sum of Total		Department		
4	Month	Store	Books	CDs	DVDs
5	October	1	5400	9600	4800
6		2	7000	11200	9200
7		3	9200	7400	9600
8		4	3600	10400	3600

	A	B	C	D
1	Store	Month	Department	Total
2	3	October	CDs	7400
3				

Figure 31-7. If you double-click cell D7 in the PivotTable at the left, the details of this data item open in a new worksheet, shown on the right.

Hiding and Showing Details

PivotTables present data at many levels—first outer fields are displayed, and then inner fields are repeated for each outer field. This structure helps you see how the fields relate, but sometimes it can make your PivotTable a bit too complex for easy viewing or printing. Also, you might want to reduce the table to display only subtotals and totals and hide details that make up these totals. Figure 31-8 shows a PivotTable with a Store outer field and Month inner fields, which are repeated for each Store field.

			Department				
3	Sum of Total		Department				
4	Store	Month	Books	CDs	DVDs	Misc	Grand Total
5	1	October	5400	9600	4800	3000	22800
6		November	5400	9600	4200	3600	22800
7		December	5100	9600	5800	2000	22500
8	1 Total		15900	28800	14800	8600	68100
9	2	October	7000	11200	9200	2400	29800
10		November	1680	1920	2400	600	6600
11		December	1800	4800	2520	2280	11400
12	2 Total		10480	17920	14120	5280	47800
13	3	October	9200	7400	9600	1800	28000
14		November	3600	5400	1020	2760	12780
15		December	4400	2310	2090	3300	12100
16	3 Total		17200	15110	12710	7860	52880

Figure 31-8. This PivotTable has an outer field, Store, and inner fields showing monthly details for each store.

Although you might want to view the breakdown in data for each month at certain times, at others you might want to hide it. To do this, double-click one of the Store fields. If you double-click the field containing 1, the details for this store will be hidden and the table will display as shown next. You can use this method to hide the details of any of the outer fields. To show the detailed data again, simply double-click on the same field, and the details will be displayed. Alternatively, you can click the field once, and then click either the Hide Detail or Show Detail button on the PivotTable toolbar to collapse or expand the field display.

3	Sum of Total		Department				
4	Store	Month	Books	CDs	DVDs	Misc	Grand Total
5	1		15900	28800	14800	8600	68100
6	2	October	7000	11200	9200	2400	29800
7		November	1680	1920	2400	600	6600
8		December	1800	4800	2520	2280	11400
9	2 Total		10480	17920	14120	5280	47800
10	3	October	9200	7400	9600	1800	28000
11		November	3600	5400	1020	2760	12780
12		December	4400	2310	2090	3300	12100
13	3 Total		17200	15110	12710	7860	52880
14	4	October	3600	10400	3600	4600	22200
15		November	1540	1760	2200	550	6050
16		December	1650	4950	935	2530	10065

Using Page Fields

Page fields enable you to break your table into smaller, simpler tables by removing one or more fields from the row or column sections. When you use a page field, you filter the data in your PivotTable and choose which item in the page field is displayed. Page fields are useful when you want to have a simple table with fewer levels of hierarchy. Page fields allow you to view only one item at a time; for example, one of several months, departments, or stores.

To use a page field, simply drag one of your fields to the Drop Page Fields Here section. Figure 31-9 shows what this looks like for our example. As you can see, the Month field is used as a page field, and data for October is displayed. The table below the page field shows the remaining fields; in this case, sales by store and by department. You can choose to view a different *page,* or item, by selecting it from the Page Field pop-up menu. If you choose (Show All), the table will display totals for all items in the page field.

2	Month	October ⬍				
3						
4	Sum of Total	Department				
5	Store	Books	CDs	DVDs	Misc	Grand Total
6	1	5400	9600	4800	3000	22800
7	2	7000	11200	9200	2400	29800
8	3	9200	7400	9600	1800	28000
9	4	3600	10400	3600	4600	22200
10	5	5800	8200	11200	2800	28000
11	6	6400	7600	11400	2400	27800
12	7	3600	2280	9200	7400	22480
13	8	5400	9600	5800	2000	22800
14	9	3600	10200	12800	3600	30200
15	10	4600	10800	7800	2400	25600
16	Grand Total	54600	87280	85400	32400	259680

Figure 31-9. The Month field of this table is used as a page field and displays data only for the selected month.

Formatting PivotTables

When you create a new PivotTable, Excel applies default formatting to the table, placing borders around different cells and items to set off the contents of the fields, the subtotals, and the totals. These borders are applied each time the table is pivoted or refreshed; if you remove them, say to print your PivotTable, they will reappear the next time you make a change to the table. You can, however, change the formatting of your PivotTable in many ways, using the Formatting Palette. If this palette is not visible, choose View, Formatting Palette to display it. You can apply formatting to PivotTables the same way you do to normal Excel worksheets.

For more information on formatting cells with the Formatting Palette, see "Using the Formatting Palette," page 628. For more general information on formatting worksheets, see Chapter 26, "Mastering Worksheet Formatting."

Notes on Formatting PivotTables

Not all Excel formatting works with PivotTables. Here is a brief overview of things you need to know about formatting PivotTables:

● Most formatting is retained when you change your PivotTable as long as the Preserve Formatting option has been selected (this is selected by default). If your formatting is not retained, make sure that this option is selected. To do this, choose the PivotTable menu on the PivotTable toolbar, and then select Table Options. In the Format Options section, select Preserve Formatting.

● Don't use conditional formatting or data validation in your PivotTable. Though conditional formatting might work, you might get unpredictable results and your formatting will not be retained if you pivot the table.

● Cell borders are redrawn each time you change the layout of your PivotTable. If you remove or change borders to print your table, the next time you pivot it they will return to the default style.

● To apply formatting to all the pages of a PivotTable with page fields, choose (Show All) from the page field pop-up menu. Any formatting you apply will affect all the pages. If there is no (Show All) menu item, you will need to select each page and apply formatting one page at a time.

If you want to remove all formatting, including borders, follow these steps:

1 Click anywhere in your table, choose PivotTable on the PivotTable toolbar, and then select Table Options.

2 Clear the AutoFormat Table check box. Click OK.

3 Click anywhere in your table, and choose Format, AutoFormat.

4 In the AutoFormat dialog, scroll down to the bottom of the Table Format list, and select None. Click OK.

Using AutoFormat

You can use AutoFormat to quickly apply formatting to your tables. AutoFormat gives you a set of predefined table formats, including fonts, styles, and cell colors. To apply AutoFormat to a PivotTable, click anywhere in the table, choose Format, AutoFormat, and select one of the table formats in the Table Format list. Click OK.

For more on using AutoFormat, see "Letting AutoFormat Do It," page 630.

Hiding or Displaying Grand Totals

When you create a PivotTable, grand totals for rows and columns are displayed by default. Though in most cases you will want totals to be displayed, you can choose to turn them off if you wish. To do this, click anywhere in your PivotTable, and then choose Table Options from the PivotTable menu on the PivotTable toolbar.

The Format Options section of this dialog enables you to choose whether you want to display grand totals for columns or rows. To hide these totals, clear the Grand Totals For Columns and Grand Totals For Rows check boxes, and click OK. To display them again, select these check boxes again.

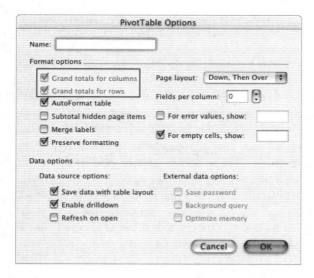

Changing PivotTable Field Settings

When you create a PivotTable, the default settings calculate totals and subtotals of the different fields, in rows and columns, and display all the items within each field. But you can change these settings, as well as several others, for any field. To change field settings, click in a field, and then click the Field Settings button on the PivotTable toolbar. The following dialog appears.

744

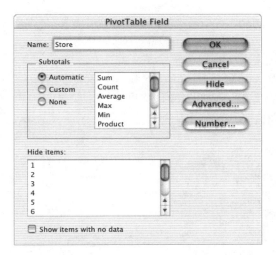

This dialog lets you change the functions used for subtotals, by choosing a function in the Subtotals section, or turn off subtotals by selecting the None option. The Automatic subtotal setting sums the values in number cells and counts the number of text cells. You can also hide any of the items in a field by clicking one of the items in the Hide Items list, and then clicking OK to close the dialog. You can select multiple items by clicking the first item, holding down the Shift key, and clicking the last item you want to select. You can select nonadjacent items by clicking the first item, holding down the Command key, and clicking other items. You can hide the entire field by clicking the Hide button. The only way to unhide the field is to drag the field from the toolbar again.

You can set the number format for the selected field by clicking the Number button, which opens the Number tab of the Format Cells dialog. The Number button is not displayed if you choose a text field.

For more information on number formats, see "Specifying Number Formats," page 612.

If you click the Advanced button, you can access several advanced options. Some of these options let you choose how external data is handled, and others let you choose sort and display options.

Using Custom Calculations

In addition to the basic summary functions available, you can also choose from a set of custom calculations in your PivotTables. To do this, follow these steps:

1 Select any cell in the data area of your table, and then click the Field Settings button on the PivotTable toolbar.

2 Click Options in the PivotTable Field dialog, and this dialog expands to show additional calculation options.

3 In the Show Data As section, a pop-up menu lets you choose from nine options. Select the one you want to use, and then click OK.

With these calculations you can display data as a percentage of a row, column, or total; as a running total; as a percentage of a specific field; as a difference; or as a difference in percent of a specific field.

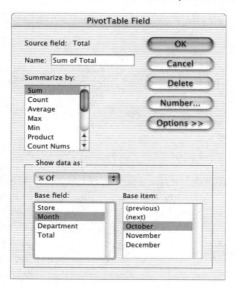

Changing Field Names

When you create a PivotTable, Excel names the table's fields according to the column headers in the source data used, and the items according to the data items in the source data. To change the field names, select the cell containing the name you want to change, and type the new name into the Formula field on the Formula Bar. Press Return, and the name is changed.

Creating Charts from PivotTables

PivotTables are like any other data in an Excel worksheet, and you can make all kinds of charts from these tables. However, you must prepare your PivotTable so the chart can be used properly. If you merely make a chart from the table in its default presentation, with subtotals and totals, these summary totals will appear in the chart and skew its presentation (unless, of course, you want the totals to be displayed). To turn off subtotals, select each field, and click the Field Settings button. Select None in the Subtotals section, and then click OK. If you make a chart now, only the data will be displayed.

For more information on charts, see Chapter 29, "Analyzing and Presenting Data with Charts."

note Most of the functions are the same between the Macintosh and Windows versions of Excel, but one useful function is missing: PivotChart Reports. In Excel for Windows, you can create a PivotChart and then move the fields around in it, as you do in a PivotTable. When you make changes to the PivotChart, these changes are made automatically to the PivotTable. PivotCharts offer a visual approach to PivotTables, enhancing your ability to examine your data. Perhaps in a future version of Excel this function will be available for Macintosh users.

Grouping and Ungrouping Data

When Excel creates a PivotTable, it subtotals inner field items within each outer field, but sometimes you might want to change which subtotals are displayed. Excel lets you *group* items together, to create new subgroups within fields and display subtotals for different groupings of items rather than entire fields.

Figure 31-10 shows an example of grouped subtotals. The table shown in Figure 31-9 on page 742 contains a list of 10 different stores, numbered from 1 to 10. These stores are grouped in two new groups, one containing the first five stores and one containing the second five stores. Rather than display the data for each store separately you can choose to display it as subtotals for each group.

	A	B	C	D	E	F
1	Month	October				
2						
3	Sum of Total	Department				
4	Store2	Books	CDs	DVDs	Misc	Grand Total
5	Group1	31000	46800	38400	14600	130800
6	Group2	23600	40480	47000	17800	128880
7	Grand Total	54600	87280	85400	32400	259680

Figure 31-10. This table shows the sales figures for 10 stores subtotaled in two groups.

To group items in a PivotTable, select the items you want to group, and Control+click one of the selected items. A contextual menu opens. Choose Group And Outline, Group, and your selection will be grouped. When items are grouped, a new field header is added to your PivotTable, and a new button is added to the PivotTable toolbar. You can move this group around as you would any other field, or remove it from the PivotTable by dragging it out of the table. By default, this field is named <field>2, where <field> is the name of the original field containing the items. But you can change this name by double-clicking the field header and entering a new name in the PivotTable Field dialog that opens.

To ungroup items, Control+click an item in the group. Choose Group And Outline, Ungroup from the contextual menu; your selection will be ungrouped, and its button will disappear from the PivotTable toolbar.

Performing What-If Analysis

What if you want to know how much money you can borrow with payments of a certain amount per month? Or if you want to know how many units of a product you must sell to reach the break-even point? Or if you want to solve an equation with two variables when you know the answer and one of the variables? Excel's What-if functions give you advanced tools for analyzing data and forecasting from it and for solving problems and determining values.

Using Data Tables

A data table shows how one or two variables change the results of a formula. With a data table, you can calculate a series of possible results using different values so that you can see how these values affect the results. A simple example is making calculations using interest rates—you can use a data table to calculate investments or loans using a range of interest rates to see how changing rates affect yields.

Creating a Simple Data Table

You can use a simple data table to examine the impact of a change in a single variable on data. Say, for example, that you want to quickly see how different interest rates affect a loan. First, enter the values you want to examine—the interest rates—down column A, as shown in Figure 31-11. Then type the formula in the cell above the first value and to the right of the column of values. The formula used here is =PMT(A3/12,120,B2). This is the PMT function, which calculates loan payments, based on a loan amount, an interest rate, and a number of payments. In this example, the number of payments is 120, or 10 years. B2 is the cell containing the principal of the loan. The interest rate is A3/12; that is, the annual interest rate divided by 12 to obtain a monthly rate. Cell A3, which is an empty cell, is the *input cell*. This cell is used as a placeholder for Excel's data table function. This can be any blank cell in the worksheet, and you specify this cell when creating the data table. Note that the result given in cell B3, the cell containing this formula, is a dummy result that has no value in your actual calculations.

◇	A	B	C
1			
2	**Amount**	$100,000.00	
3		-$833.33	
4	5.00%		
5	5.50%		
6	6.00%		
7	6.50%		
8	7.00%		
9	7.50%		
10	8.00%		
11			

Figure 31-11. This simple example is ready to be changed into a data table.

Follow these steps to create the data table:

1 Select the cells you want to use to make up your data table. In Figure 31-11, you would select cells A3 to B10. This is the smallest range that includes both

748

the formula and values being substituted. You don't want to select row 2, which contains the loan principal. This is referenced in the formula but is not a part of the data table.

2 Choose Data, Table to open the Table dialog. You will use this dialog to specify the input cell, which you chose when laying out your data. Because the example is in column form—that is, the different values used in the table are all in a column—you must use the Column Input Cell field.

3 Click in the Column Input Cell field, and then click your input cell. The cell reference appears; in this example it is cell A3. Figure 31-12 shows the Table dialog after the cell has been clicked.

4 Click OK.

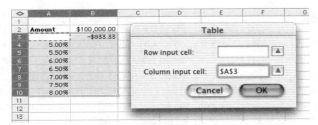

Figure 31-12. You specify the input cell in the Table dialog.

Excel calculates the data table results by applying the values you entered to the formula in cell B3. It enters the *array* formula (a formula that acts on two or more sets of values), =(TABLE(,A3)), in each of the result cells in the *results range* B4:B10 and displays the results of your formula in each of the corresponding cells. (Note that, in this example, the results are negative numbers because they represent money being paid out.) You can now change the interest rate in any of the cells in column A and obtain new monthly payment amounts in column B.

Copying and Clearing Results from a Data Table

When you copy the results from a data table and paste them in a new location, only the values are pasted, not the formulas, unlike most calculation results in Excel worksheets. You cannot copy the results range and have it recalculate in a different location, nor can you move the results range. The data table is frozen in its form. If you want to change the layout, or move the cells of part of the data table, you must clear it and recalculate it. You can, however, select the entire data table and move it to a new location. If you do this, the results will remain accurate.

Because a data table calculates results in an array, they are all interrelated. You cannot merely clear the result from a single cell, but must clear the entire results range. To do this, select the results range, and then Control+click in your selection to open the contextual menu. Choose Clear Contents, and the results range will be cleared.

Troubleshooting

My worksheet containing a data table is calculated slowly.

If you have a complex worksheet containing a data table, and make changes to the worksheet, the data table is recalculated each time any changes are made to the worksheet, whether they affect the data table or not. If this is too slow, you can turn off automatic calculation by choosing Excel, Preferences, and then clicking the Calculation category. Select the Automatic Except Tables check box, and click OK. Now when you do want to update a data table, you'll need to select its result cells and then click Command+ equal sign.

Using Goal Seek

In most cases, when working with data on worksheets, you have a set of values and want to summarize them or make calculations to find their relationships. That is, you have x and y and want to find z, as in the equation $x + y = z$. But sometimes you might want to find out what y is in such an equation. Excel enables you to solve such equations easily using the Goal Seek function. You set up a formula, tell Excel what the result is, and it generates a *goal*, a value that fits your formula. It basically tries out different values until it finds the right one, a process that would take you quite some time if you had to do it manually.

Here is a simple example to show how this works. I am 42 years old and would like to know how much money I need to put aside every month to have $1,000,000 when I reach my planned retirement age of 65. I can't simply divide $1,000,000 by the number of months and use the result ($3,623.19) as my contribution amount, because the interest that is added to the principal reduces the amount I will have to contribute (fortunately!).

To calculate this type of problem, and to have Excel come up with the result, you need to use the FV (future value) function. This function calculates the future value of an investment based on constant payments and a fixed interest rate. (Although one cannot assume that the interest rate will be fixed over such a long period, choosing a conservative rate should come close to the average over time.) The syntax for the FV function is

FV(rate,nper,pmt,pv,type)

where *rate* is the interest rate; *nper* is the total number of payment periods; and *pmt* is the amount of each payment. Two of these arguments, *pv* and *type,* are optional. The argument *pv* is the present value, used to calculate an annuity which already has an amount of principal. The *type* parameter specifies when payments are due; if it is 0, payments are made at the end of the period, if it is 1 they are made at the beginning of the period. If omitted, the type is considered to be 0. To use Excel's Goal Seek feature to find the correct monthly savings for this example, follow these steps:

1 Set up a worksheet similar to that shown in Figure 31-13. Enter labels for the monthly amount invested, the number of years, the interest rate, and the desired total at age 65.

2 You must enter values in all the cells used in your formula before using the Goal Seek function. Enter –$1000 or any negative amount in cell C2; this value is a negative number because it represents money being paid out. You can use any amount because the value in this cell will change when you run Goal Seek.

3 Enter the number of years in cell C3. This is 65 minus your age.

4 Enter the interest rate in cell C4. For this example, I am assuming an average rate of 5% over the entire period, but if you are optimistic (or pessimistic) you can use a higher or lower rate.

5 Cell C5 contains your formula, which you should type as follows:
=FV(C4/12;C3*12;C2)

- ■ The first argument, C4/12, is the annual interest rate divided by 12 to give a monthly rate.

- ■ The second argument, C3*12, is the number of years times 12 to give the total number of monthly payments.

- ■ The final argument, C2, is the monthly amount invested.

◇	A	B	C
1			
2	Monthly amount invested		-$1,000.00
3	Number of years		23
4	Interest rate		5.00%
5	Total at age 65		$516,157.53
6			

Figure 31-13. This is how the worksheet looks before using the Goal Seek feature.

6 You now want to find the amount in cell C2 that will give you a total of $1,000,000 in cell C5. Select the cell containing the formula, in this case C5. Choose Tools, Goal Seek.

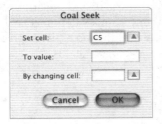

7 In the dialog that appears, enter the cell containing the formula in the Set Cell field (entered already because it was selected when you opened the dialog). In the To Value field, enter the desired value. In this example you want to reach $1,000,000, so enter that amount. The By Changing Cell field is where you choose the cell that will change. In this case it is the monthly amount invested, or cell C2. After you have entered this data, click OK.

8 The Goal Seek Status dialog is displayed as Excel iterates through the possibilities and then displays the solution, entering the correct value in the selected cell. Click OK, and the goal value will be entered into the cell, and the correct total will display. As you can see here, at 5% interest, over 23 years, it will take an investment of $1,937.39 per month to become a millionaire at age 65.

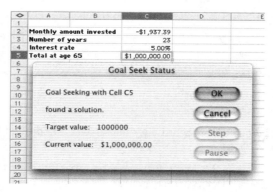

> **tip** You can also choose to step through the calculation one iteration at a time by clicking the Step button in the Goal Seek Status dialog.

Comparing Goals with Multiple Values

The Goal Seek feature can only calculate one formula at a time, with only one goal. It cannot compare results using multiple values. If you want to use the retirement fund example, but compare the results using different interest rates, you cannot do so in just one step. You can, however, copy your data range and run another goal seek. If you want to make the same calculations using different values—say a different number of years or interest rate—simply copy your data range, paste it next to your original data, and change the variable you want to compare. Your formula will immediately calculate the total with the new value. Then, run the Goal Seek function as in the preceding example. Excel will calculate this new value based on the data it contains.

	A	B	C	D
1				
2	Monthly amount invested		-$1,937.39	-$1,688.47
3	Number of years		23	23
4	Interest rate		5.00%	6.00%
5	Total at age 65		$1,000,000.00	$1,000,000.00

If you want to try out many different values, you should create scenarios with your data, discussed next. Although scenarios do not perform Goal Seek operations, they do enable you to quickly examine many different possibilities for your values.

> **tip** **Pause the Goal Seek function**
>
> Excel's Goal Seek function is very powerful: it can calculate the most complex formulas using many variables and functions. In most cases, given the speed of today's computers, Goal Seek will return a result very quickly. But, in some rare cases, this will take several seconds. If your calculation is taking more time than you have, you can use the Goal Seek Status dialog to pause the calculation.

Using Scenarios

Excel's Goal Seek feature enables you to find a missing value in a formula, as seen in the preceding section. But if you want to make a forecast with multiple values or variables, scenarios are what you need. Not only can scenarios let you work with up to 32 variables, but they also let you set constraints for your data. To explore the possibilities with your retirement fund contributions, for example, you could make several scenarios using different monthly investments and interest rates.

A *scenario* is a set of input values that Excel saves, and that you can easily change in your worksheet in order to examine the effects of the new values. You can save dozens of different scenarios, based on different prices, interest rates, variables, or other data. Each time you save a scenario, Excel records its data and results, and you can go through your scenarios to see how changes in different variables affect your results.

Creating a Scenario

Let's say you want to project how your savings will grow until your retirement. As in the preceding retirement fund example, you want to see how different monthly investments and different interest rates will lead to different amounts of capital after this period. You can also change the length of the period, or any combination of the three variables used. To make these projections, you will use the FV function to calculate the future value of an investment with regular payments and a fixed interest rate. The formula for this calculation is discussed in "Using Goal Seek," page 750.

Follow these steps to create the scenario:

1. Create a worksheet like the one shown next. Unlike the example in Figure 31-13 on page 751, where Goal Seek was used to find the monthly payments needed to reach $1,000,000 at age 65, this calculation starts with a more basic assumption: monthly investments of $500 will be made, at 5% fixed interest. (Note that the monthly amount invested is a negative number, because this represents money being paid out.)

◇	A	B	C
1			
2	Monthly amount invested		-$500.00
3	Number of years		23
4	Interest rate		5.00%
5	Total at age 65		$258,078.76
6			

2 To create a scenario using a different interest rate, select the cell containing the interest rate amount, and then choose Tools, Scenarios. The Scenario Manager appears, which you can use to create, edit, and delete scenarios and to choose which scenario is displayed.

3 Click Add. In the Add Scenario dialog, enter a name for your scenario, and enter comments, if you want. Excel automatically enters Created by... with the user's name and date, but you can put whatever you want here. If you want to change several cells in the scenario, click in the Changing Cells field, and then select the cells in your worksheet. In this example, only one cell will change.

4 Click OK, and the Scenario Values dialog appears. Enter the values for each of the changing cells in this dialog. Because the values are already in this first scenario, Excel enters them. When you create additional scenarios, you will change the values.

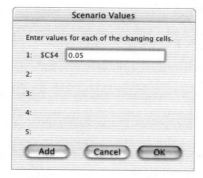

5 Click OK and the Scenario Manager opens with your scenario shown in the list of scenarios. Repeat the same operation to create new scenarios. When you have created several scenarios, they are all displayed in the Scenario Manager, as shown in Figure 31-14.

Figure 31-14. The Scenario Manager shows the three scenarios that have been created on this worksheet.

Browsing Scenarios

The Scenario Manager is your nerve center for working with scenarios. All the scenarios you create on a worksheet are recorded there, and you change the display of your data by selecting a scenario in the Scenario Manager. To select a scenario, choose Tools, Scenario when your active worksheet contains scenarios. To view one of your scenarios, select it in the Scenarios list, and then click Show. If your data does not take up too much space, you can even browse your scenarios and look at the changes in data with the Scenario Manager open, as shown in Figure 31-15.

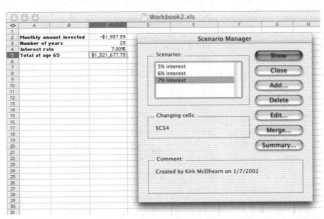

Figure 31-15. The Scenario Manager lets you choose different scenarios while your data is visible in the background.

InsideOut

Adjust your worksheet to display scenarios and view data simultaneously

As mentioned earlier, you can display your scenarios and view your data at the same time. This method works best if your data does not take up much room on your worksheet. If you have a large block of data, you might have trouble viewing it and your scenarios at the same time. You might also run into trouble if you have selected a cell that is far away from the data before opening the Scenario Manager, because Excel scrolls the worksheet to center the selected column in the worksheet window when you open the Scenario Manager. The logic behind this is probably to center the cell you want to view. So, to make sure you can see your data correctly, select a cell in your data, or a cell in the center of the worksheet display, before opening the Scenario Manager. You can't scroll the worksheet when the Scenario Manager is open, so you will have to close it before scrolling to view your data.

Browsing Your Scenarios with One Click

You have to admit it, the way Excel lets you change scenarios is a bit clunky. You need to open a dialog, and then choose your scenario. If your data does not take up a lot of space, you can browse through your scenarios with the Scenario Manager open, but, if not, you need to close it, and then open it again to change to another scenario.

If you use scenarios often, there is an easy way to browse through them with a single click: just add the Scenario button to one of your toolbars. To do this, choose Tools, Customize, select the Commands tab, and then click Tools in the Categories list. Find the Scenario button, about halfway down the Commands list, and drag it to one of your toolbars. You can change its width if you want, by clicking one end of the button and dragging it. Click OK.

Now, whenever you want to switch scenarios, just choose one from this button's pop-up menu.

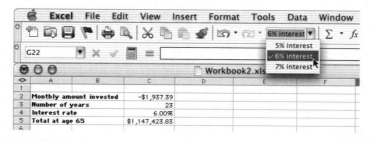

Creating Scenario Reports

If you have created several scenarios and want to examine them all together, or print them out to show others or add to a report, you can create *scenario reports,* which are tables showing all of your scenarios. The Scenario Report function lays out your data as a PivotTable or in a neat, preformatted table, which you can then change in any way you want.

To create a scenario report, choose Tools, Scenario, and click Summary. The Scenario Summary dialog lets you choose from two report types: a Scenario Summary, which is a simple table, or a Scenario PivotTable. If you choose the Scenario Summary, Excel creates a table on a new worksheet, named Scenario Summary, whose data is already laid out and grouped, as shown in Figure 31-16. You can change any of the formatting in this table and add data to it or remove data from it. This table is not frozen; it is prepared using the data in your scenarios, but is not linked to them directly. It shows the data in your changing cells and the result cells, but not all of the data in your calculations. It also shows the name of each scenario and any comments, such as the name of the person who created the scenario and the date.

Figure 31-16. You can change any of the cells in this Scenario Summary table and also show and hide grouped data.

> For more information on working with grouped data, see "Grouping and Outlining Data," page 675.

If you choose Scenario PivotTable from the Scenario Summary dialog, Excel creates a PivotTable, on a new worksheet called Scenario PivotTable, that shows your scenarios by displaying the different possibilities according to the changing cells.

> For more information on using PivotTables, see "Creating PivotTables," page 729.

Merging Scenarios

If you have several scenarios that use the same data and layout but are on other worksheets in your workbook or are in different workbooks, you can *merge* them, that is, import them all into your active worksheet. This is very useful if other colleagues are working with similar data and creating different projections. Once you have merged these scenarios, you can create scenario reports using all of them.

To merge scenarios, follow these steps:

1 Make the target worksheet—the one where you want all the scenarios to end up—active, and open all the workbooks containing the scenarios you want to merge.

2 Choose Tools, Scenario to open the Scenario Manager.

3 Click Merge, and the Merge Scenarios dialog opens.

4 Select the workbook and then the worksheet containing the scenarios to merge, and then click OK.

You can repeat this operation for as many workbooks and worksheets as you want to merge. You can also merge other Scenario Summary reports and Scenario PivotTables.

> **note** Though you can merge scenarios whose layout does not exactly match yours, this can often lead to data being placed in the wrong locations, especially with complex scenarios. The best way to avoid this problem is to create a blank worksheet that contains the cells and formulas to be used and to distribute it to the other people who will be creating scenarios. You can then be sure that all the data will fit in the right locations when you merge scenarios.

Adding, Deleting, and Editing Scenarios

The Scenario Manager lets you control all of the scenarios in each of your worksheets. You can add, delete, and edit scenarios from this dialog. Choose Tools, Scenario to open the Scenario Manager. To delete a scenario, click its name in the Scenarios list, and then click Delete. To edit a scenario, click its name in the Scenarios list, and then click Edit. The Edit Scenario dialog opens. You can modify the scenario name, the changing cells, and the comments. Click OK when you are finished.

Working with the Solver

Of all Excel's forecasting and problem-solving tools, the Solver is the most powerful and the most complex. The Goal Seek function works fine with one-variable problems, and scenarios let you calculate results of more complex problems with a variety of data input sets. But the Solver lets you make projections and forecasts that involve multi-variable problems with constraints applied to any of the variables, and come up with optimum solutions using different combinations of variables.

> **note** The Solver is an add-in that is installed by the Office Value Pack. If you don't see the Solver command on the Tools menu, run the Value Pack Installer from the Office CD.

Setting up a Problem for the Solver

The Solver finds the optimum value for variables affecting one cell on a worksheet; this cell is called the *target cell,* and it must contain a formula that refers to other cells whose values can change. These are called *changing* or *adjustable cells.* When the Solver makes its calculations, it tries out many different combinations of these adjustable cells to reach the optimum value in the target cell. In a way, this is making backward calculations, similar to what the Goal Seek function does, except that the Solver works with many variables that can have *constraints,* which are predetermined limits. These constraints can be fixed values, but they can also be formulas referring to other cells. For example, one variable could have a constraint that is a percentage of another variable, and another could be limited to the sum of two or more cells.

Suppose a computer dealer has rented a booth at a big weekend computer fair. He is selling many items, but is counting most on selling memory and hard drives. He knows his prices, and knows that, for some items, he has a limited stock and will not be able to meet the demand entirely. He needs to sell a total of $50,000 of material to cover all of his costs—the cost for the booth, travel expenses, hotels, and meals. He wants to be able to project his sales and total income based on these figures, in order to find a break-even point for the entire weekend.

To set up a problem for the Solver, first enter all of your data and labels, create your formulas, and make sure you have a well-defined target cell. In Figure 31-17, the example problem is laid out using dummy values for the number of units sold for each of the items—although you could also enter zeros for all of the Units Sold cells—and the target cell is cell F16, which contains a sum of the Total column values for each of the items sold. Each cell in the Total column contains a simple formula that multiplies the unit price by the number of units sold.

	A	B	C	D	E	F
1						
2						
3		Item			Unit price	Units sold	Total
4						
5		128 K memory chips		$23.00	50	$1,150.00
6		256 K memory chips		$55.00	50	$2,750.00
7		512 K memory chips		$95.00	50	$4,750.00
8						
9		20 GB hard drives		$109.00	50	$5,450.00
10		40 GB hard drives		$135.00	40	$5,400.00
11		60 GB hard drives		$175.00	30	$5,250.00
12		80 GB hard drives		$229.00	25	$5,725.00
13		100 GB hard drives		$279.00	20	$5,580.00
14						
15						
16				Total Income		$36,055.00
17						

Figure 31-17. The worksheet's values will change as the Solver works through the problem.

In another section of the worksheet, you need to enter any constraints that apply to the variables in your problem. In this case, the only constraints are those of stock—the computer dealer will have a limited amount of stock for each item, and even though he knows he will not sell all of his stock, he knows that some items will be likely to sell out. He therefore needs to set his stock as constraints for each item he is going to sell.

These constraints can be placed anywhere on the worksheet, and it is best to label them so they can be changed easily if necessary, as shown in Figure 31-18.

Constraints	
128 K memory chips	200
256 K memory chips	60
512 K memory chips	30
20 GB hard drives	70
40 GB hard drives	70
60 GB hard drives	40
80 GB hard drives	20
100 GB hard drives	12

Figure 31-18. These constraints limit the number of units of each item that can be sold.

Running the Solver

Now that your worksheet is ready, you will run the Solver to calculate how many units of each item the computer dealer must sell to reach his goal of $50,000 total sales. The Solver will figure out a set of values that satisfy your equation. To run the Solver, do the following:

1 Click the target cell to activate it. This is the cell containing the formula that uses the variables you want the Solver to determine. Choose Tools, Solver.

2 In the Solver Parameters dialog you will enter all of the cells and constraints to be used in your problem. The Set Target Cell field contains the reference of the target cell that you selected in step 1. If you wish to change this cell, or if you didn't select the target cell before opening this dialog, you can change it here. The Equal To field contains the target value. For this problem, you will enter 50,000, but you can enter any amount, or select Max or Min to have the solver find maximum or minimum values.

3 The By Changing Cells field contains the changing cells in your worksheet. If you click Guess, Excel will examine the worksheet and make its best guess as to which are the changing cells. In this example, Excel does not find the right cells, as shown next—it selects two ranges of cells including both the unit price and the number of units sold. You therefore need to enter **$E$5:$E$7,$E$9:$E$13**.

InsideOut

Edit changing cells manually in the Solver Parameters dialog.

When you want to edit the changing cells in the Solver Parameters dialog, you must edit them manually. Unlike other text fields where you enter cell references, the By Changing Cells field doesn't include a handy Collapse Dialog button to make the dialog roll up so that you can select the cells. Where did it go? Who forgot it? I don't know, but Windows versions of Excel certainly have one, although Excel 2001 doesn't. This is a real problem and should be fixed, because it should be easier to select these cells.

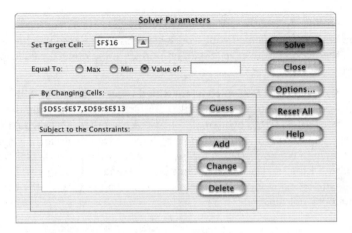

4 You now choose which constraints you wish to apply to the Solver's calculations. In this example, the constraints were entered in a different location on the worksheet. To add constraints for a cell, click Add. The Add Constraint dialog opens. There are two fields in this dialog—Cell Reference and Constraint—and one operator. The Cell Reference is the cell that is to be constrained, and the Constraint is the cell, range, value, or formula that you want to use as a constraint. The operator lets you choose from <=, =, >=, int (integer) and bin (binary).

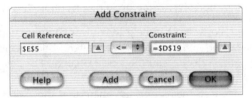

5 Click in the Cell Reference field, and then click the cell you want to constrain. Click in the Constraint field, and then enter the constraint. For this example, we select cell D19, which contains one of the constraints we entered on the worksheet. In this example, you could add constraints for each of the Units Sold cells, based on your inventory, interrelationships between the supply of one item and another, and so forth. The more you can constrain the range of values to closely model your real-world situation, the more accurate the solution is likely to be. Select the operator, in this case, <=, and then click OK if this is the only constraint you want to add, or click Add to save this constraint and add additional constraints without returning to the Solver Parameters dialog.

6 When you have entered all your constraints and returned to the Solver Parameters dialog, you can run the Solver to get answers to your problem. Click Solve, and the Solver will start calculating your problem. The time it takes to come up with an answer depends on the complexity of the problem. For a problem like this, the answer should display in just a few seconds.

7 When the Solver has found an answer, it displays the Solver Results dialog and enters its answers in your worksheet. This dialog lets you choose whether to keep the Solver's solution or restore the original values. Make your choice and click OK.

8 The Solver does its best to come up with an optimum answer, but, at times, this answer does not fit your problem perfectly. In this example, the Solver seems to have started by assuming that the computer dealer would sell out of the highest priced items but not the lower priced items such as memory, as shown in Figure 31-19. In reality, the dealer knows that he will probably sell out of the smaller memory cards and the smaller hard drives. Because there are so many variables—there are eight changing cells—the Solver's solution is not ideal.

Item	Unit price	Units sold	Total
128 K memory chips	$23.00	18	$418.49
256 K memory chips	$55.00	44	$2,393.04
512 K memory chips	$95.00	75	$7,139.56
20 GB hard drives	$109.00	86	$9,398.91
40 GB hard drives	$135.00	70	$9,450.00
60 GB hard drives	$175.00	50	$8,750.00
80 GB hard drives	$229.00	30	$6,870.00
100 GB hard drives	$279.00	20	$5,580.00
	Total Income		$50,000.00

Figure 31-19. Although the Solver came up with a solution, it is not ideal.

9 You can edit any of your constraints to help the Solver come up with a better solution. Select Tools, Solver, and the Solver Parameters dialog appears. To edit one of the constraints, select it and then click Change. For this example, we will change the constraints of cells E5 and E6—the 128-KB and 256-KB memory cards—to be equal to their stock, assuming that they will sell out. Then we will do the same for the 20-GB hard drives, in cell E9. After making these changes, click Solve. The Solver displays a much more realistic solution to the problem, as shown in Figure 31-20, and the dealer will know how many units he needs to sell to break even.

Item	Unit price	Units sold	Total
128 K memory chips	$23.00	230	$5,290.00
256 K memory chips	$55.00	150	$8,250.00
512 K memory chips	$95.00	70	$6,605.25
20 GB hard drives	$109.00	90	$9,810.00
40 GB hard drives	$135.00	62	$8,371.02
60 GB hard drives	$175.00	40	$6,936.89
80 GB hard drives	$229.00	16	$3,765.31
100 GB hard drives	$279.00	3	$971.54
	Total Income		$50,000.00

Figure 31-20. This solution is much better, because some of the constraints were modified to reflect more realistic assumptions.

> **tip**   **Go further with the Solver**
>
> The Solver is a very complex and powerful tool, and a full presentation of this function is beyond the scope of this book. Excel's online help will give you much more information if you want to go further. You can also check out the sample worksheets included with Excel to see how different Solver problems are set up. For more on these sample worksheets, see the online help topic "Solver Sample Worksheets." These worksheets are installed as part of the Office Value Pack. They are found under the Programmability item in the Value Pack Installer and are called Solver Examples. The Solver Samples workbook contains six Solver examples, each of which contains a Solver problem with explanations and indications for the target cell, changing cells, and constraints.

Troubleshooting

The Solver stops before finding a solution.

If the Solver does not find a solution within its iteration limit—the limit to the number of tries it should make—or time limit, it will stop. If this occurs, you might try entering values in the changing cells that are fairly close to what you think the solution is. Then the Solver won't have to try as many solutions to find a good one. If this doesn't help, you can change the Iteration and Max Time settings in the Solver Parameters dialog. Click Options, change these settings, and try running the Solver again.

Collaborating with Colleagues

The rise of the Internet in recent years has changed the way people work with data. Only a few years ago, if you created a report or projection with a spreadsheet program, you would probably have printed out the worksheets and sent them by mail to colleagues or clients for them to review, comment, or edit. You would then make changes to your original file from their comments on paper printouts. At best, you might have sent your spreadsheets back and forth to colleagues on floppy disks. Now that e-mail and networks are easily accessible, you can not only send files in a few seconds, but also share active files over a company network or over the Internet, so that your colleagues and clients can work on your files along with you.

This new ease of collaboration naturally requires special functions to help you share workbooks, protect ones you don't want people to change, and manage comments and changes made by others. This chapter shows you the many Microsoft Excel X tools for collaborating with others, working with comments and changes in your workbooks, sharing and protecting worksheets and workbooks, and how to share Excel documents on the Web, by saving them as HTML pages.

Sharing a Workbook

The simplest way to share a workbook with other users is to send it by e-mail, or post it to a network file server where other users can open or copy the file and work on it. If you share workbooks in this manner, you will need to review the different workbooks and integrate the changes made by other users into a single copy of the original workbook. One way to do this is to merge workbooks.

For more information on merging workbooks, see "Merging Workbooks," page 775.

If you and your colleagues keep files on a network file server, or if files on your computer are accessible to others over a network, you can save workbooks as *shared workbooks*. You can even store shared workbooks on the Internet, so that even geographically separated users can work together with the same files. When you do this, other users can make changes to your files—they can change data, formatting, layout, and formulas.

Shared workbooks allow several people to work on the same file simultaneously, making changes to the workbook. Though this calls for a certain amount of rigor among the users, sharing a workbook enables you and others to make changes or additions to a file at the same time. When you share a workbook, Excel tracks changes, to ensure that you don't get confused as to who has changed what data or formulas.

When you're setting up a shared workbook, you'll want to establish some rules with your coworkers about how each person will use the workbook, and while designing the workbook, you'll want to keep sharing in mind. For example, you might assign particular worksheets in the workbook to be the responsibility of specific coworkers, and agree that changes to those worksheets will only be made by the person to whom the worksheet is assigned.

note You can share workbooks with users who don't have Excel X, but they must use Excel 98 or later for Macintosh or Excel 97 or later for Windows.

To share a workbook with other users, follow these steps:

1 Open the workbook you want to share. If the workbook is on another computer on your network, you will have to mount the network volume containing the workbook.

For more information about mounting network volumes in Mac OS X, switch to the Finder and choose Help, Mac Help. In the Mac Help window, type **Connecting to network file servers**, and click Ask.

2 Choose Tools, Share Workbook; the Share Workbook dialog appears.

3 Select Allow Changes By More Than One User At The Same Time.

4 Click OK, and the workbook's title bar will now have the word *Shared* in brackets after the file name, as shown in Figure 32-1.

When other users open the shared workbook, they will see the same data and layout that appeared in the last saved version of the original workbook. The title bar will show that the workbook is shared, and they will be able to make changes to the workbook.

It's important to note that changes are only displayed to users after they save their file. This means that if you have a file open, and another user makes changes and saves the file, you will not see the changes until the next time you save your file, either manually or automatically. But remember that you are both working on the same file—Excel records a history of changes to the file, and, even though users might see different data displayed as they edit the file, all the original data and changes are recorded.

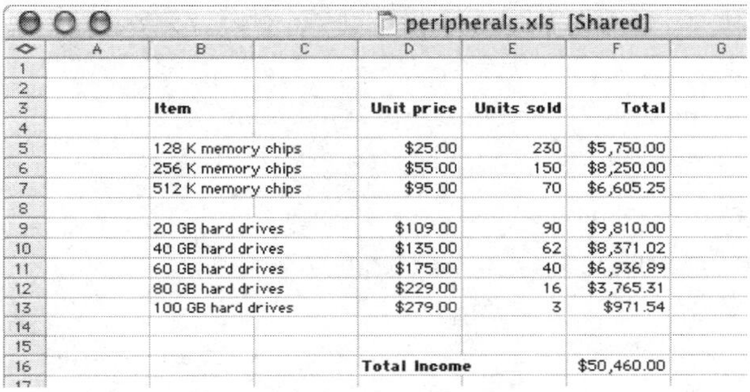

Figure 32-1. This workbook is shared—if you see [Shared] in the title bar, sharing is active.

When another user makes changes to your file, and you save the file, Excel displays a dialog informing you that other changes were made. Each change made to the worksheet is indicated by outlined cells containing comments. In Figure 32-2, another user changed the value in cell D5. The outline around the cell shows this, and a comment is attached to the cell. To view this comment, move the pointer over the triangle in the upper left corner of the cell. As you can see, this comment tells you the name of the user and the date and time that the change was made, as well as what was changed. Excel records all these changes, and you can review them and decide which changes to keep and which to delete.

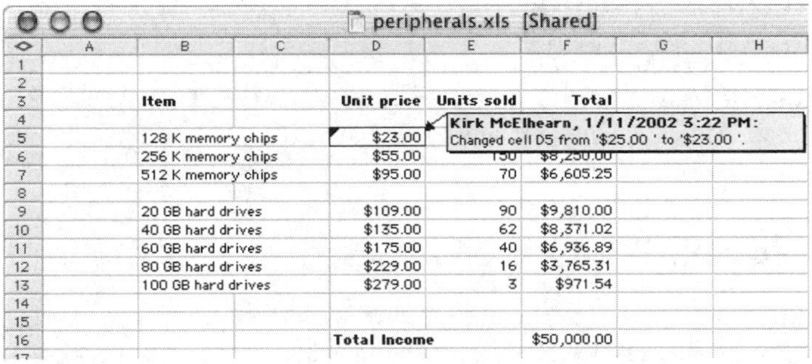

Figure 32-2. Excel displays a comment box when you move the pointer over the upper left corner of a changed cell.

Limitations of Shared Workbooks

Although users can make many changes to shared workbooks, they do not have access to all the myriad functions and features available in Excel. Here are some of the things that you can't do with shared workbooks:

- Merge cells
- Insert or delete blocks of cells (although you can insert rows or columns)
- Delete worksheets
- Change dialogs or menus (by customizing a workbook)
- Define or apply conditional formatting
- Define or change data validation
- Create or edit charts, pictures, objects, or hyperlinks
- Use drawing tools
- Protect individual worksheets or an entire workbook with a password
- Save, view, or edit scenarios
- Insert lists
- Group or outline data
- Insert automatic subtotals
- Create or refresh data tables
- Create PivotTables or edit the layout of existing PivotTables
- Write, edit, view, or assign macros
- Modify or delete arrays

Stopping Workbook Sharing

To stop sharing a workbook, choose Tools, Share Workbook; the Share Workbook dialog appears. Clear the Allow Changes By More Than One User At The Same Time check box. Click OK, and the workbook's title bar will no longer have the word *Shared* in brackets after the file name.

Using Advanced Sharing Options

If you click the Advanced tab of the Share Workbook dialog, you can change some options concerning the way Excel handles changes in your shared workbooks. The Track Changes section lets you choose how long Excel keeps the change history and whether it is kept at all. The Update Changes section lets you decide when changes are updated and whether you see all changes or only those of other users. The Conflicting

Changes Between Users section lets you control the way conflicting changes—changes made to the same worksheet elements by more than one user—are handled. You can also choose whether print settings and filter settings are saved for each user.

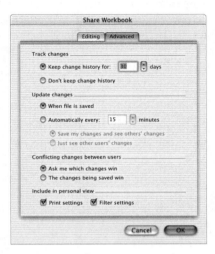

tip Because worksheet changes aren't shared until the worksheet is saved, it's a good idea to have Excel automatically save changes in the Update Changes section of the Share Workbook dialog. This way your coworkers get frequent updates of the changes you make.

Troubleshooting

I can't open shared workbooks.

The most common problem that prevents users from opening shared workbooks is that they do not have sufficient file sharing privileges. If you or another user has problems, make sure the user has been assigned the appropriate sharing privileges for the file, the folder containing it, and the network volume containing both. Under Mac OS X (and also Mac OS 9), you can check privileges by selecting a file or folder in the Finder, pressing Command+I, and then choosing Privileges from the pop-up menu. Make sure that Read & Write privileges are granted to the user or group. See the Mac OS X online help for more on setting file sharing privileges. If the file you are trying to open is on another operating system—such as Windows, or a UNIX-type file server—check the online help for that operating system. In some cases, you might need additional software to connect to network volumes running on other computing platforms. Check with your network administrator for more details.

Tracking Changes

When working with shared workbooks, it is important for the owner of a workbook to be able to track and edit changes made by each participant, and to decide which changes to accept and reject. Because Excel saves a full history of all changes made, the workbook owner can review these changes and decide, for each one, whether to accept it or not. You can choose to track changes in a workbook that is already shared, or you can turn on change tracking and workbook sharing at the same time.

To start tracking changes, follow these steps:

1 Choose Tools, Track Changes, Highlight Changes.

2 In the Highlight Changes dialog, select Track Changes While Editing, as shown in Figure 32-3.

Figure 32-3. The Highlight Changes dialog is where you can choose to track changes to your worksheet.

3 You have three choices in the Highlight Which Changes section of the dialog:

- **When** lets you choose all changes, changes that are not yet reviewed, changes made since a date you specify, or changes made since you last saved.

- **Who** lets you choose everyone, everyone but yourself, or a specific user.

- **Where** lets you choose a specific cell or range in the workbook.

4 Select Highlight Changes On Screen, and click OK.

5 If you want to create a single list of all your changes, called the *change history*, choose Tools, Track Changes, Highlight Changes again immediately, and select List Changes On A New Sheet, which will add a new worksheet to your workbook containing the change history. Then click OK.

> **note** The List Changes On A New Sheet button will appear dimmed until you start tracking changes, which is why you have to reopen the Highlight Changes dialog.

Reviewing Tracked Changes

To review changes, choose Tools, Track Changes, and select Accept Or Reject Changes. A dialog opens, in which you can choose which changes to edit, as shown in Figure 32-4.

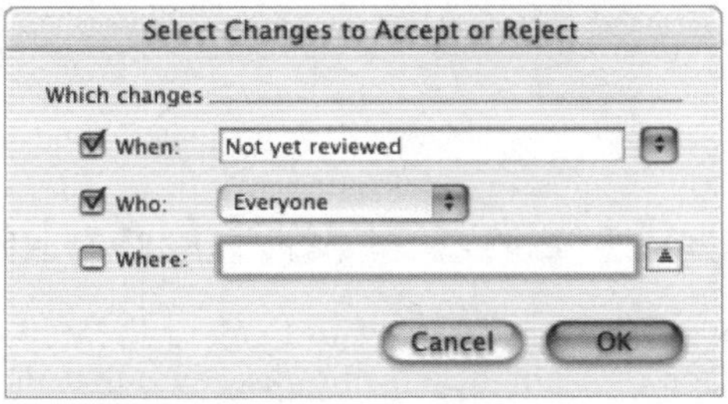

Figure 32-4. Choose which changes you want to review in this dialog.

After you make your choices, click OK, and the Accept Or Reject Changes dialog opens.

Excel displays each change in the Accept Or Reject Changes dialog, as shown in Figure 32-5. The information displayed here is the same as in the comment attached to the changed cell (see Figure 32-2 on page 767): the user name, the date and time, and the exact change that was made. You can accept or reject each individual change by clicking Accept or Reject, you can choose Accept All or Reject All to process all changes in one step, or you can stop editing changes by clicking Close.

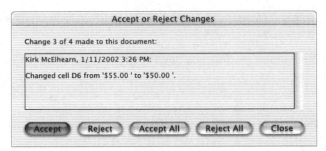

Figure 32-5. Excel displays this detailed information for each change.

InsideOut

Track changes you make to your own workbook

Although Excel's Track Changes feature is designed to track changes made by several users, you can use it to keep an audit trail of changes you make to your own workbooks. Share a workbook, as explained earlier, and Excel will track changes you make. You can set the number of days changes are recorded by choosing Tools, Share Workbook and clicking the Advanced tab. Set a new number of days in the Keep Change History For field, and click OK. You can revert to earlier versions of your data at any time, although it takes a bit of manipulation with the Accept Or Reject Changes dialog. Oh, you might like to know that you can only keep the change history for up to 32,767 days.

Protecting Worksheets and Workbooks

When you send workbooks to other users, you might want to allow them to make all the changes they want. But sometimes, you might want to make sure that the workbooks are not changed at all; you might want users to be able to view your workbooks but not edit them. Excel has a set of protection functions that enable you to choose what you protect—worksheets or workbooks—and give you the capability of protecting certain elements in your worksheets and workbooks.

Excel offers two levels of protection. The basic protection merely locks worksheet and workbook elements until protection is removed. This protection can be enabled or disabled by any user, and is designed to protect the elements of worksheets and workbooks from accidental changes when viewing or browsing them. The second level of protection involves applying a password to a worksheet or workbook. If you protect files using a password, only users with the password will be able to unprotect the workbook or worksheet. This form of protection is much more secure than the first.

caution If you do use a password, make sure you don't forget it; if you do, there's no way to get around the password protection, and you'll lose whatever level of access to the file that you set.

Protecting Worksheets

To protect an active worksheet, choose Tools, Protection and select Protect Sheet. You can use the Protect Sheet dialog to protect the worksheet's contents, objects, and scenarios. By default, all three of these elements are selected. If you don't want to protect all these elements, clear the appropriate check boxes.

Here is how each of the three elements protect your worksheet or workbook:

- **Contents.** When you protect the contents of a worksheet, users cannot make changes to any cells, view any hidden rows or columns, view hidden formulas, or make changes to items on chart sheets.

> For more information on hiding rows or columns, see "Hiding and Unhiding Rows and Columns," page 606.

- **Objects.** When you protect the objects of a worksheet, users cannot make changes to any graphic objects, including charts and text boxes; change the formatting of embedded charts; make changes to graphic objects on chart sheets; or add or edit comments.

- **Scenarios.** When you protect worksheet scenarios, users cannot change or delete any scenarios or view any hidden scenarios.

Protecting Workbooks

To protect a workbook, choose Tools, Protection and select Protect Workbook. In the Protect Workbook dialog you can choose to protect the workbook's structure and its windows. By default, Structure is selected.

You can select either or both of these options:

- **Structure.** When you protect the structure of a workbook, users cannot make any changes to the worksheets contained in the workbook: they cannot move, copy, add, or delete worksheets or view hidden worksheets. They can't display source data for PivotTable items, nor can they display page field pages on different worksheets. They also cannot create summary reports using the Scenario Manager, nor use any tools from the Analysis Toolkit that place results on new worksheets.

- **Windows.** When you protect a workbook's windows, users can't move or resize the windows when the workbook is opened.

Troubleshooting

Protect Worksheet and Protect Workbook commands are unavailable.

If you want to protect a worksheet or workbook and find that the commands to do this appear dimmed on the menu, it is because you are trying to protect a shared workbook. Because a shared workbook is, by its very nature, accessible to others, Excel will not let you protect any part of it, even if you are the only user working on the file. You must turn off sharing for the workbook before you can apply protection. But remember that the change history is deleted once you stop sharing the workbook.

For more information on removing sharing from a workbook, see "Stopping Workbook Sharing," page 768.

Protecting and Sharing Workbooks

If you wish to share a workbook and make sure that no one can remove its change history, choose Tools, Protection, Protect And Share Workbook. The Protect Shared Workbook dialog lets you start sharing a workbook and will prevent users from deleting the change history; optionally, you can add a password. Users can make the same changes as with normal workbook sharing—but this keeps them from deleting the change history. Select the Sharing With Track Changes check box, and then, if you want, enter a password. Only users with the password will be able to do anything that deletes the change history.

Troubleshooting

I can't change the length of the change history in a protected and shared workbook.

When you choose the Protect And Share Workbook command, Excel begins sharing the workbook using the most recently applied settings for sharing workbooks, set on the Advanced tab of the Share Workbook dialog. If you want to change the length of the change history, you need to either set this number of days before protecting and sharing the workbook, or remove the protection to change the number of days.

For more information on setting the length of change history, see "Using Advanced Sharing Options," page 768.

Using a Password to Protect a Workbook

The highest level of protection you can set for a workbook is to protect it with a password. If you do this, users need to know the password to open the file and view it. This is independent of whether you have protected worksheet or workbook elements—you can have a password to open and view a file, and another password to protect individual elements of the worksheet.

To apply a password to a workbook, choose File, Save As, and then click Options. In the resulting Save Options dialog, you can apply two separate passwords: one to open the file and one to modify it. Enter your passwords, and then click OK, and go on and save a new, password-protected copy of the file. Remember that when you choose Save As, the original file is not changed, so the original file will not be password protected. This is a safeguard, though; it allows you to keep a copy, which you do not distribute to others, that can be accessed without a password. In any case, make sure you don't forget the passwords you assign to the file.

Merging Workbooks

If you want several people to work on a workbook you create, and then send their copies back to you, you can easily view and incorporate all of their changes by merging workbooks. This might be easier than sharing a workbook—to share workbooks, all users need access to the same file server. Users working in locations with no direct network connection might not be able to access files on servers.

Start by making a master copy of the workbook you want to distribute, and then share the workbook; you can only merge files that have been shared. The two features are closely interrelated, because they both depend on maintaining a change history.

You should make sure that the number of days set for the change history is sufficient. By default, Excel saves the change history for 30 days. If you are not sure that the other users will return the workbooks to you within 30 days, change this number before sharing the workbook. Any changes that go beyond this number of days will be lost.

> For more information on setting the number of days for the change history, see "Using Advanced Sharing Options," page 768.

Make sure that none of the users are going to change any of the layout or formatting—you can protect worksheet and workbook elements if you want to make sure of this, but be aware that there are certain limitations as to what they can and cannot do with protected files. Once you have set up the workbook so it can later be merged, distribute copies of the workbook to your coworkers.

After the users have made their changes to the workbook data, have them send you the various files so that you can merge them. To merge these workbooks, do the following:

1 Open your copy of the workbook, which is the one you will use as the master workbook. The changes the other users made will be copied to the master workbook; the other workbooks will not be changed.

2 Choose Tools, Merge Workbooks, and select the first file to merge from the Select File To Merge Into Current Workbook dialog.

3 Continue choosing additional workbooks one at a time until they have all been merged.

Now that you have merged your workbooks, all the other users' changes have been integrated into your master workbook, but none of them have been validated yet. To view these changes, and to decide which to accept and which to reject, follow the instructions presented in "Reviewing Tracked Changes," page 771. For each element changed in the workbook, Excel will display all of the changes made, by each user; you can choose which of these changes you want to incorporate into your master workbook.

Adding and Reviewing Cell Comments

Adding comments to cells is an excellent way for colleagues to share feedback on workbooks, their layout, and the data and information they contain, as well as to provide instructions and explanations for users who will be entering data into your workbooks. You can attach comments to individual cells, so that your comments are displayed next to the material they apply to. These comments appear in yellow text boxes when you move the pointer over a cell containing a comment, as shown in Figure 32-6.

Item	Unit price	Units sold	Total
128 K memory chips	$23.00	227	Kirk McElhearn: This figure is way too low. We need more sales!
256 K memory chips	$50.00	129	
512 K memory chips	$90.00	68	$6,120.00
20 GB hard drives	$109.00	54	$5,886.00
40 GB hard drives	$135.00	46	$6,210.00
60 GB hard drives	$175.00	23	$4,025.00
80 GB hard drives	$229.00	12	$2,748.00
100 GB hard drives	$279.00	3	$971.54
	Total Income		$37,631.54

Figure 32-6. Use comments to explain, inform, or comment on data and information in your worksheets.

Adding Cell Comments

To add comments to a worksheet, click the cell you want to attach the comment to, and then choose Insert, Comment. A Comment box appears with your name in bold. Type your comment, and then click anywhere on the worksheet. A red triangle appears in the upper right corner of the cell, indicating that a comment is attached to the cell. To display this comment, simply move the pointer over this triangle; the comment displays as a ScreenTip. Note that although you can only add one comment to a cell, this comment can be as long as you want. To add a new paragraph to a comment, press Return. To change the size of the comment box (irrespective of the amount of text it contains), drag one of the handles around the box's border.

The name displayed in bold in the comment box is the name entered in Excel's Preferences dialog. To change this name, select Excel, Preferences, and then select the General category, and type a new name in the User Name field. You might want to have your own name, your name and title, or your company or department name, depending on who will be reading the comments. If you don't want your name to display at all, simply select it in the comment box when entering your comment, and delete it. Your name will not be included in the comment box, but, when the comment is active, Excel will still display the name of the user who wrote the comment in the status bar at the bottom of the window. To be truly anonymous, return to the Preferences dialog and type just a space in the User Name field. Now both the comment and the status bar will reveal only a blank contributor.

Editing and Removing Cell Comments

If you add a comment to a cell, and then select it and choose the Insert menu, you will see that the Comment menu item has changed, and now displays Edit Comment. Choose this, and the Comment box will become active. You can edit the comment by adding, deleting, or changing any of its text.

Troubleshooting

I can't edit some comments in my shared workbook.

If your workbook is shared, you will not be able to edit comments added by other users. If you are sure you no longer need this workbook to be shared, and do not need to keep the change history, stop sharing it and you will be able to edit all of its comments.

For more information on removing sharing from a workbook, see "Stopping Workbook Sharing," page 768.

To remove a comment from a cell, Control+click on the cell and choose Delete Comment from the contextual menu. Another way to do the job is to click the cell containing the comment you want to remove, and then choose Insert, Edit Comment. Click the hatched border around the cell, and press Delete to remove the comment.

Hiding Cell Comments

Excel lets you choose how comments are displayed for all workbooks. Choose Excel, Preferences, and then click the View category. There are three choices for displaying comments:

- **None.** If you choose None, neither comments nor red triangle indicators will be displayed. To see the comments attached to a worksheet, you will have to choose View, Comments.

- **Comment Indicator Only.** If you choose Comment Indicator Only, Excel displays a red triangle indicator and displays the Comment box when you move the pointer over the indicator. This is the default setting.

- **Comment & Indicator.** If you choose Comment & Indicator, all comments and indicators are displayed. This is useful when you want to edit all of your comments or view all the comments added by other users.

It should be noted that these last two preferences do the same thing as choosing View, Comments. When comments are displayed in this manner, it is the same as choosing Comment & Indicator, and choosing this from the menu also changes the preferences. If you decide to stop viewing comments, choose View, Comments again, and the preferences and display return to the default setting of the comment indicator only.

> **tip**   **Hide individual cell comments**
>
> If you have displayed all comments, and want to hide a comment attached to a single cell, Control+click a cell, and choose Hide Comment from the contextual menu. If you later want to display all hidden comments, including those you have hidden individually, choose View, Comment twice. Note that a hidden comment is not truly hidden from curious eyes, because moving the pointer over the red triangle will make the comment appear even after it's been "hidden."

Reviewing Cell Comments

One easy way to review all comments is to choose View, Comments, and have Excel display all comments. However, if a worksheet contains many comments, they might overlap, making them difficult to read. The best way to review many comments is to use the Reviewing toolbar. Choose View, Toolbars, and then select Reviewing. The Reviewing toolbar, shown in Figure 32-7, contains buttons that enable you to work with comments quickly and easily, by moving from one comment to another, editing and deleting comments.

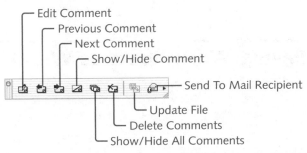

Figure 32-7.   The Reviewing toolbar gives you quick and easy access to comments.

The Reviewing toolbar contains the following buttons:

- **Edit Comment.** Click this button to edit the active comment.

- **Previous Comment.** Click this button to go to the previous comment.

- **Next Comment.** Click this button to go to the next comment.

- **Show Comment.** Click this button to show the comment in a cell if comments are hidden. If the comment is already displayed, this button changes to Hide Comment and hides the cell's comment.

- **Show All Comments.** Click this button to show all comments. If comments are already displayed, this button changes to Hide All Comments.

- **Delete Comment.** Click this button to delete the comment in the active cell.

- **Update File.** Click this button to update a shared workbook.

- **Send To Mail Recipient.** Click this button to send the active workbook by e-mail, as an attachment.

For more information on sending Excel workbooks by e-mail, see "Sending Excel Documents via E-Mail," page 574.

Sharing Excel Documents on the Web

In addition to the many functions that enable you to share Excel workbooks with other users and colleagues, you can share your documents with others via the Web, or on a company intranet, giving access even to users who don't have a copy of Excel. Excel documents shared in this manner can be displayed by any Web browser, and closely resemble your original worksheets, but of course can't be edited in the Web browser. You can update these files easily by automatically saving your worksheets as Web pages.

Limitations to Saving Worksheets as Web Pages

You must bear in mind that not all the elements of your worksheets can be published on the Web. Because not all functions and features can be translated into HTML code, there are many limitations. The following elements are not retained when saving worksheets as Web pages:

- Auditing tracer arrows
- Data validation restrictions and messages
- Distributed alignment
- Indented text
- Named cells or named ranges
- Pattern fills
- Printing and page setup features
- Shared workbook information

The following elements are converted to their current values when saving a worksheet as a Web page:

- **1904 date system.** Dates displayed remain the same, but serial numbers for dates are not retained.
- **Array formulas**

- **Charts.** You can save charts as graphics that are displayed on Web pages. Chart information is not retained.
- **Conditional formatting.** Cell formatting is retained, but is no longer conditional.
- **External data ranges.** You cannot refresh from the source data.
- **Labels in formulas**
- **Named constant values**
- **R1C1 reference style**
- **References to data on other worksheets**
- **Subtotals.** Formulas are not retained.
- **Web queries**

In addition, these elements are changed as follows:

- **Outlining.** Collapsed rows are displayed as hidden. Expanded rows are displayed normally.
- **Password protection.** Data in password-protected worksheets and workbooks can be saved as a Web page, but passwords are not retained.
- **PivotTable Reports.** PivotTable values and formatting are converted for display on the Web, but PivotTable information and functionality are not retained.
- **Precision as displayed.** Precision as displayed value is saved, but settings are not retained.
- **Rotated or vertical text.** Text that has been reoriented is converted to horizontal text.
- **Wrapped text in cells.** Text is displayed correctly, but settings are not retained in HTML.

Previewing Excel Documents as Web Pages

Before saving an Excel worksheet or workbook as a Web page, it is a good idea to preview it in a Web browser. This way you can make sure that everything you want to display is visible and that your formatting is correct. You can toggle between Excel and your Web browser as you make changes to your worksheets to see how they display as Web pages.

To preview your worksheet or workbook as a Web page, choose File, Web Page Preview. Excel opens your default Web browser and displays the current page. If your workbook contains only one worksheet, or has only one sheet with data, your browser displays the worksheet as a single Web page. If several worksheets in your workbook contain data, your browser displays each worksheet with frames: the lower frame contains sheet tabs, like the ones at the bottom of every Excel window, to navigate among the pages, as shown in Figure 32-8 on the next page.

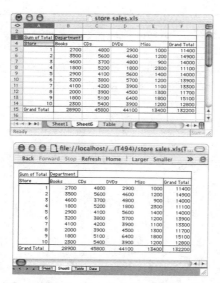

Figure 32-8. Excel displays a workbook containing several worksheets as a frameset with buttons as sheet tabs.

Saving Excel Documents as Web Pages

To save a worksheet or workbook as a Web page, follow these steps:

1 Choose File, Save As Web Page.

2 Choose the location for the files. If you want to save them to your hard disk to upload them later to a Web server, choose the location. If you want to save them directly to a folder on a Web server on your network or intranet, make sure you know the exact folder you need to use.

3 In both cases, you have the choice between saving a workbook or an individual worksheet (if your workbook contains multiple worksheets). To save an entire workbook, select Workbook as shown here; to save only the active worksheet, select Sheet.

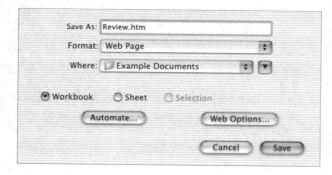

4 Optionally, click the Web Options button to set attributes for your Web page. The dialog that opens contains the following tabs:

- **General tab.** Here you can set a title and keywords for the Web page.

- **Files tab.** On this tab you can choose to update links when saving the file.

- **Pictures tab.** Here you can choose several options for graphics, such as allowing PNG as an output format and selecting a target monitor size.

- **Encoding tab.** This tab lets you change the language and character encoding if necessary (it usually isn't).

5 Click OK.

Excel saves either one file (if you save a worksheet) or a starting file and a folder of supporting files (if you save a workbook). In addition, if there are any charts or graphics in your worksheet or workbook, Excel saves these in the same folder. Files are saved with their names and the extension.htm, and supporting files are saved in a folder with the name of the file, followed by _files. So, if you save a file called Sales, Excel saves a base file called Sales.htm, and a folder called Sales_files.

---

tip **Tweak Excel's HTML code**

If you are good with HTML code, or if you have an HTML editor, you can change the formatting of any HTML pages generated by Excel. Remember that if you save only a worksheet there is only one HTML file, but if you save an entire workbook, there is a main file plus a folder containing supporting files.

Generating Web Pages Automatically

If you have an Excel workbook that you want to save as a Web page, and it contains data that is often updated, you can set Excel to generate Web pages automatically. This enables you to update the Web pages either every time you save the file, or according to a fixed schedule. Generating Web pages automatically ensures that other users will have almost real-time access to the data and information in this file over the Web or an intranet.

To automatically generate Web pages, follow these steps:

1 Choose File, Save As Web Page.

2 Click the Automate button on the Save As sheet to bring up the Automate dialog, shown in Figure 32-9 on the next page. By default, the Never option is selected. If you want Excel to generate Web pages every time the file is saved, select Every Time This Workbook Is Saved and click OK. Then skip to step 6. If you want to have these Web pages generated at regular intervals, select According To A Set Schedule, and continue with step 3.

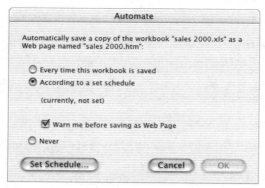

Figure 32-9. You can choose to have Excel generate Web pages automatically.

3 If you choose to have Web pages generated according to a set schedule, an additional option becomes available. Excel will display a warning before generating Web pages if you select Warn Me Before Saving As Web Page.

4 To choose when these Web pages are generated, click Set Schedule. The Recurring Schedule dialog opens.

5 Choose how often you want Excel to generate Web pages. This can be daily, weekly, monthly, or yearly, or it can occur every week (or number of weeks) on a given day or days. You can also set a start and end date for Web page generation. If you do this, Excel will only save your workbook as Web pages between these two dates and times. Click OK when you have set your schedule, and click OK in the Automate dialog to record your automatic Web page generation options.

6 Click Save to generate your Web pages.

784

Working with Hyperlinks

Although Excel workbooks are the best way to present data and information that fits into cells, tables, and charts, sometimes you want to add other information—texts or images—to your workbooks. You can certainly add this type of content, but it does not always fit well into a worksheet. For this reason, Excel lets you add *hyperlinks* to your worksheets. These are links, like those on Web pages, to other files. You can add hyperlinks to Web URLs, to other files on your computer or a network file server, to other locations in the current document; you can even add links that create new e-mail messages when a user clicks them.

Hyperlinks are useful when you want to attach additional information to your worksheets without loading them up with lots of extraneous information. Say you have a product catalog, with hundreds of different products and their prices. You can add hyperlinks to the product numbers or descriptions that open pictures of the items. Or, if you have a workbook with sales figures for different stores, sectors, salespeople, or product categories, you can add hyperlinks to other worksheets giving detailed information. You can also add hyperlinks to Web sites or files on your company's intranet, so that users can find background information on the data in your worksheets.

Adding Hyperlinks to Worksheets

Excel's Hyperlink feature enables you to add hyperlinks to your worksheets quickly and easily. Simply select the cell you want to add the hyperlink to and choose Insert, Hyperlink. The Insert Hyperlink dialog appears. As shown in Figure 32-10, this dialog contains several tabs for creating different types of links.

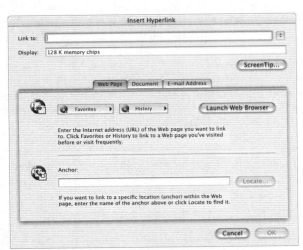

Figure 32-10. The Insert Hyperlink dialog lets you choose from many types of links.

Hyperlinks display in blue, underlined text, like the default setting in any Web browser. When a user moves the pointer over a hyperlink, the pointer changes to a hand, and a ScreenTip shows the address of the link (unless you've specified different ScreenTip text in the Insert Hyperlink dialog), as shown here:

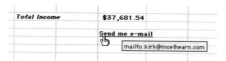

---

tip **Control+click to edit links**

The only way to edit a link is to open the Insert Hyperlink dialog. But, if you click a cell containing a link to activate it, you won't be able to choose this menu item because the link will send you immediately to a Web page or file. To get to the Insert Hyperlink dialog without activating the link, hold down the Control key, click a cell containing a link, and choose Hyperlink from the contextual menu.

Linking to a Web Page

To add a hyperlink to a Web page, you can enter its URL in the Link To field of the Insert Hyperlink dialog, if you know it. (If you enter a URL manually, you must include **http://** or **ftp://** in the URL, or Excel will think it is a link to a local file on your hard disk.) You can also choose a Web page from Internet Explorer's Favorites list by selecting from the Favorites pop-up menu, or from your browser's history by choosing a page from the History pop-up menu. If you are not sure of the exact URL you want to use, click the Launch Web Browser button to launch your browser and find the page. You can then select it from the History pop-up menu.

When you select a link, Excel inserts the name of the Web page in the Display field. Unfortunately, this is not what you usually want to display. You will need to retype the cell's contents if that is what you want displayed; if you do want the Web page's name displayed, leave this field as is. If you want a ScreenTip to display (in Internet Explorer 4 or later), click ScreenTip, and enter the text you want to be displayed.

---

tip Though ScreenTips in hyperlinks are usually for the benefit of readers on Web pages, you can also use them to add directions or descriptions of the hyperlink to people using the link in the Excel worksheet.

For more information on saving workbooks as Web pages, see "Saving Excel Documents as Web Pages," page 782.

When adding a hyperlink to a Web page, you can choose to set the link to go to a specific part of the document, or *anchor*. In the Anchor section of the dialog, click the Locate button. Excel will tell your Web browser to load the page, and, if the page contains anchors, you will be able to select one of them. If you want to link to specific parts of your Web pages, and the pages do not contain anchors, you must insert anchors in the pages using an HTML editor.

InsideOut

Negotiate limitations on hyperlinks in worksheets

There are limitations on where you can add hyperlinks to your worksheet data in Excel. For example, you cannot add hyperlinks to a shared workbook. If you want to add hyperlinks to this workbook you will have to turn off sharing first, but, if you do, you will lose the workbook's change history. You also cannot add hyperlinks to charts, but you can add them to graphic objects added to charts.

PivotTable cells are off-limits for hyperlinks as well. If you need to add hyperlinks to a worksheet with a PivotTable, you can always make a separate cell range containing links that repeat the names of the items you want to add links to. It is best to do this on a separate worksheet—when pivoting the PivotTable, Excel rearranges the data and might overwrite the cells containing the links.

Linking to a Document

To add a hyperlink to a document, choose Insert, Hyperlink and click the Document tab. Select a document from your favorites by clicking the Favorites pop-up menu, or click Select to browse your computer, or your network, to find the document you want to link to. When a user clicks a link to a document, the application required to display that document will open it. You have to make sure that other users have this application, or they will not be able to view the linked document.

When adding a hyperlink to a document, you can choose to set the link to go to a specific part of the document, or an *anchor*. In the Anchor section of the dialog, click the Locate button. You can click Cell Reference and type in a specific cell reference, or click Defined Name and select the name of a cell or range of cells. You can select an anchor to the current workbook or you can link to another Excel workbook and set an anchor in that file. The anchor feature works with Excel files only.

Linking to an E-Mail Address

If you add a hyperlink to an e-mail address, when someone clicks the link their e-mail program will open automatically and create a new message to the e-mail address you entered in the link. To add a hyperlink to an e-mail address, choose Insert Hyperlink, and click the E-Mail Address tab. You can type the e-mail address you want to use in the To field or choose a recently used address from the Recent Addresses pop-up menu. If you need to find an address in your e-mail program, click Launch E-Mail Application, find the address, and copy it. Then come back to Excel, and paste it into the To field. You can also enter a subject for the message in the Subject field. If you save your workbook as a Web page, some browsers will be able to pass the subject on to their e-mail program, but others might not.

InsideOut

Remove former hyperlink formatting along with the link

When you create a hyperlink in a cell, Excel formats the cell to make it resemble a link in a Web browser. The text is blue and underlined, and, when you have visited the link, it changes color, as it would in a browser. If you select a cell containing a hyperlink and press Delete, the cell's contents are removed, but not the formatting. If you then enter data in the cell, it will take on the blue, underlined formatting and most likely confuse you or others. To erase a cell's contents, link, and formatting, select Edit, Clear, All.

Assigning Hyperlinks to Graphics

To add a hyperlink to a graphic, simply select the graphic you want to add the hyperlink to, and choose Insert, Hyperlink. The Insert Hyperlink dialog appears. Follow the instructions in the previous sections to add a hyperlink pointing to a Web page, document, or e-mail address.

Customizing and Automating Excel

As we have seen in the previous chapters about Microsoft Excel X, there are hundreds of features and functions available to crunch numbers, organize data, and present information. Unfortunately, not all of these functions are available with just a click of the mouse or a keyboard shortcut. Some require you to choose from menus and submenus, and others make you go through several levels of dialogs. If you perform certain tasks frequently, wading through Excel's interface can begin to take up too much of your workday.

Like Microsoft Word X, you can customize Excel to gain quick access to the functions and features you use most. You can customize toolbars, make your own keyboard shortcuts, and change menus to fit the way you work. This gives you added flexibility and increases your productivity. You can also use macros to automate common tasks, and even add some functions that are missing from the program. This chapter will show you how to use Excel your way, how to customize its interface, and how to get started using macros to make the program do even more.

Customizing Excel Toolbars

Toolbars are everywhere in Microsoft Office v. X, and Excel is no exception. Not only are there basic toolbars, which are displayed all the time, but many Excel functions, when invoked, open their own special toolbars as well. You can choose to display a wide variety of toolbars, and have them visible at all times, or only show them when you want. But you can also customize your Excel toolbars, adding or removing buttons, and even create custom toolbars that hold only the commands you want.

For information on the limitations in customizing Office v. X programs, see "Customization Limitations," page 46.

Adding Buttons to Toolbars

Although Excel's toolbars include lots of buttons—too many for some users—you might find that a certain toolbar is missing the one button you really need. You can add and remove toolbar buttons, and you can move them around, to position them better, add separators, or even add menus to toolbars. These actions are described in detail in Chapter 4, "Office v. X: Do It Your Way."

For more information on adding buttons to toolbars, see "Adding a Button to a Toolbar," page 48. For information on removing buttons from toolbars, see "Removing a Button from a Toolbar," page 50. To find out how to move, copy, and separate buttons on toolbars, see "Moving, Copying, and Separating Toolbar Buttons," page 50.

Adding Menus to Toolbars

Excel, like the other Office v. X programs that allow toolbar customization, treats the menu bar as a toolbar, and allows you to add menus to toolbars, giving you an even higher level of customization than most programs. Some buttons that you can add to toolbars are actually pop-up menus; when you click these buttons they let you choose from several features or options. There are two types of buttons like this: The first, like the Font, Style, or Zoom button, gives you access to a group of settings. These buttons appear on the Commands tab of the Customize dialog, under their different menus, with rectangles next to their names indicating that they are fields, as shown in Figure 33-1.

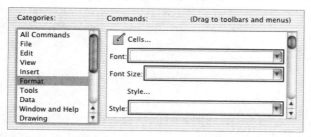

Figure 33-1. The Font, Font Size, and Style buttons, shown here on the Commands tab of the Customize dialog, are actually pop-up menus that let you choose from a list of elements.

The second type of menu button, Excel's built-in menus, includes two types of menus. The first type of menu includes the general menus found in the menu bar: File, Edit, View, and so forth. You can add any of these as buttons to an existing toolbar or create a new toolbar with them. The second type of built-in menu includes submenus from the main Excel menus, such as the Toolbars submenu, the Track Changes submenu, and so on. All these built-in menus and submenus appear in the Customize dialog with triangles after them, indicating that other menu items display when they are clicked, as shown in Figure 33-2.

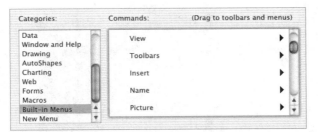

Figure 33-2. These built-in menus include the main Excel menus—View and Insert—and submenus, such as Toolbars, Name, and Picture.

To add one of these menus to a toolbar, do the following:

1 Choose Tools, Customize to display the Customize dialog, shown in Figure 33-3. Click the Commands tab, if it isn't already displayed.

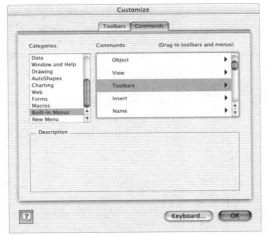

Figure 33-3. On the Commands tab of the Customize dialog you can choose any Excel command to add to a toolbar.

2 Find the menu you want to add to a toolbar. In this example, we are going to add the Toolbar menu to the Standard toolbar. In the Categories list, click Built-In Menus.

3 Click the Toolbars menu in the Commands section, and drag it to the Standard toolbar at the position you want.

4 Click OK in the Customize dialog to add the Toolbars button to the Standard toolbar. Click this button to open a menu that will show or hide any of the basic toolbars, as shown in Figure 33-4 on the next page.

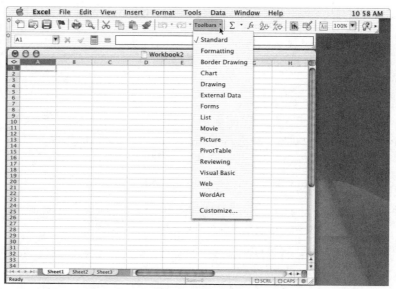

Figure 33-4. With the Toolbars button on the Standard toolbar, you can save one click each time you want to show or hide a toolbar.

For more information on adding menus and custom menus to toolbars, see "Adding Menus to a Toolbar," page 51.

Creating Custom Toolbars

Although Excel has plenty of toolbars, and together they give you quick access to most Excel functions and features, you probably use certain features more often than others. You can save a lot of time by grouping these features all on one custom toolbar. Or, you can make a toolbar with just one button on it, giving you access to a specific built-in menu. To create your own custom toolbar, do the following:

1 Choose Tools, Customize to display the Customize dialog. Click the Toolbars tab, if it isn't already displayed.

2 Click New. Enter a name for your toolbar in the New Toolbar dialog. Excel adds this to the toolbar list, and selects it with a check mark to display it. A new, very small toolbar appears on your screen, as shown in Figure 33-5.

3 To add buttons to this toolbar, click the Commands tab, find the command you want to add, and drag it to the toolbar. Repeat until you have populated the toolbar with the buttons you want.

4 Click OK to close the Customize dialog.

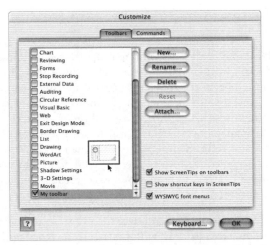

Figure 33-5. When you create a new toolbar, it starts out very small.

If you make a custom toolbar that contains only a menu, you will have one-click access to the functions and features in this menu. Figure 33-6 shows one example of this: a custom toolbar contains the Toolbars menu, which you can access by clicking the Toolbars button. You can make several small toolbars, each with just one or a few buttons, or you can make one larger custom toolbar.

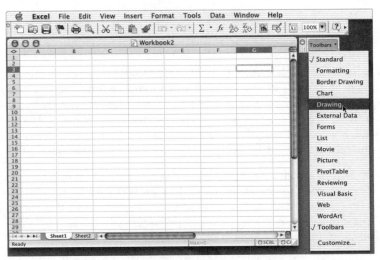

Figure 33-6. When you add a menu or submenu to a toolbar, you get one-click access to its commands.

Chapter 33

Using Excel Macros

In spite of Excel's many functions and features, you might discover something that's missing, or something that doesn't work exactly the way you want. Although such customization as setting your own keyboard shortcuts or creating your own toolbars can help you go further with Excel, the ultimate customization comes from Excel *macros*. A macro is a set of commands that run when you tell them to. Excel macros are written in a programming language called Visual Basic for Applications (VBA). You can create macros in two ways: you can either write your own in the Visual Basic Editor, or you can turn on Excel's macro recorder to record your actions as you perform a series of steps to accomplish a task. In either case, Excel creates a macro that you can run whenever you need to perform the task.

Excel macros give you a very high degree of control over the program and what it can do for you. One of the most useful ways to work with macros is to record tasks that contain several steps that you carry out often. Instead of having to perform the same actions every time—opening dialogs, selecting options, clicking buttons, and so forth—you can just run a macro to do all these things for you. You can also assign macros to toolbar buttons, so you can run them with a single click, or assign keyboard shortcuts to macros, so you can run them by pressing a couple of keys.

> For more information on using toolbar buttons to run macros, see "Assigning Macros to Toolbar Buttons," page 800.

Recording Macros

Before recording a macro, think about the task you want to accomplish, and plan the different steps in advance. If you undo actions, or change things several times to get them right, Excel will record all of these steps, which would obviously be wasted effort when you run the macro. But, if you pause or hesitate between steps, this time will not be recorded. Macros run as fast as your computer allows; much faster than when you click buttons and type text yourself.

In Chapter 24, you saw how changing custom views can be a bit of a headache. You need to choose View, Custom Views, select the view you want to use, and then click OK. Each time you want to change views you need to go through this dialog. In the following example you can record a simple macro that will change custom views with a keyboard shortcut.

Before you can create this macro, you need to create a couple of custom views in a workbook. In this example, the workbook will have two custom views: a normal view, showing the default view of the worksheet, and a four-pane view, showing the worksheet split into four panes. Figure 33-7 shows this second view.

> For more information on creating custom views, see "Getting Different Views," page 572.

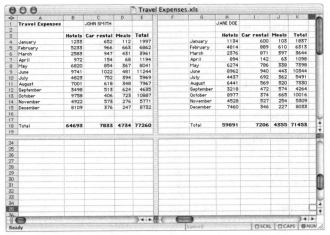

Figure 33-7. After creating this four-pane view, a simple macro can be created to switch to it.

To complete this example, follow these steps:

1 Open a workbook, and save the normal view as a custom view (View, Custom Views, Add). Then divide the workbook into four panes, and save this view as another custom view.

2 Return to the normal view. With the workbook in its normal view, you will record a macro to switch to the four-pane view. Choose Tools, Macro, Record New Macro. The Record Macro dialog appears, as shown in Figure 33-8.

Figure 33-8. Enter a name for your macro and a shortcut key before you start recording the macro.

3 Enter a name for your macro in the Macro Name field; a shortcut key, if you want to run it from the keyboard; and a description that reminds you what the macro does, if you want, in the Description field. A pop-up menu lets you choose where to store the macro. You have three possibilities:

■ **This Workbook.** This option stores the macro in the active workbook. This is useful if you don't want to use the macro when working with other workbooks, or if you want to send it, with a workbook, to someone else.

■ **New Workbook.** This option enables you to create a new workbook in which to store the macro, but this is only useful if the macro is not linked to any data specific to the active workbook, or if you want to attach it to a blank workbook to send to someone.

■ **Personal Macro Workbook.** This option makes the macro available at all times. The Personal Macro Workbook is a blank workbook, which is saved in the Applications/Microsoft Office X/Office/Startup/Excel folder and used as a repository to store macros. If you choose to save your macro in the Personal Macro Workbook, and have not done so before, Excel will create this file for you. When you quit Excel, a dialog will ask whether you want to save the changes you made to the Personal Macro Workbook. Click Save.

> **note** Excel limits you in your choice of names for macros. The first character of the macro name must be a letter, and other characters can be letters, numbers, or underscore characters. You can't use spaces in macro names; use underscores instead to separate words.

4 Click OK in the Record Macro dialog to start recording your macro. Excel goes into recording mode, and everything you do is recorded in your macro until you tell Excel to stop recording. Excel also displays a toolbar with the Stop Recording button and another button for selecting Relative References. The status bar at the bottom of the window, if visible, also shows that Excel is recording, as shown in Figure 33-9.

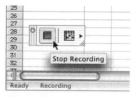

Figure 33-9. The status bar shows that Excel is recording, and the Stop Recording toolbar floats over the active window.

5 Now, perform all of the actions you want to record. For this example, we choose View, Custom views, select 4 Pane View, and then click Show. The worksheet view changes to the four-pane view, as shown in Figure 33-7 on the preceding page.

6 Click the Stop Recording button to stop recording your actions. Your macro is saved with the keyboard shortcut you assigned.

---

tip **Use complementary macros to do and undo complex tasks**

Some macros, such as the one in the preceding example, perform tasks that need additional actions to undo them. In this case, we chose a custom view, and can now use a keyboard shortcut to switch to that view. But you cannot go back to the normal view without choosing View, Custom Views and selecting the Normal view. If you want to toggle between views, create another macro that displays the Normal view.

Running Macros

If you have recorded or written a macro, and assigned a keyboard shortcut to it, the easiest way to run it is simply to press the shortcut keys. This runs the macro immediately without you having to choose any menu items or click in any dialogs.

If you didn't assign a keyboard shortcut to a macro and want to do so, see "Changing Macro Keyboard Shortcuts," on the next page.

You can also run macros from the Macro menu. Do the following:

1 Choose Tools, Macro, Macros. The Macro dialog opens, listing all the macros in all open workbooks, as shown in Figure 33-10 on the next page. You can choose to display macros in a specific workbook by selecting it from the Macros In pop-up menu.

2 Click one of the macros in the list to select it, and then click Run, and the macro will run.

---

tip **Stop macros in their tracks**

If you have a macro that is taking too long to run, and you want to stop it, simply press the Esc key. If you have a file with macros that are set to run automatically when the file opens, and want to deactivate them when opening the file, press the Shift key while double-clicking the file.

Chapter 33

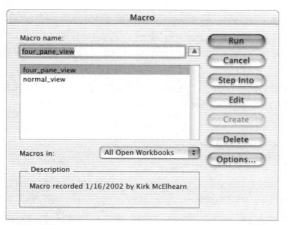

Figure 33-10. The Macro dialog enables you to run, edit, and delete macros.

Troubleshooting

I can't undo my Excel macros.

When you run a macro in Excel, you will find that you can't undo it. There is no work-around for this; you cannot undo macros. So, if you are planning to run a complex macro that will change a lot of your formatting or alter your data, think ahead. Save your workbook before running the macro, and then, after you run it, if you don't want to keep the changes, close the workbook without saving. Reopen your workbook, and it will be in the state it was in when you saved it just before running the macro.

If you have any macros that execute when you open a file, it's obvious that you can't save the file beforehand. But you can stop the macro from executing by holding down the Shift key while opening the file.

Changing Macro Keyboard Shortcuts

Though you can set a keyboard shortcut when recording a macro, you might want to change that shortcut at a later time. Follow these steps:

1 Choose Tools, Macro, Macros to open the Macro dialog.

2 Click one of the macros to select it, and then click Options.

3 Change the shortcut key in the Macro Options dialog.

Relative and Absolute References in Macros

As you can see in Figure 33-9, the Stop Recording toolbar has two buttons: one to stop recording, and the other to set relative references. When you record a macro, Excel uses absolute cell references by default. So, if you click in cell D4, copy its contents, click the next cell to the right, and then paste, Excel records that you copied the contents of cell D4 and pasted it in cell D5. If you then run this macro, Excel will take the contents of cell D4 and paste it in cell D5. But, you might want a macro to copy the contents of the currently selected cell and move it one cell to the right, no matter which cell is active in your worksheet.

To do this, click the Relative Reference button as soon as the Stop Recording toolbar appears, before doing anything else. When the button appears pressed in, or darker, relative references are turned on. Excel will now treat all the cell references in your macro as relative references, and carry out its operations accordingly.

For more information on relative and absolute references, see "Working with Relative and Absolute References," page 654.

If you don't change cells while recording your macro, Excel won't see the difference between absolute and relative references. Say you want to record a macro to turn text bold, italic, and underlined. Activate a cell, start recording, and apply these three styles. Stop recording, and then select a different cell and run the macro. You will see that, even though you didn't select relative references, Excel will apply the style changes to the active cell, not the absolute reference of the cell that was active when you recorded the macro. Excel does not use cell references except when needed. It records all actions in the active cell until you change cells, and then it records the reference of the cell you move to. Record the same macro, and, after applying the bold, italic, and underline styles, click in a different cell, and then stop recording. When you run this macro, Excel will apply the styles to the active cell, wherever it is on the worksheet, and then move to the absolute cell you clicked in at the end of the macro.

Note that using relative references can lead to errors. If, in the preceding example, you paste something into a cell to the left of the active cell, and the active cell is in column A, then Excel will not be able to find a cell on the worksheet that is the correct distance from the initial cell; it calculates the *offset* from the active cell and finds that it is out of range and returns an error. Macro writing is full of trial and error.

InsideOut

Work within Excel keyboard shortcut limitations

If you're more used to customizing keyboard shortcuts in Word than in Excel (most people are), there are a few things you should look out for. First, Excel lets you assign keyboard shortcuts using the combination of the Option and Command keys together with another key. But not all keys are available. Some are reserved by Mac OS X, and others by Excel. If you choose a conflicting keyboard shortcut, Excel displays a dialog telling you to assign a different key. Second, Excel doesn't let you customize keyboard shortcuts for macros in the Customize dialog, as does Word (and as you do for non-macro shortcuts in Excel). You must use the Options button in Excel's Macros dialog, or assign the keyboard shortcut when you record the macro.

Assigning Macros to Toolbar Buttons

Another way to run macros quickly is to assign them to toolbar buttons. You can either add buttons to existing toolbars or create a custom toolbar just for your macros.

For more information on adding buttons to toolbars, see "Adding Buttons to Toolbars," page 790. For more information on creating your own toolbars, see "Creating Custom Toolbars," page 792.

Adding a button to a toolbar is covered in detail in "Adding a Button to a Toolbar," page 48. To add a button to a toolbar for a macro, follow these steps:

1 Choose Tools, Customize, and select the Commands tab.

2 Select the Macros category, and drag the Custom Button command (it shows up with a default icon, a smiley face) to your toolbar.

3 Close the Customize dialog by clicking OK.

4 Move the pointer over the button on the toolbar, and Control+click the button to open the contextual menu.

5 Choose Assign Macro from the contextual menu, and select the macro you want to use.

It is much easier to know which macro your button activates if you display it's name in the button. The little smiley face is nice, but it doesn't tell you much about what is behind it. To add a name to a custom button, follow these steps:

1 Control+click one of your custom buttons, and then choose Properties from the contextual menu. The Command Properties dialog appears, as shown next:

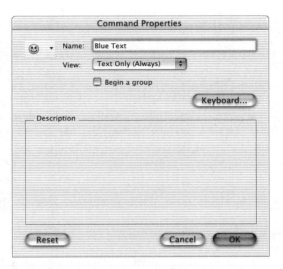

2 Enter a name in the Name field and select Text Only (Always) from the View pop-up menu to display the name you enter instead of the smiley face icon. If you want to show both the name and an icon, select Image And Text.

3 If you chose to display an icon with your text name, you can change the icon that will be displayed by clicking the pop-up menu next to the icon and selecting one of more than 40 icons.

Figure 33-11 shows the result of adding two buttons, one with a text name and one with an icon.

Figure 33-11. This toolbar has two custom buttons: the first shows the name of the macro, the second the default smiley face button.

Excel Macro Virus Protection

Excel, like Word, is an Office program that is vulnerable to VBA Macro viruses (for a detailed discussion of macro viruses, see "Avoiding Macro Viruses," page 391). Like Word, Excel has built-in protection against macro viruses. Choose Excel, Preferences, and then click the General category. Select the Macro Virus Protection check box. When this protection is enabled, Excel will display an alert each time you open a file containing a macro. You can choose to enable or disable macros on a file-by-file basis.

Note that when you disable macros in this manner, you can only disable macros written in Visual Basic for Applications. Excel can run another type of macro, written in Excel version 4 macro language (XLM macros). If a workbook has this type of macro, only the Auto_Open macro will be disabled; other XLM macros will not.

Chapter 33

Writing Macros with Visual Basic

If you want to go further with Excel macros, you can write them using Visual Basic for Applications and the Visual Basic Editor. VBA is a programming language that enables you to interact with Excel and other Office programs, and gives you a great deal of power and flexibility in working with data. VBA can do far more than Excel formulas or functions; it can control program operations as well as work with data, giving you a wide range of possibilities. But VBA can be very complex, and, like all programming languages, has a pretty steep learning curve.

> VBA is a programming language that is beyond the scope of this book. If you want to learn how to write programs and macros with Visual Basic, see the many books published about it, including the books published by Microsoft Press, listed at *http://mspress.microsoft.com.*

The following example will show you how to create a macro using the Visual Basic Editor, which is the interface you use when writing Visual Basic macros. The Visual Basic Editor is a separate program that opens when you choose it from an Excel, Word, or Microsoft PowerPoint X menu. It contains its own interface, which is similar to that of other Office programs, as well as online help to guide you in working with macros. The macro in this example will add a useful function that does not exist in Excel: it sorts worksheets in a workbook alphanumerically. When you have a lot of worksheets in a workbook, and want to sort them, you need to move the sheets around manually, but this macro will do it for you in a jiffy.

1 Open a new workbook. Choose Tools, Macro, and then select Visual Basic Editor. The Visual Basic Editor opens and displays a blank project.

2 In the Projects window, double-click the line marked Sheet1(Sheet1) to display its Code window, as shown in Figure 33-12.

> **note** When you write a Visual Basic macro, it is stored in a subroutine, which is part of a module. *Subroutines* are closed sets of programming instructions and are delimited by the statements Sub and End Sub. A *module* is a group of related subroutines. The Code window is where you enter programming code, and it displays text in two ways: green text for lines containing comments, and black and blue text for commands and statements. (Words in blue are special programming keywords used in Visual Basic. When you type these words, the Visual Basic Editor changes them to blue automatically.) To enter a comment, begin a line with an apostrophe (') and the Visual Basic Editor will display the text in green. Comments are useful to explain what macros are doing, or to document them.

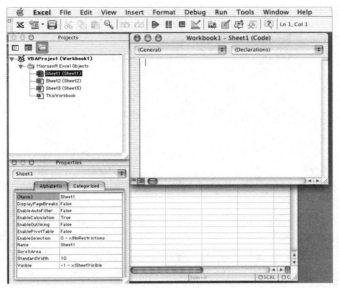

Figure 33-12. When you open the Visual Basic Editor, a blank project is displayed.

3 To begin writing a macro, you must type *Sub*, followed by a space and a name that you want to attribute to the subroutine. In this example, the subroutine is called SortSheets. Type **Sub SortSheets** and press Return; the Visual Basic Editor adds parentheses after the name, adds *End Sub* two lines below, and moves the insertion point to the blank line between these two lines, as shown in Figure 33-13.

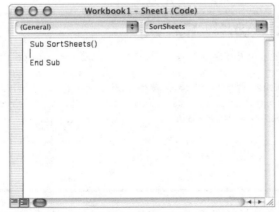

Figure 33-13. The Code window of a new macro is ready for subroutine statements to be added between the Sub and End Sub statements.

4   The code required for this macro is as follows. Type it in the Code window between the Sub and End Sub lines.

```
Dim i As Integer, j As Integer
For i = 1 To Sheets.Count
For j = 1 To Sheets.Count - 1
If UCase$(Sheets(j).Name) > UCase$(Sheets(j + 1).Name) Then
Sheets(j).Move After:=Sheets(j + 1)
End If
Next j
Next I
```

5   Press Command+S to save your macro. It will be saved in the active worksheet.

6   To test your macro, click the worksheet, and drag one of the sheet tabs out of order. Click back in the Code window, and choose Run, Run Sub/UserForm.

7   You might see a bit of activity in the worksheet window as it is redrawn. Click in this window to examine the results: the sheet tabs are now in alpha-numeric order.

8   Click back in the Code window, and choose Excel, Close And Return To Microsoft Excel to close the Visual Basic Editor.

Because you wrote this macro in a blank worksheet, you might want to copy it to another worksheet, either your Personal Macro Workbook, or another workbook.

For more information on copying macros, see "Copying Macros," opposite.

Using REALbasic with Excel

One of the new features in Office v. X is support for REALbasic. This powerful, easy-to-use programming environment enables users to create stand-alone applications and customize other applications, such as Excel. Microsoft worked closely with REAL Software Inc. to ensure integration of REALbasic into Office v. X. For more information about using REALBasic, see "Using REALbasic for Automation," page 399.

A trial version of REALbasic is included with the Value Pack on the Microsoft Office v. X CD. For more information on using REALbasic with Excel, see the online help topic "About REALbasic."

Editing Macros

Whether you write your own macros or record your actions, you might want to edit your macros at some point. When recording macros, you might discover that you have added unnecessary steps, or you might decide that, in a 37-step macro, you only need 35 of the steps. You can make changes to your Excel macro code easily with the Visual Basic Editor. Rather than re-record the macro, which can be time-consuming, it is easier to edit the macro and remove the steps you don't want.

To edit a macro, choose Tools, Macro, Macros. The Macro dialog opens, as shown in Figure 33-10, on page 798. Find the macro you want to edit—the Macros In pop-up menu lets you choose from All Open Workbooks, This Workbook, or Personal Macro Workbook, and also lists each workbook that is open. Click the macro name in the list, and click Edit. This opens the macro in the Visual Basic Editor.

Using the Personal Macro Workbook

The Personal Macro Workbook is a special workbook that holds macros. It you have previously created it, this workbook opens automatically when you launch Excel, but it is hidden. You can run macros from the Personal Macro Workbook either by using keyboard shortcuts or from the Macro menu.

You can copy and edit macros contained in the Personal Macro Workbook, but, to do this, you must unhide it by choosing Window, Unhide, selecting Personal Macro Workbook, and clicking OK. Make sure you hide this workbook when you are finished. Otherwise, it will open visibly every time you launch Excel.

Copying Macros

Because Excel stores macros in workbooks, you can only use them if they are in an open workbook. This can be the active workbook, any other open workbook, or your Personal Macro Workbook. But you might want to copy a macro into a worksheet to distribute it to other users. This is especially the case if you save your macros in your Personal Macro Workbook. When you edit a macro with the Visual Basic Editor, you can copy it into another file to distribute it to other users. This is a slightly involved process, however.

1   To copy a macro from one workbook to another, you will need to use two workbooks, which we will call Workbook 1 and Workbook 2. The first, Workbook 1, contains the macro you want to copy into the second.

2   With Workbook 2 active, record a macro that does anything—say, click in a cell and press Command+B to make bold text—as explained earlier in "Recording Macros," page 794. Make sure you save this macro in Workbook 2. This is a dummy macro that you will need in this worksheet to copy into. It doesn't matter what you record, as long as you create a macro. Give it any name you want.

Chapter 33

3 Without closing Workbook 2, open Workbook 1, choose Tools, Macro, and then select Macros. The Macro dialog opens, as shown in Figure 33-10, on page 798.

4 Find the macro you want to copy. You might have to select Workbook 1 in the pop-up menu to see it. Click the macro name in the list, and click Edit. The Visual Basic Editor opens.

5 The Code window (shown in Figure 33-13, on page 803) contains the code for your macro. Select all the text in this window, and copy it.

6 Locate the Visual Basic Editor's Projects window. This will show all available VBA Projects—the different workbooks open—with their macros, which are listed as modules. The macro you have just copied will be shown as a module in Workbook 1, and the dummy macro you recorded in Workbook 2 will show as Module1 under VBAProject (Workbook2.xls), as shown in Figure 33-14.

7 Double-click Module1 under VBAProject (Workbook2.xls). Its code window appears.

8 Select all the text in the Code window, and press Command+V to paste the macro you copied in step 5.

9 Press Command+Q to quit the Visual Basic Editor and return to Excel.

10 Check to make sure that your macro was copied correctly. Choose Tools, Macro, Macros. Select Workbook 2, and you will see your macro is now in this workbook. You will notice that its name is whatever was after the word *Sub* in the first line of the macro code. The only way to change the name is to edit the macro and change the name contained after the word *Sub*.

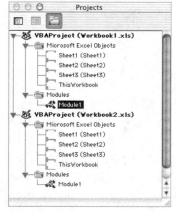

Figure 33-14. The Projects window of the Visual Basic Editor shows all the macros (modules) in your open files.

Chapter 33

InsideOut

Don't look for the Organizer to manage your macros in Excel

If you are used to working with Word, and you use macros, you know about using the Organizer's Macro Project Items tab. This simple dialog enables you to move and copy macros between files. This way you can add macros to files you are sending to others, or remove macros in your files. Excel does not have this feature, probably because it uses a Personal Macro Workbook. Although this is very practical for users, because it incites them to organize all their macros in one place, it is a hassle if you want to attach a macro to a file and send the file to someone. The way to do this is to copy the macro while in the Visual Basic Editor, as explained earlier, and paste it into another file, creating a new macro. For most users, this is a headache, because not that many people get their hands dirty and use the Visual Basic Editor. It would be a very good idea if the Macro Organizer were available in Excel as well.

Copying Macros without Using the Visual Basic Editor

The way to copy macros in Excel, as described earlier, is not only complex, but it requires that you be comfortable with a programming environment, the Visual Basic Editor. Although this is the only "official" way to copy macros from one Excel file to another, there is another way you can do this.

1 In the Mac OS X Finder, locate and select the file that contains the macro you want to use. Generally, this macro is either in your Personal Macro Workbook or in a separate workbook, if you saved it there. The Personal Macro Workbook is stored in the Applications/Microsoft Office X/Office/Startup/Excel folder.

2 Still in the Finder, duplicate this file by choosing File, Duplicate. Mac OS X will make a copy of the file, called file_name copy.

3 Open the copied file. If this is your Personal Macro Workbook, this file contains no data—it is a default workbook with empty worksheets. If this is a normal workbook, it will probably contain data. If so, erase all the data, and delete any unnecessary worksheets. You want to create a blank workbook that contains no data, but contains the macro you want to use.

For more information on erasing data, see "Deleting Cells and Clearing Cell Data," page 602. For more on deleting worksheets, see "Adding and Deleting Worksheets," page 562.

4 Now that you have a blank workbook, make sure that it contains only the macro or macros you want to use. Choose Tools, Macro, and then select Macros. In the Macro dialog (shown in Figure 33-10, on page 798), delete all the macros you don't want in this workbook, and then click OK. This is especially important if you use a lot of macros and you copy the Personal Macro Workbook.

Chapter 33

You will now have a blank workbook containing only the macro or macros you want. Rename it as you wish. You can use this workbook as you would any other, adding and formatting data, and send it to other users. It will contain whichever macros they need to use with your data.

Using Add-ins

Excel's architecture allows you to use *add-ins*, or additional files containing advanced functions that are not part of Excel's basic toolkit. Some add-ins are installed by default and the Microsoft Office v. X CD contains several add-ins as part of the Value Pack; others are available as commercial programs, freeware, or shareware. Table 33-1 lists the add-ins that are included in the Value Pack.

Table 33-1. Add-ins Included with the Office v. X Value Pack

Add-In	Function
Analysis Toolpak	Provides additional advanced statistical and engineering functions.
Analysis Toolpak VBA	Makes available the Analysis Toolpak functions to Visual Basic.
HTML Add-in	Supports macros written in Excel 98 using the HTMLConvert function.
Lookup Wizard	Helps you create formulas to find data in lists.
Report Manager	Enables you to print reports with a series of views and scenarios.
Set Language	Enables you to change the proofing language in Excel worksheets. You only need this if you are working in a language different from that of Office v. X, or if you are using multiple languages in your worksheets.
Solver	Helps you use a variety of numeric methods for equation solving and optimization.

To install any or all of these add-ins, run the Value Pack Installer on the Microsoft Office v. X CD and select Excel Add-Ins on the installation screen, to install them all, or click the disclosure triangle to display all the add-ins and select only the ones you want to use.

Loading and Unloading Add-ins

After you install Excel add-ins you need to load them into Excel to be able to use them. To do this, choose Tools, Add-Ins. The Add-Ins dialog opens, as shown in Figure 33-15, showing a list of all the add-ins found on your computer in the Applications/Microsoft Office X/Office/Add-Ins folder. To load any or all of these add-ins, select the check boxes next to their names, and click OK. If you want to load an add-in that is not in the default folder, click Select, and browse until you find the add-in, and then click Open to add it to the Add-Ins Available list.

Because add-ins use memory, you can unload them and free memory by clearing their check boxes in the Add-Ins dialog and clicking OK.

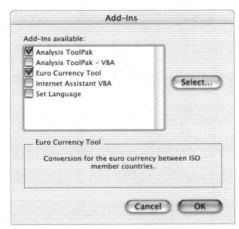

Figure 33-15. Choose which add-ins you want Excel to load by selecting them in this dialog.

When Excel add-ins are loaded, they either add menu commands or functions to the program. Many add-ins, such as the Solver, Analysis Toolpak, and Lookup Wizard, add menu commands to the Tools menu and might not be listed in the Add-Ins dialog. To use them, see the appropriate help topics or instructions provided with the add-in.

Troubleshooting

Excel can't find an add-in.

When you install add-ins, Excel keeps track of where they are located. By default, any add-ins you install using the Value Pack Installer are placed in the Applications/ Microsoft Office X/Office/Add-Ins folder, but you can load add-ins from any location. If an add-in is moved, deleted, or renamed, Excel will not be able to find it and will display an alert when you start up the program. Check the locations of your add-ins. If one of the Value Pack add-ins cannot be found, reinstall it using the Value Pack Installer. If another add-in cannot be found, search for it and reinstall it. It's a good idea to avoid needing to search for an add-in by storing all the add-ins you're using in the Microsoft Office X/Office/Add-Ins folder.

Part 5

PowerPoint

Chapter 34

PowerPoint Essentials

Microsoft PowerPoint X is *presentation software*, which helps you explain your ideas and present information to large or small groups of people. Presentations can be displayed as slide shows, distributed over the Internet, or printed as handouts, and they can include text, graphics, photos, animations, video, charts, and special effects. As a Microsoft Office v. X component, PowerPoint can incorporate information from other Office programs, such as Microsoft Excel X worksheets or Microsoft Word X documents. You can also embed slides from PowerPoint presentations within Excel or Word.

Each presentation consists of a series of slides, containing information that's formatted as an outline. You can use outlines from Word, or you can enter all the text directly into PowerPoint, using either PowerPoint's built-in outliner or by typing right on the slides. The steps in creating a presentation are as follows:

1 Create a new presentation document.

2 Add slides as required to hold all the information you want to present.

3 Choose a design template for the presentation, if desired, or apply your own design formatting.

4 Choose a layout for each slide that incorporates the elements you want to include.

5 Add text by typing or pasting.

6 Add graphics and other elements, including charts, animations, hyperlinks, or video and audio clips.

When all the slides are in place and all text and other elements have been placed in slides, you can add advanced formatting, such as transitions between slides, and then prepare the presentation for delivery. (These topics are covered in Chapters 35 through 39.) If you haven't used PowerPoint before, this chapter is a good place to start. Here you'll find an introductory tour of the program's workflow and features. You'll learn

- How the PowerPoint workspace is laid out
- Where to find the tools and commands you'll use most often
- How to create a presentation
- How to edit and check the spelling of a presentation's text
- How to distribute your presentations via e-mail
- How to flag a presentation so you can return to finish it later on

The PowerPoint Workspace

PowerPoint's interface is similar to that of other Office v. X programs, as shown in Figure 34-1. When you begin working on a presentation, you'll see typical elements on your screen: a menu bar, toolbars, the Formatting Palette, and of course a document window. As you grow used to PowerPoint, you'll evolve your own way of interacting with the program; some users love to create their own toolbars, whereas others find it more efficient to learn and use all the program's keyboard shortcuts.

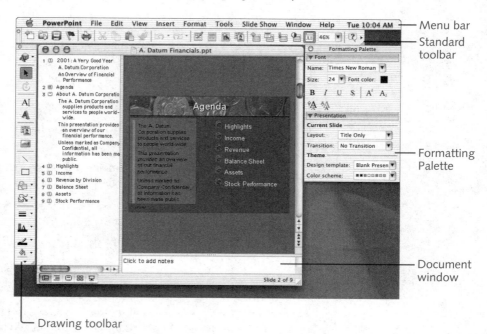

Figure 34-1. The PowerPoint interface is designed to look familiar to users of any Office program.

Chapter 34

> **tip** You can create custom toolbars and assign your own keyboard shortcuts to commands you use often. See Chapter 4, "Office v. X: Do It Your Way," for instructions.

Formatting Palette

PowerPoint's "smart" Formatting Palette changes to match what you're doing. For example, when you're editing text, the palette contains options for font, type size, line spacing, and the like. When you select a graphic, the palette changes to display options for fill and line, size, and animation. The palette's options are divided into sections that you can show or hide by clicking the section's title, as shown in Figure 34-2.

Figure 34-2. The sections within the Formatting Palette enable you to concentrate on the formatting options you want to use at any given time.

Document Window

The PowerPoint document window consists of three areas that you can show or hide using different views (for details, see the next section, "PowerPoint Views"). Figure 34-3 on the next page shows a typical working setup in the Normal three-pane view; here you can see the following elements of the window:

- On the left, the outline pane shows a constantly updated view of the presentation's structure and text, as determined by the headings and text you enter. You can create slides and watch the outline grow, or you can write an outline and have PowerPoint build slides based on it.

Part 5: PowerPoint

Outline pane   Slide pane

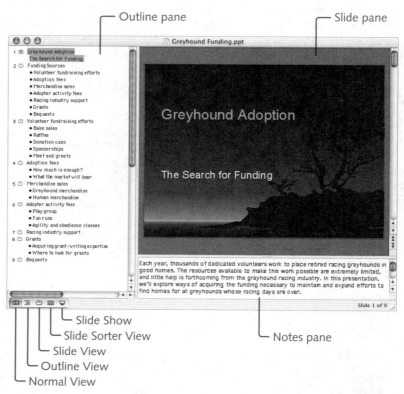

Slide Show
Slide Sorter View   Notes pane
Slide View
Outline View
Normal View

Figure 34-3. Each document window can display the presentation's slides, the outline on which the presentation is based, and notes about each slide. Buttons enable you to quickly switch views.

● On the right, the slide pane shows the current slide. You can move from slide to slide using the scroll bar on the right edge of the window or by clicking any heading in the outline pane to move to that slide.

● At the bottom of the window, the notes pane provides a place for you to enter private information about each slide: source information, thoughts about future additions, or notations for the presentation's narration. These notes can be printed as part of speaker's notes.

For more information about speaker's notes and printing, see Chapter 37, "Preparing to Present."

PowerPoint Views

As you work on a presentation, you'll probably use all six views provided for the document window. You can switch views by clicking one of the five buttons at the bottom left corner of the window (shown in Figure 34-3) or by choosing a view option from the View menu. Your choices are as follows:

- **Normal.** The default view shows the presentation's outline on the left, the current slide on the right, and notes for that slide below the slide.

- **Outline.** This view doesn't have a command in the View menu; it shows the outline in a large pane with small panes to the right showing thumbnail versions of the slides and the notes.

- **Slide.** With this view you can display the current slide while hiding the outline and notes panes.

- **Slide Sorter.** In Slide Sorter view you can rearrange slides by dragging and dropping them into a different order. Each slide is displayed as a thumbnail accompanied by the slide's number and its display time, if you've assigned times to your slides.

For more information about using the slide sorter, see "Rearranging Slides with the Slide Sorter," page 857. "Setting Slide Timing," page 894, contains details about setting slide timing.

- **Notes Page.** There's no button in the document window for this view, but you can get there by choosing View, Notes Page. You'll find it useful if you're preparing extensive narration for a presentation; the current slide is displayed at the top of the window, with a large area for your notes below it.

- **Slide Show.** With this view, you can preview your presentation; you also use this view to actually give the presentation. You can get here by clicking the Slide Show button in the document window, by choosing View, Slide Show, or by choosing Slide Show, View Show. This final option starts the slide show at the beginning instead of at the currently selected slide. Once you've started the slide show, you can use a contextual menu to control it or end it; Control+click to display a menu with navigation options.

See Table 38-1, "Slide Show Keyboard Commands," page 902, for a list of keyboard shortcuts to make it easier to view a slide show.

Anatomy of a Slide

To simplify slide layout, PowerPoint offers you standardized "slots" into which you can put text, graphics, or other elements on each slide, as shown in Figure 34-4 on the next page. These slots are arranged into preset layouts, and each slide is based on one of these layouts. The elements contained in each layout are as follows:

- **Background.** You can use the predefined background colors and graphics, or you can delete them and add your own.

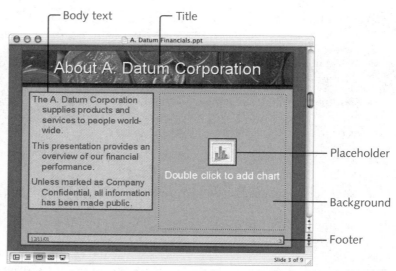

Figure 34-4. A typical PowerPoint layout can be modified to your heart's content, but it always starts out with a selection of these basic elements.

- **Title.** Each slide layout, except for Blank, includes a title that corresponds to a main heading in the presentation's outline.

- **Body text.** The slide's text boxes can include bulleted and numbered lists, image captions, or paragraph text.

- **Placeholders.** Dotted-line rectangles indicate places where you can add objects such as images, charts, and media clips to a slide.

- **Header and footer.** Each slide can contain a header, a footer, or both. Headers (at the top of each slide) and footers (at the bottom of each slide) can contain slide numbers, the date and time, or any other information about the presentation.

Once you've created a slide, you can modify its layout in two ways: by applying a new slide layout from PowerPoint's layout library, or by dragging to move or resize the elements it contains—text boxes and placeholders for graphics, charts, and more. When rearranging a slide's layout, click on a corner to resize an object, and click the side of an object to move the object.

To learn more about the various elements that a slide can contain, turn to Chapter 35, "Enhanced Presentation Formatting."

Creating Presentations

The first time you start PowerPoint, you'll see the Project Gallery, shown in Figure 34-5, where you can indicate what kind of document you want to create and choose a template on which it will be based. To create a presentation, you have three choices:

- Start with a design template to build a presentation based on one of the professionally designed templates included with Office.

- Create a blank document and design your presentation from scratch.

- Use the AutoContent Wizard to walk you quickly through the steps of designing a presentation.

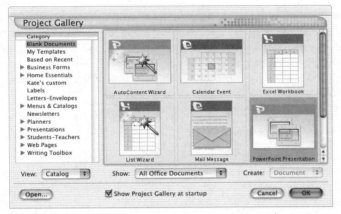

Figure 34-5. Using the Project Gallery, you can choose to create any kind of Office document, not just a new PowerPoint presentation.

Which option you choose might depend on how evolved your concept of the presentation is before you start. If you know exactly what you want, both in terms of content and design, you'll probably opt to use a design template. If you want to experiment with different colors, graphics, and content, a blank document can be your blank canvas. And if you need help determining the presentation's content, the AutoContent Wizard is a good way to get started. The following sections explain how to create a presentation using each of these methods.

> **tip** If you don't want to see the Project Gallery every time PowerPoint starts, clear the Show Project Gallery At Startup check box.

Starting with a Design Template

PowerPoint's design templates include prespecified background images, color schemes, and fonts chosen to harmonize with each other. The designs have descriptive names that might help you decide which designs are appropriate for your presentation. Follow these steps to create a presentation using a design template:

1 If the Project Gallery isn't visible, choose File, Project Gallery.

2 Click the disclosure triangle next to Presentations in the Category list on the left side of the Project Gallery.

3 Click either Content or Designs, and then double-click to choose a template on the right. Scroll to see additional choices.

Beginning with a design template is the best choice for most presentations, because many of the design choices are done for you; all you need do is concentrate on content. Content templates contain predesigned formats and color schemes like design templates, but they also contain content that can help you to get started on your presentations. For example, the template entitled "Facilitating a Meeting" contains content from Dale Carnegie Training that outlines the meeting facilitation process.

---

tip   **Keep track of your presentation's fonts**

To make sure that you'll have the correct fonts installed, the design templates are created using basic, fairly generic fonts. A quick way to make a template your own is to change its fonts to something more interesting (but still legible), as well as switching its color palette. But if you do change fonts, make sure that the computer you'll use for presenting has the same fonts; otherwise the presentation might not look right.

Once you've chosen a design, it's automatically applied to each slide you add to the presentation, with appropriate modifications for the layout of each slide, as shown in Figure 34-6. This neat trick is accomplished through the use of *masters,* which are analogous to master pages in a page layout application. Each design has masters for title slides, regular slides, handouts (thumbnails of the slides), and notes (each slide appears above that slide's associated notes).

---

note   You can change the design of individual slides by applying a different design to a slide, modifying or deleting individual elements of a slide's design, or modifying a slide's master. To learn how to customize your presentation designs, turn to Chapter 35, "Enhanced Presentation Formatting."

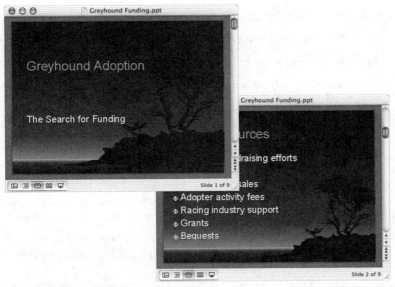

Figure 34-6. If you're using the Island design, the tree graphic is larger on a title slide (top) than on a text-only slide (bottom).

Starting with a Blank Presentation

If you prefer to start your presentation from scratch, with no predetermined design template, the possibilities are nearly limitless. You can determine the presentation's background pattern or image, its color palette, and its fonts. One reason for starting from scratch might be to create a presentation design that matches your corporate identity materials; you can use corporate colors and fonts and add your company logo. Use one of these procedures to create a new blank presentation:

- If the Project Gallery is visible, click Blank Documents in the Category list on the left, and then double-click PowerPoint Presentation in the window on the right.

- If the Project Gallery is not visible, choose File, New Presentation or press Command+N. A new presentation window will appear, and the New Slide dialog will appear. See "Adding Slides," page 824, for more information about using this dialog.

A blank presentation document has a white background, with basic fonts applied to a single title slide. You can modify these elements in whatever way you wish. Here are a few suggestions that might help you in designing your presentations:

- Don't use more than three fonts in a single presentation.

- As much as possible, stay within font families—use bold, italic, and regular versions of the same font.

- Avoid ornate fonts—simpler is better for legibility.

- When in doubt about text size, go larger rather than smaller.

- Make sure there's plenty of contrast between the text and the background.

- Cool colors such as blue and green are easier on the eyes than warm ones such as red and yellow.

- Minimize the number of colors you use; again, use lighter and darker variations of the same color as much as possible.

- Use bright colors in small doses for emphasis.

- Because some people have trouble distinguishing between them, avoid using these color combinations: red and green, brown and green, blue and black, and blue and purple.

- The more text your presentation contains, the simpler the background should be—it's hard to read text over a busy, complex background image.

> For more information about advanced formatting for your presentations, see Chapter 35, "Enhanced Presentation Formatting." To learn about adding graphics and other elements to your presentations, turn to Chapter 36, "Illustrating the Presentation."

Using the AutoContent Wizard

The AutoContent Wizard takes design templates one step further, helping you organize your content as well as providing a selection of preset designs for your presentation. Here's how you create a new presentation with the AutoContent Wizard:

1. In the Project Gallery, double-click AutoContent Wizard to begin creating your presentation.

2. On the Presentation Type page of the wizard, choose a category that describes your presentation.

3. Select a presentation type from the list below the Category menu, shown in Figure 34-7, and then click Next.

4. On the Presentation Media page, choose how you will deliver your presentation (on-screen, as overhead transparencies, or as 35 mm slides), click Yes or No to indicate whether you will need printed handouts, and then click Next.

5. On the wizard's Presentation Title And Footers page, enter a title for the presentation and the name of the person who will deliver the presentation.

6. Add any other information about the presentation that you want to include on its title slide.

Chapter 34: PowerPoint Essentials

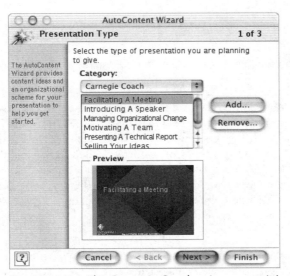

Figure 34-7. The Carnegie Coach category contains presentations on ways to manage and inspire employees.

7 If you want to use footers on your slides, enter the footer text and select Slide Number and Date Last Updated, as shown in Figure 34-8, and then click Finish.

Figure 34-8. Footer text might include an organization name or the presentation's title.

8 When the presentation opens in a new untitled window, choose File, Save to save the file with a new name.

9 Change the presentation's generic content to the information you want to include.

Step 9 is where the AutoContent Wizard really shines. Presentations created this way are already filled with text, rather than being blank, as shown in Figure 34-9. The text guides you in adding your own content with headings such as "How Did This Happen?" in a presentation based on the "Communicating Bad News" template, followed by bullet points including "Any relevant history, facts, or strategies" and "Original assumptions that are no longer valid." Be sure to check the notes pane for each slide as well; you'll sometimes find helpful suggestions for making sure you include all the necessary information in your presentation.

You might be able to use much of the automatically inserted text as-is, and you can add any text and new slides you need. Although AutoContent Wizard presentations don't include images, charts, or other elements besides text, you can add these, too. And of course you can customize the presentation's appearance in any way you like; turn to Chapter 35, "Enhanced Presentation Formatting," for more information.

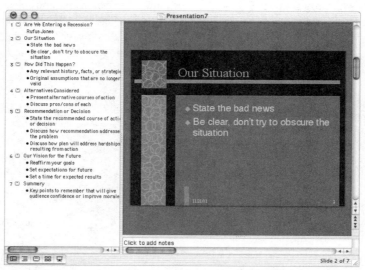

Figure 34-9. Each AutoContent Wizard presentation is structured to accommodate the kind of information that will normally be included in a presentation of that type.

Adding Slides

No matter how you opt to create your presentation, you'll probably need to add slides to it at some point. For example, even if the AutoContent Wizard creates just the right number of slides for you, it's a common practice to repeat your title slide at the end of a presentation and follow that with a blank slide to make sure you don't "click out" of your presentation and leave viewers staring at your computer's desktop.

> **tip** Another good slide to end your presentation is one with your contact information, so that your audience can follow up with comments about your talk. The feedback will help you do an even better presentation next time.

Adding slides is a simple task: Simply click the slide you want to precede to the new slide, and choose Insert, New Slide, or press Control+M. The New Slide dialog, shown in Figure 34-10, displays different layouts (including Blank) that you can apply to the new slide. Choose the one that matches your desired layout most closely, and click OK. After the slide is created, you can enter text, rearrange elements, and apply any local formatting overrides that you want (such as that blank background for the presentation's final slide).

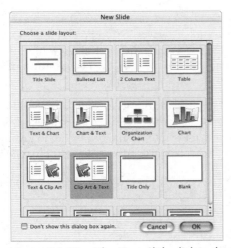

Figure 34-10.   The New Slide dialog shows 24 predesigned layouts.

InsideOut

Learn PowerPoint X's new shortcut keys for Mac OS X

Like all of the other Office v. X applications, some of PowerPoint X's keyboard short-cuts have been rearranged as part of the suite's conversion to Mac OS X. In order to comply with Mac OS X's new Aqua interface guidelines, long-standing shortcuts have changed where they conflict with standard Aqua shortcuts. For instance, PowerPoint's New Slide shortcut is now Control+M, because Command+M, the shortcut in previous versions, is reserved by Aqua for minimizing the current window to the OS X Dock.

Adding Text to Presentations

Once you have created a presentation and chosen a design, you can enter the text of your presentation. You can type text directly into the text boxes on each slide, or you can focus on the presentation's structure by adding text in the outline pane.

Writing Presentations in the Outline Pane

Behind every good presentation is an outline, and Outline view is PowerPoint's secret weapon for making better presentations. Even if you never work directly in the outline pane, the outline is always there, keeping your presentation text structured and logical. The beauty of working in Outline view is that it enables you to edit the content of your presentation without focusing on the presentation's appearance, as you inevitably do when you add text in Slide view. Although you still see a miniature color preview pane of the slide you're working on, the focus is on the text. And after all, isn't the content of your presentation its most important aspect?

If you're used to working in Word's Outline view, you'll find PowerPoint's Outline view a familiar friend. Switch to Outline view by clicking the Outline View button at the bottom of the document window. The outline pane grows to take up most of the window, while the slide and notes panes shrink and slide to the right.

Regardless of the view you're using, changing text in the outline pane also changes it in the slide pane, and vice versa. PowerPoint's Outline view uses the same keyboard shortcuts that work in Word, such as Tab to demote a topic and Shift+Tab to promote it. If you prefer to use the mouse instead of the keyboard, choose View, Toolbars, Outlining to display the Outlining toolbar, shown here:

The toolbar contains the following buttons:

- **Promote and Demote.** Click Promote to change a heading to a higher outline level or Demote to move it to a lower outline level.

- **Move Up and Move Down.** Move Up literally moves a heading, its subheads, and their associated text up to precede the previous heading section in the outline, whereas Move Down moves the section down to follow the next section.

- **Collapse and Expand.** Collapsing a section hides (but doesn't delete) all but its main head; click Expand to show its subsections again.

- **Collapse All and Expand All.** These buttons collapse or expand all the sections in the entire outline.

- **Show Formatting.** Ordinarily, text formatting such as different fonts or colors isn't visible in the outline pane; click this button to see text formatting for outline sections. Click again to hide the text formatting.

Entering Text Directly on Slides

The alternative to working in the outline pane is to enter text on each slide. This is a good option when the presentation's structure is simple and easy to keep track of, as well as if you want to keep close tabs on the length of each heading or text section. For most presentations, you'll switch back and forth between the outline pane and the slide pane to enter text.

To enter text on a slide, follow these steps:

1 First switch to Normal or Slide view, then make sure that the slide has the layout you want to use; move and resize any elements that aren't to your liking.

2 Click in a text box and begin typing. The placeholder text disappears, replaced by the text you enter.

3 For bullet points, press Return to start a new point. The bullet is added at the beginning of each line automatically.

4 Click anywhere outside the text box to deselect the text box and see the results.

PowerPoint automatically resizes text as you type to fit on the slide. This feature, AutoFit Text, watches as you type, and automatically changes the line spacing, then the font size, and then both (if necessary) so that the text fits into the text box. PowerPoint also assumes that your text will consist of titles and bulleted text. You can override both of these settings; turn to Chapter 35, "Enhanced Presentation Formatting" for more information.

Text Editing

Text editing in PowerPoint works similarly to text editing in Word, particularly Word's Outline view. To change text, you can drag to select it, or you can position the insertion point before or after it and use the Del or Delete key, respectively. You can cut or copy selected text and paste text that you have cut or copied onto the Clipboard.

A key part of editing text is positioning your insertion point where you need it. PowerPoint provides both mouse- and keyboard-based navigation. To use the mouse, simply click to place your insertion point. If you're a good typist, however, it's usually faster to move around using keyboard shortcuts, as follows:

● Press Home or End to move to the beginning or end of a line, respectively.

● Press Shift+Home or Shift+End to select a line above or below the current one, respectively.

● Press Shift+Command and the Left, Right, Up, or Down Arrow key to select one word to the left or right of the insertion point or one line above or below the insertion point, respectively.

To move text around within a presentation, you have two choices: cut and paste it, or drag and drop it. Dragging and dropping is especially effective in the outline pane, where placing the pointer to the left of an entry turns it into a four-headed arrow. Click this special pointer to select the entire entry, and then drag it to a new location. To delete text, select it and press Delete; to delete an entire slide, click anywhere within its image in the slide pane, or click its icon in the outline pane, and choose Edit, Delete Slide.

Checking Spelling

Checking the spelling in your presentations is an important quality control step. PowerPoint offers two ways to check spelling: all at once, or constantly as you type.

> **note** You can only check the spelling of PowerPoint text. Text in graphics, charts, or WordArt images will be ignored by PowerPoint's spelling checker.

To check spelling all at once, choose Tools, Spelling. If PowerPoint doesn't find any spelling errors, you're done—the next thing you'll see is a dialog that says "The spelling check is complete." Congratulations! If PowerPoint finds a word that it doesn't recognize, you'll see the Spelling And Grammar dialog, shown in Figure 34-11, which prompts you to correct the word (you can select from the suggested alternatives) or confirm that the word is spelled the way you want it. There are two possibilities:

- If the word is correct, click Ignore (to skip it this time) or Ignore All (to also skip future occurrences in the document).

- If the word is incorrect, choose the correct word from the list or type a correction and click Change (to change this occurrence) or Change All (to change this word throughout the presentation.

When you get to a word that you use often but that PowerPoint doesn't recognize, click Add to add the word to your custom dictionary. From now on, PowerPoint will recognize the word as being spelled correctly.

> **tip** **Add words directly to your custom dictionary**
>
> You can open your custom dictionary and type or paste words directly into it in Microsoft Word. For example, you can add lists of employees or your company's products to your dictionary. The custom dictionary can be found in the Users/*username*/ Library/Preferences/Microsoft folder. You'll need to choose All Documents from the Show pop-up menu in the Open dialog before you can click the Custom Dictionary file to open it. And when you save the file, you'll see a dialog asking whether you want to continue saving the file in the Speller Custom Dictionary format; just click Yes.

Chapter 34: PowerPoint Essentials

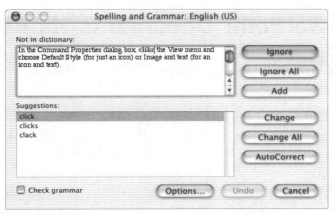

Figure 34-11. The AutoCorrect button in the Spelling And Grammar dialog instantly replaces all questionable words with PowerPoint's best guess as to what the words should be—use it with care and don't be afraid to undo if the results are not what you want.

If you prefer to correct spelling errors as you go, choose PowerPoint, Preferences and click the Spelling tab. Select the Check Spelling As You Type check box. Then select the other options you want to use.

---

tip **Check spelling in multiple languages**

If your presentation contains text from other languages, you can check the spelling of that text using the appropriate dictionary. First, make sure you've installed the Value Pack from your Microsoft Office v. X CD to add the relevant language dictionaries. Then, select the text and choose Tools, Language. Specify the language of the selected text, and click OK. The next time you check spelling, PowerPoint will use the appropriate language dictionary to check text from each language included in your presentation.

When you close the Preferences dialog and return to your presentation, you might see words with squiggly red underlines—these are the words that PowerPoint doesn't recognize. To correct them (or confirm them as already correct), select an underlined word and choose Tools, Spelling. PowerPoint steps you through the document the same way it does during a manual spelling check, giving you the option of correcting the words it doesn't recognize, ignoring them, or adding them to your custom dictionary.

---

tip An even faster way to correct misspelled text is to Control+click on the squiggly red underlined word, which opens a contextual menu that includes other possible spellings.

Chapter 34

Sending PowerPoint Documents via E-Mail

Assuming you're using one of the e-mail clients that Office can interact with, PowerPoint makes it easy to share presentations with colleagues via e-mail. Follow these steps:

1 Open the presentation you want to send.

2 If necessary, resave the file with a .ppt file name extension to make sure it can be opened by users on all platforms, as shown in Figure 34-12.

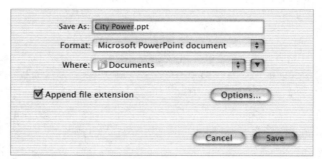

Figure 34-12. Select Append File Extension to add the correct file name extension to your presentation file.

3 Choose File, Send To, Mail Recipient.

4 Address and send the e-mail message as you ordinarily would; PowerPoint automatically attaches the presentation file to the message.

If the Mail Recipient command isn't available, it's because Office isn't able to work with your e-mail software. The programs Office can interact with include the native Mac OS X versions of Microsoft Entourage and Eudora, and Apple's Mail. If you use a different program, or if your e-mail program runs under the Classic Mac OS, PowerPoint can't automatically e-mail presentation files, but you can still manually attach them to e-mail messages.

Flagging Presentations for Follow-Up

If you want to set aside a presentation and come back to work on it later, you can flag it for follow-up. When you flag a presentation, you create an Office Notifications reminder, shown in Figure 34-13, that appears at the scheduled time to remind you to get back to work. Office Notifications uses Entourage's events database for its scheduling, but you can use the Flag For Follow Up feature even if you don't use Entourage to manage your own calendar and to-do lists.

Figure 34-13. In the Office Notifications dialog, you can click the name of the presentation file to reopen it and resume your work.

To learn more about creating reminders with Entourage, see "Creating and Editing Calendar Events," page 514.

To flag a presentation for follow-up, follow these steps:

1 Choose Tools, Flag For Follow Up, or click the Flag For Follow Up button on the Standard toolbar.

2 Choose a date and time for Office Notifications to remind you to return to the presentation.

3 Click OK.

When the presentation is done, you can remove the flag by choosing Tools, Flag For Follow Up again and clearing the check box. If you rename a flagged presentation, you'll still get a reminder. If you delete it or move it to another hard drive, however, Office Notifications won't be able to find it and you won't see a reminder.

Chapter 34

Chapter 35

Enhanced Presentation Formatting

Communicating with your audience means making your presentation both clear and compelling. Once you've created a presentation's content, you can increase its impact with advanced formatting techniques that enable you to increase readability, ensure consistency, improve navigation, and add pizzazz. It's important to consider the effect of each formatting decision on the presentation as a whole; always keep in mind the overall impression you want to create in the minds of the audience.

Consistency is one of the keys to good information design, and Microsoft PowerPoint X's slide and page masters and Replace Fonts command enable you to keep your slide designs consistent throughout an entire presentation. Other special formatting, such as backgrounds and animation effects, can be applied to one, some, or all of the slides in a presentation with just a few clicks, making it easy to add variety within the presentation.

In this chapter, you'll learn about

- Formatting headers and footers
- Using the Formatting Palette
- Applying text formatting to words and paragraphs
- Adding hyperlinks, text boxes, and other slide elements
- Inserting comments

833

- Modifying slide and page masters
- Applying different slide layouts and templates
- Using animation in your presentations
- Rearranging and previewing your slides

Working with Headers and Footers

Like running headers and footers in books, PowerPoint headers and footers enable you to display the same information at the top or bottom of each page or slide. Slides can have only footers, whereas notes and handout pages can have headers and footers. Each header or footer can contain standardized information such as the page number or a date, as well as information such as the name of your company, your name, or the event name.

As you work in the Header And Footer dialog, the Preview area shows the default location of the placeholder for each element. You can resize the elements and move them around on the slide master, and you can also change the text formatting of each element (see "Using Master Items," page 846 for more information). To change the contents of headers or footers, follow these steps:

1 Choose View, Header And Footer, and click the Slide tab or the Notes And Handouts tab.

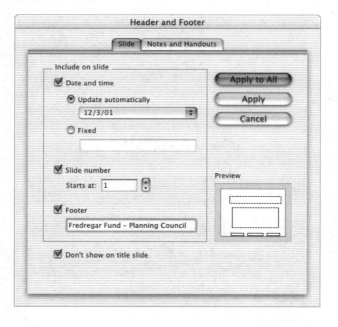

2 Select the Date And Time check box to display the date and time on the slide. Choose Update Automatically and select a format, or choose Fixed and enter the date.

3 Select the Header check box (only on the Notes And Handouts tab) to add custom text, and enter the text.

4 Select the Slide Number (on the Slide tab) or the Page Number (on the Notes And Handouts tab) check box to number each slide or page. If you want to start numbering at something other than 1, enter a number in the Starts At box.

5 Select the Footer check box to add custom text, and type your footer text.

---

tip **Use footers for boilerplate text**

The Footer field can contain about 250 characters, many more than are required for the usual name or title information. This enables you to use a footer to hold legal disclaimers, copyright notices, or other longer selections of boilerplate text.

---

6 On the Slide tab, select the Don't Show On Title Slide check box to leave the footer off the first slide in the presentation.

7 Click Apply To All to add the header or footer to every page or slide; on the Slide tab you can click Apply to add the footer to the current slide only.

Using the Formatting Palette

The Formatting Palette, shown in Figure 35-1 on the next page, pulls together formatting options from throughout PowerPoint into a comprehensive, neatly organized palette that changes to show only the options that apply to the selected object. For example, when text is selected, the Formatting Palette contains six sections: Font, Bullets And Numbering, Alignment And Spacing, Animation, Hyperlink, and Presentation. When a drawing object is selected, sections labeled Size and Fill And Line are added. If you insert a picture, a Picture section appears on the Formatting Palette. Clicking any of these section titles opens that section of the palette to display the options in that category.

To display the Formatting Palette, choose View, Formatting Palette, or click the Formatting Palette button on the Standard toolbar. Click the palette's close button to hide it. The Formatting Palette is most useful, however, if it's always on your screen—so if you're trying to save screen space, your best bet is simply to click the palette's section titles to close less-used sections and minimize the palette's size.

Figure 35-1. All the Formatting Palette's sections can be hidden to save space.

---

tip   **Dock the Formatting Palette to keep it in place**

Another good way to keep the Formatting Palette out of your way is to dock it to the side of the screen. Like PowerPoint's toolbars, the Formatting Palette sticks to the side of your screen if you drag it near the edge, even when it changes sizes as different sections are displayed.

Formatting Text

One of the quickest ways to make a presentation design truly your own is to use PowerPoint's formatting features to change the font, size, style, and color of the text on your slides. You can use the Formatting Palette's Font and Alignment And Spacing sections, the Font dialog accessible via the Format menu, or the buttons on the Formatting toolbar—all three methods allow you to make many of the same changes (though for extensive font formatting, the Font dialog provides the most comprehensive set of options). The Font dialog and the Formatting toolbar are shown in Figure 35-2.

Here's the procedure you'll follow to format a section of text:

1 Click anywhere in the text box.

2 To change the entire contents of the box, click again at its edge to select the whole box. To change only some of the box's contents, select only the text you want to format.

Chapter 35: Enhanced Presentation Formatting

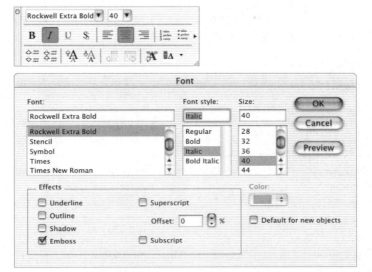

Figure 35-2. The options on the Formatting toolbar (top) include many of the same features as those in the font section of the Font dialog (bottom).

3 Choose the new formatting options:

- **Font.** Choose a font from the menu.

- **Size.** Enter a point size between 1 and 3,413, or choose a preset size.

- **Style.** Choose to make text regular, bold, italic, bold italic, underlined, shadowed, outlined, embossed, superscript, subscript, or a combination of these.

- **Color.** Choose a font color from the presentation's existing color palette or choose the More Colors option to pick your own color.

> See "Applying Color Schemes and Backgrounds," page 851, to learn more about working with PowerPoint's color schemes.

Changing Text Alignment, Indentation, and Spacing

The font, size, and style of text are all character-level attributes, but all text also has paragraph-level attributes: settings that are the same throughout each paragraph. These include the text alignment, its indentation with respect to margins, and its line and paragraph spacing.

PowerPoint's titles are usually center aligned, and body text is flush left, but you can change these settings to suit your design. To align text, click the appropriate button in the Alignment And Spacing section of the Formatting Palette or on the Formatting toolbar, or use keyboard shortcuts, as follows:

- **Left:** Command+L
- **Right:** Command+R
- **Center:** Command+E
- **Justified:** Command+J

> **tip** Use the Formatting Palette if you want to set the vertical alignment within a text box; the Alignment And Spacing section contains buttons for top, center, and bottom alignment.

PowerPoint includes a ruler designed to show you the measurements of a page and allow you to adjust the position of text with respect to its left margin. Follow these steps:

1 To see the ruler, choose View, Ruler.

2 Click in the text you want to adjust. Triangular indent markers appear at the left edge of the ruler.

3 Drag the upper indent marker left or right to adjust the indent of the first line of the selected paragraph.

4 Drag the lower indent marker to indent the remaining lines of the paragraph. This also sets the tab location for the paragraph's first line, ensuring that all text in a bulleted list will align correctly.

5 To move both indent markers at the same time, drag the square marker at the base of the lower indent marker.

For maximum legibility, it's important to use the right amount of line spacing for blocks of text. You can adjust the line spacing of text paragraphs quickly in the Formatting Palette by clicking its Increase Paragraph Spacing and Decrease Paragraph Spacing buttons in the Alignment And Spacing section. For finer control, along with the ability to add extra space between paragraphs, choose Format, Line Spacing and enter numerical spacing values. You can specify spacing in terms of points, the same units used for font size—there are 72 points to the inch—or in terms of lines, relative to the selected paragraph's font size. A line spacing value of 1 line for a block of 14-point text is equivalent to 14 points plus a few more points to keep one line from touching another.

> **tip** **Avoid redundant design in paragraphs**
>
> Indenting the first line of a paragraph and adding space above it serve the same purpose—distinguishing it from the preceding paragraph—so most designers agree that doing both adds unnecessary clutter to a design.

Replacing Fonts

If you want to change a particular font throughout your presentation, you can do so quickly:

1 Choose Format, Replace Fonts to open the Replace Font dialog.

2 Choose a font from the Replace pop-up menu.

> **note** All the fonts currently used in the presentation are listed in the Replace menu.

3 Choose a new font from the With pop-up menu.

4 Click Replace to change the font throughout the document, and then click Close.

Using the Replace Font dialog is a good way to make sure that your presentation's design stays consistent throughout, and it's much faster than changing the font used in individual text boxes.

Using Bulleted and Numbered Text

To conform to the outline that underlies every presentation, PowerPoint assumes that text other than titles will be part of a list, either bulleted or numbered. When you use the program's default layouts for your slides, the text boxes are already formatted as bulleted lists. If you want to use regular body text, you have two options:

- Remove the bullets from existing text by selecting the text and clicking the Bullets button in the Bullets And Numbering section of the Formatting Palette. The button appears darker when bulleted text is selected; clicking the button turns off the bullets and the button appears lighter.

- Add your own text boxes; text in newly created text boxes isn't formatted with bullets or numbers. To add a text box, see "Adding Text Boxes," page 844.

Chapter 35

If you want your list to be numbered or lettered, select the list, and choose a different Style option in the Bullets And Numbering section of the Formatting Palette or by choosing Format, Bullets And Numbering. The Formatting Palette contains Promote and Demote buttons to change the outline level of the selected text, whereas the Bullets And Numbering dialog on the Format menu includes the option to start a list at a number other than 1, as shown in Figure 35-3.

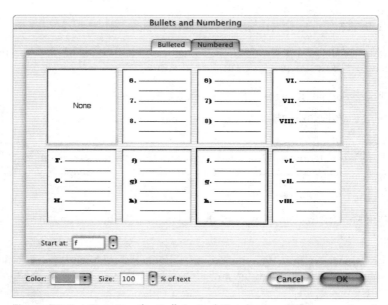

Figure 35-3. By using the Bullets And Numbering dialog, you can start a numbered or lettered list at any point.

> **tip** Text in the Bullets And Numbering dialog is shown in the same font and style that the text box is set to, so you can preview what your bullets or numbers will look like.

You can use the Bullets And Numbering dialog to choose a different bullet style, color, or size (measured as a percentage of the text size). Or you can use a custom graphic or special character as a bullet by following these steps:

1 Select the text box or the text where you want to use the special bullet.

2 Choose Format, Bullets And Numbering and click the Bulleted tab.

3 Click Character to choose a special text character for a bullet, and then choose the font, character, size, and color you want to use.

4 Click Picture to use a picture as the bullet, and then locate and double-click the picture you want.

Using the Format Painter

You can copy text formatting (as well as object formatting, such as color or line width) to other text or objects by invoking the Format Painter. Here's how:

1 Click the item that contains the formatting you want to duplicate.

2 Click the Format Painter button on the Standard toolbar.

3 Click the item you want the formatting copied to.

> **tip** To use the Format Painter to apply formatting to more than one object or text selection, double-click the Format Painter button in step 2 of the preceding process instead of clicking once. This locks the tool on. When you're finished applying formatting, click the Format Painter button once to turn it off.

Adding Hyperlinks

Hyperlinks within a PowerPoint presentation can take the user to a particular slide, a custom show, another presentation, a Microsoft Word X or Microsoft Excel X document, a Web page, or create an e-mail message. Any text, table, picture, or graphic can be hyperlinked, but if you want to use standard symbols for "next," "back," and other common hyperlink functions, you can insert PowerPoint's action buttons. They're designed with an inactive state and an active state that makes them look "pressed" when the user clicks them. Here's how to add an action button:

1 Go to the slide where you want to place the button, or, to place a button on every slide, go to the slide master.

To learn about using slide masters, see "Using Master Items," page 846.

2 Choose Slide Show, Action Buttons, and choose the button you want to insert.

3 Click to place a button at the desired location in the default size, or click and drag to define the size of the button as you place it. Hold down the Shift key as you drag if you want to retain the button's default proportions.

> **tip** The yellow diamond-shaped selection handle changes the bevel of the button's edges; try it for a different look.

4 When the Action Settings dialog appears, select the Mouse Click tab if you want the link to be activated when the user clicks it, or the Mouse Over tab if you want it to become active as soon as the user's pointer passes over it.

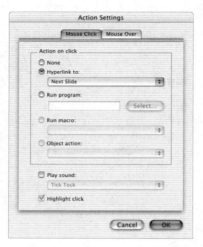

5 The Action On Click section (or the Action On Mouse Over section) will already be set to carry out the default action for the button you chose, but you can change the action if you want.

6 To give your users audible feedback when they click the button, select the Play Sound check box, and choose a sound from the pop-up menu. Then click OK.

The prefab action buttons are best suited for presentations with a wide range of user experience levels—their generic designs will be recognizable to most people. If they don't suit your needs, however, you can use regular hyperlinks to perform similar functions, as well as a range of other functions. To turn an existing graphic, image, or selection of text into a hyperlink, follow these steps:

1 Select the object or text.

2 Choose Insert, Hyperlink to open the Insert Hyperlink dialog.

3 In the Insert Hyperlink dialog, click one of these tabs for the kind of link you want to insert:

■ **Web Page.** Type a Web address or choose one from the Favorites or History pop-up menu, as shown in Figure 35-4.

■ **Document.** Click Select to choose the document that you want to link to. If you move the document later on, you'll need to go back and edit the link to point to the file's new location.

Chapter 35: Enhanced Presentation Formatting

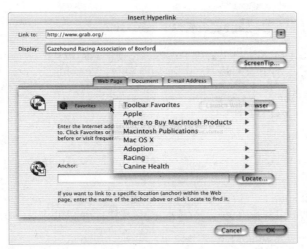

Figure 35-4. All the Web sites in Internet Explorer's Favorites list are available in the Insert Hyperlink dialog.

■ **E-Mail Address.** Type an e-mail address (perhaps your own so you can collect feedback or orders from your presentation), and enter a Subject line for the e-mail message that will be created when a user clicks this link.

4 If you're linking to a Web page or document and want the link to go to a specific location within the destination, click Locate in the Anchor section to choose an anchor.

5 Click OK to apply the hyperlink to the selected object or text.

Like World Wide Web links, text hyperlinks in PowerPoint are underlined and colored with a contrasting hue to ensure that the user can pick them out of the surrounding text. The color depends on the current color scheme, and it changes after a link has been activated so that the user can tell which links have already been followed.

To edit a hyperlink after you create it, Control+click the object, and select Hyperlink, Edit Hyperlink. You can change the type of link or its destination.

tip Hyperlinks are inactive when you're working on a presentation; to test them, select Slide Show, and click each link to make sure it works as intended. See "Previewing the Presentation," page 896, for more information.

Adding Text Boxes

PowerPoint's predesigned slide layouts provide a good starting point for most presentations, but they don't always fit the bill. You can modify the prefab layouts or create your own by adding your own text boxes and other objects. Here's how:

1 Select Insert, Text Box.

2 To add a single line of text, click and start typing.

3 To add one or more paragraphs of text, click and drag to define the shape of the text box, and then start typing.

4 To change the shape of a text box, click to select it, open the Drawing toolbar, if necessary, and choose Draw, Change AutoShape from the toolbar.

5 Choose a category of shapes from the submenu, and then choose a shape for the text box.

Attaching Comments to Slides

If you're working as part of a team to create a presentation, you might want to insert notes to other team members. Comments are electronic "sticky notes" that you can place anywhere on your slides. They also come in handy for reminding yourself of missing or questionable info or keeping track of where you left off work. Comment boxes are always labeled with the name of the person who added the comment. This helps get around the fact that PowerPoint, unlike Word and Excel, doesn't have a function to track changes.

> **tip** You can choose a font, size, and color for the text in a comment box in the same way that you'd format any other text on a slide; see "Formatting Text," page 836, for more information.

Here's how you can insert a comment on the current slide:

1 Choose Insert, Comment. Doing so automatically displays any existing comments that were previously hidden.

2 Type your comment, and then click anywhere else on the slide to deselect the comment box.

3 Click the border of the note and drag the comment box to a convenient location on the slide.

Chapter 35: Enhanced Presentation Formatting

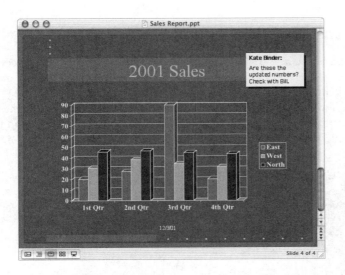

Choose View, Toolbars, Reviewing to show the Reviewing toolbar, which contains three buttons for use with comments:

- **Insert Comment.** Click this button to add a comment box to the current slide. This has the same effect as clicking Insert, Comment from the PowerPoint menu.

- **Show/Hide Comments.** Hide comments or show them again with this button—use this function when you want to see the presentation without extraneous clutter.

- **Send To Mail Recipient (As Attachment).** Use this button to send a presentation to a colleague for review. (See "Sending PowerPoint Documents via E-Mail," page 830, to learn how to e-mail Office documents.)

Chapter 35

Using Master Items

Consistency is one of the keys to good design—and consistency is what masters are all about. A master in PowerPoint is analogous to a master page in a page layout application; it contains items that look the same on each slide, handout, or note that you apply it to, as shown in Figure 35-5. In PowerPoint, masters also enable you to set the style for title and body text; you can choose different text attributes for each level in the presentation's underlying outline.

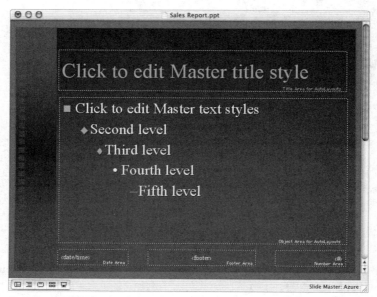

Figure 35-5. The background and the coordinating graphic on the left, as well as the footer elements, remain the same on every slide associated with this master.

You can use four kinds of masters: slide, title, notes, and handout. Each master can contain several elements, or placeholders, including title, text, date, slide number, header, and footer. The notes and handout masters have special placeholders for the thumbnail images of slides that they contain, as shown in Figure 35-6. By default, a new master has all of the placeholders for its master type. You can delete any placeholder on a master by clicking it and pressing Delete. To put a placeholder back if you decide you want to use it, view the master you want to restore, and then choose Format, Master Layout (or Notes Master Layout or Handout Master Layout). Select the check boxes next to the elements you want to insert, and click OK.

Chapter 35: Enhanced Presentation Formatting

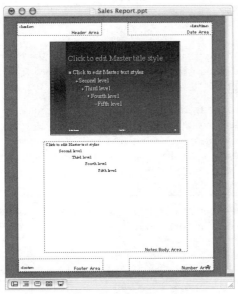

Figure 35-6. Like handout masters, notes masters are formatted as pages instead of as slides, because notes pages are meant to be printed.

You can't select master items on a slide, note, or handout; to change their size, position, or format, you must view the master for that slide, note, or handout and make the changes there. When you modify a master, your changes are applied to each slide based on that master.

new feature! For the first time, PowerPoint X supports multiple slide and title masters in a single presentation. This feature enables you to change backgrounds and the default size and position of placeholder elements by simply applying a different master to a slide. To create a new master, you need to apply a new design template to a selection of slides (see "Applying Slide Templates," page 850) or copy slides into your presentation from another presentation that uses a different design.

Editing Slide and Title Masters

Most of the slides in your presentation are based on the slide master. It contains a title text box and one for body text, as well as whatever other elements you choose to use, such as a footer, a date, and a slide number. Here's how you can modify it:

1 Choose View, Master, Slide Master.

2 Click the edge of any element to select it, so that you can resize it or move it.

3 Click in any text paragraph, and drag to select it, so that you can change its text format. (For more information, see "Formatting Text," page 836.)

4 Choose Format, Slide Design to apply a new design template to the master or to reapply the original design template. (For details, see "Applying Slide Templates," later in this chapter.)

5 Choose Format, Slide Background to change the slide's background color, or choose Format, Slide Color Scheme to change the slide's entire color scheme. (For more information, see "Applying Color Schemes and Backgrounds," page 851). Clicking the Apply button will change just the current slide; clicking Apply To All will change all the slides in the presentation.

> **tip** If you want the title master to have different text attributes from the slide master, be sure to edit the slide master first. The title master inherits all the text attributes from the slide master, including text font, size, and style.

Editing Notes and Handout Masters

If you plan to use notes and handout pages, you can customize their design using the notes and handout masters. The procedure is the same as for modifying slide and title masters, with a couple of exceptions:

● Notes masters contain a placeholder for the slide image at the top of the page, with a text area below it containing placeholder text for five levels of note text. You can resize and reposition both of these boxes; hold down the Shift key as you resize to maintain the original proportions.

● Handout masters also contain placeholders for slide thumbnails, but you can't edit them directly. The Handout Master toolbar appears when you view a handout master, with buttons for different thumbnail layouts that fit varying numbers of thumbnails on each page, as shown in Figure 35-7. Click the buttons to change the layout of the thumbnails; the other objects on the master can be moved and modified in the regular way.

> **tip** If you plan to print your notes and handouts, you'll probably want to stick to white for the slide background color to make sure they're easy to read.

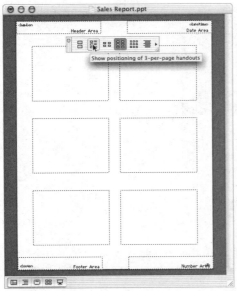

Figure 35-7. The Handout Master toolbar has buttons for five different slide image layouts and an outline layout.

Changing Slide Layouts

Although you're free to rearrange elements on a slide as much as you want, PowerPoint provides 24 prebuilt layouts that you can use either as-is or as starting points to design your own slide layouts. These are the layouts you'll see when you insert a new slide in your presentation. If you decide to change a slide's layout after creating it, follow these steps:

1 If you want to change more than one slide at a time, switch to Slide Sorter view and Shift+click each of the slides you want to change. Otherwise, just view the slide you want to change.

2 Choose Format, Slide Layout.

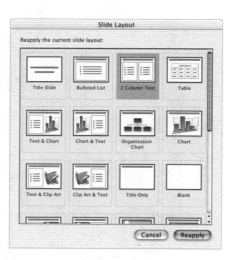

3 Click Reapply to return the slide to the original version of its current layout, or choose another layout, and click Apply to change the slide's layout.

Applying Slide Templates

Just as you can change a slide's layout after you create it, you can also change a presentation's design template after the presentation document is created. You can apply the new template to one slide, multiple slides, or the entire presentation. Follow these steps:

1 If you want to modify only some of the presentation's slides, switch to Slide Sorter view, and select the slides to change. Shift+click slide thumbnails to select multiple slides.

2 To change all the slides, click anywhere outside the current slide to deselect it.

3 Click the Presentation section on the Formatting Palette to expand it (if you're in Slide Sorter mode, Presentation will be the only section visible).

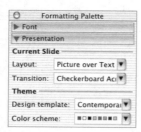

Chapter 35

4 Choose a new design template from the pop-up menu. It's applied to the selected slides or, if no slides are selected, to all the slides in the presentation. If you're not in Slide Sorter view, you'll be asked to confirm whether you want to apply it to all slides or only the currently displayed slide.

> **note** Proceed with caution—many of PowerPoint's included design templates clash with other templates, and your presentation might look disjointed and unprofessional if it uses disparate templates.

> **tip** **Save your design in a new template**
>
> If you've modified your presentation's design, you can save your changes as a new design template so that you can base future presentations on the same design. Choose File, Save As, and select Design Template from the Format pop-up menu. By default, the file location changes to My Templates; design templates saved in this folder appear under the My Templates category in the Project Gallery.

Applying Color Schemes and Backgrounds

Each design template includes several alternative color schemes. PowerPoint color schemes contain eight colors that are used for the presentation's background, text, lines, shadows, fills, accents, and hyperlinks. The built-in color schemes for PowerPoint design templates generally include at least one dark background, one light background, and one grayscale version.

> **tip** **Match your color scheme to your presentation medium**
>
> It's best to use a dark background with light text and graphics if you'll be giving your presentation in a dark room (as a slide show). Do the opposite if you're creating overheads or a printed document—stick with light backgrounds and dark contrasting elements.

It's easy to switch color schemes to vary the look of a presentation; follow these steps:

1 If you want to modify only some of the presentation's slides, switch to Slide Sorter view, and select the slides to change.

2 To change all the slides, click anywhere outside the current slide to deselect it.

Chapter 35

3 Click Presentation on the Formatting Palette.

4 Choose a new color scheme from the pop-up menu. It's applied to the selected slides or, if no slides are selected, to all the slides in the presentation.

5 If you want to create your own color scheme, choose Custom Scheme from the pop-up menu.

6 Click the Custom tab in the Color Scheme dialog, and double-click the current color for each of the eight color elements you want to change. Then choose a new color in the Color Picker, shown in Figure 35-8.

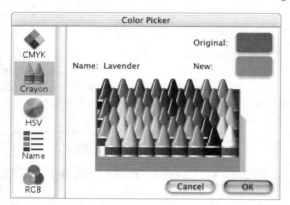

Figure 35-8. When you're editing colors, you can choose from a variety of color pickers by clicking in the left side of the Color Picker dialog.

7 Click Preview in the Color Scheme dialog to see how the new scheme will look, and then click Apply or Apply To All.

> **tip** If you develop a color scheme that you particularly like, or one that matches your corporate colors, you can save it as a standard scheme for that design template by clicking Add As Standard Scheme on the Custom tab of the Color Scheme dialog.

Another way to customize a presentation is to change its background. In addition to the background color included in the current color scheme, slide backgrounds can contain gradients, textures, patterns, or pictures. To change the elements used in your presentation's background, follow these steps:

1 Choose Format, Slide Background.

2 In the Background dialog, open the pop-up menu at the bottom of the Background Fill section, and choose Fill Effects.

Chapter 35: Enhanced Presentation Formatting

3 In the Fill Effects dialog, choose from four types of fill: gradient, texture, pattern, or picture (you can use only one fill type at a time).

■ On the Gradient tab, choose a shading style and variant. You can also change the gradient colors and (new in PowerPoint X) adjust its transparency.

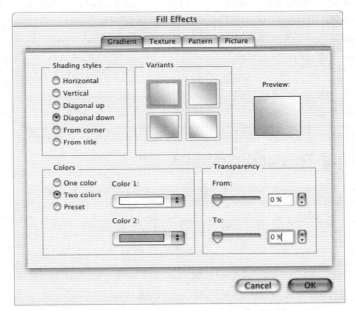

■ On the Texture tab, choose a texture, or click Other Texture to load one from a graphics file. For example, you could scan cloth, metal, or natural objects such as leaves to form a texture for your slide backgrounds.

■ On the Pattern tab, choose a pattern, and then select foreground and background colors from the pop-up menus.

■ On the Picture tab, click Select Picture to choose an image file.

4 Click OK to return to the Slide Background dialog.

5 Click Preview to see how the new background will look, and then click Apply or Apply To All.

> To learn more about using images in PowerPoint, including the supported file formats, turn to "Managing Images," page 859.

Animating the Presentation

One of the advantages of computerized presentations over conventional slide shows is that you're not restricted to using static text and graphics. Animations can energize a presentation and help you focus viewers' attention on the key points you want to make. You can apply animation to text and objects on your slides, and you can use animated transitions to move from each slide to the next.

---

tip **Use animation sparingly**

Keep in mind that, like overly bright colors and busy graphics, animations can distract from the content of your presentation. Be sure not to overdo them, or your audience will run screaming from the room—usually not a sign of a successful presentation!

Animating Text and Graphics

You can animate how text and objects enter and exit a slide. You can set text to appear by the letter, by the word, or a paragraph at a time. You can also have graphic images appear progressively on your slide. Follow these steps to get started:

1 Go to the slide that has the text or graphics you want to animate.

2 Choose Slide Show, Animations, Custom.

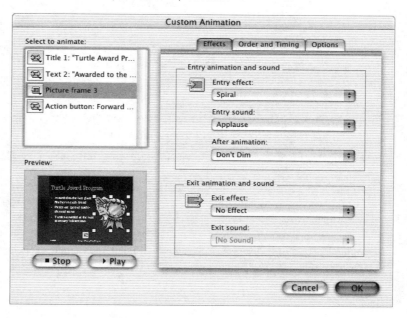

3 Choose the text or graphic you want to animate from the Select To Animate list.

4 On the Effects tab, from the Entry Effect pop-up menu, choose an animation and, optionally, choose a sound from the Entry Sound pop-up menu. This animation and sound will play as the slide displays.

5 From the After Animation pop-up menu, choose an option for the action that will take place when the animation is complete.

6 To add another animation that will play as the viewer leaves the slide, make selections in the Exit Effect and Exit Sound pop-up menus.

7 Select the Order And Timing tab, which lists all the animations applied to objects on the current slide.

  ■ To change the order of the animations, select one in the Animation Order list, and use the arrow buttons to move it before or after another animation.

  ■ To determine how an animation is activated, select it in the list, and set the options in the Start Animation section.

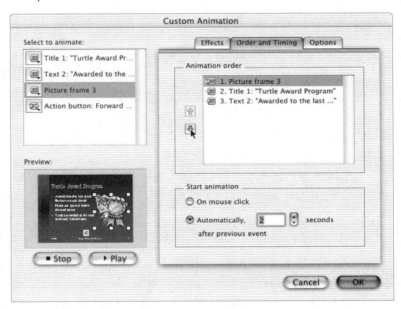

8 Click the Options tab (not available for graphics), and set display options for the entry and exit animations, and then click Play to see the animation. Note that the options available on this tab vary according to the type of object you're animating.

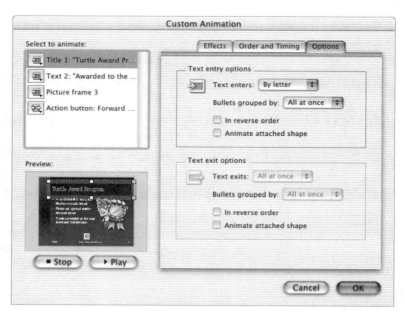

9 Click OK when you're happy with the results of your settings.

tip To play an animation at any time, choose Slide Show, Animation Preview. The animation plays on a thumbnail version of the slide on the Animation Preview palette. Click the thumbnail to play the slide again.

Setting Slide Transitions

Transitions between slides can subtly (or not so subtly) enhance the effect of your presentation's design. You can add transitions to one or more slides at one time using Normal view or Slide Sorter view, and PowerPoint includes dozens of special transition effects to choose from. As with animations on slides, less is more when choosing transitions, because flashy transitions can quickly grow tiring to an audience. Follow these steps:

1 Switch to Slide Sorter view, and choose one or more slides to add a transition to. Shift+click to select multiple slides.

2 Choose Slide Show, Slide Transition.

3 In the Effect section, select a transition effect from the pop-up menu and a speed.

4 If desired, choose a sound to play in conjunction with the visual effect. Select Loop Until Next if you want the sound to continue playing as long as the slide is on the screen.

5 Click Apply to add the transition to the selected slides or Apply To All to add it to the entire presentation.

Rearranging Slides with the Slide Sorter

Whenever you're working with more than one slide at a time, the Slide Sorter view, shown in Figure 35-9 on the next page, helps you manipulate only the slides you want to affect. In this view, you see thumbnail views of all the slides in your presentation, and you can rearrange them in several ways, as follows:

● Double-click a slide to switch to Normal view and display that slide.

● Drag slides to change their order.

● Select a slide and press Delete to remove it from the presentation.

Figure 35-9. The Slide Sorter enables you to drag and drop your slides into any order.

The Slide Sorter toolbar, which automatically appears when you switch to Slide Sorter view, contains several functions from the Slide Show menu: the Slide Transition button, the Slide Transition Effects pop-up menu, the Hide Slide button, and the Rehearse Timings button. Its final button, Show Formatting, enables you to show or hide the presentation's text and images, leaving only the slide titles. This is useful for when you want to move slides around in your presentation, and want to focus on the slide order without being distracted by the slide content. It also makes moving slides faster, since PowerPoint doesn't have to redraw all of the slide content when you make a change.

Chapter 36

Illustrating the Presentation

Images are an important part of any presentation. Some information is better presented in a graphic form—and some people better understand information when it's shown graphically. A Microsoft PowerPoint X presentation can include several different kinds of non-textual information: clip art, scanned images, sound effects, music, animations, movies, charts, graphs, equations, and WordArt. You can think of a presentation as a container for all these kinds of information. PowerPoint can work with a large variety of file formats, and many of these objects can be edited in their original programs and instantly updated with a new version in the presentation. In this chapter, you'll learn about

- Adding scanned images and clip art to presentations

- Working with transparency effects

- Creating and using WordArt

- Working with AutoShapes

- Adding sound effects, movies, and animations to presentations

- Including charts, tables, and equations in presentations

Managing Images

In PowerPoint, there are two kinds of images. *Drawings* are created with PowerPoint tools and are part of your presentation; they include AutoShapes, curves, lines, freeform shapes, and WordArt (text that is colored, reshaped, and ornamented to form artwork). You can also import drawings created in

859

other programs, such as Adobe Illustrator, Deneba's Canvas, or even the AppleWorks drawing module. Drawings are *vector images*, meaning they are made up of individual objects, such as lines, arcs, and polygons that can be stretched, scaled, or otherwise modified. The other kind of image, *pictures,* are also known as bitmaps. A *bitmap* is an image composed entirely of rows and columns of dots having such attributes as color and transparency, such as scanned images and photographs. Files created in programs such as Adobe Photoshop or the AppleWorks painting module are bitmapped images.

Adding Pictures and Clip Art

There are two ways to add pictures to a PowerPoint presentation: using the Clip Gallery or importing graphics files directly. The Clip Gallery starts out with a selection of artwork that comes with Microsoft Office v. X, and you can add your own files as well as search for more artwork online and add it directly to the Clip Gallery. If you plan to use artwork more than once, you should store it in the Clip Gallery. On the other hand, artwork you know you won't need to use again can be imported directly into your presentation from any location on your hard drive, from a connected scanner, or from a digital camera.

> **tip** Artwork in the PICT format, such as the clip art in the Clip Gallery, can be ungrouped and modified right in PowerPoint, just as though you'd drawn it using PowerPoint's tools.

Using the Clip Gallery

The artwork included with Office v. X is found in the Clip Gallery, which resembles the Project Gallery. To insert artwork from the Clip Gallery, follow these steps:

1 Choose Insert, Picture, Clip Art to open the Clip Gallery.

2 Choose a category from the list on the left side of the Clip Gallery, or type a keyword in the Search box to look for art relating to a particular topic.

3 To search for more images in Design Gallery Live, Microsoft's online image collection for Office, click Online. Follow the instructions on the Web site; downloaded images are added to the Favorites category in the Clip Gallery.

> **note** You must have a Web browser installed and an active Internet connection to use Design Gallery Live. For more information about using Design Gallery Live, see "Getting More Pictures Online," page 235.

4 To see a larger version of an image, click to select the image, and then select the Preview check box. (Clear the check box to close the Preview window.)

5 When you've found the image you want to use, click to select it, and then click Insert to add it to the current slide.

> **note** Unlike the Project Gallery, the Clip Gallery can remain open while you work.

> You can store your own artwork files in the Clip Gallery along with the provided image collection. For more information, see "Adding Images to the Clip Gallery," page 239.

Importing Pictures

When the picture you want to use is not in the Clip Gallery, you can import it directly. Here's how:

1 Choose Insert, Picture, From File (or if you're capturing the picture from a connected peripheral, choose Insert, Picture, From Scanner Or Camera).

2 Navigate to the picture file you want to use.

3 If the picture file might be changed during the course of your project, and you want the version in your presentation to update automatically, then select the Link To File check box. To copy a file you link into the same folder as your presentation folder, select the Save With Document check box.

4 Click Insert.

> **note** If you choose to link to the original image file, be sure to copy the file along with the presentation if you move the presentation document to another computer or e-mail it to another person.

Chapter 36

Setting Picture Effects and Transparency

When you select a picture, the Formatting Palette adds a new section labeled Picture, as shown in Figure 36-1.

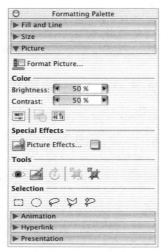

Figure 36-1. Although it doesn't contain all the tools you can use to modify pictures, the Formatting Palette is a good starting point for modifying images in PowerPoint.

Using the tools on the Formatting Palette, you can change the color and contrast of the selected image, apply special effects to it, rotate it, crop it, and more. Here's what you'll find in the Picture section of the Formatting Palette:

● The Format Picture button opens the Format Picture dialog. On the Picture tab, you can crop an image's dimensions numerically and use Brightness, Contrast, and Image Control settings. You can click the Recolor button to change the colors in the picture (if it was created in an Office application or if it was saved in PICT format).

For more information about the other tabs in the Format Picture dialog, see "Using the Format Picture Dialog," page 251.

● The Color area in the Picture section of the Formatting Palette contains Brightness and Contrast sliders, which enable you to brighten up images as a quick fix. Also included are Color Adjustment, Set Transparent Color, and Image Control buttons, with which you can, respectively, change an image's color balance; make solid-colored sections of the image (usually its background) transparent; and convert an image to grayscale, black and white, or a watermark.

- The Special Effects area contains only two buttons; with the Picture Effects button, you can apply image filters such as Chrome or Watercolor to images, and the Shadow button contains options for a number of different shadow styles that you can apply behind images.

- The Tools area includes the Fix Red Eye, Remove Scratch, Free Rotate, Cutout, and Crop buttons. The first three buttons do exactly what their names suggest, whereas the Cutout button enables you to select an area of the image and hide the rest of the image. With the Crop button, you can drag the corners of the image to accomplish the same thing, working from the outside in.

- The Selection area contains five different selection tools, with which you can designate what area of an image you want to change. The Rectangular Marquee and Oval Marquee tools draw rectangles and ovals, respectively, whereas the Lasso tool enables you to select any shape you can draw. The Polygonal Lasso tool is for selecting irregular but straight-sided areas by clicking at each corner, and the Magic Lasso tool helps you trace objects within the image by finding the edges where one color contrasts with another.

> **tip** When you're using the Magic Lasso, drag slowly and carefully, watching the gray selection preview that forms in the tool's path. Click every so often to "set" the selection up to that point, because the selection preview changes as you move around the image.

Making an Imported Drawing Editable

Ordinarily, you can't edit drawings imported into PowerPoint from other programs—the shapes of their component objects are determined when they're saved as graphics files, and that's the end of it. However, you *can* convert such images into PowerPoint drawing objects, after which you'll be able to edit them just as though they'd been created in PowerPoint in the first place. To do so, click the Draw button on the Drawing toolbar, and choose Ungroup. Click Yes in the confirmation dialog, and you're all set. Once ungrouped, the picture is broken into its component parts, each of which you can resize, reshape, or recolor according to your needs.

An ungrouped picture can contain many small shapes. To avoid separating the picture's component shapes, it's a good idea to select all the shapes and group them again once you're done modifying them. The handy Regroup command allows you to select just one object, and PowerPoint will regroup it with all of the other objects with which it was previously grouped. Click the Draw button on the Drawing toolbar, and choose Regroup; although this won't return the picture to its former status, it will enable you to move all the picture's parts as one unit.

Inserting WordArt

WordArt is ideal for creating logos and jazzing up presentation headings. With WordArt, you can add punch to your text, as shown in Figure 36-2, by coloring it; applying 3-D and shadow effects; and changing its shape by stretching it, skewing it, and rotating it. You can create WordArt based on existing text, or you can create a new WordArt object like this one:

Figure 36-2. It would take several steps to create this effect in an illustration application, but you can achieve it in one operation using WordArt.

Follow these steps to create a new WordArt element:

1 Click the Insert WordArt button on the Drawing toolbar.

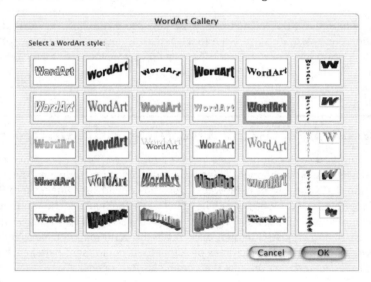

2 Choose a style from the WordArt Gallery, and click OK. Don't worry about the colors you see; you can change your WordArt object's colors later.

3 Choose a font, point size, and style, and enter the text you want to use, and then click OK.

> **tip** If the text you want to use in WordArt already exists in your presentation, you can create a new WordArt object from it without modifying or deleting the text itself. Simply select the text before clicking the Insert WordArt button.

4 The WordArt element is placed on the current slide and selected, and the WordArt toolbar appears. You can move the object around the slide, copy and paste it to a different slide, and resize it by dragging its selection handles. To make other changes, choose one of these options:

- To edit the text in a WordArt element, double-click it, make your changes in the resulting dialog, and then click OK.

- To modify other WordArt attributes, such as the color, click Format WordArt on the WordArt toolbar.

- To change the WordArt style of an existing object, select the object, click WordArt Gallery on the WordArt toolbar, and then choose another style and click OK.

Changes you've made to the object's size or color are retained when you edit its text, but not if you use the WordArt Gallery to choose a new style. You can change the object's shape without changing its style by clicking the WordArt Shape button on the WordArt toolbar and choosing a shape option.

---

caution   WordArt isn't really text—PowerPoint treats a WordArt object as a picture. This means that WordArt isn't included in your presentation's outline, and it isn't checked for correct spelling, so you'll need to proofread it carefully before finalizing your presentation.

Inserting Scanned Images

If the image you want to use exists only on paper, you can scan it directly from PowerPoint. You must have a scanner, of course, and the scanning software that came with it—either a TWAIN module or a Photoshop plug-in—must be installed. Follow these steps to scan an image:

1 Go to the slide where you want to insert the image.

2 Choose Insert, Picture, From Scanner Or Camera.

3 Select your scanner from the Device pop-up menu, and click Acquire.

4 Your scanner software is automatically launched; scan the image as you normally would. When it's scanned, PowerPoint places it on the current slide.

Troubleshooting

PowerPoint says no scanner is installed.

There are a few reasons you might see an error message stating that no scanner is installed when you try to scan an image:

● The scanner's software drivers might not be installed. Make sure that you have Mac OS X software for your scanner model, and check the manufacturer's Web site to make sure you have the latest version of the software. If not, download the new version, and follow the instructions to install it.

● The scanner software might not be a TWAIN module or a Photoshop plug-in; these are the only kinds of scanner software that PowerPoint can interact with.

● It might sound obvious, but be sure the scanner is turned on and connected to your Mac.

Adding AutoShapes

Can't draw a straight line, much less an octagon or a trapezoid? Don't worry—that's what AutoShapes are for. These ready-made shapes include rectangles and circles as well as more complex shapes (including both octagons and trapezoids), lines and connectors, arrows, flowchart symbols, stars, banners, and callout boxes. To draw an AutoShape, follow these steps:

1 Click the AutoShapes button on the Drawing toolbar, and choose a shape from one of the submenus.

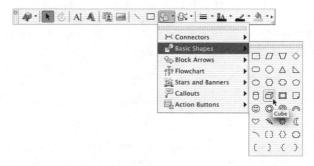

2 Click your slide to insert the shape at the default size, or click and drag to define the size of the shape yourself.

3 To add text to the AutoShape, click the shape and enter your text. You can't add text to lines or connectors.

4 To color the AutoShape, use the Fill and Line controls on the Formatting Palette.

Adding Media Files

Like pictures, media files originate outside of PowerPoint; they include sound, digital video, and animation files. Also like pictures, they must be saved in the correct file format before you can insert them in a presentation. Sounds, movies, and animations can play automatically when the slide is first viewed, or they can be represented by a clickable icon, so that they only play if the viewer triggers them.

Adding Sounds

Adding music, sound effects, or vocal annotations to a presentation gives it a whole new dimension. Follow these steps to add a sound file to your presentation:

1 Go to the slide where you want to add the sound.

2 Choose Insert, Movies And Sounds, Sound From File.

3 Navigate to the file you want to use, and click Insert.

4 In the dialog, click Yes to play the sound automatically whenever this slide is displayed during a slide show; click No if you want the viewer to click the sound's icon to play it.

5 Move or resize the sound icon as desired; double-click it to play the sound.

---

tip **Use the Clip Gallery for sound files**

You can also insert sounds from the Clip Gallery. It already contains some sounds, and you can add your own sounds for quick access to frequently used sound files. To insert a sound from the Clip Gallery, choose Insert, Movies And Sounds, Sound From Gallery. Select the sound you want to use, and then click Insert to add it to your presentation.

InsideOut

Set sound options after inserting a sound from the Clip Gallery

When you insert sounds from the Clip Gallery, you won't see the dialog asking whether you want the sound to play on entry to the slide or only on a mouse click. You can set this behavior after the sound is inserted by choosing Slide Show, Animations, Custom. Select the sound file you want to change, click the Options tab, and select the Play Using Animation Order check box. For more about using the Animations dialog, see "Animating Text and Graphics," page 854.

Adding Movie Files

You can include movies—digital video files—to your presentations in several formats: QuickTime, QuickTime VR, MPEG, and AVI. Remember that movies are never copied into a presentation; they're always linked to the original file, to avoid making presentation files too big. Because the file is linked, you need to keep the original file with the presentation file to be able to play it. Follow these steps to add a movie to your presentation:

1 Go to the slide where you want to add the movie.

2 Choose Insert, Movies And Sounds, Movie From File.

3 Navigate to the file you want to use, select it, and then click Choose.

4 In the dialog, click Yes to play the movie automatically whenever this slide is displayed during a slide show; click No if you want the viewer to double-click the movie to play it.

5 Click the movie to select it and use the selection handles to resize it as desired, or click and drag to move it; double-click to play the movie.

Resizing Movies

You can resize movies by dragging their corner handles, just like any element on a slide. But video files have preset sizes at which they'll play best, so you'll achieve better results if you let PowerPoint calculate the appropriate size for the monitor on which the presentation will be played. Follow these steps to resize a movie:

1 Select the movie you want to resize.

2 Choose Format, Picture, or click the Format Picture button on the Movie toolbar, which appears when a movie is selected.

3 On the Size tab, select the Best Scale For Slide Show check box.

4 Choose the resolution of the destination monitor, and click OK.

Like sounds, movies can also be stored in the Clip Gallery; to access them, choose Insert, Movies And Sounds, Movie From Gallery. The Clip Gallery also lists animations known as animated GIFs; those are discussed in the next section.

InsideOut

Rescale your movie—again

Due to an apparent bug in PowerPoint, the Best Scale For Slide Show check box will be cleared the next time you open the Format Picture dialog, even though the movie won't be rescaled. To make changes, select the check box again, and choose the resolution of the destination monitor from the pop-up menu.

note AVI video files are a movie format used on the Windows operating system. When you first import AVI files into your presentation, PowerPoint converts the AVI file into QuickTime format.

Adding Animations

Animated GIF files are small graphics files that contain multiple versions of a picture that a program such as PowerPoint or a Web browser displays in quick succession. You most often see animated GIFs on the Web, but you can use them in PowerPoint to spark up a presentation, either as illustrations or as buttons. Follow these steps to add an animation to your presentation:

1 Display the slide where you want to add the animation.

2 Choose Insert, Picture, From File.

3 Navigate to the file you want to use, and click Insert.

4 Move or resize the image as desired; double-click it to play the animation.

To preview a GIF animation, click the Slide Show button at the bottom of the document window.

Working with Charts

Charts, especially when combined with graphics and colored with bright or contrasting colors, are a great tool for communicating relationships among numbers, as shown in Figure 36-3. When you want to explain financial information, explore demographics, or show how trends change over time, a chart is the right tool.

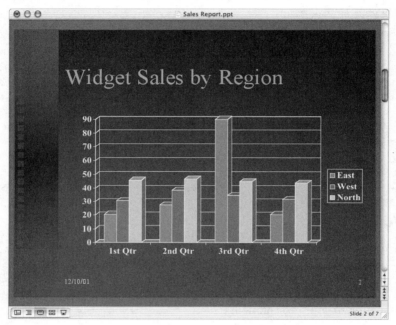

Figure 36-3. Graphs are automatically colored to coordinate with the current design template.

Inserting Charts in PowerPoint

You can insert charts in PowerPoint presentations using Microsoft Graph, a separate Office v. X program that is automatically started up inside PowerPoint when you choose the Insert Chart command. Graph has an interface much like that in Microsoft Excel X, enabling you to work in a familiar environment as you enter the data on which all charts are based.

1 Choose Insert, Chart to open a sample datasheet and its associated chart.

○ ○ ○		Graph in Sales Report.ppt – Datasheet				
		A	**B**	**C**	**D**	**E**
		1st Qtr	2nd Qtr	3rd Qtr	4th Qtr	
1	East	20.4	27.4	90	20.4	
2	West	30.6	38.6	34.6	31.6	
3	North	45.9	46.9	45	43.9	
4						
5						
6						

2 Click in the datasheet window, and enter your data. Place axis labels in the unnumbered row at the top of the window, and row labels in the unlettered column at the left side of the window. Then enter numerical values in the numbered and lettered cells.

Data entry in Graph works the same way it does in Excel, except that you must enter all the data yourself—formulas aren't supported. To learn about entering data in a grid, turn to "Entering Information in Cells," page 592.

3 Choose a chart type from the Chart Type pop-up menu on the Standard toolbar, or choose Chart, Chart Type for more options and a description of each type.

4 Choose Chart, Chart Options to set the chart's title, the number of axes, gridline types, legend position, data labels, and, on the Data Table tab, whether to display the data in table form.

The Chart Type and Chart Options dialogs are identical to their counterparts in Excel. For more information on choosing the right chart type for your data and selecting chart options, see "Understanding Chart Types," page 687, and "Chart Formatting," page 695.

5 When you're done formatting the chart, choose Graph, Quit And Return To (your file name is included in the command), or press Command+Q.

6 In PowerPoint, click and drag to move the chart around on the slide, or drag a selection handle to resize it.

7 To change the chart's data, type, or formatting options, double-click it and follow steps 2 through 5 again.

tip **Animate your chart**

You can animate a chart so that when the slide is first viewed, the chart is built up piece by piece. Select the chart, and choose Slide Show, Animations, Custom. Click the Options tab, and choose an option under Introduce Chart Elements.

Creating Charts Based on Excel Worksheets

If the data on which you want to base a chart already exists as an Excel worksheet, you can bring that data into Graph and work with it there to create a chart. Follow these steps:

1 Click Insert Chart on the Standard toolbar.

2 Click anywhere in the datasheet window in Graph.

3 Select the cell where you want the upper left cell of the new data to be placed.

4 Choose File, Import File.

5 Navigate to the Excel document you want to import, and click Choose.

6 In the Import Data Options dialog, choose which sheet you want to import.

7 Choose Entire Sheet or Range. If you want to import only part of the worksheet, enter the range of cells you want to include, from the upper left cell through the lower right cell, in the form A1:C8.

8 Select Overwrite Existing Cells to replace all existing data on the datasheet with the imported data.

> **caution**   Selecting the Overwrite Existing Cells check box will delete *all* data on the existing datasheet, not only the values in cells now taken up by the imported Excel data. Don't select this check box unless you're sure you don't want to use any of the existing data.

Inserting Charts from Excel

If you've already created a chart in Excel itself, you can copy that chart into PowerPoint. Follow these steps:

1 Open Excel, and open the workbook containing the chart.

2 Select an embedded chart or select the chart tab of a chart on its own sheet, and press Command+C to copy it.

3 Switch to PowerPoint, and go to the slide where you want to insert the chart.

4 Choose Edit, Paste Special.

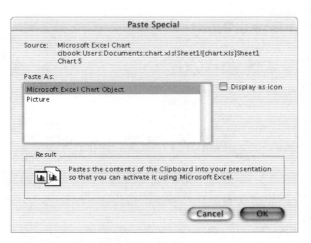

5 Select Microsoft Excel Chart Object, and click OK.

6 Drag the chart to reposition it on the slide, and drag a corner handle to resize it.

7 If you want to change the data on which the chart is based, double-click it to return to Excel. Click the appropriate tab to edit the chart or the worksheet data itself.

InsideOut

Finalize charts and data before inserting them into PowerPoint

When you return to Excel to edit a chart by double-clicking the chart in PowerPoint, the chart and worksheet that are embedded in the presentation open in a small window—not the original Excel spreadsheet. Because the chart is no longer linked to the original Excel document, changing the data will not update the chart. You might want to wait to insert charts until you're sure their data won't change.

Working with Tables

Tables are a structured way of presenting lists and comparing or contrasting information. Their concise columnar structure makes them easy to read and lends itself to presentations. In PowerPoint, you can create your own tables or incorporate existing tables from Microsoft Word X or Excel.

Creating Tables in PowerPoint

PowerPoint tables are similar to Word tables or Excel spreadsheets. Keep in mind, however, that tables in presentations should be smaller and simpler than those you might use in a printed document. Figure 36-4 shows an example of a simple table appropriate for a PowerPoint presentation.

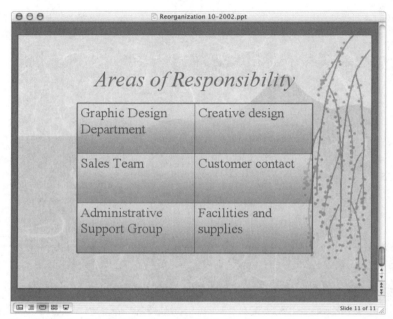

Figure 36-4. Try to keep PowerPoint tables to no more than two or three columns and rows to avoid overwhelming the viewer.

Follow this procedure to insert a table in your presentation:

1 Click the Insert Table button on the Standard toolbar.

2 Drag through the pop-up menu to indicate how many rows and columns you want the table to have.

3 Release the mouse button when the grid has the right number of rows and columns.

4 Click in the table's first cell to enter text, and press Tab to move to the next cell when you're done.

Unlike a Word table, a PowerPoint table is a free-floating object that isn't embedded within text boxes. You can drag its borders to move the table on a slide, and you can drag its selection handles to resize it.

InsideOut

Change the size of table cells

PowerPoint enlarges table cells when you add text and reduces their size when you remove text. Although you can't change this behavior, you can shrink table rows by reducing the table text's font size. You can also click and drag a row border downward to force the row to a larger height, or drag a column border sideways to enlarge the column.

The Table toolbar appears when a table is selected; it contains several useful functions for formatting tables, as follows:

● Click the Draw Table button, and draw with the Pencil tool to define split cells, or click the Eraser button, and drag the Eraser tool over cell borders to merge cells.

● Click one of the three vertical alignment buttons to align text at the top, middle, or bottom of its cell.

note Table heads are usually aligned at the bottom of their cells, whereas table text is usually top-aligned or centered vertically.

● Set table border attributes using the Border Width, Border Style, and Border Color pop-up menus, and click the Outside Borders button to choose which sides of a cell or group of cells should have borders.

● Use the Fill tool to add shading or color to cells to make them stand out from the rest of the table.

● Click the Table button to open the Table menu, and choose a command to add, insert, delete, merge, split, or select rows, columns, cells, or the whole table.

tip **Rotate column headers to fit more text**

If the text of your table's column headers is much wider than the columns themselves, consider rotating the text 90°. To rotate text in a table, select it and choose Format, Table. Select the Text Box tab, and select the Rotate Text Within Cell By 90 Degrees check box.

Inserting Word or Excel Tables

PowerPoint's table tools are suited to creating basic tables. For more complex tables, you can use Word or Excel and paste the tables into your PowerPoint presentation. For

Chapter 36

tables with specialized text formatting, you should use Word; you'll find it easier to format bulleted lists, custom tabs, numbering, and hanging indents in a word processor, and Word's table tools enable more extensive individual cell formatting and diagonally split cells. Calculations and charts within tables, on the other hand, are best done in Excel, which also enables you to sort and search data as you create your tables.

To insert a Word or Excel table in a PowerPoint presentation, follow these steps:

1 Select the table in Word or a range of cells in Excel.

2 Copy it by choosing Edit, Copy or pressing Command+C.

3 Switch to PowerPoint, and display the slide where you want to insert the table.

4 Paste the table by performing one of the following actions:

- For Word tables, choose Edit, Paste.

- For Excel tables, choose Edit, Paste Special, and choose Microsoft Excel Worksheet Object.

Once you've pasted Word and Excel tables into a presentation, you can edit and format them as you would tables created in PowerPoint.

---

tip **Paste Excel data as text or as a live worksheet based on the contents**

You can include Excel worksheet cells in a presentation in two different ways—as a table (select Formatted Text in the Paste Special dialog) or as a spreadsheet object (select Microsoft Excel Worksheet Object in the Paste Special dialog)—but how do you decide which option to use? If the data you're working with is more textual than mathematical and is unlikely to change, then use a table so that you'll be able to format the data easily in PowerPoint. If the data is financial or mathematical and might change over time, then use a spreadsheet so that you can return to Excel and work with the data easily.

Adding Other Objects to Slides

Special objects such as equations and organization charts (often called "org" charts) can also be included as part of your presentation. Both are created and edited in special Office programs rather than directly in PowerPoint.

Inserting Equations

You can add a mathematical equation to a presentation much the same way you would add one to a Word document. Follow these steps:

1 Go to the slide where you want to insert the equation.

Chapter 36: Illustrating the Presentation

2 Choose Insert, Object.

3 In the Insert Object dialog, choose Microsoft Equation and click OK.

---

note If you don't see Microsoft Equation in the Insert Object dialog's list, you'll need to use the Value Pack Installer on your Microsoft Office v. X CD to install Equation Editor.

---

4 Create the equation in Equation Editor.

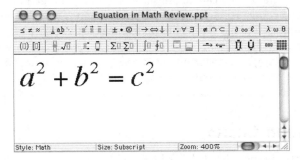

To learn more about creating equations, turn to "Using the Equation Editor," page 224.

---

5 Choose Equation Editor, Quit Equation Editor to return to PowerPoint and have the equation inserted on the current slide.

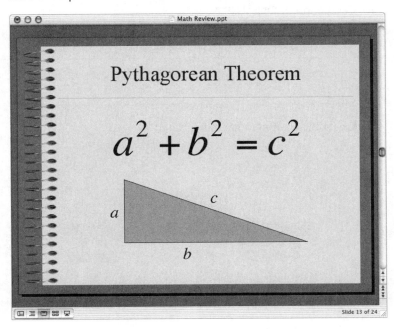

Chapter 36

6 To edit the equation after placing it in PowerPoint, double-click to reopen it in Equation Editor.

InsideOut

Use MathType to set your equations like a pro

Equation Editor is based on MathType, a program from Design Science, Inc. MathType has an enhanced feature set and can be used with any design program to create professionally formatted equations. Among other enhancements, MathType enables you to save equation format settings in separate preference files so that you can switch from one to another or share settings across a workgroup, and it can save equations as EPS files for typesetting in a PostScript workflow. For more information, see the MathType Web site: *http://www.mathtype.com*.

Adding Organization Charts

Organization charts are specialized charts intended to show the hierarchy and relationships of people within an organization, and Office v. X includes a special program for creating them. Here's how to add an organization chart to your presentation:

1 Go to the slide where you want to insert the organization chart.

2 Choose Insert, Object.

3 In the Insert Object dialog, choose Microsoft Organization Chart and click OK.

note If you don't see Microsoft Organization Chart in the Insert Object dialog's list, you'll need to use the Value Pack Installer on your Microsoft Office v. X CD to install it.

4 Create the chart in Organization Chart.

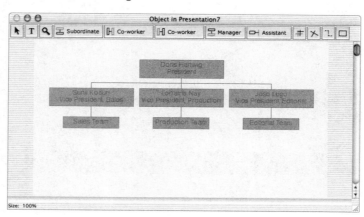

Chapter 36: Illustrating the Presentation

For more information on creating organization charts, see "Using Microsoft Organization Chart," page 260.

5 Choose File, Update and Return To [presentation name], or press Command+W, to return to PowerPoint and insert the chart on the current slide.

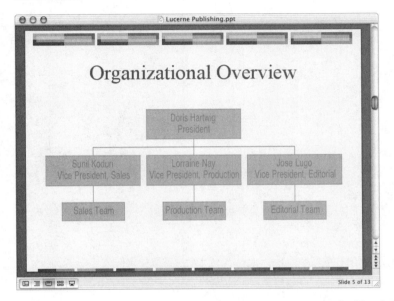

6 To edit the organization chart after placing it in PowerPoint, double-click to reopen it in Organization Chart.

---

tip   **Create organization charts in record time**

If you expect to be working heavily with organization charts during a particular work session, press Command+Option+S to update the organization chart in the presentation, then switch back to PowerPoint with the Dock without quitting Organization Chart. The next time you insert a chart, you won't have to wait for the program to start up.

Chapter 37

Preparing to Present

After you've designed your presentation and added all the content you want it to include, you're almost ready to present it. Before you get started, though, you'll need to make some decisions about how it will be presented and finalize its form for the venue you've chosen. For example, if you want the presentation to stand on its own, you can record your narration and include it in the Microsoft PowerPoint X file. For kiosk presentations, which must run on demand for anyone who walks by, you'll need to create a self-running presentation and determine how each transition to the next slide should be triggered.

In this chapter, you'll learn about

- Creating notes to guide you during your presentation
- Creating audience handouts
- Printing your presentation
- Recording narration
- Creating custom combinations of slides ("custom shows")
- Setting up your presentation to run unattended
- Previewing your work

Creating Speaker Notes

You can use speaker notes as a supplementary handout for your audience or just as a guide to yourself while you're giving the presentation. Two PowerPoint views show notes: Normal view and Notes Page view.

In Normal view, you can see the notes pane on the right side of the window below the slide. To enter notes, click in the notes pane; the placeholder text ("Click to add notes") disappears as soon as you begin typing. As you type, you might need to enlarge the notes pane so that you can see all of your text; to resize it, click and drag at the top of the notes pane.

If you're entering a lot of text in the notes area, you'll probably find it easier to switch to Notes Page view by choosing View, Notes Page. In this view, shown in Figure 37-1, each slide appears at the top of a page with a large area for notes below it.

You can edit the master for the Notes Page view to change the size of the slide image or the notes text area and add other elements. Follow these steps:

1 Choose View, Master, Notes Master.

2 Move and resize the slide image and notes box as desired.

3 Click an object and drag to move it.

4 Click an object, and drag its selection handles to resize it.

5 If you want, add other elements to the master:

■ To add a graphic to the master, choose Insert, Picture, Clip Art to add a graphic from the Clip Gallery, or choose Insert, Picture, From File to import a graphics file.

For more information about adding graphics files to your presentations, see "Managing Images," page 709.

■ To add header or footer lines to the master, choose View, Header And Footer, and click the Notes And Handouts tab. Select the check boxes next to the elements you want to add, and fill in the necessary information.

6 Choose View, Notes Page to see the results of your changes.

tip   Put your stamp on notes pages

Adding your company logo or another graphic to notes pages is a good way to "brand" them, especially if you plan to use them as handouts. You can also use the header and footer areas to add your company name and contact information, including toll-free phone numbers and Web site addresses.

Chapter 37: Preparing to Present

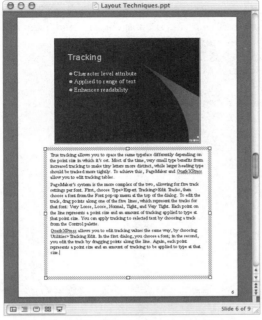

Figure 37-1. The layout of your notes pages is determined by the notes master.

Creating Handouts

Handouts enable you to give your audience a copy of your presentation to take away with them. Each handout page includes multiple thumbnail images of the slides in your presentation, arranged in different configurations as follows:

- Two slides per page, one above the other

- Three slides per page, with ruled lines next to each slide for easy note-taking by audience members

- Four slides per page, two across and two down

- Six slides per page, two across and three down

- Nine slides per page, three across and three down

- Outline only (no slide images)

The slide and notes areas on these handout layouts can't be changed, but you can add header and footer elements or insert elements such as clip art, if you can find space for them. Here's how to choose and modify the handout master:

1 Choose View, Master, Handout Master.

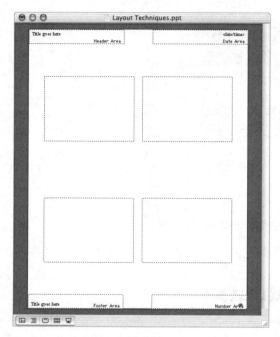

2 Choose a layout by clicking one of the buttons on the Handout Master toolbar.

3 If you want, add other elements to the master:

■ To add a graphic to the master, choose Insert, Picture, Clip Art to add a graphic from the Clip Gallery, or choose Insert, Picture, From File to import a graphics file.

One reason why you might want to add a graphic to the handout master would be to add a watermark to the handouts. For example, if you have a presentation for a limited audience, you can use WordArt to place a Confidential label on the handout master. Then use PowerPoint's graphic transparency tools to give the WordArt about 90% transparency, turning it into a watermark. For more information about making graphics transparent in PowerPoint, see "Setting Picture Effects and Transparency," page 862.

Chapter 37: Preparing to Present

■ To add header or footer lines to the master, choose View, Header And Footer, and click the Notes And Handouts tab. Select the check boxes next to the elements you want to add, and fill in the necessary information.

If you're not ready to commit your handouts to paper, you can use Mac OS X's built-in Print Preview feature to see how they'll look without printing them. Choose File, Print, and make your selections in the Print dialog. Select the Microsoft PowerPoint category and choose one of the handout layouts from the Print What pop-up menu. Then, instead of clicking the Print button, click Preview. PowerPoint will create the preview file and open it in Mac OS X's included Preview program. As an extra bonus, the preview file is in the widely used PDF (Portable Document Format) format, so it can be saved, renamed, or sent via e-mail just like any other PDF file.

4 Print the handouts to see the results of your changes, and distribute to your audience.

InsideOut

Make sure you've chosen the correct handout layout before printing

Unfortunately, when printing handouts, PowerPoint doesn't remember the current layout used on the handout master, so be sure to specify the layout you want used in the Print dialog. Make your selections, including the handout layout you want to use from the Microsoft PowerPoint category of the Print dialog, and then click Print.

Printing Your Presentation

You can print presentations in color, grayscale, or black and white. You can also print specific slides, handouts, notes pages, or outline pages. Depending on your needs, you can print any of the following elements of a presentation:

- Some or all of the slides themselves
- Handouts (slide thumbnails) with varying numbers of slides on each page
- The notes you entered in the notes pane
- The underlying outline from your presentation, in text form with no slide images

> **tip** Even if the presentation will be a slide show rather than a printed document, printing slides is a good way to proof them. Things look different on paper than on-screen, enabling you to catch errors you might otherwise miss.

Printing Speaker Notes and Handouts

Notes and handouts are meant to be printed, which is why their masters are proportioned like letter-size pages instead of like slides. To print notes pages or handouts, follow these steps:

1 Choose File, Print or press Command+P.

2 If you have more than one printer, choose the one you want to use from the Printer pop-up menu at the top of the Print dialog.

3 From the Print Features pop-up menu (the menu that initially displays the Copies & Pages pane), choose Microsoft PowerPoint to see PowerPoint's printing options.

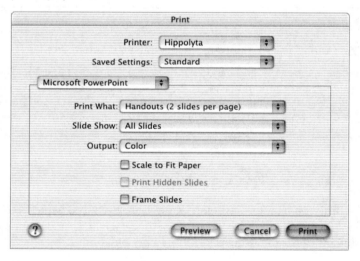

4 Choose Notes or one of the five handouts options from the Print What pop-up menu. The handouts options will all print with the same headers, footers, and other elements on the handout master; only the number of slide images per page will change.

5 Choose a color mode from the Output pop-up menu: Color, Grayscale, or Black And White.

6 Select Scale To Fit Paper to enlarge or reduce the notes or handout layout to fill the size of the paper in your printer.

7 Click Print.

Printing Slides

If you plan to give your presentation as overhead transparencies or as a paper print-out, you can print it in color, grayscale, or black and white. Follow these steps to print slides:

1 In Slide Sorter view, select the slides you want to print, or leave all the slides unselected to print the whole presentation. If you won't be printing only selected slides, you can print from any view.

2 Choose File, Print or press Command+P.

3 If you have more than one printer, choose the one you want to use from the Printer pop-up menu at the top of the Print dialog.

4 In the Copies & Pages pane of the Print dialog, select All in the Slides area to print the entire presentation, specify a range of slides to print, or select Selected Slides to print the slides you selected in step 1.

5 Switch from the Copies & Pages category to the Microsoft PowerPoint category to see PowerPoint's printing options.

6 Choose Slides from the Print What pop-up menu.

7 If you've created custom shows within your presentation, you can choose which show you want to print from the Slide Show menu. If there are no custom shows in your presentation file, the only choice in this menu will be All Slides.

8 Choose a color mode from the Output pop-up menu: Color, Grayscale, or Black And White.

9 Select Scale To Fit Paper to enlarge or reduce the slides to fill the paper in your printer.

10 Click Print.

To learn more about custom shows, which contain subsets of the slides in your presentation that are targeted toward specific audiences, turn to "Creating Custom Shows," page 890.

tip **Convert from PowerPoint to Acrobat format**

You can turn your PowerPoint presentation into an Adobe PDF file by selecting the Output Options category in the Print dialog and selecting the Save As File check box. Choose PDF from the Format pop-up menu. Once your presentation is in Adobe PDF format, you can open it and enhance it in the full version of Acrobat to add annotations, hyperlinks, and other effects.

Previewing Your Presentation in Grayscale

When you print a color document on a grayscale printer, the result might not be what you expect. In grayscale output, all text, lines, and box frames are black and all slide backgrounds are white. Special effects such as text shadows and embossing are hidden. Grayscale objects include box fills (including patterns), object shadows, bitmapped images, and charts. These objects are the ones whose grayscale settings you're most likely to need to change.

The good news is that you can preview and change the way objects print in grayscale. Follow these steps:

1 Choose View, Grayscale.

2 Check each slide to make sure it looks the way you want it to.

3 For objects that don't show up well, Control+click, and choose an option from the Grayscale Settings submenu on the contextual menu. (The Grayscale Settings menu is not available from Slide Sorter view.)

The changes you make in Grayscale view don't affect the way objects look or print in color.

Recording Narration

Recorded narration is primarily used for self-running or Web-based presentations, to take the place of a live speaker. It can also be used to record a presentation as you give it so that others can view the presentation later on, or so that you can review your performance afterward. You can record narration for your entire presentation, or you can add comments to individual slides that are played when the user clicks a sound icon.

For information about creating and printing speaker notes, see "Creating Speaker Notes," page 881.

note You'll need a microphone and a sound-capable Macintosh with built-in or external speakers to record and play back narration.

Before recording your narration, you'll need to plan what you'll say about each slide; you might want to write a script, or you might prefer to speak extemporaneously and simply refer to your speaker notes. Follow these steps to record narration for your presentation:

1 Choose Slide Show, Record Narration.

2 In the Record Narration dialog, make sure that the Sound Input Device and Input Source settings are correct and match your computer's hardware setup.

Chapter 37: Preparing to Present

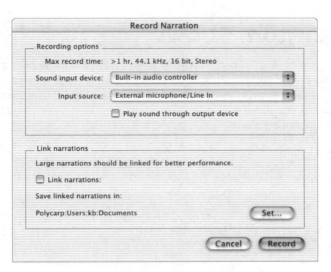

3 Select the Link Narrations check box if you anticipate that the narration will be long; this setting stores the recorded narration in a separate file that's linked to the presentation, rather than embedding it in the PowerPoint file.

4 Click Record to view the first slide and begin your narration.

5 When you have completed the narration for the first slide, click anywhere on the screen to move to the next slide.

6 To pause the recording, Control+click anywhere in the slide window, and choose Pause Narration on the contextual menu. To start again press Control+click and choose Resume Narration.

7 When you reach the end of the presentation, click Yes in the dialog to save your narration and the slide timings, or click No to save the narration only.

8 If you chose to save your timings, in the next dialog, click Yes to review the timings for your slides, or click No to return to the view you were using before beginning the narration.

The slide timings generated while you record narration consist of the time each slide was displayed on the screen before you clicked to move to the next slide. When the slide show is played, PowerPoint will use this timing information to determine how long to display each slide. If you want to change it, you can do so in Slide Sorter view by choosing View, Slide Sorter.

To learn about creating presentations that can be triggered by the user to run by themselves, and about editing slide timings, turn to "Creating Self-Running Presentations," page 893.

Creating Custom Shows

Custom shows are useful when you plan to give more than one similar presentation. You can include the slides for all your presentations within one presentation document and create a custom show for each version of the presentation. Custom shows can overlap, so that some slides within the document can be included in each show, whereas others can be unique.

To create a custom show, follow these steps:

1 Choose Slide Show, Custom Shows.

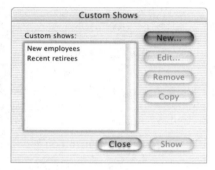

2 Click New.

3 Enter a descriptive name for the show, and choose which slides you want it to include:

> ▨ Double-click a slide title to add the slide to the custom show.

> ▨ Add a range of slides to the custom show by clicking the first slide, Shift+clicking the last slide in the group, and then clicking Add.

> ▨ Add nonconsecutive slides by Command+clicking each one, and then click Add to add them to the custom show.

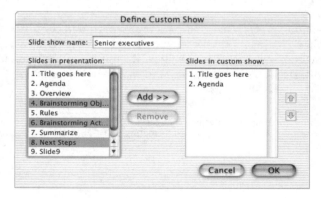

Chapter 37: Preparing to Present

4 Click OK.

5 To preview a custom show, click its name and click Show.

6 Click Close to return to your presentation.

Another way to use custom shows is to include in them only the slides that are different. In this case, you can present the common slides, and then switch to a custom show partway through the presentation. If your entire presentation is included in the custom show, then you can set up the custom show before you begin the presentation. Here are your choices for invoking a custom show:

● Set up the show beforehand. Choose Slide Show, Set Up Show. In the Slides section of the dialog, shown in Figure 37-2, select Custom Show, select the show you want to play, and then click OK.

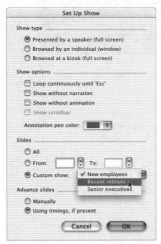

Figure 37-2. The custom show you choose stays selected until you change it, even if you close the PowerPoint file.

● Switch to a custom show during the presentation. Control+click the current slide, choose Go, Custom Show, and select the custom show from the contextual menu.

● Switch to a custom show by clicking a button on the last common slide. Create a button on the slide (see "Switching Custom Shows with the Click of a Button," on next page), and click it to begin the show, as shown in Figure 37-3 on the next page.

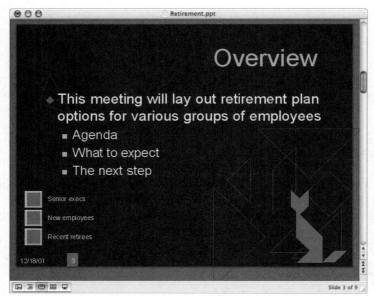

Figure 37-3. The three buttons at the lower left corner of this slide are programmed to branch off to three different custom shows.

Switching Custom Shows with the Click of a Button

You can add one or more buttons to a slide to create a branching-off point for activating one or more custom shows. Follow these steps:

1 Choose Slide Show, Action Buttons, Custom.

2 Draw a button on the slide, and label it with the appropriate text for the custom show you want to launch.

3 In the Action Settings dialog, click Hyperlink To, and choose Custom Show from the pop-up menu.

4 In the Link To Custom Show dialog, select the show you want the button to activate, and click OK.

5 Click OK to return to your presentation.

Using a button to switch shows enables you to customize your presentation on the fly. For example, if you don't have time to specify a custom show ahead of time, you can start the presentation and choose a custom show when you get to the branching-off point by clicking a button. You might also use this technique if you want to choose a custom show based on audience reaction to the first part of your presentation.

To learn more about action buttons and the functions you can assign to them, refer to "Adding Hyperlinks," page 841.

Creating Self-Running Presentations

You can set up a PowerPoint presentation to run unattended for use in a kiosk, trade show booth, or similar situation. A self-running presentation can be operated manually, with mouse clicks, or it can run automatically, switching from one slide to the next at intervals you specify. If a self-running presentation requires narration, you can record the narration (see "Recording Narration," page 888).

Making a Presentation Self-Running

Any presentation can be turned into a self-running presentation, although some presentation designs are better suited to unattended operation than others. Self-running presentations should generally be relatively fast-paced, so that they hold their audiences, and they might need to be designed with no user interaction required, in cases where it's not advisable to allow viewers access to the Macintosh's keyboard and mouse.

To make your presentation self-running, follow these steps:

1 Open the presentation document.

2 Choose Slide Show, Set Up Show.

3 Select Browsed At A Kiosk (Full Screen), which automatically selects Loop Continuously Until "Esc" in the Show Options section of the dialog.

4 Select the appropriate check boxes in the Show Options section if you want the show to be displayed without narration or animations.

5 Select which slides to include in the presentation: all of them, a specified range, or a custom show.

6 Choose an option for advancing from one slide to the next, either Manually (using mouse clicks) or Using Timings, If Present (automatically at scheduled intervals).

7 Click OK to return to the presentation.

See "Setting Slide Timings," on the next page, to learn how to determine the amount of time that each slide is displayed.

Playing a Self-Running Presentation

To play a self-running presentation, choose Slide Show, View Show. Press the Esc key to stop it at any point. If you don't want viewers to be able to stop the presentation, be sure to control access to your Macintosh's keyboard. And for kiosks, it's a good idea to set slide timings so that viewers don't have to use the mouse to advance the presentation. If you keep viewers from accessing the mouse, you'll also need to make sure your presentation doesn't use clickable hyperlinks.

Troubleshooting

Pressing Esc doesn't work to stop a presentation.

If you press Esc while running a self-running presentation, but it doesn't stop, you probably have Speech Recognition turned on. The Esc key is the default key to turn on listening, but you can change it or turn off Speech Recognition by choosing the Apple menu, System Preferences, and clicking Speech. Select the Speech Recognition tab to make these changes.

Setting Slide Timings

If you want the slides in your presentation to advance automatically, with no intervention from you or the viewer, you need to determine how long each slide should be displayed before switching to the next one. You can set slide timings automatically, in one of two ways, or manually.

note When you record narration for your presentation, PowerPoint tracks slide timings as you do so and gives you the option to save the slide timings that you used during the recording process. If you've already recorded narration and saved the timings, then you'll see the time values below each slide in Slide Sorter view.

Rehearsing Timings

If you're not sure how long it will take to complete your narration for each slide, PowerPoint can determine the slide timings while you rehearse your narration. Follow these steps:

1 Choose Slide Show, Rehearse Timings to begin the rehearsal.

2 Read the narration for the first slide, or simply watch the timer displayed in the lower right corner of the document window.

3 When the slide has been displayed for the appropriate length of time, press the Right Arrow key to move to the next slide and repeat the timing process.

4 At the end of the slide show, click Yes if you are happy with the slide timings, or click No if you want to record a new set.

> **tip** When you're rehearsing timings, it's a good idea to read your narration just as you would during the presentation. Stand up or sit up straight, breathe normally, and speak clearly without rushing.

Setting Slide Timings Manually

Whether or not you've already recorded slide timings, you can set the timing manually for each slide in Slide Sorter view. Follow these steps:

1 Choose View, Slide Sorter, or click the Slide Sorter View button at the bottom of the document window.

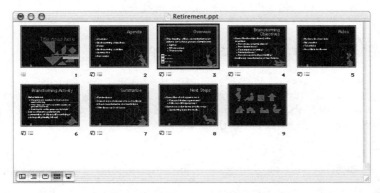

2 Select one or more slides for which you want to set timing.

3 Choose Slide Show, Slide Transition.

4 In the Advance Slide area of the Slide Transition dialog, select Automatically After and enter the number of seconds you want the slide to be displayed.

InsideOut

Select only one Advance Slide option

You might think that selecting On Mouse Click as well as Automatically would enable you to override the slide's timing by clicking to advance to the next slide. And so it does—unless your presentation is self-running, in which case the Automatically setting overrides the On Mouse Click setting. The solution is to use one or the other setting, but not both, on self-running presentations.

5 Click Apply to make the change for the selected slides, or click Apply To All to make the change for each slide in the presentation.

Previewing the Presentation

As you work to create a presentation, you'll want to view all or part of it many times to gauge the effect of the changes you make. The easiest way to preview your work is to view the slide show. What you'll see when you select View, Slide Show depends on which view you're using at the time you switch:

- If you're in Slide Sorter view, with one or more slides selected, PowerPoint starts the slide show preview with the earliest of the selected slides.

- If you're in Normal view or Slide view, the preview begins with the current slide.

Either way, you can end the slide show by pressing Esc.

Chapter 38

Giving the Presentation

Your presentation is complete: its design, content, and navigation elements are all in place. But your work isn't done; now it's time to give the presentation. First, you'll need to decide how you want the project presented: as a full-screen presentation on a kiosk or projector, or within a document window that can be moved around the user's screen. If you'll be giving the presentation live, rather than making it available as a self-playing presentation, you'll need to know how to control the presentation with the keyboard and mouse. And, depending on the design of your presentation, you might need to move around within it and add notes and annotations to it as it runs.

In this chapter, you'll learn about the following:

- Starting your presentation and advancing through it

- Navigating through a presentation as you're giving it

- Hiding and displaying slides

- Making use of action buttons to trigger events

- Annotating your slides as you speak

- Making notes as you give a presentation

Running the Presentation

You can begin running a presentation in two ways: from the Finder or from within Microsoft PowerPoint X. If your presentation document is already open in PowerPoint, you can start the show by clicking the Slide Show button in the lower left of the PowerPoint window; choosing View, Slide Show; or by choosing Slide Show, View Show. To start a presentation from the Finder, you can set your presentation file to run the slide show automatically when it opens. Follow these steps:

1 With your presentation file open in PowerPoint, first save the file to incorporate any changes in the original version.

2 Then choose File, Save As, and enter a name for the new copy of the file.

3 From the Format pop-up menu, choose PowerPoint Show.

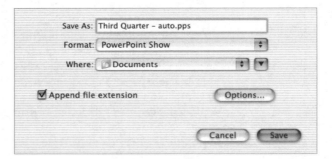

4 Click Save.

---

tip   **Keep a working copy of your presentation**

You can save the new PowerPoint Show file over the working copy of your presentation, with the same name, but it's generally better to preserve the working copy for future editing and create a new file in PowerPoint Show format. That way, you don't have to stop the slide show each time you open the file before you can do any work on it.

Before you begin the presentation (or before you save it in PowerPoint Show format), you'll need to set it up for the appropriate venue. Choose Slide Show, Set Up Show to see your three choices:

● **Presented By A Speaker (Full Screen).** With this choice, the presentation takes up the entire screen, and no menu bars or palettes are visible. This is the mode you'll want to use when you're projecting the presentation onto a screen.

Chapter 38: Giving the Presentation

- **Browsed By An Individual (Window).** If you select this option, the presentation plays within a window, with the user's other windows and desktop visible around it. Choose this option if you are creating a presentation that will be viewed on the Web or an intranet. An abbreviated menu bar contains navigation commands that enable the viewer to move through the show and edit, copy, or print slides.

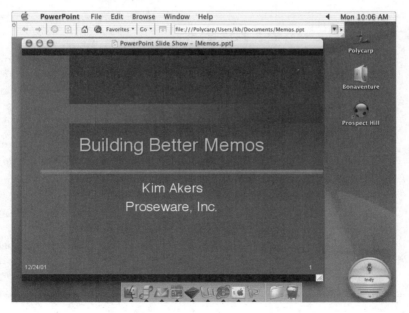

● **Browsed At A Kiosk (Full Screen).** The third option creates a self-running presentation that will run over and over again until it's stopped manually (by pressing the Esc key). The viewer won't be able to use the menu bar or most keyboard commands to interrupt the presentation.

> To learn more about creating a self-running presentation, turn to "Creating Self-Running Presentations," page 893.

---

tip **Make good use of two monitors**

If the Macintosh system (usually a portable Macintosh, such as a PowerBook or iBook) on which you'll be giving presentations is configured to use two monitors, you can run your slide show in full-screen mode on one monitor while the other monitor displays another view, such as Normal, Notes Page, or Outline view. With this setup, you can see your notes or outline, but your audience sees only the slides. To set up a presentation to run this way, choose Slide Show, Set Up Show. Click Screen in the Set Up Show dialog, and then select the monitor on which you want the slide show to play. Note that this won't work if the Macintosh is using video mirroring mode, in which the image on the laptop's built-in monitor is replicated on the external monitor. Note also that the Screen button only appears when more than one monitor is attached.

Public Speaking Precepts

The more presentations you give, the better you'll become at both presentation design and public speaking. Whether you're a presentation newbie or a seasoned pro who could use a little brush-up, the following tips can help you develop into the presentation guru you always hoped you'd be.

● Check out the presentation venue ahead of time so you'll be more comfortable there. Sit or stand where you'll be when you're speaking, and make sure that your chair, stool, or podium is adjusted the way you want it; do the same with the microphone, if you'll be using one.

● Visualize your success before you begin: imagine yourself speaking well, see the audience's interest in the topic, and hear their applause. The power of positive thinking really can help you get in the groove.

● Remember that the audience members are on your side. They're there to hear what you have to say—they want you to do well so that they can learn what you know about the topic.

- If you have a chance to greet some of the audience members as they enter the room, do so—you'll find it's easier to speak to people you know, however slight the acquaintance.

- If you're nervous, don't mention it—if the audience doesn't already know, then you're home free, and if they've noticed, what's the point of mentioning it?

- Focus your mind on the subject of your presentation, not on the audience. This will help avert your nervousness, and your enthusiasm and intensity will engage the audience's interest.

- Make sure the most important information in your presentation is clear to your audience, and don't shy away from repeating it. Start out by explaining what you're going to tell your audience, then present your information, and then close with a summary of the presentation.

- Don't read straight from a script—use your notes and slides as prompts. Repeating a script word-for-word is likely to make you sound dry, dull, and over-rehearsed.

- Don't overdo comedy. If something you want to say lends itself to a short joke or even just a wry look, that's fine, but most of us aren't professional comedians, and our audiences don't expect us to force humor into a presentation where it doesn't belong.

- Stick to your allotted time—practice your presentation beforehand to make sure you don't run over.

- At the end of the presentation, if the format allows, make yourself available to take questions, speak to individuals in the audience, and get feedback. Be sure to provide contact information so that your audience can reach you later on.

tip **Enhance your presentations with a few gadgets**

If you like to roam around the stage or room as you speak, you might want to buy yourself a Keyspan Digital Media Remote. This device is a powerful infrared remote that enables you to control multimedia computer applications like PowerPoint X in the same way you control a TV set. It has 17 keys and comes with "key maps" for popular applications, including PowerPoint, plus you can program it to support your own favorite functions. Find out more at *www.keyspan.com*. Another gadget you might find useful is a laser pointer; they've gotten quite inexpensive, and they're much more precise than pointing your finger (not to mention more polite). You can pick one up at any office supply store.

Controlling the Presentation with the Keyboard

In PowerPoint, as in any Macintosh program, you can choose to control the program from the keyboard or with the mouse by clicking buttons or choosing from menus. When you're running a presentation, however, navigating through it with a mouse might distract your audience from your presentation because anything you can control with a mouse click will be visible on-screen to your audience. Using keyboard commands can reduce distraction and make your navigation—and your presentation—more seamless.

Table 38-1 lists the ways you can move from one slide to another or perform other functions within a running presentation using the keyboard. These keyboard-based navigation commands work only when the slide show is playing, and unusually, most of them don't require holding down a modifier key, such as the Command key. To see a list of useful commands while you're running a show, press the Help key on your keyboard.

> **tip** If your keyboard doesn't have a Help key (Macintosh portables, with their smaller keyboards, don't), press the ? key to bring up the Help screen.

Table 38-1. **Slide Show Keyboard Commands**

Shortcut Key	Action
N, Return, Page Down, Right Arrow, Down Arrow, Return, or Spacebar	Play next animation or move to next slide
P, Page Up, Left Arrow, Up Arrow, or Delete	Go back to previous animation or previous slide
<number>+Return	Go to slide <number>
B or Period	Pause slide show and display black screen
W or Comma	Pause slide show and display white screen
S or Plus Sign	Stop or restart automatic slide show
Control+Shift+S	Play slide show from beginning
Control+Shift+B	Play slide show from current slide
Esc, Command+Period, or Hyphen	End slide show
E	Erase on-screen annotations

(continued)

Table 38-1. *(continued)*

Shortcut Key	Action
H	Go to next hidden slide
T	Set new slide timing while rehearsing
O	Use original slide timing while rehearsing
M	Use mouse clicks to go to next slide while rehearsing
Command+P	Show hidden pointer and/or change pointer to pen
Command+A	Show hidden pointer and/or change pointer to arrow
Control+H	Hide pointer and button immediately
Command+U	Show pointer and button for 10 seconds
A or = (equal sign)	Show or hide arrow pointer
Help or ?	Display Help window

---

tip   **Pause to answer questions or take a break**

Two of the most useful functions in Table 38-1 are easy to overlook: the pause commands. Press B or W to pause your slide show when you want to answer audience questions or even take an intermission. B switches the screen to black, and W switches it to white.

Hiding and Showing Slides

You can opt to leave slides out of a given presentation by hiding them when you set up your presentation. A hidden slide won't display during the slide show or when you run a presentation by choosing Slide Show, View Show, but hidden slides remain part of your presentation document and can be restored to visibility at any time, even on the fly while giving a presentation. Here are the ways you can control hidden slides:

- To hide a slide, go to that slide before you give the presentation and choose Slide Show, Hide Slide.

- To show a hidden slide while you're editing the presentation, choose Slide Show, Hide Slide again to clear the Hide Slide check box.

- To show a hidden slide while you're giving a presentation, go to the slide *before* the hidden slide, Control+click, and then choose Go, Hidden Slide.

Overview

You can see at a glance which slides in a presentation are hidden by switching to Slide Sorter view. Each hidden slide's slide number will be enclosed in a box with a diagonal line through it, as shown here:

Annotating the Presentation with the Pen

As you give your presentation, you can "draw" on the on-screen slides using an electronic pen, in the same way you'd use a marker to draw on an overhead transparency. The advantage of marking up slides electronically is that your annotations are temporary—they're cleared away when you move to the next slide. Follow these steps to use the pen while you're giving a presentation:

1 Control+click anywhere on the current slide to display the contextual menu, and then choose Pointer Options, Pen. (If you don't want to make any additional pen settings, you can use the keyboard shortcut instead, Command+P.)

2 Click and drag to draw on the slide.

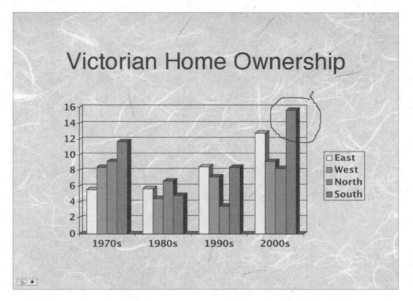

3 To draw in another color, Control+click on the slide, and choose Pointer Options, Pen Color, and then choose a color from the submenu.

4 To erase your marks, press E.

5 To move to the next slide, press Spacebar or Return.

The pointer stays a pen until you choose another option from the Pointer Options submenu, or until you click Command+A to return to the arrow pointer.

---

tip   **Optimize your results with the pen**

If you've ever tried to draw freehand shapes with a mouse, you know that the ease with which you use the pen depends in part on what kind of pointing device your computer has. It's almost impossible to use the pen with a trackball, whereas a mouse or a trackpad will yield somewhat better results. For the maximum ease in drawing with the pen, try using a graphics tablet with a cordless stylus. These are now available in relatively inexpensive packages that include a tablet that plugs into a laptop's USB port, the stylus, and a cordless mouse that also works on the tablet.

Chapter 38

Taking Notes with the Meeting Minder

With PowerPoint X's Meeting Minder feature, you can keep meeting minutes and make
a list of later actions to take while you're giving a presentation. When the presentation
is done, an extra slide is added showing any action items you created, and you can
export your notes and action items to Microsoft Word X. Follow these steps to use
the Meeting Minder:

1 During the presentation, Control+click anywhere on the current slide to
display the contextual menu, and choose Meeting Minder.

2 Click the Meeting Minutes tab and enter your notes.

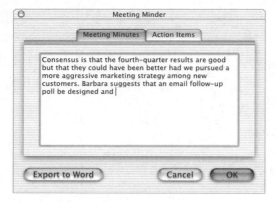

3 Click the Action Items tab, and enter your action items as follows:

■ Enter the "to-do" text in the Description field.

■ Enter the name of the person responsible for the task.

■ Choose a due date.

■ Click Add to finalize the action item.

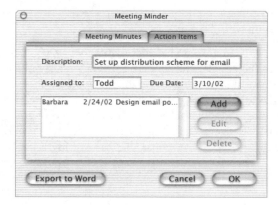

4 When you're done entering information in Meeting Minder, click the Export To Word button to send all your notes and action items to a new Word document, as shown in Figure 38-1.

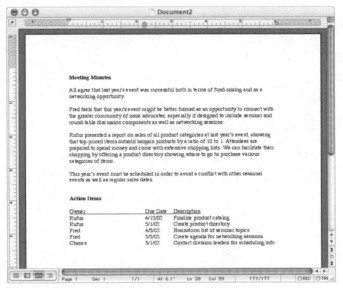

Figure 38-1. Meeting Minder notes exported to Word can form the basis for your meeting minutes.

If you end or close the presentation without having exported your Meeting Minder notes, PowerPoint asks whether you want to discard them or export them.

note If you're thinking, "I should be able to turn these action items into tasks in Entourage—you're not the only one. PowerPoint 2002 for Windows enables users to send action items to Outlook (the Office XP analog to Entourage), so there's hope that someday Macintosh users will be able to do the same with Entourage.

Once you've exported your notes to Word, you can edit the document as you would any Word document: change the font, size, and other formatting, add your company's logo, and more. You can also edit the text; however, remember that it's a one-way trip from PowerPoint to Word—you can't transfer the edited text back to PowerPoint, because it's intended to be a record of one event or meeting.

Chapter 39

Presenting Everywhere

Some presentations stay right in your computer, where you created them. Others are called to venture out into the world, either as presentation files or in another format that can be shared with people in venues other than PowerPoint itself. There are several ways to get your presentation out to your audience, wherever they might be. You can save it as a PowerPoint presentation and send it off to other PowerPoint users or write it to a CD. Alternatively, you can turn it into a movie or a Web site. Or, if you want to give the presentation in a place where you can't use your computer, you can turn the presentation into traditional overheads or slides.

In this chapter, you'll learn how to

- Create a PowerPoint Package that contains all the files needed to run your presentation
- Create a PowerPoint Movie
- Turn your presentation into a Web site
- Order slides or overheads of your presentation

Packaging Your PowerPoint Files

By the time you're finished putting together a presentation, it might contain files from all over your hard drive, or even from elsewhere on your network, especially if you've used QuickTime movies or other rich media as part of your presentation. If you want to transfer the presentation to a different computer (perhaps so you can work on it at home), burn it to a CD, or send it to a colleague, you will need to collect all those files and send

909

them along with the presentation. That's what PowerPoint Packages are all about. A PowerPoint Package includes a copy of your presentation as well as all its linked files, such as pictures, sounds, movies, and hyperlinked files.

Creating a PowerPoint Package is simple; follow these steps:

1 Choose File, Save As.

2 From the Format pop-up menu, choose PowerPoint Package.

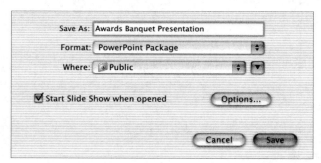

3 If you want the presentation to start playing as soon as the recipient opens the file, select Start Slide Show When Opened.

> **note** If you choose the Start Slide Show When Opened option, the PowerPoint file itself will be saved in PowerPoint Show format with a .pps file name extension, and will run as soon as you open it.

4 Enter a name, and choose a location for the package.

5 Click Save.

The resulting PowerPoint Package is actually a folder containing the presentation file and all of the constituent files needed to play it. The files in the PowerPoint Package folder are copies of the originals, so you can just delete the Package folder once you've copied it to its destination. Once the Package is created, you can burn it to a CD, send it via e-mail, or copy it to a network server.

Saving Presentations as QuickTime Movies

A PowerPoint Movie is a compact video file, in QuickTime format, of your presentation that you can play on any computer, send via e-mail, or integrate into another movie or a Web page. To create a PowerPoint Movie, you don't use the Save As command, but rather a special Make Movie command. Follow these steps:

Chapter 39: Presenting Everywhere

> **tip** **Try to use QuickTime transitions in your movie**
>
> If you know your presentation is destined to be saved as a PowerPoint Movie, consider using QuickTime transitions; that way you know that the transitions will be the same in the movie as they are in the presentation. For more information on using QuickTime transitions, see Chapter 36 "Illustrating the Presentation."

1 Choose File, Make Movie.

2 If you want to change or double-check the movie settings (it's always a good idea to do so), select Adjust Settings, and then click Next to bring up the Movie Options dialog.

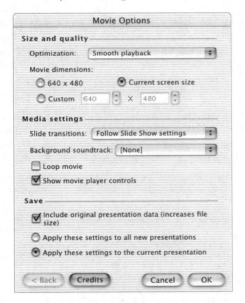

3 In the Movie Options dialog, you can change the following settings:

- ■ **Size And Quality.** Choose an Optimization option and a Movie Dimensions setting. Larger dimensions and quality-oriented Optimization settings increase the size of the movie file.

- ■ **Media Settings.** Choose a Slide Transitions option—you can stick with the transitions the presentation currently uses or substitute one of QuickTime's built-in transitions to save space. You can also choose a sound file to be used as a background soundtrack. Select Loop Movie (to repeat it until the file is closed); select Show Movie Player Controls to give the viewer access to basic playback controls.

■ **Save.** Select the Include Original Presentation Data check box to save a copy of the PowerPoint file along with the movie file, and then choose whether your changes will be applied to the current file only or saved for use with future movie files.

4 Optionally, click Credits and add the credit information if you want the movie to have credits for director, producer, copyright, and performers; after you have made your selections, click OK.

5 Enter a name for your movie, and choose a location for it.

6 Click Append File Extension if you want to add a file name extension to the file.

7 Click Save.

PowerPoint Movies are saved in QuickTime format, Apple's proprietary movie format. They can be viewed using QuickTime Player (which is already installed on your Macintosh) or by using the QuickTime plug-in for the major Web browsers and the Windows platform.

---

tip **Shun transitions and animations to keep your movie file small**

If you want to keep your movie to a minimal file size, delete all transitions between slides and eschew animations. How much difference can a few transitions make? A simple nine-slide presentation with simple Wipe transitions between slides might produce an 8.4-MB movie file; with no transitions, the same movie is about 1.5 MB.

For Award-Winning Movies

When setting up your presentation, follow these do's and don'ts to produce the best results when saving PowerPoint Movies:

● Do stick to a single slide master; PowerPoint uses only the first title master and the first slide master for all slides in the presentation, so there's no point to using alternative masters.

● Do use navigation buttons on your slide master if you want the movie's viewer to be able to view the movie slide by slide. Otherwise, only automatic slide changes will be included in your movie.

For more information on creating navigation buttons, see "Adding Hyperlinks," page 841.

● Don't use the following hyperlink and action settings: Mouse Over action settings; Hyperlink To Last Slide Viewed; Hyperlink To End Show; Hyperlink To Custom Show; Hyperlink To Other PowerPoint Presentation; Hyperlink To

Chapter 39: Presenting Everywhere

Other File; Hyperlink To E-Mail Address; Run Program; Run Macro; Object Action; Play Sound; or Highlight Click. These settings work fine in regular presentations, but they don't translate to QuickTime movie format.

● Don't use the following animations: Blinds; Box; Checkerboard; Dissolve; Peek In/Peek Out; Random Bars; Strips; or Wipe. Again, these animations won't look good (or in some cases, won't work at all) in movie format.

● Don't use the following movie and sound settings: While Playing, Continue Slide Show; Stop Playing, After A Specific Number Of Slides; Loop Until Stopped; Hide While Not Playing; or CD Track As Background Soundtrack. These settings aren't supported in PowerPoint Movies.

Turning Your Presentation into a Web Site

A PowerPoint presentation can easily be turned into a Web site, to be used on its own or as part of a larger site. PowerPoint uses HTML frames to construct a Web page that looks much like Normal view in PowerPoint itself, as shown in Figure 39-1.

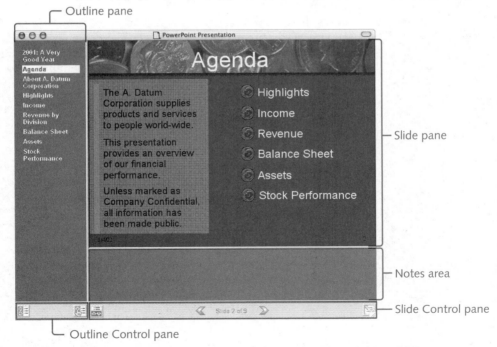

Figure 39-1. When viewing a PowerPoint presentation in a Web browser, you can use the buttons in the Outline Control pane to expand or hide the outline, and use the Slide Control pane buttons to advance through the slides.

The Web page contains a list of all the presentation's slides at the left, which the viewer can turn into a complete outline of the slide titles and the slide text with the click of a button. The slides are displayed in the window's main area at the right. Text is rendered as HTML text, whereas graphs and images are converted to graphics in Web formats, such as JPEG, GIF, or PNG. You can even choose to display your notes text below each slide.

Follow these steps to create a Web site from a presentation:

1 Choose File, Save As Web Page.

2 Click Web Options to customize Web site settings on these five dialog tabs:

■ **General.** Here you can assign a title and search engine keywords to the Web presentation; the title will appear at the top of the Web browser window, while the keywords will be hidden in the HTML and won't be visible within the presentation.

> **tip** Choose your keywords carefully, because they will be indexed by search engines if your presentation is available publicly on the Web. If your presentation will only be seen on an intranet within your company, you probably don't need keywords.

■ **Files.** On this tab, you can make sure that all linked files are updated before the Web presentation is created, and you can choose to include a copy of the original PowerPoint file with the new Web files so that the recipient can edit it. The three check boxes at the bottom of the tab enable you to choose how compatible your Web presentation will be with older or nonstandard Web browsers.

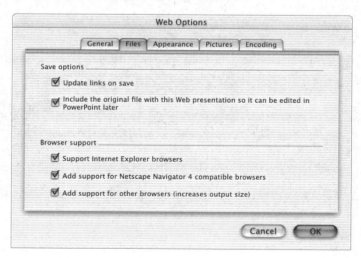

914

Chapter 39: Presenting Everywhere

> **note** Selecting all three of the compatibility check boxes will ensure that your presentation uses extra HTML code, thereby making it more likely to be viewable by most Web browsers. The drawback is that your presentation will be a bit bigger and slower to load.

- **Appearance.** These options control how the Web presentation looks, including the size of its window, the format and location of its navigation elements, and the text and page background colors used. Here you can also determine whether your notes text is included in the Web presentation.

- **Pictures.** Here you can allow or disallow the use of PNG as a format for the graphics that make up part of the Web presentation and determine the ideal monitor size for the presentation. PNG is not supported by older (pre–version 4 of both Internet Explorer and Netscape) browsers, so clear this check box to ensure maximum compatibility. Use the Screen Size pop-up menu to set the expected screen size, measured in popular monitor resolutions, that the Web presentation will be viewed on.

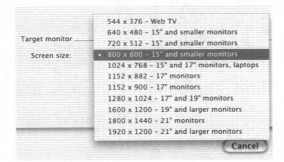

> **tip** **Avoid big Web presentations**
>
> Unless you know for certain that your viewers will be using monitors with large screen resolutions, it's better to be conservative and stick with either 800x600 or 1024x768. Otherwise, the viewer will have to scroll the browser window to see all of each slide, which is a big inconvenience.

- **Encoding.** Use this tab to set the appropriate text encoding setting, which is dependent on the language and computer platform of your target audience.

3 Click OK to close the Web Options dialog, and enter a name for the Web page file that will be the presentation's starting point.

4 Click Save.

Saving a presentation as a Web page creates a start page file and a folder full of ancillary files—the graphics, navigation elements, and slide pages that make up the presentation itself. To view the presentation, open the start page file, which has the name you assign to it in the Save As Web Page dialog, and click the links to view the presentation slides.

---

caution You need to keep the start page and its companion folder together to be able to view the presentation; the start page file itself doesn't contain the presentation slides.

Troubleshooting

The images in my PowerPoint presentation don't look right in the Web presentation.

If graphics appear too large in the Web presentation window, go back to the Web Options dialog, and choose a smaller monitor size on the Pictures tab.

If a "broken image" placeholder symbol appears instead of one of your images, the image file might have been removed from its folder. Check to make sure it's still where PowerPoint put it when the presentation was saved.

If the image file is in the correct place, but you still see a broken image placeholder or the image just doesn't appear at all, you might have allowed PowerPoint to use the PNG format for graphics, which isn't supported by all Web browsers. Resave the Web presentation with this option turned off.

Turning Your Presentation into Overheads or Slides

Strange as it might seem in this era of seemingly ubiquitous computers, you might at some point need to give a presentation without one. In this case, you'll use an overhead projector or a slide projector to display the slides in your presentation on a screen.

Printing Overheads

You can make overhead transparencies yourself, using a laser or inkjet printer with special overhead media. Follow the instructions that came with your printer to load the transparency media into the printer's paper tray, making sure that the printable side is facing the right way. Before printing your slides, choose File, Page Setup and choose Overheads as the medium you'll be using in the Slides Sized For pop-up menu, as shown in Figure 39-2. Then make sure that the pages are oriented correctly with respect to the slides—you might need to switch to Landscape orientation.

Chapter 39: Presenting Everywhere

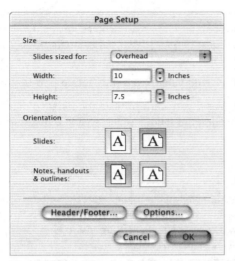

Figure 39-2. The Page Setup dialog enables you to format your presentation for its final destination; in this case, overheads.

When you're ready to print, follow these steps:

1 Choose File, Print or press Command+P.

2 Choose a color or grayscale printer from the Printer pop-up menu.

3 From the Print Features pop-up menu, which initially displays Copies & Pages, choose Microsoft PowerPoint.

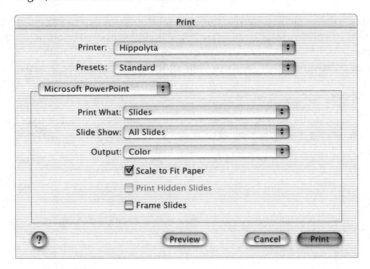

4 Choose Slides (Without Animations) from the Print What pop-up menu, and then choose All Slides or a custom show from the Slide Show pop-up menu.

Chapter 39

> **note** If you have no animations in your presentation, the menu choice in step 4 will be simply Slides, not Slides (With Animations) or Slides (Without Animations).

    5 Choose Color, Grayscale, or Black And White from the Output pop-up menu.

    6 Select the appropriate check boxes if you want to scale the slides to match the size of the transparency media, print hidden slides, or add a box frame around each slide.

    7 Click Print.

> **tip** Although you don't have to use transparency media made by your printer's manufacturer, make sure that you use media labeled for the type of printer you'll be using: inkjet or laser. You certainly don't want plastic sheets melting inside your laser printer, or inkjet ink running off plastic sheets designed for a laser printer.

Ordering Slides

To generate 35 mm slides from a computer, you need a device called a film recorder, which can be quite expensive. Most people have slides output by a print shop or graphic arts service bureau. Prices, quality, and turnaround times vary, so you'll want to check around before placing an order for slides. Many companies that supply slides can accept electronic file submissions—in other words, you can upload your files to their Web sites—and then return your slides via express shipment.

If you're working with a service bureau that does a lot of PowerPoint work, you might not need to prepare your presentation file in any special way. Some output bureaus, however, might want you to submit graphics files instead of a native PowerPoint file. You can create graphics files from your slides by following these steps:

    1 Choose File, Save As.

    2 Enter a name for the graphics files; PowerPoint will create a folder with this name and place the slide graphics in it.

Chapter 39: Presenting Everywhere

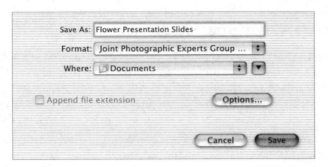

3 Choose a format from the Format pop-up menu; consult your output bureau for the correct format. The available graphic formats are PICT, JPEG, PNG, GIF, BMP, or TIFF.

4 Click Options.

5 In the Save Slides As Graphics File section, choose the resolutions, image size, and compression options you want. Again, consult your output bureau for the correct settings.

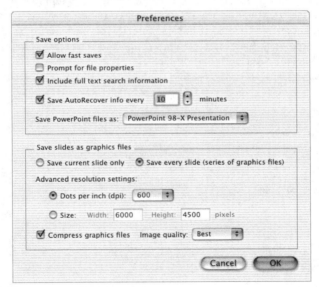

6 Select Save Every Slide to save each slide in your presentation as a separate file, and then click OK.

7 Click Save.

Working with Genigraphics

If you're located in the U.S., you can use PowerPoint X's built-in connection to Genigraphics, a large service bureau that specializes in supplying slides and other output from PowerPoint presentations. You can place your order and send your file directly to Genigraphics over the Internet, or you can request information from the company. All this takes place via a wizard that you activate by choosing File, Send To, Genigraphics.

Note that the Genigraphics Wizard isn't installed with PowerPoint by default. You'll need to install it from the Value Pack on the Microsoft Office v. X CD. You'll know that the wizard hasn't been installed if the Genigraphics choice under File, Send To appears dimmed.

When you have Genigraphics output files, you send the files to Genigraphics electronically, and the resulting output is delivered to you as soon as the next day. You have a choice of turnaround times, with higher prices for quicker turnaround, and you can choose from slides, overhead transparencies, glossy color printouts, and plain color printouts. Genigraphics also supplies poster and presentation boards.

The Genigraphics Wizard really just acts as a link to the Genigraphics Web site, and you might find that the link doesn't work and you end up with a page telling you "The page cannot be found." If this happens to you, just start over at the Genigraphics home page (*www.genigraphics.com*), and click Order Online to place your order and upload your presentation file.

Index to Troubleshooting Topics

Index to Troubleshooting Topics

Index to Troubleshooting Topics

T

W

Index

About the Authors

Tom Negrino is a book author and Contributing Editor to *Macworld* magazine. He has written three other books on Microsoft Office. He also co-authored the best-selling *JavaScript Visual Quickstart Guide, 4th Edition,* as well as several other books on Quicken and Internet topics. Tom began his writing career in 1985 with *MacGuide* magazine, joining the *Macworld* ranks in 1987. He is a frequent speaker at Macworld Expo and other industry conferences, and is a member of the Web Standards Project's Steering Committee. He lives with his wife and son in Northern California's wine country.

Kirk McElhearn is a freelance technical writer, journalist, and translator. He has written user manuals for many popular Macintosh programs, as well as technical documentation for Windows and Linux programs. As a journalist, he has written articles for a variety of publications, including the premier Macintosh e-zine *TidBITS*. And as a translator, he works for some of the world's leading computer and telecommunications companies. A native New Yorker, he has lived in France for almost two decades and currently lives in Guillestre, a village in the French Alps.

Kate Binder is a Mac geek and desktop publishing expert whose books include *The Complete Idiot's Guide to Mac OS X, Easy Adobe Photoshop 6,* and *Teach Yourself QuarkXPress 4 in 14 Days.* When she's not writing or editing books, she provides print and electronic production services to magazine, newspaper, Web, and book publishers. Her favorite Mac is her PowerBook 2400c, but she lives and dies by her very shiny G4 Power Mac. Kate lives and works in Nashua, New Hampshire, with her husband and partner, Don Fluckinger, and five retired racing greyhounds.

Curtis Frye, a freelance writer from Portland, Oregon, is the author of six books, co-author of three books, and creator of three online courses. His most recent books for Microsoft Press are *Microsoft Excel Version 2002 Step by Step, Microsoft Access Version 2002 Plain & Simple, Microsoft Office XP Step by Step* (co-author), and *Microsoft Excel Version 2002 Plain & Simple* (co-author). He is keenly interested in the societal impact of technology, writing *Privacy-Enhanced Business* for Quorum Books and editing *Technology & Society Book Reviews.*

The manuscript for this book was prepared and galleyed using Microsoft Word. Pages were composed by Microsoft Press using Adobe PageMaker 6.52 for Windows, with text in Minion and display type in Syntax. Composed pages were delivered to the printer as electronic prepress files.

coverdesigner
GIRVIN/Strategic Branding & Design

coverillustrator
Todd Daman

interiorgraphicdesigner
James D. Kramer

productionservices
Publishing.com

projectmanager
Curtis Philips

copyeditor
Erin Milnes

composition/graphics
Lisa Bellomo and Jordana Glenn

proofreader
Andrea Fox

indexer
Rebecca Plunkett

Get a **Free**
e-mail newsletter, updates,
special offers, links to related books,
and more when you
register on line!

Register your Microsoft Press® title on our Web site and you'll get a FREE subscription to our e-mail newsletter, *Microsoft Press Book Connections.* You'll find out about newly released and upcoming books and learning tools, online events, software downloads, special offers and coupons for Microsoft Press customers, and information about major Microsoft® product releases. You can also read useful additional information about all the titles we publish, such as detailed book descriptions, tables of contents and indexes, sample chapters, links to related books and book series, author biographies, and reviews by other customers.

Registration is easy. Just visit this Web page and fill in your information:

http://www.microsoft.com/mspress/register

Microsoft®

- -

Proof of Purchase

Use this page as proof of purchase if participating in a promotion or rebate offer on this title. Proof of purchase must be used in conjunction with other proof(s) of payment such as your dated sales receipt—see offer details.

Microsoft® Office v. X for Mac Inside Out
0-7356-1628-0

CUSTOMER NAME

Microsoft Press, PO Box 97017, Redmond, WA 98073-9830